Globe.

"NEITHER ADVISE NOR SUBMIT TO ARBITRARY MEASURES.—Junius."

SIX DOLLARS PER ANNUM;
SINGLE NUMBERS 3c.

...AY, JULY 1, 1867.　　　　WHOLE NO. 5385

...ll now it numbers ...llion.

...EWFOUNDLAND and ...D, which have not ...r the Dominion of ...y allude with the ...former Island was ...1497, and called ...he name given to ...language. During ...ury, though the ...and was claimed by ...various countries ...a of its fisheries ; ...year 1610 that an ...o form an actual ...ry. In that year, ...of Bristol, with ...ved from James I. ...em to settle that ...uch arrangements ...ee the exclusive ...er along its coasts. ...Vaughan settled a ...uthern part of the ...orge Calvert, after ...founded a Roman ...he called Avalon. ...century, France ...the possession of ...by the treaty of ...all other parts of ...been occupied by ...ceded Great Britain. ...climate Newfoundland ...for agriculture, its pro- ...bee, great as that of ...rican colonies. ...ugh those respects : ...mmense fishing ...hradle of a hardy ...hom we trust we ...satisfaction of ...tish American ...EDWARD ISLAND ...bin 1497, on the ...) and received ...John's Island, ...until 1799, when, ...au, it was changed ...honour of the ...Commander of the ...In 1758, when ...e and was trans- ...Edand, its popu- ...00. In 1768, it re- ...overnment, having ...hed Nova Scotia. ...color has been se- ...nfortunate sys- ...hich ates from its ...ts population now, ...adred years, scarce- ...ome of our larger ...ies. It has, how- ...loverner, a Cabinet ...tive council, and a ...and, in short, the ...Provincial Govern-

...RITISH COLUMBIA is ...recapitulation in a ...t. It dates from ...on Fraser's River, ...r only a single de- ...NORTH-WEST, the ...s of rival companies ...m the theme of an ...But its history as a ...d-by. It is admit- ...Dominion of Cana- ...us are filled by in- ...history yet to be ...VER SETTLEMENT, ...n be received into ...interesting his- ...wide subject with

and Mr. John A. Macdonald succeeded in getting together a Cabinet, to which the Reform party felt it their duty to give the strongest possible opposition. On the re-assembling of Parliament, after minis-ters had returned from their elections, the Government found themselves in much the same predicament as the Macdonald-Dorion Administration had been at the commencement of the session ; but with this difference, that whereas the latter had a majority of one or two, the former were in a minority of about the same proportions. They struggled on for a few weeks, during which period Mr. Brown's Constitutional Committee sat with closed doors. It was composed of leading members of the House on both sides of politics, and a very free inter-change of opinion took place. In the course of the discussions it appeared pro-bable that a union of parties might be ef-fected for the purpose of grappling with the constitutional difficulties pointed out in the before-mentioned despatch. On the 14th of June the Committee presented their report, which stated that a strong " feeling was found to exist among the " members of the Committee in favour " of changes in the direction of a Fede-" rative system, applied either to Canada " alone or to the whole British North " American Provinces, and such progress " has been made as to warrant the Com-" mittee in recommending that the sub-" ject be again referred to a Committee " at the next session of Parliament." This report had been adopted in the Committee by a vote of 12 to 3 the nays being Hon. John A. Macdonald, Hon. John S Macdonald, and Mr. Sco-ble. By the force of events, the question was put in the way of settlement, sooner than had been contemplated by the com-mittee, when they recommended their re-appointment in the following session. Affairs were brought to a crisis on the evening of the very day on which the committee had presented their report, by a vote of censure on the Administration being carried by a majority of two. At-tempts were made by them to detach some members of the Opposition ; but they failed, and a dissolution of Parlia-ment appeared to be imminent, although a general election had taken place in the previous year. The opportunity seemed a favourable one for attempting a solution of the constitutional difficulty, and over-tures by Mr. Brown, on behalf of the Re-form party, were met by Mr. John A. Macdonald, with a greater cordiality than could have been anticipated, judging from his vote a few days before against the re-port of the Committee. The result of the negotiations was the formation of a Coalition Government, pledged to seek the settlement forever of our sectional troubles, in the direction which had been pointed out by the Constitutional Com-mittee. Messrs. Brown, Mowat, and McDougall, on behalf of the Reform party of Upper Canada, joined the Cabi-net under the Premiership of Sir E. P. Tache. The policy of the new Ministry was accepted by the majority of the mem-bers of the House—only a very few Upper Canadian members joining the larger part of the Rouge party of Lower Canada in objecting to it.

It happened that, while the leading statesmen of Canada were considering the possibility of bringing about a Fede-ral union of the Provinces, the Legisla-tures of Nova Scotia, New Brunswick, and Prince Edward Island were endea-vouring to bring about a union among ... September, authorized to discuss

Union were almost unanimously adopted; but no steps were taken to carry the principle into practical effect, as regarded that Island. The little Island of Prince Edward repudiated the action of its delegates at the Quebec Conference, and did not, like New Brunswick, take a wiser second thought. It has chosen for the present to remain out of the Union—to its own loss we should fancy, rather than that of Confederacy.

Arrangements were made early in June, 1866, for the assembly in London of a Conference of Delegates from the several Provinces, to determine the precise terms of the Bill giving effect to the Union of British America, to be submitted for adoption by the Imperial Parliament. Delegates were duly appointed by the Governments of Canada, Nova Scotia, and New Brunswick, and an agreement was made that they should all sail for Eng-land about midsummer. The delegates from the Lower Provinces on their part, fulfilled this agreement, but they had to wait several months for the arrival of the Canadians, and the Conference was not organized till the 4th December. In con-sequence of this delay, the Confederation measure, instead of being carried through the Imperial Parliament, in 1866, as it might have been, was not submitted to that body till the session of 1867.

The Imperial Parliament assembled on the 5th of February. On the 7th, the Bill for the Confederation of the Pro-vinces was introduced by the then Colo-nial Secretary, the Earl of Carnarvon. On the 19th, it had its second reading ; on the 22nd passed through Committee of the Whole, and on the 26th February was read a third time. Having been immedi-ately taken down to the House of Com-mons, it was moved to a second reading in that body, on the 28th February ; and, after an interesting debate, in the course of which there was scarcely any opposition given to the measure except by Mr. Bright, who made a somewhat carping, ill-natured anti-Colonial speech, the motion was agreed to without a divi-sion. It passed through Committee on the 4th March. Mr. Aytoun, the member for Kirkcaldy, spoke against the proposed guarantee for an Intercolonial Railroad loan, but did not on this occasion press to a vote an amendment hostile to that guarantee, of which he had given notice. On the 8th March, it was read a third time, and finally passed by the House of Commons without a debate. On the 12th, certain amendments which had been made by the Commons were agreed to by the Lords; and on the 28th March it received the Royal assent, and became a law of the empire.

On the day on which the Confederation Bill received the Royal assent, Mr. Ad-derly introduced into the House of Com-mons, resolutions for the guarantee of a three million sterling loan on behalf of the Intercolonial Railway, which, after a debate, were agreed to on a division of 247 to 67. A Bill founded on the resolutions was introduced, and read a first time on the following day, March 29th ; and, having been duly carried through the House of Commons, was read a third time in the House of Lords, on the 11th of April.

Meanwhile, the opponents of Confeder-ation in Nova Scotia had made another and final effort to obtain an expression of opinion against the measure. The Nova Scotian Legislature assembled on the 18th March, and an assembled on ...echo the Governor's congratulations on

isthmus connects it at its south-eastern extremity with Nova Scotia. On the east its coasts are washed by the waters of the Gulf of St. Lawrence, and on the south by those of the Bay of Fundy. Its area is 27,105 square miles.

Nova Scotia, previous to 1770, comprehended also Prince Ed-ward Island, and the territory which now forms the Province of New Bruns-wick. In that year, Prince Edward Is-land was separated from Nova Scotia, and in 1783, New Brunswick and the Island of Cape Breton were also separated. In the year 1820, however, Cape Breton was re-annexed. Nova Scotia lies within the latitudes of 43 ° and 46 ° north, and the longitudes of 61 ° and 67 ° west. It is about 320 miles long (from east to west) with an average breadth of 70 miles. Its greatest width is about 100 miles. The coast of Nova Scotia being everywhere indented by arms of the sea, no part of it is more than 20 miles dis-tant from salt water. Its area, including Cape Breton, is 18,660 square miles.

The area of the four Provinces, consti-tuting the new Dominion, may therefore be stated as follows :—

	Square Miles.
Ontario,	121,260
Quebec,	210,020
New Brunswick,	27,105
Nova Scotia,	18,660
Total,	**377,045**

The Province of Ontario, exceeds, in its dimensions, those of Great Britain and and Ireland, which are 119,924 square miles. The Province of Quebec has an area almost equal to that of France, which is 211,862 square miles. Nova Scotia is as large as the kingdom of Greece, and New Brunswick is equal in extent to Denmark and Switzerland combined.

If we add the area of Prince Edward Island, 2,100 square miles ; that of New-foundland, 40,200 square miles ; that of British Columbia, 200,000 square miles ; and that of the Hudson's Bay and North West Territories, 2,750,000 square miles —we will have as the total area of the countries which will probably at no distant day be included in the Dominion of Canada, the enormous extent of 3,389,-345 square miles—nearly three times the extent of territory embraced in the Em-pire of China, with its four hundred millions of inhabitants—and greater by 400,000 square miles than the whole territory of the United States.

POPULATION.

According to the census taken in 1861, the population of the four Provinces now embraced within the Dominion of Canada, was then found to be—

Upper Canada	1,396,091
Lower Canada	1,111,566
New Brunswick	252,047
Nova Scotia	330,857
Total	**3,090,561**

That these figures have been very con-siderably increased during the last six and a half years, there cannot be a doubt. Since the previous census, the population had been increasing in the respective Provinces at the annual rate of—

In Upper Canada	4 3⁄4 per cent.
" Lower Canada	2.50 "
" New Brunswick	2.60 "
" Nova Scotia	1.82 "

Assuming that the same rate of ...

BROWN of The Globe. VOL. TWO

To my children

BROWN

of

The Globe.

VOL. TWO

Statesman of

Confederation

1860-1880

J. M. S. Careless

TORONTO

The Macmillan Company
of Canada Limited
1963

PRINTED IN CANADA
T. H. Best Printing Company Limited
Don Mills, Ontario

Contents

Illustrations

Preface

This is the second and concluding volume on the life of George Brown, 1818-1880, Canadian journalist and Liberal party leader. The first volume, which ran to the end of 1859, dealt with Brown's Scottish boyhood, his first years in North America spent in New York, and his removal to Canada in 1843. It described his founding of the Toronto *Globe* in 1844, and his entrance into active politics on the Reform side; his first election to parliament in 1851, and his rise to the leadership of the powerful Reform or Liberal party of Upper Canada, generally known as the Clear Grits, during the sectional conflict of the 1850s. From that point on, the present study traces Brown's growing association with the movement for the confederation of the British North American colonies, which became the all-embracing issue of the decade of the sixties. It particularly emphasizes his contribution to the Confederation movement, for, as Lord Monck, Canada's Governor-General of the time, declared himself, George Brown was "*the* man" whose conduct made the union of British North America feasible.

A man's life is not lived at the same pace and pitch throughout. For the historian, not all parts of his life-span are of equal significance. Thus this volume particularly concentrates on the period between 1860 and the establishment of Confederation in 1867 as years in which Brown reached the peak of his achievement. Yet the years that followed, until his death in 1880, were by no means a mere epilogue to the parliamentary career he relinquished in 1867. His continued influence in the Liberal party and his power on the *Globe* gave him an important role in the newly-created Canadian federal union. Brown's post-Confederation activities have much interest in themselves, as this present volume tries to show.

But above all, it tries to give George Brown his due weight in the story of Confederation, an endeavour greatly aided by the discovery of his private papers, now in the Public Archives of Canada. Brown has sorely needed re-examination. It is all too clear how stiff and meagre is the part he plays in popular Canadian tradition regarding Confederation. One simple indication is that he is generally envisaged among the "Fathers" of Confederation as a stern, white-headed Old Testament patriarch – instead of the vigorous, exuberant man of forty-five that he was at the time. His greatest adversary and essential partner in Confederation, John A. Macdonald, has now received a full and deserved restoration in Professor D. G. Creighton's monumental biography. But George Brown no less deserves rescuing from the indifference and near-ignorance that Canadians so often display about their past. This book may not achieve the rescue. But at least it will have tried.

The list of those to whom I am indebted for aid in the preparation of this work is largely the same as for its predecessor; yet this in no way decreases my gratitude, or my pleasure in acknowledging the debt. Foremost on the list again are Mrs. G. M. Brown and Mr. G. E. Brown of Ichrachan House, Taynuilt, Argyll, Scotland, who permitted me to stay with them while examining a trunkful of George Brown's private papers, and then allowed the whole valuable collection to be deposited in the Public Archives of Canada. But for their hospitality, generosity, and understanding, this biography would hardly have been possible. Next, assuredly, to be acknowledged is the always ready help provided by Dr. Kaye Lamb and his staff at the Public Archives of Canada, and the equally ready assistance of Dr. G. W. Spragge and his staff at the Provincial Archives of Ontario. I have every reason to know how much, indeed, the Canadian historian owes to the archival institutions of this country.

I have received valuable aid also at the Toronto Central Public Library, and at the Legislative Library of Ontario, where even after years of continued reappearance I seem never to have worn out my welcome. Among individuals (outside of institutions, I almost feel constrained to add) I must particularly acknowledge the generous interest of Professor Peter Waite of Dalhousie University, who has repeatedly sent me valuable items of information stemming from his own important researches in the Confederation period. Other individuals – especially Mr. Hugh McKanday of the Toronto *Globe and Mail*, members of the Brown family, and my own colleagues in the Department of History at the University of Toronto – will, I trust, accept a collective acknowledgement, and not consider my thanks in any sense diminished by it.

Finally, I am very glad to express my thanks once more for the financial grant received from the Rockefeller Corporation through the University of Toronto Committee administering Rockefeller funds, which helped support my basic research for this study in Scotland and England during 1955-6. And I am no less happy to recognize the aid received directly from the University of Toronto, which gave me leave of absence during the period mentioned and further assisted me by supporting additional researches in Ottawa and elsewhere in Canada, as well as providing funds towards meeting the costs of the preparation of my completed manuscript.

February 17, 1963   J. M. S. Careless

Leader in Trouble

I

That year, New Year's Day fell on a Sunday, and there were no papers out on the quiet streets of Toronto, sparkling in bright snow and sunlight. Down town on King Street the *Globe* office stood shuttered and deserted, as church-goers hurried by to morning services. Its proprietor, George Brown, the Reform political leader, was no doubt at Knox Church himself that morning, and home afterwards with his parents to spend the rest of the day in proper Scots fashion, welcoming New Year's callers to the Church Street house. But when at last the bell on St. Lawrence Hall announced to a frozen midnight that the first day of 1860 was ended, then the nearby premises of the Toronto *Globe* came suddenly to life. The Sabbath was over; the gaslight blazed; the presses pounded. Brown had his regular New Year survey to produce, already set up before the holiday, and his journal always came out on time. By 4:00 a.m. it was done. The carts were at the door for the opening issue of 1860. The citizens of Toronto – and, by Grand Trunk, Great Western, and Northern railways, the people of Canada West – would soon read the prognostications of the most powerful newspaper in British North America: George Brown's *Globe*.

What were the prospects for the year to come? What might the 1860s bring to the United Province of Canada? The *Globe* was wisely circumspect as it viewed the horizons. "Who can tell," it propounded cautiously, "that in 1859 some seed was not sown which, as the years roll round will gradually develop to the glory or dishonour of our province."[1] Some seeds, indeed, were obvious to speculate upon. There was the policy that had been adopted under Brown's leadership at the huge Reform party convention in Toronto, back in November, which called for the federation of the two sections of the province, Canada East and Canada West, to end their angry conflict within the existing Canadian union. There was, besides, the plan put forward by the governing Liberal-Conservative Coalition for a federal union of all the provinces of British North America. But months earlier the government had virtually abandoned as premature the idea of a general confederation, had dropped it into the limbo of pious wishes. And the Reform opposition's proposal for a dual federation had yet to meet its test in parliament. None could say which seed might grow, to transform the small colonial world of Canada within the years ahead.

At least the outlook in the world abroad seemed promising. In Russia, old Crimean War enemy, a reforming Czar was occupied with freeing the serfs; there, undoubtedly, liberty and progress were sweeping forward. In France, Napoleon III had evidently given up the quest for glory that had led him into war with Austria for the liberation of Italy, and bloodied 1859 with the mass slaughter of Magenta and Solferino. As for Great Britain, it now appeared that she had fully recovered from the double blows of trade depression and the Indian Mutiny. Once more she stood at the peak of industrial and imperial supremacy. Victoria's wide empire, the *Globe* assured its readers, was stable and secure about the world.

Canadians that January might well congratulate themselves on the comforting solidity of the Victorian empire – at least, whenever they looked south across their borders to a sorely troubled United States. The republic was still deep in the storm let loose by John Brown's wild raid on Harper's Ferry, in a fanatic, futile attempt to raise a slave revolt in Virginia. The would-be liberator had been hanged only a few weeks before, and all the violent passions of the conflict over slavery had raged about his death. He was hero and martyr to Northern abolitionists: madman and monster to Southern slave-holders. His soul assuredly would go marching on – in an abolitionist crusading song that rang ominously with the tramp of armies.

From Canada, the Toronto *Globe* regarded the bitter American controversy with keen sympathy for the cause of abolitionism. Its owner, after all, was a prominent member of the city's vigorous Anti-Slavery Society. Nevertheless, his paper recognized that the Harper's Ferry raid had been hopelessly misguided; and George Brown had himself obtained a legal opinion from Oliver Mowat, his close colleague in the Reform party and associate in the Anti-Slavery Society, affirming that the charge of treason against the raiders would have been upheld in Canadian courts.[2] Whatever the rights of the case, the future looked grim enough for the United States. "We take our leave of 1859," the *Globe* sombrely closed its survey of the American scene, "with threats of disunion ringing in our ears."[3]

Compared with the sectional strife in the American union, the problems facing Canada looked by no means so explosive. Yet here, too – as Brown and the *Globe* would emphasize – the Canadian union that had been formed in 1841 from the two old provinces of Upper and Lower Canada was racked with sectional discord. Canada West and East were not just halves of the United Province. They were still Upper and Lower Canada to their inhabitants; two widely divergent communities, the one dominated by English-speaking Protestants, the other by French-speaking Roman Catholics, and effectively divided within a common frame of government by the scheme of equal representation that gave the same number of parliamentary seats to each section. The discord between them had reached new heights of vehemence during 1859. It showed no sign of lessening, as Upper Canadians hotly denounced what they regarded as eastern domination of the union, and Lower Canadians grimly resisted any change that might place them in the power of a hostile West.

As the western Reform organ sharply presented it, the chief British province in America lay divided, distracted, and cast down.[4] A good harvest had helped the slow and partial recovery from the severe depression of 1857-8; yet it seemed that the heady, boundless optimism of the railway boom of the earlier fifties would never return. Railways had been built; population and economic complexity had grown; but a disappointed, disunited Canada was still little more than a thin margin of settlement in the enormous wilderness of British America. And yet, in spite of every problem, Brown's *Globe* looked forward manfully to the 1860s. "Our belief," it said conclusively, "that Canada contains within herself elements of progress which will yet place her among the foremost nations of the world, is not one jot abated."[5] Was this that wishful thinking called nationalism, which still might put its mark upon the next decade?

A time of the making of nations. Though this was barely foreshadowed, such would the sixties be. In Europe, a united Italy would arise from the bravura of Garibaldi and the calculations of Cavour, even as Bismarck worked towards that German national unity destined to upset the power balance of the world. In the United States, nationalism would triumph, in appalling cost of civil war, and establish the modern centralized republic. And in British North America itself, internal crisis and external threat, dreams and near-desperation, would at last move the provinces into a federal union, the broad continental basis for a Canadian nation-state. There were transforming years ahead, and they would work upon George Brown. The strongest exponent of Upper Canada sectionalism would become an all-

important builder of the new national design. The moulder and
leader of the Clear Grit Reform party of Canada West would
exercise a potent influence on Liberalism in the federal Dominion to be proclaimed in 1867. But in the more immediate future
lay fresh political defeats and hard new personal trials. Like
any other man, Brown was the more fortunate not to see ahead
too clearly.

Not that he would have felt great need of foreknowledge:
"Sufficient unto the day" had always been his motto. Now, as
1860 opened, he showed no real anxiety for great events impending, good or bad. He was attending closely to the *Globe*, preparing hopefully for the next political campaign, rejoicing at the
re-election of Toronto's Reform mayor, Adam Wilson. Quite
probably he went a few days later to nearby Newmarket, to
stand with party stalwarts in a swirling snow-storm as Wilson
was also declared victor in the North York by-election, which
was held to fill the parliamentary vacancy left by the death of
old Joseph Hartman, one of the early Clear Grit Liberals.[6]

Perhaps, as well, he improved his otherwise hard-working
bachelor existence with evenings at the winter lecture series in
St. Lawrence Hall, where distinguished visitors such as Horace
Greeley and Ralph Waldo Emerson were currently enlightening
Toronto society. At any rate, he was there to introduce Greeley's
address on "Great Men".[7] And his massive six-foot figure
loomed up as familiarly among the lecture-going *élite* at St.
Lawrence Hall, at the Music Hall, or at the Lyceum, as it did
in the busy crowd on King Street, when he strode along to the
Globe office or the St. Charles restaurant, long arms swinging,
a ready smile for an acquaintance on his eager, expressive face.
He was forty-one. His red hair was fading somewhat into brown,
and had sufficiently receded that a hostile observer could unkindly term him "a hungry-looking, bald-headed individual".[8]
Still, Brown's long, strong features, powerful jaw, and piercing
blue eyes might well have appeared hungry-looking to the
aforesaid observer (one Captain Rhys), seeing that the Captain's
calm proposal that the *Globe* print his theatrical posters on credit
had been indignantly rejected.[9]

In fact, however, Brown was his old vigorous self: decided in
his likes and dislikes, equally decided in revealing them. There
was no guile in his make-up; and his normal good nature, tran-
sparent kindness, and cheerful laughter far outbalanced his
sudden bursts of indignation or the aggressive urgency and
fervour of his will. His was a forthright, frank simplicity, ruled
by a powerful conscience and quick emotions. "Do as you feel
right," he said, "and you will be sure to be right."[10] Of course

he could be fiercely uncompromising, imperious, dogmatic. But he was loved and admired by his personal friends and political followers; and there were few indeed of his enemies who did not feel a deep, reluctant respect for him.

His health now appeared fully recovered after the exhaustion and depression of the preceding summer. His optimism and cheerful self-assurance were wholly restored. In short, this much was certain: that as George Brown moved forward into a new era, his confidence in the future was – in the *Globe*'s own announcement – "not one jot abated".

2

Brown had more to announce that January in his paper. He had been busy for weeks at the office on the latest large-scale project to improve the *Globe*, and the journal bowed in the new year in what it modestly called "the handsomest new dress yet".[11] This was the result of a new font of copper-faced type, of the most modern cut, specially cast for it by James Connor and Sons of New York.[12] Henceforth Brown could crowd still more into the *Globe*'s four large pages of nine columns each, yet still keep them legible and attractive. More notable still, he had bought a second big double-cylinder Taylor press. Each of them could print 3,000 sheets an hour; and he had the only two in the British provinces. To complement the presses he had installed a remarkable new folding machine from Philadelphia, as used in some of the larger American printing offices, that could fold the sheets as fast as the Taylor presses could throw them off. The *Globe* could now print, fold, and mail 3,000 papers an hour with only six employees in the press room, most of them boys. The new machinery, Brown calculated, should save enough to pay its cost within a year.[13] He was really ushering in the age of the big mechanized press in Canada – although the conservative-minded printers' trade would prove none too appreciative of his policy.[14]

In part the pressure of circulation, and in part the hope for more, had dictated this large investment in improvement. The *Globe*'s daily, tri-weekly, and weekly editions now sold well over 20,000 copies.[15] Before the following year was out, they would claim more than 30,000.[16] This, in a city of some 40,000 people and an Upper Canada of approximately a million and a quarter, was a significant figure indeed, especially when the newspaper "clubs" across the West passed each copy of the *Globe* from hand to hand among a devout body of the faithful. Moreover, the influence of the country's largest newspaper was vital to George Brown's political career. Hence politics as well as business impelled his new programme of expansion, venturesome as it might be in such dull times. Yet it had always worked before. Better facilities and faster publication would stimulate greater circulation, while greater circulation would bring more advertising revenue to meet the costs – and still wider public influence for the *Globe*.

In any case, the paper was still Brown's first love, whatever he might do himself in politics as leader of Upper Canada's Reform party. Of course, by this time his role on the *Globe* was far removed from the personal journalism of an earlier day. He was the newspaper publisher, the director of a major business enterprise, not the editor-proprietor who virtually produced a journal on his own, as he and his father, Peter, had done when the *Globe* first began, over a decade before. Now he employed a sizeable staff of editorial writers and reporters, all under the efficient supervision of his sensitive, keen-minded brother, Gordon. For some years past, in fact, it had been Gordon's distinguished and dependable talents as an editor that had largely enabled George Brown to carry on his parliamentary career.[17]

Yet – as now – whenever George was home in Toronto, he was back again at the *Globe* office: up in the third-floor editorial rooms in shirt-sleeves, bristling with enthusiasms, full of expansive gestures, and frequently smudged with printer's ink from the sheaves of sticky proofs he fingered. His parliamentary life still seemed a temporary avocation, however pressing it might grow at times. He stepped back easily and whole-heartedly into editorial writing and direction, and, above all, into the making of policy. Indeed, the major matters of policy and business management had never left his hands.[18] The *Globe*'s present programme of expansion was decidedly his own.

It had been no light matter for Brown to undertake costly improvements in the paper at this moment, not merely because of the still-lingering depression, but because another of his loves, his estate at Bothwell in Kent County, also insistently demanded money. He had found it hard enough to hold on to his extensive property in Upper Canada's far south-west. The lack of cash available in the bad times, and his inability to collect debts owed to him on his lands, had forced him to give some of it up. Only that January he advertised the cabinet factory at Bothwell for sale, and with it an assortment of completed furniture valued at $10,000.[19] Still, he clung to his farm and village lots, his sawmills, and his timber interests there.

American lumber dealers, moreover, had promised him good prices for all the sawn hardwood his mills could deliver through the winter.[20] Accordingly, in mid-December the "Laird of Bothwell" had made a brief trip to Montreal in order to arrange a bank credit of $20,000 to finance the season's operations. There he had opened negotiations through Luther Holton, his old friend and fellow-Liberal prominent in Montreal business circles, and had finally obtained the necessary credit from Edmunstone, Allan and Company, a commercial house accustomed to these transactions in the lumber trade. Brown had to mortgage his Bothwell property and agree to pay back the funds advanced as the proceeds from his lumber sales came in.[21] But he now could saw some four or five million feet of hardwood. And so his mills were steaming full blast as the winter wore on. It was a large undertaking, but the chance seemed good that he could sustain his Bothwell interests successfully.

He had quite a different sort of interest far to the north-west. Here lay that spacious inland empire beyond the Lakes which the Hudson's Bay Company controlled, and which George Brown strenuously urged Canada to acquire. He and his journal had eagerly supported Toronto's efforts to open effective communications with the North West, to extend Upper Canadian interests westward and to make the city the metropolis of a vast new hinterland. Brown still hoped for great things from the North West Transportation Company, founded in Toronto by a group of leading business men, including several of his Liberal associates. And though its promoters had so far had little return from their attempts to develop the transit trade across the Upper Lakes, the *Globe* in January of 1860 was confidently predicting imperial assistance for the company and declaring that these "pioneers of modern northwestern enterprise" would yet obtain a contract to carry the mails as far as the Pacific slopes of British Columbia.[22]

Be that as it may, another Toronto venture into the North West had apparently succeeded. At the Red River, the one pocket of settlement in the Hudson's Bay territory, two young Toronto journalists, William Buckingham and William Coldwell, had recently established the first newspaper in the inland country. Their *Nor'Wester* would agitate for the annexation of the western lands to Canada, and it was not surprising that the *Globe* should run frequent excerpts from its pages. Buckingham, indeed, had been Brown's prize parliamentary reporter before going west, and Coldwell would be received into the *Globe* staff on his return from distant Red River.[23]

The two had journeyed to the Hudson's Bay territory the previous autumn, travelling overland from St. Paul, Minnesota, by Red River cart, their precious type and press in a wagon drawn by two yoke of oxen. The *Globe* fully reported all their adventures: the passages through river, swamp, and prairie fire, and the near-disaster at the outset, when their oxen ran away with the wagon and spent an entire day lumbering in a mad circuit around St. Paul before the men were able to catch them.[24] But at length the pioneer printers had reached the Red River and set up shop. On January 26, 1860, when the north-western mails were in, the *Globe* proudly presented the contents of the first issue of the *Nor'Wester*.

The issue also provided a noteworthy disclosure, which came in a published letter from A. K. Isbister, the Red River's expatriate son in England, who for years had been lobbying at the Colonial Office for the ending of Hudson's Bay rule. Isbister reported gleanings from an interview he had had with Sir Edward Bulwer Lytton, till lately the Colonial Secretary. It seemed that when George Etienne Cartier, the Liberal-Conservative premier of Canada, had recently visited England, he had persuaded Lytton that the annexation of the North West to Canada was inconceivable. "He told him very frankly that, as the head of the Lower Canada party, any proposal of the kind would meet with his determined opposition – as it would be putting a political extinguisher on the party and the province he represented."[25] Here was plain indication that Lower Canadian fears of being swamped by an expanding Upper Canada were preventing the acquisition of the North West – that Lower Canada most decidedly was directing the government of the United Province in its own sectional interest!

One might note, of course, that the report of what Cartier had said was at least third-hand, that Lytton would hardly have conveyed Cartier's words direct to Isbister, and that even if this were the view of the Lower Canadian government leader, it was no more sectional than the belief among Upper Canadians that gaining the North West would markedly enhance their own strength and influence. These, however, were not the *Globe*'s concerns. What was important was north-western expansion in itself; and whether Isbister's story stemmed from Colonial Office gossip or not, it seemed sharply to illuminate the Canadian government's apathy in regard to the North West.

Obviously, the ministry had hung back. Its Upper Canadian members might make resounding speeches to their constituents on expansion; the cabinet might talk of western boundary claims and send an exploring party to the Hudson's Bay territory; but these were mere sops to Upper Canada. The Liberal-Conservative ministers had taken no effective steps to secure the North

West. Instead they had passed quibbling resolutions through the Assembly to evade the Colonial Office's proposal that Canada test her claim to the territory in the courts, and had rejected any other action as premature. In all this, Lower Canada's antipathy to westward expansion had been more than suspected. But now — now here was a vivid illustration of how its power in the Canadian union flatly prohibited a vital advance.

That was enough for the *Globe*. Cartier might also have told Lytton (so Isbister had added) that he *could* conceive of a separate province being erected in the North West which might some day form part of a British North American federation. Yet to Brown and his journal this was all one with the ministry's shelved policy of confederation — a useful dodge, a vague, high-sounding reference to the indefinite future, invoked when necessary to avoid practical action now. The paper saw the meaning before it quite simply: "The North West territory lies open before us — a field white for the harvest. We must not enter upon it; Lower Canadian interests forbid it."[26]

It was just one more aspect of Lower Canadian domination: the baneful consequence of a union based on equal parliamentary representation, which prevented the more populous Upper Canada from exercising its proper weight of numbers, while effectively throwing the balance of power to the close-knit French-Canadian community of Lower Canada. "Both the British and French in Lower Canada persist in ruling us," the *Globe* added bitterly.[27] The English minority in the East were in the main as guilty, since they had helped to maintain Lower Canadian ascendancy for their own commercial reasons, and ridden rough-shod over western rights. Worst of all, however, were those Upper Canadian supporters of the governing coalition, the Conservative forces led by John A. Macdonald — mere hired "sepoys" in George Brown's opinion.[28] For they had sold out their own community for government posts and patronage, and a share in the iniquitous régime.

In short, to Brown and his journal, the failure to open the North West was only a further sign of the power of Lower Canada over the present Canadian union. It was only part of a malign pattern of politics that imposed high tariffs, compensation for French-Canadian seigneurial rights, ruinous Grand Trunk railway bills, separate-school measures — and always the reign of extravagance and venality — on an Upper Canadian majority in complete defiance of its will. The whole thing was insufferable! The union must be changed! Changed to a federal form that would give each Canada a government of its own to look after its essential interests, while leaving matters of joint concern to a central authority. This was the moral and the message that the *Globe* once more pressed upon its followers as the winter days wore on. Plainly the political pot was coming to the boil again, as Brown briskly reheated the whole issue of constitutional change.

3

Another parliamentary session was approaching. Upper Canada's Liberals had to be prepared to push their fundamental answer to the problems of the union, the resolutions adopted by the Toronto Convention of 1859 for a federation of the two Canadas. The Constitutional Reform Association set up at that great November meeting was busy reorganizing the party for victory, rebuilding Reform committees from the central executive in Toronto to the farthest outlying township. At the Association's headquarters on Melinda Street, Brown and Oliver Mowat worked closely with its enterprising secretary, William McDougall, drafting the formal address that was designed to lay the Convention platform before the people and urge them to petition parliament on its behalf.[29] And then on February 15, Brown and his Toronto party colleagues met as the central executive committee, to approve with due solemnity the completed Address of the Constitutional Reform Association.[30]

As printed and circulated throughout the West, its four giant sheets were packed with small type and statistics, under heavy black headings that variously proclaimed: "Injustice to Upper Canada in Parliamentary Representation – Upper Canada Pays Seventy Per Cent of the National Taxation – Lower Canada Rules Upper Canada Even in Local Matters", and finally, "The True Remedy" – the Reform Convention's plan.[31] The plan, however, was given in little more detail than in the original key resolution passed by that body, which had called for separate provincial governments to control "all matters of a local or sectional character" and for "some joint authority" to deal with affairs in common.[32]

The vagueness of that latter phrase had, of course, been necessitated at the Convention by the widespread sentiment among its back-bench members for a peremptory dissolution of the union, "pure and simple". Those who, like Brown, recognized the fundamental value of a union of the Canadas – whatever the faults of the existing one – had been forced to minimize the role of any new central government in order to bring the dissolutionists to accept a policy of federation. It was still wise not to say too much about the policy that might rouse the "pure and simple" faction still strong in the agrarian West beyond Toronto. It was best, in fact, to present grievances in detail and federal union only in principle.

Nevertheless, the Constitutional Reform Address did state that the functions of the proposed joint authority should be "clearly laid down – let its powers be strictly confined to speci-fied duties". Furthermore, the written constitution that would define the limits of federal authority was to forbid the central government to incur new debt or increase taxes beyond the level necessary to meet existing obligations and discharge its specific functions. Even though the central power was not spelled out, therefore, Brown, Mowat, McDougall, and the other Toronto leaders clearly envisaged a sharply limited federation. They were not just seeking to appease dissolutionists in the party. Concerned as they were with Upper Canada's rights, and alarmed as they were by the present piling up of public debt, it was only natural that they should place their main emphasis on new provincial governments that were to be as inexpensive and as close to the people as possible.

The grand Address was warmly hailed by the Reform press across the West. Excitement and hope rose quickly to a peak, as the *Globe* ran the whole thing as a supplement on February 22, and again went through the case for constitutional change. Parliament was only days away; the Address promised that a vigorous effort would be made to secure the Convention plan once the legislature gathered in Quebec on the twenty-eighth. After four years in Toronto, the travelling capital of the United Province had now returned to the eastern city, to stay until the buildings at the newly chosen permanent seat of government, Ottawa, had been completed. This might take some time yet: the Minister of Public Works, John Rose, had only recently turned a frozen sod (with difficulty) to mark the beginning of Ottawa's expensive edifices.[33] Accordingly, George Brown once more set out for a session in Quebec, a day or so before its opening, with the prime aim of pursuing there the policy of the Reform Con-vention and Address.

Essentially it was his programme. True, William McDougall, one of the best minds in the party, had moved the crucial reso-lution for a joint authority at the Toronto Convention, and much of the Address had come from his hand. Staid but capable Oliver Mowat was no less thoroughly behind it. But it was Brown beyond all others who had swung western Reformers from their earlier insistence on representation by population to the remedy of federation, and away from dissolution of the union – Brown who had worked to save both the unity of his party and the unity of the St. Lawrence lands through a federal plan for Canada. His own future as party leader and the future of Upper Canada Liberalism were tied to the Convention scheme. A great deal could turn on the course of events at Quebec.

Aboard the clattering Grand Trunk, as Brown weighed the possibilities, he could hardly have expected to pass his plan on its first introduction into parliament. His Liberal-Conservative opponents were in power, after all. They controlled a safe majority of seats in the House, and had done so ever since the failure of that brief Reform fling at power, the Brown-Dorion ministry of 1858. Furthermore, the two segments of the Liberal opposition, Brown's own Upper Canada contingent and the *Rouges* of Lower Canada under Antoine Aimé Dorion, had known anything but close relations since their disputes over compensation for seigneurial rights during the session of 1859. At its end, they had been left virtually separate, if co-belligerent, bodies. Nevertheless, Brown had kept the friendship and sympathy of the two chief eastern Liberal figures – the judicious, high-minded Dorion, and that lively, irrepressible Irishman, D'Arcy McGee. Moreover, through his intimacy with Luther Holton, an astute and influential Liberal partisan in Montreal, he had another close channel of communication with the *Rouges*, even though Holton had not yet re-entered parliament since his defeat two years before.

It did seem possible, at least, that *Rouges* and Brownite Reformers could combine behind a demand for federating the two Canadas. It was Dorion who had first raised the idea in parliament in 1856. And, shortly before the Upper Canada Reform Convention of 1859 had gathered, the Liberal M.P.s of Lower Canada had met in their own caucus to hear a report drafted first by Holton and signed by four prominent parliamentary members (Dorion, McGee, Dessaulles, and Drummond), recommending that federation of the two Canadas become their party's policy.[34] The report was not officially adopted; and certainly the small eastern caucus was not the counterpart of the western mass party gathering. Still, it was evident that the *Rouge* leaders themselves looked to federation, and reasonable to believe that they could bring most or many of their followers to its support. Further still, other members of the House who were dissatisfied with the government's own lack of clear-cut policy, though uncertain yet of an alternative, might also be won over to the idea of a federalized Canadian union, if it could gain a strong vote in parliament.

That was the true consideration: not necessarily to defeat the ministry and carry the Convention plan at first try but to get a strong vote for it. Then it might build up in the House. Then it might win the next election, and carry a new parliament in its favour. But the first essential for a strong vote lay in the united support of the Upper Canada Reformers themselves. And it was by no means assured that George Brown's own followers in the Assembly would stay solidly behind him on this question.

Really, the western party front had only been formed three years earlier, from Liberal factions that had joined in the "Reform Alliance" under Brown's strong impetus and carried the elections of 1857-8 in Upper Canada. He had undoubtedly had to use all his skill and forcefulness to keep the factions together at the Convention of 1859. Perhaps, indeed, the apparent unity of Reform (with no government patronage to weld it) was largely a tribute to his forcefulness – and to the persuasive publicity of the *Globe*. Yet there still existed three main elements within Upper Canada Reform: Clear Grit radicalism, whose roots were deep in the agrarian western peninsula; Brownite Liberalism, focused on Toronto though spread across the West; and "moderate" Reformism, more in evidence eastward from the city, and particularly in the constituencies along the Upper St. Lawrence River, a region dominated by the proud and prickly John Sandfield Macdonald, who before Brown's rise had been the top contender for party leadership.

Of these three factions, the Brownite Liberals had plainly become the strongest: that group best characterized by its un-wavering devotion to the pronouncements and principles of the *Globe*. In fact, the acceptance of Brown as party leader by radicals to the left and moderates to the right was above all a recognition of the predominance of his own faithful following. Clear Grit radicalism, moreover, had been successfully held under control by the Toronto Brownite leaders, a fact marked at the Convention by the defeat of radical hopes for dissolution and "organic changes" – the remaking of the constitution on the American pattern of elective, democratic institutions.

The old drive of Grit agrarian democracy in truth had lost much force. The original Clear Grit champions had either withdrawn from politics, like John Rolph and William Lyon Mackenzie, or grown progressively more moderate, like William McDougall and Malcolm Cameron. They had found no real successors. The most promising new radical spokesman, the journalist George Sheppard, had been outplayed at the Convention and effectively muzzled thereafter in his writings for the *Globe*.[35] The unhappy Sheppard had departed the *Globe* office in January of 1860 (with a bland farewell editorial of praise

written by George Brown) to take more congenial employment
on the Hamilton *Times*.[36] He was soon to leave an unresponsive
Canada for the United States. It seemed he lacked the courage
of his political convictions; he had chopped and changed about,
and always it was the party or the country that had failed him.
Able as he was, Sheppard did not have the fibre for consistent
leadership.

Thus, lacking real direction, radicalism had become subdued.
Increasingly its adherents were merging into the Brownite
Liberal following. Thus, too, the *Globe* at last grew willing to
use the name "Clear Grit" for the whole Upper Canada Reform
party.[37] Initially the term distinguished the radical faction alone,
whose American democratic tendencies the *Globe* had fervently
deplored. It was the Liberal-Conservative press that had freely
applied "Clear Grit" to the general mass of Western Reformers,
helpfully implying that they were all ultras and republicans at
heart, while Brown's journal had naturally shunned the title
for that very reason. But now the name was safe enough. The
Upper Canada Liberals could be "the Grits" henceforth, as far
as the *Globe* was concerned.

Nevertheless, the old Grit radicalism had by no means wholly
disappeared; and, in particular, the dissolutionist sentiment with
which it had been associated was still a powerful undercurrent
in western popular feeling. Should federation not look strong
in parliament, therefore, dissolutionism might surge forth in
Upper Canada once more. Western impatience might yet threaten
Liberal unity with a radical revival on the left. Brown could
not wholly dismiss that possibility.

More possible at the moment, however, was a party split on
the right. Moderate Reformers in Upper Canada still toyed
with the idea of applying representation by population, or the
double majority (Sandfield Macdonald's pet scheme), to the
existing union. They might have been swept along by the Convention's uproarious acceptance of the joint authority principle,
yet afterwards they wondered if so great a change were really
necessary. Some moderate politicians such as Michael Foley
might even have worked with Brown throughout the party meeting, but this rather in an effort to avoid the still more drastic
policy of dissolution than from any ardent desire for federal
union.[38] Furthermore, there were a few moderate M.P.s, such
as Sandfield Macdonald, who had not attended the Convention
at all and could well consider themselves not bound by it. For
the party democracy had little coercive power over the loose
parliamentary Reform front of that day.

Moderates, too, the true descendants of Francis Hincks, were often inclined to that worthy's view that it was more important to have a winning Liberal government than a losing Liberal principle. Here was further cause to wonder whether they would shy from Brown's direction if he pushed them too fast at the federation hurdle in parliament. Actually this right wing was the smallest of the three elements in Upper Canada Reform. Hence the party leader could reasonably count on holding behind him a large majority of western Liberal members, of the left as well as the centre. But would this be enough? Could he afford any split at all, or even rumours of dissension within his party's ranks? What then would happen to a strong vote for federation – to the Convention policy and his leadership? These were the problems George Brown brought with him when he finally arrived in Quebec for the ticklish session of 1860.

4

Temporary accommodation had been prepared for the provincial parliament until the new Ottawa capital was ready. The buildings previously provided for the legislature in the old French city had been destroyed by fire: both the former Lower Canada parliament buildings and their successors. (Incidentally, the Governor-General's residence, Spencer Wood, also burned down the night after the session of 1860 opened, to round out a distinctly gloomy record.)[39] Yet the temporary arrangements made for parliament seemed quite satisfactory – in a brand new building that would become the post office when the capital had moved. It stood on a commanding eminence near the Prescott Gate, looking down the great sweep of the ice-bound St. Lawrence; a plain but ample structure with a front of the best white brick, its more humble red-brick rear plastered over to match.[40]

Inside, the Assembly chamber was shorter but broader than that in Toronto.[41] It was embellished with portraits of past speakers, hung on the front of narrow galleries that ran around three sides. The one hundred and thirty members arrayed below – sixty-five from each section – were seated much as in Toronto. Premier Cartier, galvanically active, and his Minister of Finance, portly Alexander Galt, shared a desk in the front rank on the government side; the mass of Cartier's *Bleu* supporters from Lower Canada ranged behind them. As leader of the Upper Canadian half of the cabinet, John A. Macdonald also had a desk in the front row. Here was the master-politician, still Brown's greatest foe – easy, smiling, and adroit, and as deadly effective as ever.

On the opposite side of the House, Brown and Dorion also shared a front-row desk, as the opposition leaders of West and East. Foley and McDougall were in the same line, Mowat behind Brown and Dorion, McGee and Sandfield Macdonald somewhat more removed. The opposition forces comprised some forty-nine members: thirty-four of them Upper Canada Reformers, ten *Rouges*, and the remainder, more independent Liberals from Lower Canada. The ministerial side numbered about seventy-five: thirty-three being French-Canadian *Bleus*; sixteen, English-speaking Lower Canadians; twenty-three, John A. Macdonald's Conservatives from Upper Canada; and the rest, the few western Coalition Liberals remaining with the government.[42] It was hard to define the fringes remaining on either side, however. In those days of weaker party discipline there were usually quite a number of uncertain votes, as the independent or converted, or the merely disappointed, shifted back and forth. Hence Macdonald's manoeuvring and managing abilities were at such a premium; and hence George Brown might hope to gain significant additions in a well-staged vote on federation.

The opening ceremonies went off smoothly on February 28. The day was wonderfully warm and sunny, and melting waters gushed down the steep and narrow roadways of Quebec.[43] The Speech from the Throne, read by Governor-General Sir Edmund Head, held no surprises. The forthcoming visit of His Royal Highness the Prince of Wales was officially announced for the summer. The rest was serene platitude, with no mention of the general British North American union that the government had once proposed. The House trooped back into its own chamber, fussily marshalled into place by the Speaker, Henry Smith, a perfect zealot for dress and drill who performed at the opening in lace ruffles at neck and wrist – and had ordered a full-bottomed wig from England.[44] Then, as soon as they were settled, Brown rose to give a formal notice of motion. On the earliest day possible, he announced briskly, he would move two resolutions, the first and fifth adopted at the recent Reform Convention in Toronto, declaring that the existing legislative union of the Canadas had failed, and demanding federation under a joint authority in its stead.[45] There was a burst of scornful laughter from the ministerial benches, but it rapidly died out. The House adjourned soon afterwards, full of conjecture as to the outcome of Brown's swift move.

The next morning, the first western Reform caucus of the

session met behind closed doors.[46] Immediately there was trouble. Some of the moderate members expressed doubts as to the wisdom of moving the Convention resolutions in parliament directly. It was all very well, they contended, to adopt the Convention platform as a unifying statement of aims and ideals; but to press it in the existing House would be to cut off Upper Canada Reform from those who were disgusted with the present administration but not yet ready to transform the union. Far better to warn that if misgovernment did not cease the Convention plan would be insisted on. Then there would be room to compromise with potential allies and, above all, to gain more Lower Canadian support.[47]

But those who held with Brown believed that the very purpose of the party was to transform the union, that misgovernment was inherent in its nature, and that further warnings were quite meaningless. Better, indeed, to push to the issue at once, and, if the first try failed, to push again — rather than postpone a test that the electorate expected, and fritter away reputation and support in chasing useless superficial compromises.[48] It was the age-old political debate between compelling principle and temporizing opportunism; or between self-defeating inflexibility and wise adjustment to realities, depending on the side one argued for.

Brown had expected trouble. There were already rumours abroad of reluctance and backsliding in some Reform circles, even as parliament assembled.[49] For that very reason, and to commit the party definitely, he had immediately given notice of his motion.[50] It was a bold move, and an imperious one. It brought an excited protest in the caucus (from those disposed in any case to hang back) that he had acted without authorization. Brown's reply was wholly typical. Though admitting the general need for consultation, he was forthright, single-minded — and again imperious. "In this particular case," he said emphatically, "there is no room for parley or modification — and whatever may be the result, these resolutions must be moved."[51]

He could also note that he was the party's chosen leader; that the caucus had unanimously confirmed him in authority at the end of the preceding session, when he had offered to step down for any more desirable candidate;[52] that the fullest possible party meeting had adopted the resolutions; and that, further, the party's new official organization, the Constitutional Reform Association, had embodied them in its Address with the promise that they would be introduced in parliament. What more authorization could one possibly want? Why not act on the patently obvious?

All this was true. Unfortunately it was just as true that the Reform party organization in Upper Canada could not direct the parliamentary caucus at Quebec. The underlying rifts were there still; and Brown had not succeeded, as he had hoped, in vaulting over them in one quick leap. Furthermore, the political skills he unquestionably displayed in shaping public opinion or managing huge popular meetings did not include the restraint, finesse, and shrewd understanding of differing viewpoints that were so necessary in this affair. He could deal far better with a roaring audience of a thousand than a roomful of restless politicians. Still, for the time being the trouble was allayed. The question of authorization was let drop with Brown's acknowledgement of its general necessity. And the resolutions were not introduced on March 5 as had been announced, on the ground that a number of the western members still had not reached Quebec.[53] One, John Sheridan Hogan, never did arrive. Months later his body was found in the Don River near Toronto: he had been killed in a highway robbery.[54]

In any case, nothing had been settled. Brown and many with him were unshaken in their determination to bring in the constitutional resolutions. A week or two of March passed by, while parliamentary business went forward uneventfully, and the Reform opposition strove earnestly to keep its internal problems under control. Meanwhile, however, the ministerial press had picked up the scent. The Toronto *Leader*, chief government organ in the West, gleefully reported "a terrible row" in the Grit caucus over the resolutions and Brown's leadership. Nothing had been heard since of his motion. "Why the delay?" it asked sweetly.[55] Furthermore, two prominent western Reform journals, the Hamilton *Times* and London *Free Press*, which the year before had questioned Brown's suitability as leader, returned to their refrain.[56] The old "moderate" charges, in fact, were being raised again: that Brown was too extreme to head the party, that Lower Canadians would not work with him, and hence that he was keeping Liberalism out of office.

At the other, the radical, end of the scale, dissolutionists were capturing local party meetings in the western peninsula – since they found Brown's federation policy too tame, too much concerned with maintaining ties with Lower Canada![57] That primeval Clear Grit, Charles Clarke, was writing vigorous new *Reformator* letters to the press.[58] His friend George Sheppard confidently informed him, "The 'joint authority' commands no respect anywhere."[59] Sheppard could perceive a dissolutionist reaction rising, and the coming overthrow of Brown. No doubt the wish bore some relation to the thought; and no doubt the lead the Hamilton *Times* was taking in attacking Brown bore some relation to the fact that its editor, George Sheppard, now had the chance of getting a little of his own back.

Brown was being threatened from both sides; but in Quebec the threat from the moderates seemed far more serious. It was said that five members of the Reform caucus who looked to Sandfield Macdonald would vote against the Convention resolutions if introduced.[60] The *Leader* heard that others would abstain.[61] Foley was a dubious quantity: moderates considered him a likely successor to Brown. Malcolm Cameron had even raised his name in caucus at the end of the previous session, although Foley had then denied any desire to lead.[62] Whether or not he had aspirations, or could be drafted, he was a natural rallying point for antagonism to the Convention plan. Foley was hearty, companionable, and clever. He had some of the charm and eloquence of his compatriot McGee, though not his breadth of intellect or force of character. Associated with him, moreover, was another prominent Reform figure, Skeffington Connor, Solicitor-General in the late Brown-Dorion government. Connor's habit of speaking as if about to burst into tears had not made him one of the party's best parliamentary orators;[63] but he was of old and respected Liberal lineage – had helped to found the *Globe*, in fact. In consequence, the prospect of revolt loomed large in George Brown's party. It could very well doom the policy of federation before it even reached the House.

5

To meet the crisis, the leader called a special caucus. It sat for days through the middle of March in rooms provided at the Collège de Laval, wrangling desperately over the Convention resolutions, as the moderates again insisted on postponement in order to conciliate Lower Canada and to gain a chance at office.[64] At least, in opposing such a weak-kneed policy, Grit radicals made common cause with Brownite Liberals; and thus Brown was effectively relieved from further dangers on the left. But rebellion on the right was coming to a head. "We have had sharp work in our own ranks here," he reported wrathfully on March 28 to Alexander Mackenzie, his old associate in Sarnia. "Sandfield Macdonald we expected nothing of, but Foley and Connor have acted badly as can be."[65] Frightened to death at the prospect of having to declare themselves on the resolutions, they were seeking to get rid of him, to form a new "humbug alliance". They were "snakes in the grass", Brown fumed, "who will make their spring the first moment they dare."[66]

He sprang first. He boldly placed his resignation in the hands of the caucus, and offered to make way for a moderate to lead the party.[67] It was a flat challenge to a test of strength. He would even resign his seat, Brown said positively, if it could be shown that without him Lower Canadians would join a government based on Reform principles.[68] Thus openly confronted, the moderates rapidly gave way. They had to. They were compelled to recognize that without George Brown the Liberals had no chance at all in Upper Canada, whatever the support they might collect in Lower Canada. The moderates had to make do with Brown, because they could not do without him. He towered over all conceivable rivals in the party.

But they did not yield gracefully or willingly. Brown's peremptory gesture of resignation was too much like pointing a gun that one knows to be loaded. It was still more like a pistol to the head when the reassured leader asked the caucus that the general declaration that he should not resign be put in the form of a definite vote of confidence, in order to stop all further dissension. At this, Sandfield Macdonald, Foley, and Connor hotly protested, and Foley and Connor marched angrily from the room.[69] Then the motion carried unanimously, even Sandfield voting for it – though the Cornwall *Freeholder*, his organ, ingeniously explained later that this had been tantamount to asserting that, since George Brown had got the party into such a mess, he should have the responsibility of getting them out of it![70]

Now the caucus also endorsed the Convention resolutions, although Sandfield and four others voted against them, and five would still not be committed.[71] If Brown had won a victory by the end of March, it had been at grave cost. The cost was not so much in party unity, for he had confirmed his policy and his leadership, and the remaining rebels were too weak to disturb either of them in parliament. Yet this forced acknowledgement could not make the moderates warm supporters in the House; inevitably, any prospects for a strong vote on federation had been sadly damaged. Furthermore, the disagreeable Reform quarrels could not be tucked from sight. The *Globe* itself was forced to print a full account of the goings-on at the caucus to offset the lurid reports pieced together by the ministerial papers.[72] The Upper Canada Liberals had not only lost morale in the dissensions and delay: they were left acutely embarrassed as well. And there was not much chance now that any outside support would rally to them in a vote on federation – not when they had so much difficulty in getting on with it themselves.

Brown's health had suffered under the strain.[73] Apparently he had not recovered as fully from his ills of the previous year as it had appeared, and his heavy financial commitments at the *Globe* and Bothwell may also have been weighing on his mind. Fortunately parliament's Easter recess intervened in early April, so that he could hope to recuperate before bringing in the resolutions at long last. When the House reassembled on April 11, however, the senior member for Toronto did not appear.[74] He did not return to parliament until the eighteenth, and then he had to request that the resolutions be postponed, as he was too unwell to speak to them.[75] His own condition caused only a brief further delay; but Sandfield Macdonald, Foley, and Connor sought still more postponements – while an amused and wholly confident government side urged that the famous Convention measures be introduced. There were violent moments, too, when an exasperated Brown and a defiant Foley attacked each other heatedly in debate, while Sandfield, forever armed against the world, swung fiercely and indiscriminately at both sides of the House.[76] Things could hardly have gone worse.

It was not until the night of April 30 that the ill-fated resolutions finally came before the assembly, and Brown, in introducing them, rose to make one of his giant speeches.[77] He spoke from eight till well past midnight, to a full house and crowded galleries. Yet somehow it was not an outstanding effort. He spread himself, as usual, on the ills of the union, but without really catching fire; and his treatment of the remedy, federation under joint authority, was almost perfunctory – general, short, and by way of a postscript. It was almost as if he himself had lost heart in the project after all the trials, frustrations, and disappointments of the past two months. He was doing his part, but as a duty; failure was foredoomed. There would be no strong vote, he could not help but see.

Indeed, the whole debate was an anticlimax, compared with the intense discussions that had raged within Upper Canada Reform. As it transpired, federation had come in under the worst auspices of delay and discord, and the government side had scarcely to take it seriously at all. The debate on the resolutions went on sporadically over several days, with few prominent speakers from ministerial ranks and a good many extraneous comments from back-benchers. For the opposition, McGee and McDougall spoke well in behalf of federation; Dorion and Mowat endorsed it; Sandfield Macdonald used the opportunity to preach the double majority again. For the government, Benjamin of North Hastings, past Grand Master of the Orange Order, really expressed the ministerial view when he condemned joint authority as government by commission and asked why a union of twenty years' standing should be destroyed for "a miserable, juggling expression".[78] The votes taken on May 7 settled the matter conclusively: 66 to 27 against ending the present union; 74 to 32 against federation under some joint authority.[79]

When Brown looked more closely at the votes, he might still extract some small comfort. He had kept an Upper Canadian majority in both cases: the western vote on the two resolutions had gone in their favour 25 to 22, and 23 to 22. Ministerial boasts that Reform would lose its ascendancy in the West had not proved true, even though the division had finally been brought on by the government at a time when several Grits – who afterwards declared that they would have supported the resolutions – had been out of the House, not expecting a decision. Actually Brown had suffered very few defections. Only three Reformers, all from eastern Upper Canada, had ultimately voted against them, while Sandfield Macdonald had been markedly absent. Surprisingly enough, Foley and Connor had swallowed their anger and pride, and their speeches, to vote in favour of the measures, and so for Brown's policies at the end.[80]

Nevertheless, it was equally plain that the programme of constitutional change had attracted few votes beyond Brown's own following, and precious few indeed from Lower Canada. Only nine from the eastern section had supported federation.[81] The proposal had made no headway there – no doubt because the time that might have been spent by Upper Canada Liberals in spreading better understanding eastward had been taken up in their own internal squabbles. Yet western Reformers, in reaction, would fall back still more upon themselves.[82] Why, they might argue, follow a policy that presumed on eastern support, as federation did? The West must return to its own wrongs, to its own demands, and make its own reforming forces so strong that none would dare deny them.

Obviously the federation principle had failed, even while the *Globe* tried to put the best face on it and announced that "the great question of constitutional change has passed its first parliamentary ordeal".[83] How far was it Brown's fault? He had hoped too much; he had acted too precipitately at the outset, in gambling on a quick introduction of the Convention's resolutions while the enthusiasm roused by that meeting still seemed strong. It was an ineptly calculated risk and it displayed his leadership at its faultiest. Here his chief failings as a politician were all revealed: over-confidence, impatience, and imperiousness, and then sheer inability to woo and win – to persuade and conciliate instead of ordering and insisting. Brown, the strong, far-sighted director of the Convention of 1859, and Brown, the hasty, uncompromising dictator of the caucus of 1860, were two aspects of the same man.

Yet not everything was lost. The party still held together; even the malcontents were still in association. Nor could Brown be fairly blamed for their own sizeable contribution of distrust and envy, backsliding and postponement, their placing of obstacles without offering any really positive alternatives. Furthermore, the idea of federation in Reform circles was far from dead. It had been filed away, like British North American union among Conservatives, for future reference if it ever should seem feasible. And George Brown's main share in stamping that idea on his party at the Convention, in the Address, and during the session of 1860, would be remembered long after his failure with the resolutions in that year had been forgotten. The *Globe*, summing up, wrote undismayed: "The joint authority will be established, and Upper Canada will become the centre, at no distant day, of a British Confederation extending from the Rocky Mountains to the Banks of Newfoundland."[84]

6

However important, the constitutional problem was not Brown's only preoccupation in parliament that hectic spring. An old concern of his, the university question, had appeared once more. The provincial university, the secular and state-endowed University of Toronto, was under new attacks from religious denominations with colleges of their own to maintain, on the grounds that the university had lowered standards and wasted funds, and, worst of all, had not left a surplus from the public endowment that could be divided among the denominational colleges. A select committee of nine had been named by parliament to investigate.[85] George Brown was one of a varied membership that included Foley, Malcolm Cameron, and John A. Macdonald. Party lines did not necessarily hold on the question, however; for the committee hearings that began in March and ran through April often found Cameron and Macdonald ranged on one side, Brown and the Conservative William Cayley on the other. Certainly there was no doubt where Brown's own sympathies would lie, as the champion of non-sectarian public education at all levels, and a firm believer in one strong central university. He was in close accord with the two chief witnesses for the University of Toronto at the hearings: John Langton, its Vice-Chancellor, and Daniel Wilson, Professor of History and English Literature in University College, the University's actual teaching institution.

Brown, in fact, was particularly in accord with Wilson, an Edinburgh Scot like himself, who had once been his schoolmate at the Edinburgh High School.[86] Early in the year, when complaints against the university were being prepared for presentation to parliament, he and Wilson had conferred on the troubles ahead. The crux of the problem was that the existing University Act, that of 1853, had made a vague provision for the distribution of surplus income from the university endowment among "affiliated" colleges. There had been no surplus yet – and there was no clear indication that any funds at all had to go to the colleges by right. But when denominational interests, pinched by the depression, eyed Toronto's fine new stone buildings in Queen's Park, their sense of deprivation grew righteously acute. The powerful Wesleyan Methodist Conference that maintained Victoria College had been particularly aroused. It took the lead in memorializing against the unjust Toronto monopoly.

Recognizing the extent of the danger to the provincial institution, Brown himself, in discussion with Wilson, was even willing to consider providing new professorial chairs in the denominational colleges at public expense, in order to ease their need for funds and take the pressure off the central university. But Daniel Wilson argued that admitting the principle of public grants to sectarian institutions could only imperil the whole endowment: "Why not divide it among the claimants? – and so away goes the noblest provision ever made for an unsectarian provincial system of collegiate education."[87]

When, therefore, the university committee met, Brown, urged on by Wilson, stood four-square for the integrity of Toronto university, academic as well as financial.[88] But the attacking denominational forces had the province's most potent educational personage on their side: the weighty Dr. Egerton Ryerson, a Methodist minister and one-time principal of Victoria, Chief Superintendent of Education for Upper Canada, and an old foe of George Brown's. Having submitted a written statement to the committee, Ryerson gave his evidence with all the emotional oratory and polemical zeal that had made him so powerful a controversialist. He attacked Toronto's disgraceful lowering of standards, which allowed an "unprecedented system of options" through the introduction of modern languages and natural science, and permitted half the time of its professors to be spent in tutoring honours students, instead of properly allotting their full attention to all the undergraduates for "critical exposition and drilling".[89] He attacked the university's lavish expenditures, particularly on buildings comparable in Toronto, he said, to St. Peter's in Rome. And he freely painted the staff of University College as "a family compact" engaged in the Senate in voting salary increases for one another.[90] Altogether, his was a strong performance.

Thus, when George Brown cross-examined Superintendent Ryerson in mid-April, it was like a bout between well-matched heavy-weights. Details of the record, questions of motive, personalities, flew fast. By an intensive use of university records Brown pressed Ryerson well back on a number of his sweeping charges, though the latter repeatedly evaded telling blows by failing to remember the episode in question.[91] Thereafter, too, the doctor submitted fresh statements with new interpretations to meet Brown's countercharges. At the end both sides claimed victory. The *Globe* deemed Ryerson "thoroughly roasted", while Ryerson attributed his triumph to divine aid.[92] The truth was that neither hardened battler had really been hurt.

In fact, after all the sound and fury, the whole investigation ended without a decision. There were two draft reports for and against the university given to the press, but neither of them was adopted by the committee or presented to parliament – which rose in any case on May 19.[93] The committee was too divided to decide, and so was the ministry itself. If John A. Macdonald favoured Ryerson and the denominational colleges, there were those in his own party, like Cayley, who did not. Undoubtedly the ministerialists did not feel so secure in office that they could afford to press so controversial an issue. Indeed, the fizzling-out of the university question was one more consequence of the weakness and division in government under the existing Canadian union.

Both the university interests and those of the colleges were, of course, left unsatisfied. In early May, Wilson entreated Brown without success to push the committee to a decision, in order to erase Ryerson's "most unscrupulous misrepresentations and falsehoods" and remove the stain that he had placed on the character of the whole Toronto staff – "arraigned before a Committee of your House as so many knaves".[94] On the other hand, the colleges were left with no answers to their complaints and still without funds forthcoming. Yet for Brown, at least, the contest was not without significance. He had helped keep the central University of Toronto intact; he had fought one more

round with Egerton Ryerson; and he had left a powerful
Methodist element with rankling memories of his opposition to
the interests of Victoria College.

The pace seemed quieter once Brown was back in Toronto
with the *Globe*. Soon, however, the summer calm was broken by
a stiff exchange of letters between John Sandfield Macdonald
and himself, letters fully published in the *Globe* in June and
July.[95] The argument was an old one, concerning what the
former Brown-Dorion government had meant to do to provide
compensation for the abolition of seigneurial rights in Lower
Canada. As an ex-member of that short-lived cabinet, Sandfield
had recently made known that it would have paid compensation
from the general provincial funds – as the Liberal-Conservative
ministry had done – whereas Brown, with Dorion's concur-
rence, had always held that only Lower Canadian resources had
been earmarked for that purpose. Sandfield's assertion could not
be treated as a chance remark. It was too well calculated both to
win him "moderate" friends in Lower Canada and to embarrass
George Brown among the western Grits. The party leader
naturally pressed for a retraction. He was refused. A dispute
developed in a series of bristling open letters arguing over what
had been intended by the Brown-Dorion ministers, and who had
said what. In effect, the bare façade of common party allegiance
was only maintained by the two writers' avoiding words quite so
explicit as "liar" and "cheat".

It would seem, however, that the leader had the better of it.
While Sandfield cited memories of what had been agreed on at
private party conclaves, Brown rested his case on verifiable facts
as to what the people concerned had stated in parliament, and
how they had cast votes there. Here, indeed, he neatly caught
Sandfield out. When the pride of Cornwall categorically denied
that he had ever voted with Brown for the principle that compensation should come from Lower Canadian funds alone, the
latter supplied the relevant and incriminating page reference
from the Journals of the House. The vote in question had been
inadvertently omitted from the Journals' index for 1859 –
and Brown's effective deduction was that Sandfield, doing his
research too hastily, had concluded from not finding an entry in
the index that it was safe to deny the vote![96]

In any case, if this was a victory, and a necessary victory for
Brown, it was a small unedifying one that only revealed how
wide the breaches in Liberalism were. Nor had he enjoyed the
contest. During the course of the exchange with Sandfield, he
wrote gloomily to his confidant, Luther Holton, "I have hesitated about answering, simply because if I do I must show him

up as the most unprincipled scoundrel that ever got into the position he occupies – and I have had so much disagreeable personal work to do that I shrank from assailing so old an acquaintance in such a fashion."[97]

Only a few weeks later the troubled Brown was swept into still another dispute – a much more personal one this time, involving his own financial affairs. At the end of July, the ministerial press suddenly pounced on the $20,000 credit he had obtained from Edmunstone, Allan and Company the previous winter to finance his lumber operations at Bothwell. They luridly presented it as a $20,000 bribe from the Montreal Steamship Company to purchase his support for a shipping subsidy bill in parliament.[98] The basis for so startling a charge was the fact that Edmunstone and Allan, merchants, shipbuilders, and brokers, were also the chief interest behind the shipping company more familiarly known as "the Allan line"; and, that spring, parliament had put through a bill to increase the line's transatlantic subsidy. Brown's own negotiations with the firm could hardly have been kept secret, what with the various agents and brokers concerned, and his need to arrange a mortgage on Bothwell as security for the funds advanced. But now it seemed that the time had come to uncover and use "that twenty thousand dollars" against the paragon of Reform virtue. The government papers went eagerly to work.

Brown's continuing troubles with the moderates in his party were plain enough. Any doubts raised as to his political morality could only embarrass the Reform leader further, and especially might rouse those left-wing Clear Grits who had almost a conditioned, mouth-watering reflex to the bare mention of the word "corruption". As if by set design, through early August, journals from Quebec and Montreal to Hamilton and London raised such an entanglement of inferences based on presumptions against Brown, that their original guesses began to look like fact; and the *Globe* and its master were furiously battling what another age would call a smear campaign.

In vain did the *Globe* and its allies point out that Allan and Company had provided the $20,000 credit in a regular business transaction months before the subsidy bill had been drafted by the government. They were the same concern that wanted the bill, came the reply: hence Brown was guilty, by association. In vain did the *Globe* recall the patent fact that Brown had actually spoken and voted against the measure. His votes and speeches, retorted the Toronto *Leader*, had been "so severely innocent, so cruelly harmless" that they had obviously been pre-arranged.[99] Seemingly, he had not tried hard enough to hinder the bill's

passage by the government majority. Thus he again was guilty
– by imputation.

And when the *Globe* reiterated that the money had been an
ordinary commercial credit for the export of goods, backed by
"ample securities", the Quebec *Morning Chronicle* affected to
believe that the only goods paid for had been George Brown's
brains; while the London *Prototype* bluntly doubted that he
could have had ample securities to offer – "if current reports
as to the financial standing of the hon. member are to be relied
on".[100] Now, indeed, the campaign broadened to attack Brown's
whole business reputation. The *Leader* was especially extreme.
And who was its editor now? Why, George Sheppard, who had
moved there when the backers of his Hamilton *Times* had failed.
"In Bothwell," said the *Leader* vengefully, "schoolboys make
kite-tails of Brown's 'ample securities'," while in Toronto, "Mr.
Brown's business character and standing are matters of common
gossip...we know of no man so reckless and few so unprincipled
in his business transactions."[101] Sheppard threw in new charges
for good measure: that the *Globe* owner had filled his pockets
as Minister of Finance in 1858 (surely a record for two days in
office), that three banks had recently paid him sums ranging
from $8,000 to $20,000 for "patriotic services" – and, at the
same time, that no bank would give him facilities for his debts.[102]
The *Leader* even demanded a parliamentary inquiry!

Altogether, it was a shot-gun blast of defamation, which
seemed likely to injure if it did not kill. Of course, there was
not much new in this procedure to the rowdy provincial press of
either side. But the point that grew increasingly apparent here
was how little fact Brown's defamers had to go on in making
their vague charges, whereas the *Globe*'s own accusations had
normally been much better grounded and thus much more devastating in their total effect. In this instance, within three weeks
Brown was able to collect and publish documents and letters
clearly demonstrating that the $20,000 was truly a commercial
credit for lumber that was really being cut, and that there was
no cause for believing that he had received special favours from
Allan and Company or done any in return.[103] The ministerial
press turned off to other issues, naturally claiming to be un-
convinced, while Sheppard (now "disgusted with my Canadian
experiences") left the *Leader* and the country for the United
States.[104]

Unquestionably, however, some harm had been done George
Brown, although it was more personal than political. His finances
could hardly be in an easy condition now. He had already put a
decided strain on them by his improvements at the *Globe* and his

large indebtedness at Bothwell. And the systematic press abuse had not enhanced his credit standing: inevitably some doubts would cling. Concerned about his personal reputation – which always mattered fiercely to him – and concerned over his business affairs, the Reform leader was still in no position to improve his party cause.

7

Perhaps it had been a concerted plan to disable him politically by distracting him with business troubles. At any rate, Brown grimly agreed afterwards with a sympathetic Holton that it had been "a regularly got-up attack". Apologizing as usual for being slow to write, he added soberly, "I am indeed incorrigible in the matter of correspondence – and the knowledge of that fact makes another argument in favour of my getting out of public life – which I very much long to do."[105]

Yet a different and pleasantly exciting distraction soon appeared. Edward, Prince of Wales, the twenty-year-old heir to the throne of empire, was now *en route* to Canada for the eagerly anticipated royal visit. When he landed at Quebec on August 18, in stifling heat, Brown went there to greet him with the other members of the loyal and perspiring legislature.[106] As Canada's first royal tour moved grandly forward, all eyes were fastened on its heavy daily schedule of public welcomes and processions, official receptions and farewells: partly because reverence for the Crown and belief in the British connection were real indeed; partly because Canada itself was on display, a Canada enjoying its first great chance for self-appreciation. But the sharp strains and conflicts within the province could only be momentarily obscured by the radiance of this princely visit, as briefly dazzling as the late summer sun. Suddenly, at Kingston early in September, they broke through.

Kingston was an Orange Conservative stronghold: the very citadel of Upper Canada Conservatism. The Orangemen of Kingston had erected a splendid arch, suitably adorned with Orange emblems, to welcome the Prince with all the loyalty due from British subjects, but specially claimed by the Orange Order as its own particular prerogative. Yet while this loyal and Protestant order was lawful in Canada, in Great Britain it was still an illegal body, a secret society linked with age-old Irish troubles. And the Duke of Newcastle, now Colonial Secretary, who was travelling with the young Prince as his official guardian, was determined that Her Majesty's government should not be embarrassed by Her Majesty's heir's recognizing this disreputable and proscribed organization in any way.[107]

The Orangemen of Kingston were no less determined to display their loyalty and themselves; and to their loyalism was added a righteously indignant Protestantism, mindful that in French Lower Canada the Prince had received the leaders of Roman Catholic bodies readily enough. Again the rallying cries of race and religion were sounded, as Kingston stood defiantly to its Orange arch and banners. On September 5, therefore, the royal steamer moved on past the town, bearing Prince and Duke away uncompromised, but leaving the Orangemen to an angry anticlimax, Kingston merchants and mamas to deepest disappointment, and John A. Macdonald and his Conservative colleagues in Upper Canada to no little embarrassment of their own.

As party leaders they were committed to the Orange Order, which provided them with so much organized and lusty election support. But as provincial ministers they were inevitably involved in the official repudiation of Orangeism, whether it was a matter of high imperial policy or not. Nor did the Orange issue stop at Kingston, for, as the tour went on across the West (still amid most loyal enthusiasm), Orangemen several times sought to entice the Prince under their arches, and the Duke repeatedly had to take hurried evasive action to save his bewildered charge.

The game was played in Toronto, for example. As the royal party drove to St. James' Cathedral on Sunday morning, they had suddenly to swerve from an arch where a portrait of William of Orange, patron saint of the Order, had unaccountably appeared.[108] Newcastle had angry words for Mayor Wilson afterwards; but otherwise the Toronto visit went ecstatically, for no one blamed the young Prince for his mentor's policy.[109] George Brown himself was proudly with the official group at the grand Yacht Club regatta on September 11.[110] Moreover, the decorations at the *Globe* office were quite outstanding in a city that outdid itself in welcoming display. There were flags and patriotic mottoes all across the *Globe*'s façade, an arc of illuminated globes along the top, and, within it, Prince of Wales plumes done in coloured gaslights, to shine out resplendently in red, white, and blue.[111]

Meanwhile, however, the clamour of Conservatives against their own ministerial leaders continued to rise: a most enjoyable and heartening spectacle for Brown. The *Globe* exploited it to the full, condemning Orangemen for their traditional rowdyism while conceding their legal position in Canada; censuring the

Colonial Secretary's high-handedness, but largely forgiving it on grounds of ignorance; and reserving the chief blame for Macdonald and Co. who, as the responsible ministers in the province, should have foreseen the inevitable situation in Upper Canada and given full and proper advice to the Crown.[112]

Yet even in these circumstances Brown did not change his fundamental stand on the Orange Order. He had always held it a disorderly, disruptive force that made for sectarian violence, not religious liberty, and did the cause of Protestantism far more harm than good.[113] He had said so even during the height of his campaign against Roman Catholic power in the early fifties. Now, however, it was still possible to repudiate Orange excesses in the *Globe* as "utterly indefensible", and yet point out why the troubles had occurred, and, above all, to inveigh against the government's failure to prevent them – through incompetence, spinelessness, and total disregard for the interests of Upper Canada. It was an old trumpet call; but the enemy had suffered a severe blow. They were faltering badly, in fact, and Brown knew it.[114]

This was the auspicious moment to take to the public platform again. Before the Prince had left the province, within a few days of his Toronto visit, the Liberal leader was off to Galt to address a major Reform demonstration there. There were flags, bands, and a gala parade on that sparkling early autumn day, for this was a major party occasion.[115] Brown rose to it with his best soul-stirring oratory, denouncing all the evils of misgovernment and the failings of the union, and calling once again for the Convention remedy of federation. But as he held forth, someone in the audience broke in to question his alliance with D'Arcy McGee, the Lower Canadian Roman Catholic Irish leader – a query doubtlessly inspired by the wave of Protestant anger sweeping Upper Canada at the contrast in the official treatment accorded Roman Catholic organizations in the East and the Orange Order in the West. Brown's reply was prompt and plain. He paid warm tribute to McGee's abilities, emphatically declaring, "I would rather a thousand times act with Mr. McGee than the dough-faced Protestants that misrepresent Upper Canada!"[116] Clearly the Orange furore was not going to lead him to any out-and-out campaign for "Protestant union".

McGee responded gratefully when he heard of the Galt speech: "I have to thank you for the exceedingly kind mention you there made of myself. Its boldness was worthy of you, and its kindness far more than I invited."[117] For his own part, Brown told Luther Holton: "The Galt affair . . . has done much good already. I owe that fellow who cried 'What about McGee?'

something handsome. It was the very chance I have been seeking for a long while. I hope I have done McGee justice – I
intended to do it as handsomely as possible, for indeed he is a
noble fellow and deserves a generous return."[118] He admitted
that his own inclination was to "pitch right into the mêlée on the
Protestant side – but some of our friends are weak brethren,
and I do not wish, if it can be avoided, to weaken McGee's
position."[119] In short, for the sake of the party, he still hoped to
keep ties with eastern Liberalism through his likeable Roman
Catholic ally. He rather expected that the western Conservatives would themselves try to "get up a great Protestant cry",
but did not fear it; nor "the Orange game of John A.", who
was working manfully by this time to redeem himself with his
outraged Orange supporters.[120]

Truly, the tide seemed to have swung back to Reform that
autumn. Orangemen massing at St. Lawrence Hall in Toronto,
early in October, proved they were not yet mollified. They
flatly denounced the Liberal-Conservative government, while
the *Globe* beamed.[121] Moreover, in the elections under way that
month for a portion of the Legislative Council seats, Reformers
made increasing headway in Upper Canada. Malcolm Cameron,
for one, gained a Council place, while the Lambton seat he thus
vacated in the Assembly was taken shortly afterwards by an old
Sarnia friend of Brown's, Hope Mackenzie, Alexander's brother.
Meanwhile, the harvest was good; business looked more encouraging, and Brown went down to Bothwell for several busy
weeks.

But now the Conservative ministers launched a counter-
offensive. Led by John A. Macdonald, they opened an extensive
speaking tour across the West. It was a sign of the Conservatives' alarm that they thus took to stumping the country, a
practice they had previously regarded as rather low and Liberal,
if not downright radical and republican. Brown's answer was a
counter-offensive of his own. If the ministers were going to
invade the West beyond Toronto, his prime domain, he would
foray eastward into the more Tory half of Upper Canada. On
through November the opposing stump campaigns went noisily
forward: Brown in Napanee and Kingston, Macdonald in
Brantford, London, and other western points. Of course, they
also switched back and forth to repair damage. Brown dashed up
to London, for example, and Macdonald down to Kingston in
his turn.

The Liberal leader's own best effort came in Kingston on the
night of November 22, speaking deep in enemy country, and to
an audience in Kingston's massive limestone City Hall that was

notably full of Orangemen. He took a lighter vein, but talked up boldly, as he compared himself to a Presbyterian minister preaching in the Vatican ("by invitation of its inmates"), and brightly observed, "In the West we look upon Kingston as the Ultima Thule of political hopelessness!"[122] He did not expect them to vote out Macdonald, he said frankly: Kingstonians were only aroused now because "your own toes have been trodden on". Yet this should simply bring home to them how much the government had ignored the basic interests and feelings of Upper Canada. And while Orangemen had not been on the side of civil and religious liberty thus far, they now might recognize how these had suffered under a Conservative ministry subservient to Lower Canadian masters for the past six years. He won a vote of approval at the end, probably given more for his manner than his message. But that in itself was satisfying.

By December, however, George Brown was running down, tired not only by the exertions of his campaign, but by the weight of business problems besides. "I have twenty times more on my hands than one man ought to have," he told Alexander Mackenzie, "and some six or eight Tory counties have invited me to speak."[123] Again it appeared that he had not really regained all his old stamina after his period of exhaustion in 1859; and 1860 had proved trying enough itself. Still, the Conservatives had by this time closed their campaign, so that he could also call a halt. But here business affairs intervened once more, to keep him from a rest. He had to go down to New York for the *Globe* in the second week in December, and was detained there for the rest of the month, only arriving back in Toronto in early January of 1861.[124]

One unfortunate consequence was that he was too late to attend a particularly large Liberal rally in Norfolk County, graced by the chief men of the party and designed to counter whatever effect the Cartier-Macdonald ministers might have had in the West. Michael Foley, who had arranged the Norfolk gathering, sent him a tart note of complaint. Brown returned a stiff and far from apologetic reply.[125] Their relations had evidently not improved much since their open clash at the last parliamentary session.

The party leader had other invitations to address public meetings throughout the opening weeks of 1861, far more than he could hope to accept.[126] Reform constituencies were holding gatherings of their own across Upper Canada, trying to sustain the tide that had been running against the ministry in the months before. Yet now, it seemed, that tide was ebbing, without any significant achievement, for now the angers roused in Upper

Canada during the royal visit had lost their force, and the Conservative leaders had largely managed to quiet their following
again. It was not likely that Reform had lost its superior
strength in the West; but in the absence of either a parliamentary session or a general election (which the government would
scarcely have wanted to call) the Liberals had not been able to
utilize their moment of advantage to make significant new
gains. A general election would have to come later in 1861,
since parliament's term would expire with the next session. But
in January of that year no one yet could say which side would
prove to have gained or lost the more on balance during the
twelve months preceding.

And yet, on balance, George Brown had personally lost
ground. He was quite well enough aware of it to wonder again
whether this was not the time to retire from politics. Once, near
the turn of the year, he sat down to draft a letter announcing his
withdrawal, and addressed it to his colleague Oliver Mowat.
"My dear Mowat," he began, "I need not remind you of my
determination to retire from parliamentary life at the earliest
possible moment, and that for the last three years nothing has
prevented my doing so except the fear that new combinations
might result from my retirement highly injurious to the cause
we have so much at heart. I think, however, that the moment
has come when I may retire, not only without fear of that
danger, but with the probability that my doing so may largely
conduce to secure the great ends we have been fighting for. You
must have observed that throughout their whole tour in Upper
Canada the one end and aim of the members of the administration has been to excite personal hostility to myself and revive the
feelings inspired by the fierce party contests of past years. . . ."[127]
But he left the draft unfinished, his mind still not made up.

As an alternative, a tired, uncertain, and discouraged Brown
asked Luther Holton what he would say to his own running off
to Europe to be absent for the coming session – a purely temporary withdrawal. His friend quite understood: "The temptation to allow those who are ceaselessly denouncing you as the
great obstacle to the success of the party to try their hands is I
admit very strong, but they are a mere handful." A leader could
simply not leave his followers "like sheep without a shepherd".
Unless, said Holton more sharply, "you were to assume your
definite retirement from public life, which of course you do not
and must not think of".[128]

And there it was. Nevertheless, as 1861 began, Brown still
had the defeat of his essential policy, the Toronto Convention
scheme, hanging over him, the dissensions in his party to reckon

with, and the shortcomings in his own course of leadership to face. He still might experience grave financial difficulties if business did not definitely recover, since his own resources were so obviously stretched thin. Finally, his health was again unsettled; he was worn and worried. The Liberal leader was in serious trouble, and trouble could yet become disaster.

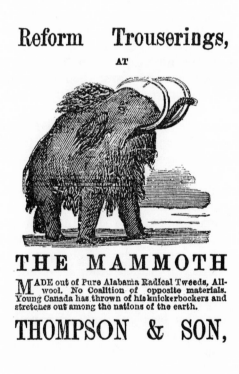

Reform   Trouserings,

AT

THE MAMMOTH

MADE out of Pure Alabama Radical Tweeds, All-wool. No Coalition of opposite materials. Young Canada has thrown of his knickerbockers and stretches out among the nations of the earth.

THOMPSON & SON,

Captain on the Side-lines

I

"Looking southward, we see no streak of blue sky; all is gloomy, dark, threatening. A fierce civil war, unlike anything ever experienced on this continent, seems inevitable."[1] So judged the *Globe* in January of 1861, as with awed fascination it watched the slow, inexorable movement of the United States to apparent self-destruction. There was little else in the papers for weeks: Canadians, Brown among them, were tensely conscious of the storm so near. Abolitionist sympathies strong in Canada, close business connections, ties of family and friendship: all linked them with the mounting tragedy in the republic; and they were no less concerned about their own future in North America. As the *Globe* expressed it, "There is little danger that the tide of war will overflow its legitimate boundaries and deluge us. But who can tell what questions will arise, what international difficulties will spring up during a long civil war among thirty-two millions of people in our immediate vicinity?"[2]

Brown watched the deadly pattern unfolding month by month and week by week: in November of 1860, the election of the Republican president, Abraham Lincoln, in the face of the implacable hostility of Southern slave interests; in December, the secession of slave-holding South Carolina; in January, four more states seceding; and, early in February, the creation of a southern Confederacy to which other slave states would soon adhere. At times there were lulls in the progress of what the *Globe* had already begun to call the "second American Revolution".[3] Then there were brief moments of hope for negotiation, for settlement or compromise, or at any rate for the peaceful parting of two American republics. But the quick-rising hopes soon faded, and seldom did Brown himself believe in them.

Secession, he saw, was a revolutionary right: it could only be maintained by arms. The North would not and could not let the Southern states withdraw from the sovereign entity of the Union; the South would have to fight to gain its independence.[4]

Besides, there was another reason why the Confederacy should not be permitted to go its own way: "The existence of a professedly Christian and civilized nation of men-stealers is a disgrace not only to America but to the whole world, and however strong the measures which the men of the North take for breaking it down, they will confer an inestimable benefit on the human race at large."[5]

Lincoln's inauguration on March 4, however, did not bring the violent outbreak feared. Again for a moment there was relief, talk of a revival of goodwill; and then came a seeming doldrum period, the kind a later age would miscall "phoney war". Yet, though the guns did not sound until the Confederate assault on Fort Sumter in Charleston harbour on April 12, nothing for two months before made their explosion less inevitable. For Brown and the *Globe*, convinced since early January that war would come, this was an interlude that altered nothing. There was sure to be a long and brutal conflict when the adversaries were ready.[6] Meanwhile, there was another question at home to be considered.

The decennial census of the United Province of Canada was under way. Soon there should be certain proof of Upper Canada's claim to a far greater rate of growth than Lower Canada during the past decade. The census of 1851 had shown the western section of the union to have the larger population, and everything since then had indicated that its lead had steadily increased. That lead, of course, had been the basis of western demands for representation according to population, both as a practical necessity and a moral right. Nevertheless, it had been possible for Canada East to argue that the West's apparent greater rate of growth was a passing phenomenon and no reason for a fundamental change in the constitution; that the next census would show a different situation; or at least that there should be no change in the equal division of parliamentary seats until the census of 1861 confirmed whether the western section really did contain a notably larger population. Now the time for the crucial count had at last arrived. It was only to be expected that as local returns started to come out in February the press of both sections would teem with estimates and predictions, counterestimates and refutations.

The *Globe* itself was emphatic on the outcome of the census: the West's predominance was a foregone conclusion. Even early in January, when preparations for counting heads were just beginning, Brown's paper had confidently declared: "It is evident that we are rapidly approaching a solution of the differences between Upper and Lower Canada. The census settles the question.'" It would be impossible to deny the right of representation by population any longer – and this was "the keystone of the Reform arch, as well as the lever by which the structure is to be raised".[8]

It seemed that Brown was bringing out and dusting off his old solution for the troubles of the Canadian union, now that the Toronto Convention plan of dual federation had failed in parliament. To a considerable extent he was. "Rep by pop" had a simplicity and a direct appeal that was lacking in the more complicated and less comprehended concept of federation. Besides, there was the census to give it new opportunity and well-nigh irresistible argument. Furthermore, it had been winning converts among Upper Canada Conservatives, as they came to share the western Reformers' disgust with a union dominated by Lower Canadian interests – though they would not go so far as to turn towards George Brown as a result. It was evident that right-wing Tories, especially, were reverting to old anti-French antipathies; so much so that some Conservative papers even sought to claim that the Upper Canada members of the government were not really opposed to rep by pop, but only waiting for the right time to bring it forward.[9] From all this, then, it appeared to be only sound strategy for Brown to take up the cause of representation by population once again. The potential support it could win and the expectations of the census both demanded it.

Yet this was not wholly a change in policy. Brown had never dropped rep by pop earlier, but had rather included it in the Convention scheme of federation as the underlying principle of the new governments that were to be established. He did not drop the federal idea now, but rather appended it to rep by pop as a means by which special interests – that is, French Lower Canada's – might henceforth be safeguarded. It was a change of emphasis and priority, more than of policy, in his continuing quest for justice in the Canadian union.

At the Convention of 1859, the sixth and last of the resolutions there adopted had stated that no federal government that was not based on the principle of representation by population would be acceptable to Upper Canada Reformers.[10] Now, in 1861, the *Globe* declared that rep by pop was "the principle governing all their arrangements and a mighty weapon to secure the object they have in view".[11] But the final objective, it said, remained the same: a federal union of the two Canadas, with the North West added – and with the prospect that the Maritime Provinces might ultimately join, if poor communications and mutual lack of interest were one day overcome.[12] In short, rep by pop was still conceived as linked with and leading to a scheme of federation.

Nevertheless, if this was only a change in priority, it undoubtedly put federation well into the background, since for all immediate purposes Brown and the *Globe* once more concentrated on winning representation by population within the existing Canadian union. Indeed, it seemed almost like old times in the United Province, as on the one side the demand for rep by pop went up again, and on the other the old cry of "maintain the union" was heard anew. The more sweeping proposals for constitutional reform were all in abeyance now. If Grit Liberals had laid aside dual federation, and dissolution was a static force among an unreconstructed radical rearguard, so the ministerial ranks were silent on the grand design for British North American confederation. During their recent western speaking tour, moreover, Macdonald and his colleagues had said little or nothing about a general federation. Instead they had harped stirringly on the preservation of the existing union against the disruption designed by Brown. And when that same autumn the Premier of New Brunswick, Leonard Tilley, had visited Canada to discuss the question of British North American union informally with the Canadian ministers, he found them too busy even to take up the subject of his visit. He had returned to Fredericton sharply noting that the experience had "not in any way strengthened my desire for union" – and that "there appears less prospect of arriving at a satisfactory solution of this than I formerly anticipated".[13] Politics in Canada were apparently back in their old groove. It might take strong pressure – perhaps something like the impact of the American war – to bring them out of it.

The census and rep by pop; rep by pop and the census: that was the programme Brown now set for his paper, whenever there was time to turn from the American crisis. "HAS A CENSUS PAPER BEEN LEFT AT YOUR HOUSE?" the *Globe* demanded in large black type, reminiscent of the style in which it so often urged Reform electors to go out and die voting.[14] As the Upper Canada figures came in, it published them like so many triumphant election returns, noting jubilantly that in newer western counties the rate of increase since the last census had reached as high as 450 per cent, and, as well, that Lower Canadian papers were now falling silent on their earlier confident prophecies of parity with the West.[15] It really did seem evident that the final population figures would give Upper Canada a commanding lead – nearly a million and a half to a little over a million.[16] Although the completed census would probably not be published before the next session of parliament was over, it was equally probable that the proceedings of the session would be greatly affected by awareness of the coming results. The House would have to give full consideration to the question of representation by population. To prepare for that debate, and for the elections that must follow the session, was now Brown's prime concern.

Or, rather, it should have been. It was announced late in February that parliament would meet on March 16. Brown should have used the remaining time to tighten the Liberal press and party organization behind the renewed demand for rep by pop. There should have been a string of powerful *Globe* editorials for reprinting throughout the satellite party papers, and more of his glowing speeches at Reform meetings to rouse the electors and keep their representatives in line. That, at least, had been the usual practice. But it was markedly absent this time. For the leader was seriously ill; he could not fulfil commitments. The *Globe* gradually lost way. George Brown's health had finally collapsed from constant strain. He had gone down with pleurisy at the very moment when his leadership was most required.[17]

His health had been declining for some weeks, and still he forced himself to work at the *Globe* office. But, on March 2, he had to take to bed and admit to "severe indisposition" – which rapidly became far worse.[18] "The disease," he said later, "had fastened on me long before it became fully developed, and was undoubtedly caused by the great exertions I had to make to put my house in order – for there was no mercy."[19] He had had to strive so long and hard with financial problems, had never been really free of them since the onset of the depression in 1857. And, in the last year, there had been the costly outlay on the *Globe,* the mortgaging of Bothwell for the $20,000 loan, the slander that this had roused, and the further strain put on his credit and his feelings through the purposeful attacks on his business reputation.

Political troubles and his recent busy speaking tour had scarcely lightened George Brown's load. Moreover, at the close of navigation the outlook for the Canadian lumber trade had been gloomy in the extreme, for the American market had seemed to freeze with panic in the mounting secession crisis – a matter of particular concern to the owner of the Bothwell mills. With the approach of spring, however, and gathering military preparations, trade had begun to come to life again; in fact, there would soon be a rising war-time market in the northern states. Furthermore, Brown's expensive improvements in the *Globe* by now seemed to be justifying themselves: at all events, by April of 1861 that paper was apologizing for temporary delays in delivery caused by a forty-per-cent increase in circulation.[20] And so its proprietor shortly could give thanks "that I was not driven to my bed until the ship was safe inside the breakers in comparatively smoother waters than it has known for years".[21]

But by that time all the damage had been done. Luther Holton put it simply: "You have spent so much of your apparently exhaustless energy that you have overwrought the machine."[22] At forty-two, Brown, worn out with business worry and with the outpouring of vitality on so many projects, had finally broken a constitution that had once seemed indestructible. Of course, he had been ill before. But never for so long, or with such lasting effect.

2

For two months and more he lay in the quiet house on Church Street, solicitously tended by his elderly parents, his sister Isabella, and sister-in-law Sarah, while physicians consulted over him and friends called by to learn of his condition. The actual peak of his illness passed fairly early, and when the severe inflammation had subsided Brown briefly felt that he would be up and doing in a few days. Yet this, he found, "was only the buoyancy of fever; as it lowered, my utter prostration soon appeared."[23] He was prescribed the proper nourishing foods, but could not digest them. He had to go on a debilitating Victorian regimen of "stimulants", and continued terribly weak, subject to a racking cough that would not leave him. At length, by early May, the patient had improved enough to drive out in the carriage for an hour a day in the mild spring air. Still, his weakness was such that when after nine weeks he tried to put pen to paper, it was − he said − "like the scrawl of an old man of eighty".[24]

Gradually strength returned, until he was able to bear the fatigue of a journey to Clifton Springs, a highly regarded health resort near Rochester, to take its water-cure and convalesce for a week or two further − though he would later claim that "fresh air, beefsteaks and London porter set me up".[25] Early in June he could at last go back to the *Globe* office for light duties, while still not fully recovered.[26] And in the meantime he had missed the entire parliamentary session.

The House had no less missed him. It had been a dull, incon-

sequential sitting. One Liberal comrade wrote to him from
Quebec: "Your absence has in a party sense been useful. It has
demonstrated to all that you are a *political necessity*, and not a
'governmental impossibility'! Even ministerialists admit that
the House is without interest when it is without Brown."[27] Representation by population had certainly been debated; and while it
had been lost, 67 to 49, the wholly Upper Canadian vote supporting it had included a number of Conservatives. Hence the
government had wisely declared that the principle was not a
"cabinet question", thus allowing their followers to go two ways
upon it, and avoiding for themselves the consequences of a nasty
split. But in the absence of the senior member for Toronto no one
had effectively exploited the situation. In fact, the best speech on
rep by pop was made by Premier Cartier, a five-hour oration that
decisively and defiantly rejected it, despite Upper Canada's now
admitted lead of more than a quarter of a million people. Cartier
condemned the proposal utterly, both as principle and practice,
declaring in one fervent passage that "the codfish of Gaspé Bay
should also be represented, as well as the 250,000 Clear Grits of
Western Canada":[28] a highly quotable remark that did not endear
him to Upper Canadian Liberals, though it well might to their
newspaper editors.

Otherwise, the session mainly showed the ineptitude of the
Reform opposition, once more demonstrating that if some of the
party could not do with Brown, none could do without him. They
were an oddly uncertain group, deprived of the man they had
come so greatly to rely on. William McDougall, who was still
writing for the *Globe*, when he could, reported back to the invalid
in Toronto to reveal the indecision and weakness of the rather
chastened bunch of Grits in parliament.[29] "There is no one on
our side," he lamented, "who will really go into a fight of this
kind with vigour and skill. Mowat is too wishy-washy and
besides is friendly to John A. personally. Connor might be
inclined to work to pay him off for his attack . . . but he is not
well posted and too indolent. . . ."[30] Then there was the lack of
leadership: "I have tried to push out Mowat, but he is afraid –
wants the leadership *put to commission*." Accordingly, a "sort of
committee of safety" of four or five had been recommended,
though McDougall personally preferred to accept Dorion as
nominal leader.[31]

In any case, Michael Foley was out of the running, although
by a good speech on the address he had "re-established himself
somewhat in the confidence of the party". There was still the
suspicion that he would intrigue with the unpredictable Sandfield
Macdonald – besides a problem of his recurrent drinking

bouts.[32] Mowat also wrote, reporting that Foley's drinking had grown "very bad", adding a bit piously: "Poor fellow, he is always so mortified afterwards."[33]

Still further, there was no effective critic of the ministry's vulnerable financial policies; in Brown's absence, Finance Minister Galt would have it all his own way. The party, said McDougall dolefully, had "no man of commercial training combined with political knowledge and speaking talent, but yourself".[34] If there were men like William Howland with the requisite business background, they lacked force in talking to the House; Holton would have been invaluable, but was still out of parliament – and so on.[35] The dismal picture might have given Brown the satisfaction of seeing how much he was needed; but it was small comfort for him, fretting helplessly in Toronto, to watch the whole session being thrown away.

And then, early in June, parliament was dissolved and a general election called. Reformers wanted George Brown; his Toronto constituency besought him to run again. He would have to go into the battle weak and unready as he was, with a party that he had not been able to pull together again, and, indeed, that had never fully recovered from the defeats and dissensions of the previous year. He had seldom entered an election campaign under less favourable auspices.

On June 7, the Toronto Reform Association called a general meeting in the Mechanics' Institute to nominate candidates for the city's two parliamentary seats, now denominated East Toronto and West Toronto.[36] The full turn-out that packed the lecture room that night included such local party notables as McDougall, Howland, and Adam Wilson, the member for North York and former mayor who had been asked to stand for West Toronto. And there was also the city's Reform representative in the late parliament, George Brown, there to be nominated for the constituency of East Toronto. As he rose to speak in this first public appearance since his illness, its mark was plain upon him. There was no dramatic change; his tall, erect figure had not noticeably wasted, his red-brown hair had not turned grey, his deep voice had lost none of its resonance. Yet he was obviously weak – "I doubt if my physicians approve of my being here tonight," he observed, explaining that he would not talk long in order to save his strength.[37] Above all, his speech did not climb and soar, and at the end he apologized for a lame performance. He also made clear that it was obligation, not enthusiasm, that impelled him. This was surely not the old Brown.

"With perfect frankness and sincerity," he said, "were I at liberty to follow my own inclination at this moment, I would not be a candidate for election on the present occasion. After twenty years of unremitting toil I feel the preservation of my health demands a period of relaxation. And most gladly would I now retire from parliamentary life – at least for a season. But I feel in this I cannot be my own master. Political connections and ties have grown up around me which I cannot sever in a day. And there are responsibilities which, when public men assume them, must not be shrunk from – at any sacrifice to themselves. At such a moment I cannot think it would be right in me to withdraw from the good cause any service I can render it."[38] It was a lofty declaration that brought cheers; but it was scarcely in the spirit that wins elections.

The candidate went off to the country for a few more days of rest before beginning his campaign, and returned on June 17 to speak to the largest indoor political meeting yet held in Toronto, before a Liberal audience of one thousand in St. Lawrence Hall. Mowat and Connor spoke also, but the chief effort was Brown's. This time there was nothing faltering or resigned about him, as he held forth on the population question and the wrongs done Upper Canada. She had 60,000 more inhabitants than Lower Canada in 1851, he proclaimed, had waited ten years under eastern domination, now had five times that lead – and still was denied justice! Were 300,000 westerners to remain disfranchised – because of the treachery of John A. Macdonald and his clique?[39] It was all rapturously received. In fact, Brown's old vitality seemed to come flooding back that evening, stirred as he was by the big, excited audience.

Just two nights later he was back at the hall again, to address a very different meeting in company with his Conservative opponent in the election, John Crawford.[40] It was a gathering of both parties, the kind of situation made for trouble. Reformers filled the back of the main floor and the gallery, but in the front and around the platform sat a solid phalanx of Conservatives, a band of some thirty to forty rowdies noisily prominent among them. As soon as Mayor Bowes had opened the proceedings, the meeting began to fall apart. Amid hoots and catcalls, a shaky Mr. Allan tried stumblingly to introduce George Brown – then had his notes snatched away by Tories clambering onto the platform. The two candidates came forward; a wild contest of cheers and jeers filled the hall. Allan was still trying, and the Mayor was already calling frantically for an adjournment, when the fun-loving roughs still on the platform tried to push Brown off as he arrived. He fought back; more of them rushed up; over went the Mayor's table; down to the reporters' desk below crashed Brown; while Grits howling vengeance came racing down the aisles.

Highland blood up, torn coat flapping fiercely, Brown led a Liberal charge that almost reconquered the platform. But out stepped Constable Jones of the Grand Trunk, and with a huge push tumbled them all back to the floor. For good measure his friend Murphy swung at Brown's head with a cudgel, but Brown had rammed his hat on in the first attack and the blow only smashed a good Victorian top-hat – a useful safety helmet for the politics of the day. At this point the police arrived, and the Mayor managed to convince the candidates that it was useless to go on. The rival forces marched out, the Reformers chanting, "On to the *Globe*!" There on the steps of the office their battered leader addressed them, ruined hat, ripped coat and all. He appeared "considerably exhausted", the press remarked next day.[41]

Thereafter the campaign was less strenuous, though the round of smaller meetings at taverns and hotels was taxing enough for Brown. Moreover, it was not going very well. He could not make the efforts he once could; his meetings were fewer and shorter. Then on June 28 he lost the show of hands at the official public nomination of the opposing candidates (still deemed a matter of considerable psychological importance), apparently because the Conservatives had brought in a large body of their West Toronto voters to strengthen their showing in the East Toronto test.[42] A long procession of Grand Trunk employees also appeared with banners flying to support Crawford, the son of one director of the line and the partner of another.[43]

The Reform contender launched into a last urgent rush of meetings before the two days of voting began on July 5. But when the polls closed on that date he was thirty-four votes behind.[44] This was the ominous, the often fatal sign: undecided electors had their minds made up for them by the outcome of the first day of polling. At the end of the second day George Brown was in the minority by 191.[45] He was beaten. He had entered parliament in the elections of 1851; he left it in elections just ten years later.

There were good reasons for Brown's defeat, among them his failure to accomplish his policies since the last general election. He had failed to establish a lasting ministry in 1858 and to achieve representation by population. He had failed to advance his federation scheme in 1860, and again had not settled the discords in the union – nor even in his own party. Now Conservatives like Crawford, who himself espoused rep by pop, were contending that they could meet Upper Canada's needs far better than the Grits, since they assuredly had proved that they could win and hold power in the country.[46] Then, too, there was the fact that, if Brown's alliance with McGee might bring him some

Roman Catholic support, his earlier record still kept other Roman Catholics away from him. Finally, a powerful pivot group in West Toronto, the Methodists, remembered his stand in opposition to Victoria and to denominational colleges generally on the university committee of 1860. They paid him back at the polls.[47]

Beyond all this, however, was the fact of Brown's illness, which had kept him out of the last session, made him a reluctant candidate, and vitiated much of his effort at campaigning. Nevertheless, after the initial shock of disappointment, the defeated candidate showed small regret for what might have been. His speech to the crowd at the official declarations on July 11, in the hot sun outside Toronto's City Hall, was almost thankful, and certainly amiable. "I believe there has never been an election conducted in this or any constituency more satisfactory for both parties than this has been," he told the crowd around him, charitably ignoring the recent battle at St. Lawrence Hall. "Mr. Crawford and I went into the contest good personal friends and I hope we come out of it as cordial as ever."[48]

Of course, he added, he regretted the result, for the sake of the friends who had supported and worked for him, and for the sake of the cause he fought for; but personally he was overjoyed that henceforth he could attend to his health and his personal interests. "I have now faithfully discharged my duty to my party – my defeat has opened up the way for my retirement without dishonour – and I mean to take advantage of it!"[49] So passed George Brown, M.P.P. It remained to be seen how long his retirement might last, and to what use he would put his new freedom.

3

The whole election had been a disappointment for the western Reform party. Both Toronto seats were gone, for Adam Wilson had lost, as well as Brown. Mowat, a Kingstonian in origin, though now identified with Toronto, had also failed to capture his native city from John A. Macdonald, and several other old reliable Brownites had not been re-elected. Still, it had by no means been a Liberal rout. While there were a number of new men and moderates who were claimed by both sides, the strength of government and opposition would likely be close to equal in Upper Canada: thirty definite ministerialists to twenty-nine decided Reformers, with the remainder probably dividing to give a narrow margin of support to the government.[50] Moreover, Mowat and Wilson had both been returned in their old ridings of South Ontario and North York, each having run in two constituencies; and other prominent Liberals, such as McDougall, Howland, Connor, Foley, and Sandfield Macdonald, were safely back. It was worthy of comment, besides, that George Brown's old lieutenant in Lambton County, the faithful Alexander Mackenzie, had now won entrance to parliament, replacing his brother Hope for Lambton when ill-health forced the latter to retire.

Nevertheless, the Grit Liberals had not only failed to increase their power in parliament, but also lost their clear majority of Upper Canada's seats. What had caused the set-back? To some extent, the same things that had worked to defeat their leader personally: the failure to achieve Reform policies since 1858, the damaging disputes in the party in 1860, and Brown's own inability to give leadership in 1861. Then the Reform thrust for rep by pop had lost some of its efficacy, since the government had made it an "open" question in the election, thus enabling individual western Conservative candidates to advocate it for themselves, even if their cabinet leaders did not. But finally, the Grits in the last session had presented the ministry with a splendid stick to use against their own heads – and used it was, to the full. It had been William McDougall's doing, once again too quick in his own cock-sure cleverness for the good of his party.

Carried away by a need for emphasis during the debate on rep by pop, McDougall had darkly warned that Upper Canadians had waited ten years for justice, and would not wait another ten. They might "look below the border for relief".[51] The government benches had been shocked, too horribly shocked to accept any explanations for the remark. Why spoil a good thing? It was ideal for elections, as John A. Macdonald saw. He informed Egerton Ryerson, just before the campaign began: "The cry is 'Union', 'No looking to Washington', and 'University Reform'."[52] Here was something for everybody, even for the disgruntled Methodist supporters of Victoria College. And "No looking to Washington", loudly reiterated, effectively blackened the Reform crusade for Upper Canada's rights, whether it made sense or not. Besides, the appeal to British loyalty overrode any lingering Orange resentments of the ministry left over from the Prince's visit. That University Reform was even emptier of meaning, of course, was neither here nor there.[53] The point was, the slogans worked.

And so the Liberal-Conservatives checked the trend towards

the steady increase of Reform power in Upper Canada – temporarily, as it turned out. In Lower Canada, however, the elections had been far less favourable to the Coalition forces. If giving a nod to rep by pop had won the Liberal-Conservatives votes in the West, it had lost them votes in the East, where French Canadians, facing the stark facts of the census, dreaded the least concession to a principle that would inevitably swamp them.[54] Cartier's powerful block of *Bleus* had shrunk from forty-eight to some thirty-five, and the regular Lower Canadian opposition had gone up from fifteen to twenty-six or so.[55] Yet this did not mean that the *Rouges* had been greatly strengthened thereby. Dorion himself had been defeated, though McGee was safe. No, eastern Reformers who had been associated, however loosely, with a western party that demanded rep by pop had not done well in a keenly anxious French Canada, determined to defend race, language, and religion.

Instead, it was moderate Liberals and dissentient *Bleus* who had swelled the eastern opposition: men dissatisfied with Cartier's leadership, not by any means because they would concede representation by population, but because they feared lest Cartier's own bold but intransigent conduct might actually point the way to that disaster.[56] His typical response to debate on the representation question had been to settle it with big battalions. His classic contemptuous answer to vexing opposition attacks – "call in the members" – wholly expressed his own forthright fighting spirit. But some Lower Canadians had apparently come to feel that this stark exemplification of the power of eastern votes would ultimately unite the whole West in anger, until the demand for rep by pop could no longer be resisted. During the last session, in fact, McDougall had noted the growth of discontent with Cartier in French-speaking circles, and reported it to Brown.[57] One likely focus for it might be Louis Victor Sicotte, a prominent if crotchety oppositionist who had once been a *Rouge*, was then a Coalition minister, and now might best be termed a moderate Liberal of a shimmering shade of mauve.

All in all, if Brown and his friends had not triumphed in the election, then neither had Macdonald and Cartier. They were in office still; they had an over-all majority. But their failure to win decisively in Upper Canada, their crumbling position in Lower, meant that the movement of only a few of their more uncertain supporters into opposition could bring the Coalition crashing down at last. With this in mind, accordingly, and at the behest of his own followers, George Brown made certain political inquiries of Dorion by letter, shortly after the elections closed in mid-July. Neither man would be in the next House.

They had each refused to take other "safe" seats offered them. Yet they were still the Liberal leaders for the present, and hence conducted the negotiations.

The western captain carefully outlined the Upper Canadian balance of seats as it now appeared, and asked Dorion for a similar assessment of the situation in Lower Canada. Could a common opposition policy be adopted, one that could swing over the uncertain quantities in the Assembly by its very display of unity — and thus turn out the ministry? To secure a solid western following, there was really only one line such a policy could take: reform of the representative system. "The Upper Canada Reformers," Brown noted, "can enter no government that is not pledged to take up this question with the sincere determination of framing a measure that, while assuring justice to the 300,000 unrepresented people of U.C., will at the same time protect your countrymen from that interference with their local matters so much dreaded or affected to be dreaded."[58]

Dorion sent back both a personal letter and an official party answer. The first was a friendly return to Brown's own private covering note. The second was a flat rejection of the western leader's proposal for the renewal of Reform unity. "The great and perhaps only difficulty in the way of that united party," he asserted formally, "is, as you are aware, the question of representation. There is no party in Lower Canada who while in opposition could attempt to submit a proposition or agree to a plan for the settlement of this question on a basis which would meet the views of the Upper Canada majority without completely destroying itself as a party. The difficulties are now much greater than they were in 1858."[59] In other words, the results of the census had hardened Lower Canadian opinion far beyond the time of the Brown-Dorion administration, when that government had actually combined the leaders of both sections of Liberalism behind an agreement on rep by pop. Furthermore, as Dorion went on to observe, the Coalition ministers were now claiming in Lower Canada that they had beaten the evil scheme, and that it surely would be abandoned. "I can well conceive the advantages of having an opposition united on all questions of public policy," he concluded, "but with the present feeling in Lower Canada the difficulties appear to be insuperable."[60]

The *Rouge* leader's personal letter in no way differed from this unhopeful stand; but the comments he added were illuminating. Brown had privately urged him to re-enter the House, even to take the Upper Canadian seat of North Waterloo — one of two constituencies won by Foley.[61] But the calm, perceptive Dorion had no intention of seeking a place in this new parliament. He expected no good from it. For, if the existing government fell, some other attempt at meaningless coalition would only follow; and then, as he said, "failure and confusion until the parties are thoroughly reorganized through another appeal to the people".[62] It was wise to stay outside until the current tendencies had played themselves out. "This parliament will not last long, and it is better for us that the moderates of all shades should try their hands, in order that the country should be convinced of their incompetency to settle the difficulties accumulated by seven years of mismanagement."[63]

Here was shrewd prediction and advice, a sound answer to Brown's gesture for Liberal unity. The time was not right. The next period properly belonged to moderates who abjured constitutional change: the Sandfield Macdonalds and Louis Sicottes, who thought that new men in a new combination, freed from the "extremists", could somehow satisfy both sections and make the present union work. Let the moderate men try, and in trying prove their bankruptcy – along with that of the union itself. Brown could afford to wait. He could no longer be used as an excuse for the persistence of sectional friction, the reputed trouble-maker blamed for all the discord in the union's politics. Dorion had given him a further excellent reason for retirement.

He had made his gesture for party reconstruction. He now withdrew from further political activity, refusing invitations to party rallies in August on the grounds that the Toronto election had "relieved me of public responsibility, and I think it best to enjoy the full benefit of the period of relaxing at my disposal".[64] That is, he would relax from politics, so far as the owner of the *Globe* and the ertswhile leader of Reform could ever find this possible.

4

Wonderful changes were occurring in Upper Canada's far south-west, Brown's favourite countryside. Oilfields were being developed not twenty miles from Sarnia in Lambton County, his old constituency, and near Bothwell in the adjoining county of Kent: the settlement that had grown up out of his own estate. In September, the *Globe* ran a series of long articles on the "Oil Region" that was rapidly coming into production.[65] "Rock oil" – petroleum – had gained a new significance in two short years since 1859, when Edwin Drake had drilled a well in Pennsyl-

vania to tap rich sources far underground. Henceforth, instead
of the limited, scanty offerings of shallow pools and hand-dug
wells, drilled wells promised to provide an ample flow of petroleum for commercial uses: above all, to replace the whale-oil of
a lamp-lit civilization. The resulting boom in rock oil had
brought a spate of advertisements in the Canadian press
("Beauty, Brilliancy, Economy – NOT Explosive") and produced a flurry of well-drilling in Upper Canada in those parts
where surface oil pools had long been known and utilized.[66]

Enniskillen Township in Lambton and lands along the
Thames a few miles from Bothwell were notable areas of this
kind. Here Indians had prized the dark and scummy oil pools
for their medicinal value, and had dipped blankets in their
surface, wringing them out to obtain the oil. It was said that
natives who swallowed this "lion's grease" never took the cholera
– or rather, never died of cholera, which was not quite the
same thing.[67] But now this land of pools was prized far more
highly, as, in happy bewilderment, settlers who had replaced
the wandering Indians saw speculators lease portions of their
farms and drill wells in frantic haste. An ugly litter of rough
pole derricks, squat black oil vats, piles of barrels, and greasy
mounds of mud spread out through clearings in the still-enclos-
ing forests. The creak of the wooden treadles that drove the
drills continued day and night, and always there was the harsh
smell of oil and escaping gas.

Men with packsacks were tramping to the "oil springs" to
make their fortunes.[68] Teamsters were making theirs, as they
hauled wagon-loads of barrelled oil down jolting, rutted trails
to the railway line, where the Great Western's new oil cars were
waiting. Plank roads were going in; taverns and hotels were
going up. The far south-west was entering on a land boom
greater than anything it had yet known. And Bothwell, on the
railway, was ideally situated to enjoy it – there where Brown's
own lands lay. There could be little question now about his
credit, or the value of his holdings. The new questions facing
him were what to buy and when to sell, and when the boom
might reach its peak.

He bought 400 more acres, and for the time being held on.[69]
Apart from his sawmills, he enjoyed the working and developing of his Bothwell farm; in any case, the boom was still too
young to foresee how it might grow in that quarter. No doubt,
he went up to Kent and Lambton to watch the developments for
himself. In October, at any rate, he could see them gain fresh
impetus from the application of the new Pennsylvania technique
of deep drilling.[70] Wells were being sunk beyond 200 feet now,

instead of less than 100, and were producing a continuous flow of oil in large quantities. The remaining problems were the market and the price. Thanks to the lack of sufficient Canadian refineries, American imports were largely supplying the province's needs, and Canadian crude was worth but six and a half cents a gallon at railhead.

It was natural that Brown's *Globe* should hail the building of new refineries in Sarnia, London, Toronto, and elsewhere, and deem it "suicidal" for Torontonians with sensitive noses to try to block the building of still another refinery in the city.[71] It mused besides on the full meaning of the "recent remarkable discoveries" in the western peninsula. Where would they all lead? "We are apparently only at the beginning of a very remarkable change in the arrangements of civilized man for illuminating the darkness of the night – but none can say how far the revolution will go."[72] No one, indeed, could then have measured the oil revolution. Yet Canada, and Brown, were caught up in its first stirrings.

They were also caught up in something far less attractive and more ominous that autumn: the reverberations of the American Civil War. It had never been far from mind since the fighting had started in the spring. For Canadians, it was like a deep, unceasing drum-beat in the background: sometimes drowned by their own outcries over the census, rep by pop, or the general elections; sometimes swelling in its own crescendos, as during the first great battle of Bull Run in late July. Yet always it was there. Nor was it merely that Canadians were front-row spectators of an immense conflict. The war was rousing old antagonisms between the United States and Britain, between Americans and British subjects in America. And, more and more, the problem of their own defence began to loom as a serious question for Canadians, as the war and growing international tension went onward without sign of end.

They had lost much of their initial sympathy for the Northern cause, which had largely been based on their own strong aversion to slavery. When it became apparent that Lincoln and the Republicans did not, after all, intend to fight a war to free the slaves but rather to preserve the American union, the Canadians had felt disgruntled and confused. Many asked why it had been right for the thirteen original colonies to declare their independence, but wrong for the southern states to do the same. Some degree of sentiment favourable to the South emerged: either for resolute men struggling for their liberty, or for discontented states that had proved that the sprawling democratic republic was inherently unsound and must collapse. In short, either the left or right in Canadian political opinion could turn pro-Southern, though the trend became more noticeable in the Conservative press. Furthermore, the colonial views might often echo those of the Mother country, where the governing classes decidedly sympathized with the "gentlemanly" South — although leading British middle-class Liberals like Richard Cobden and John Bright, with strong working-class support, maintained their faith in the democracy of the American North, and in its ultimate decision to abolish slavery.[73]

There were other reasons, too, for a Canadian reaction against the North. The Americans' rather irritating tendency to identify their own purposes with Divine plan had led them to angry denunciations of the British, who at home and in America had not shown proper willingness to aid the sword of the Lord in putting down most foul rebellion.[74] They had not opened the colonies' skimpy stock of arms for Northern use; they had even presumed to invoke neutrality in the struggle.[75] And mounting American resentment showed itself further in renewed talk of wresting British North America from England. The powerful New York *Herald* had pushed the project quite cold-bloodedly, either as a means of reuniting the divided states in a war against the old national enemy, or as a consolation prize to the North for letting the South go.[76] This sort of talk might be discounted as so much American press bluster, except that it expressed a genuine growth of animosity to Britain in the United States. It even seemed to be reflected in the policies of Lincoln's Secretary of State, William Seward, who in the early months of the war toyed with notions of his own for exploiting anti-British sentiment, and by no means kept them hidden.[77]

Consequently, as British-American relations deteriorated almost steadily throughout 1861, and as Canadian and American newspapers snapped at each other across the border, it was all the more noteworthy that the largest provincial journal, George Brown's *Globe*, continued to support the North in the Civil War. Not that his paper failed to criticize the Americans, to answer their attacks on Britain, or to scorn their wild proposals to annex Canada. Yet, like Brown's own archetypes of middle-class British Liberalism, Cobden and Bright, the *Globe* continued to believe in the essential rightness of the Northern cause, and in the absence of any real grounds for a war between Britain and the United States.

Plainly, the explanation lay in Brown himself. His personal and business ties with the Northern states were many; and he had repeatedly visited New York, not only to transact *Globe* business but also to stay with his sister and brother-in-law, Jane and

George Mackenzie, who were firmly rooted in that city. Furthermore, his first six years in America, spent in New York, had
given him a deep appreciation of the ordinary American's sense
of freedom, his self-reliance and innate decency, even though
the excessive sweep of elective institutions might make his democratic government unstable or irresponsible. But despite the
shortcomings of republican rule, Brown as a Liberal warmly
believed in the value of the huge American democratic experi-
ment for all mankind.[78] It must not fail. And, inevitably, the
blot of slavery must be erased from it. His own abolitionism,
begun in youth in Scotland, had simply been made more ardent
by his years in the United States. Certainly it did not flag in
Canada thereafter, as his prominent part in Toronto's Anti-
Slavery Society made fully evident.

Thus it was that Brown and his journal stayed firmly by the
North in battle: because it fought to save a vast enterprise of
freedom, and because it would yet become the means of expung-
ing slavery from half a continent. They denied that the chaotic
Federal retreat from Bull Run meant that the fight would soon
end in Confederate victory. They assured exulting pro-Southern
journals in Canada that there still would be a desperate struggle,
but that the North would win.[79] They discounted alarmist talk
of the danger of invasion, and of the Federals' plans to turn
their armies against the British provinces when the Civil War
was over, contending that the United States was bending all its
energies to the internal conflict, and would have had quite
enough of warfare when that was done.[80] By these determined
efforts Brown and his paper did much to sustain pro-Northern
opinion in Canada. Others did so as well, for the North had by
no means lost all its support in the province. Yet the *Globe*'s
influence was so extensive that it must have played a major part
in countering pro-Southern leanings among Canadians. It was no
easy part, in any case – especially when, in mid-November
1861, a major crisis suddenly broke out between the United
States and Britain.

The Federal frigate *San Jacinto* had stopped the British mail
steamer *Trent* in mid-Atlantic, and high-handedly seized two
Confederate commissioners aboard, Mason and Slidell, who
were being sent as their government's emissaries to France and
England. It was a blatant violation of neutral rights; but the
Northern press, eager for a hero at a dull moment in the war,
loudly applauded gallant Captain Wilkes of the *San Jacinto*.
On the other hand, when the news reached England on November 27, the British press howled quite as loudly over the outrage
to the British flag, never so sacred as on the high seas. It was a

dangerous situation, if scarcely worth a war. Yet the United States government was all but committed by the surge of anti-British public feeling, and the British government could hardly do less than demand that the insolent republic surrender the two commissioners.

British North America learned of the *Trent* affair before England did, and loyally and utterly condemned Captain Wilkes. There was indignant, gusty talk of the need for Britain to teach the Yankees a lesson, but at first no widespread expectation of war. The *Globe* itself, while denouncing the Wilkes coup as wrong and stupid ("a bit of bravado – a foolish flout"), held that neither Britain nor the United States wanted war, and saw the "only possible danger" in popular hysteria.[81] Earnestly it counselled moderation, cautious waiting at least till Britain's official response could be made known.[82] Yet as Canadians awaited that response through tense days in early December, the pro-Southern papers were anything but moderate; and, as anti-British diatribes mounted in the neighbouring American press, the colonists grew sharply aware of how thoroughly exposed their own position was beside the armed and hostile republic. "The cry of war rings throughout the land," the *Globe* uneasily admitted on December 10. "At the corner of every street you hear excited discussions as to the Mason and Slidell outrage, the next news from England, the erection of forts, and the problems of a fight with the Americans."

If it had to come, those who had tried hardest for peace would not be slow to draw the sword.[83] So Brown resolutely affirmed; but, in the meantime, he turned his journal against the recklessly pro-Southern papers in the province (mainly Conservative), bitterly attacking them for war-mongering.[84] The most fire-eating of all was the largest ministerial journal, the *Leader*; and its replies to Brown were quite as strong as his attacks. There was good cause, too. Charles Lindsey, for years and with only a few breaks the chief editor of the *Leader*, had had to step aside again through illness. And who had replaced him? George Sheppard, who had recently returned to Canada a violent Southern partisan, after writing for secessionist papers in Washington at the close of 1860, and thereafter in Richmond, the capital of the Confederate States of America.[85] "Jeff Davis's Agent", the *Globe* bluntly named him.[86] The Brown-Sheppard feud was readily renewed, and swiftly it descended to personalities.

Brown was "disloyal", a shameless Yankee-lover pandering to the North.[87] Sheppard was a miserable turncoat, a one-time annexationist who was still quite prepared to see Canada destroyed.[88] The *Globe* traced Sheppard's many shifts and swings, the number of papers that had died under him. The *Leader* printed old and new charges against Brown: that he had absconded from Scotland, defrauded creditors in New York, intrigued "with a foreign government", and was now debt-ridden and insolvent.[89] Brown promptly brought an action of libel against the *Leader*'s owner, James Beaty.[90] And as the North-South conflict raged between the two chief newspapers of Upper Canada, it seemed that the *Trent* affair might almost be forgotten in their vicarious Civil War at home.

Meanwhile, however, the crisis was coming to a head. The anxiously awaited news from Britain at last arrived in Canada on December 16 – by courtesy of George Brown: he had bought exclusive Canadian telegraph rights for the occasion.[91] When the fast steamship *Europa* docked in New York with the crucial report of Britain's official rejoinder to the *Trent* affair, the *Globe* gave it to the Canadian people before any other paper or official source. Its headlines were black, in type and meaning: "Intelligence Very Warlike!" "Law Officers Declare Seizure Illegal! – Reparations Demanded! – 10,000 troops for Canada!"[92] Nevertheless, Brown's paper still dared hope that war would be avoided, for it observed that the precise British demands on the American government would not be known until presented at Washington. If Britain asked, quite justly, for the surrender of the Confederate commissioners, then surely the United States would have the good sense to accede?[93]

Hence there was more waiting. But now war fever was at a peak on both sides of the Canadian-American border, and Brown and his journal no longer wholly escaped it. As British troopships steamed full speed westward against the freezing of the St. Lawrence, and as the Canadian government called for 40,000 volunteers, the *Globe* was vigorously exhorting: "Boats for the Lakes, Men for the Boats" – conscious that Upper Canada might only be saved from American conquest by a re-established Great Lakes fleet.[94] "Form, Riflemen, Form", it cried, while in the general turmoil the old crumbling fort at Toronto was hurriedly reoccupied and repaired.[95] Sir Fenwick Williams, commander of the forces in British North America, advocated sinking block-ships across Toronto Harbour.[96] Port Dover was planning heavy fortifications; Simcoe and Dundas sought batteries of artillery, while throughout the province hastily armed militiamen were drilling.[97] It was a grimly ominous, cold Christmas, as the *Globe* wondered gloomily how many now at the fireside would be in the battlefield next year.[98] Still, it talked bravely of peaceful settlement, and of certain British victory if war should really come. But its fears for Canada were much in evidence indeed.

Then suddenly, on December 30, "Peace!" The peril was over: "All doubt is at an end." Britain in a judiciously worded note had asked for the release of Mason and Slidell. The American government, no less judiciously, had accepted that necessity. Canada was jubilant – but much, much more relieved. And so, of course, were Brown and the *Globe*, who now found salutary lessons in the vanishing crisis. Canadians, they said with satisfaction, could see in Britain's swift dispatch of troops a sure and ample pledge of aid, if war should ever threaten them again. Americans would understand that Canada stood solidly with Britain, and Britain with her – that talk of annexation, willing or otherwise, was futile. And the British equally should recognize that Canada, which would bear the brunt of conflict and destruction if the Empire ever warred with the United States, stood staunchly ready to accept her role.[99] This last, indeed, was almost the prime consideration, as Brown and the paper reflected on the defence question, which the *Trent* affair had thrust into the foreground and which seemed likely to remain there, as long as the Civil War and its accompanying stress should last.

5

There was a major public meeting in Toronto on December 31, to discuss the problem of colonial defence; but Brown did not attend. He was ill again, confined to his room for nearly two weeks more.[100] Conceivably, the strain of the crisis and perhaps the row with Sheppard had proved too much for his health. Yet there were some consolations. Early in January of 1862, the *Leader* announced that Mr. Sheppard had left its employ and ran an article disclaiming any governmental responsibility for its own late incendiary career.[101] It was apparent that Sheppard's course as editor had not been much appreciated either by proprietor James Beaty, who faced a suit for libel, or by a weak coalition ministry that had sufficient troubles without being stamped as far more warlike than the imperial government itself. The ill-fated Sheppard moved on again, this time to try his luck in Lower Canada at Quebec. But soon there would be one more shift, to the New York *Times*, where at last he would find an enduring haven for his undoubted journalistic talents.[102]

The libel action came up in February, when Adam Wilson

and Skeffington Connor argued the plaintiff's case before the justices.[103] Beaty, through his lawyer, M. C. Cameron, retracted most of the charges that had been made; namely, that Brown had skipped from Edinburgh with the money of widows and orphans, that he had intrigued with a foreign (presumably the American) government, that he had exploited friends to raise money for himself and now was hopelessly in debt. "Defrauding" American creditors was reduced to leaving New York without paying all his debts. On this and a charge of "swindling" in four minor business transactions they stood ready to justify a case. The justices rejected the first plea a few weeks later, and the second was set aside by mutual agreement.[104] Thus the grand press libel suit evaporated, like so many others of the day. But Brown had forced his attackers to give most of their ground, and once more exhibited his own swift readiness to fight for his personal reputation.

Of much more public interest through the troubled winter of 1862 was the question of colonial defence. As a postscript, or perhaps an anticlimax, to the *Trent* affair, the troops sent from Britain to reinforce the small imperial garrison of regulars continued to arrive throughout January and February. The bulk of them had been compelled to land in Maritime ports because of the St. Lawrence ice barrier, and to proceed to Canada in long sleigh convoys through the empty, snowy wilderness of upland New Brunswick. The lack of effective year-round communications between Canada and Britain's Atlantic provinces was thus graphically displayed.

The long-debated project for an Intercolonial Railway to join Halifax with Quebec received new impetus from this practical indication of its need. The scheme had never completely lapsed, ever since the breakdown of negotiations between the British American provinces and the imperial government in 1851 had led instead to the building of Canada's own Grand Trunk. There had been further Intercolonial missions to the Mother Country in the decade thereafter, largely pressed by Maritime enthusiasts – and explained by the Toronto *Globe* as chiefly useful for "the possible presentation at court of Mrs. Bluenose and the Misses Bluenose".[105] But now it seemed that both the colonies and Britain might be readier to shoulder the heavy financial outlay for such a line, because of its political and military value. Actually, there was an Intercolonial mission waiting on the Colonial Office when the *Trent* affair occurred, and the delegates had not been slow to point out the necessity of the railway for successful British North American defence.[106]

If Brown had not necessarily opposed the Intercolonial in

itself, he had given it a very low priority. Now in February of 1862, as the ministerial press was exclaiming over the project, he used the *Globe* to criticize its "fictitious importance".[107] It would no doubt serve to tighten "the friendly bonds which already unite us to our kindly fellow countrymen", and could be a boon to Nova Scotia and New Brunswick.[108] Yet the line would never be a great highway to the sea: the St. Lawrence furnished that. And, while it would have some military merit, the Americans still might cut it at the narrow neck of land where Quebec met New Brunswick. Above all, the huge costs to Canada of building such a line would be a poor exchange for her development towards the North West: "The Red River route has a ten times better claim than the country through which the Intercolonial Railroad passes," declared the *Globe* emphatically.[109]

That was the crux of it. George Brown would not have eastern extension at the cost of westward expansion. His faith in the North West and Canada's future there was quite as strong as ever. The *Globe* had never ceased to run articles on the value of the North West beyond the Lakes, and now on the mounting dangers of American penetration into that region. Moreover, there was cause indeed to think that the Intercolonial scheme would either replace or still further postpone Canada's acquisition of the Hudson's Bay territories. The governing Coalition had shown little real concern – and, in French Canada, actual distaste – for North West expansion. Yet the Montreal business power associated with the government might contemplate the extension of its empire into the nearby Maritimes. More specifically, the huge bankrupt Grand Trunk enterprise was hopefully viewing the Intercolonial as a means of redeeming itself – at further substantial cost to the taxpayer.[110]

The new president of Grand Trunk, Edward Watkin, a clever, confident Englishman most appreciative of his own abilities, had recently come out to view the "organized mess" of the railway (his own term), and concluded that its one salvation lay in dazzling extensions to east and west, until it became the first transcontinental line linking Europe and the Orient across America.[111] But the opening step would be eastward extension, through having the Intercolonial built jointly by the provinces with imperial support. Consequently, Brown still further refused to sanction the Intercolonial as essential to colonial development or defence. He cherished too many suspicions of costly Grand Trunk projects, and of the patriotic and plausible Mr. Watkin, who, as the *Globe* averred, "fanned the flame which is always kept burning on the railway altars in Halifax and Saint John [until] the conflagration has spread through three provinces".[112]

Brown's own concern for defence lay with measures more immediately needed to protect the long inland flank of Canada, that is, with the provision of an effective militia force to supplement the British regulars in the country.[113] At present the colonial force existed largely on paper, the "sedentary militia" in which all able-bodied male inhabitants were enrolled, and which had met and drilled – more or less – once a year on the annual muster day. There was, besides, a small body of active militia with a little more claim to training, exemplified in the local volunteer companies that had been hurriedly embodied during the *Trent* crisis. But clearly the entire militia system needed overhauling, to provide for an efficient active force on a province-wide foundation. To that end, a militia commission had been named in January of 1862 by the new Governor-General, Lord Monck, who had replaced Sir Edmund Head shortly before the *Trent* affair. While it studied the problem in order to prepare for new militia legislation, the Canadian press and public concerned themselves with the drilling of the volunteer companies, and the proper principles of military organization.[114]

Brown recognized the importance of sound military organization. He saw that the early course of the American war had demonstrated the fallacy of believing that free citizens bearing arms made soldiers in themselves. That February he wrote thoughtfully to Luther Holton, who was far more uncritically pro-Northern than himself: "After all, have not the events of the past few months rather lowered your estimate of our neighbours? Has it not shown that there is something more needed to make up a great people than sharpness in business and agreeable social qualities? Has it not raised your estimate of the value of military power; of the faculty of commanding masses of men? Has it not proved the advantages of the people being taught to obey those placed in authority over them? I wish we had a chance to talk this over."[115]

On the other hand, while he wanted a thoroughly trained militia, it was to be based on volunteering. "The volunteer system," he asserted, "which has been attended with such wonderful success in Britain, is equally well adapted to Canada."[116] Furthermore, while provincials should look "to the Volunteer Force to meet the invader", it was clear that the militia's task would still be to assist, not to replace, the British regular.[117] In short, Brown still foresaw only a limited peace-time military commitment for Canada, the provision of a select and well-trained volunteer militia – all, in any case, that a small colonial population could afford.[118]

Conceiving as he did that any possible war with the United

States would arise through the clash of American with imperial, not provincial, interests, there seemed little wrong with the view that the primary task of defending Canada remained with Great Britain.[119] The colony was proud and happy to see the imperial bond retained. She would fight for it, accept her chances of wartime devastation. But she was still a colony, guided by a great power that controlled foreign policy and thus had the first responsibility for its consequences.[120] In this, Brown's concept of the imperial relationship, there was no desire to foist all obligations off on Britain, nor any wish for a larger scope for Canada in managing her own affairs. He simply took the situation as it was, while the colony was weak and the Mother Country strong, and assumed a division of the duties of colonial defence, with the Canadians clearly taking the secondary part. His assumptions might look reasonable enough. But they would be sharply tested before the Civil War was over.

6

A bill to reorganize the militia would come before the next session of parliament; and parliament was now called for March 20. Before that date, however, the discussion of defence measures had largely subsided, not to regain prominence until the Militia Bill was actually introduced. Tensions with the United States had slackened for the time being, and there were interesting domestic developments to capture Canadian attention once more.

The difficulties of the Cartier-Macdonald régime were now fully in the open. They centred in Upper Canada, where John A. Macdonald was again facing the need to reconstruct the western half of the ministry. Three of his ministers, Vankoughnet, Ross, and Morrison, were thoroughly used up and anxious to retire. Morrison, in fact, had not managed to get himself a seat in parliament in more than two years of trying. Really, Macdonald had gone through an amazing string of colleagues in keeping office since 1854. As the *Globe* unkindly put it, "Mr. Macdonald is a kind of political ogre who demands a virgin reputation every year at least, to satisfy his needs, and casts aside his victim when every shred of popularity and character has disappeared."[121] The Attorney-General's critical problem, however, was not just the need for "fresh new eggs, after the old are sucked dry".[122] It was to deal with the embarrassing growth of sentiment for representation by population among his own Conservative following.

Macdonald himself still wholly rejected the principle, almost as strenuously as his Lower Canadian associates in government; but increasingly his own party was dividing on the issue. To hold it together, he might well have to take pledged advocates of rep by pop into the cabinet, dangerous as that would seem to the taut and suspicious *Bleus* of Lower Canada. If he did not do so, John Hillyard Cameron might gain control of the rep-by-pop Conservatives: Cameron, the powerful right-wing Tory who had once been his closest rival for party leadership, and who had now returned to politics and become Orange Grand Master besides. The result could well be a fatal split in Conservatism, and the consequent fall of the Liberal-Conservative Coalition that had ruled virtually without a break for the past eight years.

Ever since the previous summer's elections the western government leader had faced this problem, but delayed as long as he dared. Now, as parliament assembled in Quebec, and there were still no new ministers, he could procrastinate no longer. While the *Globe* hopefully announced that he was at Bull Run – or perhaps Waterloo – Macdonald made his changes.[123] Vankoughnet, Morrison, and Ross readily resigned, the first two going to their just reward, the judicial bench, the third to spend more time at his Grand Trunk offices as president of the railway's Canadian board. And three rep-by-pop Conservatives were sworn in: John Carling, James Patton, and John Beverley Robinson. Yet, as Macdonald assured the House, this did not involve a change in government policy. Representation by population remained an open question for all to vote on as they would. In short, he was on a tight-rope, but still had hopes of walking it.

The Reformers naturally sought to push him off, by bringing up rep by pop to divide and distress the ministerial forces. Foley had now been officially named leader by the party caucus, though his role seemed largely nominal. (Indeed, William McDougall wrote Brown: "You must lead still, or we will make a poor fight.")[124] It was actually McDougall who took the initiative in parliament in pressing rep by pop, even driving on Foley and his friends. John Hillyard Cameron brought in a similar motion. After sharp debate, both measures were defeated on April 1 by the united weight of Lower Canada; but there were only sixteen western votes behind the ministry on each motion.[125] Upper Canada itself gave a solid majority of twenty-seven for reform in the representation. Party lines were dissolving in sheer sectionalism, and surely neither the Cartier-Macdonald government nor the union itself could carry on much longer.

At this point the militia commission made public its report. It called for an active force of 50,000 men, a reserve of the same number, and, moreover, accepted the principle of draft or conscription when necessary to secure the requisite contingents from country districts. Canadians generally were surprised, even startled, by the size of the scheme, and its recognition of a principle that they regarded as both alien and ineffective. Publishing the report on April 10, the *Globe* was still more emphatic. It could not believe that the government could contemplate a bill on this cumbersome basis, and, above all, load such heavy new expenses on debt-burdened Canada. It might do for the British exchequer, but for the empty provincial treasury it was "totally indefensible", far beyond the country's capabilities and duty.[126] Plainly, the militia legislation would have a hard time, especially when a critical phase in Canadian-American relations had passed, and there was no longer the sense of imminent war abroad.

Nevertheless, on May 2, John A. Macdonald brought in the required Militia Bill, doubling in another post as the new Minister of Militia Affairs. He was suavely and carefully vague on details, on precise costs; but, under relentless opposition probing, the government had to admit that the first year of the scheme alone would cost close to half a million dollars.[127] The country was startled anew; the bill made little progress. The *Globe* gleefully reported that it had "stuck in the mud".[128] Meanwhile, the by-elections for the new western ministers were held, and one of them, James Patton, was defeated. This came partly through the intervention of George Brown who, urged by his party, briefly stepped off the side-lines to speak in the campaign.[129] A weak and battered ministry was in its last extremity. And, if it fell, the Militia Bill would be only the occasion, not the cause.

It did fall. On May 20, when Macdonald moved the second reading of the Militia Bill, the ministry lost the vote without debate, 61 to 54.[130] Essentially it lost because a group of *Bleus* abandoned it to vote with the opposition, themselves convinced that the scheme was excessive, extravagant, and wrong in principle – but also probably resenting the inroads rep by pop had made in western ministerial ranks.[131] Edward Watkin of the Grand Trunk was at the House the next day, when the Liberal-Conservative government resigned, and just afterwards button-holed a furious ex-premier, George Etienne Cartier, to express his regret. Replied Cartier with eyes flashing and fists clenched: "Well, I have saved the honour of my country against those Grits and *Rouges – traîtres, traîtres*."[132] But, Watkin noted, "Mr. J. A. Macdonald, afterwards, took the matter very quietly, merely remarking that the slightest tact might have prevented the occurrence."[133] Whatever the case, both the passionate and the politic were out of office at last. It remained to be seen what new combination could be put together to run the province.

7

It might appear that the most likely way to form a new administration would be to call on the leader of the largest Liberal group in opposition, Michael Foley. But Foley, who had only been awarded the leadership after Mowat and McDougall had both refused it, had pretty conclusively proved his incapacity for command during the session, and ended in violent, open quarrels with his colleagues.[134] Yet it still seemed strange when the Governor-General instead approached Sandfield Macdonald, that temperamental, stiff-necked individualist who was, as he rather prided himself, a kind of political Ishmaelite in Upper Canada Reform. Nevertheless, perhaps his very isolation would make it easier for a new combination to gather around him. In any event, he was more than willing to try.

Certainly the Lower Canada opposition would not have joined readily with any thoroughgoing Grit Liberal, and whole-hearted advocate of rep by pop. And Sandfield Macdonald, of course, was not only an Upper Canada Reformer of undoubted seniority and standing, but also a tireless champion of his own pet scheme for keeping the existing union operating – the double majority principle. There was another possible explanation for his choice, a more Machiavellian one: that Cartier and John A. Macdonald, as retiring ministers, had advised the governor to call on Sandfield partly in an attempt to head off rep by pop, and partly in the expectation that he would have to call in Conservatives to fill out the Upper Canadian half of his ministry – so that, to all intents and purposes, the old Coalition rule would return once more.

Thoughts such as these must have run through George Brown's mind when on Wednesday, May 21, he learned by telegraph of Sandfield's opening negotiations at Quebec with Foley, McDougall, and Louis Sicotte for Lower Canada.[135] In the two days following, the Montreal Telegraph Company's line flashed a series of important messages back and forth between Quebec and *Globe* headquarters in Toronto. McDougall wired his former leader and old master on the journal, asking for advice. Should he enter a cabinet formed "on opposition principles?"[136] Brown, waiting for more news, which was coming through in snatches from the *Globe*'s Quebec reporter, J. K.

Edwards, hedged carefully, not yet certain of what this new ministry might mean. He could not advise McDougall on his own decision, he wired back; yet if reliable Reformers should compose the cabinet, and "policy on the representation question is satisfactory, I will cordially support the government".[137]

But then came a telegram from Edwards, giving both the settled list of ministers and a statement of the proposed government's policy received direct from Sandfield Macdonald.[138] McDougall, Foley, Howland, and Adam Wilson were all going in – and had agreed that representation by population would be dropped! Swiftly Brown cancelled his pledge of support. "Are you all mad there?" he telegraphed incredulously.[139] McDougall returned: "Not mad. If get fair play can make great reforms. Have done best possible as friends here believe you could not do more except allow corruptionists return. Do you advise this? Party after full discussion unanimously agree we ought to go in."[140]

The next few days brought a clearer picture, as Brown's Liberal associates at Quebec sent him long and rather defensive letters, all hastening to explain to the man who was still the party overlord – and controller of the potent *Globe* – the reasons why they had set aside their chief party principle. There had been an Upper Canada Reform caucus on May 23, which had approved the new ministry, or at least conceded it "a fair and liberal trial".[141] This, it seemed, was as far as the confused and reluctant Grits would go. It was a close vote, and far from the "unanimous" agreement that McDougall had breezily indicated. Summing up by mail, Edwards reported: "The party generally are surprised at McDougall and feel he has given them a hard dose to swallow, and their only reason for going into it is because they think anything is better than the late government."[142]

That, moreover, was the line taken by Oliver Mowat in writing to the *Globe* owner immediately after the caucus. Brown had confidence in Mowat. Foley had always been willing to enter a "moderate" Liberal government, constitutional reform or no, while Howland and Wilson were weak enough to be swayed in that direction. As for McDougall, inherently hasty and over-optimistic, he was simply doing what he had done years before, when in 1851 he had pushed the original Clear Grits into a futile combination with moderate Hincksites in a mistaken belief that once in power they could achieve "great reforms". Yet if the competent, substantial Mowat – rather stuffy perhaps, but wholly sound on rep by pop – could in any way accept this new and clearly retrogressive ministry, then possibly Brown might also swallow it.

Decidedly, Mowat was far from happy over the Sandfield

Macdonald–Sicotte administration. "On R by P," he noted gravely, "the new cabinet has a worse policy than the old."[143] The former at least had made it an open question, while this one would vote "all intentions inexpedient on the subject". Still, the issue for the moment, as Mowat saw it, was whether to sustain a cabinet drawn entirely from the opposition or to allow the old gang back. At the least, he expected such disclosures now from the investigation of the public accounts as would ruin the prestige of the former lot forever. Furthermore, he held that "no govt. to carry R. by P. could just now be formed".[144] Rep by pop would not die, he said; he and other Grits had explicitly informed the new ministers that they would press it unyieldingly. All in all, this was the only possible choice in a choice of evils: to accept a régime of the moderates for the present.

Correspondents other than Mowat argued more positively in favour of the Macdonald-Sicotte ministry. From the Upper House, Fergusson Blair (who had changed his name from simpler days when he was A. J. Fergusson, and George Brown's first follower in parliament) expressed his confidence that on everything but the representation question the government would prove excellent – "and the reign of corruption be brought to a close".[145] But probably Brown paid more attention to his old Lambton agent, Alexander Mackenzie, who, while still "a full private of recent standing" in parliament, had zealously identified himself as "an out-and-outer".[146] Mackenzie would accept the new Reform cabinet, bad as it was, because he believed that Sandfield Macdonald's original aim had been to bring Conservatives into a coalition with him. "I am tolerably well satisfied," he asserted, "that the only part of the *plan* which failed was the introduction of the intended Tory constituent."[147] Hence it was necessary to stand by the present set in office, and watch Sandfield like a hawk.

With this Brown had to rest for the moment. He did not question the integrity of those who approved the new ministry, though he continued to doubt their judgment. The *Globe* still condemned the abandoning of rep by pop, refusing to believe that better arrangements could not have been made if Upper Canadians had held to their principles.[148] Particularly it attacked "the monstrous doctrine" of the double majority set forth in the new cabinet's official statement of policy.[149] This viewed the union as a sort of bastard federation, wherein the particular affairs of each section would be managed in parliament by its own sectional majority, and no local legislation would be forced on either Canada against the majority vote of its own representatives. Perhaps the end was right; but the method was wrong. It offered the worst of two worlds: neither a true federation nor yet a real legislative union. Apart from that, the principle was clumsy and impractical, for it could well require a government to base itself on two antagonistic sectional majorities: Grits and *Bleus*, for instance – a position of paralysis, to say the least.

In any event, Brown had not yet made peace with his four Upper Canada associates who had jumped so readily into office alongside Sandfield Macdonald. On May 29, Foley and Wilson came to see him in Toronto and spent five hours explaining, until nearly one in the morning.[150] They must have looked and felt like schoolboys caught cheating, as they sat in the great man's study, a mixture of apology, penitence, and badgered defiance, enduring the lashing scorn of his tongue and the piercing thrust of his indignant questions. Yet they had to endure it, if for no other reason than that they faced by-elections as new members of the government and could hardly hope to be returned by western Reformers without the backing, or at least the tacit acceptance, of George Brown and the *Globe*.

As soon as they had gone, Brown poured out his feelings to one friend who had not been at all involved in the doings at Quebec: to Luther Holton, like himself still out of parliament although often urged to return. "The conclusion I have come to from all that they have told me," he wrote disgustedly, "is that a greater set of jackasses . . . was never got by accident into the government of any country."[151] They had told him that the cabinet's own so-called constitutional policy would be placed in formal resolutions before the next session of parliament, and ("Would you believe it?") vowed that "they themselves will do their utmost to have representation by population made part of the scheme, and if necessary will resign or take any other course the party will desire!"[152]

He would have given anything to have Holton there with him: "It is so hard to tell how to act. There is no doubt that if I go into it and stump the four counties three of them at any rate can be beaten! But it will split the party, and bring on once more a most disagreeable personal warfare, which I wish to avoid of all things. I am keenly desirous of sticking to my business for a couple of years, and especially of getting off to England for a few months. To go into such a fight would knock everything on the head. But then – if we don't kill them, won't their conduct kill us as a party?"[153]

He remained in his unsettled state a day or two longer, while Holton wrote to say that he could not manage to come up, and McDougall arrived in Toronto to make his explanations in turn.[154] McDougall (who "felt his oats", Brown thought) admitted that

he looked on the present ministry as a makeshift, and was willing
like the others to agree that when resolutions on the constitution
did come before the next session they would follow the course
the party then might ask of them, even at the risk of losing
office.[155] But while Foley and Wilson were ready to put such
a declaration in their election addresses, McDougall, far more
sure of himself and less awed by Brown, positively refused to
have it included in his own or any other.[156]

Thus Brown was still left to his decision – and, as he told
Holton, with only his brother Gordon to consult.[157] The two of
them deliberated long hours at the *Globe* office on what was best
to do: "Start candidates against all four and run out as many of
them as possible, or permit them to go in unopposed, and hold
them up to the mark under the stimulus of bit and spur?"[158]
Finally, they determined on the latter course. "We shall quickly
fall into the attitude of independent but hearty support on all
but the one question," Brown asserted. "I will ask no favours
from them for myself or others, and will stand ready heartily to
aid them to the best of my ability, with the one reservation that
on the constitutional question they are to be coerced on every
occasion."[159] By early June the *Globe* was again fixed on course,
as it declared succinctly of the Macdonald-Sicotte cabinet: "They
will earn no popularity by their constitutional doctrines; they
must rest for success on their administrative virtues."[160]

Two things especially had decided Brown: the first, that to
oppose the ministers would split the party, not merely in a few
constituencies, but all over the province, which was assuredly a
grave responsibility to face.[161] As for the second, even if he did
divide the party, it would be to little purpose unless he himself
ran to provide new leadership – and this he was determined not
to do.[162] He still intended to stay out of parliament until his
health was fully restored. He meant to take the trip to Britain
that he had been planning for months past, and for which he had
booked passage in the Montreal Steamship Company's *Anglo-
Saxon*, sailing from Quebec on July 12.[163]

He was free for his first return in twenty-five years. His
business interests had recovered; the *Globe*'s circulation, at over
31,000, was three times larger than that of any other paper in
Canada.[164] He had successfully launched an evening edition in
the winter, and Bothwell was on the rising curve of a land
boom.[165] No, politics would positively not be allowed to interfere with his personal plans. Let the Macdonald-Sicotte venture
have its day. There would be occasion enough to deal with it on
his return.

Accordingly, the next few weeks were chiefly spent preparing for departure: a week at Bothwell, final arrangements at the Church Street house and at the *Globe* office, where Gordon would keep things running for the coming four or five months. His parents would stay behind in Toronto, where his sister Isabella, Gordon, and their families would look after them. They were too old and infirm now to face the strain of an Atlantic crossing, which could still be thoroughly arduous, even in the new age of steam. Early in July, he said his good-byes and set out alone for Quebec. Yet, even as he left, politics pursued him. There was an odd little incident in Kingston on July 11, as he was *en route* from Toronto to take ship.

There he was approached by a certain David Shaw, who desired some conversation with him on the subject of constitutional reform. Shaw purported to be an emissary from – John A. Macdonald! At any rate, he gave Brown the surprising information that the defeated Conservative leader was now prepared to advocate representation by population, and to co-operate with any party in order to carry that measure.[166] Brown must have been amazed, though he may have conjectured that Macdonald, out of power, weakened by the growth of rep by pop in his own party, and casting about for some new coalition to upset the double-majority ministry, might well be applying an American maxim not unknown to the political art; namely, "If you can't lick 'em, join 'em."

Whatever the explanation, Brown's reply was safe enough. He would be delighted, he said, to see an understanding reached at last between the two great parties of Upper Canada to achieve rep by pop. He suggested that it might be done through both Conservatives and Reformers pledging themselves not to support any government that refused to adopt this principle, and that, when a crisis followed, whichever party was called to form a government should be sustained by the other until the principle was carried.[167] Here was a simple plan for achieving constitutional reform without coalition, which he would again put forward under other circumstances two years hence. But certainly, a coalition of the parties was far from his mind.

He had left the country before Shaw could carry negotiations further. When, however, the latter did so by mail, Brown had further cause to be amazed. Now the presumed emissary reported that John A. Macdonald "was animated with the most friendly desire to co-operate with you in every possible way" – that he accepted *Brown*'s proposal to act with him on the basis of rep by pop or any other question – and that both partners should bring their own best followers with them, "forming therefrom one strong party".[168] Was John A. Macdonald seriously prepared to combine with his most obvious foe, and to espouse the very policy he had so vigorously opposed? Brown might reflect that this was exactly what Macdonald had done in the case of Francis Hincks and the secularization of the clergy reserves eight years before. But perhaps Shaw was exaggerating, even though he said that Macdonald had "instructed" him to make the offer.[169] Or, more likely, perhaps Macdonald was merely playing his old amiable game of throwing out lines to the opposition, suggesting alliances that might never come off, but that could at least bring him information on the state of the enemy.

One thing was sure: Brown's stiff response to Shaw, making plain that he had never for a moment considered a coalition of parties – "which I regard as demoralizing and from which I am persuaded the right feeling of the country would revolt".[170] He would not work with Macdonald inside a party combination; he would not play his game at all. In fact, he went still further. "I did not contemplate renewing friendly personal intercourse with Mr. Macdonald," he wrote bluntly. "A public man has no right to permit his personal feelings to prevent his meeting any-one on public business in a recognized public capacity. But Mr. Macdonald has made charges against me of a character that until entirely withdrawn must debar any other than parliamentary intercourse between us."[171]

The old rancorous accusations were still remembered: Macdonald's blackening charges of perjury, falsification of records, and suborning of witnesses, which he had levied in parliament in 1856 against Brown's conduct on the Penitentiary Commission – charges he had never retracted, although the evidence taken at the subsequent committee of inquiry had shown how ground-less they were. In any case, Brown's message ended the dubious intervention of David Shaw. The returning Scot was far too much caught up in the visit to his homeland to spend time in weighing all the implications of the strange little episode.

He landed on July 23, 1862, at Liverpool, the same port from which he had sailed for America with his father in 1837.[172] He had left at eighteen, impoverished, in a crowded emigrant sailing vessel. He had returned at forty-three in a first-class mail steamer, the owner of a great newspaper and a valuable estate, a dominant figure in Canadian affairs. Meanwhile, the guns were roaring in Virginia in the York Peninsula campaign. And in Britain, the press was questioning the very worth of a colony like Canada, that had refused to pass an urgently needed militia measure, to guard against the threat that war might spread.

The Remaking of George Brown

I

Like any proper traveller, Brown had planned a wide itinerary for the British Isles. Thus D'Arcy McGee had furnished him with a letter to an editor friend in Dublin and listed all the sights to see there – from the grave of Daniel O'Connell to the cattle in Phoenix Park.[1] But as a returning native Brown meant to spend much of his time in old surroundings; in London, where he had once worked with the city agents of his father's firm, and, of course, in Edinburgh, the scene of his boyhood. He set out for London first. And as soon as he had reached the smoke and splendour of the metropolis he went off to Westminster to hear the House of Commons debate of July 25.[2]

This, however, was more than a colonial politician's exercise in filial piety. Parliament was just then discussing the highly interesting topic of Canadian defence. The House of Lords had debated the matter a few days before, and consequently Brown had missed the remarks of the Colonial Secretary himself, the Duke of Newcastle. But, watching from the gallery in the Commons chamber, he could follow some of the leading public figures of the empire as they expressed their opinions on his province: Palmerston, the aged but thoroughly agile Liberal Prime Minister, Thomas Baring, head of one of Britain's greatest banking firms, and Benjamin Disraeli, the skilful House leader of the Conservative opposition, supported by Sir Charles Adderley, prominent Conservative critic on imperial affairs.

Half-unknown Canada was momentarily receiving a singular amount of attention in Great Britain. For when the news of the defeat of the colony's Militia Bill had reached England, it caused a good deal of surprise and indignation, the latter most warmly voiced in the press by the mighty London *Times*, self-appointed to the task of prescribing policy for Britain and the world. Heedless of the widespread view in Canada that the late Militia Bill had been ineffective, extravagant, and based on a wrong principle, *The Times*, with much of British opinion behind it, saw only a supine and ungrateful colony that had readily accepted some 12,000 imperial troops but would do nothing to defend itself.[3] And this was a judgment that played readily into the hands of the vociferous anti-imperialist or separatist faction in Britain, which regarded colonies only as unnecessary burdens to be thrown off.

Moreover, whether separatist or not, there were sizeable elements in both British parties that objected to the heavy weight of imperial expenses and looked to see them reduced. The outcry over Canada spurred them anew to demand that self-governing colonies take on greater responsibility for their own defence. Indeed, they might easily be led to doubt the whole value of supporting dependencies that would not share properly in their own protection. It was a serious problem; and so it appeared to Brown, who hoped to see Canada grow up within the British Empire, not cut off from it, and who regarded Britain's aid and protection as vital to British North America for some indeterminate time to come. Nevertheless, convinced as he was that the likelihood of an American war was not really great, and that the causes of such a conflict would in any case arise between Britain and the United States, he still believed that the main responsibility for defence should lie with the mother country – that a smaller Militia Bill, within Canada's means and already projected by the Sandfield Macdonald ministry, would be a fair and sufficient recognition of the colony's obligations.[4]

Brown's real concern, in fact, was whether the British government would be swept by the passing wave of resentment against Canada into an anti-imperial frame of mind. Hence he followed the debate in the British House keenly, to hear the different viewpoints presented there. Old J. A. Roebuck, the engrained radical, was the most sweeping, as he fumed: "I want the Canadians clearly to understand that England would not be sorry to see them depart from her tomorrow."[5] Adderley, the Conservative, was hardly less sweeping as he scathingly declared that Canada wanted only the cash that the British redcoats spent, that she was indefensible, and (somewhat illogically) that she should be told to defend herself or Britain would recall the troops. But the Conservative leader, Disraeli, affirmed that he would keep Canada, while complaining that self-defence should have been made a condition of her receiving responsible government in the first place. And Baring and a string of others expressed their confidence that Canada would yet do her duty. Most important of all, Palmerston also made plain that the British people had a solemn obligation to preserve their "fellow subjects", despite the fact that local dissensions had for the moment kept the provincials from acting in their own behalf.[6] All in all, Brown could conclude, in mixed annoyance and relief, that Canada had friends enough, although few were ardent and none seemed to understand the true reasons for the fate of the Militia Bill.

As he went about London in the days that followed, widely received and entertained in both political and business circles, he discovered how little indeed was known about Canada. "The ignorance of English politicians about Canadian affairs," he decided, "is about as astounding as the helpless dependence of the capitalists on the nod of a few bell-wethers."[7] But he was glad to learn how things were actually handled at the centre of empire: "It is very funny, and very instructive!"[8] At the same time he found the feeling against the United States in the London world he moved in "something horrible – and it is as senseless as it is bitter".[9] As for the policy of *The Times*, he wrote to Holton: "It seems to be nothing but a mean pandering to the passions of the people, without regard to the hostile feeling that will arise in future years between the nations."[10]

Nevertheless, the Canadian visitor could only appreciate the ready kindness he was shown on every hand, even among those city business men deeply involved in financing the ruinous Grand Trunk Railway. "The truths told by the *Globe* in the last ten years," Brown noted dryly, "have not prevented the Barings, and Glyns and Chapmans etc., being very civil – and those who escaped Grand Trunk benefits particularly so."[11] In truth, he was perhaps disposed to be a little more civil to the Grand Trunk himself, since the recent reform and reorganization that Edward Watkin had sought to carry through would take the railway somewhat out of Canadian politics and put it more effectively under a directing board representing the major British interests behind the Company. Furthermore, that spring the *Globe* had welcomed the appointment of C. J. Brydges as the new Canadian general manager of the line. He was known as an efficient and experienced railway man, having been manager of the well-run Great Western, in which capacity George Brown had long had business dealings with him over Bothwell.[12]

Yet Brown still remained suspicious of the ultimate aims of Grand Trunk enterprise, fearful that its plans for recovery and extension would again turn out to be at public expense, that they would mean still further raids on the debt-encumbered Canadian treasury. It was, no doubt, in a mood of considerable scepticism that he went along to a crowded meeting of Grand Trunk shareholders, held in the well-known London Tavern on August 8.[13] Its purpose was to ratify new arrangements that Watkin had negotiated with the Canadian government to enable the railway to continue operating. Thomas Baring presided as Chairman of the Board, while Brown joined the throng of some 800 unhappy but still hopeful investors, as they listened to speeches by leading Grand Trunk financiers. Watkin was the most effective, deftly switching from talk of staving off foreclosure on the railway to bold pronouncements on completing its "original design", a line to the Atlantic through British territory, to be complemented thereafter by a line to the Pacific. At the end, he won his ratification by a large majority, and the shareholders dispersed, presumably comforted and heartened. But the Canadian Reformer, lacking enthusiasm for railway extension so brightly promised out of bankruptcy, only had his doubts confirmed.

He learned, however, that hopes for railway expansion were echoed in high places, when the Duke of Newcastle requested his presence at an interview in Downing Street. Brown must have been impressed to have the Colonial Secretary lay the imperial government's considerations frankly before him; "a most satisfactory interview", he termed it.[14] Emphatically, he told Holton: "Whatever small politicians and the London *Times* may say, you may depend on this – that the government and the leaders of the opposition perfectly understand our position, and have no thought of changing the relation between Canada and the Mother Country. On the contrary, the members of the government (with the exception of Gladstone) are set upon the intercolonial road and a grand transit route across the continent!"[15] If the imperial power were behind the scheme, might this not change its prospects? And if the North West were thus to be opened, might not the railway to the Atlantic be managed as well?

One thing at least Brown felt was certain gain, after his discussions with Newcastle. "His scruples about Rep by Pop are gone entirely," he reported happily, "and it would have done even Sandfield good to hear his ideas on the absurdity of the double majority."[16] There was another good sign. Alexander Galt, Canada's former Minister of Finance, was in England that same summer; Brown at last made peace with his old enemy, whose financial policies he had so often led in criticizing. And Galt, he found, "goes in now for constitutional changes *stiff*".[17] Prospects for altering the Canadian union were looking better and better.

A month and more thus passed in England, though marred by the poignant news that his mother had died suddenly but peacefully while his ship had been at sea. "But for the sad thought," he recorded, "that never more will I see my beloved Mother –

ever recurring – my visit would have been one of intense pleasure throughout."[18] He had enjoyed being a welcomed visitor
and privileged observer, and had no less benefited from exchang-
ing views in the spacious atmosphere of London, so different
from the cramped confinement of a colony. None the less, the
stamp of Canada was on him strongly, and most clearly in his
resentment of the widespread lack of comprehension in the
motherland of his country across the Atlantic. He declined
repeated invitations to speak, for, as he said stoutly: "I have no
idea of *defending* Canada before the English people, and defence would be the only possible attitude at this moment."[19]
Even when he moved on to his native Scotland early in September, and wandered through "the old loved spots" in Edinburgh,
he felt no impulse to turn back from the land of his adoption.
"I needed nothing to 'reconcile' me to Canada," George Brown
wrote, "but after all I have seen, I say now as earnestly as ever –
Canada for me!"[20]

2

In Edinburgh there were many friends, of course, and many
happy meetings with old cronies – although he found that "the
sad, sad blanks tell the tale of twenty-five years".[21] Yet one
connection here that Brown renewed began to take on growing
significance as the days went by: his link with the Nelsons, the
wealthy Edinburgh publishing family whose handsome, hos-
pitable mansion, Abden House in the suburb of Newington, was
a substantial indication of the achievements of their big Hope
Park printing works near by. William and Thomas Nelson, sons
of the first Thomas Nelson, the late founder of the firm, had
been George Brown's schoolmates at the high school many years
before.[22] Brown had run into Tom Nelson in London, in fact,
and the latter had written to his sister Anne at Abden House
that it was "not unlikely that George Brown of Toronto will
come and spend a week with us".[23] He did come to stay, and did
not move far away thereafter. For in Anne Nelson he found an
attraction that would not let him go. Suddenly, surprisingly, the
confirmed bachelor of forty-three was falling very much in love.

Anne was worth it; she was entirely worth it. Some ten years
his junior, she was light-hearted, lively, and engaging, yet no
less intelligent and firm-minded for that. Her glossy dark hair
was pulled back tightly in the heavy chignon of the 1860s from

her glowing, fair-complexioned Scottish countenance, her clear
eyes shone warmly, her sensitive mouth smiled easily. She loved
company and busy activity, but best of all her affectionate nature
loved the intimate group of family and friends that gathered at
Abden House. George Brown himself, happiest in a close-knit
group of family intimates, could readily feel at home among
the cordial Nelsons – and above all in Anne's presence. She
was the charming centre of a companionable circle that included
her older brothers, William and Tom, the younger John and
James, and her sister Jessie.

Anne, however, was far more than the devoted, contented
daughter of a prosperous Edinburgh household, and Brown
admired her all the more for it. She was quite widely travelled
and certainly well cultivated. She had studied in Germany, knew
the language, and still kept in touch with German friends in
Heidelberg.[24] She had lived in Paris in her early twenties, and
had written a conscientious journal of her grand tour from Paris
to Avignon, Marseilles, and Nice, from Genoa to Milan and
Switzerland, and on through Germany down the Rhine to the
Low Countries.[25] Thanks, indeed, to her family's wealth, she
could keep up her European contacts, and accompany her brother
James on later continental visits. And of course there were regular trips down to London. In short, hers was far from a narrow
or secluded Victorian female existence.

Perhaps it was still surprising in that age that she had not
already married, for, cultivated or not, Anne was no prim,
learned spinster. Actually, the Nelsons had not married early,
perhaps because of the very closeness of the clan, sufficient among
themselves, and in this rather like George Brown's own domestic
circle. Yet more surprising was the fact that, although Anne
and George had each apparently settled into an enduring single
state in their own families, within five weeks of the almost chance
encounter between the Edinburgh publisher's daughter and the
visiting journalist from Canada, they had definitely resolved on
marriage. One of Anne's friends complained urgently from
France, "Though you have told me *the* thing, viz. that he is
unquestionably the right man, you have stopped there regarding
his name, appearance – and have left me in utter ignorance!"[26]

Assuredly Anne had decided for herself. She always knew her
own mind, and while she would accept the lead of someone she
respected, loved, and trusted, she still meant to share in the
making of decisions. No doubt as a capable, keen-witted individual, with a place in society of her own, she had examined George
Brown critically enough – this unknown quantity from the
distant colonies. But he stood up very well under examination,

as a staunch Liberal and Free Kirk Scot of her own Edinburgh background, wholly acceptable to her family, a man of undoubted power and prestige in Canada, and well-to-do besides. After all, these things mattered to a mature young woman, past any likely tendency to calf-love. But more important, surely, were George's tall, commanding presence, kindly good nature, quick laugh, and eager, voluble conversation that would reveal high ideals and sensitive dreams to the right kind of woman. She was that kind. The decade's difference in their ages did not matter, for their ideas and sympathies were in essential harmony. And, being both decisive, they saw no reason for delay. On an evening early in October, as they walked along the twilight shore of the Firth of Clyde, she agreed to marry him.[27] It would turn out to be the climactic step in George Brown's life.

He had gone with the Nelsons for a late holiday on Arran (Gaelic for "the lofty isle"), the picturesquely rugged island in the Firth of Clyde that was already noted as a summer resort. Here Anne and he spent a brief, idyllic courtship – here in the soft radiance of the warm west coast, where summer still lingered and where the glens of Arran tumbled down to quiet inlets of the sea. There was one day that stood out particularly in their memory, the day of their expedition to Lochranza at the far northern end of the island, when together they paused at such an inlet to watch a boy sailing on a plank in the shining, placid water, while a tiny white sailboat passed silently by.[28] It was nothing and it was everything: a moment they would long hold in memory, because it was so completely their own.

It was afterwards, when they had just returned to Greenock (where John Nelson had his church as a Free Kirk minister), that George Brown asked Anne to marry him. This, too, he well recalled thereafter – "the dinner at John's, the hope and the fear, the despair and the joy, changing every hour – until all was settled in that delightful walk along the shore".[29] For, marvellously, Anne had accepted him, and they could announce the monumental fact to the family. They began at once on plans for the wedding, and for George's return to Canada with his bride.

Naturally, the arrangements could not be concluded overnight. Time was needed to prepare for a sizeable company to attend the wedding, to collect a properly complete trousseau for a bride departing for the wild New World, and to arrange for the voyage itself. Tom Nelson would accompany them to Canada; they would sail in the *Scotia* for New York early in December. But, meanwhile, there was a month and more before the wedding would take place.

They were back in Edinburgh now, and no doubt George

Brown was of little more use than any other bridegroom before the wedding. He wrote affectionate little notes to Anne when they both came down with mild chills and worried about each other.[30] He visited Alloa, his birthplace, some miles up the firth from Edinburgh.[31] And he went back to London to deal with business for the *Globe* (probably to arrange more English correspondence for it), as well as to keep another appointment with the Duke of Newcastle.[32] And then, at last, it was November 27, his wedding-day.

John Nelson officiated; Abden House was crammed with guests for the occasion.[33] There was music and singing to follow; but the newly married couple left early by carriage in a sparkling fresh snow-fall, ostensibly bound for York. (Anne's mother wrote just afterwards: "My firm belief is you did not go very far from Edinburgh – we will find out bye and bye.")[34] John Nelson gaily threw snowballs at George Brown as they departed – and was only sorry that his target was wearing a travelling cap instead of his new tall hat.[35] A week later, Mr. and Mrs. Brown returned from their honeymoon to rejoin the Nelsons at Liverpool, this time to say good-bye and make ready to embark. On December 6, they and Tom Nelson were aboard the *Scotia* as she steamed out towards the wintry North Atlantic.[36]

Only one thing could have qualified George Brown's complete happiness at that moment: the aching knowledge that his own mother would not be there at home to greet his bride. Yet he was sailing back to North America a different man from him who had disembarked in Liverpool a few months before: married, deeply contented, and very much in love.

3

It was a rough crossing. There were headwinds and much pitching about. Tom was miserably sea-sick, as were almost all the passengers, but George and Anne, with some special dispensation for the newly married, were wonderfully well, enjoying every minute of the voyage.[37] They landed in New York on December 19, and naturally went to stay with George and Jane Mackenzie at their house on Seventh Avenue.[38] A few days later the Browns and Tom Nelson went on by rail, but stopped, quite naturally again, to visit Niagara Falls – indeed, spent Christmas there.[39] Then on the twenty-sixth they caught the Great Western for Toronto. But when they reached Hamilton at six that evening,

a large party of George Brown's Toronto friends came throng-
ing festively aboard and bundled them off to a special train hired
for the occasion. Among the group were Oliver Mowat, William
McMaster and John McMurrich – two leading Toronto Liberal business men, recently elected to the Legislative Council –
and Thomas Swinyard, the managing director of the Great
Western.[40] They told the surprised Brown and his still more
startled wife that a huge public reception had been planned to
greet them at their final destination.

At Toronto it was pouring rain; yet, none the less, as their
special pulled into the Union Depot at seven-thirty, they found
a mass of more than 5,000 people of all political opinions,
jammed around the station in the wet black night to welcome
them home.[41] It was a triumphant, moving moment. Toronto
was emphatically proud to have George Brown back; even his
enemies had missed him. For the time being, differences, antipathies, were forgotten, as Grits and Tories, Orangemen and
Catholics, lustily cheered the great man of the *Globe*. Oliver
Mowat and the city alderman ushered him to the rear of the
Depot to present a formal address from the citizens, while his
wife was taken to a carriage. Brown was loudly called on to
reply. He answered briefly, thanking them all for the "magnificent reception – as unexpected as it is gratifying", and adding
warmly: "I can only say that after six months' visit to the noblest
and best governed land on earth, I feel more than ever the
necessity for Upper Canadians of all shades of political opinion
to unite heartily in advancing the great interests of our country –
to forget the minor differences which have so long separated
us."[42] Then he, too, was taken to the carriage, to be escorted in
a flaring torchlight procession through the rain and darkness to
the home on Church Street.

There were bands blaring "Hail to the Chief", and, for Anne,
"Annie Laurie" and "Flowers of Edinburgh".[43] There were
hundreds of hissing torches, Roman candles, and rockets; the
streets were lit like day. Cheering wildly, the crowd pushed
along the greasy sidewalks and muddy roadways, and people
thrust heads and waving handkerchiefs out of upstairs windows
everywhere along the route. The noise, the stark contrasts of
light and darkness, the great distorted shadows on the buildings
– it was all thoroughly exciting for Anne, but bewildering and
a little frightening too. Of course she had known that her husband was a powerful figure in provincial public life. But the
fierce clamour, the near-frenzy that so frequently surrounded
public men in Canada, she could hardly have surmised. She
would never be really at ease with George Brown's political

career, and perhaps her sense that Canadian politics were in some way a strange and savage rival pulling at him began in this torchlit, tumultuous night introduction to her new homeland.

At the doorway of 204 Church Street, Brown turned to answer insistent calls for some final remarks. He spoke his thanks again, and again significantly referred to the need for unity he saw on his return. "I come back," he earnestly proclaimed, "with vastly enlarged views of the greatness of England and the British people. I come back too with a better knowledge of public affairs and with a more ardent desire to serve . . . I trust that in all the public movements we make in Upper Canada we will pay more regard to the lessons read to us by the mother land – and that whenever the great interests of Canada are at risk, we will forget our merely political partisanship and rally round the cause of our country."[44] That, he said, would be his new motto. Would he remember it? Here was a speculation for the future.

His father, Peter Brown, white-haired and frail, was waiting for him in the house – waiting there alone, without his wife of nearly fifty years. Tom Nelson noted George's swift greeting: "Just, 'O father!' Not another word. I saw the tear in his eye and respected him for it."[45] But now father and son who had always meant so much to each other were reunited. And now, as well, there was a new era beginning in the Brown home, as Anne moved easily and affectionately into possession. The journeying and receiving were done. The next step was to pick up the ordinary threads of daily life.

One of the first tasks was to answer the messages of welcome and felicitation that had come streaming in. "Many thanks for your kind congratulations," George Brown replied to Luther Holton a few days after his return, "and I assure you my friends may well congratulate me, for I am a new man in mind and body and as happy as the day is long!"[46] He was cheerfully occupied with suppers and receptions, as he proudly introduced his wife into Toronto society, and at home he delighted in each cosy domestic detail of his new existence. He had slipped almost eagerly out of the ways of bachelorhood. Restored in health, he seemed to pour his old accustomed gusto into his marriage – all his whole-hearted capacity for enjoyment. Perhaps because marriage had come late, he prized it the more. And always there was a recurring sense of wonder and gratitude that this could have happened to him, that Anne was his. He could laugh aloud at the very joy of it.

Surely, he was a new man – and most of the remaking was Anne's work. Oliver Mowat would one day write to her: "Since you became his wife, the softer side of his nature has been developed under your loving influence – himself becoming an increasingly gentle, kind and considerate person."[47] Yet Brown had changed in other ways as well. For one thing, his long ill-health had left a mark. True, he was well again, brimming once more with vigour and enthusiasm. But he would never have the old copious quantities of energy to burn, and, what is more, he seemed to realize it. He would seldom drive himself as hard as he had before, carrying on four or five jobs at once for months on end. He appeared less impetuous and impatient; he could even become detached, at times almost easy-going. Possibly his new engrossing centre of interest, his marriage, had much to do with this. Nevertheless, there was also some diminishing of his restless physical vitality (not that, compared with other men, he had grown quiet or sober!), and the fact that henceforth he was often subject to painful attacks of sciatica also seemed to point to some definite change in his constitution.[48] More than marriage was altering George Brown.

Another influence stemmed from his experience in Britain. As he had indicated in his own words, his British visit had brought him a new sense of scale, of dimension in politics. He had seen Canada's problems against a background of imperial issues at the very focus of the world. He had been struck by British ignorance of Canada, but no less struck by the magnitude and power of Britain's political and economic life. And so the vehement battles of Canadian politics, once so all-absorbing, could come to seem more like parochial quarrelling – "merely partisanship".[49] Brown would not and could not throw off the views and habits of a lifetime. He believed intensely that honest politics and true patriotism lay in the maintenance of strong party principles; he would return repeatedly to attacks upon the expediency and corruption that pretended to some higher political morality than strict party loyalty. None the less, his mind had been opened to a possibility that for truly great ends it could be right to sink grave party differences. An able but restricted colonial politician had gained a new awareness that compromise and conciliation might be the way of constructive statesmanship.

Nor would the state of Brown's own fortunes be without effect. He was becoming a decidedly wealthy man. Anne had brought with her a dowry of $120,000.[50] His holdings at Bothwell would soon be valued at more than twice that amount, and there was still the *Globe*, in a flourishing condition.[51] In Canada of the day, these total assets meant substantial wealth indeed. Previously, Brown had achieved business prominence and owned much property, but he had rarely known financial ease. Now there was far less strain of business problems tugging at him;

and in this way, too, he could relax somewhat. He could afford to take his time and push less hard.

Altogether, this new Brown was a broader, more mellowed, less demanding individual. Of course he had not wholly altered. Directness, force, fire, determination, still were all present, and dogmatism and over-confidence might show themselves again. What mattered, however, was that Brown's whole personality had been modified, if not shaped anew. And how much it mattered would be revealed by the events of the next two years.

4

The question now was, what should he do about politics? Before he had left Canada the previous summer, George Brown had planned to return to parliament after his holiday was over. For, however much a burden public life had seemed at times, he still had felt its obligations as unfinished business, and unquestionably he had known excitement and gratification as well as duty and dedication in his political career. Even at the time of his defeat in the elections of 1861, he had spoken only of staying out of parliament for the present. In fact, when he had gone to England, the *Globe* had announced that his intention was to seek re-election on his return to Canada, once a suitable opportunity should present itself.[52]

But that had been announced in August 1862. By January 1863, the new Brown had other ideas, and was by no means ready to return to parliament at all. He told Holton: "Entirely re-established in body and mind as I am, and free from nearly all business retardments, I have no desire whatever to enter parliamentary life, and would much rather accomplish through others what the country wants than be a prominent participant myself."[53] Doubtless he meant to work through his position of power at the *Globe* office. In any case, it seemed he felt no yearning for his former role as party leader. He had, he said, "chalked out a course for myself pretty clearly".[54] Perhaps he would be the judicious director off the parliamentary stage – the wire-puller behind the scenes, critics might charge. Yet, whatever happened, it appeared unlikely that Brown would pursue any course leading to the commanding position he had held in the Upper Canada Reform party between 1854 and 1861. He would be a power in Liberalism, but not an active commander – an overlord, perhaps, but not a captain in the field.

The reasons for the change were plain enough: his moderated outlook, his greater detachment, and, above all, his marriage. Past memories of all he had disliked in public life combined with his present consciousness of happiness, and made him shrink from the thought of losing one moment with Anne for the dubious pleasures of parliamentary existence: the bitter wrangles, the frustrations and disappointments, the long night hours, the loneliness of life in rented rooms at distant Quebec. In all this, the contrast between George Brown and his greatest rival, John A. Macdonald, was strikingly revealed. Brown did enjoy being with people, but in small circles of friends, and especially in his own home. He found little ease or pleasure in convivial evenings with political cronies at hotels or inns. Macdonald, on the other hand, not only had a natural zest for cameraderie, but also through his own domestic tragedy – the illness and death of his invalid wife – had long lacked any real home life, and had almost been forced to dwell in the public and political world.

Brown, however, cherished his own private world and meant to hold on to it. Furthermore, Anne herself wanted no less strongly to keep him with her.[55] She did not comprehend the power of political demands, and what she saw of them repelled her: the noise, the violence, and the passions. Why should George go back to these, subject himself again to strain, abuse, and shock? He was a notably successful journalist; the *Globe* was his first care; and certainly they had money and position enough. No doubt, she did not actually demand of him that he stay out of public life. She was strong-minded, but not domineering, and would do as he wished in all the big things. But in this case she had only to reinforce his own wishes and confirm his own desire to stay home. Let others, who cared to, think that they were running Canada!

All this was true. Still, what should he do about politics – about the deep sectional discord in the Canadian union that still demanded remedy, the inept moderate Liberal government that hoped to find the solution in the futile double-majority principle; the inflated talk of an Intercolonial Railway, egged on by Grand Trunk interests, and the pressing need, instead, to acquire the North West before the Americans thrust into it? And what of the campaign for reform of the union that Brown had led in parliament for nearly a decade? Could he really withdraw now, before these issues had been settled, the answers gained? Could he work as effectively for them from the outside?

In a sense, duty and determination pushed him forward while inclination and contentment held him back. But there was more to it than this. Brown, after all, had been deeply involved in active politics for years and he had unswervingly pursued a certain set of goals: reform of the union, justice for Upper Canada, north-west expansion. He was still too involved, whatever he might think and say – still too intent on seeing these goals achieved – to leave the uncompleted work to other hands. He had a good idea of his own value, and he had his characteristic single-minded concentration on ends. He felt that he was still needed. Not even Anne and all his devotion to their marriage could overcome that innermost conviction. Hence, almost against his will, as the opening weeks of 1863 passed by, he became more and more persuaded that he should stand for re-election to parliament.

There was no real self-deception here. George Brown sincerely did not want to leave so much that he prized for so much that he detested. Yet the feeling of urgent need impelled him, especially as he saw the Macdonald-Sicotte government making ready to meet the legislature with little more to offer than a more limited Militia Bill and their hopeless double-majority notion. If there was any self-deception in his thinking, it might have been in his growing conviction that he would be indispensable to the Reform cause in parliament under such a fumbling régime. Yet was his conviction wrong?

On February 12, the day parliament opened, Brown wrote to Holton: "I confess I view the position of our party with some alarm – more alarm than I have felt in ten years. Ministers may get their supporters to vote down rep by pop, or they may treat their voting on that question with indifference – but the country will not do so. . . . Divisions will spring up – in every store and bar room of Upper Canada the contest will be waged . . . one set will be pitted against the other – and when the election comes, the result will be seen. I have no desire to enter parliament. On the contrary, nothing but the strongest sense of duty would tempt me into it at present – but sometimes when I think of the gulf before us, I am almost tempted to wish myself once more in the House."[56]

Hastily he added: "A little reflection, however, soon brings me back stronger than ever for quiet and happiness."[57] But Holton, who had now returned to parliament himself, having been elected to the upper chamber, at once answered, expressing his own anxiety to see Brown in the Assembly "at the earliest possible moment", and reported on a movement at Quebec to secure him an immediate nomination in South Oxford.[58] This Liberal seat had been vacated through Skeffington Connor's appointment to the judicial bench. Leading Reformers in the constituency had already written to urge Brown to run. He had declined, but evidently on the ground that he knew "less of South

Oxford perhaps than of any county west of Belleville" – hardly an indication that he was against the very idea of running.[59] "Were I desirous of going in," he mused, "I suppose I could do so by stumping the county. . . . A little stumping would, I dare say, make the thing sure enough."[60] In reality he had almost decided already as he weighed the challenging situation in the riding: the fact that he knew only Ingersoll in South Oxford (which had been Francis Hincks's old stamping-ground), although North Oxford had been familiar territory to him since his electioneering there back in 1847.[61]

And so Brown's resolution to stay out of parliament finally broke down. Pushed by his own feelings, pulled by the insistence of his political associates, he accepted a requisition signed by more than a thousand Liberals of South Oxford. The *Globe* announced his decision on February 26. Anne wisely did not stand in the way, however much she must have regretted the move. Nevertheless, her husband took up the candidacy assuring her that this was only a temporary return, and he meant it: "I am into it for this struggle."[62] He would stay to resolve the issues to which he was committed. As ever, he was in politics for a purpose, not for a career.

In any event, his returning to political life under these conditions, and with this attitude, still further indicated that a much more detached Brown would sit in parliament. He would sit there with one eye on the clock, waiting for debates to end, writing letters to Anne at his desk in the chamber and thinking of home, repeatedly restless for the business of the session to be wound up. Moreover, he intended to remain a semi-independent back-bencher, or at least to function in the House apart from the front-bench Liberal leaders. In other words, if Brown did feel obliged to return to parliament, he had still not given up the idea he had expressed to Holton; of seeking rather to "accomplish through others what the country wants, than be a prominent participant myself".[63] If this could be done at all, assuredly the old George Brown, the urgent, authoritarian commander of other years, could not have managed it. But perhaps the new one might bring it off – and then be able to escape joyfully from public duty, back to Anne and home.

5

"My Dearest Anne: Well, I am fairly into it – and I do assure you I wish I were once more quietly home in Church Street by your side. I find a wonderful change in my feelings about all this since the olden time. I am persuaded that had I stayed out of it for a year longer I would never have returned."[64] It was a note scribbled from Ingersoll on the night of February 25, as Brown's by-election campaign got under way. His only adversary was Warden Bodwell – a Reformer himself, for the constituency was so solidly Reform – a locally prominent politician whose main hope of winning rested on the appeal of the resident against the outsider. Of course, the moderates, some Conservatives, and the old anti-Brown friends of Hincks backed Bodwell. Their chances did not seem bright, however, when at the nomination meeting their own man endorsed Brown's two-hour speech on the state of public affairs and, somewhat over-awed, chiefly pleaded that he was the local choice.[65]

The campaign that followed was swift, by no means bitter, and hardly in doubt for a moment. "It is very pleasant to find how kind every one is to me," Brown remarked. "Not a harsh word except for coming to drive out Bodwell – and Bodwell himself is compelled to say all sorts of kind things."[66] He gave his best none the less: up till two in the morning and off at seven in chill but clear weather, to talk here, move on eight miles and talk there: at Norwich and Woodstock, Otterville and Tillson-burg. He thought the outcome safe enough. "Twist and turn it every way, I don't think it possible he can beat me."[67] Still, he asked Anne to pass on word to Gordon that the *Globe* should talk moderately about the contest. "We will crow when victory is won."[68]

The polls came on March 5 and 6, and from the start Brown commanded a sure majority.[69] When the official declaration was held at Hillman's Corners a few days later, the member-elect again struck the note of conciliation. He was specially gratified, he said, by the "kindly feeling which has been manifested throughout".[70] He thanked those Conservatives who had voted for him, moreover, proclaiming it a sign that "Upper Cana-dians were coming to a right sense of their position, and would not permit partisanship to prevent a settlement of the great questions now under discussion".[71] There was a victory banquet at the Royal Hotel in Ingersoll that night.[72] Then he went back to Toronto, where Anne was fretting for his return.

By this time, since parliament was soon to adjourn for a three-week recess, it was hardly worth while for Brown to set out for Quebec. Instead, he paid a visit to Bothwell in early April, to see to his property there before taking up his parliamentary post. Now the south-western countryside was warming into spring. It was mild, clear weather, and the laird greatly enjoyed his rambles through the greening fields, watching the ploughing and examining the sheep and cattle with a would-be professional eye.[73] Beyond this, there was the land boom. "The oil wells are a great fact," he told Anne. "There seems no doubt that oil in any quantity will be had here. Many people arrive daily from different quarters to inquire into the prospects, and already three or four new companies have been formed to open wells. Every dwelling house in the village is occupied. . . . Three vacant taverns are anxiously inquired after."[74]

But soon it was time to go back to Toronto and make ready for the trip to parliament. There was a brighter side to it, however: Anne would accompany her husband for this first return. They would be together in Quebec. They would also stop *en route* in Montreal to visit the Holtons, so that Mrs. Brown could meet Mrs. Holton and the children.[75] Accordingly, the session had already recommenced when the member for South Oxford and his wife finally established themselves in comfortable rooms at Mrs. Steele's residential house in the Lower Canadian capital.[76]

Brown found the Sandfield Macdonald–Sicotte government deep in difficulty when he arrived. Indeed, it had known little else since its constitution the previous summer. In the Lower Canadian half of the ministry Sicotte had managed to include McGee and Dorion, bringing the latter back into parliament in June of 1862. Yet the long-time *Rouge* leader had not been comfortable in office, even though there was no barrier of principle to keep him or McGee from the cabinet. The eastern Liberals had not been committed to any set policy of constitutional reform, much less to rep by pop. Dorion, however, was firmly devoted to the cause of retrenchment and hostile to railway entanglements. When in September the government had adopted expensive proposals actually to build the Intercolonial Railway, he had very soon resigned, and efforts made in January of 1863 to win him back had failed.[77]

The ministry, in fact, had made rather a mess of its Intercolonial policy. At Quebec, in September 1862, an interprovincial conference of the governments of Canada, New Brunswick, and Nova Scotia had agreed to send new delegations to negotiate with the imperial authorities for an Intercolonial railway, and had even agreed on a provisional sharing of the costs. Doubtless there was mounting popular interest in the project in Canada, particularly in the East, and doubtless it found Liberal as well as Conservative advocates. D'Arcy McGee was one, impressed as he was with the need of effective communications for development and defence.[78] The ministry, moreover, took the line that the Intercolonial was necessary as a *quid pro quo* for further imperial military aid; Canada must prove that she would take her own share of burdens.

Nevertheless, it was still a shock when a government that had proclaimed rigid retrenchment boldly announced a huge new programme of railway expansion, and when ministers who had won office by defeating a militia bill because it far exceeded the needs of defence now urged defence needs as justification for their costly railway. Upper Canadian Reformers, who had accepted the Macdonald-Sicotte régime because it at least promised an end to Coalition extravagance and Grand Trunk railway jobs, were particularly upset. Consequently, even while Howland and Sicotte were being sent to London as Canadian delegates to negotiate on the Intercolonial, Sandfield Macdonald and Co. realized that they had gone too far. They could not hope to keep western Reform votes on an Intercolonial bill. And so the Canadian delegates in London suddenly broke off the successfully advancing negotiations, on the pretext that a sinking fund proposed by the imperial government to safeguard the financing of the line was unacceptable. When they returned home at the beginning of 1863, the Macdonald-Sicotte ministry had been saved from its blunder at the cost of a bad taste in everyone's mouth – and a bad reputation for Canadian probity in the angry and disgruntled Maritime Provinces.

Then, when parliament opened in February, the government went still further in its career of alienating friends and disillusioning people. Naturally, the representation question at once came up. Some western Conservatives moved rep-by-pop amendments in an attempt to embarrass the ministry. As could be expected, their motions were readily defeated by a solid block of Lower Canadians voting in combination with the western moderates.[79] But what was more significant, the Macdonald-Sicotte ministers did not introduce their own resolutions on the double-majority principle, promised on their taking office. The fact was that they did not dare to. There were too many hostile interests, Reform and Conservative, which, though mutually opposed, would assuredly combine to defeat resolutions on the double majority. And so the government strove to avoid the whole issue, and Sandfield Macdonald used all his undoubted resources of peppery courage, biting wit, and parliamentary strategem just to keep his administration alive. Now, however, came the fatal mistake, the result of a new separate-schools bill put forward by Richard Scott, member for Ottawa and a Roman Catholic.

Scott had been introducing similar measures since 1860, to remove certain anomalies in the provisions for Roman Catholic state-supported schools and round out Catholic educational rights in Upper Canada. He had made little headway until 1862, when John A. Macdonald, Chief Superintendent Ryerson, and the Catholic hierarchy reached agreement on a modified bill, which was then brought in by Scott. But on the fall of the Cartier-Macdonald régime he had withdrawn his measure, presumably because the new Macdonald-Sicotte government had promised him better consideration at the next session, when they were more prepared.[80]

Sandfield Macdonald himself, though a Roman Catholic, was no great believer in separate schools. But his cabinet contained their most eloquent and devoted champion, D'Arcy McGee, who endorsed Scott's bill as a government measure designed to bring final settlement to the perennial schools question.[81] Sicotte, another Lower Canadian, was no less eager to settle Upper Canada's school affairs.[82] Consequently, when the bill came before parliament in March of 1863, it was bound to involve the ministry deeply, and no less to revive bitter religious controversies over education. In general, it made only minor adjustments and small enlargements to the scope of Catholic schools. Yet an Upper Canadian Protestant majority stood flatly opposed, precisely because they did not believe that these would be final adjustments, but merely further nibbles at Upper Canada's public-school system, just as previous "final" claims had been. The fact that a leading Roman Catholic organ, the *Canadian Freeman*, declared Scott's bill only an instalment did not prove this opposition wholly wrong.[83] Two years later, indeed, new "final" terms would be demanded.

As a result, the Scott bill was hotly contested in parliament, and a whole series of amendments put forward, which were only overcome by majorities dependent on the votes of French Catholic Canada. It passed its third reading on March 13 by a vote of 76 to 31.[84] Yet this decisive vote was most instructive. Upper Canada itself had definitely rejected the measure, 31 to 22; and the twenty-two western members who had supported it were all Conservatives except for one Liberal and three ministers.[85] Several things accordingly were clear. First, the Upper Canada Reform party had voted overwhelmingly against the cabinet on an actual ministerial measure. Second, Lower Canadian domination had been demonstrated once more, for the West now had another school act by virtue of eastern votes. And, third, the Macdonald-Sicotte ministry had ignored – no, flatly contradicted – its own doctrine of the double majority by forcing a measure on one-half of Canada against the clearly expressed will of that section. It, too, had had to govern by using Lower Canada against Upper.

The "moderate" government did not resign, but it was

doomed. Its *raison d'être* had proved void and meaningless. In short, the sectional differences had exposed the double-majority principle as the impossibility it was: the Canadian union could not be maintained on such a basis. Constitutional reform was only made the more inevitable – as George Brown would have predicted long before.

6

These events had occurred before parliament's recess, and before Brown rejoined the House in mid-April. In consequence, he had played no part in the fight over the Scott bill, although there was no doubt where he stood, especially when the *Globe* condemned the measure as heralding a new assault upon the national school system.[86] Nevertheless, he had not been personally entangled, and certainly this time moderates could not hold George Brown's "extremism" responsible for any of the difficulties in governing the union. Instead, they had been shown rather clearly that sectarian and sectional problems existed quite independent of him.

During his first few weeks back, Brown took only a minor part in debates, as he felt out both sides of this parliament. He took time as well to go with Anne on a spring excursion to Montmorency Falls in company with Malcolm Cameron and Egerton Ryerson's daughter – a rather oddly assorted group.[87] Cameron, by now a virtually nominal Liberal in the Upper House, was in confidential communication with John A. Macdonald, and sent him a report on Brown. "Nothing is nearer to his heart," judged Cameron, "than to upset the ship, but it is to him impossible unless Rep by Pop is got over."[88] Actually, this was not very sensational information. Brown had made no secret of his dislike for the existing ministry, nor of his reluctance to turn it out merely to bring back the old gang without advancing rep by pop. The *Globe* had said so; he had said so himself in South Oxford. He had recently remarked to Holton on the ministry's deplorable career: "How John A. must be chuckling! I confess I can hardly make out whether he and Sandfield are working together or not."[89]

He would soon have the chance, however, to register his views of Sandfield's government. On May 1, urged on by impatient followers, John A. Macdonald finally struck the blow that had been impending for weeks. He moved a direct vote of no confidence in the administration, "as at present constituted".[90] But it was a motion that condemned the ministry's composition rather than its programme (which, in point of fact, was not very different from that of the old Coalition), and seemed to imply that a suitably reconstituted cabinet might prove quite acceptable to the Conservatives. Undoubtedly it looked like the old Macdonald game of dealing in men rather than measures. It might even point the way to an alliance between the two Macdonalds, Sandfield and John A., which Grit Liberals had often apprehended.[91]

Brown himself had heard a few weeks earlier that this very combination was in prospect.[92] And on the other side of politics, that remarkably partisan civil servant, Egerton Ryerson, expressed to John A. Macdonald his own wish for such a happy consummation.[93] The play conceivably would run as follows: many Grits, disgusted with Sandfield's ministry, would vote against it on a test of confidence; whereupon, in no less angry disgust, Sandfield and those he could carry with him would join forces with John A. Macdonald, Cartier and Co. The old firm would not only come back in: it would come back stronger than ever, while the Reform party would be split again and left in shattered opposition. In short, there was a chance here for a new coalition coup as dazzling as that of 1854, with Sandfield Macdonald cast in the role Francis Hincks had played.

And again, as in 1854, a great deal would turn on George Brown's course of action. Now, as then, he was outside the Reform ministry, yet potentially the chief focus of sentiment within the Upper Canada party. Would he once more, as in 1854, vote with Conservatives for the sake of demolishing an unprincipled Liberal government — and thus open the way for a new moderate-Liberal and Conservative combination? He would not, for this was a different Brown. He was just as desirous as ever of seeing party principles sustained, but now his view was broader, his recognition of political realities sharper. In fact, he meant to challenge John A. Macdonald at his own game: to see the ministry reconstituted, but as he, George Brown, wanted it. First, therefore, Sandfield must be maintained in office, and then steered to true paths of Reform.

And so, as the debate on the motion of no confidence proceeded, the member for South Oxford was distinctly restrained. He waited, took the opinions of his Reform colleagues, yet kept his own counsels. Then, as the debate moved to a close on Thursday evening, May 7, he rose to speak. It was a strong speech, but not the old impassioned sort: blunt rather than fiery, measured and deliberate.[94] He criticized the course of the government in evading constitutional reform; he also criticized the Conservative non-confidence motion which had equally evaded the real question at issue, the future of the union itself. The best answer to that question, he asserted, was still the federation plan of the Toronto Convention. Again Brown read its resolutions. He assured Lower Canadians of guarantees for their security under any measure of constitutional reform; he fully acknowledged the problems of language and race in the union, no less than the need for rep by pop. And, finally, he declared that while a change of system must come, he still preferred the existing government to the last. He preferred, he said, to keep the Conservatives still in opposition to reflect on their past misdeeds, until they showed more convincing signs of a change of heart!

This was the right note at the decisive time. The angriest Grit could follow Brown in supporting the moderate Liberal ministers as the lesser evil, while echoing his frank warning that "he would kill them off when he could do better".[95] When the vote was taken shortly afterwards, it seemed that the member for South Oxford had made his case. True, the ministry was beaten, 59 to 64, because there were still a small number of defections – enough in a closely balanced House to bring it to defeat.[96] Yet this was no resounding triumph for John A. Macdonald. In fact, the government carried a majority within Upper Canada; the Grits went overwhelmingly with Brown to support Sandfield's régime. Hence, if the Liberal ministry had not been saved, the Liberal party had been. There had been no significant split in Upper Canadian Reform. Moreover, even John A.'s limited success soon proved hollow, for Sandfield asked the Governor-General for a dissolution of parliament and a new general election, and, unlike Sir Edmund Head in 1858, Lord Monck immediately granted the request. Now it was the Conservatives' turn to rail against a governor-general, as on May 12 parliament was prorogued and the members left Quebec to prepare for new election campaigns.

The night before prorogation, Brown drafted a full, confidential report to his brother Gordon, explaining the events behind the scenes, as he traced the course he had followed on the motion of no confidence.[97] "I sounded out our fellows," he began directly, "and discovered that I could carry with me a respectable division of them for the motion. Still there would be a larger section against it, and a rupture of the party [would] ensue. A coalition of John S. and John A. would have followed immediately. Our party would have been broken up, Rep by Pop would have been indefinitely postponed, and I blamed for the whole. On the contrary, if I carried through the ministry,

I felt that I would be master of the situation. And so it has proved."

"I kept perfectly secret," he continued, "how I intended to vote – with a view to frighten Sandfield into modifying his policy, as well as to induce the opposition to speak out on Rep by Pop. . . . Consequently, my speech excited consternation in the Tory ranks – they fully calculated on my support." On the other hand, the Reformers had been delighted with his remarks – "and are ready to stand by me unitedly in our future policy". Yet another dividend had been secured. Sandfield Macdonald had given him "express assurance that if he had an Upper Canadian majority he would entirely change his policy and reconstruct his government so as to make it as acceptable as possible to Dorion and myself". In fact, as soon as the vote had been declared, Sandfield had sent to Brown asking his aid in a reconstruction of the ministry.

Yet George Brown still intended to work through others. "I replied that I could not go into a government under any circumstance, but that I would heartily aid as an outsider. What then would I advise? . . . Make Dorion leader in Lower Canada, take in Mowat and other reliables, pitch over the Intercolonial . . . and cut down the expenditure to the lowest shilling. Then give us an acceptable policy on Rep by Pop, and all will be right." And this Sandfield Macdonald had fully agreed to do, so conclusive was Brown's victory!

There had probably been another influence working on Sandfield besides, although Brown had not known of it at first. It was the Governor-General, Lord Monck, himself, who only the week before had had a significant interview at his own request with the member for South Oxford. They had been together for over two hours, discussing "all sorts of things".[98] "He was amazingly frank, straightforward and kind in all that passed," Brown reported. "He admitted all the evils I complained of, felt strongly the necessity of remedying them – admitted I was seeking the right remedy, and put the question direct, 'Mr. Brown, could you repeat what you did in 1858 – would Mr. Dorion go with you to the extent he then did?' I explained to him the change in circumstances, but expressed my belief that a satisfactory government might even now be formed. It seems that I had no sooner left him than he sent for Sandfield, told him that there was great force in what I said – that sooner or later my views must be carried out, and (I gather from what Sandfield has let fall bit by bit) strongly advised him to throw himself into the hands of Dorion and myself."[99]

Whether or not this last conjecture was correct, it was apparent that the burly, likeable Monck – so different from the prim, pedantic Head – had made a conquest. It was one of much importance, for Brown had gained a confidence in this governor's understanding of Canada's needs that would further affect his own course in politics. It seemed evident, too, that Monck had made a very different assessment of the potentialities of the short-lived Brown-Dorion government of 1858 than Head had done; and that was both vastly encouraging and pleasantly soothing to a still-felt wound. At any rate, from this moment on, Brown with good cause believed in Monck's recognition of the necessity for constitutional reform.

The governor was willing; Sandfield was willing; the problem now was to reconstruct the government in order to carry out reform. A meeting was arranged between the premier and Brown, Mowat, Dorion, and Holton. The group foregathered. "I took the lead," said Brown, "as *amicus curiae*."[100] At first all went well, as he asked for Dorion to have *carte blanche* in Lower Canada, and for a thorough change in the Upper Canadian half of the ministry – though Sandfield Macdonald here won an agreement that McDougall must be kept in, lest he "create a row and damage the administration from the start". Various policies were rapidly settled, until at length they came to the critical question of rep by pop. Sandfield again professed his own willingness to concede it, but hit shrewdly at the crucial point: "I will do whatever Dorion and Holton say they can carry the elections with."

"Very good." [So Brown recorded it.] "What say you, Dorion?" "I say that it can be made an open question, but nothing more can be done without destroying us in Lower Canada." They were at the old stumbling-block again, the old barrier to reform of the union. Brown did his best. "I put the matter in every way – urged and hotter urged, but to no avail. They would not budge." The meeting was adjourned to give everyone time to consider, while Sandfield warned ominously that if the negotiations failed he would "make the same offer elsewhere – and it will be accepted". Dorion equally declared that, if agreement broke down, "he and his friends would feel at liberty to form combinations with any other party in U.C." "Certainly – we never thought otherwise," replied George Brown.

Fair words – but he was facing a new crisis, a new threat of Reform disunity and collapse. Again he recognized reality. It was better to have rep by pop once more an open question than to leave the Grits in isolation, confronting some new party combination in power. He decided to bow to the terms set by Dorion and Holton in their own realistic appraisal of the Lower Canadian situation. "I became perfectly satisfied," he told his brother, "that we ought to accept. We would have in the L.C. section the men most friendly to Rep by Pop. If it cannot be got from them, it can be got from none." Besides, although the Grits might sweep Upper Canada in the coming elections, what good would it do if they had no friends in the East? "Who should we look to to help us in L.C.? Recollect that many of our best friends are frightened at (I had almost said tired of) the policy of coercion."

Here was a remarkable admission from the once unyielding champion of Upper Canadian sectionalism, who earlier had held that it would be sufficient to unite all Upper Canada behind the demand for representation by population in order to overawe Lower Canada and force her to give way. Now he acknowledged the need for Lower Canadian help – that coercion could not be enough. Truly he had changed! Yet there was another reason, besides, for hopefully accepting half a loaf: "This is not to be forgotten, that the Governor is thoroughly with us – and this is half the battle."[101]

Now arrangements for the reconstructed ministry could be speedily concluded. By May 16, the Sandfield Macdonald–Dorion cabinet had been announced. Dorion had brought in a completely new eastern section, consisting of himself and Holton, Thibaudeau, Letellier de St. Just, Huntington, and Drummond. In the West, Foley and Wilson were dropped, while Howland now became Receiver-General. He was replaced as Minister of Finance by Holton, who would now leave the Council and seek re-election to the House: a man of much stronger character and speaking power, and one whose reputation as a leading business man stood at least as high as Howland's. The other western ministers, besides Sandfield Macdonald and McDougall, were Mowat, Fergusson Blair, and Lewis Wallbridge. It was a definite shift leftward of the moderates.

About the only serious loss in the change was D'Arcy McGee, whose strong advocacy of the Intercolonial had weakened his ties with Dorion while his renewed efforts for separate schools had loosened them with Brown. Brown, however, continued to hold his personal regard for McGee, though the latter felt bitter enough at being excluded from Dorion's section of the cabinet. As for the real cabinet-maker, George Brown, he was thankfully back in Toronto now, entirely persuaded that "my course has been right throughout".[102] That much had not changed, at any rate.

7

At last there was a strong Liberal ministry — full of real Reformers, both East and West. Now everything depended on the elections. If they could carry them, then the problems of the union might finally be ended. Justice could be brought to Upper Canada, security to Lower. That was Brown's great hope, as he went up to South Oxford to begin his own campaign for re-election.

His nomination speech in Ingersoll's Town Hall on May 19 showed his wider concern for both Canadas, as he frankly told his audience of western Grits: "It was perfectly impossible to make representation by population a cabinet question and carry the elections in Lower Canada."[103] He succeeded in convincing them, too, for this time the Reformers of South Oxford supported him without division from the start.

The Conservatives put up a man against him, Dr. Cook, who had been a Hincksite member for the constituency from 1854 to 1857. Yet he was so slight a threat that Brown even took time to tour through North Oxford as well, on behalf of Hope Mackenzie, the Grit candidate there. Indeed, it was like the strenuous old days, as he campaigned on horseback into the back concessions, or talked till two in the morning at one meeting, then drove till broad daylight for the next, trying to snatch some sleep in a swaying, bouncing carriage, half frozen in the unseasonably cold night.[104] But in the end victory came easily. When the polls closed on June 16, Brown had received nearly ten times his opponent's votes.[105] Hope Mackenzie swept North Oxford as well. The tide was running strongly with the Grits.

That was evident throughout Upper Canada. When all the returns were made, by July 4, it appeared that Reformers had taken some forty seats in the West, Liberal-Conservatives only twenty-two.[106] All the old Grit stalwarts had been returned, and more added. Toronto, for example, had been recaptured from the Tories, and now was represented by John Macdonald and A. M. Smith, two wealthy Liberal business men. The triumph of Reform, the rout of John A. Macdonald, was above all a vote for representation by population, the great theme of the Upper Canada campaign. But it also reflected the West's acute dissatisfaction with Macdonald Conservatism, which had had nothing more to offer but another round in the threadbare game of ins and outs. Whatever the rep-by-pop protestations of individual Conservatives, their leaders had merely proposed to put the old Coalition back in office to sustain the inequitable union of the Canadas; and that union had just given renewed proof of the inequity that enabled an over-represented Lower Canada to impose laws on Upper Canada by the passage of the Scott Act. Under these circumstances indignant Upper Canadians had pinned their hopes for relief on the Reform party, which Brown had kept united. Grit Liberalism, in consequence, had never looked more close-knit, confident, and powerful.

Yet the Reform triumph was sadly incomplete. Victory in the West was counteracted by defeat in the East. Liberals had done as badly in Lower Canada as they had done well in Upper Canada. In the East, only twenty-four *Rouges*, led by Dorion and Holton, were returned, to about thirty-four *Bleus* under Cartier.[107] Of course, there were a number of more-or-less Liberals in between, whose very uncertainty meant that the eastern party strength could not be calculated exactly. Yet it was probable that many or most of them would vote with the *Bleus*: notably Sicotte, McGee, and their colleagues, whose resentment at being dropped from the ministry could well carry them into active opposition.

The force that had swung Lower Canada against Reform was the very counterpart to that which had won victory in Upper Canada: reaction to rep by pop. As the West was roused to make a new attack on the existing union, the East was roused as strongly to protect the position it enjoyed there, and which it so much dreaded to lose. Accordingly, French Canadians had looked to their tried *Bleu* defenders, not to *Rouge* allies of the menacing Grits. Dorion's reasoned oratory proved just as vain as Brown's talk of guarantees for French Canada, when "notre langue, nos institutions, et nos lois" seemed once again in peril. And so one fervent sectionalism simply balanced and offset the other. A dominant block of Grit Liberals confronted a dominant block of *Bleus*, and this could mean the inability of either side in parliament to govern. Sheer deadlock was in prospect.

Brown saw the pattern emerging when he wrote to Holton on June 26, by which time the election returns were all but complete. "We have been as successful as we could hope to be," he soberly asserted — "and now begins the real trouble. . . . I need not remind you that our very success in Upper Canada and the complete rout of the old corruptionists have rendered our future course more difficult than before."[108] No longer could the threat that John A. and Co. might return to power be used to dissuade eager Upper Canadian Reformers from demanding constitutional reform forthwith — and "the vote for rep by pop will be almost unanimous on the part of the U.C. members".[109]

Yet events in Lower Canada had by no means gone as they should. The key centre of Montreal, for instance, had just rejected both Dorion and Holton.[110] They would take other, safer seats — but it was sharp warning that, if the West should insist on action, the East would not at all be ready. And what then?

"What is to be done?" Brown asked Holton. "Look the case fairly in the face — or wait the event? The former is very difficult after what occurred in Montreal — and the latter may throw the Reform party into a defensive attitude not advantageous on such a question." His own opinion favoured an immediate summoning of parliament for a short session. "Announce that it is for the Supplies and the Militia Bill alone — push them through in ten days — and call us at the regular time — end of January. This will give you a chance of feeling the temper of the House . . . and it will enable you to prepare your plans coolly and considerately before your trial next winter."[111] It seemed good advice under the circumstances. The Macdonald-Dorion government resolved to summon the new parliament for a brief meeting in August.

But before this meeting occurred, George Brown had suffered a deep personal loss. On June 30, his father died, just the day after his seventy-ninth birthday.[112] The old man had failed badly in the past year, ever since he had lost his own devoted wife, Marianne, in the previous July. Yet Peter's warm good humour, his lifetime habit of scholarly reading, and his keen interest in events about him, had not failed, even during his final illness. He had been re-elected to the governing committee of the Anti-Slavery Society only months before, and on fine days his well-known figure could still be seen out on the streets of Toronto, leaning heavily on his son's arm.[113] The comradeship that began in George's childhood had not lapsed for a moment. They had come to America together, gone into journalism together as partners in New York; moved to Toronto and established the *Globe* together; and, through all the years, George Brown had never ceased to discuss his business and political affairs with his father. Thomas Nelson, who had known Peter Brown only in his last days, had found him "one of the most interesting old men I have ever met".[114] Lovingly George Brown recorded his passing:

"He faced death fearlessly and rejoicingly. He asked the medical attendant, 'Doctor, is this death?' 'Yes, Mr. Brown.' 'Will it be soon, Doctor?' 'Very soon, Mr. Brown.' 'Ah well, I am ready. I will soon be with dear Mother and Katie.' Then he prayed fervently for a few seconds. I never saw Christianity *lived out* in such a way before. Were it not for parting with dear, dear Anne, I could die tomorrow without a pang, could I die such a death as his."[115] From now on, he would need Anne more than ever.

Before the end of July, Brown was back at Bothwell, trying to keep busy every moment, hard at work from six in the morning to ten at night, examining the crops, the stock, and the buildings on his property, planning new operations with his agent, Captain John Taylor – arranging the fall work, settling with the hands, and making up the books.[116] There was 350 tons of hay in the barns, and much more to come. He was out in the fields as much as possible, helping to bring it in. But the physical labour revived him in body and spirit. "You will hardly know me when I return," he told his wife, "from the expanded sunburnt look of my handsome visage. I have a very nice little cap, but it has no brim and the face suffers."[117] Early in August he returned to Toronto, to prepare to leave for Quebec and parliament. Anne was to accompany him again.

Parliament opened on August 13, and a Reform caucus was at once held to nominate a candidate for Speaker of the new House. George Brown was its unanimous choice. Yet he expressed a "strong unwillingness" to serve unless his friends insisted.[118] He urged persuasively instead that a candidate be chosen who would draw the most Lower Canadian votes – again his compelling concern – and thus it was resolved to leave the matter to consultations between Brown and the ministry. They ended in a decision to put forward Lewis Wallbridge, a lawyer with a good knowledge of French, although his taking office as Speaker would necessitate replacing him in his post as Solicitor-General West. Wallbridge won election in the House, 66 to 58.[119] The comparative closeness of this opening vote, while no surprise, was not a good augury for the new Macdonald-Dorion régime, especially when Lower Canada had voted 40 to 23 against it. Now, in fact, it was the East that was being ruled by a western majority.

From that moment the situation grew steadily worse. The Address announcing government policy was a mild affair, since this was meant to be a short business session: the supplies, a bankruptcy bill, and a fairly non-controversial militia bill that the late Macdonald-Sicotte cabinet had not had time to pass. None the less, two of the displaced Liberal ministers, Sicotte and Foley, smarting to retaliate, moved want of confidence, and were only beaten 63 to 60.[120] From then on, there was virtually constant warfare, as the opposition moved one no-confidence measure after another, dragging the "short" session on all through September. Of course, the problem was that the combined Conservative-*Bleu* opposition was nearly as strong as the government forces. Cartier's eastern strength made up for John A. Macdonald's western weakness, especially when a disgruntled handful of moderates was added to it.

The government did its best. Sicotte, at least, was got out of the way by an appointment to the bench. The *Globe* talked of more reconstructions, admitting that a ministry with a bare majority could not in any case attempt basic reforms, and conceding that it was no better to have an Upper Canadian sectional majority dominating Lower Canada against its will than vice versa.[121] But a newly hopeful and reinvigorated Macdonald-Cartier phalanx tried every means to pull the government down, as the *Globe* turned gloomily to discourse on "The Spirit of Faction".[122] Somehow, by early October, the supplies were passed and the Militia Bill enacted: a permanent replacement for the temporary measure already put through by the Macdonald-Sicotte ministry in 1862, which now added 10,000 more men to the 25,000 under arms, wholly on a volunteer basis. Yet a final want-of-confidence motion by Alexander Galt was only fought out on October 7, when Brown eloquently defended the ministry.[123] Again, the government was saved by only three votes. Fortunately the session closed a few days later.

It was clear, however, that the Reform administration now had just this margin of two or three votes to count on. Gordon Brown tried to put a good face on it in the *Globe*, congratulating the ministry on a successful first testing, predicting new accessions of strength at the next session.[124] But the truth was that a chance vote might topple the shaky Grit-*Rouge* régime; and even if it did endure, it could hardly envisage gaining sufficient strength to move on to constitutional changes.

Accordingly, it was all the more significant that George Brown had given notice on August 14 of a motion which he had never had the opportunity to move, but which he recalled to the House on October 12, just before the hard-fought session ended.[125] It embodied a wholly new approach to the question of changing the constitution of the union. Instead of demanding rep by pop or even dual federation, and instead of taking any partisan line, it called for a general, impartial canvassing by a committee of the House of all the various remedies proposed for dealing with the problems of the Canadian union, with a view to issuing a considered report upon that subject. Furthermore, to avoid stirring up more partisan arguments over the ills to be dealt with, and who was to blame, Brown had grounded his motion on officially recorded facts. It began by reciting in preamble the words of a dispatch to the Colonial Office of February 2, 1859, which in turn embodied the memorial that Messrs. Cartier, Galt, and Ross had drawn up in October of 1858, when they had been in London as Canadian government delegates to discuss the proposal for a general federation of the British North American provinces.[126]

This was the abortive confederation project adopted, though soon abandoned, by the Cartier-Macdonald ministry at its inception in mid-1858. But, if the project had been shortly dropped by the Liberal-Conservative government, there was no question that their own dispatch had squarely acknowledged the problems of the Canadian union; namely, that grave difficulties of government were yearly growing worse, because of sectional differences and "the evils of internal dissension", and that a remedy was necessary in order to remove these difficulties forever. Beyond all question, the dispatch of 1859 had recognized the need for change. And it was a shrewd stroke on Brown's part to recall it now in 1863 and use it as authority for his own motion, especially when it had been framed by his opponents.

Accordingly, he intended to move "that a Select Committee of thirteen members be appointed to enquire and report on the important subjects embraced in the said dispatch, and the best means of remedying the evils therein set forth."[127] That was all. Simple, clear, hard to oppose, and with no sting or stigma in it. Yet it would prove the key to the log jam, the way out for the Province of Canada to a constructive and far broader future.

Though he had not been able to introduce his resolution into this turbulent autumn session for want of time, George Brown assured the House that he would bring it up at the next meeting of parliament. He spoke calmly and moderately, as he admitted that, while his side had kept command, it was neither "convenient nor desirable" that the present state of affairs should continue, and that "the strongest efforts should be made to secure for the government not only an Upper Canadian but a Lower Canadian majority".[128] Hence he would propose his committee, to be chosen from the leading men of both sides of parliament, to discuss the whole question of sectional relations "separated from the assertion of any dogma or principle", and thus the work of settlement by this or another government might be "immensely facilitated and advanced". It was a gesture of careful, even patient, statesmanship.

He had come to it gradually over the past few months, as he had faced up to the failure of the reconstructed Liberal ministry and the ensuing elections to provide any solution for the fundamental problem of the Canadian union. If the double majority and the rule of the moderates had failed within the year, it seemed no less apparent that rep by pop and the Grit-*Rouge* combination were unlikely in themselves to find success. And so Brown had charted out a new way, for trial at the next session in 1864.

This new way was in keeping with the change that had occurred in him during the past fifteen months. It was in keeping with his effort at greater detachment in politics, with the wider outlook he seemed to have acquired, and with his expressed desire to reduce the heat of partisan emotions. Moreover, George Brown still hoped to find the end of his own political career. He wrote to Anne's mother at that moment: "I am half sorry I came back into parliament – and yet it would have been difficult for my political friends to get along without me under present circumstances. Anne says, however, I am not to run again – and as I always do as she tells me – why I suppose this parliamentary life will not trouble us long."[129] His resolution, and his whole approach, were those of a man looking for a way out.

But there had been another side to the noisy ordeal at Quebec, the time he had spent there with Anne: the parties with the Mowats, with Dorion, Holton, and their friends; the river excursions in the summer, the Sunday walks along the ramparts, and their quiet wanderings above the town in the cool of autumn. They had stood together to watch the endless panorama of the St. Lawrence, a water-plain of clearest blue between hills bright with autumn foliage, criss-crossed by puffing little steamers gay with flags and dotted with the white sails of tall square-riggers bound inward from the sea.[130] Now it was time to leave; but Brown would most happily remember this particular parliamentary session. Anne would not be with him at the next one. She was expecting their first child that winter.

He made ready to leave for home, "frisky as a young kitten".[131] They were back in Toronto, as October passed into November, following another visit with the Holtons in Montreal.[132] By then George Brown was probably as much concerned with the coming event in his own family as with the future of the province. In both cases, however, it was still the time of waiting. And as for politics, there was little yet to suggest that a climactic era for British North America lay just ahead, or, similarly, that the most important period in Brown's life lay just before him. Nevertheless, the full consequences of the remaking of George Brown were soon to be revealed – in the remaking of Canada itself.

Initiator of Union

I

Gettysburg on July 3, Vicksburg on the fourth – within two summer days of 1863 the turning-point of the American Civil War had come. In the east, the greatest Confederate drive northward had been smashed outside an obscure Pennsylvania town. In the west, the South's last stronghold on the Mississippi had fallen, leaving the Confederacy cut in two. From this time forward, the eventual triumph of Union arms grew steadily more apparent. And the question of union in British North America grew more compelling than ever before.

It grew not merely through the fear that a victorious North might soon be free to work off an accumulation of anti-British feelings against the provinces. It grew as well because an enormous new power had arisen on the continent. A scantily armed, loose-knit band of states had been transformed into a centralized national republic, its industrial might advancing as irresistibly as its armies. Who could stand against it in North America? If the Confederacy, which had once seemed likely to divide the continent with the United States, was now striving grimly against ultimate defeat and extinction, what future was there for a little group of weak and separate provinces and the wilderness of British territory beyond? Unite, or be engulfed sooner or later: these were alternatives that would rise with increasing clarity before British North Americans, as the Civil War passed its bloody crest of decision.

Some had seen and stressed the alternatives before now, D'Arcy McGee for one. George Brown, however, firmly believing that the United States had no desire to undertake another war against Britain and her colonies, was more concerned to combat the panic-mongers of the anti-Northern press in Canada than to heed the long-run threat to separate existence raised by the growth of American power. Yet, while he normally remained sceptical of the likelihood of actual American attack, in one respect he fully recognized a danger from the great republic –

from the very numbers, wealth, and energy that would make an armed invasion virtually unnecessary, as the United States advanced its influence into the unorganized, underdeveloped British North West. Here, where the stakes were almost half a continent itself, he plainly realized the need for effective British North American union. He had for years; but now he realized it with mounting urgency.[1]

None the less, among Canadians generally, the call to combine or die had yet to be felt as critically urgent. The full significance of Gettysburg and Vicksburg took time to become explicit. Moreover, since warlike excitement over the *Trent* affair had subsided at the end of 1861, no comparable crisis had arisen in Anglo-American relations. But after Gettysburg a change was coming. And it was bound to come, as increasingly desperate Southerners sought to use Canada as a base of operations to strike at the United States from the rear.

There were some 15,000 Southern refugees or escaped soldiers in the British provinces in 1863[2] – or perhaps 100,000; no one could say for certain. Brown was well acquainted with their headquarters at the Queen's Hotel in Toronto, and the St. Lawrence Hall in Montreal, and the *Globe* made frequent references to "Southern activities" in Canada. From these centres Confederate agents circulated, dispensing funds, shaping grand designs to raid Detroit and Chicago or to free the prisoners of war in the big Federal camp on Johnson's Island, across Lake Erie near Sandusky. At first, in these plans, they sought to observe Canadian neutrality; but later they evinced far less concern. For the ominous truth was that raids engineered in Canada might do much more than divert some Northern strength to guard against attacks from the rear. They might well embroil the British provinces in war with the United States and realize the South's long-cherished dream of drawing Britain into the struggle alongside the Confederacy. Soon, indeed, there would be dangerous new strains on Anglo-American relations, strains originating on the borders of Canada herself.

A foretaste of trouble came early in November 1863. A scheme for a Confederate raid on Johnson's Island was uncovered by provincial authorities anxious to protect Canadian neutrality, and was immediately reported to Washington. The surprise attack was averted just in time. Canada's good faith was proved, and for the moment American relations were kept safe enough. Yet there was shock in the *Globe* headlines of November 13, when the late-night telegraph flashed the first reports of the attempt that had been frustrated: "Filibusterism on the Border! A Secesh Plot! Buffalo and Detroit Threatened!" And, while afterwards Brown's journal was glad to note that Canada was free of any complicity, it was sharp to tell Southern refugees that Canadians had no desire to see the war extended, and would not permit armed bands to organize upon their soil.[3]

At the time, however, the abortive raid still seemed an isolated episode to Brown. It was the same with an incident in the Lower Provinces a few weeks later, when a Confederate plot launched in New Brunswick (and involving several New Brunswickers and Nova Scotians) brought about the seizure of the New York-to-Portland coasting vessel *Chesapeake* by Southern raiders. The *Chesapeake* was soon recaptured by Federal warships, within Nova Scotian waters. Hence Maritimers were soon caught up in bitter exchanges with the Northern press, as they denounced the violation of their neutrality, and were denounced in turn for giving aid and shelter to Confederate "pirates". That the issue did not become a second *Trent* affair was chiefly owing to restraint and good sense both in Washington and London. But the *Globe* condemned Confederate authorities for "deliberately and of premeditation" making a base of British American soil. "British neutrality must be preserved," was its reading of the lesson, although it thought that Americans should realize that the true blame lay with the South.[4]

Yet if Brown did not yet comprehend the full potential threat in border friction with the United States, he was already concerned about the possible effects that mounting American animosity might have on trade relations; that is, on the future of the Reciprocity Treaty of 1854 between the American republic and the British provinces. That agreement would run until 1865, and then could be either renewed or terminated on a year's notice. Without doubt, Canada would seek its renewal. The free trade in natural products provided by the treaty had been richly beneficial in opening American markets for Canadian lumber, livestock, and farm produce. Many American interests had also benefited by the ease of exchange across the border. But there were other interests in the much larger, more complex republic that saw little worth in reciprocity: the strong high-tariff forces of the middle Atlantic states, for instance, or the powerful American manufacturers who considered that the degree of tariff protection that had been given to incipient Canadian industry under Galt's budgets of 1858 and '59 contravened the spirit if not the letter of the agreement, and left it of benefit only to Canada.

American criticisms of the Reciprocity Treaty had consequently been growing in the past few years, as the time for its renewal approached. Now its critics could exploit the antagonism to everything British roused by the Civil War; and, more particularly, popular indignation with the British provinces evoked by border incidents. The complaisant colonists might well be punished by being deprived of the privileges of reciprocity – the advantages of a one-sided treaty, as its American opponents portrayed it. Here was a nice juxtaposition of political emotion and economic interest. There was even danger that American hostility might go as far as cancelling the bonding system, which ensured Canada of access to the ocean through United States ports when winter closed hers in. Like most Canadians, therefore, Brown had good reason to worry over trade prospects, as the decisive year for the treaty, 1864, drew near.

He had upheld reciprocity ever since the ending of the old imperial controls over colonial commerce in 1849 had made a trade agreement possible with the United States. He upheld it in theory as a good Victorian free-trade liberal, to whom any lowering of "artificial" trade barriers brought closer accord with the natural economic harmony of the universe. He upheld it in fact because Canada was essentially a country of primary producers, whose chief products had access to the broad American market under the Treaty of 1854. Furthermore, the statistics of mounting trade with the United States since the agreement began seemed to show its value beyond question, while in the present years of booming war-time demand its worth looked greater than ever. Thus Brown's private conclusion: "The importance to Canada of maintaining the Treaty can hardly be overrated."[5]

Nevertheless, he believed as strongly that the Treaty was equally valuable to the United States.[6] What true Cobdenite Liberal could believe anything else than that the freeing of trade benefited both parties to the exchange? He wholly denied the American claim that Canada enjoyed a credit balance under reciprocity, though he realized that such a claim might doom the treaty in the United States. Canadians, therefore, had particular reason to make clear that they were not the sole gainers through reciprocity – above all, that it was not vital to their very economic existence, as Americans were all too ready to assume. It was only sensible in seeking a bargain not to play into the other party's hands. It was sensible, and it was right: however much a boon to Canada reciprocity might be, the province could exist without it. Brown had made that assertion in the *Globe* even as the treaty was signed in 1854.[7] He said so once again, now that its continuance was in question.

His paper raised the point in answer to "one of the ablest and most liberal American journals", the Chicago *Tribune*, which supported the treaty but feared that the expression of anti-

Northern views in Canada would endanger its renewal. Stoutly the *Globe* replied, "If the Americans imagine that Canadians for the sake of Reciprocity will abandon their right to discuss questions with which the whole world is ringing, to maintain such opinions as please them, they make a wonderful mistake. The Canadian people can by no means be driven into a corner in dealing with this Reciprocity matter – but can live and prosper without Reciprocity."[8] It was a bold front, but the truth was that Brown and the *Globe* still had their hearts set on the renewal of the treaty.

Yet the question of reciprocity also involved the other British provinces that were partners to the agreement. In fact, the issues that were crowding in on Brown by the opening of 1864 were broad, general ones that affected British North America as a whole. The future of provincial trade, the border problems, the impact of the Civil War in its decisive stage: all called for viewpoints wider than any single province could provide. Danger, and the need for a united response, were in the air together. They pressed him to think of union. And besides all this, there was the ever-present question of the North West, where George Brown had long asserted that the future of all British America must lie.[9]

2

In the previous summer (1863) a group of British financiers had bought control of the Hudson's Bay Company for a million and a half pounds, and Watkin, the aggressive president of the Grand Trunk, had figured prominently in the transaction. Its hopeful significance, as Brown could clearly see, was that the title to the North West had now been transferred from old, unchanging fur monopolists to a powerful group of business men particularly concerned to open up the territory and develop a transit route to the Pacific.[10] Watkin still had his starry vision of building the bankrupt Grand Trunk into a huge all-British transcontinental system, which would require both the Intercolonial railway to the Maritimes and communications across the western plains to British Columbia – the first phase here to be by wagon road and a telegraph line. Indeed, in 1862 Brown had had three meetings to discuss British North American development with the grandiose promoter in London – and they had disagreed on practically everything, "except on the subject of opening up the North West territories".[11]

Since then, Watkin had been in Canada to pursue that very subject, and had found that Sandfield Macdonald, Cartier, and John A. Macdonald all shared his own view that a separate Crown Colony could be erected in the territory. Yet Brown, of course, held out for its annexation to Canada. He and Watkin had had another stiff interview; for each of them had formed a thoroughly low opinion of the other – the narrow, intransigent Clear Grit, to Watkin; the brash embodiment of Grand Trunk waste, to Brown.[12] Nevertheless the Reform politician could at least expect new developments in the North West under a reorganized Hudson's Bay Company, especially when he was sure that Newcastle, the Colonial Secretary, was himself strongly interested in opening the territory.[13] Here, then, was another item on the agenda for 1864, and all the more reason to urge that Canada should press her own claims to the North West, lest British capitalists, if not Americans, develop that vast region purely in their private interests and leave Canadians virtually as poor relations cut off from their natural inheritance.

As for the Americans, their threat to the North West was all too evident. "Cooped up as Canada is between lake, river and the frozen North," the *Globe* declared, "should all the rest of the continent fall into the possession of the Americans, she will become of the smallest importance."[14] Brown heard of alarming plans for the extension of the St. Paul and Anoka Railway northward into British territory, right to Fort Garry: "Once let the railway be built, and the whole country, cut off from any but a roundabout and costly communication with Canada, will speedily become Americanized. . . . We believe that the movement which has now been instituted for the purpose of facilitating communication between the Red River and the State of Minnesota is nothing more or less than the handing over of the vast North West Territory, not only commercially but politically, to the United States."[15] The issue was one of basic continental strategy: the competition between north-south and east-west designs for the communications and control of western British North America.

And yet this issue, like the others that were forcing themselves on Brown, could still not be considered central to his thinking. His primary concern remained what it had always been: reform of the existing Canadian union through settling the representation question; it was just over ten years since he had first moved representation by population in parliament. No, these broader and external questions acted, rather, on his mind from the periphery. In consequence, however, they worked to expand its horizons, leading him increasingly to view reform of the Canadian union in the full context of the development of British North America. They served to stimulate that wider sense of statesmanship already revealed in his proposal for a select committee to examine every aspect of the constitutional question. In a very real way Brown was what he had always been: a leader of Upper Canadian sectionalism, pre-eminently devoted to the "rights of Upper Canada". Yet, in no less real a fashion, he was prepared by this time to integrate that sectionalism into a design for a great new national structure. And since any new British North American state must rest on the integration of disparate regions, sections, and cultures, his position was itself a thoroughly realistic one.

One necessary aspect of this realism was a clear recognition that the French-Canadian community had as much right to maintain sectional interests in a new union as Upper Canada had. Brown had now abandoned his earlier presumption that French Canadians would be assimilated; in fact, he had abandoned the belief that at first had underlain his advocacy of rep by pop: that there was no reason to have a sectional line dividing Canada in two, or to regard the inhabitants of the East as in any way requiring different institutions from those of the West.[16] It would be wrong to say that he had come to understand the French Canadians or even to appreciate their devotion to customs, faith, and culture, which to him still appeared unprogressive and priest-ridden. Nevertheless (and this was highly important), he was prepared at the least to let the French-speaking community go its own way, to concede the cultural duality of Canada, and, at the most, to see valuable attributes in the French Canadians that made possible a constructive future partnership of peoples.

This change in his thinking, increasingly in evidence since his marriage and return from Britain, was best exemplified in the Globe, which, as always, reflected George Brown's leading opinions and set them before the country. It ran a number of articles, some probably by Brown himself, on the relations of the two communities in Canada. No doubt the aim was partly to calm Lower Canadian fears of rep by pop. But the articles constituted a public commitment to a line of policy for Brown, often couched in language so forthright that it would be hard to say that he was merely wooing French Canada with soft blandishments. His recognition of facts was rather the significant thing.

"For all we care," the Globe now announced, "the French Canadians may retain their language, laws and institutions till the end of the world. The employment of their language in parliamentary proceedings may involve some expense, but no one would think of giving deep offence to the French people in order to save a few thousand dollars or pounds per annum. The laws of Lower Canada are very good laws, as far as we can judge, and nobody desires to change them. The institutions, so long as they please the people of Lower Canada, will remain unchanged, for no one in Upper Canada takes any interest in them."[17] As for any complaint against the Roman Catholic hierarchy, it was not at all that they had worked ill in Lower Canada, but that they had sought to interfere with the institutions of Upper Canada — an interference that had to be resisted.

Furthermore, the frequent charge that the *Globe* considered French Canadians an inferior race that must inevitably succumb was sheer political libel, a device employed to weaken Brown's allies in the East in the same way as the "No looking to Washington" cry had been used against the western Grits. Quite bluntly, the journal reversed the accusation. It was the French Canadians who thought they were superior: "They attribute all to jealousy of their superior institutions, and behind this impassable barrier entrench themselves against the assaults of reason and experience."[18] But, in any case, the real question at issue was not the superiority or inferiority of the French, but their power — their power to dominate the union, which had to be removed without any subsequent domination being imposed on them instead.

"By their bond of a common nationality," the *Globe* declared, "the French Canadians will always possess power in Canada greater in proportion to their numbers than the British population. We do not object to that. Let them make all they can out of it. But let them not expect to govern us by a minority. As to the merely sectional and commercial differences between Upper and Lower Canada, there is not one which cannot be fought out in the legislative arena without an atom of bitterness. . . . Upper Canada has not the slightest objection to allowing Lower Canada to manage her own affairs. If she will consent to leave us alone we have no desire to interfere between priest and people in Lower Canada. . . . But let us endeavour in carrying on the affairs of our common country to arrive at some basis on which we all may stand in peace and contentment. We see no insuperable difficulty in the way of this result, and shall not cease to strive for its accomplishment."[19]

Going further, Brown's journal set forth the qualities of the French Canadians that could make them worthy partners in the development of this common country — "naturally industrious, frugal, temperate, handy, ingenious, and under favorable circumstances, enterprising". Indeed, "the French Canadian has penetrated every part of the American continent. In the West as well as the Eastern States you find him, and he is beloved and respected wherever he goes."[20] Not so energetic or ambitious as the Anglo-Saxon, he was more uniformly successful. If at home his agriculture was deficient, his technical skills and education limited, it was only because of his self-imposed isolation. "The pride of race is strong in the French Canadian, but it is a false pride when it leads him not to deeds which show his superiority over his neighbours, but on the contrary compels him to shut himself up in a cold and barren corner of a vast and fertile continent, afraid lest if he venture forth, some portion of his individuality may be lost in the vigorous life around him."[21] The *Globe* eagerly urged him forth instead. "We ask the opening of a vast territory, from which will flow a great stream of traffic through the St. Lawrence, fertilizing its exhausted shores, and affording the French race an opportunity for developing the rare qualities which they possess, such as even the early pioneers of New France never imagined."[22]

As the Grit organ saw it, it was precisely because of this bright prospect that the great majority of Upper Canadians desired "to see Upper Canada not only united with Lower Canada, but with all the other British American territories adjacent".[23] And French Canadians had no reason to fear being swamped in such a combination: "No one will dream of one government for the Gut of Canso and the Saskatchewan River, or even for the St. Lawrence and Lake Winnipeg."[24] The *Globe*, in short, was recognizing the need for a general federal scheme of government.

But how would representation by population fit into such a scheme? It would be a basic requirement in any federal union, the first ingredient of its general government – the essential prerequisite to settle the wrongs done Upper Canada. "Before entering into new alliances," affirmed the *Globe*, "it should be the effort of Upper Canadians to regulate the affairs of their own province, to obtain representation by population, to open the North West territory so that, when federation of all the British American provinces does come, it may be formed with Upper Canada as the central figure of the group of states, with western adjuncts as well as eastern."[25] Here, accordingly, sectional and national aspirations were again combined in Brownite thinking; yet once more this was a not unrealistic forecast of the Canadian federal structure that would actually emerge.

Such was the position George Brown had reached by 1864. Still seeking the reform of the Canadian union, he was prepared to accept the dualism of French- and English-speaking communities, and to comprehend it through the federal principle. He was willing to see that principle extended to bring all the British provinces together. He was concerned with the underlying economic problem, heedful of American reactions, keenly anxious to gain the West. In sum, Brown was ready for his greatest role: as the initiator of British North American union.

3

Public affairs, however, gave way to other considerations in mid-January of 1864. On the twelfth, Anne Brown gave birth to a daughter, a thoroughly healthy and wholly wonderful little girl, to be christened Margaret after Anne's mother. At forty-five George Brown took eagerly to fatherhood, doting, fussing, full of plans for his wife and family. They would move into a new home; they would make a trip back to Scotland in the summer to display their child to admiring relatives. His private world had seemed complete before, but now he found it had a new dimension, now that "Baby Maggie" had brought "a vast addition to our happiness".[26]

Then, on January 15, another birth occurred, this time at the *Globe* office. The *Canada Farmer*, "a fortnightly journal of agricultural, horticultural and rural affairs", came into existence, edited by W. F. Clarke of Guelph, an experienced agricultural writer and journalist.[27] Brown was broadening his enterprise again, providing, in fact, a periodical specifically designed for his already wide following in the Upper Canadian countryside. It was a sound move that would pay for itself many times over. "It has evidently met a want much felt," the owner happily concluded, as hundreds of subscriptions came in daily.[28] The *Canada Farmer* would indeed become a familiar part of rural life in a much larger Canada, extending far across the western plains.

But public problems could not be left for long. One of them, the Reciprocity Treaty, Brown took up with Luther Holton as Minister of Finance, in his worry lest the Americans announce their intention to end that agreement. "It appears to me that none of you are sufficiently awake about it," he wrote anxiously on January 19. "I confess I see very serious trouble ahead if *notice* of the repeal is given. Such a feeling will be manifested here as will determine the Americans to repeal it. . . . I do think you are taking on you a very serious responsibility in not opening negotiations at Washington. . . . It would be a thousandfold easier to negotiate before notice than after."[29]

Holton no doubt reported these views to the prime minister.
At any rate, just two days later Sandfield Macdonald offered
Brown an assignment as a "quasi-political" Canadian agent to
spend some months in Washington and sound out, in an unofficial
way, the parties concerned there with the treaty.[30] "By the freedom of the intercourse thus afforded," Macdonald noted a bit
stiffly, "it is considered that the prejudices against the treaty
would be greatly modified." His colleagues had all pointed to
Brown as eminently qualified for the task. "I am authorized,"
he continued, "to bespeak your co-operation in any way you may
feel disposed to lend it towards maintaining the Treaty as it is,
or if that should be impossible, to combat for the best terms that
could be agreed upon as the basis for a fresh Treaty."[31]

But Brown declined the offer. It was certainly not that he
underestimated the need for such a mission: "I do think the
clamour against the Treaty has been allowed to go too long
unchecked," he replied to Macdonald, as he advised immediate
steps to make plain to Congress and its all-important committees
how much the United States had also gained from the agreement.[32] On the contrary, he thought the question of such moment
that an unofficial Canadian emissary would not be good enough.
Actual negotiations with the American government in any case
would have to rest with the British minister in Washington,
Lord Lyons. Hence, in Brown's judgment, the best course would
be to keep Lyons in constant touch with the views and wishes of
the Canadian government through stationing one of its members
in Washington, and, because of both his commercial training
and his position as Minister of Finance, Luther Holton was the
ideal man to send. "The matter is of such vast importance to the
Province, I think *no consideration* should prevent Mr. Holton
from assuming this duty at once."[33]

He would be only too happy to co-operate with Holton,
Brown added, though he could not see his own way clear now to
leaving Canada for any lengthy period. Perhaps there was also
the thought in the back of Brown's mind that Sandfield Macdonald's offer might merely be a dodge to remove a difficult
party presence from the next session of parliament – a thought
that gained substance when the premier failed to send Holton or
anybody else to Washington. For the fact remained that although
George Brown and his paper had supported the remade Macdonald government with a fair degree of cordiality, the Toronto
press lord was both too strong and too independent for Sandfield's complete ease of mind.

Moreover, in the past few months Brown had been in considerable disagreement with one aspect of the government's

financial policy, and carrying on a sustained private argument by letter with Holton himself. The dispute arose from the latter's decision to transfer the government's account from the Bank of Upper Canada to the Bank of Montreal, which constituted a grave blow to the West's chief banking institution. The Finance Minister explained that the move was wholly due to the inadequate resources of the Bank of Upper Canada, and professed his confidence that Brown, as "a keen-eyed man of business", would understand.[34] But the other rose vigorously to defend the Toronto bank, denying the necessity for the transfer and deploring the additional power to be given to "a Montreal institution, soul and body, and most hostile to Upper Canada interests".[35] Brown was simply jealous of "the real metropolis of the country", Holton retorted.[36] Opposing sectional viewpoints had come between two old associates; they argued sharply and at length. Their exchange never became acrimonious, however, nor was it public. At the end, in January, they simply agreed to disagree.[37] Thus their friendship was not shaken, and in other respects they continued in accord. Nevertheless, Brown's connections with the Macdonald-Dorion ministry were not strengthened by his conviction that it had carried through a financial policy seriously damaging to the best interests of the section he represented.

Then too, the government had still failed to press the North West question; its negotiations with Watkin and his associates had so far done nothing to open the territory or remove the dead hand of the Hudson's Bay monopoly. Nor had it acted to arrange for moving the seat of government from Quebec back to Toronto again, as it should have, since the new Ottawa capital would not be ready for three more years. But worst of all, it had lost an important by-election quite unnecessarily, at a time when the close balance of the opposing parties in parliament made such a loss serious indeed.

The contest in question was held in South Leeds in late January to return A. N. Richards, recently appointed as Solicitor-General West in place of Lewis Wallbridge, who had been named Speaker of the House. Richards was a Sandfield Macdonald man from Macdonald's eastern bailiwick in Upper Canada, whereas Wallbridge had shared the outlook of the western Grit majority. Before the election, Brown protested to Holton, "I think the appointment was a very wrong one. . . . Richards holds, and did hold, all the views of the Macdonald-Sicotte ministry. Mowat and Wallbridge were taken specially in to give confidence to those who did not hold those views – and Wallbridge's successor should certainly have been of like opinions."[38] Unfair or not, the appointment clearly proved impolitic. Instead of choosing a Grit Liberal in a safe, solidly Grit western seat, Sandfield, in his short-sighted desire to strengthen his own following in the cabinet, had opened a contest in a far from secure eastern constituency. Moreover, John A. Macdonald and D'Arcy McGee descended together on South Leeds: the former in a keen awareness of the chance to reduce the narrow governmental lead, the latter in a burning desire to pay back Sandfield and Co. for tossing him out of the ministry.[39] The conjunction of these first-class political talents turned the trick – and a dangerous bond was established between two formerly fierce enemies. The Conservative candidate, D. F. Jones, was elected in South Leeds. The narrow margin of the Macdonald-Dorion ministry in parliament grew even narrower.

Brown's annoyance was to be expected: "Here is a pretty mess! Perhaps Sandfield will now have his eyes slightly opened to the fact that it is only on thoroughly Liberal constituencies the government can rely when the pinch comes."[40] Furthermore, he was astounded to learn from Holton that Sandfield was now claiming that he, Brown, had agreed to Richards's appointment in the first place! It was true, George Brown admitted, that he had discerned some time before that Sandfield had really had his eye on Richards, and had not spoken specifically against him then. "It was not for me to say that Richards' appointment would be a gross injustice and breach of our understanding at the formation of the government, while Sandfield was protesting all the time that he had no thought of appointing him and would do nothing without letting me know."[41] But Brown grew still more annoyed when Holton in return feared that his allegiance might be wandering.[42] In some warmth he answered: "Must I, whether I honestly can do so or not, approve of the course of the government on the Bank matter – the Seat-of-Government matter, the Reciprocity matter, the South Leeds election – the North West matter – on all of which I was consulted after the thing was done, or when it was too late to do anything? And because I do not and cannot approve of the course of the government on these things – does it follow that I will not stick to my party? . . . I think Mowat and you should not have allowed matters to get into the shape they have. I have done my duty in urging you both and warning you of the coming trouble – from my point of view. You have not seen proper to go upon it. But I don't 'take the pet' on that account. The question is not what I think ought to have been, and might have been – but *what is*. It is impossible in my opinion – however we up here may exert ourselves – to get through the coming session. I see you don't think so. Well, I sincerely hope you may prove right – for a break-up now is not only to lose the reins but ruin the party up here. I don't want that. And little respect as I have for a portion of the gov't., I can't separate them from the great Reform party."[43]

This was early in February, and the *Globe* had already made clear to the public that it considered Richards's defeat a grave blow to a tottering administration. Michael Foley, like McGee, was fixed now in vengeful opposition. The further loss of Richards would leave the ministry virtually at the mercy of a few near-nonentities when parliament met on February 19 — men who still had stayed outside the major party blocks, and whose chief claim to attention lay in their ability to throw the thin edge of power in either direction.[44] Although the Grit Liberals were still the largest single block of any party, the outlook gave no reason for enthusiasm. And that fact, coupled with George Brown's disillusionment with the enfeebled Macdonald-Dorion régime, inevitably made him more independent, more detached in outlook than ever. He could profess his devotion to the Liberal cause and still mean it. But he foresaw a "break-up", and was not far from accepting it. "Don't you regret you had not made a stand before this?" he asked Holton.[45] Each event in sequence, it seemed, was pushing him further and further along an individual course of action.

John A. Macdonald sensed it. He might not understand it; he could not know where it might lead; but his acute political perception and inherent readiness to exploit any opening led him to a careful probing of Brown's intentions through C. J. Brydges, the general manager of the Grand Trunk.[46] Brydges was about the only Grand Trunk representative who might speak easily to Brown, owing to their friendly relations during the former's years on the Great Western. Now in mid-February of 1864, as Brown came down to Quebec, Brydges approached him with a proposal that was strikingly indicative of the close relationship between the Grand Trunk interests, the reorganized Hudson's Bay Company, and, of course, Edward Watkin's pet project, the Intercolonial.

As Brydges afterwards reported the encounter to Macdonald, he had offered Brown the chairmanship of the Canada Board of the Hudson's Bay Company — "at which I think he was a good deal impressed".[47] At the same time the Grand Trunk representative had made plain to him that nothing could be done about the North West unless the Intercolonial project were accepted too. It was a valid point. Westward expansion and eastern extension should go hand in hand, not impede one another by fruitless competition. Just as Grand Trunk interests had recognized that to accomplish the Intercolonial scheme required a continental plan of through communications, so Brown had to realize that effective measures to gain the North West also involved accepting the railway to the Atlantic. "On the latter point," said Brydges significantly, "he is *much* mollified. Thinks that the action of the Yankees about reciprocity and bonding has put an entirely new phase on the question, and that it ought now to be seriously taken into consideration."[48] In short, Brown was growing prepared for the Intercolonial.

Significantly, too, regarding the existing government, Brydges noted: "He is very angry with the present men and thinks that they will sink, but believes that he could propound a policy that would save them."[49] Brydges did not elicit that policy; but most probably it included federation. Even the preceding October, the Grit leader had told D'Arcy McGee that he would approve a federal union either of the Canadas or of all the provinces in order to "eliminate the present sectional antagonism".[50] Now, as Brydges noted, Brown did not apparently object to "the marrying of the North West and the Intercolonial", but wanted a wider solution – "an omnibus arrangement" – that would include a settlement of the representation issue as well as western and eastern extension, not to mention a lowering of the tariff. "He would support such a programme, and thinks it could be carried."[51] Indeed, it would be. Carried to achieve the confederation of British North America.

For the present, however, the programme remained simply in Brown's mind. He promised only to think over Brydges's offer of the Hudson's Bay post, and John A. Macdonald did not bother to pursue the approach further. He himself was not ready for such an "omnibus arrangement" as Brown projected – above all, not for the constitutional settlement. Macdonald was still engrossed in the barren politics of the existing union, still totting up votes to devise another of its endless, empty ministerial combinations. Brydges's report on Brown had not disclosed anything of practical value for this end. And yet it had revealed that George Brown was ready to support the essential programme of Confederation before the close of February of 1864 – before what proved to be the final round of the old political game in the Canadian union was fairly under way.

4

The opening weeks of parliament consisted of mere sparring. The Speech from the Throne on February 19 had not enunciated any bold policies, since Sandfield Macdonald's government obviously meant to walk as gingerly as possible through the almost equally divided House. The opposition, on the other hand, was disposed not to seek a decisive division until the ministry had introduced its main measures. Consequently, the debate over the Address in Reply, which lasted till March 2, chiefly concerned personalities, not policies, and lavished mutual recriminations without any test of confidence being called. The fact was that both sides were hanging back, waiting for all the members to arrive, trying to net the last loose fish, calculating and re-calculating the probable vote. It might go either way; no one could be quite sure. Only one thing was certain: the parliamentary air was crackling with strain, as deadlock ruled the Province of Canada.

Yet through it all Brown kept his measure of detachment. He made no speech in the debate on the address. As it rose angrily about him, he sat in his place in the House devotedly writing home to Anne: "Already I long to be back with you and will grudge every day I am kept from your side. . . . Don't fail to write me every day, if only a single line to tell me you and baby are well. Tell me all about your doings and baby's – the smallest incident will be anxiously perused."[52] He was not even in the chamber for some of the fiercest episodes. He told Anne on February 25, "There was an awful scene of abuse in the House last night. McGee, O'Halloran, Ferguson and others pitching into each other like fury. Fortunately I stayed home to nurse my leg [sciatica was troubling him], played a couple of games of chess with John Macdonald [member for West Toronto] and went off to bed at one o'clock. . . . The debates so far have not had one hour of practical common sense in them. . . . There ought to be a shake-up and I hope there will be."[53]

Nor had he thoughts of office in a reconstructed government. "Gordon is entirely wrong in fancying that I would for a moment entertain the idea of 'going in'. Lots of people here talk of that, but nothing would tempt me to commit such an act of folly. No, my Anne, we will pay off all our debts, have two or three years quiet enjoyment with our little pet, lessen our labour – and then *perhaps* think of such work. But now – it would be arrant folly. At any time, it would be – well I won't moralize. But *you* are so ambitious!"[54]

His thoughts for the future turned instead to their projected trip to Scotland, which Anne referred to diffidently, fearful, no doubt, that George's political commitments might yet prevent it. Affectionately he answered, " 'If we should go home in the summer' . . . I can fancy the half-pleasure, half-sadness with which that 'if' was written. I believe, Anne, you are the best wife that ever lived. You think it will be inconvenient for me to cross the herring pond this summer – and you are constantly saying kind little things to make it easy for me to say so. But Madam, you may as well make up your mind to the fact at once. There are others concerned besides you and me and Baby. Our words are pledged to go, and go we shall."[55]

The fiercely partisan debate wound on. Once he would have plunged into it with zest. Now he found it boring. "Rose," he reported, "has just risen to speak and he has said the only sensible thing that has yet been uttered. . . . He hoped that the debate would now be brought to a close without further waste of time – and that we may get to the business of the country."[56] As for Cartier's savage attack, that stung government members to fury: "Would you believe it? . . . The little wretch screetched – is that the way to spell it? – thirteen hours in one speech! They used to charge me with being long-winded – but Cartier outdoes all the world, past present or to come."[57] He could not even view all his opponents with the old hot antagonism. He sent Anne a photograph of his former political ally McGee, who apparently felt much the same way towards him. "I enclose you a carte of D'Arcy McGee, and I think you will say that he never looked so well in his life. It was a great thing in him to give it to me – but I believe he does not think me quite as bad as the rest of the ministerial party – but rather as a redeeming point."[58]

He stayed quietly by himself as much as possible, often in his lodgings at Mrs. Langlois's waiting for his wife's letters. "Near three o'clock," he wrote, "and Anne's letter not come! That horrid Grand Trunk. For the last two hours every foot on the stairs has made my heart beat a little faster – there come my letters – but it always goes past, and I go back to work again. Perhaps you won't believe it, but I am very industrious these days. Never go out till the House meets and work like a beaver at letters and all sorts of things. I have a very comfortable room, indeed, with a glorious view of the St. Charles, and I read a little, write a good deal, look out a little, and think and muse about darling Anne and our little Baby all the while. You won't be vexed if I confess that I am not a bit unhappy – separated though we are?"[59]

The debate on the address at last concluded, the assembly turned to its committee work, and George Brown found quite enough to keep him busy. "They have put me on all the leading committees," he announced, " – on eleven I think – and I expect to do some good work upon them. The members (even the French) are all very kind and civil to me this session – particularly so – and I find it very pleasant."[60] So the days went by. The heavy snows of Quebec melted in a sudden gush of early spring, and Brown momentarily gave way to his impatience with politics, his longing to be home with his wife and family. "I hate this parliamentary work. . . . I think what a fool I am to be here."[61]

But then, on the night of March 14, he had his chance to move the resolution for his own select committee to investigate the constitutional problem, the resolution he had announced the previous autumn but not found opportunity to introduce. Now he made his first real speech of the session on that subject, and it was a short, conciliatory one for him. He had not replied to unfounded charges, made during the address, that he had abandoned rep by pop, Brown explained, because he had wanted to lay this motion before the House free from all party feeling; he stood here tonight as an independent member. Similarly, he had framed his resolution "in the least possible objectionable shape", by basing it on "the words of the honourable gentlemen opposite, given as sworn advisers to the Crown".[62] The reference, of course, was to the dispatch of the Cartier-Macdonald ministers that had declared the steady growth of sectional discords in the Canadian union to be "fraught with great danger", and recognized the need for "a remedy for a state of things that is yearly becoming worse".[63] Relying on that declaration, said Brown, "I simply ask the House to say that a great evil exists, that a remedy must be found, and to appoint a committee to consider what that remedy should be."[64]

He went on to outline once again the ills and injustices of the existing system. As he finished, a French Canadian member, Joseph Perrault, was on his feet to urge instead that parliament seek an imperial bill that would enshrine equal representation in the Canadian union forever: "As long as Lower Canada is Lower Canada, it cannot concede representation by population!"[65] Then Alexander Galt rose to speak against Brown's committee, asserting that he still held to the idea of a general confederation, but that it was up to the government to initiate any action on the constitutional question.[66] A western Grit, John Scoble, was all for rep by pop and condemned the very idea of federation, which had failed so signally in the United States.[67] And, following this, John A. Macdonald congratulated Scoble on his remarks, at least as far as the failure of the federal system in the United States was concerned. Any future British North American union must be "a complete union", he contended: "We should have a legislative union in fact, in principle, and in practice."[68] "That is not my policy," interjected Cartier, hastily repudiating this backsliding from the former government's principle of general federation.[69] But Macdonald quickly swung away to accuse Brown of deserting rep by pop as futile, and to label his committee as a mere dodge towards that end: "He now desires to burke it in committee in order to get rid of it altogether!"[70]

Cartier next opposed the motion; Mowat and Alexander Mackenzie supported it. And Brown at the end showed some of his former fire as he answered Macdonald's charges of apostasy. "These miserable personal attacks," he thundered, "were all that the honorable member could resort to in order to divert attention from the important question before the House – on which he has not expressed an opinion!" Scornfully he pointed to Macdonald's denial of the Conservatives' own doctrine of general federation – "but one specimen of his own want of any fixed principle in politics".[71] Once again the old antagonism, the old lack of comprehension, had come between the two men. Macdonald could not or would not see that Brown, far from evading or abandoning the representation issue, was wholly fixed upon its settlement. Brown would not or could not see that Macdonald's desire for a strong, complete union, far from indicating lack of principle, was a constant factor in his politics throughout.

In any event, the motion had taken up an evening sitting without coming to a vote. Debate upon it was adjourned for a week, but Brown was far from discouraged. He told Anne in some satisfaction next day, "I was delivered from my responsibility on the representation question last night – having spoken out my whole mind on the subject. I spoke, for once, an hour, and kept the rapt attention of the house the whole time." However, "The opposition took a wretched course in the debate. Galt, Cartier and John A., throwing aside entirely the importance of the subject, attempted to turn it off on miserable personal questions of inconsistency – John A. was especially mean and contemptible. He attacked Mowat and myself very bitterly – but I think he got it back with interest. . . . I don't think we will carry the committee, but we will have at any rate a large vote upon it."[72]

Perhaps Brown was a prejudiced witness on his own behalf. Yet an equally prejudiced witness on the other side offered proof of the change that had come over him. The parliamentary correspondent of the *Leader* gave no friendly report of Brown's speech on the resolution – but was no less revealing for all that. The member for South Oxford, he found, had been "dull, gentle as a sucking dove. . . . There was not one word in his speech about 'Lower Canadian domination', not one word about the grasping hierarchy of Lower Canada, not one word of threat that if Rep by Pop were not granted there would be a revolution, . . . not one syllable to show that the same bloodthirsty spirit, so to speak, pervaded his bosom." Undoubtedly this was "a great transformation".[73] In fact, the savage Brown had been strangely tame throughout, until, at the close, he had referred to the hostile commercial policy of the United States. Then, "in marked heroics", he had entreated the people of Canada to cast off party prejudices and "stand shoulder to shoulder to fight their own battle for progress and prosperity, and if need be, to meet and do their best unitedly to repel a common foe". In this passage, thought the *Leader* correspondent, the Clear Grit chieftain had shown some of his wonted energy and warmth. But, of course, everyone agreed that he had lost his hold.

Here, suddenly, the issue lapsed. There was no more time for further consideration of Brown's motion. The inevitable crisis had at last arrived for the Macdonald-Dorion government, and everything else was put aside. For weeks now, Sandfield Macdonald had been striving hard behind the scene to find just one or two votes more. He even sought to reconstruct his government to include the majority group of French Canadians, and to that end approached without success Sir Etienne Taché, venerable member of the Legislative Council who once had headed Liberal-Conservative Coalition cabinets in 1856 and 1857.[74] The opposition was now eager for the test. But Sandfield would not face it. Although it seemed that he still might win by a majority of two or three, he refused to try to carry on a ministerial programme with such a bare, uncertain margin. Rumours of a government crisis were spreading through Quebec by March 18.[75] Three days later Sandfield resigned. All was in flux again, as Governor-General Monck entrusted one politician after another with the task of forming a new ministry, and, one after another, they reported the failure of their negotiations.

Fergusson Blair, a western Liberal, tried to form a new combination of parties. So did Alexander Campbell, an Upper Canada Conservative and John A. Macdonald's old law partner. Cartier failed, and Dorion as well, and Monck turned in near-desperation to Taché. Taché himself now looked to that highly experienced cabinet-maker, John A. Macdonald, who was game for one more try. His skill at length succeeded, and on March 30, the Taché-Macdonald government was announced.

To all intents and purposes, however, it was the old Liberal-Conservative Coalition back in office.[76] Macdonald, Cartier, and Galt were there in their commanding positions, as Attorneys-General West and East and Minister of Finance respectively.

True, two erstwhile Liberals, McGee and Foley, gave the ministry some new blood from the other party — but this too was thoroughly in keeping with John A.'s long practice of grafting fresh shoots on to the Coalition stock. And while the cabinet also included such a relative independent as Campbell, and such an old "moderate" friend of the Queen's government as Isaac Buchanan, this did not alter the fact that government again rested on the well-tried alliance of Lower Canadian *Bleus* and Upper Canadian Conservatives. The *Globe* put it with characteristic simplicity: "Every one of the chief actors of the old Corruptionist Company is there in full life. The change is merely in the scene-shifters and candle-snuffers."[77]

Ministries based on the western majority and the eastern minority had failed. Now the eastern majority and western minority would try once more, to see if they could manage any better to control a deadlocked House. Parliament was adjourned on March 31, so that the new ministers could meet their by-elections. George Brown went home quite sure that they had no answer, and that his own approach, through the select committee, promised the only solution to political paralysis in Canada.

5

His brother Gordon had been ill, and, catching cold before his full recovery, was very ill again.[78] He would not be able to manage the *Globe* for some time — a further reason for George Brown to welcome the parliamentary adjournment, apart from being home with his family. April, then, was spent fairly quietly in Toronto, about the only excitement being furnished by the by-elections. Michael Foley's drew the most attention, for western Reformers were determined to defeat the deserter who had once been nominally their party leader. Alexander Mackenzie and Archibald McKellar — Brown's two devoted agents in old campaigns in the West, who now had made names of their own in parliament — invaded Foley's home constituency of North Waterloo. Foley had had a good deal of personal popularity in Waterloo, but it was strongly Grit as well, and Mackenzie's and McKellar's intervention decisively turned the trick.[79] Poor Foley's political career was finished, though to a considerable extent he had drunk away his own earlier promise. As for the Taché-Macdonald ministry, this defeat promised to be as damaging in the closely balanced House as Richards's had been for the previous cabinet. The new Conservative combination was likely to do no better than the former Liberal régime, when parliament met again on May 3.

Brown, however, was too busy in Toronto and at Bothwell to return to Quebec in time for the opening. He had been forced to alter the plans he and Anne had made to leave for Scotland in June. It was obvious that he could not go while politics were still in such a turmoil. Parliament might sit for some time yet, and a new election could very well be called. Consequently Anne and the baby would have to go without him, and he would follow when he could. But, since Gordon was to take a sea voyage to recover his health, Anne could accompany him across the ocean. The changed arrangements were effected. His wife and brother would sail from New York at the beginning of June.

It was May 11, therefore, before George Brown arrived back in Quebec. He saw the same unending, exhausting, futile spectacle of deadlock. No ministerial programme could be carried, yet the House sat till dawn, for days in a row. As for the Reformers, he found "the party in an uproar, dissatisfied with the conduct of the leading men and urgent for a test vote".[80] The late ministers could not supply effective command. Sandfield had plainly failed; Mowat lacked sufficient stature; McDougall was still in disgrace with many western Grits for calmly dropping rep by pop to take office in the late Macdonald-Sicotte double-majority régime. Under these circumstances, Upper Canada Liberals would inevitably turn to Brown. Without his seeking it or in any way desiring it, the role of party leader was again before him.

At the same time the Grits and *Rouges* were drifting apart, now that their brief joint sojourn on the government benches was over. There was no conscious clash or cleavage, but Grit Reformers could see the inability of their eastern allies to supply them with any real support, while *Rouges* might no less consider that the scantiness of their numbers in Lower Canada was due to the western company they kept. A few weeks earlier, Luther Holton had expressed to Brown his disgust that the negotiations to rebuild the Liberal ministry had "proceeded on the assumption that we, the Lower Canadian minority, were the difficulty, whereas *our* weakness arises wholly from our persistently striving to stand on ground that would enable us to act with the U.C. majority".[81] He even chided Brown for "squinting" at the notion that the western Liberals should seek new allies from the dominant eastern group – from the *Bleus* themselves! For, while speaking to his resolution for the select committee, had not Brown actually advised Sandfield to "apply to the leaders of the L.C. majority"?[82]

Indeed he had: in the sense that, in urging the settlement of the constitutional issue, he had appealed for the majorities of both sections to stop continually frustrating one another, and join instead to end the sectional conflict once and for all.[83] But he certainly had not proposed another old-style coalition just to keep the present union going. Nevertheless, it was true that Brown realized the need for the Grits somehow to reach the majority group of the French Canadians, and it was equally true that Holton might discern in him a shifting away from *Rouge* allies who were virtually powerless to affect the future course of government. And so, from this time on, there was a distance growing between the two strong Liberals. Their personal friendship was too deep-rooted to be seriously threatened, but politically they had less and less in common.

Brown was contemplating whole new dimensions in politics. Holton still could not see much beyond the present system. The Montreal Liberal drew back towards the confines of the English-speaking minority in Canada East, uneasy for its future under any new pattern of government. But the western Reformer, determined as he was on fundamental change, was ready to pursue it even if it led away from Holton and Dorion towards an inveterate enemy, George Etienne Cartier.

It seemed, however, that the next immediate item of business would be the want-of-confidence vote, which both Reform contingents were eager to force as soon as possible. In the meantime, Anne's husband spent all the time he could in writing letters home. He had a room now in the St. Louis Hotel, across the hall from Oliver Mowat. He could sit at his writing desk and look out on the harbour, and hear the sailors' chants from below the cliff, as the sails were clewed up and the ships anchored in the east wind.[84] He stopped to drive out to Cap Rouge with Mowat and Holton, and came back invigorated, despite the chill breeze and rainy, blustery weather.[85] But still he fretted. "It does seem such preposterous folly to be wasting time here when I might be enjoying myself with you and baby, and making money 'to buy a coo'."[86]

On May 16, he announced the opening of the confidence debate, though he expected a defeat by one to three votes. "Things here are very unsatisfactory," he declared. "No one sees his way out of the mess — and there is no way but my way — *rep by pop*."[87] But there was an intriguing new point. "There is great talk today of a coalition — and what do you think? Why, that in order to make the coalition successful the Imperial Government are to offer me the governorship of one of the British Colonies! I have been gravely asked today by several if it is

true that I have been offered it and whether I would accept!!
What do *you* say, Madam? Will you consent to be 'Her Excel-
lency, the Governess of the Windward Islands' – or of the
Province of British Columbia? My reply was, and I think my
Anne will endorse it, that I would rather be the proprietor of the
Globe newspaper for a few years, than the Governor General of
Canada, much less a trumpery little province. But I need hardly
tell you that the thing has no foundation – beyond *sounding*
what could be done to get me out of the way and let mischief
go on."[88] Nevertheless, talk of such things continued, and was
openly voiced in parliament.

Dorion's no-confidence motion was defeated, but only by two
votes. The narrow decision made further assaults on the government the more certain. Before they began, however, Brown at
last had the opportunity to proceed with his resolution for the
constitutional committee. It came before the House again on
the afternoon of May 18. Once more he spoke only briefly,
stressing that he had not abandoned representation by population
but believed it must be at the basis of any constitutional change,
yet telling the members from Lower Canada that his motion
expressed his willingness to go into the issue from their point of
view as well as his own.[89] This set the mood for an assembly
now gravely worried by the impasse in politics. Instead of
charges and rebuttals, this time there was sober, serious discussion of the constitutional framework. "We had a capital debate,"
Brown was glad to tell Anne that evening, "the best debate on
the question we ever had in parliament, calm, temperate and to
the point." He was cautiously, but almost wistfully, hopeful.
"I feel a very great desire to carry my motion. I would give a
good large sum to carry it. It would be the first vote ever carried
in parliament in favour of constitutional change – and even
that would be some satisfaction after my long fight for it. But
I have taken care not to set my heart upon success."[90]

Marvellously, however, he did succeed. When the vote was
taken the next day, the motion passed, 59 to 48: a clear majority
for basic change.[91] It was comprised of Upper Canadian Reformers and Conservatives generally, with a few Lower Canadian votes from both camps. The negative side largely consisted
of French-Canadian members, understandably holding out to
the last against a reconstruction of the union. But it included a
notable trio besides: Galt, John A. Macdonald – and Luther
Holton. Brown was jubilant. "It was indeed a great success," he
informed Anne afterwards, "and took Cartier, Macdonald and
Co. by intense surprise. They had no conception that there was
a probability of my motion being carried. It has excited great

discussion this morning, and my committee had its first meeting at noon today."[92]

The resolution had established a committee of twenty, with the member for South Oxford as chairman. He had chosen nineteen prominent members of the House, men representing every opinion on the constitution: from proponents of the union as it stood, through advocates of rep by pop and "joint authority", to those who argued for general federation – or even dissolution. Sixteen of the nineteen met more or less willingly with the chairman in a committee chamber of the parliament buildings on May 20. Galt, Chapais, and Hillyard Cameron were unavoidably absent; but those present included Cartier, John A. Macdonald and Sandfield Macdonald, Dorion, Cauchon and McGee, Holton, Mowat and McKellar.[93] Brown began the meeting significantly and typically. He strode to the door, locked it, and pocketed the key. "Now gentlemen," he said emphatically, "you must talk about this matter, as you cannot leave this room without coming to me."[94]

At its end, he judged it "a very useful and harmonious discussion".[95] They went over the general outlines of the constitutional problem and considered questions of procedure. A subcommittee was set up to draft formal proposals to present to the main body; it was composed of Brown, Cauchon, McDougall, and Dunkin, a Lower Canadian Conservative of fairly independent views. They put their list before the full committee on May 23.[96] Since, however, the proceedings were kept closed and confidential, one may only conjecture that the proposals submitted covered the gamut of suggested reforms – double majority, dual federation, and all. Yet the secrecy enjoined upon the committee was surely a wise provision. It prevented mere talk for the record and long arguments about consistency, and removed both the restraints of party obligations and the need to make political capital. At last opposing politicians with long and often bitter experience of government under the union of the Canadas could join in deliberate, dispassionate discussion of its problems. Undoubtedly the gathering of these twenty leaders in Canadian political life to exchange views on the constitution had consequences for their mutual education and enlargement – consequences that could be profound for the subsequent development of British North America. And the credit for their meeting was George Brown's.

There were eight meetings in all, conducted throughout, it was reported, "frankly and in a spirit of compromise".[97] What different view might Brown thus gain of Cartier – no longer the irascible foe across the House whose favourite defence was

slashing attack? What broader opinion might Cartier form of
Brown, now that he was not roaring out the public anger and
private prejudices of Upper Canada? And what impressions were
left with John A. Macdonald regarding the prospects for newly
constructive future combinations — or with Galt or McGee for
realizing a grand colonial union? New impressions could not
help but emerge, as this committee of the *élite* worked earnestly
and constructively towards some common agreement on the constitutional question, conscious always of the unresolved crisis
that hung so darkly over Canada.

The real task before them was to settle on some second-choice
proposal that might prove broadly acceptable, after the first
choice of this or that element was in turn rejected by the rest.
For if the double majority might suit Lower Canadians as well
as Sandfield Macdonald, neither the Grits nor John A. Macdonald would stomach it; while, if John Hillyard Cameron as
well as Brown would put rep by pop first, Cartier, Dorion, and
other Lower Canadians would, of course, resist it. As for the two
extremes, dissolution and continuing the present union, they
would find still more opponents and fewer supporters. This left
federal union, deemed costly and clumsy by some, Yankee and
ineffectual by others, but, in view of all the difficulties, still a
possible means of achieving the double purpose of giving Upper
Canada her rights and protecting Lower Canada in hers. It would
be a reluctant choice in some quarters, particularly for French
Canadians still fearful of leaving the security of equal representation for an uncertain federal future. It said much for their
own realism and ability to compromise that they made the choice,
and that, as a result, *Bleu* leaders such as Cartier and Chapais
signified their willingness to proceed with constitutional change
on the federal principle.

And so this highly influential body came finally to a report,
which Brown delivered to the House on June 14. "The committee," he announced, "have endeavoured to find some solution
for existing difficulties likely to receive the assent of both sections
of the province. A strong feeling was found to exist among
members of the committee in favour of changes in the direction
of a federative system, applied either to Canada alone or to the
whole British North American Provinces; and such progress
has been made as to warrant the committee in recommending
that the subject be again referred to a committee at the next
session of parliament."[98] A fairly vague statement, obviously;
a somewhat brief report of progress. No attempt had been made
to choose between a dual and a general federation, for that might
have split the committee and prevented even this limited

achievement. Yet, limited or not, it represented a tremendous gain.

The "Parliamentary Reform Committee", as the *Globe* liked to call it, had made progress for the first time in bringing the opposed sectional forces together.[99] Hearteningly, it expected that progress would continue. It had produced a vital measure of agreement; brought enemies to look to federal union as the answer to deadlock. It had offered new hope and a way out. The variety of names appended to its report further showed its significance: among them, Brown and Cartier, Mowat and Galt, Cameron and Chapais. There were just three committee members who insisted on signing their names in opposition: John Scoble, the western Grit who still would not yield the primacy of rep by pop; Sandfield Macdonald, who similarly kept to his old intransigence; and John A. Macdonald, who even now rejected the federal principle, and at this late date refused to join in the movement for constitutional change.[100] But as for Brown, through his committee he had provided the jumping-off point for Confederation.

6

The committee did not report till June 14, because of Brown's absence from Quebec at the end of May and during the first week of June. He had managed to arrange a pair with Alexander Morris, member for Lanark (quite a friendly chap for a Conservative), so that he could return to Toronto to look after Anne's departure for Scotland.[101] There was, in fact, something of a lull in parliament's activities over the end of May, as now by common consent other members also paired off and left the capital to catch up on their private business.

After a brief stop in Toronto, Brown took Anne and the baby down to New York to stay at the Astor House. Gordon and his wife, Sarah, went with them.[102] There was shopping to be done there for the new home on Wellington Street that the George Browns planned to occupy after Anne's return from Scotland. There was wallpaper to look for and furnishings to select, and Anne left her husband a whole series of wifely commissions on unfinished items.[103] Then, on June 1, she and Gordon set sail. George and Sarah saw them off, and set out back to Toronto. "We got safely ensconced in a sleeping-car," Brown wrote in the first letter he sent his wife across the ocean, "and were soon sweeping along the Banks of the Hudson northwards." The river scenery was enchanting in the clear summer night – "but for the wandering of our thoughts seaward. . . ." Still, he estimated hopefully, "the session will not likely last more than ten days."[104]

He changed his mind on reaching Quebec on June 7: "there is no prospect of an immediate termination to the session," he now recognized. "Ministers are very weak and dare hardly make a motion – but there is an unwillingness among the opposition to push things to extremities."[105] It was as if the Reformers feared to bring down the Taché-Macdonald ministry because they did not know what else could follow except another feeble and short-lived régime. The sittings continued at interminable length, as the government sought at least to carry the House through the supplies. They sat till four in the morning on Friday, June 10 (George Brown got home in daylight), then were called into session on Saturday again, though everyone was so sleepy that very little was accomplished.[106] Brown went off for a drive afterwards with Alexander Morris – "that set us up a little".[107] He got on well with this party opponent, who was an ardent advocate himself of both western expansion and general confederation.

He missed Anne deeply, but he refused to be gloomy, as instead he thought upon her own joy at reaching her old home in Scotland: "I picture your investment while I write in the drawing room at Abden House, surrounded by old friends come to rejoice with you at your escape from the savage land! I think I hear you sticking up for Canada against all comers, and only hope Canada's maligners will be as unreasonable as possible in their arguments!"[108] He was too busy in any case for despondency. Aside from the long sessions at the Assembly, there were the meetings of his constitutional committee, and some four or five other committees to attend every morning.[109] He found time, however, to go to a grand concert at the Music Hall, escorting Mrs. Mowat, since Oliver was ill with a sore throat. They sat in a vacant row of seats normally reserved for the Governor-General. "If you had only seen the crop of glasses directed at us when we took our seats, from Madame Duval downwards!" he told Anne gleefully.[110]

Yet now the ministry was nearing the end of its tenuous existence, as the Liberals decided to move definitely to its defeat. They had managed to win over two men in the middle, Dunkin and Rankin of Essex. They could be almost certain of bringing down the government.[111] On June 14, as the House opened, Brown read the report of his constitutional committee, and soon afterwards, debate began on the latest no-confidence motion,

brought by Dorion and McDougall. It was all over with surprising speed, for the government put up scarcely more than
token resistance. The vote was called, the ministry was beaten
by the predictable two votes, and the House stood adjourned
before midnight.[112] The Taché-Macdonald ministry had failed.
The old Coalition had failed once more. Yet what would replace
it? Long after the gas had been turned down, excited little
groups of members stayed on the floor, anxiously discussing what
might happen next.

Four ministries within two years! A constant succession of
political crises, an inability to get even ordinary parliamentary
business done, while extraordinary problems of North West
expansion, American relations, and commercial policy grew ever
larger and more urgent. There would no doubt be a dissolution
and a new election, but how would that help? There had been
two elections within the past three years to no avail, and no
reason to think that another would alter the pattern of solidly
opposed sectional blocks which, under equal representation, had
paralysed the Canadian union. There must be fundamental
change. It was past denial. And George Brown's committee, in
a report delivered on that very day, had pointed to the answer:
federal union, backed by both sides in parliament. This latest
crisis, in fact, need not mark the complete futility of the existing
system. Its very urgency provided the ideal opportunity for
ending the ruinous defects in government once and for all – for
creating a strong régime supported by both parties, dedicated at
last to remaking the constitution.

That was Brown's own swift perception.[113] He had won assent
to the idea of constitutional reform at exactly the right time.
Now he took the initiative to ensure its realization. That night
of June 14, and the morning after, he put a startling proposal
before some of his Conservative opponents. He told them that
the crisis could be utilized to settle the constitutional question
forever, and, boldly, incisively, offered to co-operate with the
present government or any other, if it would honestly seek to
realize that purpose. Particularly, he spoke to Alexander Morris,
who eagerly agreed that the crisis could be turned to great
advantage.[114] He saw John Henry Pope as well, member for
Compton, Canada East.[115] Would Brown authorize them to
convey his views to the ministers, they asked. He would indeed.
They must have gone out quivering with the import of their
mission.

That afternoon, June 15, the House met briefly so that John
A. Macdonald could ask for an adjournment while the cabinet
consulted with the Governor-General. On the Reform side,

Sandfield Macdonald was disposed to be difficult, plainly hoping to force the ministers to resign at once, in order to prevent them from obtaining a dissolution and appealing to the country as the government.[116] Brown, however, disagreed. He showed no desire to kill them, and instead expressed the wish that "they would take the fullest time to consider" their future course.[117] The ministers gained their adjournment. He gained his purpose of keeping the case open, to enable them to come to terms if they would.

And here he secured a most important ally: the Governor-General himself. Macdonald and Cartier, the real government leaders, would find Lord Monck ready to grant the dissolution they advised. But before acting on it, he suggested that they should first apply to opposition spokesmen to see if a reconstruction of the ministry was not possible.[118] Of course, Monck was inevitably aware of the talk of new coalitions, in the air for weeks, and now would hear of Brown's overtures to individual Conservatives. Besides, according to George Brown himself, the Governor-General had recognized the necessity of constitutional change more than a year before, in the interview they had had in May of 1863.[119] At any rate, Monck's suggestion fitted in admirably with Brown's own desires. In consequence, the Liberal-Conservative ministers had the proposal to work with their arch-enemy presented from two directions at once – from the governor, and from Alexander Morris and Pope – at a time when dissolution seemed to promise nothing but useless election costs. Should they try this drastically different course?

In one sense, perhaps, it was not all that different. The Liberal-Conservative leaders had been reconstructing coalition régimes for years, and had brought many a powerful opponent into camp and cabinet. What was really different this time was that reconstruction would mean their acting on the constitutional question. At last, however, they were ready to act. The hopelessness of the existing situation could hardly be gainsaid. Galt and Cartier were prepared for a change, as their signatures on the constitutional committee report had witnessed. But what of Macdonald, who had rejected that report? Co-premier of a now-defeated administration, with steadily shrinking minority support in the western half of the union, he explained to a party follower afterwards: "As leader of the Conservatives in Upper Canada, I then had the option of forming a coalition government or of handing over the administration of affairs to the Grit party for the next ten years."[120] Macdonald was always ready to meet realities.

The next day, he met them. About three o'clock, just as parliament was assembling to hear and grant another request for an adjournment, the buzzing House observed the unusual spectacle of George Brown and John A. Macdonald in brief conversation in the middle of the floor. Would Brown object to meeting with Galt and himself for discussion, Macdonald inquired? "Certainly not," said Brown.[121] A meeting was arranged for the following afternoon, June 17, at Brown's quarters in the St. Louis Hotel. The negotiations were officially under way. They were coming to him – as he told Anne triumphantly – "*on the basis of settling the constitutional difficulties between Upper and Lower Canada*".[122] He had not won yet; but this much was wonderful itself.

At one o'clock on the seventeenth, he received the two government emissaries in his pleasant room that overlooked the harbour. The meeting began coldly but courteously, with mutual assurances that only extreme urgency would ever have brought them together. They were formally charged, Macdonald and Galt declared, to invite Brown's aid "in strengthening the administration with a view to the settlement of the sectional difficulties of Upper and Lower Canada".[123] If the administration would pledge itself to bring in a measure to that end next session, he replied, he would cordially co-operate and induce his friends to do so. But, both on personal grounds and because "the public mind would be shocked", he could not undertake to enter the government himself.[124] Here was the first hurdle. The ministers thought naturally in terms of coalition; Brown as naturally abhorred it, and wanted to give outside support. Yet Macdonald rejoined that he must be in the cabinet, as a necessary guarantee.

Perhaps Brown rose to pace the floor – his usual habit when faced with a stiff problem. At any rate, he proposed, and they agreed, to leave personal considerations aside for the present, while they examined what the basis of the constitutional settlement should be. Macdonald and Galt put forward the federation of British North America. Brown countered with representation by population. A general confederation, he said, ought to come and would come ere long, but there were so many parties to be consulted that its adoption was too uncertain now to make it a remedy that Upper Canada could accept. Rep by pop, they said in turn, could not be carried by any government, and they could not accede to it. Another hurdle. But Macdonald and Galt were already offering the way around it – the one he had provided himself: "Unless a basis could be found in the federative principle suggested by the report of Mr. Brown's committee, it did not appear that anything could be settled."[125]

He could readily agree with that. Applied to the Canadian

union, the federal principle would meet the essential ends of
rep by pop. Brown had so contended ever since he had shaped
the Reform Convention programme of 1859. All he needed to
ensure now was its application to Canada's urgent sectional problems first – a dual Canadian federation must come first. There
was nothing wrong with general federation in itself, he reaffirmed, but its probable delay must not afford another excuse
for failing to deal with Canada's internal difficulties directly.
They were still debating this point of priority when three o'clock
drew near, and it was time to go to the House. They had made
a significant and highly encouraging advance towards agreement.
It was certainly sufficient to announce to parliament, in order to
gain a still longer adjournment and allow the talks to go on to
a conclusion.

The House was full, the galleries jammed. There was breathless anxiety to catch every word as John A. Macdonald rose to
make a dramatic announcement. The cabinet had received the
governor's consent to a dissolution, he declared, but first had
sought to consult a leading member of the opposition with a view
to reconstructing the ministry. In this it had made such progress
that he thought the grave step of dissolution could be avoided
(Hear, hear!). Then, savouring the surprise, he ended: "I
would only add that the honourable gentleman with whom the
Finance Minister and myself have conferred – is the member
for South Oxford."[126]

There were gasps of wonder and astonishment. Sandfield
Macdonald was agitated, McDougall frowning. "It's one of
John A.'s coups!" exclaimed a believer; "We have them in a
trap now," declared another hopefully.[127] But there were other
more generous exclamations of approval and relief. Then Brown
stood up, wholly conscious of the exceptional nature of this
moment and this venture. With all his force he emphasized it.
He was certain, he said fervently, that no one in this House
could think the ministers ever could have consulted him, or he
conferred with them, but under the most exceptional circumstances. "When the repeated endeavours year after year to get
a strong government formed have resulted in constant failure,
and we now stand ranged, Upper Canada and Lower Canada, in
such an attitude that no dissolution or dozen of dissolutions is
likely to bring about a satisfactory change, I am bound to say
that the honourable gentlemen opposite are approaching this question with candour and frankness worthy of men occupying their
position . . . and I do hope that the honourable members will
approach it with but one desire: to consider the interests of both
sections of the Province, and to find a settlement of our difficulties!"[128]

The Speaker left the chair. The pent-up excitement burst in a torrent of cheers from both sides of the House and from the galleries as well. Joseph Dufresne, *Bleu* member for Montcalm, rushed impulsively across the floor to clasp George Brown's hand.[129] He responded warmly, his face quickly glowing with smiles. Everyone clustered round, laughing and shouting; the visitors poured down from the galleries and mingled with the exultant groups on the floor. The long tension of deadlock had been broken, and they rightly gave the credit to George Brown. "You never saw such a scene," he wrote to Anne at 1:00 a.m. that night. "But" (added "your own sleepy husband") "as the whole thing may fail, we will not count our chickens just yet."[130] The normally hostile parliamentary correspondent of the *Leader*, who had witnessed the proceedings, was somewhat less restrained. "Events which occurred today," he announced, "may be pregnant with results of vastly greater importance than perhaps ever befell Canada."[131]

7

The next day, Saturday the eighteenth, was filled with comings and goings as the negotiations went on intensively. At ten in the morning, Macdonald and Galt again saw Brown at the St. Louis Hotel; afterwards he talked with some of his party friends.[132] At one, the conference was resumed in the Executive Council Chambers, Cartier for the first time joining his two colleagues.[133] The ardent *Bleu* leader, it was said, looked carefully to see that the *Rouges* Dorion and Holton were not in train behind his old western enemy, then heartily embraced him and swore friendship.[134] And so the meetings continued, until, by Monday afternoon, June 20, terms had at last been worked out, ready for reference to the party caucuses on either side.

There was hard bargaining, as could only be expected. The first issue, of course, was whether the greater or the smaller federation should be the prime objective of the reconstructed government. Brown still put the federal union of the Canadas first, with provision for the admission of "the Great North West" and the Maritime Provinces when practicable.[135] There was little so far, and certainly nothing concrete, to show that British North American union was any more immediately feasible in 1864 than it had been in 1858, and he feared to take constitutional reform up a blind alley where it might be lost. He was impatient to exploit this present opportunity to dispose

of the sectional problem, lest the mood of willingness to tackle
it should vanish in the days to come.

The ministers' hopes were perhaps greater than his, but they
had other valid motives for seeking general federation and
avoiding, if possible, a federation of the Canadas alone. From
Cartier's viewpoint, French Canada's inevitable minority position in any future union would be more bearable if there were
Maritime and perhaps western representatives as well to offset
the ascendancy of Upper Canada. From Macdonald's viewpoint,
a federation merely of the Canadas was a backward step, a
loosening of the bonds of legislative union that he had so diligently defended. But, sharp critic of federation though he was,
Macdonald could at least find the principle endurable if it meant
the extension of British union over a broad new area; while the
central government of a great new federal state might be made
as strong as possible to avoid the errors of the American example,
now plunged in civil war. These urgings could be quite as compelling as Brown's. The important thing, however, was that
there was the desire on either side to find a compromise.

Thus, after a good deal of discussion and drafting of statements, it was agreed, on the one hand, that the new government
should pledge itself to bring in a measure at the next session of
parliament to introduce the federal principle into Canada,
coupled with provisions for subsequently incorporating the
Maritimes and the North West; and, on the other, that the
ministry should meanwhile send representatives to the Lower
Provinces and to England to seek consent for an immediate
union of all British North America on the same federal basis.[136]
Accordingly, Brown was assured of a settlement of the Canadian
sectional problem. He had not expected legislation in this dying
session, in any case; it would take time to design. The pledge of
it for a year hence was the vital accomplishment. At the same
time, Macdonald, Cartier, and Galt would have the opportunity
in the months ahead to try for the general federation they
espoused. Perhaps, if anything, Brown had the best of the
bargain. The Liberal-Conservatives had now agreed to accept
dual federation, if necessary, while he had no objection at all to
the broader union − if it *could* prove practicable. It would give
him all he wanted, and much more. Still, the other bargainers
also had what they wanted, since they held that general federation assuredly was feasible, and the new régime was going to
pursue it first. An ideal compromise, when all participants could
feel that they had won!

It was more difficult, however, to agree on the make-up of
the new administration. In the first place, how should the Upper
Canada Reformers be linked with it? The Lower Canada Re-

formers, at any rate, would not be: after the opening of the negotiations Brown had tried to persuade Dorion and Holton to support them, but to no avail.[137] The breach between him and his old eastern allies was steadily widening. Yet as regards the Grits, the Conservative ministers were quite ready to have them take some of the cabinet seats, and were even determined that George Brown should occupy one of them as the best assurance for the support of the powerful mass of western Liberals.[138] He himself would have preferred to see Reform stay wholly outside the government (and thus uncompromised by coalition), merely backing it on the constitutional issue.[139] But on consulting his own party associates, Brown found them insistent on a share of the cabinet posts, and he yielded reluctantly to the idea of full-fledged coalition.[140] Nevertheless, he remained equally insistent that he would not take office himself.[141] Everything he believed about the evils of coalitions would come back to haunt him; he would have to join a group of politicians he had bitterly attacked, among whom was John A. Macdonald, still separated from him by a deep personal grudge. Besides, he would have to give up his hopes of soon leaving parliamentary life – and even, probably, his eager wish to get away within a few weeks to join Anne in Scotland.

It was consequently easier to proceed with the question of how many seats Reformers should hold in a coalition government than to deal with his personal role. Yet here too there was difficulty. Brown asked for half the cabinet, on the ground that the Liberal side in parliament was actually in the majority, having defeated the Conservative forces: specifically he asked for four Upper Canadian seats, two Lower.[142] The others demurred: the eastern half of the ministry was secure already, and it was essential that no change should make the party led by Taché and Cartier feel that its rights were not fully protected. Macdonald similarly declared that his own Conservatives in parliament would withdraw their support from the government if his places were cut to two in the western half of the cabinet. He was prepared, however, to offer Brown an equal division of the Upper Canada seats; three each for Grits and Conservatives.[143]

It was not an equitable division, considering the much larger numbers of the western Reformers in the House – but was it worth upsetting a plan that had gone so far and that promised so much, for the sake of one cabinet post? Brown withdrew to see Lord Monck and consult his friends, though actually he was the more concerned over the firm ministerial demand that he himself take one of the places proposed. He felt "very nervous and stupid" under the strain.[144]

The negotiations reached a climax. He had the ministers'

written pledge for constitutional reform, their offer of three cabinet posts. Macdonald, Cartier, and Co. had really done their part now; the rest was up to him and his party. It was late in the warm afternoon of June 20. While waiting in the Governor-General's office, he scribbled a hasty note to Anne: "I have closed the negotiations for the construction of a new government pledged to carry constitutional changes – and I have the offer of office for myself and two others to be named by me. I call a meeting of the party tonight to accept or reject this offer – and I must abide by its determinations. I am deeply distressed at having this matter thrust on me now – but dare not refuse the responsibility with such vast interests at stake. How I do wish you had been here to advise me! You cannot tell how I wish you had been. But never mind, I will try to do my duty to the country in such a manner as you, my dearest Anne, will not be ashamed of."[145]

The full Reform caucus, however, could not be gathered until the following morning. At eleven o'clock on June 21, thirty-nine of the forty-one Upper Canada Reform members met in excited anticipation at the Kent House, to consider the proposed terms as Brown reported them.[146] Hope Mackenzie at once moved approval of their leader's course (for now they so regarded him) and of the project for federation that he outlined. The motion passed with no negative votes, but with five abstentions, one of them by Sandfield Macdonald. Then Sandfield himself moved that at least three opposition members should enter the government, though Alexander Mackenzie in amendment called for only outside support. Voted on as alternatives, there was a solid twenty-six for the former proposition, eleven for the latter – notably including Brown, Mowat, and Mc-Kellar, as well as the two Mackenzies. Obviously, some of the strongest Grits in the party shared their chief's misgivings about coalitions, especially one with John A. Macdonald. But now it was unanimously resolved that Brown should join the ministry, to complete the enterprise he had begun.[147] Supplied with these clear expressions of his party's wishes, the Grit leader returned to conclude arrangements with the Liberal-Conservative ministers.

Even now Brown strove to avoid entering the cabinet, tried various tacks in new meetings with the other side.[148] Was it, he asked, a *sine qua non* that he should enter? Yes, came the flat reply. He wrestled with the problem all the rest of the day, and through the morning of the twenty-second. He took opinions widely, saw Lord Monck again, read letters that were coming in now from every quarter urging him to join. A former associate, D'Arcy McGee, sent him one such note after they had talked the problem over: "How *can* you hope to secure the settlement without your own personal participation . . . ? It [the negotiation] must go on during recess and session, 'hail, rain or shine', but you unless a Minister cannot be on the spot — cannot enter the council chamber — cannot, in short, speak, think or act for yourself unless you are a member of the government. I can only add to what I might make a long letter of reasons, that should you conclude to join this government with a view to settling our great and increasing constitutional difficulties, I can assure you, you will find in me, if not a very able, certainly a very willing coadjutor."[149]

The Governor-General wrote as well: "I think," said Monck, "the success or failure of the negotiations . . . depends very much on your consenting to come into the cabinet. . . . Those who have hitherto opposed your views have consented to join with you in good faith for the purpose of extricating the Province from, what appears to me, a very perilous position. They have frankly offered to take up and endeavour to settle on principles satisfactory to all the great constitutional questions which you by your energy and ability have made your own. The details of that settlement must necessarily be the subject of grave debate in the cabinet and I confess I cannot see how you can take part in that discussion or how your opinions can be brought to bear on the arrangement of the question unless you occupy a place at the Council table."[150] It was an effective plea from a governor whom Brown respected and trusted: "He is entirely with me," he believed.[151]

He could not talk to Anne or his brother Gordon; his old comrades Dorion and Holton remained opposed. If he went in, to sit outnumbered among his enemies, he could compromise his own political position and damage his party's future. And he would at least divide the eastern and western Liberals decisively against each other. The Conservative leaders had yielded to constitutional reform; he might yield his whole political career. Who would make the greater sacrifice? But Brown was still in politics for a purpose: the remaking of the union, which he had pursued so long and so single-mindedly. If this were the only way, then his duty was to enter. This was the supreme opportunity; all possible harm had to be discounted. As he had often done, Brown, after deep and troubled pondering, made up his mind — and would not look back upon a closed issue. A little after one, on Wednesday, June 22, he told the ministers that he would sit in the cabinet.[152] The business was concluded.

Earnestly he explained himself to Anne. His own party

caucus, he began, had "passed a resolution urging me to go into the government – but that did not influence me much. Private letters from many quarters did far more. And the extreme urgency of the Governor-General did still more. . . . The thing that finally determined me, was the fact ascertained by Mowat and myself that unless we went in the whole effort for constitutional changes would break down and the enormous advantage gained by our negotiations would probably be lost. . . . We consented with great reluctance – but there was no help for it – and it was such a temptation to have possibly the power of settling the sectional troubles of Canada forever!"[153]

There would be another government now, still under the titular headship of Sir Etienne Taché, as a widely respected, permanent member of the Upper House and largely removed from active party politics. It would be established after the close of the session, which would be ended quickly, and pledged to constitutional change. It would have an overwhelming majority behind it: the big blocks of Grit and *Bleu* votes, together with the western Conservatives, leaving only the *Rouges* and a few dissentients from both sections outside. No force in parliament would be able to prevent this Taché-Macdonald-Brown government from dealing with the constitutional problem – or this truly "Great Coalition" from reconstructing Canada. Such was the combination that Brown had initiated and had now accepted, at whatever cost to his personal feelings or concern for his political standing.

8

The expectant House that met that Wednesday at last had the whole plan laid out before it. John A. Macdonald read out ministerial explanations that meticulously embodied the full story of the negotiations and the precise wording of the compact finally reached.[154] When he finished, it was up to Dorion and Holton, now virtually leading the opposition, to question and bring out the implications of this remarkable bargain, this monumental agreement. They probed at a critical point. What was involved in this phrase in the document, asked Holton, that pledged constitutional reform "according to the well understood principles of federal government"?[155] Did this mean representation based on numbers in the central legislature of a new union? He was plainly out to embarrass ministerialists who had fought rep by pop for years. Cartier answered brusquely that the honourable gentleman knew perfectly well what it meant: equality in one chamber of the federal parliament, "population and territory taken into account in the other".[156] It was an unpleasant admission for the chieftain of the *Bleus* to have to make; he got over it as quickly and as generally as he could. But now Dorion pushed further. Was the federal principle thus to mean, as in the United States, equality in the upper house – and *representation by population* in the lower? It was John A. Macdonald who swallowed the dose as fast as possible. "Yes," he said – and no more – as triumphant cheers rang from the Grits who had sought rep by pop so strenuously.[157]

Beyond doubt it was George Brown's triumph at last, but he saw no need and felt no desire to exploit it. Instead he followed with approval the further explanations Macdonald had to make, as Dorion pressed to know what Cartier had had in mind, then, when he had talked of territory as well as numbers. As his questioner surely realized, the Attorney-General West said testily, a federal system of government based representation in the lower house on population; but his colleague had properly guarded himself against the implication that everyone and anyone should henceforth have the vote.[158] Other considerations – property, territorial divisions – should affect the franchise, just as under the present provincial constitution. The Attorney-General East, the member for South Oxford, and he himself were all equally opposed to making the assertion of rep by pop the equivalent of universal suffrage. "Hear, hear!" cried Brown approvingly.[159] In no way a universal-suffrage democrat, he had always contended that rep by pop was not the dangerous Yankee democratic device Macdonald and his friends had formerly alleged. Here, too, they had come around to his own thinking; and Brown was satisfied. A principle that was thoroughly recognized by Victorian Liberals in the mother country, in reforming and redistributing seats in a British parliament based on a property franchise, would similarly be applied to the new Canadian constitution. That was all he had ever required.

But now it was Brown's turn to feel uneasy, as Dorion and Holton turned to consider his own participation in the project that had been set forth. They talked more in sorrow than in anger, and the mildness of their reproaches to a deserting comrade only made his act seem worse. Dorion was as calmly judicious as ever. He did not consider that a public man should be restrained by friendship from doing what he thought to be his duty – but he did think that Brown had yielded everything for the barest promise of the federal principle. He himself had always opposed a general federation, at least for this age, since it necessarily involved building the Intercolonial to the Maritimes to give it any reality whatever, and this was a useless railway that would cost the Canadian taxpayer some four or five million pounds. Furthermore, the company Brown would keep in the cabinet, with men he had so often denounced for gross extravagance and malpractice, did not give much promise of a grand new era of reform.[160]

The stiff, saturnine Holton said much the same, asserting that "considering speculative changes in the constitution" bore no relation to the real issue of honest, effective government, and declaring that neither the time nor popular opinion was ripe for a confederation.[161] His political relations with Brown had altered, yet, he added keenly, he hoped their personal relations would not change. His speech struck home to Brown, no less than Dorion's. Both men had recalled some of his own inner feelings about their old alliance, his doubts about his new course, and his discomfort in his new company. But if they were largely right in terms of the past, he had gone on to a new stage that they had not reached and did not comprehend.

Galt expressed it in answering the two *Rouges*, with whom he too had once been associated. Why should party foes not unite for such great objectives, he asked enthusiastically. This was an extraordinary moment, a time for purest patriotism. Let them combine to settle questions that could be settled in no other way, and separate afterwards as they would![162] From the other side, Alexander Mackenzie, the dour, devoted, cautious Grit – Galt's very opposite – took essentially the same position. He did not hold with coalitions, Mackenzie avowed, but sometimes circumstances justified, indeed demanded, them. Was not this surely such an occasion?[163]

But they were all looking to Brown. It was time for him to speak, and he was achingly conscious of his position. Whatever might be argued in his defence, he had broken with old friends to join old foes – gone against the inherent loyalties and passions of his nature. He could be charged with blatant inconsistency, after all the *Globe*'s outcries against those who joined John A. Macdonald. It could even be said that personal ambition and desire for aggrandizement had led him to sell out. Shaken by always quick emotions, Brown could hardly frame his words as he began.

For ten years, he painfully acknowledged, he had opposed the present ministers "in the most hostile manner it is possible to conceive."[164] He was all too well aware of the language he had used against coalitions, and of the suspicions of personal motives to which he was now exposed. Then, growing stronger: "But I think the House will admit that if a crisis has ever arisen in the political affairs of any country which would justify a coalition, such a crisis has arrived in the history of Canada." He had always stated that he would meet with any body of men who would try boldly and vigorously to settle the discords in the union. "The day," he said, "which I have so long expected has now arrived – and I think had I not listened to the approaches made to me by gentlemen opposite, I would have shown that I was one of the vilest hypocrites that ever entered public life."

Yet listening to these approaches had meant breaking with his allies in Lower Canada, friends he had "learned warmly to esteem, gentlemen who stood by me in times of great difficulty". He had tried; Dorion and Holton knew how he had tried; they would remember how he had repeatedly urged them to take up the representation question again. He had hoped, too, that he would have the eastern Liberals with him on his select committee. But when they had refused its findings, and when he thought of the rights that were due to Upper Canada, he knew that he could only negotiate with his ministerial opponents. Nevertheless, even after his first discussions with them, he had gone back to Dorion and Holton as old friends, to ask their co-operation in what was being proposed – without success. Personal friendship was left; he had done nothing to sever that. "Hear, Hear," responded Holton quickly.[165]

They still might say, he added, that he was merely infatuated, and had joined with party enemies for no more than a vague, undefined future possibility – "I may be told that I am of a credulous disposition." The true, authentic Brown swiftly thrust that aside: "Well, Sir, I would rather have a credulous disposition – I would rather be deceived easily and often than live constantly in an atmosphere of suspicion!" But he did not doubt the sincerity of the ministers' pledges. He paid generous tribute particularly to Cartier and Taché, as French-Canadian leaders who had had to come so far themselves to join with him. As for his own part, he had struggled desperately against entering the cabinet. "In this I have been overruled. I have been forced to accept office against my wishes and to the serious injury of my personal interests; and I think I am in a position to say to every honourable member of this house – let us try to rise superior to the pitifulness of party politics – let us unite to consider this question as a great national issue – in a manner worthy of us as a people!"

The strength of his appeal and the fervour of his own belief had restored all Brown's fluency and contagious enthusiasm.

Repeatedly the House cheered him as he swept onward, until, at last, he proudly and emphatically concluded: "I do frankly confess, Mr. Speaker, that if I never had any other parliamentary success than that which I have achieved this day in bringing about the formation of a government more powerful than any Canadian government that ever existed before – pledged to settle the alarming sectional difficulties of my country – I would have desired no greater honour for my children to keep years hence in their remembrance, than that I had a hand, however humble, in the accomplishment of that work."[166]

Immediately he finished, the House was recessed. And pandemonium broke loose once more. Amid prolonged cheering, members crowded to congratulate George Brown. He was the undoubted hero of parliament, and very soon of the press and public as well. Letters of praise poured in; the newspapers, notably the ministerial newspapers, could hardly be kind enough. Even Cartier's organ, *La Minerve*, whose view of Brown had approximated the *Globe*'s opinion of the *Bleu* leader, considered that his deed had been "truly great and admirable" – praised his "talent, business experience, knowledge of the country's resources, love of work and energy" – although it also hailed "the sincerity of Mr. Brown's repentance".[167] Brown's own spirits were thoroughly recovered. "It is great fun," he told Anne. "The unanimity of sentiment is without example in this wooden country – and were it not that I know at their exact value the worth of newspaper laudations – I might be puffed up a little in my own conceit."[168]

The business of the session now moved quickly to a close. On June 30, parliament was prorogued. The same afternoon, Brown was sworn in as President of the Council, Mowat as Postmaster-General, and McDougall as Provincial Secretary – these being the two Reform colleagues he had named to the new cabinet. There was no question of his choice of Mowat, a prominent, able, and thoroughly reliable Grit. Brown had been rather reluctant to pick McDougall, however, for he was far less reliable and had in times past been positively erratic.[169] Still, he was undoubtedly talented, and certainly a more bearable representative of moderate Reform opinion than Sandfield Macdonald would have been.

Once constituted, the new government would begin planning the drive for general British North American union. It had already been announced during the ministerial explanations in parliament that a mission would be sent to the Maritimes, and later to England, to promote that cause. The Lower Provinces, it seemed, were going to hold "a convention at Charlotte Town,

Prince Edward Island" to discuss the possibilities of union among themselves.[170] The Canadian cabinet intended to take this opportunity to lay proposals for a greater confederation before them. And this would mark the opening of a different era, of inter-provincial conferences and high state missions, of ceremony, diplomacy, and constitution-drafting.

Brown, above all, had succeeded in making this new era possible. He had ended deadlock, ensured the settlement of the sectional question, and produced a ministry dedicated to the establishment of federal union. But he had scarcely won these achievements single-handed. What of the others who shared in them – at the very least, Macdonald and Cartier?

What credit had Macdonald, first, for the all-important compact on union by the federal principle? Virtually none – until negotiations for a new régime had actually been instituted. Then he had immediately seen that this doubtful notion could be practical and successful politics, and that made all the difference. That brought his acceptance. For Macdonald was an expert on political possibilities, while at the same time he had consummate power to use them creatively. His shrewd, opportunistic improvisations had a way of becoming positive, lasting achievements. He could effectively serve his country and his party interest at once, when Brown might have trouble in keeping the two of them together. Brown would throw all his energies into seeking one objective, and, having gained it, hardly know how to reshape his thinking. Macdonald, considering many, might seek none until one was presented for him, and then he would know exactly how to use it. In fact, the one man almost began where the other left off; both were necessary complements in the movement for Confederation. That movement, moreover, would increasingly call for Macdonald's special talents: his tolerant understanding of human weaknesses and ability to work with them, his skill at genial persuasion and constructive bargaining – and always his underlying faith in a broad, strong British North American union, thoroughly active now that other men had brought union within range of the possible.

Among those others, one had a peculiarly vital role: George Etienne Cartier. Without his willingness to pledge support of the French-Canadian majority – and thereby mortgage his entire political future with his people – the new government and its project would have been wholly impossible. Essentially, it took two to end deadlock, the two who could swing the votes of the two opposed sectional majorities: Brown to make the offer, Cartier to receive it. In agreeing to that offer, the *Bleu* leader was accepting both the loss of the entrenched French position in the existing union and the establishment of rep by pop within a new federation. It was an act of highest political courage, and, one might add, of undeluded vision. Brown gained new respect and fellow-feeling for Cartier on their joining forces, for, as one sectional leader, he knew what it had cost the other to come to terms. The two of them brought the majority votes, Grits and *Bleus*, that made the Confederation ministry politically viable. It could not have existed or pursued its ends without them both.

Then there were Galt and McGee, each representing strong minorities: the English-speaking Protestants of Lower Canada, the Roman Catholic Irish of both sections. Their roles were not the critical ones, but their qualities of statesmanship were undeniably important in carrying the union movement forward through successive stages. And yet, beyond all others, there was Brown: still the key figure of them all in releasing the movement that brought about Confederation.

As far as the Province of Canada was concerned – and the dynamic power behind the movement lay in this largest, most troubled British province in America – the original design of Confederation had come from Galt in 1858; its practical execution and final realization would be Macdonald's work preeminently; and the bravest, and utterly essential act of acceptance was Cartier's. Yet, by its very nature, Cartier's act was fundamentally passive. The active force that drove the question of union to the point of decision, opened a way to decision through the constitutional committee, and then made the crucial move that transformed a blank wall of deadlock into vistas of nationhood, was George Brown – in all this, the real initiator of Confederation.[171]

Confederation Minister

I

First there were by-elections for the new Reform ministers. They necessarily delayed the coalition cabinet in drafting a plan for British North American federation to put before the Maritimes, but they offered a test, in three western constituencies at least, of public reaction to this strange new combination of thorough Conservatives and downright Grits. Brown left Quebec for Toronto the day he was sworn in, and by July 6 was in South Oxford to launch his own campaign for re-election. He was rapturously received at Ingersoll. ("Brass band, formal address, Headquarters illuminated, immense crowd," he noted.[1]) Evidently the electors were ready to approve his presence in the coalition, and to believe him when he swore that "nothing but the unspeakable importance of the settlement sought would have induced me to consent".[2] No opponent was put up; his speeches around the constituency were chiefly useful in explaining the details of the new régime to enthusiastic audiences. On July 11 he was elected by thunderous acclamation. Mowat was similarly returned in South Ontario. But in North Ontario, McDougall ran into much more difficulty, and a serious election contest threatened.

It was partly that the facile McDougall had never acquired the grip of a Brown or a Mowat on the ordinary voter, and strong Grit partisans were still suspicious of him because of his past conduct. Beyond that, however, an element of the Conservatives showed considerable reluctance to follow their own party chiefs into a compact with the Reformers. For, once the initial wonder at the Great Coalition had passed, the Conservative press and public of Upper Canada seemed less disposed to acclaim the new ministry than were the Liberals. They rather felt that Brown and his party had scored, forcing themselves and their terms on the Conservative leaders in the government. While this Tory reaction did not necessarily imply any repudiation of the projected federal union, it did help explain disgruntled criticism of aspects of that project in papers like the *Leader* or the Hamilton *Spectator*.[3] And in North Ontario it brought strong Conservative support for the candidacy of Matthew Crooks Cameron, the riding's member in 1861-3, despite every appeal from John A. Macdonald himself on behalf of William Mc-Dougall.

Macdonald undoubtedly tried by private letters and circulars to have the coalition agreement honoured in North Ontario, but he could not control the local Conservatives, despite his open assertion that government "on purely Conservative principles" was now impossible.[4] Brown went into the riding on McDougall's behalf. He spoke from Uxbridge to Cannington and Beaverton, through the intense heat of mid-July, when drought gripped the countryside, fires smouldered in the fields, and blue smoke haze hung across the woods.[5] "I never had such uphill work," he reported wearily, "and never met such personal hostility against anyone as against McD."[6]

His candidate lost, by a hundred votes; yet it could have been worse. "McDougall will get another county," Brown concluded, undismayed, "and the wheels will roll on. John A., Mowat and myself did all we could for him – and it is to be hoped that he learned a lesson which will do him good."[7] Indeed, the safer seat of North Lanark was shortly to be obtained for him. What was possibly more important was that North Ontario had seen the first practical exercise in co-operation between Brown and Macdonald. There were years of resentment and distrust to overcome, but the by-election campaign gave earnest of Macdonald's sincerity in the ministerial bargain.

There was time afterwards for a brief trip to Bothwell, and for ordering furniture for the new home on Wellington Street, to be called Oak Lodge. George Brown's letters to his wife in Scotland teemed with reports on half-tester bedsteads, corner what-nots, and music racks. Concerning Oak Lodge, the Reform leader solemnly acknowledged, "But we *must* think of wallpaper and carpets, whatever comes of the constitution."[8] He sent Anne details of the black-walnut furniture to come from Jacques and Hay, the crimson rep dining-room curtains to match the carpet from Duggan and Co. "Before I leave," he added, "I will order the painting and papering – so unless you speak soon you may be put to shame by my horrid bad taste."[9] Then he set out for Quebec, and on August 4 settled into his new quarters there as President of the Council, down to government work at last.

The next day, the full cabinet met: Brown, Mowat and Mc-Dougall, Macdonald, Campbell and Cockburn for Upper Canada; Taché, Cartier, Galt, Chapais and Langevin for Lower

Canada. Only McGee was absent. He and some forty M.P.s had gone to New Brunswick and Nova Scotia on a grand goodwill visit — as Brown told Anne — "on an excursion party at invitation of the Bluenoses".[10] That was an interesting fact itself, a sign that the Maritimers also were looking towards their fellow colonists in America. While one could not make too much of the joint invitation from the Saint John and Halifax Boards of Trade, it seemed, at any rate, to suggest some change from the indifference earlier exhibited in the Lower Provinces, when the Canadian ministry of 1858 had made its brief overture for the discussion of British North American union.

Moreover, there were reasons to expect a change: for one, the Maritime yearning for the Intercolonial, which might yet be built by a union of the provinces. There were the strains induced by the Civil War; for if the coastal provinces were less exposed than inland Canada, they too had met border trouble in the *Chesapeake* affair, and felt the danger of militant new American power. There was, besides, the possible loss of reciprocity with the United States, and thus a question of the very future of Maritime economic life. Finally, there was simply the uneasy, growing awareness that small, separate provinces might have no future at all in an age of spreading continental empires and fast rising industrialism. Considerations such as these had brought the legislatures of Nova Scotia, New Brunswick, and Prince Edward Island to take up the question of Maritime union, which might either be a benefit itself or constitute a first step to a wider colonial union. Their delegates were to begin discussions at Charlottetown on September 1, 1864. And the new Canadian government had asked and received permission to send an informal delegation of its own, to put the case for the larger union before the Maritime meetings.[11]

Consequently, the ministers at Quebec had both to formulate a general plan for the conference at Charlottetown, less than a month away, and to deal with the normal round of cabinet business, hardly touched for six weeks. Brown was thoroughly busy, presiding over cabinet meetings and attending to administrative duties. But as ever he found time for all-important family matters, delighting to hear that Maggie had acquired two teeth "without any squalling or other baby nonsense", wondering, "Did anybody besides John express astonishment at Baby being white and not having a cigar in her dear little mouth?" and ardently recording, "There is nothing in this world that is really satisfying — unmixed happiness — except Anne — my beloved Anne."[12]

The sessions in council were going harmoniously. The Liberal leader felt no doubts now of the coalition compact's being carried out in good faith. "Taché, Cartier and their colleagues", he said, "have behaved very well, and show no inclination to swerve from their bargain."[13] He now could even casually remark of a party at the Governor-General's, "John A. and I were the only civilians – we had very good fun."[14]

One lesser topic that concerned the cabinet was the matter of moving to Ottawa. They had hoped to go that autumn; Brown went to the future capital to examine the government buildings under construction and report upon the prospect. He went all over the great stone piles of half-erected Victorian Gothic, and even seeing them as they were, was highly impressed. "They are really magnificent. Fit for the British, French and Russian empires, were they all confederated! A hundred years hence the people will fancy the men of those days were giants in imagination if not in ability." He stood on the Parliament Hill of a future Canadian nation, gazing out across the Ottawa at the sunlit sweep of Gatineau hills, and judged the setting "nowhere surpassed except at Quebec – even if it is there".[15] But he still had to report that there was too much to be done to permit the capital to be transferred to Ottawa at least before the following summer.[16] Before leaving, however, he did look out for a possible house for Anne and himself to rent, and planned "to entertain the Members of Parliament handsomely next session".[17] The minister was plainly happy in his duties and his expectations – but he was plagued with sciatica, which could bring such utter agony in bed that sometimes he would scream with pain. "Fortunately the thing is not fatal," he hastened to reassure Anne, "and I am fat and strong."[18]

Back in Quebec, there was again the round of cabinet meetings. The constitutional discussions went on daily as they drafted the Confederation proposals for Charlottetown. "I do believe we will succeed," Brown buoyantly declared on August 26. "The discussion today lasted from 12 to 1/4 to 6 – and from first to last it was interesting – most deeply interesting. For perhaps the first time in my political life I indulged in a regular chuckle of gratified pride – no higher sentiment – at the thought of my presiding over such a discussion by such men – there not being one man at the table who had not openly derided the idea of such a scene ever occurring in our lifetime. I could not help recalling many furious scenes in which several of those around me had bitterly denounced me for even proposing the consideration of the very subject they were then engaged in settling under my Presidency!" He grew more serious. "It will be a tremendous thing if we accomplish it. I don't believe any of us appreciate in

The new *Globe* office of 1864

King Street, Toronto, in the 1860s

Ontario Archives

George Brown and family

Notman and Fraser, Toronto

Ellisson and Co., Quebec

Wells in the Oil Region

Luther Holton

Ontario Archives

Deadlock in Parliament: fall of Sandfield Macdonald's ministry

Ontario Archives

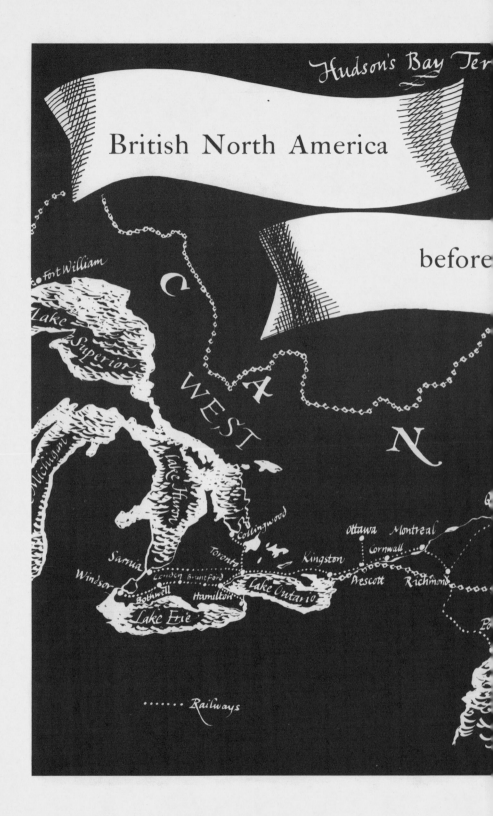

British North America

Hudson's Bay Ter

before

Fort William

C

Lake Superior

WEST

A

N

Michigan

Lake Huron

Collingwood

Ottawa Montreal

Toronto

Cornwall

Sarnia

Kingston

Windsor

London Brantford

Prescott Richmond

Bothwell

Hamilton

Lake Ontario

Po

Lake Erie

Q

.... Railways

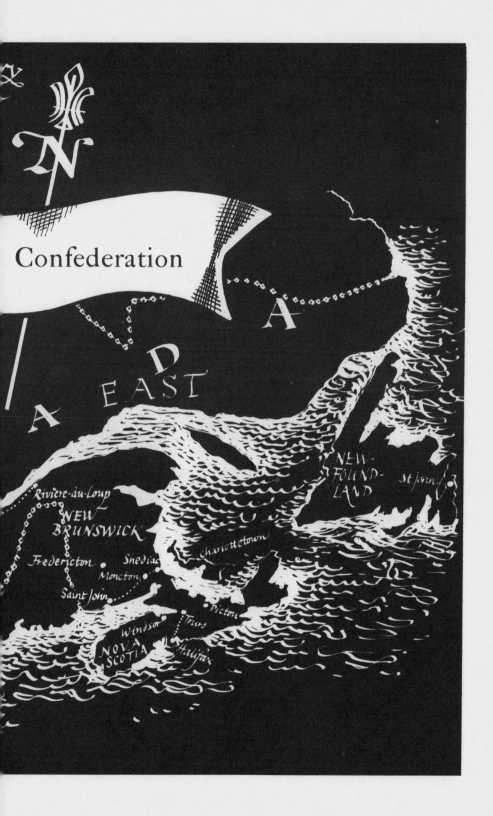

Confederation

Queen's Own Rifles during the Fenian Raid

Public Archives of Canada

The sage of the *Globe*, 1873

Public Archives of Canada

The house at Bow Park

Lambton Lodge today

Alexander Mackenzie in the 1870s

Public Archives of Canada

Brown in later years, as engraved for *Globe* readers

Toronto 'Globe'

its true importance, the immensity of the work we are engaged in."[19]

"Perhaps," he mused, "some twenty years hence people will talk of us as we talk of Lord Sydenham, Lord Durham, and the other originators of our old constitutional system. But there is one thing peculiar about our position. There is no other instance on record of a colony peacefully remodelling its own constitution — such changes have always been the work of the parent state and not of the colonists themselves. Canada is rightly setting the example of a new and better state of things."

It could not always go on so swimmingly, however. Just two days later, Brown had a very different report to make to his wife.[20] "Do you know you were very near being stripped yesterday of your honours of Presidentess of the Council?" he wrote. "Would not that have been a sad affair? It was in this way. The Council was summoned for twelve and shortly after that we were all assembled but John A. We waited for him till one — till half past one — till two — and then Galt sent off to his house specially for him. Answer — will be here immediately. Waited till half past two — no appearance. Waited till three and shortly after, John A. entered bearing symptoms of having been on a spree. He was half drunk. Lunch is always on the side table and he soon applied himself to it — and before we had well entered on the important business before us he was quite drunk with potations of ale." But, after two and a half hours of debate, they wound up their discussions of constitutional changes and agreed on the course to be followed at Charlottetown. And then the trouble broke.

Macdonald suddenly announced that he had an important matter to bring up: the dispute with the contractors for the new Parliament Buildings in Ottawa. The original contracts let under the old Cartier-Macdonald régime had been for $700,000, but when the Liberals under Sandfield Macdonald had taken office they had investigated, in their ardour to clean house, and found that $1,200,000 had been spent on works not yet half-finished, and $550,000 more was claimed. Government commissioners had reported that far from any such payment being due, the contractors had been overpaid; and there the case had rested ever since. But now the contractors were making new efforts to secure their claims — now, said Brown wryly, that their friend John A. Macdonald was back in power. "I was quite willing to send the thing to arbitration," he added, "but determined that men only of the highest character and position should be entrusted with it." Macdonald accordingly proposed to appoint three men, two of them unknown to Brown. He demurred, asking for a delay until he could make inquiries. The old suspicions and antagonisms returned glowering to the council table. But Macdonald, the worse for wear, would not be thwarted by this cross-grained Grit.

"John A. would not hear of delay and insisted loudly, fiercely, that the thing should be settled then and there. His old friends in the cabinet saw of course that he was quite wrong – but they feared to offend him and pressed for a settlement. Matters came to a point. I declared that if the thing were done then I would not sit in the council one moment longer. Mowat stood firmly by me and McDougall partly – moderately. Galt got alarmed and proposed a mode which in effect postponed the matter till Monday. I agreed to it, and the council all but John A. adopted it. It was declared carried. Thereupon John A. burst out furiously declaring that his friends had deserted him and he would not hold office another day. The council adjourned in great confusion – John A.'s friends trying to appease him."

Brown, however, was not unduly worried over the prospect. "Of course all this would have blown off easily when John A. got sober." He did not believe the proposed appointments would be pushed further; it would be too damaging to Macdonald if the whole affair went before the public – "He will not think of it when he gets sober." Nevertheless the episode had reinforced old feelings in Brown. "To say the truth," he pensively concluded, "were our visit to the Lower Provinces and to England once over, I would not care how soon a rupture came. The constitutional question would then be beyond all chance of failure – and I would be quit of company that is far from agreeable."

Yet for the time being the breach was successfully closed, after the Grit leader next day talked with Taché, Galt and Cartier, and then Lord Monck.[21] In any case, there was no more time for argument. Brown and other delegates from the cabinet were to leave that very day, August 29, for Charlottetown, aboard the Canadian government steamer *Queen Victoria*. Too much was in the balance, as Brown well knew, for minor disputes to be continued now. The harmony with which the coalition had drafted their constitutional plan was quickly restored, as they set out to present it to the Maritimes. For the Canadians had Confederation to put forward at Charlottetown, and on that proposal there were no real differences between them.

2

There were eight delegates aboard the *Queen Victoria*: Macdonald, Cartier and Galt, Brown and McDougall, McGee, Alexander Campbell and Hector Langevin. Lee, Clerk of the Executive Council, Bernard, Chief Clerk in the Attorney-General's office, and a shorthand writer completed the company.[22] They turned out to be a most congenial party; indeed, they could hardly help it, quite aside from their common sense of mission. The weather was perfect – calm, bright, and sunny – the scenery of river and gulf magnificent, the ship excellently appointed. There was a broad awning to recline under, a splendid variety of stores, unexceptionable cooking, lots of books, chessboards, and backgammon. The pleasant cruise atmosphere seemed complete when they stopped for an excursion ashore at the beautiful fishing harbour of Gaspé on August 31. The population turned out *en masse* to receive them, amidst the firing of guns and other rejoicing, and M. Le Boutillier, M.P.P., hospitably entertained them at his mansion.[23] From Gaspé they sailed on down the Gulf directly for Prince Edward Island, to arrive there on the morning of September 1.

Brown was up at four that sparkling morning to see the sunrise and enjoy a salt-water bath. They had just reached the northern tip of the Island, and soon were running along the coast of what he thought "as pretty a country as you ever put your eye upon".[24] He was captivated by the scene, as they rounded the rich green shores of Northumberland Strait. About noon they steamed up Hillsborough Bay to find Charlottetown suddenly and picturesquely spread out before them.

The *Queen Victoria* swept up majestically to anchor, and dropped the hook with naval precision. "Its man-of-war cut evidently inspired the natives with huge respect for their big brothers from Canada," said Brown complacently. "I flatter myself we did that well." Then the delegates carefully dressed themselves, and the ship's two boats were smartly lowered. "Being each duly manned with four oarsmen and a boatswain, dressed in blue uniform, hats, belts, etc. in regular style," he told Anne, "we pulled away for shore and landed like Mr. Christopher Columbus, who had the precedence of us in taking possession of portions of the American continent."

The Maritime delegates were already assembled for the Conference in the Colonial Building, the Island's parliament house on Queen's Square. There were five each from three Atlantic provinces; Newfoundland, while expressing some interest, had not been notified in time to allow it to participate. As for the Canadians, they were there merely as informal visitors. The meeting was organized at two that afternoon without them. J. H. Gray, the premier of Prince Edward Island, was named chairman; Charles Tupper and Leonard Tilley, the premiers of Nova Scotia and New Brunswick, were made joint secretaries. But once that was done, the visitors were invited to come in, and were most cordially introduced to the assembly. This first day, in fact, was mainly one of mutual greetings and opening formalities. As Brown lightly described it, "Having gone through the shake elbow and the how-d'ye-do and the fine weather – the Conference adjourned until the next morning at ten, then to meet for the serious dispatch of business."

In the evening Governor Dundas of the Island gave a dinner party in the stately little Government House beside the harbour – "the sea washing up gently to the very door". Brown thoroughly enjoyed himself; thought Dundas "a very nice fellow" and his wife most agreeable. And, for the visitor down from inland Canada there was special pleasure in a setting on the very edge of Atlantic water. "After all, Anne," said this expatriate of an island Britain, "there is something in the sea." The Maritimes were already beginning to work their charm upon him. A region hitherto unknown to Brown, and little regarded, would steadily gain interest in his eyes.

At the Conference next morning – as Brown said – "Canada opened her batteries". Cartier led off first with the general arguments in favour of Confederation.[25] Macdonald followed in much the same broad vein, with a long but effective presentation of the precedents and practices for such a union, the faults in federalism to be avoided. This occupied the rest of the session until the adjournment at three, and the Maritime delegates had done little talking themselves except to put questions for the Canadians to answer. That, indeed, would largely be true of the whole conference. But it simply demonstrated the fact that the men from the Lower Provinces had no clear plan of their own to offer, and were really less interested in the specific project of Maritime union than in the general need to do something. In this uncertain yet receptive mood they readily responded to the well-prepared, enthusiastic Canadians, who offered a grand and shining confederation as a definite proposal. No wonder, then, the unofficial delegates seized and held the initiative, and made the Charlottetown Conference a forum for their own views.

On the other hand, Prince Edward Island dispensed lavish hospitality for all. William H. Pope, Provincial Secretary in the

Island ministry, gave a sumptuous buffet at four that Friday afternoon, built on lobsters, oysters, and champagne. "This killed the day," Brown observed truthfully.[26] The well-fed delegates spent the warm, bright, moonlit evening walking, driving, or boating as the mood impelled; Brown himself sat quietly on Mr. Pope's balcony in the moonlight, "looking out on the sea in all its glory", and thinking of Anne, at Arran now, on other Atlantic shores.

On Saturday Galt occupied the Conference by describing the financial arrangements for a federal union and the way in which disparities between the provinces, and their differing requirements, might be looked after. Then it was the Canadians' turn to play hosts. All the delegates were invited to an elegant luncheon aboard the *Queen Victoria*, served to the accompaniment of more free-flowing champagne. The mood could not have been more cordial, as Cartier and Brown seized the glowing moments after lunch to win a psychological victory for Confederation. "Cartier and I made eloquent speeches – of course – and whether as a result of our eloquence or of the goodness of our champagne, the ice became completely broken, the tongues of the delegates wagged merrily, and the banns of matrimony between all the provinces of B.N.A. having been formally proclaimed and all manner of persons duly warned then and there to speak or forever after to hold their tongues – no man appeared to forbid the banns and the union was thereupon formally completed and proclaimed!" There, in the chief stateroom of the *Queen Victoria*, amid the wineglasses and cigar smoke, twenty-three men had warmly agreed to found a new nation. Other states might have a more dramatic start – but few, surely, a more enjoyable one.

That night there was another dinner party, given this time by Premier Gray of the Island. The quietness of Sunday, September 4, must have been a welcome relief, and Brown spent it at William Pope's house where he was staying. For one who so much enjoyed domesticity it was a positive pleasure to be with the Popes and their eight "strong, vigorous, intelligent and good-looking children"; to browse in their fine library, and talk about the Island with Mrs. Pope, the grand-daughter of a former governor who herself had never crossed to the mainland. Brown found it strange, but many of the inhabitants were in that same position – and were "notwithstanding amazingly civilized".

Monday was Brown's own day at the Conference. He spoke on the constitutional framework of the proposed federation, the structure of the central and local governments, the division of

powers between them, and how the judiciary should be constituted. In short, he had the all-important task of outlining the
constitution of the new union, and took the whole day in doing
it. George Coles, the Island opposition leader, entertained at
dinner afterwards, a "handsome set-out" graced by his several
attractive daughters, "well educated, well informed, and as sharp
as needles". That evening, however, Brown escaped to the ship
to play chess and take up the engrossing sport of catching lobsters over the side.

On Tuesday, the meeting earnestly debated the various
aspects of the suggested Confederation, as the Canadians closed
their case and withdrew to let the official delegates, the Maritimers, decide what should be done about the proposal that had
been made to them. Yet another party followed, given this time
by Edward Palmer, Attorney-General of Prince Edward Island,
and followed in turn by a ball at Government House. The next
morning, Wednesday the seventh, the Conference assembled to
give the Canadians their answer. It was scarcely in doubt, for
goodwill and enthusiasm, vision and optimism, continued at a
peak. "They were unanimous," recorded an exultant Brown, "in
regarding Federation of all the Provinces to be highly desirable
– *if the terms of union could be made satisfactory* – and they
were prepared to waive their own more limited question until
the details of our scheme could be more fully considered and
matured." The Conference was adjourned to meet again in
Halifax on the tenth.

But festivities continued. The Canadians received the Governor and his lady, the delegates and theirs, aboard the steamer,
though Brown was absent with a bilious attack – "the natural
result of such a round of dissipation", he admitted to Anne. On
Thursday, the visitors rode out to see the countryside and made
parting visits, and that night the Island's inhabitants gave a
grand farewell ball in the parliament building, glittering with
light, and echoing to the music of two bands. Brown, being careful, left about midnight as supper was coming on. Yet after supper, he deplored, "the Goths commenced speech-making, and
actually kept up for two hours and three-quarters – the poor
girls being condemned to listen to it all!" Then in the early
morning the whole lively party of delegates came trooping to
the ship, to embark for Pictou on their way to Halifax. And so
ended the episode of Charlottetown, the gayest whirlwind courtship in Canadian history.

From Pictou Brown went on by stage and rail across Nova
Scotia, visiting coal and gold mines, and reaching Halifax on
Saturday, September 10.[27] There was now another round of

meetings and ceremonies, and the paying and receiving of calls. The floating Conference met in the provincial legislature, and decided to float on to Saint John on the sixteenth. Meanwhile, its official members tried to grapple with the business for which they had originally been summoned, Maritime union. The Canadians, of course, were merely bystanders without significant opinion on the subject – at least, as long as it did not interfere with their own objective of confederation – though Brown himself might personally have preferred to see Maritime union accomplished, so that a strong Atlantic province might sit in a well balanced federation beside two big Canadian partners.[28] In actuality, the Maritimers' loyalty to their own provincial entities proved too deep-rooted to allow any agreement to merge them in a single Acadia. Yet those separate provincial entities still could be preserved within a confederation such as the Canadians proposed, and here was further reason to pursue that project. Accordingly, the Halifax meeting resolved to accept the Canadian invitation to another, larger conference, to be held in Quebec, on the subject of British North American federal union. Then they adjourned for Saint John.

Before leaving, however, there was a public dinner in honour of the delegates, at the Halifax Hotel on the night of September 12; this constituted the first announcement to the populace of what the Conference intended. The meetings had all been kept closed, a policy that had fostered broad, informal discussions at this initial stage, but rather annoyed the press, and produced only garbled, pieced-together guesses at proceedings. In all, ten speeches were made for public consumption at the Halifax banquet. George Brown gave one of them in reply to the toast to the delegates. Eight years after, John Hamilton Gray of New Brunswick remembered it as an address of great power, the first of the speeches made in the next few months by Confederation delegates that gave practical shape to the movement for union and definite form to the ideas that were in the air.[29]

Brown found himself unusually nervous beforehand. "People expect so much," he said.[30] But his presentation was masterly – confident, authoritative, and based on carefully collected facts, as he set forth the assets and potentialities of a British North American union. In fact, he spoke as an eager advocate of union between the Canadas and the Maritimes, now that he recognized the contributions these eastern provinces might make to a great new state in shipping and shipbuilding, ports and fisheries, population, mines and markets. For all this, an Intercolonial Railway was not too great a price to pay. The arch-Grit revealed his readiness to accept that line, now that it was a necessary part of a greater constitutional change instead of an alternative – an alternative, formerly, that had involved the expense without the achievement of union.[31]

He went on to meet various Maritime press objections already being raised against Confederation. He dealt with the contention that Canada was debt-ridden. True enough – he had often said so – but her resources were so great that the rapid growth of her population and wealth could easily overcome the debt within the next few years. He denied that a new federal state would in any way endanger the British tie: the stronger the colonies were, the better for the whole empire. And above all he denied that Confederation was a mere device to get Canada out of her own sectional difficulties, pointing out that the Canadians had already agreed to settle their internal problems in any case by means of dual federation. They had not approached the Maritimes to seek relief, he emphasized; they were fully pledged to the smaller scheme of federal union if the larger one did not proceed. "Our sole object in coming here is to say to you, 'We are about to amend our constitution, and before finally doing so, we invite you to enter with us frankly and earnestly into the inquiry – whether it would or would not be for the advantage of all the British North American colonies to be embraced under one political system.' "[32]

The answer of the Maritimers seemed quite obvious, for the decision to meet at Quebec in October was announced. There was much more said as well that night on the virtues, the expectations, and the grandeur of colonial union, while thunder rolled a deep accompaniment outside. Then the delegates broke up to move on to New Brunswick, to take the train to Windsor and the boat to Saint John. There was another banquet when they reached there on the fourteenth, and more speeches. Yet Brown was thoroughly enjoying himself as he predicted a railway from Halifax to the Pacific as the product of Confederation, and a defence force of half a million, with 70,000 marines included.[33] "The affair went off splendidly," he thought, "and we made quite an impression on the natives."[34]

He equally enjoyed the trip by river steamer up the magnificent Saint John to Fredericton, where Cartier, Galt, and himself were invited to stay at Government House as guests of Lieutenant-Governor Gordon. There was a tour and the inevitable dinner before returning, on the sixteenth, to Saint John – "a very pleasant city – the most thriving place in the Maritimes".[35] Now it was time for final leave-taking. A special train carried the Canadians that night to Shediac, where the *Queen Victoria* was waiting with steam up. "We have got on very amicably," Brown summed up, " – we Canadians – wonderfully so."[36] There was another delightful cruise back up the St. Lawrence; they reached Quebec on the morning of September 19, just three weeks to the day since their departure. "Our expedition has been all and more than we could have hoped."[37]

Indeed, it had been successful; and it had done much for Brown as well. The mission to the Lower Provinces had given him new knowledge and appreciation of this necessary seaboard for a continental union. It had shown the Maritimes that he was not a narrow western partisan, but was capable of broad national vision and constructive statesmanship – capable, in fact, of outlining the constitution for the new federal state. Now there was the task of filling in that outline and winning agreement to each detail. For, if the Charlottetown Conference had been the carefree courtship, ending in promise of marriage, the Quebec Conference would have to work out the precise and practical marriage settlement. Only then might the wedding actually take place. But, as Brown said, "We are all in favour of Federation if we can agree on conditions – and we have good hopes that we can agree. . . ."[38]

3

Everywhere in Canada there was discussion of colonial union, in anticipation of the meetings to open at Quebec on October 10. In welcoming the prospect, Brown's *Globe* did not forget an earlier cause. Confederation, it averred, would prove the means of opening the North West.[39] There might be no good reason why Canada should not secure that end without union with the Maritimes – but "practically", the chance of obtaining the first objective would be greatly enhanced by the success of the second. The achievement of eastern extension should erase all opposition to westward expansion, since Lower Canada need no longer fear the preponderance of western interests in a broader union, if the Maritime counterweight were there as well. Moreover, the necessary co-operation of the imperial government would far more likely be forthcoming if an entire British North American Confederation, rather than just one province, asked for the transfer of the West. That should permit far better terms to be reached with the Hudson's Bay Company in extinguishing its claims, and provide British financial aid for western development as well. In fact, announced the *Globe* in utter confidence, one of the first and greatest results of Confederation would be "justice" for the North West. A united government would press for it, to save that great territory from the United States.[40]

At Quebec in the meantime, Brown was "up to the ears morning, noon and night", catching up on neglected affairs.[41] He was preparing reports and drafting minutes for cabinet, presiding over long sessions as they dealt with three weeks' accumulation of business, and, at the same time, being badgered for information by correspondents from New York and London papers.[42] It seemed that British correspondents were after him particularly because his major speech in the South Oxford by-election, explaining the nature and purpose of the Confederation coalition, had received notably wide play in the newspapers of Great Britain. Anne proudly sent him cuttings: the London *Daily News* had published it in full, with a whole column of comment; the *Spectator*, the *Economist*, the *Star*, and many others gave it a large amount of space; and *The Times* obviously regarded him as the pre-eminent figure in the union movement. "Considering that they talked of your husband in a way to make even him blush," he returned brightly, "I do think it was pretty strong for you to observe that they gave 'a pretty fair view of the present state of political matters in Canada'. I am afraid my Anne has a very exaggerated view of her husband's merits – but perhaps it is well just to let her go on so while she can, puir body!"[43]

Busy or not, he was in excellent spirits. The old enemy, sciatica, had hardly troubled him since his return from the Maritimes, and had almost disappeared during that trip. He wondered whether "the riotous living of those three weeks was not the cause of his disappearance. What do you think of that as a plea for a generous table when we get back?"[44] He was even jaunty about the weather. Anne had crowed about the fine holiday weather at Arran – "Not a day lost," she had said. "Nothing about half days of umbrellas and great coats," he replied. "What would the aboriginals of Arran think of ten weeks without a drop of rain or a cloud in the sky night or day? That's a climate for you! The blessings we enjoy in Canada are unspeakable – though it must be confessed that such charming weather is hardly the thing for turnips!"[45]

There was only one cloud constantly in his own sky: the repeated postponement of his voyage to Scotland. He had first hoped to follow Anne late in June, when parliament ended; then came the coalition. He had still thought to get off before the end of summer; then came Charlottetown. And now there was the Quebec Conference to go through. Optimistically, however, he considered that it would sit only about a week, and that he would be able to sail by the *China* from New York on October 19.[46] He would not be able to leave any earlier because there was also neglected business piling up for him at Toronto.

In Toronto, not only was the Brown household to move from Church Street to Oak Lodge, but the *Globe* office was to move as well, as soon as new quarters being built for it on King Street had been completed. They were actually the product of a subscription taken up by Brown's friends during his illness and political retirement in 1861-2, in testimonial of his services in public life.[47] The funds raised – increased by his own reviving fortunes – had been sufficient to construct one of the finest press buildings in North America: three tall stories, stone-fronted, with a carved balcony and long arched windows, in the popular Tuscan manner. And this new *Globe* home on the north side of King, just east of Yonge, would be ready within weeks. Having all this on his mind, as well as affairs at Bothwell, Brown worked hard to complete his official duties at Quebec before the end of September, so that he could get through as much as possible of his own private business before the Conference met. He arrived back in Toronto by Grand Trunk at one in the morning, to find the Church Street house all lighted and his brother Gordon at the door to welcome him, fully recovered now after his own trip abroad.[48]

The house itself had been pretty thoroughly dismantled for the move. And so, when not down at the *Globe*, George Brown dwelt in empty solitude with the carpets up, the linens and drapery packed, the crockery and glass put away in barrels. "Doing Robinson Crusoe", he called it. "I breakfast at Sarah's and dine down town at a restaurant, and Sarah sends one of the girls in to make up my room. I get home in the afternoon and work without interruption. I put on my own fire, draw water and brush my boots. There was not a morsel eatable or drinkable left in the house but plum cake and two bottles of champagne! The latter are gone, and the former is fast going!"[49]

At length, towards the end of the first week in October, George and Gordon between them had the *Globe* removal fairly well in hand, and the arrangements made for the domestic move from Church Street. Gordon's family, in fact, were to take over the old house when George and Anne's belongings had gone to the new one. Early on Friday, October 7, George Brown left for Quebec, somewhat vexed that he had still not been able to settle everything, and would have to return to Toronto before setting sail. At least, his trip to Quebec was a good one, since the Grand Trunk had thoughtfully provided the President of the Council with the luxurious sleeping-car that had been built for the Prince of Wales's tour.[50] Arriving comfortably on Saturday morning, he found some of the Maritime delegates already on hand, and on Sunday the *Queen Victoria* docked with the main body, ready for the conference the next day. But Brown now feared he might not get away until a sailing on October 26, or even November 2.[51] He faced the climactic discussions of Confederation in a mood of some impatience.

At eleven o'clock on Monday morning, October 10, thirty-three delegates from Canada and the Atlantic provinces assembled in the plain white-brick parliament building that stood high on the cliffs overlooking the St. Lawrence. The *Globe* watched from Toronto. "While we all rejoice," it commented gravely, "we cannot but remember that we have arrived at the very crisis of our fate."[52]

The Conference members there that morning were those of Charlottetown, with the addition of the rest of the Canadian cabinet, two more delegates each from New Brunswick and Prince Edward Island, and now, as well, two representatives from the larger island in the Gulf, Newfoundland. They were Tory and Reform, government and opposition, and they were a wide mixture of temperament and personality: the stately Taché and the ebullient McGee, the prudent, precise Tilley and the robust, hard-driving Tupper. They gathered in the second-floor reading room of the Legislative Council, which became the Conference chamber, grouped about a long crimson-covered table – Canada at the middle, Prince Edward Island and Newfoundland ranged around one end, and Nova Scotia and New Brunswick around the other.[53] Brown's place was at the centre of the table, directly opposite the chairman of the Conference, Premier Taché. Behind the chairman, through the three arched windows of the room, he could see the view that formed a magnificent backdrop to the meetings, the superb thrust of the great river downstream to the far horizon, between banks still fired with autumn colour.

They soon disposed of procedural matters, agreeing that their deliberations should be secret, that each province should have one vote – Canada counting as two provinces – and that resolutions for discussion should be prepared in advance by the Canadian delegation.[54] Then they went rapidly to work on the substance, earnest, bearded, pragmatic men – no-nonsense Victorians – intent on finding out in short order whether a structure for confederation could actually be built. Their pace, however, was not the mark of superficiality, but rather of the ease of discussion without hampering formalities or speeches for the gallery – not to mention the hard preparatory work put in by the Canadians.

Besides, a good deal of agreement on first principles had already been achieved at Charlottetown: for example, that representation by population should be the basis of the all-important lower house in a federal parliament, and equal representation of the three sections – the two Canadas and the Maritimes – the basis of its upper chamber.[55] Furthermore, the Canadian government, having the recognized responsibility for initiating the federation proposals, had already fed a semi-official outline to the press in late September to elicit public comment. George Brown had sent his wife an advance copy for her own private perusal.[56] It set forth the division of central and local powers much as they would finally be established, affirmed that the federal institutions would still follow the British parliamentary model, and provided that the central authority would take over provincial debts and revenues, paying an allowance in return. Consequently, with all this background, and daily preparatory meetings of the Canadian cabinet in Council before the Conference opened, there was good reason for steady progress to be made.

Even the weather helped. It turned uniformly bad; the long, dry summer was over with a vengeance. Day by day now, the rains poured down on Quebec, rattling the ungainly skylight-cupolas of the Parliament Building, dropping a chill grey curtain over the St. Lawrence outside the chamber windows, drowning the brilliant colouring along its banks, yet bringing a strange return of spring-like green. In such weather, one might as well be in and working. Holiday skies and warm sunshine had fitted the gaiety of Charlottetown. Drab clouds and driving rain were not unsuited to the diligence and practicality of Quebec.

Not that it was always gravity and industry. Relief from work and weather came in the evenings in a radiant series of receptions, banquets, and balls. The Governor-General held a drawing-room for fourteen hundred in the Parliament buildings, for which both legislative chambers were re-floored and carpeted.[57] The bachelors of Quebec gave a ball that brought out such an array of local beauty that the *Globe* reporter wondered why there were any bachelors left in Quebec.[58] And members of the Canadian cabinet entertained almost nightly at the Stadacona Club. George Brown, indeed, had a special role in entertainment. He was the one Canadian minister staying in the St. Louis Hotel, where the government had housed the Maritime delegates and their wives and daughters.[59] Whenever he was not at some larger function, he did the honours as host at the Maritimers' table in the hotel. "We entertain them very grandly," he observed, " – every day they sit down to 'a company dinner' of the first class!"[60]

Meanwhile the Conference daily heard, debated, and voted on resolutions, at times amid strong arguments and serious difficulty. Nevertheless the framework of federal union was successively going up. John A. Macdonald had brought in the first resolution on the opening day, expressing the general desirability of federation. Unanimously adopted, it was built upon the next day, when Brown moved the basic resolution of Confederation. He called for "a General Government charged with matters of common interest to the whole country; and Local Governments for each of the Canadas and for the Maritime Provinces, charged with the control of local matters in their respective sections, provision being made for the admission into the Union on equitable terms of the North West Territory, British Columbia and Vancouver."[61]

"It must be a federal and not a legislative union," he emphasized. "That is the main object of my motion, together with the inclusion of the North West Provinces."[62] In that far quarter the Red River Settlement already held 12,000 people, and while bringing in British Columbia and Vancouver Island might seem "rather an extreme proposition", it would be wrong to exclude them in formulating the general scheme. "The Americans are encroaching," he said; the great West had to be secured.[63] Though Palmer of Prince Edward Island and Carter of Newfoundland demurred a little over the propriety of talking of incorporating Hudson's Bay Company territory, the continental sweep of Brown's motion was warmly endorsed by Maritimers no less than Canadians.[64] It, too, was carried unanimously. Then the meeting turned to arrange the institutions of the future general government, first dealing with the upper house. And this provided the first real problem.

Since Newfoundland had not had delegates at Charlottetown, it had not been considered in the tentative agreement reached there on equal representation of the three sections in the federal upper chamber. The Maritimers, conscious of the overwhelming number of places that populous Canada would have in the lower house, were not anxious to see Newfoundland now included within their block of seats in the upper chamber; and were hopeful, indeed, of substantially increasing their own share there. Thus, when Macdonald moved for three equal divisions of seats, Tilley countered with an amendment for twenty-four seats each for the two Canadas and thirty-two for the four Atlantic colonies. They argued over the matter for three days, but on Monday, October 17, reached a compromise – typically parliamentary in being a bit illogical and yet effective at the same time. On a motion by Brown, the principle of sectional equality in the upper house was preserved; there would be divisions of twenty-four seats each for the three regions. But beyond that, Newfoundland was, so to speak, abstracted from the Maritimes, and invited "to enter into the proposed Confederation with a representation in the Legislative Council of four members."[65]

By this time, Brown was already feeling the labour, as well as anxious to see it done. "We have had such a week of it!" he reported wearily; "Council from 9 to 11 – Conference from 11 to 4. Council again from 4 to 6 and sometimes to 7 – every day – and then letters and orders-in-council to write at night. It has been very hard work."[66] The deliberations within the Canadian cabinet itself went harmoniously enough, but he was often up till all hours afterwards, drafting the resolutions. On the seventeenth, however, because it was mail day for the Cunard steamer, he got Council to adjourn at four, so that he could enjoy his one relaxation, writing a letter to Anne.[67] "The Conference proceedings get on very well," he told her, "considering that we have a great deal of talkee-talkee, but not very much practical administrative ability among our Maritime friends. We were very near broken up over the question of the distribution of members in the Upper Chamber of the Federal Legislature – but fortunately we have this morning got the matter amicably compromised after a loss of three days."[68]

Yet other points of difficulty might well cause similar delays. He was sure now that he could not make the sailing of October 26, and even feared he might have to wait for one on November 9 or even later.[69] But, impatient as he was, Brown still knew the high importance of the meetings – and knew as well that his wife "would not wish me to imperil all my work and ruin myself with my political friends throughout the country by abandoning this great scheme at the very moment when a firm hand was most needful". He was very sure of it. "How painful, my own Anne, would have been our long separation, but for this perfect confidence that we could not misinterpret each other. For me, I enjoy continually the most agreeable quiet chuckles when I think how perfectly lovable and loving my Anne is."[70] That was the constant source of strength and refreshment for all his efforts – the private happiness he carried with him.

4

The next point of difficulty at the Conference arose almost at once. It also concerned the upper house. Should its members be elected in each province, either by popular vote or by the provincial legislatures, or appointed for life by the Crown – that is, by the central government? The division on this issue not only involved the desire of the smaller provinces to control the presumed defenders of their rights, but also a preference among some of the delegates for an elected second chamber: Canada, after all, had adopted the elective Legislative Council herself in 1856. On this point Brown disagreed with his fellow Reformers, Mowat and McDougall, and sided with Macdonald and other advocates of an appointed upper chamber.[71] He renewed the stand he had once taken against the Elective Council Bill in Canada, arguing that two elected bodies were not compatible with the structure of British responsible government.[72] To which would a ministry be responsible in case of deadlock between them? He did not, besides, consider that the federal upper house should have anything like the strong positive authority of the American Senate, since that body functioned under a very different system of government. In the British system, the second chamber had essentially a negative role; it was a safeguard, a restraint on over-hasty legislation by the popular house, and to make it elective would only be to give it false presumptions of power. In any event, the supporters of an appointed upper chamber won the day.[73] The Conference moved on to deal with the lower house in the new federal system.

Here Brown properly led the way. On October 19, he introduced a series of resolutions to establish that body on the basis of representation by population.[74] In the federal House of Commons – as it would be called – Lower Canada was to have a fixed allotment of sixty-five seats, and the other provinces would range proportionately from Upper Canada's eighty-two to Prince Edward Island's five, their numbers to be adjusted in the future according to the decennial census. It was the full embodiment of rep by pop – but it ran into trouble in a new direction, from the delegates of Prince Edward Island.

Painfully conscious of their own province's lack of numbers, they contended on no very strong ground for one more seat in the federal assembly. "We could not justify it," said Galt flatly, thinking of the effect on basic principle, while Brown pointed out that to give the Island six seats would require proportionate increases elsewhere, enlarging the House from a projected membership of 194 to an unwieldy 230.[75] Islanders of both parties had already been losing enthusiasm for confederation, as they realized how limited their own province's role would be. Now this was the conclusive issue. The Island delegation dissented in the vote that carried rep by pop, and stayed largely in a gloom of disaffection thereafter. Newfoundland, too, was a distant

and dubious quantity. Yet the chief potential partners were the
Canadas, New Brunswick, and Nova Scotia. If plans could be
completed for their union, the others might always join later.
Undeterred, the Conference accordingly went on to the next
item, the structure of the local or provincial governments in the
federation.

Once again George Brown took the lead. On October 20 he
moved "that in the Local Government there shall be but one
Legislative Chamber". These local authorities, he argued,
"should not be expensive and should not take up political matters".[76] Hence they did not need the full trappings of parliamentary rule. The single legislative chambers should be under
federally-appointed lieutenant-governors (who "would thus
bring these bodies into harmony with the general government"),
assisted by elected department heads permitted to speak but not
to vote in the assembly. The plan was an odd mixture of American and British precedents. But it was obviously not intended to
produce powerful provincial régimes.

In any case, Brown's proposal met objections enough. Cartier
thought it introduced republicanism. Tilley declared that New
Brunswick wanted to keep its existing parliamentary structure.
Tupper did agree that the local authorities should be as inexpensive as possible and their powers diminished – "but we must not
shock too largely the prejudices of the people".[77] And McCully
of Nova Scotia added firmly, "We must have miniature responsible governments."[78] Brown tried still. "Consider", he said,
"how insignificant are the matters agreed at Charlottetown to be
left to the local governments."[79] It was no use. Finally he withdrew his resolution, while McCully carried one instead, leaving
each province to design a new local legislature for itself in its
own existing parliament. At least Brown was left with the hope
that his views might yet be implemented for Upper Canada
alone. But the most important thing about them now was what
they indicated about his own concept of a federal system.

Plainly, it had changed since he had first taken up the cause
of federal union in 1859-60. The plan of the Toronto Convention, and the Constitutional Reform Address, which had followed, had decidedly stressed the role of the provincial governments in a proposed federation of the Canadas. They were to be
the chief repositories of power. Above them would merely be
"some joint authority", whose powers, as the Address had said,
should be "strictly confined to specified duties".[80] And though
in advocating such a limited federation Brown and his journal
had inevitably been influenced by their awareness that some of
their Grit supporters were dubious of even "joint authority",

their repeated assurances that the really significant régimes under dual federation would be the provincial governments had carried the ring of conviction. Why, then, the complete change? Why were Brown and the *Globe* now emphasizing that the local governments in federal union should be simple, and even non-political, that they should possess "only definite and expressly delegated powers" – and that the central government should be "sovereign, in so far as we can have 'sovereignty' here"?[81]

Perhaps the basic reason was that this was no longer a question of the federation of two Canadas, but of full British North American union – the creation of a whole new nationality. And Brown's inherent national aspirations were thoroughly awakened to that prospect. Indeed, at the Toronto Convention he had spoken ardently of future British North American nationhood, and looked forward to the day "when these northern countries shall stand out among the nations of the world as one great confederation".[82] Suddenly that day seemed close at hand. Of course the new national authority should have precedence – for, as the *Globe* put it: "It is unphilosophical that the part should be deemed greater than the whole, or that the lower should be more important than the higher."[83]

Moreover, it was no longer a question of ties merely with Lower Canada, ties that had been reins of domination. Henceforth the inhabitants of Upper Canada need not fear the ruling power of "French Canadianism".[84] It would be preserved, but equally confined within one province. Upper Canadians, then, could freely merge their interests in a broad union of several partners and accept the paramountcy of its general government. Furthermore, they could be sure of their full share of influence in that government, now that rep by pop was secured. In fact, since Upper Canada would control the largest number of federal seats, it should have corresponding power in the central sphere!

No wonder the local or provincial realm seemed of greatly reduced significance to Brown. And, in this regard, he was also influenced, surely, by his native Reform belief that all government should be restricted as far as possible in scope and cost. Some Liberal critics of the confederation scheme might attack it as extravagant. But he felt that it need not be, since the local authorities would have little to do. Their work would be "largely clerical and routine"; they could be kept small and inexpensive.[85] Hence Brown had proposed unicameral local legislatures to the Quebec Conference, and a system of government more suited to district councils than to provincial parliaments. It was not that he had turned his back on the British parliamentary system. That was reserved for the higher sphere, for the new national legislature. But it was not necessary for the provincial governments, precisely because they would not be that important.

This same attitude came out again when the Conference proceeded to discuss the division of authority between general and local governments. Far from evincing any desire to enlarge the list of provincial powers, George Brown would have been willing to reduce it. For example, he did not think that education, or property and civil rights necessarily belonged in the provincial field, though he recognized French Canada's special claim to have them in the local realm as protection for its language, laws, and institutions. Even agriculture, to be an area of concurrent jurisdiction, he thought might better be left to central control alone.[86]

Further still, George Brown was in accord with the dominant feeling in the Conference that whatever lists of subjects were drawn up, the residuary powers should lie with the general government; that is, in Confederation (unlike dual federation) the provinces should have only certain specified powers delegated to them, and the central régime keep all the rest.[87] Macdonald and others had emphasized that the chief flaw in the American federal system was the fact that the states had delegated powers to the federal government and retained the residue themselves. This had given rise to the doctrine of states' rights, carried by the South to the point of breaking up the union. But Brown would wholly agree that "a great evil in the United States, the acknowledgement of an inherent sovereign power in the separate states", above all had to be avoided.[88] British North America should reverse the United States principle, keeping any "implied power" for the general government, and securing "all those powers which will enable the legislative and administrative proceedings of the central authority to be carried out with a firm hand".[89] To the *Globe* this was the essential difference between the two federations. The Civil War had proved the inherent defect in the American system; in the new Confederation there would be no basis for any right to secede, because the general government would control "the whole nation".[90]

By this time, the Conference was into its third week, and on Tuesday, October 25, it put the final touches to the list of specified local powers as moved by Oliver Mowat. Only one major problem remained, the financial arrangements for Confederation. Galt had already introduced financial resolutions on the twenty-second to cover the transfer of debts and assets to the new federal authority, and the grants and allowances to be made in return to the provinces for the purposes of their government. But delegates from the Maritimes, where there was no system of municipal taxation such as there was in the Canadas, declared that the grants proposed for provincial administration were quite inadequate. The matter had to be referred to a special committee, composed of Galt and Brown, Tupper and Tilley, Archibald of Nova Scotia, Shea of Newfoundland, and Pope of Prince Edward Island. They threshed away at the problem until Wednesday, the twenty-sixth, when they brought in a modified set of financial resolutions that provided for additional allowances on debts to be paid to the Maritimes. These proved acceptable to all but Prince Edward Island.

The job was almost finished. There were a number of last-minute resolutions to polish off, but Thursday, October 27, would see the end of the ordeal at Quebec. Seventy-two resolutions were then to be formally adopted, to constitute the complete plan of union. It was a momentous and marathon achievement for three rainy weeks: the consequence of earnest, able men, careful preparations, and an insistent awareness, drumming with the rain, that this was the moment that must not be lost. The Conference had moved to two long sessions daily in its second week, for, tired as its members were, they were resolved to "make or break" before leaving Quebec.

The same spirit held Brown firmly, despite all yearnings to be off. Again he told his wife, "Nothing could save my reputation – more important still, nothing could even restore peace of mind and self-respect to me, were this great movement to fail in consequence of my absence at the critical moment."[91] And he correctly valued his importance to the Conference, as head of the majority party in the most populous section of British America, as well as a leading participant in the discussions by virtue of his own strong intellect and grasp of issues. Nevertheless, he still had his measure of detachment. He was still looking for a final release, as he declared, "Dearest Anne, we will finish this business up and retire on our honours if we win them – or in the consciousness of having tried to do our duty if we don't."[92]

Perhaps that detachment helped to save him from the worst strains of weariness and impatience. Throughout the Conference he retired to his inner world to write to Anne as often as he could, and, while there, resented all interruptions ("pestering", he called it).[93] He snatched quick glances at Maggie's photograph during discussions in the council chamber, showed it, and probably made a nuisance of himself on all possible occasions – as when Mrs. Pope "coaxed" him to exhibit it to the ladies of the Maritime delegates at the Executive Council's ball. "They were all perfectly charmed, and declare there never was so beautiful a photograph before!"[94]

Finally the end came. The members of the Conference actually, triumphantly, completed their agreement. On the closing day, the twenty-seventh, George Brown scribbled his own note of triumph to his wife. "All right!!! Conference through at six o'clock this evening – constitution adopted – a most creditable document – a complete reform of all the abuses and injustice we have complained of!! Is it not wonderful? French Canadianism entirely extinguished!"[95] He was just starting for Montreal on the nine o'clock train, along with Macdonald, Cartier, Galt, Chapais, and some of the Maritime delegates. "They are crying to me to hurry and my baggage is gone down. There they are again! You will say our constitution is dreadfully Tory – and so it is – *but we have the power in our hands* (if it passes), *to change it as we like*. Hurrah!"[96]

He was thinking, in all likelihood, of those eighty-two Upper Canada seats in the new federal legislature – sure to be dominated by right-minded Grits. There was joy enough in the prospect. But the more immediate joy was that the grinding Quebec Conference was over; the last great obstacles were removed that had barred his return to Anne. There would still be a host of odd jobs to clear up. But he would definitely sail on the *Persia* on November 16.

5

The delegates now went on tour, to unleash public celebrations of their accomplishment and to promote it judiciously among the people. It would first, of course, have to win the approval of the Colonial Office, and then be submitted to the various provincial legislatures, but in the last analysis popular acceptance was obviously vital. Brown's own feelings were mixed. "The Constitution is not exactly to my mind in all its details – but as a whole it is wonderful – really wonderful. When one thinks of all the fighting we have had for fifteen years – and now finds the very men who fought us every inch going far beyond what we asked – I am amazed and sometimes alarmed lest it all goes to pieces yet. We have yet to face the ordeal of public opinion in the several provinces – and sad indeed will it be if the measure is not adopted by acclamation in them all. For Upper Canada – we may well light bonfires and build monuments the day it becomes law."[97]

However, he did not accompany the delegates on their festive round of banquets and speeches in Montreal and Ottawa, but instead went directly to Toronto to finish up his own affairs. Yet he had more than personal reasons to justify his absence, since he was now to go to Britain on official business as well as to rejoin his family. Back in June, during the negotiations for the Great Coalition, it had been proposed that Brown should serve as emissary to consult with the imperial government on federation;[98] and now that the Quebec plan had been completed, his mission would naturally have much more definite significance. He should arrive in London not long after Governor-General Monck's dispatch transmitting the seventy-two Quebec resolutions had reached the Colonial Office. He would be the first to confer there on the Confederation scheme – no inconsiderable assignment, beyond all doubt.

Nevertheless, he still had a role to take in the post-Conference celebrations when the travelling delegates in due course reached Toronto. Cartier had played host in Montreal, his own realm; Macdonald, significantly, in his future domain of Ottawa. But Toronto was George Brown's affair. He was at the station, on the cold, clear night of November 2, to meet the delegates' train from Ottawa, and introduce them formally to the mayor and corporation. A torchlight procession and a large, cordial crowd noisily escorted the visitors to the Queen's Hotel.[99] There, in response to loud calls for speeches, a little group stepped out into the torchlight on the balcony above. Tilley neatly thanked his "fellow-countrymen" for their fervent welcome, and Whelan of Prince Edward Island alluded briefly to the national future before all of them.[100] Tupper stressed the strength to come from union, to meet the almost incredible transformation of the United States and protect, if need be, "hearth and homes from invasion and assault".[101] And Brown pointed glowingly to the benefits to come in canals, railways, and the opening of the North West, not to mention Toronto's again becoming the capital seat of Upper Canada's provincial government.[102] He closed the impromptu but eagerly received performance in the best way possible: by leading three roaring cheers for the Queen.

There was a grand formal luncheon in the Music Hall the next day. There it fell to Brown to make the first full public report on the scheme of union constructed at Quebec. It had originally been planned that Cartier would give an authoritative summary of the work of the Conference during the Montreal banquet, but there had not been time.[103] Then Macdonald was to present it at the Ottawa function, but when he began he had been taken suddenly ill and been unable to continue.[104] And so, at Toronto's Music Hall, after several stirring but unenlightening orations from other speakers, it was George Brown who rose, "to convey at least a general idea of the scheme which has been unanimously adopted".[105]

He lucidly described the structure of the new federal government, the planned division of powers, the proposed judicial and financial arrangements. He dealt with the major developments entailed: the Intercolonial Railway and expansion to the North West. He frankly conceded the need for the railway: "I repeat it heartily today — without the Intercolonial there could be no union of these provinces." Yet at the same time he emphasized that the Conference had "made it a condition of union that the great North West may come into the federation any time it pleases", and had further agreed that communications would be opened westward as soon as finances permitted.

There was one other important matter that had been given serious attention at the Conference. "The delegates have unanimously resolved," Brown announced, "that the United Provinces of British America shall be placed at the earliest moment in a thorough state of defence." He was not one, he said, who considered that Canada stood in danger of attack from the Americans. "I cannot doubt that they have plenty of work already on their hands — and I confess that notwithstanding the fierce ebullitions of the American press, I have faith in the good sense and good feelings of our neighbours." But he knew his fellow countrymen would not shrink from any possible threat, but "would show, in the hour of trial, that the spirit which was manifested in 1812 has not died in 1864".

Furthermore, they had a duty to defend themselves effectively. "If I am asked whether Canada, united with the Lower Provinces, is able to take upon herself a larger share of the burden of defence than she has heretofore borne, I answer without hesitation — undoubtedly 'Yes'." England could not be expected to send forces to defend the American colonies much longer, "whilst we continued developing the resources of our country and accumulating wealth untaxed for the appliances of war". Canadians, then, must be vitally interested in having the question of colonial defence re-examined and settled. They must end the false impression "that these provinces are in a naturally weak and feeble state". And so the Conference at Quebec had pledged that Confederation would bring in measures "to place ourselves on a firm and secure footing in the eyes of the world — to put our country in such a position of defence that we may fearlessly look our enemies in the face!"[106]

Brown might well have had in mind a recent border incident that had sharply underlined the need to stand prepared. Just the week before the Quebec Conference had closed, a band of Southern conspirators based in Lower Canada had suddenly swooped down on St. Albans, Vermont, robbed the banks in the dumbfounded little community, shot two men, and escaped into Canada. It was hardly a great military coup, this small-town banditry, and the raiders had been arrested as fast as they could be rounded up by provincial authorities anxious to preserve British neutrality. But the shock of the border foray brought fierce new anti-British outcries in the Northern press, while General Dix, Federal commander of the area, at once had ordered his troops to pursue the attackers into Canada if necessary. Fortunately, the prompt arrest of the raiders and the beginning of proceedings to extradite them to the United States had somewhat soothed American anger. A lengthy examination in the courts was under way even as George Brown spoke.

Yet he could still be aware that the Confederates at St. Albans had come close to starting war between Britain and the United States – and that, whether ordinary American neighbours wanted such a conflict or not, a frantic, dying Confederacy might yet precipitate it. The pattern of danger was apparent. Border conspiracy could produce a second war in America, to save the South but devastate the British provinces in the process. Certainly they must arm against the prospect, so that, as Brown declared, they might fearlessly look their enemies in the face.

His words were vigorously acclaimed. The press seized on them immediately, and spread the Toronto Music Hall speech throughout the provinces. People were making quite a fuss about it, the orator told his wife. "They say it was the best I ever made, but that is *stuff*."[107] The day following, most of the Conference delegates left Toronto for Niagara Falls. But some stayed on, and were shown over the *Globe*'s handsome new building on King Street East, now one of the sights of the city.[108] The office staff had carried through the move while Brown was at the Quebec Conference.

He had to go to Bothwell briefly; he would have to return to Quebec for a final cabinet meeting before sailing. And there was the decorating in progress at Oak Lodge. He ordered more carpeting and wallpaper, including, for Maggie's room, "a bright lively pattern for the little darling to wonder at, and a pretty border round it".[109] He dealt with the *Globe*; he wrote "half a thousand letters".[110] And still there was one more pressing problem.

The Vice-Chancellor of Upper Canada had died on October 24; Oliver Mowat had been offered the high judicial post. It was a prize hard for any lawyer to refuse, and Attorney-General

Macdonald had urged him to accept.[111] But Brown feared "that he will take it and leave me in the lurch", for Mowat had been his chief reliance in the cabinet.[112] As dependable a Reform colleague as he was capable, the astute Oliver had played a prominent part at Quebec; McDougall was not only less reliable, but more superficial besides. Now it was clear that Mowat would go. Who could replace him? Alexander Mackenzie was undoubtedly as sure a friend in George Brown's eyes, but he was still too young in parliamentary experience and standing. Brown's choice was almost inevitably William Howland, a Toronto Liberal of cabinet rank, Minister of Finance in the Macdonald-Sicotte government and Receiver-General in the Macdonald-Dorion. Howland had administrative ability as well as party stature. His trouble was that he did not perform well in close argument and could fairly readily be talked down. Altogether, it was not a strong Reform team that Brown would henceforth have to lead in the coalition. But in the hurry for his own departure, there seemed little else to do. In fact, he had to return to Quebec even before Howland had finally accepted.[113]

He reached the capital on November 9, just in time to consider a highly important document, *Report on the Defence of Canada*, submitted to the cabinet the next day.[114] Its author, Lieutenant-Colonel Jervois, had been sent out by the Colonial Office as a military expert to advise the Canadian government on the defence problem, a matter that was again much exercising the imperial authorities, as the release of victorious Northern armies from the Civil War seemed increasingly imminent, and British public opinion grew worried over even saving the imperial garrison in Canada in the event of an American attack. Jervois had met with the Canadian ministers during the Quebec Conference to discuss the military situation. His report constituted an answer to the queries they had raised. It was a pretty staggering answer, too, since the scheme of fortifications and lake gunboats he envisaged to enable relatively small forces to resist huge armies would cost the enormous sum of a million and three-quarter pounds. How could it be met?

With misgivings, the cabinet went to work to prepare their own views for the Colonial Office. They stressed Britain's major responsibility for Canada's protection, looked frankly to a sharing of the costs on that basis, and proposed that any permanent agreement on defence should wait until Confederation had been achieved.[115] In part, the ministers' reaction expressed the old, unlovable colonial tendency to pass the bill to mother; in part, perhaps, it represented an attempt to ensure British support for a speedy federation; and certainly it reflected an anxiety that anti-imperial sentiment in Britain was influencing the home government to shrug off its proper duties of defending overseas domains. Nevertheless, as evidence that the colonists were ready to do more themselves to meet the military problem – as Brown had publicly proclaimed – the ministers proposed to fortify Montreal at a cost of some two million dollars, if Britain would fortify Quebec and arm both cities. Moreover, they would bring in an appropriation for another million for the militia at the next parliamentary session.[116]

It was a good deal more than a gesture. It meant, besides, that while Brown was in England to sound out the imperial response to Confederation, he could also test it on the Canadian defence proposals, closely and naturally associated with the project of union. At the same time he was charged with another question, in the long run just as significant for the survival of an effective British North American union: the opening of negotiations at the Colonial Office for the transfer of the North West from Hudson's Bay control. Well briefed and thoroughly eager, he left Quebec for New York. On November 16, in company with Colonel Jervois, he set sail at last.[117]

The *Persia* was a fast ship. Brown went from Liverpool direct to Edinburgh for the long-delayed reunion at Abden House, to be with Anne in time to celebrate their second wedding anniversary on November 27.[118] There was Maggie also to exult over: her ability to stand alone in the corner, and other examples of unparalleled progress. Anne had got through all her "state visits". They spent a blissful week together, with the Nelsons and old friends only, before George's official business claimed him. But he promised to be back in two weeks, as he left for London "to negotiate with the Government folks in Downing Street".[119]

6

Down in London on Saturday, December 3, Brown went immediately to the Colonial Office, to be welcomed there most cordially by Edward Cardwell, who had replaced the ailing Duke of Newcastle as Colonial Secretary several months before. Cardwell kept him until half-past six in the evening, discussing Confederation. Together they went over the dispatch to go to Canada that day, replying to the Governor-General's transmission of the Quebec resolutions.[120] It fully approved the Conference plan, save for two minor qualifications regarding the right of pardon and the appointment of Legislative Councillors, put in, so it was explained to Brown, to guard against possible attacks in the British House. "A most gracious answer to our constitutional scheme," he deemed the final product. "Nothing could be more laudatory. It outdoes anything that ever went to any British colony – praises our statesmanlike discretion, loyalty and so on."[121] It was evident that the Colonial Office would be happy to back British North American union, now that the provinces had jointly taken up the cause, and now that American dangers and the burdens of colonial defence loomed so large in the eyes of the imperial parliament.

With general agreement on Confederation assured, Brown was ready to take up the particular problems of defence and the North West. Instead, he fell miserably ill. He had caught his forefinger in a door at the Quebec Conference, and now it had begun to fester under the nail. His whole arm swelled to the shoulder; he spent an excruciating sleepless night until the gathering broke at seven in the morning and gave him some relief. A visit followed to the well-known Dr. Paget, who put him on cold poultices, quinine and lots of wine, and placed his arm in a sling, until, within a day or two, he had fairly well recovered.[122]

Thus on Tuesday, December 6, the Canadian emissary was able to keep an appointment with the great William Ewart Gladstone, Chancellor of the Exchequer, the beau-ideal of Victorian Liberals everywhere, and, to Brown, "the ablest man in England".[123] It was a delightful chat, he wrote to Anne – an hour and a half of frank, straightforward discussion: "I was glad to find that we agreed in almost everything, and I was able to put him right on many points that he had not clearly understood about Canada." A little embarrassed, the colonial went on: "Do you know, it is strange but I did not feel him a tremendous length beyond me in intellect. . . . I must be dreadfully conceited . . . and though (as he remarked) we had been discussing the highest questions of statesmanship – he did not by any means drag me out of my depth." Brown stopped, shaken by his own temerity: "Don't for any sake read this to Tom or Willie, or they will think I have gone daft."[124]

Thereafter he was repeatedly at the Colonial Office with Cardwell, Sir Frederick Rogers, the Under-Secretary, and others of the permanent staff. He had conferences at the War Office, as well, on the matter of defence, and Lord John Russell summoned him to the Foreign Office to pump him on Canadian-American relations.[125] Arthur Mills, Liberal chairman of the

Commons committee on imperial defence policy, called to interview him; Adderley, chief Conservative critic on the same subject, wrote approving at least the intentions of the colonists on
defence.[126] Canada's representative had a thorough going-over
on the problem, and gave as much back in return. Undoubtedly
his resolute and forceful presentation did much to overcome the
impression still left from the Militia Bill of 1862 that Canada
would not act to defend herself, and to make clear the close
connections between defence and Confederation. "Everything
Canadian has gone up in public estimation immensely," he
observed."[127]

The outcome, though indefinite, seemed fairly satisfactory.
A final answer on the Canadian defence proposals would not be
given until January, Brown was told, but he gathered there
would be no great trouble in reaching an agreement suitable to
the province. None the less, he was considerably troubled by one
aspect of British opinion that appeared in regard to both Confederation and colonial defence. He remarked on it particularly
in a report sent back to John A. Macdonald. "There is a manifest desire in almost every quarter," he noted sombrely, "that,
ere long, the British colonies should shift for themselves, and
in some quarters evident regret that we did not declare at once
for independence. I am very sorry to observe this, but it arises,
I hope, from the fear of invasion of Canada by the United
States, and will soon pass away with the cause that excites it."[128]

Having at least cleared the ground on the defence question,
Brown turned to that of the North West. Here some ground had
been cleared already. For well over a year the Colonial Office
had been conducting its own slow-paced and tentative negotiations with Hudson's Bay officials to find out on what terms the
West might be transferred from the Company to the Crown,
so that it could be opened for settlement. The reorganized Hudson's Bay Company assuredly stood ready to cede its territories
and see a transit route to the Pacific built through them. But
equally it meant to make the cession pay, and did not intend to
yield property without full compensation. The Governor of the
Company – Brown's old friend, Sir Edmund Head – had
thus put forward a variety of imposing terms to the Colonial
Office: the grant of half the western lands and mining royalties
for the Company, at first; then 5,000 acres for every 50,000
sold by the Crown, plus five square miles for each mile of road
and telegraph built; and, finally, the whole package for a million pounds.[129]

Meanwhile, during the summer, Cardwell had suggested
that the Canadian government should send a delegate to present

its own views on negotiations for the transfer of the Hudson's Bay territory. The Charlottetown and Quebec Conferences had intervened, but Brown was now that delegate. He had come with a policy set by the coalition cabinet, which reiterated Canada's contention that the territory was hers by right of original French possession, and that the Hudson's Bay Company's title was invalid.[130] Accordingly, the Canadian position which Brown was to uphold expressed a willingness to co-operate with the British government in providing for the settlement and administration of the North West, but emphasized that the first task was the extinction of the Hudson's Bay claims – a task for the imperial authority itself. The real facts of the matter were these: Canada wanted the West, but did not want to pay for it; the Company stood firmly by its title and insisted on being paid; and the British government sought to be the honest broker only, neither meeting the costs nor testing anyone's claim.

Brown strongly argued the Canadian case at the Colonial Office. He denounced "the utterly untenable character of their pretensions"; that is, the attempts by Hudson's Bay officials to sell to Her Majesty's Government lands they did not own – at highly inflated prices, too.[131] In any event, Canada should not be asked to pay for a monopoly she had not created and did not recognize. Yet once the British government had disposed of the Hudson's Bay problem, he said, either Canada or the new Confederation would be prepared to establish effective communications with the North West and provide local government for settled areas. Again he pressed on Cardwell the need for decisive action.[132]

This was as far as the Canadian delegate could go for the present. He expressed the same views to other members of the British government, but the negotiations would obviously have to be carried on further before the three parties involved could reach an agreement. Still, Brown had accomplished two things. He had made plain Canada's insistence that the Hudson's Bay barrier must be completely removed – that there could be no partial or piecemeal arrangements for developing the North West – and he had made plain that Canada would then associate herself fully with western development, either directly or within a British North American Confederation. In short, he had materially advanced the western question towards its ultimate decision.

His work at the Colonial Office was finished by Wednesday, December 14, but there were still other things to do. He spent a full day with Arthur Mills discussing federation, for example; he breakfasted at Lord Henry Holland's, dined with Colonel

Jervois, partied with Cardwell, Attorney-General Sir Roundell Palmer, and Admiral Fanshawe.[133] The visitors and invitations kept flowing in to his quarters in the Waterloo Hotel. John Bright would dine with Mr. Brown any day he chose; Richard Cobden wanted him at Midhurst; Lady Waldegrave took him out to Strawberry Hill.[134] Anne thought he would be "put up" by all the flattering attentions heaped upon him – George was obviously getting what another age would call the full treatment.[135] Yet even the last crowning attention, a week-end with Prime Minister Lord Palmerston down at Broadlands, rather made him worry about the day he might miss in getting back to Scotland.[136] It had snowed at Broadlands. Old Pam said genially, "Brown, will you take a walk? You don't mind snow, do you?" – the pleasantry untold numbers of Englishmen have addressed to countless Canadians.[137]

He did not rejoin his family in Edinburgh until December 20, and there was less than two weeks left in their stay. George had to be back in Canada to prepare for parliament, which was to meet very early, in mid-January, to discuss the Confederation scheme. Nevertheless, they packed a good deal into the time remaining, visiting John Nelson at Greenock, celebrating Christmas at Abden House, and going to Alloa, George's birthplace, to see other old friends there. It was not easy for Anne to leave her safe, beloved circle and face winter Atlantic storms again, but they set out on the *China* on the last day of 1864. On January 13, they landed in New York, and the next night were in Toronto, settling into a fresh and glistening Oak Lodge.

7

Brown found that in his absence a full crisis had blown up in Canadian-American affairs. On December 13, the magistrate presiding in the long court wrangle over extraditing the St. Albans raiders had suddenly decided that he had no jurisdiction in the matter. A confused little man beyond his depth, "Judge" Coursol had almost taken refuge in a legal technicality raised by the defence – a seeming gap in Canada's neutrality laws. He discharged the Confederates without even binding them over to a higher court; they escaped scot-free with the stolen St. Albans bank money. Though the government offered a reward for their recapture and suspended Coursol, the harm was done.

The Americans reacted violently. While the Chicago *Tribune* lusted to dispose of Canada "as a St. Bernard would throttle a poodle pup", General Dix renewed his menacing order for pursuit across the border, and General Hooker, commanding adjacent border districts, was hot and eager for a full invasion.[138] Washington had already given notice of its intention to end the Rush-Bagot agreement restricting naval forces on the Great Lakes. Now it clamped a tight passport system along the inland boundary. From all the angry excitement in the United States, it seemed that Southern hopes of lighting war from border friction were perilously close to realization.

Hastily the Canadian government set up new detective forces to sniff out conspiracy, rushed volunteer units in mid-winter to patrol the frontiers. They offered restitution for the stolen St. Albans bank money, and began to draft a stiffer neutrality law. On the other side, moreover, the leaders of the American administration – principally Lincoln and Seward – really had no intention of letting the crumbling Confederacy achieve its one hope of salvation through a British war. They controlled their hothead generals; Canada's actions gave proof of her own desires to accommodate; and the Northern press turned back to greater battles in Virginia and Tennessee. In fact, the vehement phase of the crisis had passed before Brown's return. Nevertheless, its consequences were very much on hand to trouble him from the moment he arrived.

For one thing, the St. Albans crisis affected the defence question. It damaged the old contention that, since Canada would only become involved in war through the clash of British and foreign interests, it was primarily up to Britain to defend her. For unlike the *Trent* affair, this clash was local. If war had resulted, it would have been Canada that had involved Britain. Brown had reason to wonder whether such a fact might strengthen the anti-imperial feeling he had so recently observed in England. Would it not lend force to those who argued that self-governing colonies should bear the chief burden of their own defence – or even encourage a demand for cutting Canada adrift completely? That was the last thing he wanted. He was sure that Canada could not yet survive separate from Britain, by any means. And there was another problem, too, to worry about.

In the United States, the anger against Canada roused during the St. Albans crisis perfectly suited those powerful interests in Congress that were campaigning to abrogate the Reciprocity Treaty. Swift retribution for St. Albans lay in cutting off the trade benefits so valuable to the colonists. Perhaps it was just the climax of the congressional movement against the Treaty, but the very day that Coursol released the raiders, the House of Representatives resolved decisively for abrogation. On January 12, the Senate did the same. As a result, the Treaty would expire a year from March of 1865. Canada, and all British North America, would have to seek a new agreement, or look to very different arrangements for its trade. Brown had further reason for concern, as he reflected on the daunting prospect.

There was not much time for worrying now, however; parliament was to assemble on January 19. After only a few days in Toronto, the President of the Council set out for Quebec to meet with his cabinet colleagues just before the opening. On the nineteenth, the session that would take up the Confederation plan set to work in an atmosphere of sharp foreboding, taut with anxiety over the fate of reciprocity, the British response to the defence issue, and the American reaction when the Civil War ended, as clearly it soon must do. Along the borders chilled militiamen patrolled and waited, and banks in Brockville issued arms to guard against a rumoured reprisal for St. Albans from across the frozen St. Lawrence.[139] Never did strained times demand more statesmanlike response, as the members of Canada's legislature made ready for the weightiest parliamentary debate in the country's history.

The first matter to be dealt with was the neutrality law. A strong "Outrages Prevention Bill" was brought in and passed within two weeks, and early in February it was possible to begin discussion of the Quebec Resolutions. Macdonald opened the way on Monday the sixth, with a general outline of the Confederation plan, largely a reworking of the speeches he had given on the subject from Charlottetown to Quebec. Cartier followed the next night; Brown was to come after. But since Cartier did not leave him enough time for a major speech, and since he was not quite ready, Galt agreed to step in.[140] Thus Brown would have a whole evening sitting for himself. He worked hard on his material. "If I am in the right frame I will make a telling speech," he felt. "It is in my mind, if I can get it out."[141] On Wednesday night, February 8, at eight o'clock, he rose in a crowded House to try.

He stood in his place at the forefront of the government benches and looked out at the hushed assembly of the two Canadas, the packed, shadowy galleries beyond, and, beyond again, the snows of Quebec and the iron-hard St. Lawrence. "The scene presented by this chamber at this moment," he said with quiet emotion, "I venture to affirm has few parallels in history. One hundred years has passed away since these provinces became by conquest part of the British Empire. I speak in no boastful spirit — I desire not for a moment to excite a painful thought — what was then the fortune of war of the brave French nation might have been ours on that well-fought field. I recall those olden times merely to mark the fact that here sit today the descendants of the victors and the vanquished in the fight of 1759, with all the differences of language, religion, civil law and social habit nearly as distinctly marked as they were a century ago. Here we sit today seeking amicably to find a remedy for constitutional evils and injustice complained of — by the vanquished? No, but complained of by the conquerors! Here sit the representatives of the British population claiming justice — only justice; and here sit the representatives of the French population discussing in the French tongue whether we shall have it. One hundred years have passed away since the conquest of Quebec, but here sit the children of victor and vanquished, all avowing hearty attachment to the British crown, all earnestly deliberating how we shall best extend the blessing of British institutions — how a great people may be established on this continent in close connection with Great Britain. Where in the pages of history shall we find a parallel to this?"[142]

"Look at the map," he urged. There was Newfoundland the size of Portugal, Nova Scotia as big as Greece, New Brunswick as big as Switzerland and Denmark combined; here, Lower Canada as large as France, Upper Canada larger than the British Isles; and beyond, British Columbia equal to the Austrian Empire in extent — and the North West greater than the whole European realm of Russia! "The bold scheme in your hands is nothing else than to gather all these countries into one — to establish a government that will seek to turn the tide of European emigration into this northern half of the American continent — that will strive to develop its great natural resources — and that will endeavour to maintain liberty, and justice, and Christianity throughout the land."

Should not such a scheme fire the ambitions of every member of the House? "Does it not lift us above the petty politics of the past, and present to us high purposes and great interests that may well call forth all the intellectual ability and all the energy and enterprise to be found among us?" And one thing had to be remembered in every word uttered on this monumental project: "We cannot stand still. We cannot go back to chronic sectional hostility and discord — to a state of perpetual ministerial crisis. The events of the past eight months cannot be obliterated; the solemn admissions of men of all parties can never be erased." The existing Canadian constitution must be changed. And anyone who rejected the Quebec Resolutions must not only propose a better scheme – but one that could be carried also. Of course, he knew the present plan had failings. "It was necessarily the work of concession; not one of the thirty-three framers but had, on some points, to yield his opinions; and, for myself, I freely admit that I struggled earnestly, for days together, to have portions of the scheme amended." But granting this, granting all difficulties and defects, the design as a whole deserved support without reservation. "I believe it will accomplish all, and more than all, that we who have so long fought the battle of parliamentary reform ever hoped to see accomplished."

With fervent conviction, the Grit leader appealed to the veriest Grit, as he set forth Confederation as the complete remedy for existing problems in the Canadas, defending the equality given to Lower Canada in the federal Upper Chamber, and the acceptance of separate schools in Upper Canada as already provided under the act of 1863. Yet always he came back to the great reforms embodied in the plan: representation by population, the removing of sectional questions to provincial jurisdiction, the local management of local affairs. In fact (he said warmly), seen merely from a Canadian viewpoint, viewed only as a remedial measure, Confederation was so sound and satisfactory, "that were every word of objection urged against our union with the Maritime Provinces just and true to the very letter, I would not hesitate to adopt the union as the price of constitutional reform in Canada!"

But the objections were *not* true, Brown forcefully continued, as he turned to the broader constructive aspects of Confederation. Union with the Maritimes was so far from being a hindrance that he regarded it as "the crowning advantage of the whole scheme". He had changed his mind, he frankly admitted, since the days when he had held that general British American union, while desirable, was remote, and, being remote, could only postpone settlement of Canada's own internal problems. Now he knew the eastern provinces and the sentiments of their leaders. He knew, moreover, that circumstances had entirely altered – and they were urgent and compelling:

"A revolution has occurred in Great Britain on the subject of colonial relations to the parent state – the government of the United States has become a great warlike power – our commercial relations with the republic are seriously threatened – and every man in British North America has now placed before him for solution the practical question: What shall be done in view of the changed relations on which we are about to enter? Shall we continue to struggle along as isolated communities – or shall we unite cordially together to extend our commerce, develop the resources of our country, and to defend our soil?" What other answer was there but Confederation?

It could add nearly a million people to Canada in a single day, produce a combined market of some four million, provide a rich variety of resources, attract capital and impel development. It would supply an ice-free seacoast, and "make us the third maritime state in the world", with a total ship tonnage exceeded only by Britain and the United States. It would give a new start to immigration, and "enable us to meet without alarm the abrogation of the American reciprocity treaty". For, even if the treaty were repealed, "a fresh outlet for our commerce will be opened up to us, quite as advantageous as the American trade has ever been".

This was a heady mixture of hope and statistics, vision and enthusiasm, and its force was almost irresistible. Brown had only one main task left: to answer the opposition's demands for delay, for dissolution and a new appeal to the electors on the grounds that the Quebec plan was hasty, ill-considered, and not understood by the people. "Never, I venture to assert," he cried, "was any great measure so thoroughly understood and so cordially endorsed by the people of Canada. . . . The British government approves of it, the Legislative Council approves of it, this House almost unanimously approves of it, the press of all parties approves of it . . . only four candidates ventured to appear at the hustings in opposition to it – all of them in Lower Canada – and but two of them were elected. And yet we are to be told that we are stealing a march upon the country; and that we must dissolve the House upon it . . . at the risk of allowing political partisanship to dash the fruit from our hands at the very moment we are about to grasp it!"

He was approaching the close. In deeper, quieter tones once more, he appealed for fair consideration. "Let not honourable gentlemen approach this measure as a sharp critic deals with an abstract question, striving to point out blemishes and display his ingenuity; but let us approach it as men having but one consideration before us – the establishment of the future peace and prosperity of our country." Now came the peroration. "It may be that some among us will live to see the day when a great and powerful people may have grown up on these lands . . . and when one united government, under the British flag, shall extend from shore to shore. But who would desire to see that day, if he could not recall with satisfaction the part he took in this discussion?"

"I have done," he ended simply. "I leave the subject to the conscientious judgment of the House."

Brown had got his speech out; the chamber echoed with

cheers. It was a great speech, everyone told him, as the House broke up after midnight. "I suspect it was pretty successful,"[143] he carefully concluded the next day. But the Confederation debates, of course, did not end there. Indeed, they went on for days, and into weeks, as member after member rose to say his piece. There were trenchant speeches in opposition as well, since *Rouges* like Dorion and Holton and a scattering of dissentients from both Canadas found ample reasons to attack the Quebec Conference proposals. For inevitably the plan had flaws, as Brown had freely conceded. But what better plan – or even half as good – could be put forward? He grew increasingly annoyed by the negative, obstructionist tactics of Holton and Dorion, his former allies. The breach between them opened wide.[144]

Yet the government still held its huge, commanding majority, despite all that the *Rouges* and others, such as Sandfield Macdonald, could do. They used it to push the debates onward, until in early March, amid a wild winter blizzard, the long discussions approached their end. At half past two in the morning of March 10, 1865, the Canadian assembly approved the Quebec Resolutions, 91 to 33.[145] They would go forward in an address to the imperial parliament, requesting their enactment as the basis of a British North American federation.

Another milestone was passed on the road to constitutional settlement and new political existence. George Brown, who had done so much to bring his country down that road, felt a clear sense of climax. "Whatever happens now," he wrote to Anne, "my honour is safe in going into the coalition – and my fifteen years' labour is amply recompensed. . . . I feel now quite relieved of all anxiety as to what may hereafter happen. Come what may, I have placed the question on such a basis as must secure its early settlement."[146]

He turned to the other vital matter always before him, his life with his family. "Circumstances have separated us very much in the past year, dear Anne. . . . It was our duty to do it – and perhaps we should be happy that our sacrifices have had much effect on the welfare of half a continent. Is it not so, dearest Anne? . . . Could I possibly have abandoned the trust that has gradually grown up, and now rests upon me? Would you not like that darling little Maggie should be able twenty years hence – when we may be gone – to look back with satisfaction to the share her father had in these great events? For great they are, dearest Anne, and history will tell the tale of them."[147]

Retreat from Coalition

I

Bothwell was going. Brown had agreed to sell out to a Scottish syndicate formed to exploit the oil lands there. Negotiations for the sale had begun during his visit to Scotland, and in mid-February of 1865 he learned by letter that the purchase would go through for $250,000 cash, plus $25,000 in syndicate stock which, it was promised, would be worth five to ten times that nominal value.[1] "I was offered a million but only conditionally," Brown recorded, "and $275,000 in hand is worth a million in the bush."[2] He thought the stock would be safe enough. He was probably right, seeing that the oil properties of the Bothwell Land and Petroleum Company eventually would go to the Imperial Oil Company of Canada.[3]

Of course, it was still a wrench. "It does pain me somewhat to part with Bothwell," he wrote from Quebec in early March. "I feel a blank. It supplied relaxation when I wanted to escape from the pressure of thought about things around me. I believe thinking about Bothwell has been of essential service to my mind — and the working it out was most enjoyable. I could readily tomorrow, without regret or hesitation, give up politics and the press and go on a large farm with Anne and Baby! I might tire of it, of course — but I don't think I would."[4]

Nevertheless the passing of Bothwell would make him a decidedly rich man, possessor of one of Canada's first oil fortunes. "The sale ends all fear for the future," he told Anne jubilantly, "and leaves us open to do very many things that we would like to do."[5] They would be able to slip across the ocean whenever they liked, and properly entertain their Scottish friends on visits to Canada.[6] But Anne's reaction to the prospect was hardly what George might have hoped. Her love for her former home was poignantly strong, and she had scarcely spent more than three consecutive months with her husband in Toronto since their marriage. Even with the friends she had made there, she still did not feel fully at home. She still cherished thoughts of some day settling back in Scotland. Now George's forecast seemed to imply dwelling permanently in the Canada that he loved and she had not yet accepted. She answered him in an agitation that revealed her loneliness and sense of exile:

"My dearest George: You may think as you like, *but you must never speak of settling down here for life.* I may come to take your view of the matter but for the present you must let me indulge the hope of by and by going home and settling amongst friends there. I believe I would get quite ill if I thought anything else at present. The idea of being buried here is dreadful to me."[7]

His response was quick and affectionate. "Yes, my own Anne, you shall indulge your expectations of our going home to end our days in Scotland as much as you choose – and assuredly if after a fair trial you cannot be reconciled to Canadian life, why we will pack up bag and baggage and go off to the old sod. That was our bargain, and it will be religiously adhered to. But you have not yet seen enough of Canada to judge – and we have had too unsettled a life to give any idea of what it might be made."[8] The matter was dropped. Anne, as if a little conscience-stricken, instead sent him letters to Quebec reporting how much she was enjoying social activities and finishing the decorating of their house.[9] Yet here was further reason tugging at Brown's mind to make him restless with politics and ministerial duties: not only his new opportunity to enjoy life, but also the positive need to build a settled and contented life for Anne.

He exclaimed with her over the pleasure of seeing their new furnishings installed. "Do you know, I am vulgar enough to like all the little fuss about putting down new things. I would like, for instance, to see the mirrors put up and the chandeliers hung."[10] As for her worries over cost, "Who cares what the people say? We have only to please ourselves – and we are able to pay for what we have bought. I don't think we have been extravagant one bit."[11]

Still, there was one worrisome topic he could not avoid: the possibility that he might have to return to England on a second official mission, this time as one of a deputation that would take up the matters relating to Confederation that he had broached there: defence and the transfer of the North West, as well as the newly important problem, the future of reciprocity. He did not want to go and leave Anne again. He did not mean to; he assured her it was "impossible".[12] However, while Galt would go to England, Cartier was unwilling, and Macdonald and Taché "absolutely refused" – although a strong deputation would obviously be necessary.[13] His own Liberal followers

brought pressure on Brown.[14] He was still determined to resist
if he could. Yet even while the cabinet was considering the
question of the mission, events occurring in the Maritimes made
it more imperative than ever.

On March 4, when the Confederation debates in Canada were
drawing towards their close, Brown reported, "It looks very
much as if our new Confederation will fail in New Brunswick.
If it does so, it will fail in Nova Scotia. But I don't wonder much
at it. . . . It is a very serious matter for the Maritime provinces,
but magnificent for us."[15] The fact was that ever since the nature
of the Quebec plan had become known, doubt and criticism had
been rising in the Maritimes. It was one thing, after all, to talk
of colonial union in the abstract, and quite another to be confronted with a definite design, one embodying the unpalatable
truth that Maritime influence in Confederation would be far
outweighed by that of Canada. To Canadians, union largely
meant adding new territory at the price of an Intercolonial Railway. To Maritimers, it threatened the loss of their identity. It
was natural that they did not ask themselves what viable alternative they had for the future; what alternative they would themselves accept. New fears, old loyalties and local interests, attacks
on this specific point and that: all were expressed in a vociferous
anti-Confederation movement. And, in New Brunswick, it
seemed likely to defeat Tilley's Reform government, which
had called an election on the very question of federal union
under the Quebec scheme.

Some in Canada might condemn Tilley's want of wisdom in
putting Confederation before the people, instead of first carrying
it through a legislature he still controlled. But Brown, at least,
had known something of Tilley's reasons since the previous
November, when the Maritime Liberal leader had written to
him confidentially explaining the difficulties he was meeting in
New Brunswick. Then Tilley had informed him, "We will have
a hard fight here, many prejudices to overcome. The current of
public opinion is against us."[16] And at the same time, the term
of parliament was soon to expire. "Our general election is so
near at hand," said Tilley, "that all parties take ground that we
should have an election before submitting the question for the
decision of parliament." Still further, the Lieutenant-Governor
of the province, Arthur Gordon, appeared definitely hostile to
Confederation, believing as he did in legislative union, and above
all in Maritime union first. "I am getting no assistance from
Mr. Gordon," asserted the New Brunswick premier. "On the
contrary his course is weakening my hand and embarrassing me."
Consequently, it had been fruitless to try to reconvene a dying

parliament, and better, indeed, to go boldly as a government to the people. "I was not prepared for as much opposition as we are meeting with here," Tilley confessed, "but we must fight it through, and No Surrender be our motto."[17]

They did fight, and they lost. On March 6, the Tilley government resigned. In the light of this defeat, Tupper's Conservative régime in Nova Scotia did not even dare to put the Quebec Resolutions before the legislature, while Prince Edward Island's hostility and Newfoundland's disinterest were evident. It was a serious blow, though not yet fatal. If New Brunswick could be won back, Nova Scotia might then make a favourable decision; the others could come later. In Canada, the bad news from the Maritimes only made the government decide to wind up the Confederation debates faster and prorogue parliament without delay, so that the delegation could quickly leave for England to consult there on the changed state of the union project. "The affair in New Brunswick does not discourage us," Brown privately declared: "We shall go on just as we have been going – and push the matter to a termination. If it fails after all legitimate means have been used, we will go on with our scheme for Canada alone."[18]

Now the matter of the deputation to England had really to be settled. Brown was quite willing – more than willing – to leave it to Macdonald, Galt, and Cartier. Galt, he confided to Anne, "is *not to be trusted alone*".[19] Besides, even if Galt and Cartier should both go, Upper Canada obviously required a representative. But as for its being Macdonald – "John A's business affairs are in sad disorder, and need close attention, he says."[20] Hence the ministers debated in Council, and still reached no conclusion, while in the House members hoped it was not true that Brown had refused to go.[21] In the meantime parliament discussed defence, and, as the ministry had proposed, voted a million dollars for it in the supplies. On Saturday, March 18, the exhausting session finally ended. The members left rapidly, and some of the ministers also. By Monday the President of the Council was in almost lonely state, as he noted, "Taché is gone to St. Thomas, John A. has been tipsy since Friday, Cartier and McGee are gone to Montreal."[22] But the cabinet was soon to reassemble, to dispose of the English mission problem once and for all.

They met, in fact, the next day, and sat all the rest of the week threshing over the question. Brown found it "the gravest discussion I ever took part in".[23] He was apprehensive now as to the outcome of the mission to England, and judged that Governor-General Monck felt much the same way.[24] Britain seemed so lukewarm towards the colonies, her government so afraid to act. True, recent debates at Westminster had given reassurances (played up in the *Globe*) that she did not intend to break colonial ties, and would go to the aid of her American domains if they were attacked.[25] But at the same time, the British government had made the meagre gesture of offering only £50,000 as the first of four annual contributions towards fortifying Quebec. If there really was danger of imminent war with the United States, this was a hopelessly inadequate response. If there was not, £200,000 spread over four years was still too little and too reluctant to indicate any very warm support for the cause of colonial defence in the mother country.

Brown himself was still not greatly worried over the threat of American attack, either now or when the Civil War should end. He had discounted it both privately and publicly during the Confederation debates, even while maintaining that Canada should be armed (as the *Globe* put it) to set too sharp a hook in the bait to tempt Americans.[26] But he assuredly was worried over the belief in Britain that the danger of attack was real − that Canada, though virtually indefensible, might involve the empire in war with the United States. The British fears regarding Canada might be all too readily exploited by anti-colonial elements in the motherland, to bring about the virtual disowning of British North America. "If we do not conciliate English sentiment," the *Globe* even then was warning, "we must prepare for a new political existence."[27] Thus it was that a Canadian mission to England was of such vital importance.

At the same time, however, there was still the possibility that such a mission might fail to achieve agreement on a joint defence programme because of the unfavourable set of British opinion. And that, conceivably, could wreck the Confederation project, if the British government became convinced that it involved too costly a commitment in North America and turned from its support. "The consequences of failure on the future of the provinces may be very serious indeed," Brown asserted heavily.[28] In view of the imperial problem, then, and the rebuff in the Maritimes, might it not be as wise to reconsider the federation of the Canadas alone, in case the full Confederation became indefinitely postponed?

It was this question, as well as that of the actual make-up of the English mission, that made the cabinet discussions so grave and even critical − so critical that Galt grew ill under the strain, and Brown was ready to resign twice within six hours.[29] The stubborn refusal of both Brown and Macdonald to join the delegation, for reasons that each considered fully justified, could only revive the old antipathies between them. Macdonald had been unwell, besides facing business troubles; Brown had just returned from one mission abroad and felt he could not fairly be asked to leave his family so soon again. But while their friction would add heat to the controversy, its heart surely lay in Brown's determined attempt to obtain fresh guarantees that the smaller federation would proceed if the larger one failed – while the Conservative leaders, who had never liked dual federation, contended that such guarantees were quite unnecessary.

The peak of the crisis came on March 23, when Brown was wholly willing to withdraw from the government, and even expected a break-up.[30] Faced with that possibility, his opponents backed down, and he in turn accepted a compromise on the mission to England. He would go, and Macdonald would go also; but either one could name a substitute if at the last moment he could not leave – rather a face-saving device.[31] But further, if the mission failed, and it appeared on the delegates' return that there was no hope for Confederation, a plan for the federation of the Canadas would be prepared. Otherwise, if there was hope, they would wait until the session of 1866 to submit the lesser scheme to parliament; and if by that time Maritime objections had been removed and Confederation could continue, they would instead bring in a measure setting forth provincial constitutions for the two Canadas inside the general federal union.[32]

It was a thoroughly reasonable reassurance, that established a revised timetable for Confederation made necessary by events in the Maritime Provinces. It also answered criticism put to Brown by uneasy Grit supporters, as well as by outright *Rouge* opponents, that he was placing far too much trust in the Confederation idea and neglecting his original prime purpose, reform of the existing Canadian union. Brown himself had kept his wishes pinned to general federation, but now he had provided for the alternative. He could join the English mission with apprehension considerably allayed.

"The breezes of yesterday have all blown over," he commented, as on March 24 he busily drafted the minutes embodying the cabinet's policy.[33] On the twenty-sixth they finished up their business, and Brown set out for Toronto. The delegation was to leave early in April. With this ahead (and Anne to be prepared and comforted) the brief rift in the coalition could well be forgotten. Yet could it? Now that Brown felt that he had already accomplished much of his purpose in the ministry, by carrying the principles of constitutional reform through government and legislature, now that he had on the one hand the alluring prospect of private ease, spent in reconciling Anne happily to Canada, and, on the other hand, uninviting new tasks that meant more separation – would he remain reconciled to his place in the coalition? Or would his readiness to resign in March of 1865 be a portent for the future?

2

The Civil War was all but over, and April brought the final cataclysm. From the wire services to the *Globe* office in Toronto, George Brown could read dispatch after dispatch describing the utter ruin of the South: the fall of Richmond on the third; Lee's surrender of the exhausted, beaten Army of Northern Virginia on the ninth; and on the fourteenth, Johnston's call for armistice, as commander of the last major Confederate force in action. The victory of the Union was complete.

But, fortunately, tension between the United States and Canada had meanwhile lessened. In March, Seward had reaffirmed American willingness to maintain the Rush-Bagot convention, and had withdrawn the passport regulations on the border. And at this very juncture, when the enormous Union armies stood released from mass destruction in the South, the shock of an individual tragedy served, however paradoxically, to overcome Canadian apprehensions of the long-dreaded moment. The assassination of Abraham Lincoln on the night of April 14, 1865, evoked a swift and striking upsurge of pro-Northern sympathy throughout the province; and that sentiment was recognized in the United States, appalled by its great and sudden loss. In Toronto, the *Globe*'s excited city editor personally carried the news to Brown's home late at night, and waited while "the Chief" sat down in his study and wrote out a special editorial. The editor, John Ross Robertson, would remember that lamplit scene in later years, when he was a powerful press magnate himself, the owner of the Toronto *Evening Telegram*.[34]

There were unresolved issues on the American boundary still, and all the resentments accumulated in four war-time years of strain. Yet Brown at least could leave for England confirmed in his belief that there was no immediate military threat to Canada. Far more serious was the economic threat, since the Americans had now given formal notice of the abrogation of the Reciprocity Treaty. Could a new agreement be constructed in the year the treaty still had to run – not to mention settling Confederation, the defence issue, and the transfer of the West?

These were the goals, at any rate, as he left Toronto to sail from New York on April 19.

Galt and Cartier had gone the week before. He was aboard the *China* in company with John A. Macdonald. It might seem an uncomfortable partnership, yet Brown took it amiably and as a matter of course. Past quarrels were over, and there was no cause to raise new ones. There was, of course, that old barrier between them: Macdonald's charges of perjury, falsification, and suborning made in parliament in 1856 and never withdrawn, which, in Brown's words, had kept them earlier from "anything but parliamentary intercourse".[35] But when the Coalition of 1864 was formed, Macdonald had made Brown a promise: to make "public reparation" for his charges.[36] Obviously he was expected to retract them openly, although thus far he had not done so. It would be like Macdonald not to take the need too seriously – any more than he would now take his accusations of nine years before (just party politics) or the crotchets of that peculiar "covenanting old chap", George Brown, who needed to be humoured and cajoled.[37]

It would also be like Brown, however, to let the matter go for the time being, once he had the principle recognized and the pledge of the other to right his personal wrong. As he said later (regarding Holton): "I do so hate to be on unfriendly terms with any one."[38] True, he always had enemies enough, if for no other reasons than that his strong temper, hot tongue, and rigid stand upon convictions would make them. Nevertheless, to Brown, it was only duty that could separate him from other men – and his natural warmth consistently hoped that duty might let down the barriers. In this case it had done so; Macdonald had promised. The old grudge could be set aside, for one day John A. would acknowledge and redeem his grave error. How wrong each man was in his estimation of the other!

Now, aboard the *China*, in the holiday atmosphere of a smooth, warm passage and a group of passengers out to enjoy themselves, Brown could readily relax into informality and let his natural exuberance hold sway. They had "all sorts of cantrips" on the *China*: sword exercise, tig, throwing medicine balls, dances, concerts, and seances.[39] He could hardly be stiff with Macdonald in such circumstances, his partner in a common cause. It was almost a brief idyll of comradeship between the two most vital, mutually necessary men in Canada.

They planned to leave the ship at Queenstown and go to England via Ireland. They changed their minds, however, went on to land at Liverpool on April 30, and took the midnight mail to London.[40] They were in their suite at the Westminster Palace

Hotel at five the next morning — two small bedrooms and one good sitting room between them. Galt and Cartier had prepared the way. There was a whole list of appointments and invitations waiting.

No one could complain of the social reception given the Canadian delegates in London that brilliant May. They were out to dinner nearly every night, and usually to late parties afterwards. The Prince of Wales — Canada's royal visitor of five years before — was particularly attentive. At supper in Buckingham Palace for 2,000, he gave them entrée into the cosy inner circle of 100.[41] He invited them to private dinner parties, then kept them upstairs to all hours, smoking cigars with him, as he chatted at ease in a superb Turkish dressing-gown.[42] Peers and financial magnates sent cards and invitations, and sharp-eyed lion-huntresses bagged the Canadians for the functions of that London season.

Brown was impressed but not excited. "A few years ago I dare say I would have enjoyed it as much as anyone — but there is a lack of ambition now — a contentment with things as they are — and a hearty purpose to sit down comfortably for the rest of life with Anne and Baby."[43] He was more pleased by the progress they seemed to be making on the business of their mission. "We have taken the bull by the horns," he reported on May 6, "and have stated our position so clearly and strongly that we have carried with us every official person we have yet met."[44] The British authorities promised all legitimate aid for Confederation: "They are willing to do whatever we desire."[45] Federal union, in short, was assured imperial policy. This could be of no small consequence in the Maritimes, where, earlier, the colonial governors had generally been cold or hostile to it — particularly Gordon of New Brunswick. And so Confederation was not to be abandoned, only postponed. There would be no need yet to take up federation of the Canadas alone.

Defence, however, was a much more difficult problem. An agreement here would cost the British government money — money that would have to come from the House of Commons, where their majority was shaky and the critics of imperial expenditure were loud. There were internal dissensions in the government party between the stand-pat Whigs and the reforming, retrenching Liberal wing who looked principally to Gladstone. Then the "Canadian question" was a ticklish one in parliament, in any case, when the shadow of American power hung across the subject and memories of the rejected Militia Bill had still not wholly dissipated. As Brown saw the question of defence, their main problem was "to give courage and stamina to the ministry" – to bring them to take up publicly what they agreed to in private.[46] But even in private the powerful Chancellor of the Exchequer, Gladstone, sought determinedly to keep down imperial costs, and in his view of empire was not too far from the forthright anti-colonialism of such Manchester School Liberals as Cobden, Bright, or Professor Goldwin Smith of Oxford.

Consequently, the mission began losing headway. "In argument we always succeed," Brown noted in some exasperation, "and then comes the question of what the House of Commons will do, and what will be the effect on the elections, and how the Americans may regard such bold measures."[47] But if the Canadians could be entertained and fêted into happiness, it would surely be done. There was a state dinner at the Colonial Office, a state ball, a state concert at Buckingham Palace, and they were to be presented at court. George Brown had to "commit the enormity" of buying full-dress civil uniform – cocked hat, knee breeches, sword, and all.[48] If Anne had only been with him, the occasion might have been fun. "As it is, the thing inspires a feeling a quarter of pleasure, a quarter of bore, a half of comicality." But, he conceded to his wife, "Ladies, however, regard these things differently!"[49]

Nevertheless, he must have made an imposing figure when he appeared in his uniform at the hotel on Monday evening, May 18, and waited for the carriage to leave for Buckingham Palace before an admiring crowd of servants. "The Chambermaid's Delight", he proclaimed himself.[50] Over six feet tall, straight-backed, he towered in his ceremonial cocked hat. Large-boned but not stout, he could carry off the resplendent gold-laced coat, silk stockings, and dress sword that might seem pompous or ridiculous on other men. At forty-six, his hair was graying, but his face was strong and still unlined, his bearing vigorous, his colour healthy, his eyes their flashing blue. At this critical moment for the future of Confederation, Brown looked, and still was, in his prime.

At the gorgeously thronged and glittering throne room, the four Canadians found in some consternation that the Queen had directed they should be presented first. "Dukes and Duchesses had to give way and open up a passage for us," said Brown smugly, " – very much to their astonishment."[51] But it went off very well, as he knelt and kissed Victoria's hand, and she whispered, "I have much pleasure in seeing you here, Sir." Later, when the ceremonies were over, she rose, walked quickly up to him, and, in true royal fashion of enlightened inquiry, said to Brown, "You have been in this country before, Sir, I think?" A few words in French to Cartier, and she was gone.[52]

The mission seemed to be going better now. They had an interview with a committee of the cabinet on the nineteenth, at which Gladstone ("our great enemy") took the lead in the discussion.[53] Yet they made out the Canadian case for sharing the defence costs so completely that Brown began to hope for full success. Canada offered to spend up to a million dollars a year on training the militia, and to pay for the fortifications west of Quebec, if the British government would give the imperial guarantee for loans to meet the cost of the works, and would provide a naval force for the Great Lakes. A week later, however, when they saw the cabinet ministers again, Brown found them so frightened by their own dissensions that they would not accept their part in the proposals. "We must just make the best of it," he said philosophically; "All fear of war is supposed to be passed – and we will save our money, perhaps the very best arrangement for us."[54]

Still the negotiations dragged on: Canadian rejoinders to the British cabinet committee, more cabinet meetings to answer the rejoinders, Canadian replies to the answers, and so on. By now Brown was "fairly sick of it".[55] Of course everyone was very kind, and the social dance of the aristocracy was diverting, "but they are a different race from us, different ideas, different aspirations, and however well it may be to see what the thing is like – it takes no hold of your feelings, or even of your respect."[56] He felt so weary to be gone.

Nevertheless, he passed some time usefully and happily in shopping for Oak Lodge, buying chandeliers, silverware, plate, and crystal; he did not accept an invitation to Oxford, in fact, because he was too busy with the chandeliers.[57] The table silver would cost £250. The glassware was so expensive he was ashamed to tell Anne – "but we can afford it".[58] Then he and John A. Macdonald went to the opera together, saw *Lucretia Borgia*, and much enjoyed it.[59] And finally, on May 31, there was Derby Day.

"Like the rest of the world," said Brown, the Canadians journeyed to Epsom Downs, and went by carriage to see the fun of the road. It was a delightful day and a marvellous spectacle; he found that the reality of the Derby far surpassed its reputation. "Such a scene and such fun – such good humour and such wonderful evidences of unbounded wealth!"[60] There were half a million people swarming on the grounds. For the revels of the return journey he had a peashooter, and Macdonald furnished him with peas. As the throng of vehicles crawled in a tight, festive mass along the sixteen miles to London, Brown had a joyous time puffing away on the peashooter, through a counterfire of peas, bran bags and exploding bombs of flour.[61]

These pleasures did not lessen his annoyance over the British ministers' "miserable shuffling". Their whole effort now, he thought, was to get rid of the Canadians without trouble.[62] To prevent that, and secure at least some settlement, he and Macdonald and Galt sat down on June 1 to draft statements of what Canada was after, meaning to choose the one that read the best and submit it to the cabinet for an answer, yes or no.[63] And now the negotiations were brought to a decisive phase.

The Canadians abandoned their proposals for immediate, large-scale defence expenditure under imperial guarantee, and gave up the idea of naval armament on the Great Lakes – which would in any case contravene the Rush-Bagot agreement, once more secure. The British, in return, pledged themselves to use all their power, naval and military, to defend all parts of Canada in the event of war. Even the exposed West was not to be left unprotected. Otherwise, permanent defence arrangements would be put off until after the achievement of Confederation – which again tied the two great issues together.

Brown was far from displeased with this result. Since talk of American war seemed to have ended, Canada might well avoid taking on a burden of some five million dollars. Yet by her readiness to assume it she had proved her full willingness to do her part. "We have choked off the cry that we will do nothing towards defence," he said with decided satisfaction.[64] That should undercut the imperial retrenchers and the anti-colonialists!

At the same time, the delegates had been promised imperial help towards obtaining a new reciprocity treaty with the United States; and, even further, they had reached agreement on the transfer of the North West. Here too, it was a matter of compromise. To avoid long litigation, Canada abandoned her contention that the Hudson's Bay charter was invalid, and now stood ready to compensate the Company for its rights. But in this instance an imperial guarantee would be granted, to cover the loan required to meet the Company's claims. And the entire north-western territories would be handed over. "So we *will* be able to return with flying colours," Brown announced exultantly.[65]

This much was determined at a meeting with the imperial cabinet on June 8. The next few days settled the final agreements: Confederation, the North West, reciprocity – an understanding on defence – they had reached satisfaction on them all. Brown rapidly prepared to leave London, but first went with Cartier and Galt to a splendid dinner with the exiled French royal family, the heirs of Louis Philippe.[66] He travelled on to Edinburgh on the twelfth, to spend a few days with the Nelsons before sailing. Though Macdonald and Cartier were staying on a little longer, Brown and Galt went aboard the *Cuba* at Liverpool on June 17. He was homeward-bound at last.

3

Home not quite two weeks, he had to leave again and go to Quebec for cabinet meetings beginning on July 12. The rest of the government were to hear their report on the mission to England, and prepare it for presentation to parliament. There was to be a short summer session, since the winter one had been so hastily concluded in order to free the delegates for England. The cabinet spent only a few days in discussion and in considering measures for parliament. But while Brown was in Quebec, he looked about for a house to rent during the coming session, and hit on the Rectory House, former home of Bishop Mountain, in the square by the Anglican cathedral.[67] Anne and Maggie were to come with him this time. In fact, he was first taking them to Portland for a holiday by the sea. They would all go on to Quebec from there.

They went down to Maine by the Grand Trunk, and took George's sister Ise and her children with them, intending to stay until parliament opened on August 8.[68] A week before that date, however, Brown had to rush up to the capital because of the sudden death of the Prime Minister, Sir Etienne Taché. He was a pall-bearer at Taché's funeral in the little Lower Canadian village of St. Thomas on the hot and dusty second of August.[69] The slow solemnities marked the passing of a distinguished figure who had sat in cabinets since the days of Baldwin and Lafontaine, and in the last year had become a serene symbol of public service beyond all partisanship, presiding in grave, good-humoured tolerance over the divergent interests in the coalition. But Taché's passing also raised a crucial question. Who should succeed him as head of the government?

First thing the following morning, Brown received a request from the Governor-General to call on him at Spencer Wood. His relations with Monck were cordial and sympathetic; Brown had always felt there was a close understanding between them. He might have been presuming or flattering himself, except that Monck's letters regularly struck that note, and from the first the governor had shown keen appreciation of his views.[70] But now, as Lord Monck greeted him, he was obviously in a state of agitation — for there was a difficult task ahead.

The Governor-General stressed his "inexpressible embarrassment" (so Brown told Anne) at the situation in which he found
himself.[71] He thought it increasingly important to the country
that the present ministerial combination should continue, and
would do anything to accomplish that end. But how to do it with
the leaders of three parties in the cabinet? How to choose one
without offending the others? He had looked for a principle to
follow in his predicament, and could think of none except that
of seniority. "He was sure I understood his feeling toward me,"
Brown reported, "and what his inclination would have led him
to do, but clearly his duty compelled him to give Macdonald the
advantage of his position as the Senior Councillor in the combination."[72]

On ground of seniority, the choice was indisputable. Macdonald had first become an executive councillor in the Draper
government of 1847 and had been prime minister as early as
1857, preceding Cartier as well as Brown in both respects. Of
course, the Conservative press might later assume that Monck's
first choice was merely a recognition of the pre-eminence that
Macdonald had already acquired in the coalition. But this was
far from clear in August of 1865, when Brown himself had been
so prominent at the Confederation conferences and on missions
to England, and had also often led the House during Macdonald's absences from the last session, handling the task with
marked ability.[73] The basis of selection, as Lord Monck explained, instead sought to avoid making any comparison between
the party leaders in the existing cabinet. Yet Brown still could
not endorse it — for in any case it would plainly mean acknowledging John A. Macdonald as his political superior.

His reaction might naturally have been a welling up of *amour
propre*, or at least of the antagonism between old rivals. But why
should Brown not object, when he had strong contentions of his
own to put forward? He was sure the governor had acted con-
scientiously, he coldly acknowledged: perhaps this was the only
proper way to open negotiations.[74] There he stopped. Monck
urged him eagerly to speak out "as frankly and fully as we had
always heretofore done".[75] In that case, Brown continued (no
doubt warming as he did so), he feared the governor's policy
was seriously mistaken. The true course was not to name any one
of the three party leaders in the cabinet prime minister, but to
choose someone like Taché from the Upper House, with good
position but no marked party views, and continue the ministry
on the same basis as before. That had been the basis, indeed, on
which the coalition had been formed, and any other would have
been "indignantly rejected". Why should it be changed now?

Furthermore, Brown went on strongly, the appointment of any one of the three party chiefs would transform the cabinet from an alliance of separate interests into a fusion under one party head. His own Clear Grit supporters, *twice* as strong as Macdonald's in parliament, would never stand for it, and felt that they had sacrificed quite enough already. They would not always go on sacrificing, he said still more warmly: "The other party must not have the victory at every turn!"

Monck himself grew excited and alarmed − "entreated me every way but to *no purpose*". Brown, however, cooled off in contrast, and assured the troubled governor that he felt no personal chagrin over his course − "that I had no personal aspiration whatever," he recorded, "except to see parliamentary reform carried and get into private life at the earliest moment; that however Macdonald constructed his government − no matter who were in it − and if they pledged themselves to bring forward a measure next spring either for the greater or smaller scheme − they would have until then my hearty support." Then he tendered his resignation. Monck at once refused it, and "broke completely down, begged me to see Macdonald in the belief that if the case were presented as I had put it, Macdonald would probably accept my plan and agree to the selection of a neutral man."

Brown had gained his point, and for two reasons: because of the big western Grit majority behind him, and because he actually was so ready to resign. His attitude did not arise from petty captiousness or thwarted ambition. He had certainly not sought the premiership for himself, and giving outside support to a ministry dedicated to constitutional reform had been the very position he had wanted to occupy. And since he really did look forward to leaving public life, he was not merely making threats.

He agreed to meet Macdonald officially, but first consulted his colleagues, Howland and McDougall, and found them in entire accord.[76] Then he saw Macdonald. The amity of their English trip was gone; hard political differences had obtruded. Brown stiffly reiterated his position, claiming that the proposed cabinet change would virtually destroy the scheme of coalition and create a new government unacceptable to a large and necessary part of the present ministry's supporters. He pointed out, besides, that the three Liberals now in the cabinet already confronted nine Conservatives in key official posts, and should hardly be asked to accept a Conservative prime minister as well.[77] Macdonald as firmly contended that Taché had previously been the Conservative prime minister; that in forming the coalition the Liberals had only taken offices "that happened to be then vacant", and there was no reason to preclude a Conservative's moving up to the prime ministership, an office they already held.[78] He tried "all sorts of coaxing and wheedling" (according to Brown), but finally, recognizing that the other was adamant, swung onto a new tack and suggested Cartier as premier.[79] He, Macdonald, would step down for the sake of harmony, and propose the leading man in Lower Canada in his place.

He could scarcely have expected the gesture to succeed. Brown's arguments against Macdonald as head of the ministry would apply equally to Cartier, although an element of personal antagonism might at least be lacking. Nevertheless, the Grit leader offered to consult with his colleagues on such a proposition if it should formally be made. The long, strained interview ended. John A. went off to communicate his proposal to Monck, and no doubt to Cartier. But that evening he tried the same approach on McDougall without making headway.[80] The three Liberal ministers were in agreement. He could not divide them.

Meanwhile, as George Brown waited, he wrote to Anne – in anything but the terms to be expected from a cantankerous obstructionist threatening resignation unless he had his way. "You cannot imagine how delighted I am at the prospect of being freed from the trammels of office," he said. "I can go out with honour and success – and it will be my business to see that the great scheme does not suffer from my going."[81] Pretence? Sour grapes? Not in view of the whole pattern of Brown's behaviour and interests.

It was terribly hot. Quebec was in the middle of a heat wave, as Brown the next day, August 4, prepared the rented house for Anne's arrival. But he found time for another interview with Macdonald. "He is wonderfully modified this morning," he discovered, "and something may yet be done."[82] They were to exchange official letters. "I am half sorry that there is a chance of my not getting out of office," he added. "Public interest and personal feeling decidedly clash on this occasion."

That afternoon, by letter, Macdonald formally proposed Cartier's name, and by letter, Brown and his associates formally declared that they would regard his elevation as creating an entirely new government, although they were willing to consult with their party in regard to such a possibility.[83] This, too, was surely a gesture. Parliament was about to meet; there was no time for consultation, and perhaps the reshaping of the whole coalition. Macdonald and his colleagues abandoned their nomination of Cartier in a further note the following day.[84] Without admitting that their own claims were invalid, they proposed instead that a Legislative Councillor of long service, Sir Narcisse

Belleau, should assume the premiership. Belleau was a relative nonentity with little of Taché's former standing, but at least he had the virtue of being grey. It was the kind of neutral, nominal leadership that Brown had wanted. He wrote the same day to accept the proposition.[85] The coalition would continue as it was – triumvirate, Confederation policy, and all.

Not without reluctance, Belleau accepted his unexpected honours and was sworn in on August 7. The brief summer storm was over before parliament met, and all seemed calm again. Its meaning was considerable, however. For one thing, the crisis had made plain that the Confederation coalition had by no means done away with the struggle for political power. Macdonald wanted the leadership and looked forward to getting it, even if he realized that he would have to postpone his efforts for the time being.[86] In a manner as natural to him as breathing, he was advancing his interests over an old opponent. The fact that he effectively and sincerely identified his personal or partisan objectives with the patriotic goals of Confederation only made him the more dangerous to any rival who sought to work with him inside the government, yet not wind up under his control.

Then too, the crisis had again revealed Brown's discomfort about his own position in the ministry. When he had always denounced coalitions for the damage they did to political principle – especially any containing John A. Macdonald – it was inevitable that he should be sensitive about his role in the existing administration. Back-bench Grits were continually worried lest he be deceived by Tory wiles. *Rouges* were all too glad to exploit these worries, to warn him charitably of the dangers that he ran. During the Confederation debates, for example, Holton had recalled Brown's own words regarding the long line of gravestones of former colleagues that had studded Macdonald's progress, as he forecast the "yawning grave waiting for the noblest victim of them all".[87]

Undoubtedly, therefore, Brown was sensitive: sensitive for his own reputation and for the future of his party, both of which he had hazarded on entering the government. Consequently, he was quick to protest when more than once Macdonald "inadvertently" gave public precedence to Galt over him.[88] Small points, perhaps – but they were points of principle, always important to Brown, especially when he was constantly aware that while he controlled one of the two great power blocks in parliament, his party had only three seats to the Conservatives' nine in the cabinet. Besides, he recognized uneasily that the cabinet majority were still at the old political game of handing out jobs and favours to supporters.[89] He found himself virtually their unwilling accomplice. Still further, while he was off in London to introduce the Confederation plans to the English late in 1864, Macdonald, looking ahead, had been cementing a compact with Tupper of Nova Scotia to work together in the future.[90] From the moment the Confederation coalition had begun, in fact, John A. Macdonald had tended to treat it as a permanent political arrangement to broaden and build upon – not as a temporary armistice of parties, as Brown did.[91] Indeed, from all the circumstances, the latter well might wonder how inadvertent were Macdonald's failures to grant him due precedence in the ministry.

And so the crisis of August 1865 belonged in a wider context: that of Macdonald's natural proclivities and Brown's deep-seated misgivings. The Grit leader had entered the cabinet against all his own inclinations, pulled by the Conservatives and pushed by his own supporters. Urgent public necessities, however, had shaped the Great Coalition, and still preserved it. While they were uppermost, as at the Quebec Conference, during the Confederation debates, or on the joint mission to England, the inherent strains in that association had been kept hidden. But now the strains had sharply reappeared, and, though they were covered over once more, nothing had transpired to lessen them. Perhaps they had even been aggravated; certainly Macdonald's will to power was not likely to decrease. And, since his adversary was a man with little concern for office, but much concern for reputation, it simply was not probable that George Brown would be found in the ministry a great deal longer.

4

After this preliminary excitement, the summer session at Quebec seemed almost dull. The mission to England was discussed; the correspondence on the naming of a new prime minister was presented; the opposition made the predictable attacks and the ministry the predictable replies. Brown, for his own part, made an evident point of being conciliatory, admitting that difficulties must arise in a coalition, and adding, "Yet I must say that things have come on more successfully and agreeably than I hoped to see at the time of entering the government."[92] Parliamentary business was soon completed, and the legislature was prorogued on September 18.

In its final week a somewhat more interesting gathering was

also in session in Quebec: the Confederate Council on Commercial Treaties, formed at the behest of the imperial authority from representatives of the British American provinces under Lord Monck's presidency. This was a first fruit of the British government's agreement to do everything possible to facilitate the continuance of reciprocity with the United States. The Confederate Council was empowered to frame proposals for the renewal of the existing treaty or to advise on possible alternatives. Yet, as its name suggested, it might also prove a step towards Confederation, since it not only brought the provinces together in a common interest, but led them as well to consider the possibilities of interprovincial trade and the economic value of union, should reciprocity turn out to be no longer feasible.

This second Quebec Conference was, of course, a much more restricted assembly than the first, and consisted only of Brown and Galt for Canada, Ritchie for Nova Scotia, Wilmot for New Brunswick, Pope for Prince Edward Island, and Shea for Newfoundland.[93] Nevertheless, it was a select and weighty group concerned with a vital issue: the future livelihood of British North America. By September 18, moreover, they had adopted a significant series of resolutions as policy to be recommended to their constituent governments, and above all to the British government, which still controlled trade negotiations with foreign countries. They declared the colonies satisfied with the existing American treaty, but ready to consider proposals for its modification or extension. They urged Her Majesty's Government to seek a temporary continuation of the present treaty, if negotiations for a new one had to be undertaken and could not be concluded before the date of abrogation, March 17, 1866. And they requested Her Majesty's Government to authorize the Council's members, or a committee of them, to confer with the British Minister in Washington on negotiations with the Americans.

The Council further proposed trade missions from British North America to the West Indies and Latin America to search for new markets. Further still (and this could be important), they all agreed that, "In the event of the abolition of the treaty by the United States Government, it is the opinion of this Council that all the British North American Provinces should combine cordially together in all commercial matters and adopt such a common commercial policy as will best advance the interest of the whole."[94] That way pointed to the development of a home market, to an Intercolonial Railway that would bind it − and to the sheer necessity of Confederation.

When the Confederate Council and Parliament closed to-

gether, Brown and the Maritime delegates went on to Toronto.
The Council members were to tour Canada and visit the Provincial Exhibition, this year being held in London. But in
Toronto Brown had invited all the Maritimers to stay with him.
There was nothing he liked better than entertaining in his own
home. He had always delighted in family hospitality, his own
or anyone else's, whereas grand public functions or hotel con-
viviality generally bored him. And since his marriage he had
positively gloried in welcoming people to his home – thus the
importance of a good big house, gracious furnishings, and the
best of table appointments. Anne had to be prepared for sudden
descents with little warning. Perhaps the house would be thrown
open to give Presbyterian ministers attending the Synod a place
to sleep, to put up party friends from the West, or to fill the
place with a pack of family children, Marianne's from Woodstock, Jeanie's from New York, or Ise's and Gordon's broods
almost from next door. Or else, as at present, Brown would write
casually to tell Anne on two days' notice (she had left for
Toronto a little before), "I will bring with me Maritime delegates enough to fill the whole house. So please look out for good
servants and be ready for an invasion."[95]

When the Maritime visitors had gone home towards the end
of September, George Brown could turn to business concerns
neglected since the spring. In particular, he had to wind up his
own affairs at Bothwell, for, though the oil lands transaction had
gone through, he still had considerable property in village lots
to dispose of there, not to mention the herds and flocks from his
farm. October accordingly found him back at Bothwell, and at
London, Chatham, and Detroit as well, as he closed out his long-
standing interests in Upper Canada's south-west.

He stayed with Captain Taylor, his Bothwell agent, and for
days on end they laboured to compile and settle Brown's final
claims. His sale to the Scottish oil company had stimulated the
Bothwell boom still further; the new wells they were bringing
in only added to the speculative frenzy. Crowds thronged the
streets, avid to sell and buy: "Houses and money flying about in
thousands," Brown observed with relish; "the *fifth part* of a lot
I sold a few months ago for $200 was sold today for $1500 in
gold!"[96] New buildings were going up as if by magic, and meanwhile fortune-seekers were glad to pay any sum to sleep in
stables. One gratifying result was that persons who had bought
from George Brown years before and never completed payment,
whom he had given up long ago as bad debts, were flocking round
him demanding to settle what they owed in order to clear the
title to their lots. He and Taylor straightened out one such en-

tanglement dating back to 1855 and found $570 due, which was promptly paid over. "A very good day's work," Brown thankfully commented.[97] But after a day of this sort he was equally thankful to take brandy and water with Taylor and go off to bed. At any rate, he could tell Anne, "I shall make a very handsome thing out of my town lots – that is quite clear."[98]

It was the third week in October before he could return to Toronto. He could not stay there long, however, for events stirring in the Maritimes soon suggested that the time had come for an official Canadian agent to take another tour in that direction. The prospects for Confederation seemed to be improving there. As a member of the Confederate Council Brown might well be sent down on its business, and at the same time consult in the right quarters on the possibilities of advancing the unionist cause.

In New Brunswick, the key to British North American union, the anti-unionist government led by A. J. Smith and R. D. Wilmot was already up against a hard truth. It was easy to express provincial distrust of the Confederation scheme, but it was not so easy to find anything to put in its place. About the only positive policy that the administration had to offer was railway connection with the United States – an alternative to the Intercolonial – and this in turn would be of little value if reciprocity should not be renewed. On the one side, the anti-unionists in New Brunswick faced an indifferent American republic; on the other, an unsympathetic imperial government firmly committed to the policy of Confederation. Under the circumstances an approaching by-election in York County, New Brunswick, gave unionist forces a good opportunity to make a counter-attack on the Smith-Wilmot government, which was a combination of diverse elements joined by little more than a common antipathy to the Quebec Resolutions and the old Tilley régime.

On November 6, the York by-election was carried by the anti-government candidate, Charles Fisher, a delegate to the Quebec Conference and a friend of federal union. It was only a small break in the barrier, but it seemed a heartening sign, and the breach might grow. In fact, it might judiciously be widened. "The news from New Brunswick is glorious," cried Brown, ever the optimist, as on November 7 the Canadian cabinet met in Quebec and unanimously decided to send him on an expedition to the Maritimes.[99] He had been the first emissary of Confederation in England; now he would be the first to test the reviving chances for the project in the Atlantic provinces.

Anne Brown, at least, was not at all surprised. She had already assumed her husband would be asked. "You are a witch of a guesser," he informed her brightly, "for I am off in an hour from the moment of writing."[100] He was at Portland the day following, and in Saint John by steamer on Friday, November 10.

5

On Saturday, Brown went by special train to visit Premier Albert Smith at Moncton, as a matter of courtesy, and returned to Saint John that night.[101] He saw Robert Wilmot there; then on Monday drove sixty-five miles in a chilly open carriage to Fredericton for another meeting.[102] He was to stay with Lieutenant-Governor Gordon at Government House, and consult with this rather recent convert to Confederation, whom he had first met after the Charlottetown Conference the year before.

Gordon, of course, had then been a decided opponent of general federation and an advocate of Maritime legislative union. The two proposals were not necessarily incompatible. Indeed, Brown's *Globe* at first had hoped to see the smaller scheme accomplished in order to bring one sizeable eastern province into Confederation.[103] But the Maritimers themselves had treated the two plans as alternatives, and had readily dropped the cause of local union, which aroused little real enthusiasm, to espouse the general plan instead. Gordon, however, who disliked federation on principle (and to Brown deplored "the costly rubbish" of retaining distinct provincial governments), had wishfully believed that Maritime union could indeed have been realized – "but for the interposition of the federal scheme".[104]

He had even written Brown to that effect after the defeat of the Tilley government in March of 1865, urging, besides, that when Canada proceeded with her own constitutional reform, she should avoid the blunder of federal union. "Could not such a system of municipalities be established," Gordon had hopefully suggested, "as would preserve to Lower Canada all she can reasonably ask without impairing the efficiency and *supremacy* of the central authority?"[105] The New Brunswick governor, in fact, had shown as little appreciation of the real strength of provincial or sectional loyalties in British North America as he had of the colonials' strange preference to be guided by their own rustic politicians rather than the enlightened imperial proconsuls sent to watch over them. He was intelligent and able; but he was a natural and conceited autocrat, ill-suited to the restrictions set upon his functions by the conventions of colonial responsible government.

Yet since a recent visit to England, Arthur Gordon was a changed man — outwardly, at any rate. In response to the Canadian mission to England, the Colonial Office during the summer had emphatically informed its governors in America of Britain's "strong and deliberate opinion" that Confederation must be supported.[106] When Gordon was home on leave that autumn he had had the point impressed upon him still further. Monck was also then in Britain for a brief holiday. Gordon, he reported significantly to Brown, "has had positive instructions and has promised."[107]

Thus Brown now found in Fredericton a governor returned to duty who was obediently prepared to give his best efforts to Confederation. They made an odd combination, this elegant son of a former British prime minister, Lord Aberdeen, and the forthright western Grit — whom Gordon had secretly considered "the most dangerous and most unscrupulous demagogue in British North America".[108] That, at least, had been his opinion on first meeting Brown after the Charlottetown Conference of 1864. Of course, he had already heard Sir Edmund Head expatiate on the sore subject of an old enemy, George Brown,[109] but his own dark view at the time could well have been influenced by the knowledge that Brown was a powerful leader in the very federation movement that he, Gordon, so opposed. Moreover, the governor had in some degree blamed Brown for the discarding of Maritime union, because Upper Canada would not wait for it.[110] Yet that project had actually been discarded because it was not feasible; and it was fallacy to blame Brown, or Upper Canada for that matter, for the Maritimes' own lack of interest in union among themselves. While Gordon had still sought Maritime union, however, it had been easy for him to believe that Canadian sectionalism and self-interest had spoiled his hopes. Consequently, the jaundiced view he had acquired of Brown was not altogether surprising.

But now, by November of 1865, a good deal had been altered, and the two men were allies for Confederation. In fact, after three days of discussions with his Canadian visitor, Gordon could report to the Colonial Secretary, "Though I have not a good opinion of him, I am very ready to admit his ability and energy, and we get on capitally together."[111] Furthermore, they found themselves in almost complete agreement on strengthening the position of pro-Confederation forces in New Brunswick — although Brown perhaps might not have swallowed Gordon's bland assertion to Cardwell, "I am convinced that I can make (or buy) a union majority in the Legislature."[112]

The Canadian's own appraisal of the situation was a bit more cautious, yet no less encouraging for that. "There are great difficulties in the way of Confederation here," he noted, "but they are gradually falling away, and the progress of the public mind on the question is immense."[113] The York by-election had had an excellent effect. "All over I hear it said by everybody, were a general election to come on now, the question would be triumphantly settled. Even the present ministry of N.B., formed as it was to defeat Confederation, would take it up now, if they had the face to make such a change."[114]

There were grounds for such a sweeping statement in the unhappy quandary of the Smith-Wilmot régime. At least, there were as far as Wilmot himself was concerned. He was a leading New Brunswick politician, nominally a Liberal but a member of previous Conservative ministries, and his rejection of the Quebec Conference scheme had dealt a severe blow to its chances in the province. Recently, however, he had represented the New Brunswick government in the Confederate Council, where he had increasingly been won to the cause of federal union, thanks to his doubts that reciprocity could be renewed, and his hopes for interprovincial trade instead.[115] Brown had used his opportunities in the Council to acquaint himself with Wilmot. He was well aware of the latter's change of heart. Now he saw him again, at Saint John, and, further, managed to effect a meeting between him and his erstwhile chief opponent, Leonard Tilley. As Brown said, he brought the two strongest men in New Brunswick together; he was glad to tell Lord Monck afterwards that they were now "acting jointly for the accomplishment of Confederation".[116] Wilmot would shortly resign from the Smith government, this time to strike a shattering blow at the anti-unionist cause. Undoubtedly the Canadian emissary deserved some share of credit for the improving fortunes of Confederation in New Brunswick.

But in Nova Scotia there was less that could be done. Arriving in Halifax on November 18, Brown conferred with Tupper at his home, and met with a number of other Bluenose politicians.[117] In particular, he talked with William Annand, a prominent Liberal anti-Confederate, though he did not see the veteran leader of Nova Scotia Liberalism, Joseph Howe – who had once harped stirringly on the idea of British American union, but had sharply recoiled from the definite prospect that threatened the identity of his cherished province. To Annand, however, Brown apparently made overtures for the Liberals of Upper Canada and Nova Scotia to join forces in the cause of federal union, as he deplored the fact that thus far he had found only Conservatives to deal with in the coastal province.[118]

This might have been an attempt to match John A. Macdonald's pact with the Conservative Charles Tupper, or it may have been an effort to win Nova Scotian Reformers from their anti-union stand. But apart from Archibald and McCully – Liberal delegates to the Quebec Conference – the party in Nova Scotia was almost solidly against Confederation, and Brown's wooing failed. Here, indeed, was a lasting barrier to any hope of finding strong eastern allies for his own Grit party in the future: the fact that in the Maritimes generally, and particularly in Nova Scotia under Howe, Liberalism had become widely associated with anti-unionism, the very antithesis of Brown's own position.

In any case, as Tupper could have told him, there was little to be done in Nova Scotia now. The Confederation enterprise would have to stay in suspension there until New Brunswick had made up its mind. Accordingly, Brown left by sea for Boston a few days later, to arrive back in Canada in time for a cabinet meeting called for November 22.[119] His Maritime mission had taken just two weeks, and on the whole it had been a significant and constructive fortnight. What he met with on his return, however, was at least as significant, but would hardly prove to be constructive. In fact, it would lead to the worst crisis in the coalition ministry yet.

6

Brown learned that in his absence the Canadian government had moved on the reciprocity question without informing the other members of the Confederate Council. Negotiations had been opened with the Americans in a way he decidedly did not like. No doubt it was partly that the cabinet had acted without consulting him in a matter with which he was very much concerned. But he also opposed the line of policy that had been followed, and had sought to prevent its developing ever since the ministry had first seriously taken up the problem of opening conversations with the Americans several months before.

Back in July, following the mission to England, the Canadian cabinet had discussed sending a representative to Washington in order to sound out the prospects for a new reciprocity agreement. As Minister of Finance, Alexander Galt had then submitted a report on terms to be sought and concessions to be offered, and had suggested himself as emissary.[120] Galt, in short, had virtually proposed to initiate the negotiations right away, and not merely to ascertain United States opinion. But Brown had deemed it "the height of folly" to yield so fast and to begin by offering concessions.[121] It would only confirm the American belief that Canada had gained most from reciprocity and desperately required it. The opening gambit, he thought, should rather be, "We are satisfied to renew this Treaty as it stands – but are willing to amend it any way that is fair – What do you want?"[122] Let the Americans do some of the talking!

He had also objected to Galt's going alone as emissary. The finance minister, no stranger to self-esteem himself, concluded that Brown's objections to his person and his policy were really expressions of jealousy and his own desire to play a leading role in Washington.[123] Perhaps there was jealousy between Galt and the man who for years had been his ablest financial critic, but perhaps, as well, Brown was well qualified for the role in question. He had been one of the few outspoken champions of the Northern cause in Canada throughout the Civil War. He was *persona grata* to the Radical Republicans who dominated Congress, as a zealous abolitionist and an old acquaintance of the powerful Senator Sumner, with whom he had corresponded as far back as 1850.[124] He was known to Seward in the administration and had visited him previously in Washington,[125] and he was in touch with prominent American business men through his own business transactions, through his brother-in-law, George Mackenzie, now a well-known New York shipping magnate, and through William and Thomas Nelson, who held substantial American investments themselves.

Brown might thus have thought his claim to go to Washington was just as good as Galt's. But in any case, he would not trust the latter to be sole delegate any more than on the mission to England; Galt was too headstrong, too likely not to follow instructions but to make rash commitments of his own. And so, at the cabinet discussions in July, he had fought strenuously to bring his colleagues to agree that another member of the government should accompany the finance minister. After "a long and unpleasant debate", as Brown recorded it, Galt and Howland had been authorized to proceed to Washington together.[126] They went merely on a scouting mission, to test opinion at the American capital, not to undertake negotiations themselves.[127]

They had returned by August, in time for the brief summer session of parliament, with the impression that something could still be done to save reciprocity. Then the Confederate Council on Commercial Treaties had been established, and in September had laid down its programme for concerted action by all the provinces. In this respect, Brown had deliberately moved a resolution in the Confederate Council designed to prevent concessions' being offered to the Americans at the outset, and inviting "any reasonable proposals" by the United States instead. It had been unanimously adopted.[128] So was a resolution calling for a committee of the Council to go to Washington when the expected formal negotiations were begun. This, then, was the state of affairs in regard to reciprocity when Brown set out on his trip to the Maritimes.

The trip confirmed his opinion that the Confederate Council was of critical importance; not least, for the sake of Confederation itself. "It set every commercial man thinking of what commercial interests the colonies had in common," he wrote afterwards. "Nothing has done so much good to the cause of Confederation in the Lower Provinces as the institution of that Council."[129] At Fredericton and Halifax, moreover, he found the provincial ministers as keenly aware of the importance of the Confederate Council as they were "jealous of Canadian dictation", and relying on the assurances given to their representatives at the Council's meetings that that body would be convened again to discuss the steps to be taken with the United States as soon as the American Congress assembled.[130] Certainly, it was understood that Canada would not act further on her own.

It was true, however, that just before departing for the Maritimes Brown had attended cabinet, and there had learned from Galt that the Chairman of the United States Revenue Commission, David Wells, wanted to discuss suggestions for an extension of reciprocity that he might recommend to his government. Because it would be a dangerously delicate matter to put any such suggestions in writing, even for informal discussion, Brown himself had proposed that Galt might go as far as New York for a quiet chat with Wells.[131] That much seemed acceptable. None the less, he left for his own Maritime visit in the understanding "that nothing should be done in my absence"[132] – nothing more than unofficial, exploratory talks, that is. Of course there must be no regular negotiation instituted by Galt alone, and in contravention of the agreement of the Confederate Council on joint action.

When Brown returned from the Atlantic provinces and went to cabinet on November 22, Galt was away, but there was nothing to suggest that he was engaged on anything but his strictly limited assignment in the United States.[133] It was not until the Liberal leader was back home in Toronto that he found out otherwise; first in a press report from Washington of November 30, then in a letter from Galt himself.[134] He was amazed to learn that Canada's would-be diplomat had gone on from New York to Washington on his own – and there had conferred with McCulloch, Secretary of the Treasury, and Seward, Secretary of

State! The latter had smoothly told him that a new reciprocity treaty or an extension of the present one was out of the question, but that something might be done by joint enactment of trade concessions in the legislatures of both countries. Galt had taken to the notion, and done so much talking about terms — too much — that the Washington press had announced that Canadians were willing to meet United States requirements in settling their own customs duties![135]

Of course, this was only a press report, and probably inaccurate. Yet, quite apart from the blithe new suggestion of reciprocity by joint legislation instead of by treaty, there was the obvious fact that Galt's unauthorized initiative had already prejudiced Canada's case. And what this unilateral Canadian action might do to the entire work of the Confederate Council and the resurgent sense of unity in the British North American provinces was too upsetting to contemplate. Brown left for the next cabinet meeting on December 12, alarmed, indignant, and burning to protest.

The ministers met in Ottawa now. The government departments had been moving to the new capital ever since parliament had closed in September at Quebec. On arriving, Brown went straight to the council chamber in the half-finished Parliament Buildings, but threw them an appreciative glance on his way. "They grow upon you," he told Anne. Some of the rubbish in the central square had been cleared away; new-fallen snow concealed the rest. "The *tout ensemble* is really very fine."[136]

Reciprocity, of course, was the main matter of business. Galt presented an oral report of his doings in the United States that was really a defence of his conduct — though as the thick-set, sanguine financier held forth, it seemed that he saw nothing to regret in his activities. He explained that when he had gone to Seward and McCulloch on Wells's urging, each had declared that only reciprocal legislation could be considered, and when he found them indifferent to all the difficulties that this procedure would raise, he had gone on to discuss the terms that could jointly be enacted, including free trade in natural products and some manufactures, common access to inland waterways, reciprocal shipping rights, and assimilation of certain customs duties.[137] And for all this unwarranted bargaining Galt calmly asked a minute of Council endorsing what he had done and empowering him to continue.

Brown made a jarring reply. The finance minister, he said harshly, had acted "most indiscreetly".[138] He had had no authority to go to Washington, his approach to key American officials had been in direct opposition to the policy adopted by the Canadian government and the Confederate Council, and the proposals he had offered were utterly uncalled for. He had "flung at the heads of the Americans every concession that we had in our power to make," Brown charged bitterly. "Every suggestion he has made will be regarded as a boon we are seeking – and our eagerness in making them has evidently already shown the Americans how entirely we think ourselves at their mercy."[139] Worst still, all these gifts were for "legislative reciprocity", not for a binding treaty – mere acts of Parliament and Congress that either side might repeal at any moment! The Canadians would thus be left "dangling from year to year on the legislation of the American Congress – looking to Washington instead of to Ottawa as the controller of their commerce and prosperity."[140] Indeed, the plan was all too well suited to underlying American hopes. "Knowing as I do Seward's determination to absorb the provinces into the union," Brown added warmly, "how admirably this scheme is designed to attain his end!"

And what of the reaction in the Maritime provinces when they realized that Galt had been arranging the basis for a new reciprocity agreement without a word of consultation with them – in plain betrayal of the Confederate Council? This was what affected Brown most deeply. He felt honour-bound to stand by the assurances of united action. In his own dark view, if Galt's course were persisted in, "the result might be the loss of Confederation as well as Reciprocity."[141] And so – to bring matters to a head – if cabinet approved that policy, he must forthwith resign.

It seemed that the Upper Canada sectionalist was showing more concern for the feelings and interests of the other provinces than were Liberal-Conservative ministers of reputedly broad views on British American union. What would he do instead, they asked uncomfortably. Treat Galt's proceedings as entirely unofficial, Brown answered. Call the Confederate Council at once by telegraph, and start negotiations anew. "Make a dead-set to have this reciprocal legislation idea upset," he urged, and only in the last extremity – "after every exertion has been made to restore the proposal for a treaty" – consent even to discuss legislative reciprocity.[142] For Brown firmly believed, and strove to convince his colleagues, that Seward had merely tried that unheard-of notion on Galt to see what would happen – and had been happily surprised to see him swallow it completely. Thus the Secretary had rushed immediately to the British minister in Washington to assure him that the issue was already settled. "He struck the nail while it was hot," Brown noted caustically.[143]

His strong stand must have had effect, since, after consultation with his friends, Galt gave ground and produced a compromise proposal. His trip to Washington would be considered unofficial. He would go again, with Howland once more, and this time try for the promise of a treaty. If that failed, they would ascertain the best terms possible and report them back.[144] The exclusion of Brown from the proposed mission annoyed that member of the Confederate Council, but under the circumstances a snub from the smouldering Galt was understandable.[145] Here the issue might possibly have been settled.

Galt, however, still wanted a minute of Council passed to acknowledge his proposal, while Brown sought to keep the whole thing informal and explorative, and leave the further stages to the Confederate Council to negotiate.[146] The discussion continued on that point for several days. And the draft minute that Galt insisted on putting before the cabinet on December 18 seemed to the Liberal leader to retain most of the faults of the original proposal.[147] It still was based on the minister's November mission, and virtually approved its course. It still did not give the initiative to the Confederate Council, but would merely inform the member governments of what was intended – although Brown did manage to get a clause added to indicate that the Council should meet when Galt and Howland returned, in order to discuss their findings, while an assurance was also included that Canada did not seek to make terms separate from the other provinces.[148]

But he could not manage otherwise to alter the minute's inherent acceptance of legislative reciprocity. It still asserted as an official cabinet conclusion that "the American Government are not disposed to submit to Congress any proposal for the renewal of the Reciprocity Treaty," though Brown again contended strenuously that this was yielding the whole case in advance, and only represented Seward's successful duping of Galt.[149] Once more he fervently objected to the minute.

It was no use; he could not convince the others. They were ready to approve Galt's draft. Apparently they thought it compromise enough; probably they were not so sure that the finance minister had been duped, or that the Americans would accept a treaty. Certainly, in the final testing, they were much more likely to line up with Galt than his opponent. Party ties had their bearing, and, beyond that, Howland was a thin reed well bent in Galt's direction, while McDougall (unpredictable, but at any rate strong-minded) was out of the country on a trade mission to the West Indies. Brown was left isolated in the cabinet. The Conservative majority there was not likely to go on giving ground much longer to a single forceful Grit. By now, in fact, without any deep ill-will, both sides seem to have concluded

that they could give no more, and that the gap remaining between them could not be bargained away.

The minute was adopted. The next morning, December 19,
George Brown wrote out two documents of his own. The first
was a letter of resignation from the ministry, the second, a telegram to his wife: "Mrs. George Brown, Oak Lodge, Toronto:
Thank Providence – I am a free man once more."[150]

7

But it did not end quite there. Sir John Michel, Administrator
in Lord Monck's absence, at first refused to accept Brown's
resignation, while two of his colleagues, Cartier and Alexander
Campbell, called to see him at his room in the Russell House in
hopes of persuading him to change his mind.[151] Obviously, the
parting had not come in bitterness. Cartier made the approach to
Brown; their old enmity had been replaced by friendly personal
feelings, and a kind of tolerance for each other's flaws – Brown's
old anti-papal prejudices, and Cartier's natural zest for patronage. There had even been talk in some Conservative quarters of
a Brown-Cartier alliance once Confederation was achieved, and
the *Bleu* leader himself had seemed to entertain the prospect.[152]
At any rate, it was not entirely strange that he should be the one
to come after Brown. He missed him at the hotel, however, and
left a cordial note instead, hoping that the other might be "induced to reconsider".[153] Brown replied as amicably, but still
asserting that he could not change his views.

"I think," he said, "a very great blunder has been committed
in a matter involving the most important interests of the country,
and that the order-in-council you have passed endorses that
blunder and authorizes persistence in it." He admitted frankly
that he had been much annoyed by the slight shown him – but
all that had passed in view of the importance of the issue, too
grave for personal feeling. "I desire to leave you in perfect harmony," he assured Cartier, as he proposed that nothing be made
public on the cause of his resignation until the reciprocity question was settled, lest it affect the outcome in any way. He even
offered to give $500, and more if needed, to the fund being
raised to support the unionists' cause in New Brunswick. "In
conclusion," he wrote, "let me say that if you stick to the compact
you made with me when Sir Narcisse came into the government,
my being out will not change my course in the slightest – and

that you will have my best aid in carrying the constitutional changes we were then pledged to."[154]

Cartier answered in turn, still hopeful: "I flatter myself that after a friendly interview with you, Campbell and myself, this evening, you might be induced to change your mind."[155] But he prepared for failure, even as he acknowledged Brown's magnanimous stand. "Allow me to say to you," he ended, "that whatever may be the result of our interview this evening, I will always feel very thankful for the patriotic and generous sentiments you are so kind to express in your note to me."[156]

The interview failed, of course. Brown would not give way any more than the rest of the cabinet, each side convinced of the rightness of its case. But the whole episode made it still more clear that personal pique or jealousy had not brought about Brown's resignation. He left the coalition as he had entered it, on a question of principle; and the principle was not an excuse, but a sincerely held conviction. He was still putting first things first. He believed that constitutional reform now was safe enough. On that subject he intended fully to support the government. As he explained to Sir John Michel on submitting his resignation, "I consider the question of Confederation as of far greater consequence to this country than reciprocity negotiations. My resignation may aid in preventing their policy on the reciprocity question from being carried out – and the government should be sustained, if wrong in this, for the sake of Confederation."[157] It was not the attitude of an angry or embittered man.

Nevertheless, it was equally true that more than a disagreement over reciprocity had led to George Brown's resignation. It could almost have been expected, whenever an important issue should appear, at any time since the cabinet crisis of August 1865. All the groundwork was ready: Brown's belief after the Confederation debates, or at any rate since the June mission to England, that his essential tasks in the coalition had been fulfilled, his longing to escape official burdens, the distaste he felt for what seemed the old Conservative jobbery going on about him, and always his underlying worry that John A. Macdonald was coolly piling up party advantages – Macdonald who still had not redeemed his personal pledge to him. Undoubtedly there was true thankfulness in Brown's message to his wife: "I am a free man once more!"

His resignation was at last accepted. Howland, now the senior Liberal in the ministry, offered the vacant place to Alexander Mackenzie, who refused it after consulting with George Brown.[158] Fergusson Blair entered the government instead and the brief public excitement quickly subsided when it became clear that the Confederation coalition would not be shaken by Brown's departure. The ex-minister was home in Toronto by Christmas, drafting a many-paged letter to explain his course to Lord Monck, still overseas. "I should have much desired," replied the latter regretfully, if a bit heavily, "that your public spirit and self-sacrifice would have been rewarded by your having a personal share in an official capacity in the completion of the great work for which we have jointly laboured."[159]

By the time this answer arrived in the new year, 1866, the Canadian ministry had sent Galt and Howland back to Washington, as had been proposed. There they were joined by Smith of New Brunswick and Henry of Nova Scotia in negotiating for some degree of reciprocity. The discussions went on through January and into February. But on February 6 the provincial delegates decided that the case was hopeless, and so informed the Americans. The latter obviously had no real desire to negotiate. Their offer of free entry for only such highly important commodities as millstones, rags, gypsum, and firewood was devastating proof enough. Back at the *Globe*, Brown could nevertheless "congratulate the country on the escape it has made from an unspeakably greater evil" – economic domination by the United States through legislative reciprocity.[160] No doubt this was making the best of it, but, as he said later, "there is something more in building up a great country besides mere commercial advantages." Canada should never so tie herself by disgraceful concession as to "be bound to sail in the wake of Washington".[161]

In consequence, the Reciprocity Treaty would expire in March of 1866 without any sort of replacement. Perhaps this made the whole fuss over legislative reciprocity, and Brown's resignation, seem just a little pointless. The United States would make no breach of any kind in her tariff walls. Yet Brown's stand had still been based on his fundamental belief that it was possible to give altogether too much away for the sake of reciprocity: Canada's economic security itself. And it was still conceivable that Galt's over-eagerness to offer terms *had* helped to convince the Americans that they need concede nothing to Canada, since she was so thoroughly dependent on them. Undoubtedly expansionist ambitions were rising afresh in the United States, and one accompaniment of the Republicans' China-Wall protectionism was the notion that without reciprocity the British colonies might be forced to come within the American political system because they could not long survive outside.

At any rate, reciprocity was a closed issue for the present, and British North American union was made all the more compelling for that reason. Brown, in these early weeks of 1866, had no cause to doubt that union would succeed. The reaction he had witnessed in the Maritimes in favour of Confederation would surely grow, now that the United States had proved so unaccommodating. With Canada solidly committed, the imperial government committed, the federal plan complete in all essentials, it seemed merely a matter of time, perhaps months only, before Confederation would be realized.

And yet, by resigning now, had he lost his own share in a broader political future? Had he abdicated his own claim to power in the new federal state that he had worked to found? Perhaps he had, if he cared. If the essence of politics be the getting and keeping of power, then Brown might well have thrown the game away. He had, in fact, attained commanding power only once, in the all-important moment of mid-June 1864. He had used his power solely to ensure constitutional reform, and since then had failed to keep it − had scarcely even tried. Viewed thus, in the cool omniscience of a century after, it might appear that Brown's resignation was but the consequence of being outplayed in a power struggle that had inevitably continued, coalition or no coalition.

But perhaps the viewpoint merely determines the thing that is seen. Another perspective might equally reveal that the adaptable, pragmatic men of power seldom shape the great departures they themselves exploit. For these, the men of set purpose and ruling conviction make their essential contributions: in Canada, the Baldwins for the Hinckses, the Browns for the Macdonalds, the Woodsworths for the Kings. It is a poor country that appreciates the one without the other, that judges its leaders only by success or failure in the play of power, or by the thin and often misconceived antithesis of adaptability *versus* intransigence in public life. As for Brown himself, he saw nothing to regret. Nor need a later age regret for him.

Party Politics Again

I

The approach of spring in 1866 brought alarming new signs of American unfriendliness. The rise of the militant Fenian movement in the United States threatened British North America with actual armed attack, and, for months to come, the provinces lived in an atmosphere of swirling rumour and warlike rumblings from across the border. In the republic, the Fenian Brotherhood had first emerged as a network of secret societies dedicated to freeing Ireland from British rule, but since the Civil War one powerful faction had veered to the wildly peripheral objective of conquering Britain's colonies in America. And at the same time, Fenianism had swelled enormously with the influx of Irish-born ex-soldiers from the Northern armies, their purpose perhaps best explained in a Fenian marching song:

> *Many battles have been won,*
> *Along with the boys in blue.*
> *And we'll go and capture Canada,*
> *For we've nothing else to do.*[1]

It was a confused, vociferous movement, a mixture of farce and menace, filibusterism and burning Irish memories. Backed by washerwomen's pennies, it was led by braggarts and muddle-heads; yet there were hundreds of battle-hardened veterans in between. Its purpose might be madness, but its forays could be serious; and more serious still was the fact that the United States evidently felt little desire to ensure peaceful relations with the British provinces. Resentments left from the Civil War made Americans quite ready to watch border raids go the other way – to give the colonists a taste of St. Albans. Fenians might mass openly near the border, orate, parade, and drill to their hearts' content, even though their avowed aim was invasion of the neighbouring territory. There was little parallel here with the secret, small-scale Southern conspiracies in the colonies during the war, checked earnestly – if not always successfully – by provincial authorities trying to safeguard the boundary.

By early March, tension was soaring along the Canadian border. George Brown, down in Bothwell to observe the oil boom (which was still expanding), could tell at first hand of the anxiety in Upper Canada's exposed south-west.[2] There was, in fact, a widespread belief that the Fenians would strike on Ireland's national day, March 17. This was mostly based on rumour and the Fenians' own windy eloquence. Still, D'Arcy McGee – an ardent anti-Fenian, but with the best of contacts throughout the Irish community – told Brown he had strong evidence of raids projected for the seventeenth from both Buffalo and St. Albans. "I believe we are likely, indeed, I would say to *you* certain, to have trouble from these rascal Fenians," McGee wrote sombrely.[3] Certainly the government was apprehensive. On March 7 it called out 10,000 volunteers for frontier duty – a step the *Globe* approved as a wise precaution, as it sharply condemned the American authorities for failing to control the danger.[4]

The *Globe*'s owner was at least as apprehensive over trouble at home, in Toronto, on March 17. The large Irish element in the city was drawn more from Protestant Ulster than from the Roman Catholic South, but there were quite enough Southern Irish to make Brown and others worry about possible Fenian sympathizers in their midst. Above all, there could be bloody rioting in Toronto, if any Catholic Irishmen demonstrated for Fenianism, and it was said that Fenians would march in the city's St. Patrick's Day procession. Should such a move be timed to coincide with border raids, the results could plainly be chaotic.

Brown's worries in the matter led him to write directly to the Governor-General to seek an official proclamation forbidding Toronto's St. Patrick's Day parade.[5] Lord Monck, however, while far from unconcerned, considered that such a measure might do more harm than good. The procession was legal enough in itself; prohibiting it might actually incite violence. In any case, it was up to the local authorities to maintain order, though the governor earnestly hoped that a "contemptible minority" would not disgrace Toronto on the seventeenth.[6] Brown's own attitude might simply have expressed anti-Irish, anti-Catholic prejudice, except that D'Arcy McGee, chief spokesman for Canada's Catholic Irish, himself wanted to see the parade stopped. He had approached Bishop Lynch to prevent it, he anxiously informed Brown: "If he does not quietly do so, I really think it may be a fair subject for the Mayor's interference." With armed raids in prospect, "it cannot be tolerated that a seditious society should at one and the same time be parading our own streets – distracting or preoccupying the attention of the authorities."[7]

But nothing happened after all. March 17 passed off peacefully – tranquil at home, unthreatened from abroad. Perhaps the Canadian government's response, 10,000 strong, had cooled the Fenians; perhaps their talked-of enterprises had been only bombast, or else had collapsed of their own internal quarrels and lack of co-ordination. For the time, at any rate, Canada seemed safe enough. By the close of the month, the militia on the border could be reduced and sent home again. And for George Brown, March 19 turned out to be a much more significant date than the seventeenth. For on that day Anne gave birth to a second daughter, Catherine Edith – the "Catherine" after George's dead sister.

Now Fenianism was moving in a new direction. By early April, members of the Brotherhood were pouring into Calais and Eastport, Maine, on the New Brunswick border. Their strength grew rapidly to about five hundred in or out of uniform – some of the uniforms of their own concoction.[8] The whole district was thrown into turmoil, as Fenians chartered schooners, brought in arms and powder, and manoeuvred on the banks of the St. Croix, while on the New Brunswick side both regulars and militia were deployed. There was an abortive night landing attempted below St. Stephen, where a horseman galloped through the sleeping countryside, like Paul Revere in reverse, to warn the redcoats that the Americans were coming.[9] But apart from this, and raids boldly executed on the Indian Island custom-house, the Fenians showed more disposition for talk than for action. Towards the end of April they were running out of money. Still brandishing revolvers, they drifted noisily away.

Nevertheless, they had not been without effect on New Brunswick. Indeed, their grandiose pronouncement – issued "by order of the Republican Committee of St. John" – against "the obnoxious project of Confederation" all but applied the *coup de grâce* to the tottering cause of anti-unionism in the province.[10] Provincial patriotism, loyalty to the Crown, incipient British North American nationalism, would all respond in favour of Confederation. And as New Brunswick's reaction against Fenianism mounted, Governor Gordon improved the hour by virtually engineering the resignation of the Smith ministry. Fortunately for the federal cause, the anti-union cabinet was now so clearly in the last stages of futility that not even Gordon's abuse of his position could redeem its members. He adjourned the legislature, and dissolved it a few weeks later, and elections were called in the aftermath of Fenian excitement.

This time, surely, Confederation would win. From Canada,

Brown and the *Globe* confidently watched the campaign that opened in New Brunswick in May.[11] They were quite amenable to the Canadian parliament's being delayed until the results could be known.[12] Meanwhile, strengthened by the turn of events in the neighbouring province, Tupper in Nova Scotia introduced and carried a vaguely worded resolution that at least authorized him to renew negotiations for union. The polling in New Brunswick began late in May; and long before the last returns were in on June 12, it was apparent that the Confederates – Tilley, Wilmot, Mitchell, and Fisher – had won a triumph. Brown could rightly hail it as a full endorsement of Confederation.

But while the voting was under way in the east, Brown's attention was suddenly deflected back to his own province. It was the Fenians again: at the end of May, they had suddenly become an imminent threat to Upper Canada once more. By now the *Globe* and its contemporaries were bristling with reports of new Fenian concentrations around Buffalo, New York. Some 2,000 raiders were expected to move to Sandusky and strike from there – or else to go to Ogdensburg; stories disagreed.[13] But at 3:20 in the morning of June 1, the telegraph flashed to Toronto that a strong body of Fenians had marched out to Black Rock to cross the Niagara River before daybreak. The grand invasion, the cloudy conquest – the quite pointless raid – was under way. The *Globe* angrily expressed "our utter astonishment at the placid manner in which the American government continue to look on while our Province is being invaded, openly, defiant of their authority, by American citizens from American soil."[14]

By daylight, some 1,000 Fenians had landed and seized the little village of Fort Erie unopposed. Both regulars and volunteers were hurriedly dispatched by rail from Toronto, Hamilton, and elsewhere. Toronto was in wild excitement as the city's Queen's Own Rifles entrained, and, with them, the young men of the University and Trinity College Company, bursting to reach the battle front. It was not until the next day, however, that the troops collecting in the Niagara Peninsula reached and engaged the Fenians. On the morning of June 2, a column of some 800 volunteers advancing from Port Colborne ran into a roughly equal body of the invaders established on Limestone or Lime Ridge, several miles inland from Fort Erie. The volunteers attacked in a rush that showed more ardour than battle training, driving in the Fenian line. But disorganized by their own swift advance, and by a mistaken attempt to form up against cavalry (the Fenians had none), they broke and fell back under heavy fire. The enemy themselves retired afterwards; indeed, they could do nothing else. Strong British forces were still converging on them, while the American authorities had finally acted to prevent further reinforcements crossing the river. There was a smaller skirmish in Fort Erie that afternoon. But at night, in the early hours of June 3, the bulk of the Fenians managed hastily to re-embark from their short-lived, useless landing.

In Toronto, meanwhile, crowds thronged the down-town streets to read the latest bulletins at the press offices, and the *Globe* was feverishly running off extras to fill the avid demand for news. The clash at Lime Ridge had fallen on a Saturday; but much of the story was still to be told the day following. On that day, George Brown's instincts as a newspaperman overcame the *Globe*'s strict rule against Sunday labour. The steam presses did not turn, but a hand press kept cranking out sheets for the waiting crowd, while *Globe* correspondents down in the Niagara Peninsula sent back material in plenty.[15]

It was several days more before the extraordinary excitement in Toronto worked itself out. The civic funeral for the dead at Lime Ridge was a final release for popular emotion. There had been nine militiamen killed there, five in the Queen's Own, three of them young undergraduates of the University of Toronto. It had only been a skirmish, but a skirmish fought in defence of Canadian soil – and the response that echoed far beyond Toronto could only be called national. Here, too, the Fenians had served the cause of Confederation – by strengthening the will to union, the will to form a new nation, despite all pressures from across the boundary.

Brown felt it. "We have buried our dead," the *Globe* said soberly, "but the lesson which they have taught us will live long after all those who were present at the ceremonies have followed them to the tomb. . . . Behind the mask of sympathy for Irish wrongs there lurks a desire to force this country into a connection with their neighbours by means of border troubles. If anyone else should ever be tempted to yield to such a pressure, the recollection of the men who fell on Lime Ridge will banish forever the despicable thought. The autonomy of British America, its independence of all control save that to which its people willingly submit, is cemented by the blood shed in battle on the 2nd of June."[16]

An ill-planned thrust at the Lower Canada border was easily repulsed, and the Fenian invasion was over. The Brotherhood would sporadically cause tension and trouble for several years more, but the raid of June 1 and 2, 1866, had been the climax. "The most exciting event," the *Globe* concluded, "which we have had in Canada since the Rebellion of 1837."[17]

2

A few days later, on the eighth, the last session of the old Canadian legislature met in Ottawa, the new capital, to complete
preparations for Confederation. George Brown went up as a
private member this time, but, in or out of the government, he was
still the leading Liberal figure. His ascendancy over the Grits
had by no means passed to Howland or McDougall in the
Assembly or Fergusson Blair in the Legislative Council. The
outside support he gave the Confederation project remained
highly important to the coalition ministry, of which the *Globe*
had continued to show general approval. So far, then, Brown
had not yet really returned to party politics.

On reaching Ottawa, and testing Parliament's new Gothic
splendours, he found the acoustics bad in the Commons chamber,
but the parliamentary corridors wonderfully cool and breezy in
the summer heat of the Ottawa Valley.[18] He also found an
invitation to visit Lord Monck, and went out to Rideau Hall
for a long, informal chat on all sorts of subjects. Monck was
as cordial as ever. He not only gave Brown a free hand to make
to parliament whatever explanations of his resignation he wished,
but also asked him to consent to be a delegate to England to
see the final Confederation Bill through the imperial legislature.[19] Brown was not taken with the offer. "I did not think it
right in him to make such a suggestion at such a moment," he
confided to Anne, "and without flatly refusing gave it the
go-by."[20]

Then he had to meet with the members of the cabinet to consider the official statement to be given to the House on his leaving
the ministry. After a bit of difficulty they reached an agreement,
and on June 15 the case was put to parliament.[21] It came as no
surprise. For months it had been known that Brown had resigned
over a difference of opinion concerning reciprocity, though both
sides in the dispute had scrupulously refrained from filling in
the details. Now Macdonald spoke briefly and temperately to
describe the ministerial changes. Then Brown spoke at greater
length, outlining his arguments for a "fair treaty" of reciprocity, without altering the moderate tone.[22] Then Galt as firmly
gave his own side, while complimenting the other on the temper
of his presentation. It all went off very well – "famously,"
reported Brown; "could not be better."[23] Naturally, he was sure
he had carried the House with him in his arguments.

There was another item of unfinished business still outstanding. The day after Brown arrived, John A. Macdonald had come to his room (no doubt during the discussion of the ministerial explanations) and had shaken hands with him. It was a typically friendly, affable Macdonald gesture − but also typical was the fact that Macdonald had not yet fulfilled that promise, now of two years' standing, that he would make "public reparation" for his old personal charges. Brown shook hands, but told his visitor bluntly that unless he now made good his word, there could again be only "parliamentary communication" between them.[24] It was no less typical of Brown. He had had enough; he would wait no longer for someone who consistently failed his pledge. He could not understand what seemed to him insincerity and deception − while Macdonald may well have felt that the situation called for more humouring on a matter that was scarcely serious.

Could this strange chap really expect him to perform some grand renunciation of half-forgotten accusations made ten years before? Brown did, of course. Macdonald at least went through the motions once again. "He promised to redeem his promise immediately," George told Anne without conviction, "but I have no idea that he will do so."[25] And he did not. Here was the real and final break in Brown's association with the Conservative leader that had begun in June of 1864. The old enmity soon would reappear, and would never again depart. Macdonald seems not to have understood why.[26] Still, it might be said on Brown's behalf that he had only joined a company of former colleagues or associates of John A. Macdonald who much more bitterly believed that they had been the victims of broken promises, evasion, and duplicity.[27]

There were rumours none the less that Brown would go back into the government. ("I would as soon think of cutting off my head."[28]) The rumours may have represented wishful thinking, for he informed his wife amusedly, "The old Upper Canada Tories are talking strongly in favour of forcing me to go to London to look after U.C. interests!"[29] By now his own confidential opinion of the cabinet was sinking low indeed. He discovered them in some seamy transaction − unfortunately unspecified − and made his sentiments clear enough to Anne: "I note what you say about accepting the commission to England − but indeed my whole feelings revolt from having anything to do with such a set of scamps. You cannot believe the piece of rascality I caught them in − I will tell you of it when I get up."[30] In private, he had scarcely a good word for any of the ministers, except, notably, for Cartier.[31] Still, he sought to avoid any open rupture.

Keeping up appearances, perhaps, he dined at McDougall's with Galt and a mixed lot of government supporters – "good dinner, rather indifferently cooked – good wine"[32] – and again with Cartier, Campbell, Fergusson Blair, and John Hillyard Cameron – "We were very merry." In fact, he thought he got on well with everyone, apart from John A. and Luther Holton.[34] The clashes with Holton during the Confederation debates of the year before still estranged Brown from an old friend who had fought relentlessly against the Quebec Resolutions and against himself. But though they remained political opponents, both men were ready to forget their personal differences and end the cold stiffness between them. One day late in June, Brown made the move. As he was going into a room in the Parliament Buildings, he suddenly met Holton coming out. They looked full into each other's face – two tall men in the doorway, the lanky, dark, deliberate *Rouge*, the big, ruddy, swift-tempered Grit – and the latter said characteristically, "Well, Holton, I think we may as well talk this business out."[35] They did; each set out his bill of grievances against the other. They shook hands in forgiveness and were friends again. Brown was deeply pleased.[36] That left only Macdonald.

As for public business, however, Confederation did not seem to be moving on as fast as it should. The expected appointment of delegates to go to England with Maritime representatives had not been made at all. "We have heard nothing more of the Confederation measure," Brown wrote to his wife on June 26, "John A. having been as usual out of order." Certainly, the real head of the government now was often absent, and drinking pretty heavily, sometimes being so incapacitated in the House that he might just as well have stayed away.[37] Nor had the cabinet produced the expected scheme for the provincial constitutions of the two Canadas under Confederation. But just when Brown's scant patience with the ministry was running notably low, Galt suddenly brought in a budget that proposed sweeping and quite unexpected changes. A "sensation", the *Globe* of June 28 called it.

The finance minister had two main proposals: to reduce the tariff on manufactured goods from twenty to fifteen per cent, and to raise five million dollars by the issue of provincial bank-notes to that amount. The first might look to be acceptable to an economic Liberal such as Brown, who championed free trade in theory and the lowest possible revenue duties in practice. But Galt's reduction on manufactures would be accompanied by a million dollars' worth of new taxes to make up the loss in revenue. Hence Brown considered it an empty gesture, while the taxes themselves seemed particularly ill-designed. The second proposition was still worse. Government-issued paper money was a dangerous device in itself, and it would compete with the notes issued by the chartered banks, to weaken, if it did not overturn, the entire provincial banking system. The *Globe* launched a campaign against Galt's "reckless" budget measures. Seeing that Brown was briefly home for a parliamentary recess at the end of June, he may well have mapped it out.[38]

The recess, in fact, virtually marked a transition for George Brown, a transition back to party warfare. He was pledged still to support the coalition ministry on Confederation; he did not seek or want to bring it down. But the budget was not Confederation, and on this he was quite ready for an open break. A federal union was to all intents assured; any more delay was the fault of the ministers themselves. Why should he stay quiet now, when new issues arose? No doubt his natural combativeness and partisan spirit had been repressed about as long as possible, and to his poor opinion of the ministers and sharpening distaste for Macdonald was added an increasing care for the future of his own Liberal party. The peace he had made with Holton might also symbolize the change. If Reform had to make a stand, he might even work with members of the *Rouge* opposition, who by this time had been forced to recognize Confederation as a nearly accomplished fact.[39] And so the Liberal forces could begin looking towards party reunion, in anticipation of the day when coalition rule would be dispensed with altogether.

Accordingly, as soon as Brown was back in Ottawa on July 4, he began "confabulating" with fellow Grits, to see if the government's financial plans could be resisted.[40] "Though the coalition has evidently weakened their adherence to party bonds," he noted, "still it is obvious that the whole party with very few exceptions will go strongly for the views I have been urging on them."[41] He wanted their support for a resolution declaring Galt's budget measures "inexpedient" in view of the early accomplishment of Confederation. Probably his own prejudices against Galt, the rash, improvident minister, coloured his arguments. But there was more to them than that.

In regard to the tariff, instead of reducing expenditure, Galt had put duties on tea and tobacco, meat, dairy products, grain, and flour. These food taxes were grossly wrong in principle – "Corn Laws", Brown scathingly called them.[42] Indeed, they practically introduced agricultural protection, and that was no better than industrial protection.[43] Furthermore, the sudden slash in manufacturing duties could have a drastic effect on the business of the province.[44] And, finally, the crowning absurdity was

that the whole disturbance might recur in a few months, when
the first Confederation parliament fixed a new federal tariff.[45]
Galt might claim that his reduction would bring the Canadian
fiscal structure more nearly in line with the low-tariff Maritimes,
in anticipation of union. Brown would answer that it was best
to finish the federal constitution first, and not try to determine
the future financial system in what John A. Macdonald himself
called a "moribund Parliament".[46]

So it was with Galt's provincial note issue: the bank charters
would expire in any case in four years, and a new Confederate
parliament could use the time for working out revisions in the
banking system – instead of the present government upsetting
it in one moment by legislating five million dollars of currency
into existence.[47] As a sound Victorian Liberal, Brown deplored
state meddling with the natural laws that regulated the supply
of money. As a good Canadian Reformer, he dreaded to see
more opportunity for inflation and extravagance pass into ministerial hands. And as a prominent Toronto business man, he
feared for the chartered banks of Upper Canada, dependent on
their right to issue notes, especially when it appeared that the
only banking institution likely to gain was the affluent Bank of
Montreal, which under the plan could convert the sizeable
advances it had locked up with the government into new nego-
tiable provincial notes.[48] Thus the currency scheme was still more
suspect, since it would benefit all-too-powerful Montreal financial interests at the expense of Toronto and the West.

These were the views Brown put to parliament on July 10,
in support of the resolution against Galt's changes moved by
McGiverin, Liberal member for Lincoln. It was a steaming hot
evening. Brown gave his best in the airless chamber, and finished
exhausted, drenched with perspiration. He did not expect to
win; the government would doubtless be able to vote the motion
down and pass the budget.[49] The point was to rally as many Grits
as possible to disclaim Liberal responsibility for financial measures that had been no part of the original coalition bargain.[50]
Yet even as Brown spoke, he knew that his party would not make
the showing he had hoped for.

"The canvass of members," he bitterly observed, "has disclosed a startling amount of sordid and selfish scheming at work
and makes one very sick – sicker than ever before of parliamentary life."[51] It was like Brown, of course, to impute wrong
motives to anyone who did not pursue the obviously right policy,
his own. Yet, while the mass of back-bench Grits probably did
not share his business worries over the nature of Galt's programme, it was probably true, as well, that they had come to

value the substantial advantages of representing "government" constituencies. Without turning to Howland or McDougall as party leaders, they were prepared to heed them as Reform ministers who urged support for the cabinet's financial policy. In short, they held to the coalition on the question, and not to Brown.

Furthermore, the government promised some revisions and mollifying cuts in the estimates, and still further, seized the occasion to announce a plan for the distribution of Upper Canada's constituencies after Confederation that would satisfy the most suspicious Grit.[52] And so, after three days of debate, the motion to postpone the financial changes was lost, 28 to 83; of the twenty-eight, most were *Rouges* of the regular opposition. There were few from Upper Canada beyond Brown and his old original "Brownie" comrades, Alexander Mackenzie and Archibald McKellar.[53]

The resilient Brown was not upset long, however. He had at least influenced the government to revise its budget plans, and he had issued a clear challenge to the Reformers in the coalition to remind them of their party loyalties and principles. William McDougall, indeed, had already reacted to that challenge. He attacked Brown fiercely during the financial debate. The other deliberated on the best response: "whether to give him such a thrashing as would be a lesson to all future traitors, or to give him a down-setting in a dignified manner." He sent his wife an interesting explanation of his final choice: "Had I been unmarried, the former would certainly have been my course – but with my own Anne always in my mind, I think the reserved style will be better."[54] Party politics might return, but in all likelihood, the old fire-eating Brown of bachelor days would not.

3

Another recess followed at the peak of summer heat; and afterwards Brown found his party in more hopeful shape. "We had three divisions last night," he reported on July 25, "in which the U.C. Liberals stuck to their colours better than they formerly did."[55] McDougall and Howland, he said happily, were "awfully cut up by the votes" – McDougall threatening the Grits with dire consequences if they did not stand by the cabinet.[56] Of the twenty-nine western Reformers who had been present, seventeen had voted with Brown, nine with the two ministers.

"Half a dozen more such votes," he buoyantly predicted, "and the whole party will be reunited."[57] That very evening he had a long, confidential talk with Howland, who was most uneasy in the cabinet and might resign any day: "He sees the danger of remaining in the government, and yet has not the courage to come out. He admits that McDougall is over to the enemy holus bolus."[58]

At this point, the resolutions on the form of provincial governments for the two Canadas were at last brought forward. Partisan differences again were sunk in broad deliberations on the constitutional question. Brown's own approach was thoughtful and conciliatory. He endorsed the cabinet's proposal of a unicameral legislature for Upper Canada, agreeing with John A. Macdonald that no more was needed for a merely local authority. And he rejected Sandfield Macdonald's contention that the people should have a say in naming the governor of the province, asserting that the lieutenant-governor would stand in exactly the same position as the Governor-General stood to the people of Canada. The former would be chosen by a government responsible to the new federal parliament, just as the latter was selected by a government responsible to the parliament at Westminster. The British imperial system would simply be applied within the federation, although, of course, as part of that system, there would equally be self-government under the lieutenant-governor within the scope of provincial authority.[59]

Brown did make an attempt, as he had at the Quebec Conference, to exclude the full cabinet system from the realm of provincial government. He thought it expensive and unnecessary in the restricted local sphere, and quite sufficient to have an administration of department heads who would not be in the elected assembly, though subject to its financial control and laws. He did not at all approve of the presidential system, he quickly answered, when John A. Macdonald suggested that the member for South Oxford had the American model in mind.[60] What he wanted, rather, was something like the structure of the county councils that had already worked so well in Upper Canada. But though Macdonald might concur with the premise that provincial governments should not be much more than large municipal councils, he and the ministry were not willing to abandon the full trappings of responsible cabinet government in favour of a more local simplicity. Had they done so, indeed, Macdonald himself might have had less trouble in the future with a provincial régime at Toronto asserting virtually co-ordinate authority with that in Ottawa. But Brown's pleas for a provincial government with purposes "very clearly defined" and with "very little latitude" went unregarded.[61]

Nevertheless, he indicated that he was willing to give the proposed system a fair trial. It could always be amended later. And he restricted his discussion to Upper Canada, urging his fellow members from the western section not to vote on the constitution for the eastern section, on the grounds that this was properly a matter for the representatives of Lower Canada to settle.[62] The resolutions passed on August 2 with little trouble. Next, Canadian delegates would take the proposed local constitutions to England, in the expectation of submitting them to the imperial parliament in January or February of 1867, as part of the whole plan of Confederation.

Certainly federal union could not be settled in the current year now, for the Canadian ministry had delayed too long. A political crisis had occurred in Britain during July of 1866. The weak Whig-Liberal government of Lord John Russell and Gladstone (Palmerston was dead) had been defeated, and the Conservatives under Derby and Disraeli had taken office. The imperial parliament was thus to be prorogued on August 10. While the new British ministers were just as anxious as their predecessors to see Confederation established, the final enactment could not go forward at Westminster until the Houses met again early in the new year. At any rate, that gave plenty of time for Canadians to confer with Maritime delegates in England on necessary modifications in the original Quebec Conference plan.

One last major question now came before the dying parliament of the old Province of Canada. That chronic sectional and sectarian problem, separate schools, arose again, for one more "final settlement" before Confederation. The Quebec Resolutions had apparently made that settlement already, by leaving education in the sphere of provincial power but guaranteeing the existing school rights and privileges of the Protestant and Roman Catholic minorities of the two Canadas in the federal union to come. But the Protestants of Lower Canada, fearful of the massive French Catholic majority that would dominate their new provincial legislature, now sought a bill to confirm and extend their own separate-school rights. Galt had personally pledged himself to such a measure. Accordingly, the government introduced it, and it seemed likely to pass — when suddenly the Roman Catholics of Upper Canada demanded a similar bill. Bell of Lanark brought it in as a private member. Of the Upper Canadian ministers, only Macdonald gave his support.

It could be argued as usual (and with the usual failure to convince) that there was no valid comparison between the Roman Catholic denominational schools of the eastern majority and the non-denominational state schools of the West. It could be argued also that the Upper Canadian separate-school law had been re-made only three years before as an ostensibly final settlement. Yet it was no less understandable that western Catholics would contend that if minority school rights were going to be changed before Confederation for Lower Canada, they should be changed for Upper Canada as well. For men like Brown – and for the western majority in general – this left but one answer. No new sectarian legislation could be accepted on either side.

In the House he twice blocked the introduction of Bell's bill, stating frankly that he would use every means that parliamentary rules allowed to block it, since this was no longer a fit subject for legislation.[63] When D'Arcy McGee read him a lecture on toler-ance, Brown retorted that the honourable minister both in 1863 and 1865 had declared that he considered the separate-school question closed – but now he would use the Lower Canadian bill as a lever to open it again.[64] On this hot issue the Grits with-out question rallied against the ministry, and so did Protestant Upper Canadians generally. Howland told Brown that he was ready to resign if the bill was not dropped, though the latter hardly believed him.[65] On the other hand, if the Lower Canada bill was abandoned also, Galt would be in difficulties because of his commitment to it. "Altogether it is a proper mess these people have brought themselves into by their folly,"[66] Brown remarked to Anne. And at a time like this, with the assembly and cabinet in turmoil, Macdonald was out of action again. "John A. was drunk on Friday and Saturday and unable to attend the House. Is it not disgraceful?"[67]

On August 7, however, Macdonald announced that the minis-try would not proceed with separate-school legislation because of the Upper Canadian opposition to it. This brought Galt's resignation, because of his own pledge to the Protestants of Lower Canada, although, in speaking on that subject, he declared that he thought the government's decision wise under the cir-cumstances.[68] Brown himself spoke to praise this resignation on a point of honour, and to approve the "agreeable personal rela-tions" Galt still sought to maintain.[69] In private, however, he confided to Anne that the ex-minister was "intensely indignant at the treatment his colleagues have shown him".[70]

Little remained now but dotting i's and crossing t's to finish the work of the session. It would end on August 15, and with it a political era stretching back to the first parliament of the Cana-dian union in 1841. For close on two decades Brown had been at the centre of that era, but, far from feeling pangs over its pass-ing, he wanted only to have the work done and to leave the Assembly on the eve of Confederation. Whatever his hopes and wishes to see Liberalism strong and reunited, he still meant to make this his last parliament. He would not even wait for the official end, for the closing ceremonial of the old legislature, but would set off four days early, on August 11, to be back with his family on the week-end.

"I do feel so happy to think of it," he wrote, "and rejoice at my freedom for good and all from parliamentary responsibilities."[71] His last parliament. If a long phase in his life was ending, no one could be more pleased about it than George Brown.

4

The ensuing weeks at home were peaceful and thoroughly enjoyable: dining out with friends, Anne's croquet parties, and, above all, being with Maggie and the baby day by day. At two and a half, Maggie was already a chatterer and indisputably strong-minded – how could she be otherwise? She had renamed herself "Maddie", and baby Edith, by her best approximation, was "Oda". Young Maddie was a handful, but not to an indulgent father. "No fear but the little darling will temper down as she gets older," George Brown told Anne.[72]

Of course, he could keep busy enough just relieving his brother Gordon of some of the responsibilities at the *Globe*. He had now incorporated his newspaper enterprise; in fact, the bill establishing "The Globe Printing Company" had gone through the session just concluded.[73] The paper had become almost too big for an individual proprietorship. It seemed both sensible and right to permit its chief conductors to hold shares.[74] Moreover, Brown was thinking ahead, to assure continuity for the *Globe* and financial security for his wife and family.[75] There was no pressing need for outside capital, and the shares in the company would remain with himself, his brother, and others in the *Globe* family. Indeed, the change would hardly be felt at present, though it would provide flexibility for more expansion in the future. And it did suggest how far the big morning daily, with its thriving offshoots, the *Evening Globe*, *Weekly Globe*, and *Canada Farmer*, had grown beyond the old personal journalism of the Browns, now that it was a legal being in its own right.

But besides the *Globe*, there was Bow Park, the estate George Brown was developing in Brant County. Ever since he had sold Bothwell the year before, he had been longing for farm lands

again to give him the country life he loved: the sheer pleasure
of watching things grow, the healthy satisfaction in the work of
farming. But though money was no great problem after the
Bothwell sales, time was. It was only after he had left the government that Brown had the opportunity to look for the property
he wanted. In the spring of 1866, he had fixed on it; this time
much closer to Toronto, on the outskirts of Brantford, less than
twenty-five miles west of Hamilton and not seventy from
Toronto itself. Here the Grand River made a great loop below
Brantford, called the Oxbow Bend. And the long tongue of land
marked off by the curving river seemed the ideal site to Brown.

It was placid, prosperous farming country, green and richly
inviting. Most of it was already well cleared, though groves of
the original forest still stood, and there were stretches of dense
tanglewood, bramble, and wild grape, especially in the area
known as the "Indian farm", for this initially had been part of
the great Six Nations Indian reserve. The Oxbow lands were
fertile and well watered: warm, gravelly soil rising to the high
bluffs that hemmed the Grand to north and west, fine, easily-
worked loam in the middle, and rich alluvial bottom land along
the eastern margins.[76] Transportation was excellent. Both the
Grand Trunk and Great Western served Brantford, whose roof-
tops were visible across leafy slopes and meadows beyond the
Oxbow. Besides, the Grand River "roarers", the steamboats of
the Grand River Navigation Company, had long swept up the
Bend to Brantford, and bulky shipments could easily be sent by
water. Finally, and most important, the land here was fairly
readily available.

Much of it was owned by the Bowns, a prominent Brantford
family: Robert R. Bown, J.P., and Dr. John Y. Bown, who had
been a member for Brant since 1861 and a Liberal colleague of
Brown's, though independent in his party votes. Robert Bown
held the choice property around the end of the Oxbow, where
the road wound along the lofty river bank, past orchard and
gardens, to an unpretentious but comfortable frame cottage.
And since the Bowns were willing to sell for a good price, Brown
could acquire a sizeable, developed estate in reasonably short
order.

His initial purchase, however, made in April of 1866, was the
farm of Richard Senior, ninety-four acres on lot 16 in the Bend.[77]
Then the next month he bought R. R. Bown's properties, more
than 420 acres, comprising lots 10 to 15.[78] He went on through
the summer to buy lots 8, 17 and 18 from J. Y. Bown, and lot 9
from James Gillin.[79] Thus, by the autumn, for about $25,000,
he had a continuous holding of close on 800 acres, stretching

from the tip of the Oxbow far back towards its base; and later he would acquire lot 7 here as well.[80] That fall, he was happily occupied with plans for stocking his estate, for more clearing and draining, and for improving the buildings at Bow Park. It was like the early days at Bothwell over again, except that this time he could afford to do much more.

With all this to work on, Brown paid only cursory attention to public affairs – which were rather in the doldrums until the final Confederation conference should begin in England. There was more Fenian excitement, it is true, and the *Globe* became quite exercised over the prospect of another raid, expected late in September.[81] Fenian noises across the border turned out, however, to be chiefly for political purposes linked with the approaching Congressional elections in the United States, and Canadians soon relaxed again. But meanwhile the *Globe* campaigned against John A. Macdonald's handling of the Fenian threat as Minister of Militia, charging him with continued indecision, incompetence, and neglect – and, more specifically, with drunkenness on duty, contending that this scarce-hidden phenomenon of the last twelve years now merited public notice, since public safety was itself involved.[82] The Conservative press naturally retorted that this was mere personal vindictiveness on George Brown's part. The *Globe* answered that the managing director had never seen a word of the articles in question before their publication. They had been "conceived and written by the ordinary conductors of the *Globe*" without his suggestion – quite probably while he was taken up with the affairs of Bow Park.[83]

Nevertheless, the journal added, Mr. Brown was not seeking to avoid any responsibility, and approved every word that had been written. No doubt he did. While in the government, he had frequently seen the difficulties caused by Macdonald's drinking, and though he enjoyed a drink himself, Brown was inherently opposed to anything that seemed to be habitual intemperance. Someone like "poor Foley" he might excuse because of his earnest efforts to reform – but not a cheerfully unregenerate Macdonald! In any case, the Grit leader would feel small compunction about shifting the blame to an old enemy, who, he felt, had done it to him often enough. For instance, he had lightly commented on one of Anne's encounters with a troublesome household servant that summer: "I very much admire the idea of putting all the blame on my shoulders. You must have been studying tactics under John A. That is precisely his course when a difficulty occurs – My dear fellow – I would gladly do what you want – but that horrid fellow Brown would be down on me in the House and in the *Globe*!"[84]

Apart from Fenians and derelict Attorney-Generals, another source of excitement in September was the failure of the Bank of Upper Canada. On the eighteenth, it closed its doors in Toronto irrevocably, after more than four decades. The bank had actually been languishing ever since the government accounts had been transferred to the Bank of Montreal in 1863. But the *Globe*, with some justice, observed that any hope of obtaining new capital for Upper Canada's chief bank had been killed when Galt's scheme for government bank-notes had undermined its own right of issue.[85] Furthermore, the Bank of Montreal had precipitated the collapse by refusing to honour the notes of the western bank.[86] Brown himself was not financially involved. Yet whether or not he wrote the relevant editorials, he assuredly echoed the *Globe*'s words of sympathy for the shareholders and its hot condemnation of incapable finance ministers and a ruthless Bank of Montreal.

October brought nothing quite so stirring, as Brown visited the South Oxford Agricultural Exhibition at Norwich in his constituency, and spent time at Brantford supervising the work at Bow Park.[87] Towards the end of the month, however, he had to give more of his attention to the *Globe*. Gordon Brown's health was suffering again; he would have to take extended leave from the office. Soon, in fact, he crossed the ocean to spend six months in Paris.[88] But this was not wholly a loss, since Gordon could slip across the Channel to London from time to time to send back reports by the new transatlantic cable on the Confederation Conference when it opened. Still, it meant that George could not leave Toronto as freely until his brother returned home in the spring.

In November, the Canadian delegates at last got off to England for the meetings with the Maritimers and the British officials. There were six of them: Macdonald, Cartier, McDougall, Howland, Langevin, and Galt – the last having agreed to share in this concluding mission for Confederation. The London Conference opened on December 4, 1866. Actually, it did not produce much news, for the meetings again were held in closed session. At any rate, by Christmas the Conference had reached agreement on an amended body of resolutions, to go forward to the Colonial Office for the drafting of the Confederation Bill at last. Yet, for Canadians, the basic federal plan had already been determined at Quebec and carried through the provincial legislature in 1865. This final round of revision, essential as it might be, did not rouse public interest to the extent that the previous discussions had done.

There was a brief flurry in the press over reports that the delegates in England meant to include a clause in the Confederation Bill enabling a minority to appeal for federal intervention in the provincial sphere of education in order to safeguard separate-school rights.[89] But the excitement died inconsequentially. Obviously, nothing much could be said until the finished bill should come into public view before the imperial parliament. Even then, nothing really could be done until after the measure had come into effect, when the people of the united provinces would be able to take up any faults that had crept in during the closing stages in the drafting of the federal scheme.

That was the *Globe*'s position, and George Brown's, as this time of finishing up – this interim – moved to a quiet conclusion through December.[90] The new year would inevitably be different. It would bring the passage of the Confederation Bill, and all the change and adjustment to change that this would necessarily involve. The present coalition would lose its reason for existence with the establishment of federal union. Then normal party divisions would reappear, and Reform would have to be ready for the fight for power. Though Brown might not intend to re-enter parliament himself, he unquestionably hoped to see his ideas and his party triumph under the coming dispensation. Accordingly, as 1867 neared, he began increasingly to think on preparations for Canada's new political existence – and of the federal and provincial elections that would lie ahead.

5

"There is a lull," Brown wrote in January of 1867, "a doubt, an uncertainty – but the moment the right chord is struck, the response will be as of yore."[91] The auspices for Liberalism in the new union were excellent, he assured Luther Holton, who was now prepared to make the best of Confederation: "I quite agree with you that it would not be a bad dodge for John A's purpose to shove off the Confederation settlement – but he cannot do it. . . . And the sooner it comes, the better."[92] Brown positively exuded optimism, and did not mind emphasizing his expectations to a friend who not so long ago had sharply disagreed with him: "I never was so confident as at this moment that the movement was a right one . . . and how any Liberal politician could doubt that any settlement of the constitutional question *must* place his party in the ascendant and give a new face to the whole politics of the country, I never could understand and don't now."[93] Still,

he did concede, forgivingly, "of course you in L.C. had a difficult card to play."

The first step that he could see ahead was to stir up Reform
activity in the Upper Canadian constituencies, for three years of
coalition had left the body of the party neglected in structure
and enervated in spirit, as well as leaving its parliamentary
representatives all too free from the vigilance of their own
electorates. By mid-February, plans for local Liberal conventions were under way in county after county across Canada West,
while the *Globe* ran a regular column, headed "Organization of
the Reform Party", reporting on the movement of regeneration
that was sweeping over Upper Canada.[94] Brown, moreover, was
directly in touch with his chief party associates, and notably with
Alexander Mackenzie, by now second only to himself in the
Grit-Liberal ranks outside the ministry.

"The accounts from all sections of the province are very satisfactory," he asserted. "I fully calculate on a sweep such as the
weak-kneed sisters will be amazed at."[95] It was time, however,
to get some of the most reliable party leaders together to agree
on a programme for the developing campaign. Besides, there
were able new men anxious to join in and seek election: Edward
Blake, for instance, a distinguished Toronto lawyer and son of
a still more distinguished Reform father, William Hume Blake,
Baldwin's Solicitor-General and late Chancellor of Upper Canada. Blake, Brown told Mackenzie, "is ready and will be a host.
As a lawyer he is admirable – excellent common sense, immense
industry and great pluck. Not much of a politician, but anxious
to learn and as sharp as a needle. He has a great opinion of you,
and I am persuaded you will be immense helps to each other."[96]

They planned a quick meeting in Toronto of a few reliables
to talk the whole matter over. But meanwhile, the first news of
the proposed Confederation Bill had already given Brown some
substance for a party programme. On February 22 the *Globe*
published a résumé of the alterations made in the proposed Confederation Bill from the Quebec Resolutions: Gordon Brown
had cabled them from England.[97] Three days later the paper had
the whole text of the bill, covering page one and spilling over
onto page two. This was an advance copy, it said: there might be
verbal changes in the measure as put before the British parliament.

"The Kingdom of Canada!" announced the accompanying
Globe editorial, fully approving the proposed title of the new
union, as well as other new terms adopted – Ontario and Quebec,
Senate and House of Commons. But the increased subsidies to
be given the provinces were "preposterously unjust", while the

transfer of such matters as fisheries and penitentiaries from provincial to central jurisdiction put "a wedge of federal interference in local matters" – a prophetic cry.[98] To the *Globe*, it was unreasonable to give more money to the provinces to do less, and unwise to place affairs that were really local under federal authority, since they would only pave the way for the return of sectional jealousies, jobs and corruption in the central parliament.[99]

In regard to separate schools, the draft of the projected measure was still not wholly clear. If the only intention was that the federal government should be able to disallow a separate-school bill like any other local measure, that was quite satisfactory; but it was most unsatisfactory if the federal government instead could legislate on schools itself.[100] Still, the fact remained that this Confederation Bill was an "immense boon to the people of Upper Canada", and though some of the changes were unreasonable or unjust, the remedy lay with the electors themselves.[101] That was Brown's conclusion: elect good Liberals to remove the flaws that had entered since the Quebec Conference, and make the new machinery work to best effect.

In publishing the bill itself, the *Globe* had scooped the entire provincial press – not to mention the government of Canada, besides. Toronto, Montreal, and Ottawa were agog: the government had only received an official copy of the British North America Bill on March 1, four days after the *Globe* had printed the text and repeated editorials on it.[102] True, there were some formal differences to be found in arrangement or wording, but the *Globe*'s draft proved essentially correct in content. The other leading papers howled bitterly. The Montreal *Gazette* and the Toronto *Leader* accused Brown's journal of the worst malpractice, until one might almost gather that Gordon had burgled Colonial Office desks for his brother.[103] The accused organ, however, loftily responded that it had got the news first because, as always, it had spared neither effort nor expense. It exasperatingly urged its rivals to think on "high quarters" where the text might have been secured: "For instance, could it not have occurred to our contemporaries that a most gracious lady – but we forbear!"[104] In any event, whether mysterious benefactors or paid pilferers were involved – or, more likely, Brown's excellent political connections in London – the *Globe* had snatched British North America's biggest news story, the first report of the future Act of Confederation.

The *Leader* soon sourly pointed out that the *Globe*'s draft had called the new union the "Kingdom of Canada", whereas the official text showed that the name would be "Dominion of

Canada".[105] It even charged that Brown's report had caused such hostile American reactions to this threat of monarchism in a continent consecrated to republics that the title had had to be changed. But by this time the argument was raging in Brown's absence. He had left the office for a few days to fire a round personally in the mounting Reform campaign by addressing his own constituents in South Oxford.

His speech at Tillsonburg on March 1 confirmed the line of policy emerging in the *Globe*: praise of the Quebec Conference scheme of union, which was complete justification for the coalition of 1864; criticism of the damage done to the Quebec plan at the London Conference, which was indication that the coalition had just about outlived its usefulness.[106] Nevertheless, he emphasized that Confederation remained a vast achievement; and Reformers were best entitled to take charge of it, to operate the new government that they had so largely made possible. One thing further: Brown made public his own intention not to run again. Yet retiring from parliament did not mean withdrawal from political activity, he assured his audience. "At no election have I ever striven harder than I intend to at the coming one for the triumphant success of the great Liberal party of Upper Canada."[107]

To Holton, however, Brown confided that the election was to be the end of his political career. "My fixed determination is to see the Liberal party re-united and in the ascendant – and then make my bow as a politician. As a journalist and a citizen I hope always to be found on the right side – and heartily supporting my old friends – but I want to be free to write of men and things without control beyond that which my conscientious convictions and the interests of the country demand. To be debarred by fear of injuring the party from saying that Foley is unfit to sit in parliament and that McMonies is an old goose – makes journalism a very small business. Party leadership and the conducting of a great journal don't harmonize."[108] This was the nub of the matter: it was not solely his own desire for a quiet domesticated life or Anne's desire to have him out of politics, important as these feelings were. Had he remained a bachelor, indeed, Brown would have come to the same ultimate conclusion.

Yet the announcement at Tillsonburg that the leading Grit would not seek re-election inevitably brought protests from his colleagues and supporters. Dr. Parker, member for Wellington South, expressed his regret and astonishment, as he implored Brown to change his mind. Otherwise, he forecast sheer disaster for Reform, and the long entrenchment of its enemies in power. Present appearances, thought Parker, indicated that the first

Confederate ministry would be a coalition: "Your absence from the House of Commons will vastly assist McDougall and associates to draw a Reform support, and thus aid the immediate and permanent division of the Reform party."[109]

At the other end of Upper Canada, another old Liberal associate, blunt Donald A. Macdonald (Sandfield's more dependable brother) was quite as outspoken in deploring Brown's decision. "In my opinion, if you ever made a mistake in your life politically, this is the greatest." All the leader's efforts to rouse the party would be thrown away if he did not go into parliament himself. "Take my word for it," avowed Macdonald, "you will find that a more powerful coalition than you ever saw in this country will take place." He urged Brown to reconsider, to stand for one of the more doubtful counties. Yet he conjectured also that "the fault is not wholly with yourself, that your good and kind wife has had something to say in the matter. . . . If you consent, she has an awful responsibility resting upon her shoulders."[110]

There were more importunings, but Brown clung to his decision, while working no less earnestly to prepare his party for the coming contest.[111] A contest was certain now. In England, after passing both the houses, the British North America Act received the royal assent on March 29. The Canadian government delegates would be returning soon, and already the Conservative newspapers in the province were raising a "no party" cry, demanding that the federal union be launched free from partisan bitterness – which was to say that the present coalition leaders should continue to rule in the new Dominion of Canada.[112]

In any case, Reform nominating conventions were in full swing by this time; the *Globe* was full of reports of them through March and April. The Reform Association of Upper Canada was reconstituted as well. On April 9 its Central Executive Committee was formed at a meeting in Toronto. The membership list included names as well established in the city's business community as George Brown, John McMurrich, William McMaster, John Macdonald, and A. M. Smith, as well as newer names like Edward Blake, J. D. Edgar, and Adam Crooks.[113] The same group, it appeared, was to guide the Toronto Branch of the Reform Association, along with Gordon Brown, H. S. Howland (brother of the cabinet minister), John Taylor, William Elliott, and other owners of leading city firms.[114] Nor was it without significance that when the first general meeting of the Bank of Commerce was held a week later, as Toronto's latest answer to the Bank of Montreal, George Brown was present as a prominent shareholder, while Howland, Macdonald, Elliott, and Taylor were elected directors and McMaster was made president.[115] For Toronto's leading Liberals were concerned with both political and economic control over the West. It was quite natural that the same men should be at the core of both the western Reform party and the big new western banking institution, each of which was dedicated to gaining power in the Dominion that was so soon to be established.

It would be proclaimed the next month, on May 22, to take effect on July 1, after which the elections would ensue. The summer, then, would bring the actual test. Coalition must be ended by that time, coalition which the *Globe* now termed "the bitter price of justice to Upper Canada".[116] There was no longer the slightest reason for extending an unneeded and humiliating régime. If any Liberals sought to do so — above all, the present three Reform ministers, McDougall, Howland, and Blair — they would not be continuing coalition at all, but merely seceding from their party.[117] Thus the *Globe* enunciated the principle, as Brown made ready for another step in his preparations: the battle that must precede the election conflict, if some Reformers should still support coalition and attempt to delude the faithful with the false "no party" cry.

6

By May, it seemed altogether probable that one segment of Upper Canada Reform would try to keep the party in coalition. Several Liberal journals were arguing against withdrawing before the new constitution had been given a trial run, while the western government organ, the *Leader*, expressed a belief that Howland, McDougall, and Blair did not mean to withdraw in any case.[118] As a member of the Legislative Council, Blair posed no particular problem. He would go to the appointed federal Senate, and Brown already had no illusions about the political potency of that body of "old ladies".[119] Howland and McDougall, however, could be rallying-points for coalitionist sentiment in the party and disastrously divide Reform. McDougall had to be written off as lost, or at least unmanageable, but Brown still had slight hopes of Howland. He tried him when the latter reached Toronto on May 8, after returning from London. "My estimate of him was not elevated by my conversation," Brown informed Holton wryly. "He can't see his way — can't make up his mind exactly — John A. might do so much harm if left uncontrolled – and so forth."[120] It appeared very likely that Howland would sit with his Reform partners in the first federal cabinet, under John A. Macdonald.

In consequence, the *Globe* redoubled its efforts to convince Upper Canada Liberals that there was no excuse for a continued coalition. The Conservative call to put patriotism above party in the new régime was so much eyewash, it asserted, meant to ensure a new lease on power for John A. and Co. The normal condition of politics under free government *was* party division: "When you tell us that a coalition of men of all parties is the best possible arrangement – you give the lie to all the teachings of English history."[121] Equally false was the Tory press cry of "the union in danger", the contention that there was still an emergency requiring coalition, because Howe in Nova Scotia was leading an anti-Confederation movement against Tupper and his friends. The *Globe* agreed that Howe's course was "reckless and indefensible" – but Confederation was still an established fact; the real question now was how to run it. Those who sought a disciplined party government were in no way weakening the union. Rather, it was those who shouted "union in danger" and imputed anti-unionist sentiments to all who merely opposed the maintenance of coalition![122]

But as June approached, it seemed that stronger action would be needed to combat "no-party" arguments. The obvious answer was to hold a grand Reform gathering like the conventions of 1857 and 1859, and, like those again, designed to unify the party. In this case, however, party unity would be focused not so much on a specific set of reforming resolutions as on a general agreement that Liberals would close ranks against the principle of coalition, and fight the elections for a genuinely Liberal government. The Central Executive of the Reform Association met accordingly in early June. On the seventh a printed circular went out from its Toronto headquarters calling a general party convention in the city for June 27. "Read the enclosed circular and see if I have not given Messrs. McDougall and Howland checkmate," Brown exulted to Holton. "Things are moving on splendidly here," he added, never so happy as when in vigorous action.[123]

He was equally pleased to hear Holton report, "Our *Rouge* friends are coming round all right."[124] By now the Montreal Liberal was fully reconciled to Confederation and thought any *Rouge* movement for repeal had been prevented.[125] But even Dorion hoped to exploit the feelings against the scheme in many parts of French Canada, and the most that could be looked for from still uncertain *Rouges* was a common front against the

Macdonald coalition.[126] Brown himself did not expect a breach of three years' standing to be forgotten in a moment: "It is not perhaps desirable that the U.C. and L.C. sections of the Liberal party should all at once be perfectly allied. Let us fall into line naturally and by degrees." Yet if Dorion and Holton could come up to the Toronto Convention "by *accident* or by direct invitation . . . it would have an electric effect over the country."[127]

Holton, however, doubted that their visit at this juncture would help the cause "either here or with you".[128] Still, Brown was plainly looking to a broader goal than just the reunifying of Liberalism in Upper Canada. That was the first task; but the final goal must be a national Reform party.[129] At present, Lower Canada Liberals were too far off, while Maritime Liberals were still largely waging the battle of Confederation. Ultimately, however, all would come within one framework. Till then – as the *Globe* cautioned its own followers – "We must avoid speaking or acting as though general questions were to be settled by the voice of Upper Canada alone."[130]

At the same time, Brown hoped for broader Liberal unity in another sense: that, within Upper Canada, Roman Catholics who had traditionally been Reformers would return to the party now that the fiercely sectarian clashes of the old Canadian union were at an end. Four Catholic deputations from different parts of Upper Canada came to see him on one Saturday alone – "to make a permanent treaty for their friends with the Liberal party," Brown said. "I really believe we will poll a large majority of the Roman Catholics."[131] Perhaps he was altogether too hopeful that the mass of Catholics could so readily forget the harsh struggle over separate schools and the *Globe*'s strictures, but he was exuberantly confident of the Reform cause. In his view, a week before the Convention, "It is impossible that matters could look better than they do."[132]

In the meantime preparations for the meeting had rapidly gone ahead. As in 1859, Reformers in each Upper Canadian municipality, urban or rural, were to choose delegates up to five in number, while Reform members of parliament, Liberal editors, and, this time, party candidates, would come in their own right. By June 26 delegates were pouring into Toronto, more than 600 strong, even more than for the "Great Convention" of eight years earlier. The Music Hall on Church Street had been hired for the occasion, a capacious white-brick building that also housed the Mechanics Institute. Here the next morning proceedings would begin.

But before the Convention could open, the coalitionist forces moved quickly on their own. McDougall, Howland, and Blair had come to town themselves. On the afternoon of the twenty-sixth, they called a sudden caucus of all "loyal" Reform members of parliament; that is, of all who had voted with the government in the previous session, when Brown had made his attack on the cabinet's tariff and currency measures. And when this caucus gathered at the Queen's Hotel, the ministers boldly announced their decision to enter the new federal cabinet. They were attempting to undercut the Convention, to win a strategic victory with the party *élite*, the parliamentary members, before the mass meeting had time to start. But they failed miserably. Only thirteen Reform members turned up, six of them Legislative Councillors at that, and of the House representatives only three approved the coalition ministers' stand.[133] And so they were left as an awful example for the Convention the next day, caught in the act with jam on their fingers — the marks of a *coup* that had not succeeded.

The following morning, Thursday, June 27, the delegates presented their credentials in a cheerful bustle at the Music Hall. They were the epitome of Grit Liberalism: "the cream of Upper Canada" — so Brown enthusiastically said afterwards — "Wardens, reeves, J.P.'s, coroners, merchants, manufacturers — the pick of the local politicians, business men and professionals."[134] Of course, there were farmers, too, among these leaders of what was still essentially an agricultural community; but by and large they were men of substance centred in its prosperous towns, if not in its Toronto metropolis. For the day of the farmer, as more than voter, was past in Liberal Ontario at Confederation, poised as it was on the threshold of the industrial age.

The Convention got organized in the afternoon with only brief speeches, as William Patrick, long-time Reform member for Prescott, was named chairman, and J. D. Edgar and Samuel Spreull of the Toronto Central Executive, its secretaries. The necessary committees were established; the important one on resolutions having George Brown as chairman, as might be expected, buttressed by Alexander Mackenzie.[135] Brown explained that the Central Executive already had a draft programme of resolutions ready for the committee's consideration. There would be no lack of guidance, it appeared. Then the meeting adjourned for the committees to do their part, to take up its real work that evening. At that time, McDougall and Howland would be specially invited to appear as well. The day was rising to a climax of blistering heat. But it was safe to predict thunderstorms by night.

When the Convention reopened in a sweltering Music Hall just after seven, the resolutions were ready for debate. In general, they were fairly innocuous statements of principle, calculated to produce party harmony. Edward Blake led off with the first one, expressing satisfaction at the achievement of representation by population and "local control of local affairs". Brown moved the second, which accepted the new federal constitution "with joy", despite its defects. And there were others seeking the reunion of Protestants and Catholics and Upper and Lower Canadians in Reform, calling for reciprocity by treaty and tariff reduction, or free homesteads and the development of mineral resources. But the most significant resolution was one that condemned coalitions for inevitably lowering public morals and promoting lavish expenditure and corruption. By the time it came up for debate, about nine, Howland and McDougall had arrived. They sat uncomfortably on the platform among Brown's chief supporters, peering out in the gaslight at rows of sharply quizzical faces, as they waited for their chance to speak.

The critical resolution, which justified the Coalition of 1864 as "imperious necessity" but damned those formed for "ordinary administrative purposes", was briefly supported by John McKeown of Hamilton and eloquently endorsed by James Young of Galt. Then Howland had his turn. Obviously diffident and uneasy, he nevertheless managed to talk both moderately and firmly, and was heard with a fair degree of calm. He admitted that the compact of 1864 had achieved its purpose and was at an end, but he argued that the new Dominion government should represent the interests of all the people. Especially when New Brunswick Reformers like Tilley would sit in the cabinet, they should not be deserted there by their Liberal comrades from Upper Canada. Were Upper Canadian Reformers wholly to estrange themselves? Should it be said that they were never to be satisfied, would not live quietly under the new government they had gained? It was a good speech, but the wrong note for the Convention. It sounded like a man who had already become a Conservative at heart. Howland made no impression.

Next came William McDougall, to be greeted with hisses and groans. The chairman called for order, but McDougall, the same cock-sure McDougall, was not at all taken aback. Where Howland was defensive, he was defiant. Well built, graceful, if a bit stout now, strong-featured and with a sweeping moustache, he made an impressive figure as he boldly and ably turned to the attack. He assailed Brown's party leadership, his effort to suppress honest difference of opinion among Liberals. He denied that the Convention truly represented the party. Its mind was already made up, he bluntly asserted; the real decision on Reform policy would be made at the polls. Furthermore, the work

of the coalition was by no means finished yet. There was much
more territory to bring into Confederation, and the Dominion
government must be secure and strong in order to negotiate
effectively. Indeed, claimed McDougall, there was no alternative to coalition, for without it Ontario would face a new "eastern
domination" of Quebec and the Maritimes together. And what
did Brown and Co. offer instead? "You have nothing but a cry –
nothing but the names of men. No measure, no policy is pointed
out." Let the new government be formed as a coalition! Party
differences would re-emerge in time; but for now, the old divisions were meaningless. "Sir, Toryism and Reform and all the
rest of it are buried in the past. We have a clear slate, a *tabula
rasa*: there is the constitution – there is the machine – work it!'"

It was powerful, it was cogent; but McDougall sat down to a
new outburst of boos and jeers. Of what use was it to tell a
Reform Convention that Reform was virtually dead? He only
proved to its members that he had sold out completely, that
coalition was indeed the negation of party principles, since he
denied that any were left at all. But now George Brown stepped
forward to answer for the whole meeting. As usual, he began restrainedly, as he carefully took up Howland's and McDougall's
arguments, countering them in turn. The two were in some disagreement, he noted, as to whether the compact of 1864 was or
was not finished. Howland would renew it in any case, because
the Maritime Reformers in the coalition should not be abandoned. But he had said not a word about the Lower Canadian
Liberals, who were not included – what about abandoning them?
McDougall, on the other hand, had raised a bogey of eastern
domination. Yet now Upper Canada held the balance of power
with eighty-two federal seats. There was no need to surrender
meekly to John A. Macdonald when only a few more Liberal
seats from other provinces would ensure a majority in parliament. What policy was there then to offer? To sweep the elections! To send Upper Canada Reformers to Ottawa in such
numbers, and "prepared to make such friends as they can", that
the coalition must inevitably be replaced by Liberal rule.

Besides, as for "working the machine" – did McDougall
really think it could be worked in any way under the coalition
except the Tory way, Macdonald's way? The so-called Reform
ministers would be useless in his cabinet. If he did not force them
out, he would nullify them: "John A. Macdonald is a very astute
man," Brown noted caustically, "and knows well how to play
one colleague off against another – and if he does not succeed
in getting one in Upper Canada or Nova Scotia or New Brunswick when he wants him, he is a little more stupid than he used

to be when I was in the government." No, a new coalition was not a *tabula rasa*. It was merely the basis for Macdonald Tory rule!

By now Brown was thoroughly aroused. He paraded the platform, arms sweeping in vehement gestures as he pounded out arguments that scorched with passionate conviction.[136] He swung suddenly to face Howland and McDougall — the first tensely white, the second flushed. His powerful body stretched to fullest height; his eyes flashed; he thrust long, accusing arms towards them as he cried: "Tell us that we are now to condescend — tell me that we are to condescend — at this day, when we stand claiming credit for one of the noblest records public men ever could display before a country — that we are to go down on our knees to Mr. John A. Macdonald!"[137] The convention exploded with cheers. "Go into the same government with John A. Macdonald?" "Never! — never!" howled the audience. "Sir, I understand what degradation it was to be compelled to adopt that step by the necessity of the case, by the feeling that the interests of my country were at stake, which alone induced me ever to put my foot in that government, and glad I was when I got out of it. It was the happiest day of my life when I got out of that concern!"

The excitement was tremendous. It flamed from Brown to the audience and back again, as he unleashed their deepest feelings. To go through so much and then throw it away! "But tell me that, after we have gained the end, when we have bought it from our opponents by giving them three years of office — that we should now renew that hateful compact and put John A. Macdonald at the head of the government! If that is to be the position, gentlemen, blot out your resolutions and throw your record in the fire — before you let the Reform party take the contemptible position which this course would reduce it to!"

No more words were really needed. When the vote on the resolution was called, the whole chamber rose with a roar to support it. Only three hands dared to go up for the negative — three out of six hundred. Coalition was condemned, the ministers were irrefutably beaten, and Grit unity behind Brown had been confirmed once more.

The hot, sulphurous night session ended after one in the morning, and that of the next day was rather an anticlimax, except for a powerful speech by Alexander Mackenzie. Yet before the Convention closed on the afternoon of June 28, a resolution not on the programme was put through unanimously. It offered grateful thanks for George Brown's past services as party leader, and begged him earnestly to alter his decision not to run again. It struck at precisely the right time, while he was jubilant at the success of the party gathering and still roused by Howland's and McDougall's desertion. Brown was visibly shaken; his always quick emotions overcame him for the moment.[138] And then he agreed reluctantly to return to parliament for a short time, if, after consultation with his friends, that appeared to be necessary. The actions of the three ministers were responsible for changing his decision, he emphasized; his personal desire to stay out was just as strong as ever.[139]

Hence the Convention ended on another high note. There were loud cheers for the Queen and the new Dominion as the delegates broke up and departed. And Brown was left in both satisfaction and determination: satisfaction that the party had been renewed in full integrity, determination to win the final round, the first Dominion elections.

7

Just three days later came Dominion Day, born, in Toronto, to the midnight peal of church bells, as bonfires were set blazing in the down-town streets.[140] The night had seemed hot enough without them, when George Brown arrived at a stifling *Globe* office before midnight to prepare the leading article for next day. "Have you got any water here?" he asked Robert Gay, the night foreman.[141] "Yes, sir," responded Gay, pointing to a pail full and moving to find a pitcher and glass. But Brown had swept the pail up, and tossed off at least a quart before setting it down. Then, turning back to Gay: "What time can you catch the eastern mail? How much time can you give me?"

"Until half past two," replied the foreman. Brown took off collar, coat, and waistcoat, and went into his inner office to write. At half past two, Gay was at his door. "Mr. Brown, we'll lose the eastern mail," he warned.

"Through in a few minutes," Brown said abstractedly, busily scribbling on. A worried Gay was back in half an hour to collect what was ready for setting. "Mr. Brown, we will certainly lose the eastern mail! It's three o'clock."

"Through in a few minutes," came once more.

Another half hour, and again the foreman returned for more: "Mr. Brown, the eastern mails have gone."

"Through in a few minutes – give me a drink," was the sole reply. Outside, King Street shone in fire-light, as happy crowds made un-Toronto carnival, parading and singing through the night. Rockets burst, fire-arms clattered, and the bells of St. James' Cathedral chimed out "Hurrah for Canada" and "God Save the Queen".[142] Yet in the close little room at the *Globe* a perspiring and oblivious Brown wrote on and on. At four o'clock, Gay had to warn him that the western mails were now in doubt. Still the utterly engrossed editor, setting forth the whole history of the Confederation movement, made his automatic reply. And again at five: "Mr. Brown, the mails are *all* lost."

"Through in a few minutes."

It was light now; the fires had paled in the dawn. The last revellers had long since gone home, when a twenty-one-gun salute boomed from the Garrison to announce Confederation Day. And still Brown had not stopped writing. Six o'clock passed and seven approached; a crowd of more than 200 people was already waiting anxiously outside the *Globe*'s doors for the oracle's pronouncement on the great day.[143] At seven, a resigned, almost hopeless Gay went in again. Brown was just finishing his final sheet. "Well, there's the last of it," he said contentedly. "We've done well." They had indeed. Through the night he had written and they had set some 9,000 words – a conservative estimate – in an article that would occupy the entire first page of the *Globe* for July 1, and continue in statistics for a second page. It was the most elaborate article published in Toronto on the first day of Confederation.[144]

Now the city shimmered in bunting under a soaring July sun, as news-boys at last began crying the *Globe*'s Dominion Day edition, and Brown went home to bed. His article had not only told the story of Confederation; it had sketched the history of the provinces that had come together, outlined the commerce and resources of the new Dominion, and commented glowingly on the brilliant prospects ahead. "We hail the birthday of a new nationality," it began. "A United British America, with its four millions of people, takes its place this day among the nations of the world." And at the end it fervently wished "that the people who now or shall hereafter inhabit the Dominion of Canada ... who shall populate the northern part of the continent from the Atlantic to the Pacific, shall, under a wise and just government, reap the fruits of well directed enterprise, honest industry and religious principle ... in the blessings of health, happiness, peace and prosperity. SO MOTE IT BE."

In Ottawa that morning, the awards of birthday honours for the new Dominion were being made, as Lord Monck announced that Macdonald was now a Knight of the Bath, and Cartier, Galt, Tupper, Tilley, McDougall, and Howland, Companions of the Bath. But the man who had done more than a little to make the whole event possible was fast asleep at Oak Lodge in Toronto. Monck, however, well recognized his part. He would write to Brown: "I will confess to you that I was mortified and disappointed that circumstances had rendered it impossible for me to recommend for a share in those distinctions *the* man whose conduct in 1864 had rendered the project of union feasible."[145]

In Toronto that afternoon there were lake excursions away from dust and heat, public and private picnics in the Government Grounds or in cool, secluded groves along the Humber. There were brass bands, too, and a splendid evening concert in the Horticultural Gardens. And, as warm darkness fell, illuminations flooded colour through the city, until the climax came in the brief, triumphant glare of fireworks.[146] Toronto had rejoiced at the day whole-heartedly. So had George Brown. But he had made his own celebration at its outset — just as he had made his crucial contribution to Confederation at the beginning, not in the final stage.

8

The next day he was back at politics, reporting to Luther Holton on the success of the Toronto Convention and its excellent effect upon the country. "We hear but one cry," Brown said, " – *No coalition!*"[147] The only difficulty that he recognized was an old one: there had been comparatively few delegates from eastern Ontario at the Convention. As usual, from Toronto west the Grits had come in numbers; but representation had declined to eastward, until the Upper St. Lawrence and Ottawa Valley had hardly been represented at all. This old "Central Canada" region had fewer votes; yet Brown could scarcely afford to neglect it. What could be done? Should he deal with Sandfield Macdonald, he asked Holton.[148] That notably eccentric and cross-grained Reformer was still a power in Central Canada, but he had opposed Confederation doggedly to the very end. Was it possible to treat with him at all?

Holton in reply, however, reported on an interview he and Dorion had just had with Sandfield in Montreal. Macdonald had told them that he expected a proposal from the Coalition, which they had earnestly counselled him against accepting.[149] "I am not so sure that he will refuse their overtures," acknowledged Brown, thinking probably of Sandfield's previous tendencies to form "moderate" alliances.[150] A week later he found how right he was. Sandfield Macdonald was to be nothing else than the first premier of Ontario, and to construct the new provincial administration. From Sir John Macdonald's standpoint it was an admirable stroke. He had added strength to the "no party" coalition cry by winning over a leading Reform figure, the head of former Liberal governments and an old rival of George Brown's. In the process he had dealt a new blow at the Liberal unity in Ontario that Brown was striving to achieve.[151] Yet it was somewhat ironic that the two Macdonalds, who had both signed the report of the Select Committee of 1864 in opposition to its proposal of federation, should now be heading two of the Confederation governments. It was still more ironic when Sandfield called to his cabinet as his chief Conservative lieutenant Matthew Crooks Cameron, who had fought vigorously against Confederation right down to 1867. It showed the advantage that reformed sinners could have over the merely righteous.

Sandfield had difficulty filling up his cabinet, however. It was not till July 22 that he finally completed his "patent combination" of two Conservatives, Cameron and Carling, and two coalition Liberals, Wood and Richards, under his leadership. Meanwhile, George Brown had other and better news. It seemed that Roman Catholics in Ontario indeed were coming over to the Grits. A Catholic Convention of 200 delegates met in Toronto on July 9 and carried resolutions repudiating the Conservative party and reaffirming old Roman Catholic ties with Reform. "The fun of it is", Brown cheerfully commented, "that there has not one word passed, nor a demand been made, nor inducement sought or offered that might not be cried from any house-top in the country."[152]

Still, he was worried about the problem of the eastern Ontario counties, now that Sandfield was beyond redemption. Should he "make a raid through them" himself?[153] He had been invited to speak in several eastern constituencies. Perhaps he should move in that direction. Instead he decided on a compromise. If he had to run again, he wanted to make a test of some doubtful constituency, not take a safe place like South Oxford in the west. But it would not do for the party leader to face too great a risk of losing, or go too far from his own territory. He would run east of Toronto, then, but not very far east; in fact, he might well attempt the riding of South Ontario that had once been Oliver Mowat's seat.

Now the Conservatives held it. Their member, T. N. Gibbs, a resident and a strong man locally, would try for re-election. Yet Mowat's old supporters could surely pull Brown through, and his election in South Ontario could help Reform campaigns farther to the east. Under strong party pressure, his sense of duty combined with his confidence in a Liberal sweep to bring him to accept a requisition signed by 1,200 voters in the riding.[154] His closest lieutenant, Alexander Mackenzie, still advised against it.[155] But on July 19 the *Globe* announced that the party leader would stand in South Ontario for the Dominion parliament.

Brown opened his campaign on July 22, at Dunbarton schoolhouse, where Gibbs and a rowdy gang from Oshawa gave him a hot reception.[156] Two days later, at Brougham, Sandfield Macdonald was on hand to uphold Gibbs's cause. The only trouble was, Sandfield became so worked up in old antipathies that as well as denouncing George Brown he decried rep by pop and the new federal constitution, to Gibbs's considerable embarrassment: "made an ass of himself", Brown gloated.[157] As the round of meetings went on into August, Matthew Cameron turned up, and then McDougall was sent in.[158] At Whitby he and Brown hammered at each other from eight in the evening until three in the morning. The coalitionists were using their best strength to back up Gibbs – as Sandfield informed the greater Macdonald.[159] Brown, however, returned the compliment, and raided other critical constituencies. It was the most hectic of summers. Yet in South Ontario, across the province, and at Toronto headquarters, the Grit leader gave himself unstintingly to what he regarded as his final parliamentary effort.

At Whitby on August 19, the South Ontario nominations were held. The elections were only a week off now, and Brown went speaking daily through the dusty back concessions from Claremont to Myrtle and Columbus.[160] Polling began on Monday the twenty-sixth. At the end of that first day, the Grit candidate was ahead by a mere eleven in an extremely close contest.[161]

And on Tuesday, Gibbs rallied all his resources as a prominent local resident, sitting member, and supporter of a government that would do everything to defeat George Brown. Money was spent freely; jobs, contracts, favours were promised in profusion.[162] If only Mowat could have been there to help in his old constituency, instead of on the judges' bench! Despite all that Brown's unhappy campaign managers could do, Gibbs moved gradually into the lead. The lead mounted, slowly but steadily; nothing could check it. When the polls closed on the sultry evening of a desperate fight, the Reform chieftain had lost decisively, 875 to 971.[163]

The result showed all too plainly that South Ontario had

been an overly optimistic choice. Brown had few personal contacts of his own there, and had had to canvass personally for
votes, something he had never done before and found hard to
do now.[164] Under these circumstances, he had really chosen his
constituency too late for the full preparatory work that was
needed. Preoccupied as he was with the problems of the whole
party, the leader had not had time for a thorough campaign in
a difficult riding. Once again he had tried to do too much.

Yet the critical factor in Brown's defeat was surely a split in
the Reform vote, a far more significant factor than any ministerial spending or promises of government patronage. Despite the
Reform Convention, an element of South Ontario Liberals had
obviously heeded the "patriotic" no-party appeal and had voted
for Gibbs as the coalition candidate. Naturally the Conservatives
had done so as well; the combination had carried the election.
As a result, Brown had virtually been defeated by Reform votes
cast in the name of patriotism and union. But the worst part was
that this might be an augury for the elections as a whole.

9

From Lambton, when he heard the news, Alexander Mackenzie
sent a hurried note scrawled on a village store counter in the
midst of his own campaign. "Not very much surprised, though
deeply grieved", Mackenzie urged Brown to take another
constituency and run again, arguing that he had not lost a county
but only failed to gain one, and that the morale of the party
would suffer severely if its leader now accepted defeat.[165] But
Brown felt unshakably that he had done enough. He had firmly
meant to retire; he had been pushed into one more effort against
all his plans and wishes. The party now could surely ask no more
of him. He would still help with other elections and speak for
other candidates, but run again he would not.[166] Defeat, for him,
was both a shock and a release. After the first undoubted blow
to his proud and confident nature, he found in it a positive source
of satisfaction (whether rationalization or not), since no one
could say he had not tried devotedly for his party and fully
earned an honourable retirement.[167]

But Mackenzie may well have been right about the harm
done by Brown's withdrawal. At any rate, the elections elsewhere were going none too happily. McKellar was hard pressed
down in Kent, for example, and lost the federal seat, though he

took the provincial one. And, at the end of August, both Toronto ridings fell.[168] Brown was still giving active aid. He was in Bowmanville on September 3, to speak for Edward Blake in West Durham. Here, indeed, he came up against Sir John Macdonald, also on tour to champion candidates. Their encounter went very much as might have been expected. Macdonald would not come to the platform when called; he could not be found, in fact. He was cannily making certain that Brown would have to speak first. And Brown, running true to form, bounded up to do so, pouring his scorn on a prime minister who was afraid of a private citizen and evading the issue as always.[169] Then Macdonald appeared for the last word, now able to chaff Brown effectively without having to set forth his own policies for criticism. Still, Blake won the election – perhaps virtue did bring some reward.

But by the middle of September, when returns were all but complete, it appeared that virtue would have to bring the Reformers consolation instead. The Macdonald coalition had won a clear majority of Ontario's eighty-two federal seats, and Sandfield's "patent combination" had gained a similar margin in the provincial sphere. In Dominion elections elsewhere, the coalition had swept Quebec and taken about half the New Brunswick constituencies; and though Howe's anti-Confederate Liberals had captured all but one of Nova Scotia's federal seats, there was no question that Sir John Macdonald's first Dominion government had been resoundingly confirmed in power. When the federal parliament began its sittings in November, the Liberal opposition would be fragments, nothing more: about thirty-six Grits and some twenty *Rouges,* with Maritime "allies" who even opposed the union itself.[170] Clearly, Liberalism would have to build almost from scratch in federal politics. It was a new task in a new field, and Brown felt little desire to try it.

From his standpoint, what had happened was disaster, a bleak ending to a glowing parliamentary career. Yet, though his bright pre-election hopes had been wholly disappointed, the debacle was no real fault of his own. Unless, perhaps, for one thing: his over-confident assumption that a triumphant party Convention necessarily meant that the ordinary voters would go its way. They might, or they might not; on this point, Brown's basic limitation as a politician once more stood revealed – his readiness to jump to a conclusion that he wanted to be true. At no time had he shown that tendency more clearly than in the months before the elections of 1867.

On the other hand, the major causes for the disaster were

quite outside his control. To begin with, the Grit Liberals could have no truly alternative programme to lay before the voters, only that frequently fatal claim, "anything they can do, we can do better". There were no major grievances left (in Ontario at least) that they could turn against the government. Besides, that government enjoyed all the accrued prestige of successfully completing Confederation. Only the most faithful Grits would be likely to cast their votes against it. Brown, moreover, had inevitably cut himself off from the prestige of completing the Dominion by his own resignation from the cabinet over a year before. He had had reason to leave; but in any case, had he tried to stay in the government he would surely have been eclipsed, or finally forced out, by Canada's best in-fighter, John A. Macdonald. In fact, go or stay, Brown scarcely could have maintained his role as the initiator of Confederation. Again the problem was beyond his control.

For the times were simply out of joint for him. His political career had been built on powerful sectional grievances and an insistent demand for basic reform. But basic reform had been accomplished. The people now were swept by national aspirations, and that imponderable called patriotism gave credence to the no-party cry. Even Reformers who would normally abjure coalition were ready to give the Macdonald government the fair trial it asked. And Brownite Grits, though anything but anti-unionist, were bound to suffer from association in the public mind with Maritime Liberals who actively opposed Confederation and *Rouges* who were still unsettled.

Of course, the coalitionists exploited that association. Vote safely for Confederation, they argued – with Howland and Mc-Dougall, if not with John A. Macdonald. Enough Reformers heeded the plea to split the Upper Canada party even in its main areas of strength, far beyond South Ontario. And so the critical factor that defeated Brown personally worked to defeat his followers as well. The sage strategist, Macdonald, saw it for himself. "In the western part of Ontario," he said later, "a good many of our Conservative friends were elected by Reform aid, and by the split in the Reform ranks which the Coalition effected."[171]

And yet, if Brown, the partisan Grit leader, was out of keeping with this moment of no-party patriotism, he still was right, and Howland, McDougall, and their supporters wrong, in contending that a genuine coalition could be maintained under Macdonald's leadership. Within a year for Howland, two for McDougall, they were out of office, and the ministry was clearly what Brown had said it would be, an instrument of Conservative rule. John A. merely swallowed two more Liberal rivals; but a hard core of Reform survived with George Brown, even though in unavoidable defeat.

Perhaps he was right to retire now, from this new political era. Certainly he had accomplished the tasks that had kept him long and reluctantly in public life. Representation by population was won; Ontario had her own government for her own affairs, and due weight in a much broader union than that which had been overthrown. The North West was committed to Canada. And Brown's own national vision of a transcontinental state was well on its way to realization. Dejection at defeat much wider than his own would soon pass, to be succeeded by sheer thankfulness at having reached the end at last.[172]

Summing up, on September 25, 1867, the *Globe* necessarily found the best side. "It is a far greater credit to a public man," it said, "to have consistently fought the battle for constitutional reform to the end, than to have held office for a generation." If this was mere excuse, it still expressed the very theme of Brown's career in politics. Personal considerations aside, he would by nature have agreed with it.

He quickly took steps to enjoy his liberation. Early in October, he met briefly with Mackenzie and other chief men of the party in Toronto, and in farewell advice proposed a "quiescent" policy of watchful waiting until the first Dominion ministry got well entangled in its own rope.[173] Then on October 11, the former leader left with Anne and the children for New York, on their way to a long-promised stay in Scotland, which politics had so consistently postponed.[174]

Qualified Retirement

I

Sunday, January 5, 1868; Brown was in the library at Oak Lodge in Toronto, a good fire inside, the first thick snows of winter outside, writing to his wife, who was still in Scotland with the children.[1] Late in December he had returned to Canada, intending to rejoin his family in the spring. His brother's health was uncertain again; he could give Gordon some relief on the *Globe*, and also arrange for next year's operations at Bow Park. Beyond that, Ontario's first legislature had opened on December 27, and George Brown wanted to be on hand to follow it. For, as he had assured Alexander Mackenzie before leaving Canada in the autumn, his retiring from parliament did not mean his abandoning the Liberal cause. He would, he had promised, "work for the ascendancy of my friends federal and local as cordially and enthusiastically as ever."[2] The past leader of the Grits could still wield power in the country. In fact, as long as he controlled the potent *Globe*, he might continue to be overlord of Liberalism.

He was managing nicely in the big house, he told Anne, with a butler, a cook, and a page boy, the cook's little nephew – "Buttons – I have a Buttons!"[3] The table silver was still stored in the bank; but with pewter spoons, steel forks, and the butler standing solemnly behind Anne's empty chair, Brown felt "we get along delightfully". He was even making plans to entertain; much as he missed his family, he meant to keep fully occupied. All day he was at the *Globe* office, where business was excellent. The evenings he spent with the political society that had gathered in Toronto again, now that the first parliament in eight years sat in the old red-brick legislative buildings on Front Street.

He gave his first big dinner party on January 15 for the leading Grit Liberals in town, among them, Mackenzie, McKellar, and Blake.[4] The federal parliament was in recess, and thus Mackenzie could be present, while Blake held both a federal and a provincial seat, since dual representation was quite permissible. Three days later, Sandfield Macdonald and an assortment of Tories and Coalitionists came for dinner. Then Brown held a "grand blow-out" for Ontario's first Lieutenant-Governor, Sir Henry Stisted, and a surrounding set of dignitaries.[5] In return, he went to Sandfield's dinner for seventy, William McMaster's "awful splurge", and the Lieutenant-Governor's ball at the Music Hall.[6] "We are getting tremendously gay in Toronto," he remarked to Anne, "and invitations are now sent out on pasteboard cards engraved – think of that!"[7]

He visited Bow Park at times, but his busy party-going continued on through February. Not surprisingly, his digestion suffered, and he had to give up sugar, potatoes, and wine, and take to penitential draughts of lime-water.[8] Brown, however, had not simply been seeking amusement: his social life was a means of keeping *au courant* with the political world. In particular, he stayed in close touch with Grit inner circles. Here he still could carry a great deal of weight, especially until someone was chosen to succeed him at the head of the party.

But the retired leader did not try to direct the parliamentary Liberals from back-stage. He was too determined to keep his personal independence and freedom as a journalist to resume the responsibilities of command. Instead, he offered constant consultation and advice to the chief men – Mackenzie and McKellar, or the fast-rising Edward Blake. The leadership itself practically remained in committee, because party lines in parliament were still so confused by coalition, and because in the federal sphere the varied opposition contingents of Grits, *Rouges*, and Maritime Reformers had yet to be formed into one national Liberal party. And if in committee Brown's voice was forceful, his party heirs could not honestly complain that he sought to govern them. They might rather complain that he would do nothing but freely give advice, for he steadfastly refused every new plea to return to parliament.[9] At any rate, considering Brown's native imperiousness, he really did quite well in making the transition from director to associate, thanks above all to his determination to stay out of public life.

He still found political affairs full of interest, and even quite encouraging. Sandfield's Ontario régime was obviously weak, while in the Dominion cabinet "the feud between Cartier and Galt on the one hand and John A. on the other is open and bitter".[10] There was the problem of Nova Scotia, for example, where Howe and the ascendant anti-unionists were working vigorously to take the province out of Confederation. Someone should carry the Dominion's case to London; but Macdonald, it appeared, would not trust Galt to go without Tupper, and Galt was angrily resentful.[11] Then there was disagreement in the cabinet over the projected Intercolonial Railway. McDougall wanted a cheaper inland route, Cartier the longer north-shore line; the former, in fact, seemed to favour saving the cost altogether by letting Nova Scotia go.[12] But the worst discord of all, since it touched statesmen on their self-esteem, arose out of the honours that had been awarded at the birth of Confederation.

Macdonald, as chairman of the final London Conference that had settled the new union, had been made a Knight Commander of the Bath; the other leading figures of the Conference had only been made Companions of the Bath – no knighthoods. This far from delicate distinction particularly rankled with Galt and Cartier, who had been no more prepared than Brown to concede a superior place to Macdonald in the work of federation. Under the circumstances, George Brown was moved to write to an old opponent, for whom he had gained considerable regard during their association in the Confederation ministry, George Etienne Cartier. Brown had no direct political designs; indeed, he could write largely because he felt removed from the contrivings of political life. But undoubtedly he wanted to express a fellow-feeling to Cartier, and to drive home some of his own views while the latter was restless and disgruntled. So began a correspondence that could shake popular assumptions regarding Brown's intransigence – or Cartier's unswerving attachment to John A. Macdonald.

"I have had a longing to write to you from a good while back," Brown began, "for notwithstanding all our old battles there was nothing in our intercourse as colleagues for eighteen months that left a painful remembrance on my mind towards you personally but much that commanded my respect and esteem. . . . If then, I am now found writing to you on political matters – to you who were 'mine ancient enemy' – it is because there is one point on which an expression of opinion is specially due from me to you, and two or three points which are of such high national interest and so removed from all personal considerations that *even* I may address *even* you upon them."[13]

"Well, then," he continued, "I want first to express to you my sincere regret that the highest reward offered by the Crown for the services rendered in carrying Confederation was not offered to you as well as to Mr. John A. Macdonald. . . . No man, perhaps, is in so good a position as myself to say who contributed most towards the success of the great constitutional changes that have just been accomplished – and I have always said, and am ready to maintain, that without your aid they could not have been accomplished. Lower Canada was the difficulty in the way – and you were the only man in Lower Canada, who when the crisis arrived, had the pluck and the influence to take the bull by the horns. You ran the risk of political death by the bold course you took, Mr. Macdonald ran no risk whatever. If ever subject earned the highest reward of his sovereign, compatible with his position, you have done so."

It was frank, forthright acknowledgment. Brown was equally frank and forthright about his own part. "Of course, I believe that my fifteen years' contest for constitutional reform, and my bold action in 1864 won the battle – that you and Macdonald were made to 'move on' in spite of yourselves, to a certain extent – and that I might therefore have entered claims to honours very different from either of you." But that did not concern him: "I live very much in the consciousness of having done the work – but I don't care one straw for a ribbon or a title, as a Canadian – which I always expect and wish to be."

He turned from personal to political matters as he sought to impress on Cartier the need for making every effort to hold Nova Scotia. To allow secession would be "simply madness" that would "throw us back half a century". He was amazed at the ministry's inaction; and "this leaving unanswered the most absurd mistakes and misrepresentations – this failure of the government to take moral possession of the new province is the worst of all." A mission should go there at once: "Two or three members of your government – not Nova Scotians nor New Brunswickers, but Canadians – men who know how to speak and keep their tempers and won't be put down, should face the enemy on the ground – even yet." Furthermore, were "Howe and Co. to have the field in England entirely to themselves?" All Brown's own convictions went into the answer, as he urged, "They ought to be met and met manfully – not in the clever fashion of Dr. Tupper . . . but in a candid, statesmanlike spirit spoken in the interest of the whole British American family. . . . Not bitterly, not sneeringly, not even slightingly – but persuasively and firmly. . . . In discussion their case is quite untenable. There is no portion of the Dominion that gains so much by Confederation as Nova Scotia."

He switched to questions of banking and currency, and especially to the government's note issue, which he had opposed in 1866 as ruinous to the chartered banks, and to which he now ascribed the failure both of the Bank of Upper Canada and of the Commercial Bank late in 1867. It was far more important

that capital should be easily available to "industrial interests"
than that it be kept on hand for the exchequer through the government note scheme, just so that the finance minister need not
borrow abroad. "Draw off the floating capital of a country by
means of savings banks, exchequer bills, stock loans and legal
tenders — and you may no doubt replenish your public coffers
and save yourself humiliating applications to London bankers —
but you may at the same time lose the life blood of your industrial progress and stop many a hopeful enterprise. . . . The thing
is downright silly. We have not yet reached the day when to
import capital is an injury." A hundred years later, his argument would still have a contemporary ring.

Warmly he defended the private banking interests. "What
would Canada have been at this moment but for her banks?"
The true course was to borrow abroad, withdraw the legal tender
notes, and deposit public moneys again in the chartered banks.
For now they were all afraid of one another and the government. "Such a state of things in a young country full of natural
wealth awaiting development, and with plenty of people ready
to develop it, if they had the oil to grease the wheels, exhibits
frightful mismanagement."

But Brown had had his say. He had felt it a duty to present
these views, he told Cartier, though he did not imagine they
would have much effect. In any case, he was leaving for Scotland in six weeks or so, and planned to take his wife on a continental tour. Once, nothing would have taken him away when
issues such as these impended. "But now — while keenly alive
to all that affects the well-being of the country to which I owe
everything, and anxiously desirous of the success of Confederation — and while ever ready to give a yeoman's lift at any
moment to my old friends in the Reform party — I am not
conscious of a single personal aspiration in connection with
public affairs."

"I am no longer the slave of the lamps," he ended. "My
hours are my own. I have a happy home — always happy — a
prosperous business that occupies my thoughts sufficiently —
a beautiful property that gives me relaxation and where I hope
to welcome you someday — and the heart, I trust, to thank
God for all his blessings." He looked forward to seeing Cartier
and his wife at Bow Park in time to come. "Now that all our
electoral, educational and ecclesiastical bickerings are at an end,
would not such a visit be a pleasant thing?" Warmly he added,
"No one would be happier to see it than my good wife."

It was almost a valedictory to politics; but Cartier did not
leave the matter thus. In an equally long reply he evinced a keen

desire to do more than just exchange generalities with Brown.[14] He wanted to talk politics in private; his tone was most cordial and friendly. "I must remark to you at the outset," said Cartier, "that I felt not only pleasure but also complimented by the spirit and kind feelings which prompted you." He particularly acknowledged the satisfaction that Brown's appreciation of "the C.B. matter" gave him: "The great error and mistake in the awarding of those honours was that they were conferred solely on the consideration of the *accidental* composition of the last London Conference, and of the *accidental* chairmanship of John A. as the oldest Executive Councillor there present." Returning the favour, he declared that Galt and he had both thought that the omission of Brown's name was shameful – shameful that "your daring as *political leader* of the Reform party in Upper Canada had not been considered". He went further: "If anyone in Upper Canada deserves a proper recognition of his services in connection with the Confederation question, I say, and everyone says, that it was you." This from John A. Macdonald's long-time partner!

He agreed with Brown "that everything should be done to keep Nova Scotia in the Confederation", and further, that McDougall had no conception of its importance, or of the need to carry out the pledge to build the Intercolonial. He thanked the other for his good advice on defeating Howe. As for the banking and currency question, here Cartier was more circumspect regarding Brown's advice. "Without telling you at this moment if you are *right* or *wrong* in what you say on these subjects, I can say to you that I feel pleased and delighted to have before my eyes the view of one so conversant with these matters as you are."

Discreet flattery, perhaps, but Cartier was coming to his own point. "No man could be more useful in parliament than yourself," he wrote significantly, "and I must add to you that every day I regret that you are not a member of the House of Commons. It may be that some difficulty might spring up before *long*, and your presence in the House might be so useful, and so conducive to solve it." He no less regretted that Brown proposed leaving for Europe so soon – "I would have liked very *much* to have had a few moments of private conversation with you." He would have come to Toronto for a talk, in fact, had he not been obliged to go to Quebec for the provincial legislature. Still, they could exchange further letters before Brown left. "I take for granted Mackenzie represents your ideas in the House," Cartier added. "If you have any occasion to see him, tell him to *continue* to express himself strongly as he *does* in favour of British connection." Another odd development – the leading Quebec member of the cabinet transmitting private suggestions for a leading Grit member of the opposition!

The rest was amiable small talk as Cartier expressed his delight at Brown's happiness, his thanks for the invitation to pay a visit, and his pleasure that the Browns were to see the treasures of Rome, saved and maintained by the Vatican. "I am sure," he said playfully, "you and Mrs. Brown will exclaim, 'After all, Papacy has done a *good* thing.'" There were kisses for the children as he signed himself, "Your most devoted friend and ex-colleague, George Cartier."

There the overture rested momentarily; but Brown undoubtedly talked of it with Alexander Mackenzie a few days later, when early in March the latter stayed with him on his way to the reopening of the Ottawa parliament.[15] In fact, Blake and McKellar joined them in a party consultation. Once more they pressed Brown to take a place in parliament; a choice of two was offered to him. Once more he refused.[16] In Ottawa indeed, rumours were already spreading that the government would fall and the former Grit leader be sent for.[17] Mackenzie and his associates certainly entertained the possibility that a new alliance could be formed with Cartier and Galt in Quebec, excluding McDougall and a few Ontario Liberal followers. Yet the man vitally necessary to any such design still held back. If anything, he was giving his best attention now to adding a four-storey wing behind the *Globe* office in order to house a new rotary press too large for the existing building.[18] He was working hard to get all the arrangements made, so that he could still sail in April as planned.

The most Brown would do was to write Cartier and say that while he would not re-enter active politics himself, he would gladly support his own party in an alliance with the *Bleu* leader "on sound principles".[19] In return, the other eagerly proposed that Brown come to Ottawa for a confidential talk "on several political topics", suggesting also how the real purpose of his trip might be concealed.[20] Within a few days, however, the news of the projected visit leaked out in the capital.[21] Now cautious Alexander Mackenzie grew uncertain of its value; for now that it was known, any negotiations with Cartier might set back the work of rebuilding Reform, while their failure could be even more damaging. Accordingly, in reporting the situation in Ottawa to Brown, Mackenzie left it up to him to decide whether or not to come.[22] This was tantamount to killing the entire project. Busy at the *Globe*, eager to leave for Europe, determined not to become enmeshed in politics again, the former party leader was only too ready to drop the venture. Towards the end of March, he told Anne that between settling matters at the office and Bow Park, he had not a moment left to run to Ottawa.[23] Thereafter he ignored the whole idea.

Cartier was left to regain his equanimity in Sir John Macdonald's government. If there had been any possibility of Brown's making a startling return to politics — conceivably at the head of a Brown-Cartier government — it could never have been realized in any case, since he had no intention of trying. Yet the episode went to show two things: that Cartier, subordinated by Macdonald, did not find it inconceivable himself to approach Brown; and that Brown might still have been an effective rival to Macdonald in Dominion politics, had he wanted to be.

Early in April he completed plans for the summer work at Bow Park, dashed back to Toronto, and set out for the ocean voyage. But one thing spoiled his joy at leaving: the shocking news from Ottawa of the death of an old friend and foe — yet far more friend than foe — D'Arcy McGee, murdered by a Fenian bullet on the night of April 7.[24]

2

Reunion in Edinburgh in the spring of 1868 was quite as wonderful as always. Anne was not well, however. She had been ill intermittently since the middle of the winter and had been confined to bed for some time, although she had minimized her troubles in writing to her husband.[25] As spring turned to summer, she improved; yet it was clear that she would not be strong enough to make a continental trip. It scarcely mattered to Brown. He took a seaside villa at North Berwick for his wife and children, where they all could spend the summer, and Anne could fully recover her health.[26]

Nevertheless, he did have a brief trip to the continent on his own in late July. He had brought his sister Isabella with him from Canada, and she and a cousin, Kate Brown, were to go to take the waters at Kissingen in Bavaria, since Ise had also been ailing. Reluctantly Brown agreed to convey the ladies there, reluctantly because Anne could not go with them to make the journey worth while — for, as he said, "All things take colouring from my own Anne."[27] But on July 29 he and his party took the night boat from Dover to Ostend, and by next morning were in Brussels.

"A magnificent city," he exclaimed, "the finest city I have

ever seen – next to Edinburgh."[28] They saw all the sights, and
left next day for Cologne. Here the cathedral was superb, but
the dirt and the stench in the heat of summer were appalling:
"No wonder the plague was so severe – wonder any of them
were left."[29] The trip onward, up the Rhine by steamer, however, fulfilled all expectations of the grandeur of the river. On
August 1 they reached Kissingen, a leading international
watering-place, where Brown was pleased to note "the Czar of
all the Roosiars", Alexander III, quietly strolling on the
promenade.[30] "A queer place", he found it none the less – "a
town of hotels all built and supplied by crowds of invalids, rush-
ing to the wells – wasser, wasser – nothing but wasser!"[31]

Having settled his charges in a hotel redolent of "cold-
slaugh", he came back by Frankfurt and Bonn (where he
watched the King of Prussia arriving in state), and went on to
do more sightseeing in Cologne and Liége.[32] On August 4 he
was in Antwerp enjoying "a capital dinner and a petit bott' du
vin".[33] The day after, he was back in London, looking forward
to seeing Anne once more, and "determined to find you vastly
better and quite well".[34]

She did recover fully, as the pleasant, easy summer by the
sea wore on. On occasion Brown still had to leave "Ebenezer
Villa" for London, since he was engaged in settling a small
estate there, left to him by his mother from the Mackenzie side
of the family.[35] Moreover, when in London in September, and
not tied up with wills and lawyers, he was busy buying books –
"Such bargains and such capital books!" – for he was building
up a sizeable library for himself.[36] And so the days passed
through September, until it was time to pack up all the pur-
chases – dresses, suits, and furnishings, as well as the sets of
history, biography, and philosophy – and prepare for the
return to Canada.

Brown had made one more purchase, a finely cut new font of
type from Miller and Richard of Edinburgh.[37] The *Globe* was
in for another thorough remodelling. Back in Toronto that
autumn, he went at the task wholesale. It was as if he were
pouring all his energy and enthusiasm into the newspaper, now
that he was done with public life and had had his fill of holidays.
On October 10 a resplendent new *Daily Globe* appeared, with
bright, clean print replacing the old, worn, and blurring type;
with sharp new headings; and with the front page largely
cleared of advertisements and conspicuously featuring the latest
cable and wire reports from Europe, Ottawa, Montreal, New
York, and Halifax.

Sports news was beginning to make a definite appearance;

cricket and lacrosse matches were described. A daily "literary" column was added, and there was a regular City News section now, as well as the longer-established financial column. Through this growing trend to regular departments and features, and the change that put the biggest news on page one, the *Globe* was taking on much more resemblance to a present-day newspaper.[38] Nevertheless, the editorials on page two were as powerful and extensive as ever, even though, in this fairly quiet autumn of 1868, the paper seemed to have few consistent topics for criticism beyond the fallacies of Nova Scotia separatism and the deficiencies of the Sandfield Macdonald régime in Ontario.

Brown's improvements, however, did not end here. The *Weekly Globe* was also reorganized and given increased news content.[39] At the end of the year, the *Canada Farmer* was enlarged also.[40] Of course, he counted on increased circulation. Thus he had a new Hoe Lightning "four-feeder" press ready in the extension behind the *Globe* building: the extension he had arranged for in the spring in order to provide room not only for bigger presses but also for increased dispatch and delivery services.[41] Still further, he announced late in November that a second and even larger four-feeder press was under construction specifically for the *Weekly Globe*, and would soon be added to the spacious new press room.[42] At the same time, *Globe* branch offices were opened in Hamilton, London, and Montreal, in order to promote more advertising and circulation.[43] And then, as the crowning touch, *Globe* rates were cut. The price of the daily went down from six to five dollars for a year's subscription and from three to two cents for the individual copy.[44]

The sharp reduction was made possible by increased circulation, the *Globe* said blandly on November 4. But that early, it must have been an expression of hope rather than a statement of fact. Certainly Brown had gambled again on costly improvements, expecting that, as in times before, they would bring returns in greater circulation and consequently larger advertising revenues. Wealthy man that he was, he was in sufficient need of additional cash at the outset of the expansion scheme to place a temporary mortgage on Bow Park for $20,000.[45]

But the venture paid off magnificently. In mid-October of 1868, the *Globe* had been selling some 7,700 copies of its daily edition.[46] Within two months the sales had soared to over 15,000, and of these copies more than half went by mail and express to readers outside Toronto.[47] The climb continued. By mid-January of 1869, the circulation of the *Daily Globe* stood at 16,320, while the weekly issue, which reached the farther portions of the province and Dominion, counted 31,200 subscribers on its books.[48] Hence the *Globe*'s total circulation was nearing 48,000, and it went on mounting, although now at a slower rate. When the population of Toronto itself was not greatly over 50,000, the extent of the *Globe* empire was all the more striking. Indeed, the paper claimed that nowhere else in the world was one journal read by so large a proportion of the public.[49] Brown's drive could hardly have been more successful.

A sense of satisfaction may reasonably have coloured the *Globe*'s view of the outlook for 1869. Times were peaceful and prosperous; Toronto was enjoying a building boom. In politics, the Nova Scotian anti-Confederation movement had been decisively disappointed in its appeal to Britain, and now was falling apart. Meanwhile, Cartier and McDougall had gone to England to settle the terms with the Hudson's Bay Company on which the North West would finally be added to the Dominion. As for the government of the Dominion, "substantially the Coalition is at an end."[50] Of the Ontario Reform ministers, Howland had been appointed the second lieutenant-governor of Ontario, Blair had died in office, and McDougall was left in isolation. To all intents, the "no party" administration was a Macdonald Conservative cabinet. Yet the Liberal opposition had shown high quality in parliament – Mackenzie and Blake, Dorion and Holton, and their allies – and there was every expectation their support would grow, now that party lines were clearing again.

Brown's own relations with his party remained much as before. He refused another offer of a safe seat in Centre Wellington in January; but within the limits of political retirement and journalistic independence (the *Globe* denied that it was "the mere mouthpiece" of any party) he still co-operated closely with the parliamentary leaders of Liberalism.[51] Mackenzie kept him fully informed on Ottawa activities and often asked for his opinions. Furthermore, at week-ends, when "Mack" had not gone home to Sarnia or stayed at the capital, he might well be found in Toronto at Oak Lodge – perhaps, indeed, stretched out on the study sofa of a Sunday evening, fast asleep.[52]

Yet something, still, had changed. While Brown had been out of the country as well as out of politics for months on end, Alexander Mackenzie had inevitably been assuming leadership in his own right. The earnest, shrewd-eyed Scots Grit with the firm-clamped jaw had been a devoted lieutenant for over fifteen years; but he had never been subservient. He was too staunchly determined, too jealous of his own integrity, ever to give blind obedience. And now, thanks largely to tenacity of mind and character, and to his sharply-cutting skill in debate, Mackenzie had become leader of the Grits in parliament in everything but name. No one else had his stature. If Blake had evident ability, he was still young in experience; Mowat was on the bench; and such prominent Liberals of former days as Sandfield Macdonald, McDougall, and Howland were obviously not in the running. Nor could the *Rouges* Dorion and Holton, with their limited and still separate following, fairly be considered as alternative possibilities to Mackenzie.

In consequence, the relations of Brown and Mackenzie were bound to be altered. Yet it could not be easy for the man who had led, and by nature was impatient and commanding, to keep the change always in mind. At the same time, it was no easier for the man who had virtually assumed responsibility for the party – and was scarcely disposed to take his duties either lightly or meekly – to submit to advice or criticism that might seem too close to instruction. The important fact, however, was not that there were moments of friction, but that the two old associates got on so well in their new relationship. For there was this between them: complete trust and confidence in each other's intentions, and personal understanding and affection that only grew across the years.

In any case, for the present there was not much political activity to worry about. An uneventful Ontario session closed in January of 1869, and the federal parliament was not to meet until April 15. (In between, George Brown found time to take up a new hobby, cycling, and had a specially large bicycle built for himself.[53]) But late in March important news arrived from England.[54] The negotiations with the Hudson's Bay Company had been successfully concluded. All of Rupert's Land and the north-western territory beyond would pass to Canada, in return for compensation to the Company of £300,000 and one-twentieth of the lands in the "fertile belt" across the prairies. The terms were not what Brown might have wished. Canada was paying to extinguish claims that he had never considered valid. Still, he had recognized that the imperial government would consent to the transfer only if the Company's claims were satisfied, and £300,000 was a good deal less than the £1,000,000 that had been asked originally, when he had first opened the negotiations in London in 1864. And, as the *Globe* pointed out, the price tag on the enormous western empire was only half the cost of the Ottawa parliament buildings, one-tenth of the Intercolonial Railway, and one-fifth of what the United States had paid two years earlier for Alaska, an insignificant wasteland in comparison.[55] It was the triumphant conclusion to the campaign for the acquisition of the North West that George Brown and the Upper Canada Reform party had pursued for over a decade.

Parliament was opened in April by a new Governor-General, Sir John Young, soon to be Lord Lisgar. (Lord Monck had said his good-byes to Canada in the preceding November, with a particularly warm one to George Brown.)[56] There were matters to note, and some to deplore, in parliament's proceedings – such as the grant of increased subsidies to Nova Scotia in order to make the province sit easier in the Dominion. To Brown, the "better terms" simply undermined the financial compact reached at Quebec on which the federal union had been built, and opened the way to endless future assaults by provinces on the national treasury.[57] In fact, the Dominion's finances were already growing strained; the old Macdonald Conservative programme of buying adherence, of more borrowing and more burdens, seemed to be taking shape once more.

Of greater concern to Brown, however, was the question of organizing the north-western territories that would come into Canadian possession in the autumn. Resolutions went before the House of Commons early in June to provide for their initial administration by a governor and appointed council. There was no provision for the council to include members from the existing settlement in the North West at the Red River, nor for them to choose even one representative. The *Globe* greatly regretted it. "The people of Red River will not long submit to the proposed government," it said prophetically.[58]

Then there was the problem of access to the North West through Canadian territory. Apparently the federal government did not propose to do more than complete a "common road" from the head of Lake Superior and thence by wagon-trail and waterways to Fort Garry on the Red. Again the *Globe* deplored the meagre conception of the government's policy. The Americans had built a railway to the Pacific and were busy supplementing it. Canada could not race the United States in western development by competing against railways with a cart-road! "The railway must come, and the Dominion must aid in securing it."[59]

The session closed in June, but the North West question occupied attention throughout the summer, as the *Globe* stressed the urgency of improving the route across the wilderness of lake and forest that lay between Fort William and Fort Garry. When American rails through Minnesota could easily reach the British North West, "to dawdle, hesitate or delay for even a single year would be a blunder equal to a crime".[60] On the other hand, Brown and his paper were not wholly displeased to learn that

William McDougall would be the first Canadian governor of Rupert's Land and the north-western territory; for McDougall at least had had a long association with Canada's campaign to gain the West. If he would apply a liberal and enlightened policy in his new domain, he could redeem his lost political character, and even those who had strongly condemned him would "forgive and forget".[61]

Another matter less in the public eye also concerned George Brown that summer: the question of formally naming his successor as party leader. Alexander Mackenzie, of course, in practice led the federal Grit contingent, while Archibald McKellar served in the same way in the Ontario house. But perhaps it was time now to elect an official leader of the Liberals at Ottawa, in particular, to indicate the reconstitution of the party on a Dominion-wide basis. Luther Holton certainly felt so. He raised the matter of tighter party organization with Mackenzie, who referred it to Brown.[62] Holton, it seemed, would be willing to serve under Dorion in one nationally organized Liberal party, or under Brown, if he would return to parliament. Otherwise he aspired to the leadership himself.[63]

Brown was exceedingly dubious; dubious both that Holton would make a good leader and that the time was ripe to organize the federal party closely. As to the first, he told Mackenzie, "With all my high opinion of Holton, I am sure that such a step would greatly damage if not utterly ruin our hopes of success at the next election. What a howl would be raised!"[64] The trouble was that Holton and others of the *Rouges* were still inclined to recall their old anti-Confederation arguments, in order to say "I told you so" about the mistakes of the Dominion under Sir John Macdonald. Then, too, they were playing with ideas of Canadian independence, which Brown regarded as neither desirable nor feasible. Certainly both these themes would not make Holton or the *Rouges* popular in Ontario, or in much of Canada beyond.[65]

Similarly, he doubted whether any very close connection was yet possible between Ontario Grits and Quebec *Rouges*: "I think it would be very inexpedient to separate from them, but fancy it would be better for each party to paddle its own canoe a little longer."[66] The same conclusion would apply to the Maritime Liberals, still marked by anti-unionism, even if Mackenzie were himself elected as official leader of the whole party: "How the necessity of shaping your own course and that of your party to suit the votes and local prejudices of your allies below would embarrass us all the next election!"[67] Besides, too close contact with the *Rouges* before that election would destroy all chance of splitting off a section of the *Bleus* in Quebec.[68] In short, if Brown himself looked forward to a nationally organized Liberal party under one leadership, he did not envisage it as practicable until after the next federal contest. And then it would certainly not be constituted on a *Rouge*-radical or semi-separatist basis.

It might be useful, he conceded, for Mackenzie himself "to be *formally* elected leader of the U.C. section – but it is far better to be actual leader by force of ability than to hold it by any vote."[69] In his own view, his old lieutenant could hardly be in a stronger position than he was now, although he was best equipped to judge that for himself. Mackenzie entirely agreed with Brown. "I would scorn to be the *manufactured* figure head of the party," he returned.[70] And so things stayed as they were; Holton's proposal came to nothing. Alexander Mackenzie remained *de facto* leader of a loosely jointed federal opposition – but very much Brown's heir as the head of Ontario Grittism.

Summer was coming to an end. Brown had, no doubt, spent as much of it as possible away from Toronto at Bow Park, where Anne and the children could escape the city heat among cool, shaded slopes beside the Grand. His wife was expecting their third child. They were home in Toronto before the middle of September, for there, on September 13, a son, George Mackenzie Brown, was born.[71]

3

That autumn, Sir John finally filled the vacancies in the federal cabinet, now that the last fading flower of Ontario coalition Liberalism, McDougall, had been transplanted to the West. In came an undoubted Conservative, Alexander Morris, and two reputed Liberals, Senator James Aikins and – Sir Francis Hincks! To the *Globe*, Aikins or "some other feeble brother" from the appointed chamber carried little weight; but to claim that Hincks represented either Ontario or Liberalism was sheer fantasy.[72] He had been out of Canada and politics for the past fifteen years as Governor of Barbados and British Guiana. He had joined with Conservatives back in 1854 to form the very party that Macdonald led, in which any Hincksite element had long since been absorbed. His appointment really underlined the fact that the coalition principle had lost all meaning.

While Hincks was being found a seat, Lieutenant-Governor

McDougall had travelled west to begin his duties at the Red
River once the transfer of the territories to the Dominion had
been completed. From there, on November 13, 1869, Brown
first learned that Canada might yet face trouble before she took
possession of the North West. "A Row at the Red River",
announced the *Globe*: some of the French half-breed or *métis*
element in the population had apparently blocked McDougall's
entry into the settlement. It made a whimsical picture, the
almost-governor forced to camp in American territory just short
of his promised land![73] Nevertheless, Brown's paper assumed
that the difficulty would not last, for the half-breeds had simply
misconceived Canada's intentions. "There is nothing which
cannot be removed by the exhibition of a friendly and liberal
spirit."[74]

As the days went on, and the impasse continued, however,
Brown had to recognize that the trouble would not be settled
easily. In fact, it was mounting; the *métis* had occupied Fort
Garry unopposed. A typically imprudent and unauthorized
attempt by McDougall to raise a "loyal" force resulted only in
its ignominious capture by the *métis*. On December 8, they proclaimed a provisional government of their own. Meanwhile, the
Canadian ministry had decided not to accept transfer of the
North West in its present unsatisfactory condition, and literally
stopped payment on the compensation to the Hudson's Bay
Company. The Red River hung between two régimes: the Company's, which effectually had lapsed, and the Dominion's, which
had not begun. Under the circumstances the provisional government filled the gap in fact if not in law, led, it appeared, by
the astute young demagogue who had directed the *métis* rising,
one Louis Riell, or Riel.

There the case stood by the end of 1869. Poor William Mc-
Dougall – "William the Conquered" – returned from the
kingdom that had jointly been denied to him by the *métis* and
the Macdonald government, while at Red River, Riel appeared
to face no effective opposition. The Bay Company's old officials
and adherents were not unfriendly, because of their resentment
over annexation to Canada; the long-established Selkirk settlers
and English-speaking half-breeds accepted the situation; and
the newer Canadian element seemed cowed.

Above all, the majority at Red River felt small enthusiasm
for joining Canada without some assurance of their rights. And
in assessing the whole unfortunate muddle, Brown was not disposed to blame them; in fact, he believed that the chief responsibility for the existing stalemate lay with the Dominion government itself. "The original and fundamental error of the

government," declared the *Globe*, "lay in ignoring altogether the opinions and feelings of the inhabitants of the Selkirk Settlement."[75] The Scottish settlers and half-breeds had been jealous to secure self-government; the French element doubly so, for they feared being overrun by English-speaking new-comers. And yet the rights of the Red River people had not been acknowledged. Instead they had been given a government that was utterly out of date – a mistake the *Globe* had warned against for months before the rising began.[76] Then surveying parties, all Canadians, had entered the land, advance groups of "foreign officials" that made it seem that all good things in the colony were to go to the Canadians. "Let our readers in Ontario put themselves in the place of the people of Selkirk, and say whether they also would not have felt indignant!"[77]

Finally had come McDougall's bungling, compounded by the weak retreat of the Ottawa government in refusing to take responsibility for the North West. Riel was left free to raise any flag he pleased at Red River, and if Canadian inaction continued, extreme policies might well take control there. For inaction was a confession of weakness and an encouragement to violence. The entire mess was but "the natural fruits of official injustice and wrong, followed up by official vacillation and timidity."[78]

Now, as 1870 opened, Brown urged immediate steps to save the situation.[79] The "claim of rights" put out by the Red River inhabitants seemed reasonable enough; delegates should be sent to discuss terms with them. Canada, moreover, should honour her agreement with the Hudson's Bay Company. And then troops must go west, not in any spirit hostile to the people of Red River, but simply to make clear that the North West was a British and a Canadian possession.[80] The *Globe* was well aware by now that both American and Fenian elements were at work within the settlement to exploit the *métis* rising for their own purposes. Moreover, in the United States, expansionists were loud again, demanding the annexation of the Red River in the name of freedom, justice – and manifest destiny. It was necessary to show American "well-wishers" that they might have to fight to gain the British North West, a fact that would doubtless cool their generous sentiments.[81] A firm, strong response was no less needed to assure Red River that annexation would not be allowed, to dissuade Riel and Company from extremism, and to encourage the moderate forces in the settlement. "THE NORTH WEST MUST AND SHALL BE OURS," Brown's paper vigorously proclaimed.[82]

But equally the *Globe* insisted on self-government for the

people of the West. Things would obviously be far safer, it held, were Louis Riel the leader of the opposition or a member of the ministry in "Her Majesty's House of Commons in Rupert's Land".[83] If the inhabitants of Red River indeed were not entrusted with the responsibilities of freedom, "the Canadian Confederation will never take root in those western regions – and it may be doubted whether in that case, it ought."[84] As January and February passed, however, all the news from the little colony isolated in the prairie winter indicated that extremists held the upper hand, and were striving to force separation, or annexation to the United States. Riel in particular was acting in an arbitrary, high-handed manner. In fact, it seemed that liberty and property at Red River now hung on "the simple fiat of the great potentate of the North, Monsieur le Président Riel" – the "self-constituted autocrat of all Winnipeg".[85]

None the less, emissaries from Canada had now reached Red River to discuss a settlement, and on March 1 there was better news. A deputation from the colony would come to Ottawa to negotiate terms for its entrance into Confederation. But then, only a few days later, Brown learned of the attempt by Canadians at the Red River to rise against Riel and seize Fort Garry. The provocation had been great, his paper agreed, yet it seriously doubted that their move was well considered.[86] Their utter failure soon proved how ill considered it had been. And worse, far worse, out of this fiasco came the disastrous climax at Red River. One of the captured Canadians was tried by a summary court martial and shot: Thomas Scott, an unimportant, if unruly, prisoner, was made a grim example of Riel's authority. By his death that far-from-sovereign power was stained with a capital crime – and Canada would be divided for years to come over the retribution that the act demanded.

To the *Globe* late in March, Scott's death was certainly "foul murder".[87] But the crime would never have been committed, it argued, if Riel had not been able to count upon immunity because the Canadian government had so utterly abandoned its responsibilities.[88] Nor had Scott been killed by French Catholic half-breeds because he was an Orangeman, as many in Ontario would claim. No, it was because he was a poor man without any influence or backing that Riel had felt safe in choosing him to display his power: power that the Dominion government had actually allowed him to accumulate, by not encouraging the growth of moderating forces from the start.[89] At least now they would have to send troops. Canada would not be kicked about any longer!

Yet here the inflaming issues of "race" and religion inevitably

had entered. If, for Ontario, French Catholics had murdered
an English Protestant, in Quebec's eyes the English were
clamouring to crush the western defenders of French rights.
Brown's journal had said relatively little on the "racial" aspect
of the trouble at Red River until now, beyond briefly noting
that the French element there sought to preserve its own
identity, while its Roman Catholic clergy hoped to secure special
rights of religion and language that would create a western
Quebec.[90] But even this report, scarcely pursued, had been
largely acquired from the speeches of McDougall after his
return in February, as he vengefully sought re-election to parliament as an anti-government candidate.[91] Now, in fact, it was
the sharp reaction in the French-Canadian press that during
April brought the religious and sectional issues fully to the
Globe's attention.

The *Nouveau Monde*, it observed, had responded to Ontario
outcries against Riel by proclaiming that a new racial struggle
had begun. "Sincerely we hope that this is not the general feeling," replied the *Globe*, "and that our French compatriots have
made a great mistake."[92] When soon it appeared that *Le Pays*
and *La Minerve* were both making the North West question
one of hostility between Ontario and Quebec, the *Globe* refused
to agree.[93] Riel had unlawfully taken the life of a Canadian –
French or English did not matter – had refused to heed his
own clergy, and had acted solely for self-gratification. Where
was the racial clash in this? There was no feeling against Riel's
French followers, it declared. The West was intended for all
Canadians, and Ontario only wanted the Red River to enter
Canada with the full popular liberties she herself enjoyed.[94]
A fair argument or not, it made it apparent that Brown still did
not mean to lead the way into another sectional holy war. But
that might easily develop, as charges and recriminations were
hurled back and forth between the Canadas over the Riel affair.

It was in this angry atmosphere that talks began in Ottawa on
April 25 between the Canadian government and a delegation
from the Red River. Nevertheless, terms were reached that
would bring the settlement into Confederation as a full new
province, Manitoba, with rights for its French-speaking population guaranteed. As Brown's journal watched the progress of
the negotiations, it assuredly had hard words for Riel's schem-
ings – which had really shaped a premature demand for
provincial, not territorial, status – and for the part played by
French Catholic clergy in securing special privileges for their
flock in Manitoba.[95] But when the final Manitoba Bill stood
revealed on May 4, the *Globe*'s criticism centred chiefly on the

insignificance of the new province's area: a mere farm lot about the forks of the Red and Assiniboine that left all beyond it still as the North West Territory. Manitoba's bounds would have to be extended when the expected flood of settlers entered.[96] Quite evidently, Brown was prepared to concede the measure as a *fait accompli* and look rather to the spread of settlement to nullify the little western reserve of Quebec that it envisaged.

The Manitoba Bill still met stormy debate in parliament where the question of Scott's death fiercely bedevilled the western issue. The sudden severe illness of the Prime Minister, however, rather quelled excitement on both sides of the House, and the Bill passed on May 23. There remained the matters still of formally taking title to the North West and of sending an expeditionary force to confirm British-Canadian possession and ensure the orderly transfer of the Red River from Riel's control to the new provincial régime. These were far more than perfunctory affairs, but the crucial stage of the North West question had passed. It petered out during that summer of 1870, as the Red River accepted the constitutional settlement, the hopes of American annexationists were frustrated, and an apprehensive Riel fled the colony before the approach of a combined force of British regulars and Canadian militia. And in the East, other problems soon came to overshadow the still unsettled issue between two Canadas – that of Louis Riel, patriot or murderer.

4

Brown, of course, had merely been a commentator throughout the North West crisis; but an engrossed and influential one, affected always by two great concerns – the need to grant self-government and the need to save the West for Canada. Both ends had now been realized, and he could turn to other matters. Yet even during the worst months of crisis he had not always remained at the *Globe*. In January of 1870, for example, he had spent a week in Chicago with the inventor of the "Baines process" for rolling steel rails, which he was backing. They demonstrated it to American railroad men there, and at least obtained promises of contracts from several major American lines.[97] And in May, shortly after the Manitoba Bill was introduced, he was down in New York on *Globe* business, staying with his sister and brother-in-law, Jane and George Mackenzie.[98]

But as always, George Brown could be sure Gordon would carry on his policies in his absence. The close partnership of the brothers continued. They could share editorial control or switch it back and forth, and the paper would evince no change. Thus, late in May, Gordon could leave in turn. His health was still chronically poor. He was going to spend another summer abroad, while George once more took over solitary control.[99]

The *Globe*'s second Hoe rotary press, double the size of the first, was ready at last. Brown had it installed and in operation during June.[100] Again improvements and increased circulation seemed to go together. Tabulated daily throughout July and August, circulation rose well over 20,000 for the *Daily Globe*, and by early September reached 60,000 for all the editions combined.[101] Perhaps the Franco-Prussian War was partly responsible. At any rate, from its outbreak in July of 1870, reports of the swift, spectacular struggle completely dominated the press for months – the dazzling sequence of Prussian victories, the startling collapse of Napoleon III's empire, and then the dramatic rallying of French resistance around besieged Paris. Canadian news, other than the doings of the expedition to Red River, was almost swept aside.

Late in September Gordon returned for duty, and George Brown could be with his family at Bow Park for more than hasty visits.[102] Maddie would take him to admire their peacocks, or they would go on long tours to inspect the estate with Brontë, the dog, tours that usually ended with the little girl swung up on her father's broad shoulders. He had already done a good deal in the past four years to develop superior breeds of livestock on his farm. Now he planned to auction some of his pure-bred shorthorn cattle. On October 20, a most successful sale was held, as crowds came down on a fine autumn day to see the herds of farmer Brown.[103] He even brought the Grand Trunk to put on special trains to his station siding for the occasion – a fact that the General Manager, Brydges, gleefully drew to public attention, as proof that the railway so often attacked in the *Globe* could still be of service to its director![104]

By November, the tempo of politics was picking up, for it was known that Sandfield Macdonald intended to call an election in Ontario within the next six months. The Premier had piled up a considerable surplus in three years in office, if no very strong following, and had decided to appeal to the country on the safe ground of cash in the bank. Anyone who had axes to grind had better look to him, said Sandfield in his sharp, outspoken way.[105] The *Globe* judged that he meant to buy support, to use his surplus to divide and destroy the Reform opposition.[106]

Yet Brown was far from worried, especially now that the party in Ontario was led by Edward Blake. At thirty-six, the brilliant equity lawyer had been chosen by the provincial caucus to replace McKellar, who was anxious to step down. Brown was entirely pleased. He told a correspondent, "I have known all the public men of Canada intimately for twenty-eight years past, and I believe Edward Blake the ablest of them all."[107]

The Ontario legislature was to open on December 7. It was decided to mark the occasion with a grand Liberal demonstration in Toronto. That night, a large and lavish banquet was held in the Music Hall, accompanied by the band of the Queen's Own. George Brown sat as chairman, flanked by Blake, Mackenzie, McKellar, Senator David Christie, and all the notables of Grit Liberalism. The chairman spoke for over an hour; yet it was a mark of changing times — a slightly sad mark — that his own paper did not print even a summary of his address, though it gave the speeches of the active politicians in full.[108]

The provincial session that followed produced no particular excitement, though both sides were plainly arguing with one eye on the coming elections, and the *Globe* underlined the wrong votes of so-called coalition Liberals in a manner designed to fix them indelibly in its readers' memories. The House rose on February 15, 1871, and was shortly afterwards dissolved. The elections would take place on March 21: one of Sandfield's undoubted claims to fame was that he had put through a measure requiring all the provincial polls to be held henceforth on a single day. Mackenzie would run as well as Blake. Turning from federal politics for the moment, the Ottawa leader had agreed to be a candidate in Middlesex.

Early in March of 1871, an important development occurred in the campaign. A deputation called on Brown on behalf of a meeting of Roman Catholic electors from across the province.[109] As in 1867, some of the Catholics of Ontario were dissatisfied with their allegiance to a Conservative party that gave them little attention and was cosily entwined with the Orange Order. Need they reject the Reformers any more, now that the church-and-state issues of the old Canadian union were dead? Certainly the Grits themselves were trying to close the breach. They had put up four Catholic candidates, their opponents none.[110] And Brown had an excellent chance to help the good work forward when the Catholic deputation came to him, as the Reform leader during the past religious strife, to ask what the Liberal position was now. It enabled him to answer in a long open letter, published by the *Globe* on March 9, and widely copied.

Characteristically, his letter retracted nothing and apologized for nothing, beyond agreeing that both sides in the conflict had talked too violently, for "when men go to war, they are apt to take their gloves off." But in tracing the Reform course through the sectional and sectarian struggle in the old Province of Canada, Brown did contend that the bitter warfare had produced the happiest of results: an achievement so great that, "had the battle been ten times fiercer than it was", its accompanying evils would still sink to insignificance. "We have banished sectarian discord from our legislative and executive chambers," he proclaimed, "and have a degree of consideration for the religious views and feelings of each other that no living man ever witnessed in Canada till now." Assuredly, there was no reason now why Ontario Catholics should not rejoin a Liberal party that once they had supported strongly, in days before the Protestant-Catholic clash.

In that earlier time, Upper Canadian Catholics had been thoroughgoing Liberals, and fully shared with Protestant Reformers in fighting oligarchic government and Anglican state-church privileges. The bond might never have been broken, Brown asserted, had it not been for "the intrusion of French Canadian dictation in our affairs", during which the Catholics of the West had joined with Conservatives and French to maintain an unjust eastern domination in the mistaken belief that thereby they were upholding the best interests of their religion. But that unhappy time was past; Ontario controlled her own concerns, and had her just weight in the general union. And he would frankly ask Roman Catholics at this point, how well had they fared during their years of Conservative alliance? How many had been elected for Conservative constituencies, or even shared in the huge patronage dispensed during the period? But, said Brown, he was not trying to advise Catholics on their future course; merely to explain why there had been a breach, which need be there no more.

"All I ask," he ended, "is that they shall forget for a few minutes whose name is attached to this paper and read calmly what is written. Let them blaze away at George Brown afterwards as vigorously as they please, but let not their old feuds with him close their eyes to the interests of their country, and their own interests as a powerful section of the body politic." He himself was out of parliament and politics, he stressed, and so presented no barrier to a Catholic return to Reform. It was an effective conclusion. Catholics still might find it hard to accept George Brown, but not his successors. Furthermore, it demonstrated that Brown plainly recognized the need to dissociate the past and vanished era of Liberalism from the present. Here, in fact, was one more valid reason for his own retirement.

He had said so in the first year after Confederation, in writing to that old Reformer, Charles Clarke of Elora: "In the interest of Canada and the Reform party — it was highly expedient that I should not be in the first Parliament of the Dominion, so that old feuds might die out, and the contests of public life be freed from the bitterness that had *necessarily* grown out of the *necessarily* extreme policy forced on us to secure a reformed constitution doing justice to U.C."[111] That was still Brown's fixed position. He did not adorn his course before 1867 with any heroic Protestant lustre — and he did not regret it either. But now, in 1871, men might forget their old religious differences.

It would be impossible to measure the actual effect of Brown's letter on Roman Catholic voters. Nevertheless, it unquestionably marked a changing era in Ontario politics. For when the election of 1871 was over, Sandfield Macdonald reported to the Ottawa Macdonald chieftain regarding the Catholic vote, "two thirds of the faithful left us during the last contest, and that too without giving us the least notice".[112] Indeed, before long, Ontario Conservatives would be charging the Grits with being under Catholic influence themselves!

Despite the change, the Reform campaign in the province had been a difficult uphill fight against Sandfield's surplus, and his calling the election at the depths of spring mud, which made it hard to bring in the outlying, non-"axe-grinding" vote. But when March 21 was over, it was clear that the Blake Reformers had won the largest single group of seats in the legislature — about half the total number. Enough independents had been returned, however, that the coalition forces might still hope to stay in office by winning their support; and any politician as experienced and determined as Sandfield could be expected to try. Hence nothing would finally be decided until the Ontario house met at the usual time in the late autumn. Yet Brown felt happily confident of victory, as his attention returned to federal politics.[113]

5

The session of 1871 had opened in Ottawa in the middle of February; but it lacked Sir John Macdonald. The Prime Minister was down in Washington, serving on the Joint High Commission convened by Britain and the United States to deal with the accumulated disputes between them. Some were of particular concern to Canada also, such as the question of American access to her Atlantic coastal fisheries. One important matter was put through the Ottawa parliament in Macdonald's absence: the resolutions that would bring British Columbia into Confederation and extend Canada to the Pacific, on terms that included the completion of a transcontinental railway within ten years. In Toronto the *Globe* welcomed the accession of British Columbia; Brown had always looked for it, once the North West had been acquired. But it found the subsidy promised extravagant for so small a population, and the binding ten-year railway pledge absurd, when so little was known of the size of the task ahead.[114] The British Columbians themselves had only asked for a wagon-road at the outset. Yet the resolutions passed early in April, to herald the beginning of another era, the day of the building of the C.P.R.

In May, the proceedings of the Joint Commission in the American capital closed with the signing of the Treaty of Washington. Macdonald returned to Canada altogether conscious that, outfaced by the Americans and outweighed by the other three British commissioners, he had had to see Canadian interests sacrificed to achieve a settlement between the two great powers.[115] Canada's rich inshore fisheries had been freely opened to the United States for some unspecified future cash compensation. He had not been able to use them to bargain for a new reciprocal trade agreement. The Americans, besides, could henceforth navigate the whole St. Lawrence in perpetuity, and the "bargain" in return was similar free navigation on three Alaskan rivers. Finally, Canada's claims against the United States for Fenian damages had not even been put on the agenda, though Britain promised a grant in consolation. Fortunately for Macdonald, parliament had risen before his return. He would have a year's respite before the Canadian articles of the treaty came before the Dominion legislature for ratification. And by then, the inevitable blast of Reform indignation would have lost some of its strength, as the public's sense of outrage cooled.

For the moment, however, public feeling was high enough. The *Globe* expressed its own utter condemnation of the treaty, and George Brown personally did more. He went to Ottawa in June to call on the Governor-General. He spent two and a half hours with him, protesting the "atrocious character" of the Washington Treaty and warning of its consequences.[116] Lord Lisgar seemed frank and friendly, as he assured his visitor that he would immediately communicate these views to Mr. Gladstone, now Britain's Prime Minister. On the whole, Brown was glad that he had gone — and yet there was a most disquieting aspect to the whole interview. "*I came away, however,*" he sombrely recorded, "*with the conviction that the British government desire us to cut adrift and shift for ourselves.* He did not say so in so many words — but he kept constantly striving to get from me what I thought should be the future position of the Dominion, as its present position was 'so anomalous' and must be changed!"[117] Brown himself had no desire for change. A partnership with Britain, even a subordinated partnership for the present, was all he sought for Canada — self-government within the Empire, and room for gradual national development. He consoled himself with the thought that Gladstone and Co. were not the people of England.[118] The former might look askance at empire, in their excessive zeal to reduce costs and commitments around the world; but the British electorate would never accept a policy of casting off peoples overseas who willingly remained under the British crown.

He was at home alone now. Anne and the children had left early in June for another Scottish visit, the first in three years. He would have to join them later, because Gordon had been ill again. "No Anne in the drawing room," he said disconsolately, "no Maddie or Oda to run out and meet me on the landing, and no little fellow to make his Ba! resound through the house."[119] He shared in launching the Isolated Risks Fire Insurance Company in conjunction with William McMaster, Edward Blake, and the Conservative Alexander Campbell, all under the nominal presidency of Alexander Mackenzie.[120] He bought himself a white summer hat with an enormous brim ("look quite charming in it"), and on week-ends went for long pleasant rambles through the Indian woods at Bow Park, now in a June luxuriance of wild grape and clematis, wreathing the elders, blackberry, and brightening cherry.[121] Still, loneliness could not always be evaded.

On Dominion Day — "the dullest day I ever spent in my life" — he had to stay in town because both Gordon and his brother-in-law Tom Henning, the *Globe* treasurer, were away. He wandered through the empty, shuttered down-town streets to the *Globe* office. It, too, was deserted, and he could not bring himself to work there; his brother's and sister's houses were empty as well. He went back to his own silent home and tried half-heartedly to while the day away reading *Vanity Fair*. "What a solitary house this is without you, my dearest Anne, and our little romps. . . . You hear the clock ticking at mid-day,

and speak under your breath. I am weary to be away to you –
and have you all back."[122]

Gordon came back soon afterward, much recovered, and Brown
could look forward to leaving. He entertained the Mowats at
Bow Park, and let Mackenzie use the city house.[123] And he
received an interesting communication from South Ontario, an
address urging him to run there in the next federal election,
signed by some of his strongest opponents in 1867. "Were I telling you this as a piece of the day's news," he wrote to Anne,
"after coming in to dinner – late as usual – I fancy I hear
you saying: 'What will you do?' My answer would be: 'Do!
Do nothing.' *I shall not go back to Parliament.* But it is of
course gratifying to have these people regret what they did."[124]

It was late July, and Anne was pressing him to leave his
business ("We don't have to be wealthy"), yearning to have
him with her.[125] He sailed at the end of the month, to be in
Edinburgh by August 8.[126] They took a place at North Berwick
again, where their stay proved as delightful as before. There
was good reason for it. Brown well knew that his wife was never
so happy as in her beloved Scotland, and he revelled in her
happiness. She had adjusted to life in Canada and had good
friends there; she was devoted to her home, and to Bow Park
in particular. Nor could she bear to be without George for long.
Yet always there was a deep, recurring nostalgia for her old
home, her old friends, and her family. Longing for Abden
House, Edinburgh, and Scotland could strike her like physical
pain – even while she was as bound up in her husband as he
was in her. His life was in Canada; hers must be there also. But
he understood her feelings, nevertheless. Without any such
desire for these periodic visits to Scotland, George was warmly
glad to make them, to use his wealth and leisure to give Anne
her dearest wish. Thus these Scottish summers were idylls for
them both, different as their reasons were.

Autumn brought their return to Canada, and thrust him back
on the *Globe* in the midst of politics once more. It was provincial
affairs this time, for, as the first session of the new Ontario
assembly approached, the question as to whether the coalition
government or the Reform opposition would win the struggle
for power loomed ever larger. Sandfield Macdonald had been
judiciously dispensing patronage to secure doubtful followers,
and markedly appointing Catholics to official posts. This, he
informed Sir John, had left the Grits "flabbergasted", and
greatly pleased "the faithful".[127] By November, he was sure
he could maintain his government in the house, although there
were two by-elections and some contested election returns still

to worry about.[128] The Grits, for their part, were equally busy speech-making for the by-elections, and pushing efforts to unseat government supporters whose elections seemed especially open to charges of fraud. They, too, felt confident, as the *Globe* assured the public at large.

When the Assembly met on December 7, Blake moved an amendment to the reply to the throne speech, regretting the government's use of its railway funds. Sandfield struggled to stave off a vote; but on the fourteenth Mackenzie and McKellar moved a direct motion of no-confidence.[129] Testy, acidulous and cynical, the old premier was nothing if not game. He was ill – fatally ill, though no one knew it – yet he drew on all his power and experience to fight as hard as he had ever fought before. Matthew Crooks Cameron, his chief Conservative associate, ably supported him. Nevertheless, the flashing oratory of Blake, the relentless drive of Mackenzie, steadily wore the government down. Crowds jammed the assembly chamber to watch – Brown no doubt among them – overflowing from the galleries to the floor and even sitting on Mr. Speaker's steps.[130] When the vote at last was taken, it went 37 to 36 against the ministry.[131] That one-vote margin was crucial for Sandfield. The faint-hearted deserted him, the temporarily-won independents changed their minds. Though he still fought to stay in office, on December 19 he was crushingly defeated, 43 to 26.[132] The next day he at last gave up. Blake was called on to form a new administration, and the house stood adjourned until January.

It spelled the end of Sandfield Macdonald's career, the rejection of the coalition principle in Canada's largest province, the beginning of a Liberal régime in Ontario that would last unbroken for thirty-four years. In Ottawa, the master coalitionist was perturbed. "A most unfortunate event," Sir John considered it, "of which one cannot see the result."[133] But Grits like Brown were sure enough. Liberalism was surging forward. The next victory would come in Ottawa itself!

6

On January 18, 1872, Premier Blake met the Ontario legislature with a strong Reform cabinet that included Alexander Mackenzie, Archibald McKellar, and the prominent Roman Catholic politician Richard Scott – which signified the new connection made with Catholicism. Sure of its position, the Liberal régime set out on an active legislative programme. There were measures for roads, railways, education, social welfare, and hospitals, and also one to abolish dual representation, so that the government members themselves would have to choose between sitting at Ottawa or Toronto before the following session began. When the Assembly rose on March 2, a good deal of effective work had been done. Yet the successful session in Ontario seemed only to point to greater things. The Dominion parliament's term would end this year: there would have to be a federal election. "The close of Sir John A. Macdonald's reign is not far off," predicted the *Globe* hopefully.[134]

As March went on, Brown's journal began preparing the way for the closing session of the Ottawa parliament; above all, rewarming the Treaty of Washington, which at last would come under parliamentary debate. But before the month was over, and before the session could begin in Ottawa, Brown and the *Globe* were necessarily diverted to a problem much closer to home: nothing less than a printing strike in Toronto, which notably involved the *Globe* office.

It was the product of the Nine-Hour Movement, a widespread campaign among British and American trade unionists to cut an hour off the working-day. The movement had now come to Canada, where unionism had grown rapidly in recent prosperous years, and especially in Ontario, the leader in industrial development. Early in February, the young Toronto Trades Assembly had resolved to begin agitating for the "nine-hours system".[135] A mass meeting of workmen was held to discuss that cause in the Music Hall on February 14, presided over by J. S. Williams of the Typographical Union.[136] A month later, another meeting in the Music Hall adopted a memorial prepared by the Trades Assembly, which requested local employers to institute the nine-hour day in early June, and return an answer to the memorial by May 1.[137] As Williams of the printers' union again presided, the audience cheered a rousing call from the head of the National Labor League of the United States, the eloquent Mr. Trevallick, who told them "to trip up the law-makers", if need be — and that, when the united workers proclaimed "justice shall be done though the heavens fall, then capital yields and labour triumphs!"[138]

The printers were in the forefront of the whole movement in Toronto. Members of one of the oldest skilled trades in the city, they had organized a Typographical Society as early as 1832, and in 1866 their Society became Union No. 91 of the American National Typographical Union.[139] By 1872 they could count more than two hundred members in the newspaper, job-printing, and book-publishing offices that were an important segment of the city's business.[140] Furthermore, they had their own specific plans for improving their position. On February 17, the Typographical Union met to approve in principle an increased "scale of prices" and a fifty-four-hour week.[141] Then on February 29 they issued a circular informing their employers, the master printers of Toronto, of the new price scale and the nine-hours rule.[142] Two days later, another union meeting decided that the increase in wages and reduction of hours should be instituted on March 18, and discussed the possibility of a strike.[143] It seemed that the printers intended to put the Nine-Hour case immediately to the test, and to lead the way for the whole projected unionist offensive.

At the *Globe* office on King Street, George Brown had watched the growth of the Nine-Hour campaign with close interest and concern. His paper had not been unfriendly to the movement in its British background and first beginnings in Canada. After the Toronto trades meeting of February 14, the *Globe* had declared that reducing hours was a perfectly legitimate end, and that in the present "great prosperity" employers might well concede what they could well afford.[144] It was, however, " a question of profit and loss as between the employer and the employed; it is one that may well be discussed on social and moral grounds, but there is no law in morals or philosophy which makes eight or nine hours labour right and ten hours wrong."[145] That was the essence of it, to the *Globe*; it was not wrong for the labourer to ask — or for the business man to refuse, if he could not afford it. Nothing said that nine was "the mystical golden number and ten an abomination".[146] For Brown, consistent with his Manchester School economic liberalism, had always held that the price of labour, like any other commodity, had to be determined by the law of supply and demand operating in a completely free market.[147]

Of course, with such a view, he had never taken kindly to unions. The *Globe* had not denied the workers' right to form associations, or even their right to strike. The "principles of association" that had been applied with such good results to capital could not be called inapplicable to labour, it had said.[148] An adherent of British mid-Victorian liberalism could hardly deny the principle of freedom of association. But — and it was a large *but* — labour associations could not infringe on another basic liberal principle, freedom of contract. A union must not interfere with a non-union worker's freedom to make his own contract with an employer, nor must a strike, through suasion and intimidation, become a veritable conspiracy in restraint of trade. Accordingly, in reasoning from principles of this sort, Brown might acknowledge a union's right to exist — but very little more. It might function as a benevolent society; yet he would scarcely concede it the power it needed to ensure effective bargaining.

In this attitude to unionism, he was not very different from the bulk of employers in his day, except in two significant respects. First, his attitude was based on more than self-interest and natural class bias; it reflected an intellectually consistent set of doctrines regarding economic freedom and natural laws that he ardently believed were right and almost divinely revealed. Second, his swift, authoritative nature was no more happy to accept conditions or directions imposed by others in his business affairs than in his politics, and least of all in his newspaper office, his first love outside of his family.

It almost goes without saying, then, that Brown had fought with the printers' union before, and probably would again. The printers had struck at the *Globe* office for higher wages in 1853 and again the year after.[149] Both times the owner had kept his paper going, partly by hiring boys and young women ("Brown's harem", said the printers), though he had also made concessions to the union's demands.[150] Yet in 1854 he had even had the strike leaders arrested for conspiracy and fined a token penny each, to establish the *Globe*'s contention that the union was illegally infringing the freedom of contract — an act that might provide a precedent for other occasions.[151] In 1859 there was more friction, though less acute, when Brown and two other Toronto publishers lowered their labour rates in the bad times.[152] Then in following years relations had improved, although the *Globe* had remained officially a non-union office. There was little question that Brown generally paid good wages and was a fair employer; but he rigorously insisted on running his own concern.[153] In 1866, moreover, the union had decided that there was no quarrel left between them, and had opened the *Globe* office fully to its members.[154] And there matters had largely remained, until the movement of 1872 brought the biggest crisis of all in George Brown's relations with trade unionism.

It really began for him even before the Typographical Union issued its general circular of February 29, notifying the master printers of King Street of their new price scale and nine-hours rule. Some days earlier, a deputation of printers from the *Globe*'s own news-room had waited on the managing director to ask that their rate of pay be increased from 30¢ to 33 1/3¢ per thousand ems of type.[155] These were the night compositors, who worked overnight by gaslight to set up the next morning's daily. They were the *élite* of the trade; but as they were paid for piece-work rather than by time, the nine-hours issue was not necessarily involved in their case. In any event, Brown readily agreed to increase their rate to 33 1/3¢, to begin on March 2, although the scale at this time was still 30¢ in Montreal and 27¢ in Hamilton.[156] Obviously, however, he knew that the *Globe* could afford it. And since this was a piece rate, the question of dictating the working-time for his office – or of infringing on the "freedom" of the labour market – was not involved in the night news hands' demand.

But now came the union circular of the twenty-ninth, demanding not only the 33 1/3¢ rate for the night news hands on all the Toronto papers, but also that day compositors receive the same piece rate or else, on a time basis, work only a fifty-four-hour week.[157] Heretofore day hands at the newspaper, job-printing, or book offices had generally been paid by the ten-hour day.[158] Now they were to be paid the same for a nine-hour day: a significant jump in their wage-rate. Aside from that, working conditions for the job printers were less exacting and less arduous than for the news hands, although the same terms were now to be required for them. And beyond that again, the union's setting of the general nine-hour limit appeared to master printers of the day to be a drastic interference with their own power to control their business operations.

Perhaps the Typographical Union had been encouraged by Brown's ready granting of the increase at the *Globe* to put forward their comprehensive demands. Perhaps the negotiations at that office had been planned to open the way. Certainly the union circular made marked reference to one of the largest employers of news hands who "to his honour" had already given an increase without hesitation.[159] The master printers, however, found the announcement of shorter hours, over-all wage advances, and the tying of day hands to the night *élite* to be anything but acceptable. They met together to frame a reply; no doubt, at the *Globe*, which as the largest paper in the city, was necessarily at the strategic centre of the whole struggle, both for the union's offensive and the employers' resistance.

The latter's answer was read to a union meeting on March 13 at their own King Street quarters.[160] It conceded the 33 1/3¢ rate for night compositors throughout the city, but rejected the other provisions of the circular. And so this meeting became the critical point for all that followed, as the printers now determined to move from an announcement to an ultimatum, and to threaten a strike on March 25 if its terms were not complied with.[161] A notice of motion was already before the meeting, to stiffen its resolve and strengthen it in solidarity. As put by William de Vere Hunt, foreman of the Toronto *Leader*'s job-printing office, and signed by seventy-four day printers, it declared: "that it looks cowardly and puerile now to back down from our scale ... that we can get it now as readily as in June ... and that we are as fully entitled to a struggle for our advance as the piece hands."[162] Hunt's motion passed. With only three dissenting, the members voted to strike if necessary.[163]

Armed with this ultimatum, union delegates went to the master printers in each office. They got a chilly reception, except at the *Globe*, where the master's response was characteristically hot. Howell, the foreman of the job office who would normally deal with its employees — since George Brown kept the newspaper and job-printing operations strictly separate — was away and gravely ill.[164] Under the circumstances, Brown found the insistent union representations ill-timed in the extreme. Far from yielding, he exploded. He ordered the two men who had approached him discharged, and any others in the job office who threatened to strike.[165] And he worked with the other employers to build a common front through a Master Printers Association, which on March 19 issued its own regulations for the printing trade: 33 1/3¢ for night piece-work; 30¢ for day, or, by time, $10 for a sixty-hour week instead of $10 for fifty-four hours, as the union was demanding.[166]

On the one side, the master printers rejected any terms but their own. They agreed to pool their facilities if a strike came, and to declare their firms "non-union establishments".[167] On the other side, the union took a final strike vote on March 23, and ordered the printing offices closed to its members on Monday, March 25, at 2 a.m.[168] At the *Globe* that early morning, the union night compositors left with three cheers for the office — some indication of reluctance?[169] In any case the paper managed to appear without them, boiling with determination to shake off "the tyrannical thralldom of the Typographical Society".[170]

Assuredly the strike did not stop the flow of the printed word in Toronto. Instead it caused a flood of press debate. The *Globe* and its allies, the *Express*, the *Telegraph*, and others, seemed far from hampered, as they poured out articles on the false premises behind the strike, denying that there were any serious class differences in egalitarian Canada, such as in Great Britain, or all-powerful capitalists such as in the United States.[171] But union views found equally full expression in the Toronto *Leader*, which proclaimed the righteousness of the strike, the short-sighted selfishness of its opponents, and, above all, the iniquity of George Brown, the evil genius behind the Master

Printers Association.[172] More noteworthy, however, was the fact
that the strikers had the voice of the *Leader* at all, and that its
owner, James Beaty, alone had failed to accompany the other
master printers into their anti-union combination.

Beaty's motives were varied, and are still by no means certain. He surely felt sympathy for the unionists, matched against
intractable foes, and the *Leader*'s own version of classical eco-
nomics undoubtedly gave more scope for the rights of labour
than did the *Globe*'s. But beyond that, there were sharply
practical reasons for Beaty's not siding with Brown and the rest
of the employers. Brown was an old and bitter enemy of press
rivalry and libel suits. The *Leader* for years had been the
Globe's main opponent in Toronto, though now declining so
badly as a Conservative party organ that Sir John Macdonald
and other leading Tories were already working to establish the
Toronto *Mail* to replace it.[173] Accepting the union's case might
cost Beaty some money, but it could also put him in a very
advantageous position. While the *Globe* struggled with inadequate staff, the faltering *Leader* would have the choice of the
best printers. Furthermore, it might hope to pick up readers.
This apparently did happen to some degree, for in late March
and early April the paper was happy to publish letters and
reports on cancellations of *Globe* subscriptions and their transfer
to the *Leader*.[174]

There was also the recognized fact that Beaty, a wealthy
leather merchant and contractor, kept his paper as a side-line:
"I do not make my living by printing," he declared, as he dissociated himself from the master printers.[175] In this way, too,
he could afford to stand apart. But further, if the *Leader* was
his avocation, hobby, or his pet, it also was particularly useful
to James Beaty, Conservative politician and member for East
Toronto. Nor was it unimportant that East Toronto was one of
the very few constituencies in Canada so far where the labour
vote was sufficiently concentrated to be an important electoral
factor in spite of the qualified franchise of the time.[176] To
triumph over the *Globe*, to damage the chief Toronto Grit, to
strengthen his own position in an election inevitably close at
hand – all these were excellent reasons for Beaty's sustaining
the Typographical Union, whatever higher motives he might
have entertained as well.

Unquestionably, however, Beaty's course made it considerably harder for Brown and his allies to fight the strike. The
unionists had a good press, a strong political friend, and some
source of employment and income besides strike funds. If the
printers had failed to close the newspapers and publishing firms,

the employers were equally unable to drive the union to the wall. The unionists showed full awareness of the value of their new-found ally, for at another Nine-Hour rally in St. Lawrence Hall on April 3, James Beaty was the guest of honour. "What has produced the capital?" he cried, caught up in his new-found role. "Why, the labouring class! It is the labour put on raw material which gives all value."[177]

Meanwhile, Brown at King Street headquarters was striving diligently to bring a sufficient number of non-union printers into Toronto to break the strike. There were advertisements in the *Globe* offering jobs. He sent agents to London, Hamilton, and Woodstock; he dealt with inquiries as well from Barrie, Bothwell, and Port Dover.[178] But the strikers were working equally hard to check the use of imports and "rats" (the contemporary term for the non-striker). They, too, had agents, it appeared; among the conductors and trainmen on the Great Western, Northern, and Grand Trunk. They would report printers arriving on the trains to a union reception committee in Toronto, whereupon the latter would take the hopefuls in hand, entertain them, explain the error of their ways, and escort them to the next convenient train out.[179]

They certainly brought men who had signed agreements with Brown to break their contracts. Faced with such practices, the masters' association brought in a government detective from Ottawa in the hope of catching the vigilance committee of the union in bribery or intimidation.[180] Their "illegal and reprehensible work", fumed the *Globe*, could not be allowed to continue. The sole difficulty in filling vacancies, it said, was the dread of personal violence or persecution. "The law is perfectly clear and most effective in its operation against everything in the shape of molestation, coercion, or intimidation."[181] Indictable offences would be prosecuted!

The lines were drawn hard now, and they were spreading far beyond the original contenders. Following the two hundred printers, the book-binders had gone out on strike on March 29, and the iron trade had formed a Nine-Hour League.[182] In return, the employers of Toronto held a mass meeting of their own, to discuss the threat of a general Nine-Hour strike in June. On April 8 they issued a manifesto of defiance, signed by an impressive representation of Toronto industry.[183] And in this mood of spreading tension and angry bickering over the continued printing strike, Brown and the master printers decided on drastic action. They had taken legal counsel, and been assured that the Typographical Union could indeed be prosecuted as an "indictable conspiracy".[184] They now laid charges. Warrants were sworn out, and, on April 16, fourteen leading members of the union were arrested on grounds of conspiring to keep other workmen from their employment.

It was an extreme step, an unwise step, that might do George Brown's own cause more harm than good. Not, of course, that he was individually responsible, although the *Leader*, the union, and their friends would willingly ascribe the whole blame to him. Still, while the master printers as a group had made the move, Brown was undeniably the dominant force in their association – and the move itself did seem to show that same exasperation with determined opposition, and that same hasty, overzealous judgment, that had often been his attributes. One could add, however, that he fully believed that the printers had been acting illegally. Could they infringe on the freedom of contract and go scot-free? In the context of his time, with his own precedent of 1854 in mind – with the right to strike by no means as accepted as in a later day – Brown's part in the arrest of the union leaders was neither as unwonted nor as invidious as a later age might find it. None the less, that action had brought an entirely new phase to the printing strike, the results of which could be far broader than any altered price or time scale for the *Globe*.

7

The Ottawa parliament had opened on April 11; but Brown was still taken up with his problems in Toronto. On the eighteenth, the arrested printers were examined before Police Magistrate Macnabb, and both sides to the dispute had an impressive array of learned counsel assembled for the contest. Yet they need hardly have come at all. As soon as Kenneth Mackenzie, Q.C., acting for the master printers, had substantiated the obvious facts that there was a union and it had struck, Macnabb briskly declared that no more was necessary: a trade union was an illegal combination, and that was that. Mackenzie, rather taken aback, responded that the prosecution wished to prove overt acts by the strikers. They were separate offences, returned the magistrate flatly. Under the existing law, it was sufficient merely to prove the existence of a workmen's combination; no usage or customary acceptance of unions could in any way make their actions lawful.[185] The masters had won, hands down; yet it was not a victory they had planned for. It could prove empty indeed.

The fact was that the old common law of England was still in force in Canada; and it held labour unions to be unlawful combinations in restraint of trade. Subsequent British statutes that had recognized unions and granted them some rights had never been enacted in the North American provinces. Hence Magistrate Macnabb's opinion was well founded, however rigorously he had applied it. Nevertheless, this complete and arbitrary condemnation of the printers brought them public sympathy as the persecuted, while the master printers' own case was set aside. Their charges of coercion, inciting to violence, and the rest, were not put forward. The more than twenty witnesses they had in court were never heard.[186]

The case was adjourned till May 6, briefly resumed, and adjourned again until May 18 for a decision. Though Macnabb ruled that the printers should stand trial at the next assizes, he also observed that the law might well be changed by then.[187] In fact, it was; the prisoners were never tried. In the meantime they were out on bail with the aura of martyrs, and the masters themselves stood accused of having ruthlessly misused the law to crush their workmen, even while maintaining a combination of their own. Of course, George Brown was presented as archtyrant – a view fully publicized by the *Leader*, and by labour's own new paper, the *Ontario Workman*, as well.

And yet "the Czar of King Street" had not thought of proceeding against unions on grounds of their ancient legal disabilities. The action against the printers had really been taken under a law still in effect in England, to prevent intimidation in a strike. Associations of either men or masters were admissible to Brown – but not conspiracy or use of force. The *Globe*, in fact, made that point again early in May in regard to a local association of iron-ware manufacturers, who were seeking to exact higher prices from the saddlers who were their customers, by withholding supplies. "Prices may be raised or lowered by reason or by argument," it held, "but not by threats or tyrannical and unjust combinations which destroy the liberty of the individual."[188] The argument used here against an organization of business men Brown would equally endorse when applied to a labour union.

At any rate, the strike now quickly petered out. Perhaps both sides had been sufficiently shaken. Certainly both now were ready for discussions and concession. The employers gave some wage increases to cover the day hands, the printers gave up the strict nine-hours demand. The *Globe* by early June was even praising the "wise moderation" displayed on either side, as the union ceased to insist on "a cast-iron rule" for everyone as to the length of a day's labour, while the employers "willingly agreed" to shorten the working hours on Saturday.[189] On June 1, more-over, the union voted by more than two to one to reopen the closed offices fully and stop strike levies.[190] The great King Street strike of 1872 was officially at an end.

The whole Nine-Hour Movement was now equally petering out, and there was no more talk of a general strike in June. But aside from the fact that employers had made some concessions, there was another evident gain for the cause of unionism arising out of the printing strike. Sir John A. Macdonald had promised a measure to legalize trade unions, by making the Canadian law conform to the British. Specifically, he proposed to put into effect Gladstone's trade union legislation, enacted in Britain in 1871. The gain for labour, however, while real, was not large, since it only put Canadian unions where they assumed they had been all along. But to Macdonald, it offered easy profit in the best way possible, by stealing Liberal thunder; in this case, by adopting measures associated with the hallowed Liberal name of Gladstone. Actually, Brown and the *Globe* themselves were cool towards Gladstone's government at the moment, for ignor-ing Canadian interests in shaping the Washington Treaty. Yet there was little they could say against Macdonald's proposal. As for the Conservative leader, he had a splendid chance to be James Beaty on a grand scale: the working-man's friend, the very embodiment of his party's concern for labour.

The measure was put through before the Dominion parlia-ment rose on June 14 in expectation of the general election. And as election preparations got under way, Macdonald and the Conservatives had a further opportunity to drive home their new-found affinity for the working class. On June 19, John Hewitt, corresponding secretary of the Toronto Trades As-sembly, invited the Prime Minister to receive the grateful tribute of trade unionists in Toronto in the form of an address for himself and a golden casket for Lady Macdonald.[191] The presentation ceremony, set for July 11, was agreed to by Mac-donald, and all was ready for a touching revelation of true Tory Democracy.

It went off very well, too, at the Music Hall that night. But stories came out about the episode that soon made it look more like a well-engineered Conservative election rally. Terence Clarke, delegate of the Bricklayers Union in the Trades Assembly, began sending indignant letters to the *Globe* before the presentation occurred, to say that the whole idea of a testi-monial to Sir John had been put forward by a mysterious gentle-man who lived out of town, a "friend of labour" who refused to have his name mentioned – who had even chosen the gift and paid for it, and supplied a sketch of the address to go with it – all out of the goodness of his heart![192]

There had been no subscription taken up; the whole project had been put to the Trades Assembly at a small special meeting; and when reconsidering at the next regular meeting, on June 29, a motion to reject the whole project had only been lost by one vote. Indeed, it would still have been dropped, if Hewitt had not already committed the Trades Assembly by writing to Macdonald. But Clarke had protested heartily against this exploitation of the union movement for Conservative party purposes, and turned to reveal the inner story to the *Globe*.[193]

Naturally the Conservative press saw him simply as a Reform agent, or at least as a unionist bribed by Brown to discredit the workmen's testimonial. But in all their shocked denunciations they did not name (or deny) the unknown friend who had initiated the project and purchased the gift. Nor did they explain the strange secrecy of the proceedings, Hewitt's haste to inform Macdonald, or the supplying of a ready-made address of praise. The records of the Toronto Trades Assembly, moreover, bear out Clarke's contention as to the "stubborn opposition" there – on the grounds that Sir John Macdonald had "no great claim on the working man".[194]

Election writs were issued on July 15, however, and the affair of the Bogus Testimonial was soon submerged in general campaigning. At the *Globe*, Brown found occasion still to refer to the union question (the Grits inevitably were being called anti-labour by their foes), as he insisted that Macdonald's much-touted amendment of an obviously defective labour law was a mere election trick, "most shameless hypocrisy".[195] Yet in his paper the labour question was soon swallowed up in larger matters, such as Tory talk of protection as opposed to Liberal free trade, the Pacific railway and the Washington Treaty, the Riel case still – and always, the ineptitude of the Conservative régime, now at last to be replaced by sound Reform administration.

The *Globe* office still served virtually as Grit campaign headquarters. Hence George Brown stayed in town, while his family went to Bow Park. But he and Gordon could let each other go away for a few days' rest now and then, so that he managed to snatch several trips to the farm. The elections began in August. Daily until all hours people were scurrying in and out of the *Globe* office, reporting on progress in this constituency, asking for aid in that. When Alexander Mackenzie was away, moreover, Brown again found himself "doing leader – receiving telegrams every few minutes, arranging meetings, and despatching speakers in all directions."[196] Besides, Mackenzie had put him down to give a number of speeches himself. On August 7, the former leader was talking in Newmarket; on the 10th, addressing a party rally in Elora with that veteran Grit, Charles Clarke, now the local provincial member.[197] It really was like old times.

On August 16, he spoke for nearly two hours in the Music Hall, to help the fight against James Beaty in Toronto East.[198] But the Conservatives won a close election there, and also won Toronto West – though they lost the new seat of Toronto Centre to the Liberals. The Tories took one other urban seat, in Hamilton with an undoubted working-class candidate. [199] Elsewhere in Ontario, however, there was little labour vote as yet. Any stock the government had acquired from the Toronto printing strike and Macdonald's trade union legislation thus proved of no great consequence, after all.

Instead, it soon grew evident that the Conservatives were in serious trouble across the province. The Reform swing that had given Blake the Ontario government was being repeated in federal politics. At the *Globe*, news of victories came in almost daily, until by August 22, Brown could gladly tell his wife that "the final result does now seem doubtful".[200] Hincks had been beaten; McDougall, who had returned to the Conservative side, had been beaten; and the Grits already had gained a majority of Ontario seats, even with more constituencies still to be heard from. On August 28 came further striking news: a Liberal, John Young, had won Montreal West – and Cartier had been defeated in Montreal East! The *Globe* office was gaily illuminated that night. A procession with bands and rockets marched there, and Brown spoke jubilantly from the balcony, which no *Globe* office could afford to be without.[201] He promised Anne afterwards to bring the children the Chinese lanterns for Bow Park's harvest home.[202]

When the elections were finished, in early September, the Macdonald government held only thirty-eight seats in Ontario to the Reformers' fifty: a sizeable defeat for them in Brown's home province. They had done better elsewhere, but still not remarkably well. In Quebec the Conservatives had won thirty-eight seats to twenty-seven, seven less than in the last House. In the Maritimes, they apparently had a slight margin over the Liberals, though a number of members were still uncommitted. In the West however, Manitoba had given them three seats of its four, while British Columbia had presented all six to the government that had promised it the Pacific railway. Quebec and the West would provide Macdonald with a slim majority – but slim enough to look uncertain. Even barring some unknown catastrophe, the Conservative régime might not survive the first meeting of the new parliament.

Thus Brown had little reason to be displeased with the results, and especially with the victory in Ontario. Clearly his role in the printing strike and the union agitation of 1872 had not turned out to be of grave significance.[203] The strike and the Nine-Hour Movement had really done more to demonstrate his economic and social views than to affect his political interests.

Those interests, obviously, were still very much in being, however insistent Brown was on his retirement. He was still a leading figure in the Reform party, a prominent member of its inner circle, a powerful influence on public opinion – and his paper was stronger than ever. Some might say that if this was retirement, he had not retired very far. Nevertheless, with the passage of time, Brown inevitably had moved further back, until by now he was rather in the position of a Liberal elder statesman. And in this role he would continue to exercise his influence on Canada, in the years immediately ahead.

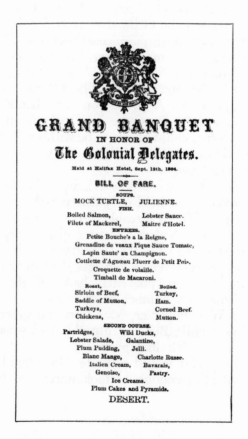

Elder Statesman

I

Brown's health had suffered again during the strenuous election summer of 1872. He never became really ill, and he kept regularly active; at fifty-three he was young for an elder states-man, after all. But two months of heat and excitement at the crowded *Globe* office — up till all hours, few regular meals — had inevitably taxed a constitution that had lost some of its earlier resiliency. The consequences appeared in digestive troubles, nagging back pains, and a state of depression and irri-tability that was quite unlike his normal bright good temper.[1] He went on a diet, and restricted himself to claret; yet basically he needed time to recuperate.[2] And so, in the weeks following the election, he was glad to rest at Bow Park.

It was sheer relaxation for him to supervise the work of the farm, to buy and sell livestock or think out more improvements. In the city he was no early riser — not after years of night work at a newspaper office. But in the country he liked nothing better than to go out very early on a clear autumn morning and cut weeds along the coach-road with a sickle, before the breakfast bell had rung.[3] He piled stones from newly-cleared fields, wan-dered with the children, went out driving with Anne. And he was luxuriously content.

Most of a tranquil early autumn was passed in this way at Bow Park, with only brief returns to Toronto, now that affairs were quiet again and either Gordon or Henning could well look after the *Globe*. George did take Anne to town for a dinner at Govern-ment House on September 25, for they were invited to be present to meet Canada's new Governor-General and his wife, the Earl and Countess of Dufferin.[4] Dufferin was paying his first state visit to Ontario, and making Toronto his residence. He liked to do things in the grand style — as befitting a very grand person — but his genial charm and generous hospitality made an excel-lent first impression.[5] Soon afterwards, Brown had his fall cattle sale to prepare for at Bow Park, which was held successfully in

mid-October despite a heavy downpour.[6] The family then returned to Toronto for the winter, and thereafter Brown visited
the farm only for brief inspections.

Back in Toronto, on October 21, he was party to a most important political conversation. He and Edward Blake called on
Oliver Mowat — to ask him to return to political life as Premier
of Ontario.[7] The legislation prohibiting dual representation was
responsible; both Premier Blake and Treasurer Mackenzie had
to choose whether they would continue in Ontario politics or in
the federal parliament, and they both preferred the larger,
national sphere.[8] But who would succeed Blake at the head of
the Ontario government? Brown decidedly was not a candidate;
Archibald McKellar had already made plain his lack of interest
in positions of command.[9] The strongest, most eminent old party
hand available was clearly Oliver Mowat, if only he could be
persuaded to return from the calm security of the judicial bench
to the heat and danger of politics.

Yet, whatever the satisfactions of the Vice-Chancellorship of
Ontario, Mowat was still a political war-horse at heart. He
showed it when he entertained the forceful pleas of Blake and
Brown, backed up the same day by a visit from Mackenzie.[10]
He proved it when, two days later, he consented to return. It was
an auspicious decision for Ontario Liberalism. Mowat might
lack Mackenzie's burning force of resolution or Blake's eloquence and brilliance; but he had more political astuteness than
the former, and a tough elasticity quite absent in the latter. In
some ways he was a local and Grit version of John A. Macdonald
— or, more conceivably, a foretaste of Mackenzie King. At any
rate, the Liberals had gained a leader who would rule Ontario
without a break until he retired undefeated in 1896.

Mowat's government, announced on October 26 amid shocked
Conservative outcries over his deserting a judicial post,[11] moved
Adam Crooks to Mackenzie's place as Provincial Treasurer,
continued McKellar and Scott in the cabinet, and brought in
Timothy Pardee as a new minister. The by-elections went off
easily; Mowat himself was acclaimed as member for North
Oxford late in November. The new ministry was solidly in office,
with the *Globe*'s blessing, and was preparing to meet the
assembly in early January, when attention reverted to Dominion
affairs once more.

The dominating question here was the Pacific railway. By the
beginning of 1873, the air was full of talk and rumours of the
plans of various sets of promoters to gain the contract for the line
to the Pacific. As the *Globe* saw it, "four railways and a bit" were
in prospect; but the chief contenders were Senator D. L. Macpherson, heading a Toronto group, and Sir Hugh Allan of

Montreal, backed by American associates.[12] Sir Hugh, however, seemed quite to expect that he would build the line, although there was no word yet of the government awarding the contract.

The word did not come till early February of 1873, when the Toronto *Mail*, the new Conservative organ in Ontario, reported that a company under Sir Hugh Allan would be granted the charter as soon as the Governor-General had returned to Ottawa.[13] It was true enough. The charter of the Canadian Pacific Railway Company, headed by Allan, was published in the *Canada Gazette* on February 20. The company was to construct the line for a grant of thirty million dollars and fifty million acres of western lands. Allan, presumably, had severed his connections with American railway interests that might make the C.P.R. merely a tributary to their lines in the United States. But there was a good deal of doubt about where he could raise the company's capital, and to what extent he was already committed to American promoters.

Accordingly, when the federal parliament opened on March 6, it met in an atmosphere of keen interest in the C.P.R. arrangements – and more than a little suspicion in Grit quarters about the nature of the transactions that had granted an enormous railway monopoly to Sir Hugh Allan and Co.[14] The Liberals at Ottawa were in fighting trim in any case, after their good showing in the 1872 elections. One sign of their new strength and solidity was the fact that they now formally elected a leader, a reluctant Alexander Mackenzie, who bowed to his sense of duty when a still more unwilling Blake refused the heavy responsibility and hard work of Dominion party leader.[15]

Parliament spent March in disposing of preliminaries. But on April 2, a Quebec Liberal, L. S. Huntington, member for Shefford, produced a startling motion for inquiry into "matters affecting the Pacific railway" – and caused a country-wide sensation.[16] As the *Globe* succinctly put it, his explosive motion simply amounted to this: "That the Prime Minister of Canada had granted the Pacific Railway in return for a bribe."[17] Allan's company was only nominally Canadian, Huntington charged, and Allan had got the Pacific charter for supplying campaign funds from his American backers to the chief Conservative ministers during the elections of 1872! "Only when the whole story is laid bare will the public be satisfied that they are not being secretly and treacherously betrayed," the *Globe* said urgently.[18] Brown was apparently unaware himself of what specific evidence Huntington had to support his demand for a committee of inquiry. But he already knew through Mackenzie that there was some cause for the demand.[19]

Yet Prime Minister Macdonald seemed to show less than

burning zeal to clear himself and his government of the sensational charge. His initial response to Huntington's motion was
merely to vote it down with the government's majority, without offering a word of reply.[20] The next day, however, in
response to the uneasiness of his own supporters, who felt that
this looked too much like suppression, Macdonald announced
that he himself would move for a select committee.[21] As
appointed on April 8, it consisted of John Hillyard Cameron,
McDonald of Pictou, and Blanchet, for the Conservatives,
Blake and Dorion for the Liberals. An "Oaths Bill" was now
put forward, to enable it to take sworn evidence. The bill
received royal assent on May 3, and not till then could the
committee plan its first meeting to hear witnesses, summoned
for May 5. But on the fourth, Sir John applied to the committee
for more delay, arguing that two important figures in the
inquiry, Cartier and J. J. C. Abbott, Allan's solicitor, were at
present out of the country.[22] McDonald of Pictou quickly produced a resolution to this very effect. The Conservative majority
on the committee carried it; the House approved it the next
day; and hence the time of reckoning was put off even further,
until July.

Meanwhile the Grit press, headed by the *Globe*, hit hard at
the "policy of delay", declaring it plain evidence of guilt.[23]
And excitement was renewed when Huntington's documentary
evidence was "impounded" by the committee on May 18. It was
a body of Allan's private correspondence that proved – so
Brown now could tell his readers – that Sir Hugh had paid out
$360,000 to the government on behalf of the Americans.[24]
Canada had been sold to United States speculators by the self-
proclaimed patriots of Confederation, and Allan was their go-
between!

But on May 21 news came of the death of Sir George Cartier
in England, where he had fruitlessly been seeking a cure for
Bright's disease. Momentarily, the turmoil over the Pacific
Scandal ceased, in the shock at the passing of one of the country's leading figures. Parliament adjourned just two days later.
It was to meet again on August 13, in order to receive the findings of the select committee.

In the interim, the battle for opinion was necessarily a newspaper conflict, as government journals strove to belittle the
entire Pacific affair, contending that it was nothing new for
business men to make campaign contributions to parties, and that
the fact that Allan might have done so in no way proved any
corrupt bargain between him and the government.[25] George
Brown, however, kept Allan's thumping $360,000 before the

public with all the power of the *Globe*. Did men make this kind of contribution without expectation of return – especially when they were seeking the Pacific contract at the same time? And did the government accept this kind of money in blissful ignorance of the donors or their interests? The very idea was ludicrous![26]

In June it was learned that the Oaths Bill had been disallowed in Britain. This gave the government new grounds for delay. When the select committee reassembled on July 2, again to begin taking evidence, McDonald moved that because of the disallowance the committee should adjourn until August 13 in order to seek new instructions from parliament.[27] The *Globe* and the Grit press protested strongly. Why could this committee not take evidence without oath, as all other parliamentary committees did? Huntington's original motion had never intended otherwise. Indeed, it now looked as if the whole Oaths Bill manoeuvre had been just another tactic for delay. Why *was* the ministry so afraid?[28]

The Liberals immediately produced their answer: a devastating retort to the latest postponement, and to Conservative contentions that no bargain had been proved between Allan and the government. On July 4 and 7, the *Globe* printed copies of Allan's correspondence with his American associates and with members of the cabinet. There in plain words was Allan's own statement to an American correspondent that he had signed an agreement with the government that gave the C.P.R. charter to a company under his presidency and control "for certain monetary considerations".[29] And there were the considerations fully spelled out: a memorandum from Cartier to Allan, for example, of initial election "requirements" that included $35,000 for Sir John, $5,000 for Cartier, and $5,000 for Langevin. There was a telegram from Macdonald to Allan just before the elections, assuring him of the government's support for his presidency of the C.P.R. – "the whole matter to be kept quiet until after the elections". And later, still more "requirements" were revealed; for instance, Macdonald's frantic telegram to Allan's solicitor, Abbott, at the tail-end of the elections: "I must have another ten thousand. Will be the last time of calling. Do not fail me."[30]

The documents were overpowering. Admittedly the Liberals could not take an unsullied line of outraged virtue, seeing that it also became clear in July that Allan's correspondence had only reached Huntington after being stolen from Abbott's office. Nevertheless, whatever pot-and-kettle calling went on in the press, and however one might minimize Conservative error and maximize Liberal connivance at theft, certain things were glaringly apparent still. At the most, the leading ministers had been guilty of gross corruption in selling the C.P.R. charter to win elections. At the least, they had displayed cynical indifference to the simplest rules of political morality by taking money for party purposes from the very men who were seeking the biggest public contract in Canadian history. Nor would it help to argue that they had taken the funds under false pretences – Allan and his friends had obviously thought that they were buying the C.P.R. And the idea that old political hands like John A. Macdonald and Cartier had sent their damning messages in thoughtless or naïve unawareness of their implications seemed too incredible for serious consideration. The more likely answer appeared to be that they had never expected to be found out.

This was the line that Brown pursued relentlessly in the *Globe* throughout July. Any plea that the money had only been given for "general purposes", said his paper flatly, "may be suggested to the marines".[31] And those who feebly argued that if Sir Hugh wanted to spend his money, he was at liberty to do so, presented "the saddest spectacle the Canadian public has ever been called upon to witness".[32] The kill seemed only a matter of time. The *Globe* was running hard for it.

But Brown himself could not keep up the pace. Perhaps because of the renewed strain and excitement at the newspaper office, his pains, digestive disorders, and depression had returned to an alarming degree.[33] Finally he decided that he should give up for a time, to go on a sea voyage, and consult the best London doctors to find if there was anything organically wrong with him.[34] Furthermore, there were matters to transact for Bow Park on the other side of the Atlantic. On July 21, therefore, he left the Pacific Scandal in mid-course, and set out alone for a brief visit to Britain. No doubt his departure at this juncture illustrated his declining personal connection with politics and the fact that the *Globe* could keep up its pressure without him. But even during his absence Brown would still have a role to play in the Scandal – for his political importance was not quite finished yet.

2

The *Globe* had opened a London office in Cheapside, and Brown made this his headquarters, after arriving from Liverpool on August 4.[35] Three days later he was able to see a doctor recommended by an old political opponent, Sir John Rose, a London banker and baronet now, and Canada's unofficial representative in England. This was Dr. Pollock, who had been Lord Metcalfe's physician in Canada thirty years before.[36] His latest Canadian patient was much impressed with him, and vastly relieved to learn, after a thorough examination, that his own troubles were simply the result of overwork. Three months off, lying on a beach reading novels, eight hours' sleep a night, good food, no physic, and "a good jorum of good wine every day" – such was Dr. Pollock's prescription. "Live well and don't think – Let that big brain of yours rest for three months!"[37] Small wonder he was a popular doctor. And George wrote jubilantly to Anne, "I know you will rejoice with me that I am not to be a croaking, disagreeable, dyspeptic old fellow, the plague of all around him and especially of his wife – yet awhile!"[38]

Now he turned to a political mission that Alexander Mackenzie had enjoined on him just before his leaving for England.[39] He was to interview the Colonial Secretary, Lord Kimberley, in order to make certain that he knew both sides of the story of the Pacific Scandal, seeing that the Crown's representative in Canada displayed marked sympathy with his existing Conservative ministers. A personal friend and fond admirer of Sir John Macdonald, Lord Dufferin had been ardently unwilling to believe wrong of him.[40] The Liberals had reason to doubt the constitutional impartiality of Canada's Governor-General, and in particular, they feared that he would continue to accede to the cabinet's evasive tactics – that he might kill the parliamentary committee of inquiry, in fact, by proroguing the legislature as soon as it reassembled on August 13.[41] Thus the importance of obtaining some assurance from Dufferin's superiors of a properly non-partisan attitude towards the Pacific case; above all, so that its investigation might effectively go forward in Canada.

Brown got his interview at the Colonial Office on August 9; and at once the value of his position outside of parliament became apparent. Lord Kimberley carefully noted that while he "could not receive any communication from the parliamentary opposition of any colony" he was ready to hear suggestions from a prominent inhabitant.[42] His visitor as carefully answered that he had not come to discuss "the painful matters that have recently occurred in Canada", or the actions of the imperial government in that connection. He merely wished to point out that it had been "almost officially" intimated in the Dominion that when parliament met on August 13 it would be prorogued without enabling the adjourned committee of inquiry to recommence its work, and without any discussion of the grave questions at issue.[43]

In response, Kimberley gave a lengthy explanation of the imperial government's position. "He laid down precisely the line of non-interference in our local matters that the Liberal party has so long maintained," Brown was glad to tell Mac-kenzie.[44] The Colonial Secretary, he added, was most guarded in assuming everyone implicated in the Scandal to be innocent until proven guilty, yet "quite acquiesced in the necessity of a full inquiry". Kimberley declared that he could not step in beforehand, in advance of the proceedings of the thirteenth, but assured Brown that the British government was well aware of their implications. The latter withdrew satisfied that "the Colonial Minister is fully posted on the whole matter, quite alive to its extreme importance, and is watching closely what goes on".[45]

Consequently, when on August 14 Brown learned by tele-gram that Dufferin had indeed immediately prorogued the reconvened Dominion parliament, he was not as upset as he might otherwise have been.[46] "I think," he said, "that when the matter is properly understood – as now it *must* be – the public feeling here will be entirely with the opposition."[47] That same day, moreover, Kimberley wrote admonishingly to Dufferin, "I cannot doubt that you are fully alive to the necessity of a thorough and immediate investigation into the astonishing charges against the ministers."[48]

Actually, the Canadian cabinet were ready by now to bow to that horrid necessity; but they still hoped to find a more favour-able instrument for their own examination than a committee of the House. They wanted a royal commission instead, which they would name, which would be outside parliament and would not report to it. Dufferin had already secretly signed the authority for such a body in early August; it now replaced the defunct parliamentary committee.[49] The spectacle of the latest "Crom-wellian prorogation", however, had not done the Dominion government's cause any good.[50] Their continued manoeuvres only seemed more damaging; and since parliament was to meet in any case for an autumn session, they would yet have to face the likelihood of a vote of censure. Meanwhile, in London, George Brown was busily exploiting the public reaction against the Canadian ministry. He breakfasted and dined with one of *The Times*'s chief political writers on the thirteenth – "and pumped the whole thing properly into him".[51] Delane, the *Times* editor, the next day promised a decided editorial based on documents that Brown supplied. Brown did his best with other papers, too (called it "putting the press men right"), and saw the *Saturday Review* and the *Spectator* come out strongly for truth and justice according to his light.[52]

These political efforts kept him in London longer than expected, and away from relaxation in Scotland. He did, however, manage to look after business for Bow Park, as he bought new breeding stock to improve his growing herd of shorthorn cattle and acquired a new Bates bull of which he was specially proud.[53] Then Brown left for two weeks in Scotland, visiting some of the Nelsons holidaying at Nairn on Moray Firth, and others in Edinburgh.[54] At length, on August 30 he took passage home, benefited in every way by a satisfying trip, and was back with his family at Bow Park before the middle of September.

A royal commission of three judges was sitting all that month, taking evidence on the Pacific Scandal. The testimony, printed daily in the press, did the government little good, even with Macdonald regularly on hand to cross-examine witnesses and to make a vigorous assertion of his own guiltlessness that culminated in a ringing declaration, "These hands are clean!" ("As clean as ever they were, at any rate," the *Globe* sourly commented, "and that is a comfort.")[55] The commission ended by simply transmitting the evidence it had collected without offering an opinion; but parliament, to meet again on October 23, was bound to make good that omission. And as October moved onward, Brown's journal was still working hard to shape the verdict, republishing long editorials from the metropolitan press of Britain, which held the charges against the Canadian ministers to be proven and deplored their sad failure to maintain the standards of British parliamentary government. As *The Times* said trenchantly, who could doubt that those who took the cash knew what it was for?[56]

Beneath all the discussion Brown saw a deeper issue, fervently expressed in a *Globe* editorial of October 21, two days before parliament's meeting. It was not too much to claim, it announced, that the world's eyes were on Canada now; and the question that faced the country was far more than the guilt or innocence of its governors. By their actions they had corrupted the electorate, degraded great national interests, forced down the whole level of public life. Parliament now must show if it grasped these frightening facts. "Shall the highest servants of the nation, the chosen advisers of the Crown, be suffered to maintain their position by selling the public interests and public lands for gold, and pandering to the lowest and most sordid motives?" If so — if ministers could thus misuse their power — "then representative institutions would be neither more nor less than a blind for a despotism erected on the ruins of public morality".

Without doubt, this was Brown's heartfelt view, and not just politics; he looked anxiously to parliament to redeem the nation. When parliament met, it faced up to the task. As fierce debate went forward on a motion of censure by Alexander Mackenzie, the sound of going in ministerial ranks grew ever more apparent. The government's majority shrank day by day; by November 3 Brown could deem its defeat assured.[57] And on the fifth, Sir John A. Macdonald recognized the inevitable and resigned, at least depriving his foes of the ultimate pleasure of pulling him down. Said the *Globe* in pious exultation, "The hand of the defiler is removed from the Ark of the Covenant."[58] The devious, unprincipled, demoralizing reign of John A. was over at last, and a crucial victory won for political integrity. It remained for the Liberals to show what they could do with it.

Alexander Mackenzie was sent for, while parliament stood adjourned. On November 7, the *Globe* could proudly announce the membership of the first federal Liberal cabinet. Mackenzie headed it, of course, and had also taken the exacting position of Minister of Public Works to set the shop in order. Blake had resolutely refused a post, until a powerful petition from the Liberal caucus (and perhaps an urgent telegram from Brown) brought him to accept the Presidency of the Council on the understanding that it would only be for a short time.[59] Dorion became Minister of Justice; but Holton refused to take the finance ministry, or any other office, for "personal reasons".[60] Hence the financial post fell to Richard Cartwright of Kingston, once a Conservative, but lately a confirmed enemy of Sir John Macdonald. Senator David Christie – an original Clear Grit, Brown's old schoolmate in Edinburgh and now a neighbour at Bow Park – became Secretary of State. Albert Smith, ex-Premier of New Brunswick, was named Minister of Marine and Fisheries, and D. A. Macdonald, Sandfield's brother, Postmaster-General. The rest of the ministers Brown had had little or no contact with. Yet he could readily acknowledge the new government to be effectively and most promisingly constructed – full of Ontario Grits as it was.

But there was one more appointment announced within a few weeks of the establishment of the Mackenzie ministry. In December, George Brown was named to a vacancy in the Senate.[61] This was a party reward that the retired politician was willing to accept. It gave him a re-entry into the world of parliament, and took him back to the capital, but only in a limited, qualified way that did not impose the heavy burdens of political life once more. The Senate was an easy-going body of appointees; he was fairly free to attend or not, as he saw fit. And though he held no high idea of the authority of the Upper Chamber, Brown could undoubtedly appreciate the dignity of the title Senator, just as he might enjoy a partial return to parliamentary debate.

Accordingly, as 1873 ended, George Brown could mark it as a year of notable transition. The Grits were in power; he was named to the Senate, the proper home for elder statesmen. And he was about to have an opportunity to enlarge on that role; this time as a diplomat and plenipotentiary for the Liberal régime that he had worked so earnestly to found.

3

On January 2, 1874, parliament was dissolved, as Alexander Mackenzie prepared to make sure of his new government by an appeal to the country. The next few weeks were full of election campaigning until the polls opened late in January in Ontario and Quebec. Then it rapidly became clear that the elections, held in the aftermath of the Pacific Scandal and in popular revulsion against the old régime, were going sweepingly in favour of the Liberals. They took all three Toronto seats, for instance; this time James Beaty was obliterated. Even by January 31 they had won decisively in Ontario and Quebec, and the returns that came in from the Maritimes and the West through early February only confirmed the fact that when the Mackenzie ministry met the new House, it would command an overwhelming majority.

Brown played no important part in the contest, except, of course, at the *Globe* office, which was busy throughout issuing broadsheets and pamphlets on the Pacific Scandal, advertised in job lots.[62] But as soon as the elections were secure, he turned his mind to a new task Mackenzie had to offer him: to reopen negotiations for reciprocity with the United States.

It would be a national triumph if the benefits of reciprocal free trade could be restored, and no less a party triumph if Liberals could succeed where Conservatives had failed. Closely associated as Brown was with the Mackenzie régime and long identified with the question of reciprocity, he was an obvious choice as emissary to Washington. "Though truculent and narrow-minded," wrote Dufferin (not one of his warmest

admirers after the *Globe*'s activities during the Pacific Scandal),
"Mr. Brown is a man of considerable force and ability, thoroughly at home in this particular subject — of which he has
made a hobby — and well regarded by the present Government of the United States."[63] Even before the new Liberal
régime had faced its general elections, in fact, Alexander Mackenzie had told the former Grit leader that Blake was coming
down to see him in Toronto to discuss "a mission we would like
you to undertake for us".[64]

Brown was more than willing to accept the assignment.
Naturally, the memory of his resignation in 1865 over the
handling of reciprocity negotiations was with him still. Here
was the chance to prove he had been right where his opponents
had been wrong. He still believed that Canada had a good deal
to offer in the way of a commercial bargain, that she need not go
to Washington cap in hand; and that Americans could be
brought to recognize the value of freer trade with Canada in
their own national interest. Beyond that, however, he saw the
possibility of acting at this particular juncture, before the terms
of the villainous Treaty of Washington had been fully carried
out.

In granting the use of Canada's Atlantic fisheries to the
Americans, the Treaty of 1871 had provided for compensation
to be paid by the United States, the amount to be determined by
a commission appointed to arbitrate the case. Why not seize
upon the fact that the commission had not yet been convened to
offer the republic access to the fisheries in return for a reciprocal trade agreement, as under the old Treaty of 1854? Brown
considered that the Americans would have to pay more than
they bargained for, under any fishery arbitration. They might
well prefer granting trade concessions to making a cash payment. At any rate, such a proposal would permit the testing of
opinion on alternatives that the United States now might accept
in the way of trade arrangements.[65]

Henry Rothery, a distinguished English jurist and Registrar
of the Admiralty Court, had been in Canada late in 1873, preparing the Canadian case for the projected fishery arbitration.
At Ottawa, the Liberal government had raised the question of
reciprocity with him; and at Toronto, on Rothery's way to
Washington, an eager Brown had strongly urged him to suggest to the American authorities the substitution of a general
commercial treaty for the fisheries settlement.[66] In January of
1874 Rothery reported to Lord Dufferin from Washington that
the Americans were indeed interested in the idea of avoiding
cash payment through some new agreement.[67] And so, as soon

as the Dominion elections seemed safe enough, the Mackenzie cabinet dispatched George Brown to the United States, to make a first informal trial of the field.

By February 9 he was in Washington,[68] then under the lax and lavish administration of Republican President Ulysses S. Grant. It was the glittering, strident era of Reconstruction and Big Business rampant in the United States. Brown found a capital of mud and half-complete magnificence, opulent and ramshackle, aspiring and corrupt. As Canada's agent, he at once set out to see as many of Washington's politicians as possible, driving about town in a resplendent brougham lined with cherry satin — complete, he noted, with "a portly dignified coloured gentleman on the dickey in full blazing livery and buttons that would fairly have stolen the heart of Ginney!"[69]

The Canadian visitor conferred as well with Rothery and the British Minister in Washington, Sir Edward Thornton; and thought the former rather vain and ignorant of "the Yankee animal", but the latter "a very quick subject".[70] He also saw Hamilton Fish, Secretary of State in Grant's administration, with whom any formal negotiations for reciprocity would have to be conducted.[71] But he concentrated on members of the Congress, whose votes would ultimately decide the fate of any agreement, talking steadily in an effort to consult all the leading figures among some 300 representatives. "Our M.P.s are not all Solons," he told his wife a little wearily, "but they are quite up to the Yankee mark."[72]

Still, the administration seemed favourable, and so did many of the most important men in Congress. The weighty Senator Sumner, an old acquaintance, was fully with him; they spent two hours together on February 12, drafting plans.[73] And it was "a great haul", Brown felt, when he won the support of Ben Butler, an unlovable but powerful Republican member of the House, who previously had been anything but friendly to the Dominion. "I was afraid to go at him," Brown confessed, "when he was brought to me at his own request . . . and we were soon as thick as thieves."[74]

All in all, results appeared to indicate that a reciprocity measure would have an excellent chance of clearing Congress. Of course, George Brown was always an enthusiast, expecting what he hoped for. "I feel confident," he finally concluded, "that were a bill for the renewal of the Reciprocity Treaty submitted to both houses next week, it would be carried."[75] Yet he did not blind himself to dangers along the way: "Whether such a bill will get before Congress and what new influences may arise to affect its chances when it does, is a different thing."[76]

He left to report to Ottawa, on February 19, feeling "matters at Washington continue as favourably as could possibly be desired".[77] Nevertheless the cautionary fear remained that "by some accident or whim the castle may be toppled over even at the last moment of completion".[78] In any case, the venture was still very much worth trying.

Mackenzie and the cabinet agreed. The next step was to request the imperial authorities to appoint a commission to negotiate officially with the United States, on which the Honourable George Brown should serve. Dufferin transmitted the request to the new Colonial Secretary, Lord Carnarvon, in the Disraeli government that had now replaced Gladstone's.[79] On into March the cables and dispatches went back and forth between Ottawa and London, as the imperial government approved the appointment of a Canadian to act as joint commissioner with Sir Edward Thornton and concurred in the naming of George Brown. Dufferin told Carnarvon that Brown had made "a very favourable impression" on Thornton – who had written to say that he would be very glad of his selection.[80] Meanwhile, the prospective Canadian commissioner made his own preparations. Anne would go with him to Washington, while Gordon would postpone a trip to California, if necessary, in order to look after the *Globe*.[81]

Brown's commission was issued on March 17; but it was well towards the end of the month before he could get away to the American capital, and settle into a suite at the Arlington with Anne. Hence he and Thornton would not formally initiate negotiations with the American Secretary of State until March 28. Yet as soon as he reached Washington, Brown recognized that things had "considerably changed" since his visit of five weeks before.[82] A fierce struggle over a bill to inflate the currency with more paper greenbacks was dominating Congress and dividing the government. There was a scandal in the Treasury over the "Sanborn contracts", further shaking Grant's rather sleazy administration. And the fact that congressional election campaigns were already in sight would scarcely encourage politicians to welcome any removal of duties from Canadian products that might make new taxes necessary. The whole mood in Washington had altered, markedly for the worse.

In consequence, Thornton had all but lost the cautious hopes he had entertained earlier.[83] He was a naturally gloomy individual, however – somewhat like Brown in physical appearance, but not at all in temperament. As for the latter, he boldly refused to be disheartened, asserting that he had calculated on difficulties like these. Yet the first draft of the report that the

Canadian representative framed to send back to the Prime Minister in Ottawa suggested a little more doubt than the firm avowal he finally transmitted.[84]

And when he and Thornton saw Mr. Secretary Fish on the twenty-eighth, Brown had to note that the chances for reciprocity looked much less hopeful: "His tone was far from being as decided as it had been to Sir Edward, Mr. Rothery or myself in our separate interviews with him in February."[85] When the two commissioners reminded the Secretary of his earlier, more positive stand, that solemn-looking but adroit official skilfully "rectified his position", assuring his visitors of his own personal desire for reciprocity but gravely refusing to say what he himself would propose to achieve it.[86] He was a difficult man to fathom, this Hamilton Fish: a personage of dignity, wealth, and family tradition, very different from the late arrivals and speculative politicians who were his colleagues in Grant's administration. At sixty-six, he was also, however, a capable and experienced foreign minister, whose heavy features and phlegmatic manner belied the keen, bargaining brain behind them. The British commissioners withdrew from their first official interview with the ponderous Mr. Fish, promising as amiably as possible to draft proposals for his consideration. Brown debated whether the Secretary "was really afraid to proceed – or playing a game for better terms?" He decided, "Probably both these considerations influenced his course."[87]

In any event, after some discussion, Brown, Thornton, and Rothery (who was still in the background) determined not to be discouraged by Fish's attitude, but to prepare a strong explanatory paper on Canada's position "fit to go before the executive, the Senate or the people", and to support it by widespread personal interviews, together with a press campaign.[88] Brown, it seemed, was quickly discovering the true scale of problems that beset the negotiator in the United States capital – and briskly reacting in the best tradition of the Washington lobbyist.

As the most forceful personality in the British team, with the strongest interest in reciprocity, the Canadian representative inevitably took the lead as negotiations proceeded. "Mr. Brown does most of the talking," Fish recorded in his own diary.[89] At the same time, however, the British Minister's dignity was a little bruised by this impetuous colonial invading the high preserves of imperial diplomacy, and Thornton had already been somewhat put off when Brown had seemed slow to join him at the start through settling his affairs at home.[90] There could be internal trouble in the mission. Furthermore, when

Albert Smith, the Minister of Fisheries, came down from Ottawa early in April, and tried fussily to guide activities for the Dominion, he soon learned that George Brown would stand no interference with his position as Canadian plenipotentiary.[91] The fisheries minister left hastily, with a flea in his ear.

Undoubtedly Brown's strong will was asserting itself again; not in any jealousy for status, but in rigorous concentration on his goal. Yet Alexander Mackenzie fully backed him in keeping the task of representing Canada to himself, and even apologized for Smith's behaviour, while Thornton came tacitly to yield the initiative to his zealous colleague.[92] Thereafter the two of them got on very well. The commission's internal frictions subsided, if its external problems remained.

The spring was cool in Washington that year, although the controversy over the currency bill was not. Times were bad. The trade slump that had followed a panic on the New York Stock Exchange the previous autumn was now being recognized as a general depression; indeed, its long-continued reign over North America and the world beyond would ultimately make it the "Great Depression" of the later nineteenth century. Under the circumstances, the advocates of greenbacks in the United States were loud in their demands for more currency inflation as the national economic cure. The question of reciprocity with Canada was bound to seem small beer by comparison – inevitably so.

But Brown had little time for such considerations, as for three weeks he worked away in the British Legation drafting a paper of proposals to lay before Fish, collecting both American and Canadian statistics on trade and compiling lengthy arguments on the subject. He finished his memorandum and sent it up to Ottawa for approval on April 22; had it back, and worked feverishly at last-minute changes over the week-end of the twenty-fifth and twenty-sixth, in order to present it to the Secretary on the Monday.[93] He was more resolute than sanguine now. The elusive Fish had to be brought to solid land. "We will go at it might and main," he told Mackenzie, "and the cry is 'Victory or Westminster Abbey!' "[94]

4

The memorandum the two British commissioners took to Secretary Fish on April 27 embodied proposals that the Canadian government had drawn up for George Brown at the outset: renewal of the Reciprocity Treaty of 1854 for twenty-one years, with free admission this time of selected manufactures as well as natural products; free access to the Canadian fisheries, instead of compensation under the Treaty of Washington; and free navigation of the Canadian canals, to be deepened for heavier traffic at Canada's expense.[95] There were other terms besides; but these were the essential inducements meant to win American agreement. Yet the Secretary viewed the document with glum disappointment, expressing his inability to see in the Brown-Thornton proposals any basis for reciprocity measure that Congress might accept.[96]

Brown sent some vivid private comments on their interview back to Lord Dufferin.[97] They not only showed frustration, but also painted a somewhat irreverent picture of their adversary: "He is very particular, is Mr. Fish. A very great man, indeed, as becomes a Secretary of State who counts his wealth by millions and is sick of public life. . . . He enters the 'audience chamber' with a very grand air — and shakes hands with great empressement — talks of the weather and every conceivable nothing until he forces you to begin — and then sets himself to negotiate with you exactly as you could fancy a great London fish-dealer, down at the seaside for the health of his brats, dickering with the fishermen of the little place he honoured with his presence — for their morning catch."

"But the funny part of it is," Brown added, "that in his own house he is courteous and affable and a most kind and entertaining host." In any case, he well knew that he had to meet the game that the spokesman of the United States was playing: "First piece of diplomacy — that only half an hour was to be allowed to us." Thornton and he protested, asked for an hour; and were informed that there was another pressing engagement at one o'clock. "Don't be shocked — " Brown told Dufferin "your ambassador had the audacity, though in the most diplomatic terms, to suggest whether the other party might not be negotiated with for 30 minutes' delay. And the great man yielded. Private secretary instructed to inform John Smith, should he present himself, that at 1:30, and no sooner, could he be admitted to the presence."

"No interpreter being at hand to translate my Scotch," Brown continued, "Sir Edward read the paper and read it well. For me nothing was left but to watch the humour of the Secretary's face, and very amusing it was. Curiosity, at first, was evidently uppermost — with a few questions thrown in jauntily to show knowledge of the subject. Presently, as the argument grew stronger, positive interest with a shadow of surprise stole over the Secretary's features and movements – and once or twice the lips opened for a question, but closed again without the utterance being completed . . . very soon Mr. Fish became completely abstracted and moody – turned in his chair uneasily – put his hand over his face – and said not a word until the paper was finished. The grand air was gone. He said: 'Well you know there is a great deal in this that is all well enough from your point of view – but I am disappointed at your proposals.' "

At which of them, they asked. "Well – the coasting trade." Joint access to the coasting trade was only a suggestion to go with the improvement of the Canadian canals, Thornton answered. What else? "Oh well, the patent clause." That was a concession to the United States – but strike it out. Anything else? "Ah well – no textiles." Free admission of textiles might cover a great deal more than Mr. Fish perhaps would want, replied Brown; but they would consider any suggestions in that direction. " 'Ah well-um-' he would read the paper carefully and see us again." He could name no day, but would try to do so that week. "And here the interview ended," said Brown wryly, "with mutual assurances of distinguished consideration."

What to make of it? Was Fish simply uninterested, really doubtful that any agreement could pass Congress – or just trying to extract the last ounce? "I have a strong suspicion that the old gentleman's 'disappointment' about our proposals," Brown averred, "arises from our frank statement in them that whatever articles were made free to the United States [in trade with Canada] must be made free to Great Britain." That is to say, Fish had hoped to gain the Canadian market for American manufactures such as textiles without having to meet British products competing on an equal basis. But Brown was firmly opposed to the idea of giving American goods a privileged position in Canada through preferential duties over British goods, or to anything like a North American customs union. Fish, he told Dufferin, might well have such a notion in mind. "If he proposes this – that we are to put on differential duties against Great Britain for the benefit of the States – I hope Thornton will let me answer in my own name for Canada, free from any constraint which his name being conjoined with mine might be supposed to have had over the character of that answer."

Yet whatever was the true explanation of Fish's attitude, the commissioners could only discover it by continuing the negotiations. "I have strong hope that Mr. Fish *must do something*," Brown declared. He still felt that a majority in the Congress were favourable in spirit, although "entirely ignorant of the facts", and that, if Fish could be induced to sign a treaty and send it forward as a government measure, it would pass the Senate. But Brown also recognized a different and ominous possibility: that Fish "may lack the courage to do this – and may propose to toss our paper before the Senate and leave action with them." Without positive endorsement by the administration, such a measure could be as good as lost.

But they must try. They must go on with the bargaining, make Fish talk, and at the same time try to bring pressure on him to induce him to sign a treaty. The interviews went on through May. The Secretary blew alternately warm and cold on detail after detail, without really approving the outline as a whole; and Brown and Thornton grew more and more convinced that "his official manner is put on for diplomatic purposes".[98] Meanwhile, the Canadian commissioner was busy showing his memorandum confidentially to leading administration supporters in both houses, and gaining their promises to urge Fish on.

Senator Conkling would do so, General Garfield, Minister Schenck, and others.[99] Anne Brown had to leave Washington to return to her children in Toronto in early May; but her husband began giving a series of intimate little political dinner parties on his own.[100] He set out as well to interview every senator personally – although the death of Charles Sumner in March had robbed him of his closest contact in the Senate. Apart from these efforts, Brown undertook to shape a broad publicity campaign for a Canadian reciprocity treaty. Through Cyrus Field, promoter of the Atlantic cable, he arranged to meet representatives of some of the leading American newspapers for a friendly dinner at Delmonico's in New York on May 2; the New York *Tribune*, Chicago *Tribune*, Louisville *Courier-Journal*, and Springfield *Republican* were among those represented.[101] He went hurrying to New York with editorials, which he succeeded in planting in the *Times*, *Tribune*, and *Herald*, and brought the Associated Press to issue what he called "my grand manifesto" throughout the papers of the country.[102] While Thornton watched the diplomatic front, Brown tried bombing in the rear.

It seemed to have its effects, not merely in favourable press comment and resolutions passed by the New York, Chicago, and other Boards of Trade, but also in more amiable treatment from Hamilton Fish.[103] "I had a most pleasant interview with Fish on Monday," Brown wrote Anne on May 21, "and his friends all say he means to sign a treaty. We will see."[104] In fact, just four days later, it appeared that a break-through had been finally made.

They still had to push for it, however. By now it really did look as if the Secretary had been playing his "humbugging game" in an attempt to have differential duties against British goods inserted into a trade agreement with Canada.[105] Accordingly, Brown and Thornton resolved to settle the issue one way or another. On May 25 they opened their discussions with Fish by asking point-blank if differential duties were a prerequisite of an agreement; for, if so, they must break off the negotiations at once. Thus faced, the Secretary gave ground remarkably – "got completely off," said Brown, "and spoke freely."[106] He reassured them of his own earnest desire for a treaty; declared that differential duties were the only sure way, but would be glad to see the Senate accept a measure without them. And he asked the British commissioners to prepare a draft agreement on the basis of Brown's memorandum, which would be sent to the Senate by the President before signing, in the same way as the Treaty of Washington.[107] Brown was jubilant: "If it goes as we have it, it will make Canada a grand country ere many years!"[108] Yet still he was careful: "But we may find it too good, and it may be smashed in the Senate, or before it reaches there."[109]

Now the drafting got under way in earnest, while the temperature in Washington climbed up through the eighties. One critical question concerned the list of manufactures proposed for free admission in the treaty, including various cotton, iron, leather, and other goods. Alexander Mackenzie feared that removing duties from such a selection would mean very considerable losses to Canada's revenue. "Big no doubt, but nothing in comparison with enormous gains," Brown telegraphed to his Prime Minister. "But never mind – we will fix it."[110] He rushed briefly up to Ottawa at the beginning of June for that very purpose. Back in Washington with amendments to the list, Brown put Ottawa's views to the Secretary of State on June 6, and won his acceptance after a hard fight. But Fish added provisos, the most serious of them the surrender of the right of passage through Nova Scotia's Gut of Canso to the United States forever.[111]

It was a matter of political feeling rather than economic consequence – the hardest kind of issue to settle. Brown was sharply worried until he hit upon a counter-demand: similar perpetual free passage through Pacific channels around the San Juan Islands, recently declared to lie in American waters.[112] That settled talk about the Gut of Canso! Other problems continued: whether the Canadian canals should be deepened to twelve or fourteen feet, whether salt and malt could be included in the free list, whether the reduction of lumber duties should be postponed. Fish still had to be pushed constantly, was still solemnly producing new demands. Brown was up at five and working till all hours, and it was well over ninety in Washington now.[113]

And time was running out as well. Congress was to adjourn on June 22; it would almost certainly not sit longer in the heat. To add to the delays produced by Fish's cavilling, Derby, the British Foreign Minister, had to have the entire text of the draft treaty cabled to him for approval – and then did not reply. "Three precious days absolutely lost because Lord Derby has not signified his assent," wrote an exasperated Brown on June 10.[114] "We have hardly a moment to spare, but still we cannot move!" Nevertheless, he still was hopeful of the Senate, if only there were time enough.[115]

In all, there were five days of suspense before Derby's consent finally arrived on June 11. Brown and Thornton went back to Fish directly, and the trouble started all over again. "This would not do and that would not do; [so Brown recorded] in short there was no hope unless we made a lot of concessions now proposed for the first time – within ten days of the adjournment of Congress!"[116] They withdrew again, "Thornton very much downcast and very mad at the old fellow." Brown's own reaction was equally typical: "My bump of hope as usual kept me from despair and determined me to make one last effort to bring Mr. Fish back to reason."[117] He should see the Secretary alone, it was decided. He called on him next morning at the State Department.

George Brown was "as grave as a parson" as he informed Fish that even if the Canadian government should agree to these latest terms, he personally would not advise, accept, or sign a treaty that was as one-sided as that which the Secretary now proposed.[118] Again a firm stand worked. "The old fellow evidently got alarmed," Brown thought, "looked a little foolish", and presumably felt that he had overplayed his hand.[119] At any rate, Fish was ready to discuss the Canadian's objections to his latest terms – eight in all. They had a long hard tussle; but "slowly and painfully, like pulling teeth", Hamilton Fish gave up six out of the eight, compromised on one and left as the only significant concession to the United States that Canada would build a canal at Caughnawaga on the St. Lawrence without any compensating measure.[120]

That should have been the end; yet it was not. Though Fish now seemed eagerly co-operative and suggested positive improvements in the treaty, Brown could not help wondering whether he was really scheming to delay them past the session:

"At his time of life, to go into so elaborate a cheat without any gain seems incredible."[121] But then on June 15 – with Congress's adjournment a week off and the treaty to go to the Senate the next day – Fish objected to a lack of uniformity in canal tolls.[122] They were at a standstill once again. It took two more days of discussion and wires to Ottawa to settle it, until at last, on June 18, the treaty actually went forward to Congress. That was on a Thursday. They had till the Monday for it to pass through the committee stage, reach the floor, and be considered – with Sunday in between!

Brown was asked to the White House on the night of the eighteenth; President Grant was most complimentary, and "broke out most enthusiastically for the Treaty".[123] The same day the Senate had considered the draft agreement in secret session, and passed it to the Committee on Foreign Relations for report. But when on the twentieth Brown was able to get a copy of the message the President had sent to the Senate with the treaty, he had to put far less stock in Grant's enthusiasm. The President's words, he thought, were fair enough – yet they had "the defect of not speaking definitely of this particular measure as his own and his government's, and calling on them to sustain his treaty".[124] Without the government's specific endorsement, Brown had to recognize that what he long had feared might indeed happen: that at this late date the Senate would not act on the measure at all, but would simply throw it over until its next session in December. "*N'importe*," he said philosophically. "We have done all we could, and the U.S. government must be responsible for what comes hereafter."[125] Characteristically, he did not intend to cry over any spilled milk.

And so, in fact, it ended – after all the effort, hopes, worries and frustration. Lacking the government *imprimatur*, the draft treaty did not invite immediate senatorial action; and the members of that important body did not intend to stay and stew in Washington debating a whole new issue when there was other weighty business to be wound up. The Foreign Relations Committee did not report on the Canadian reciprocity agreement by June 22. The session closed. Brown's treaty was left hanging.

5

The next meeting of Congress might yet approve the treaty. Until then, no more could be done. Brown had a final interview with Fish, saw a number of Congressmen – who all said that the fate of the measure had nothing to do with its merits – and prepared to leave Washington on June 25. He was far from depressed. He had hoped against hope throughout, and he was still unconquerably optimistic. He had nothing to reproach himself with; and he was going home at last.

But did the treaty really have any chance? Perhaps so – if it had been launched a few months earlier, if the depression and the currency question had not become so dominant, and if Grant's administration had not been distracted and declining when faced with this new measure that called for its endorsement. These are the "if's" of history, and of course they are imponderable. Equally, however, they point out the contingencies in history – which in this instance may serve to prevent any simple conclusion that Brown's attempt at reciprocity was foreordained to failure merely because the United States was wedded to high-tariff Republicanism. After all, the bargain of free fisheries for limited reciprocity could and did commend itself even to leading Republicans of the day.[126]

Yet had Fish, representing the Republican administration, really set out to thwart the Canadian proposal, by toying with it and delaying it to death? There was no need for him to do so. He could have broken off negotiations at a dozen points without difficulty or loss – and when the British plenipotentiaries threatened to do it instead, he yielded ground. No: it would appear that the Secretary did hope for an agreement, even after his failure to obtain differential duties. But quite evidently, he was conscious throughout of playing the better hand, meant to squeeze the utmost in concessions, and was not unduly worried as to when the treaty might reach the Senate, or how far it might be delayed there through not being a definite government commitment. In brief, if the measure honestly concerned Fish, it did not concern him very much.[127] A Canadian agreement was not a vital matter to the United States.

And that, surely, was the controlling factor. If there was no strong antagonism to the proposal, there was no strong enthusiasm either. It was worth trying for the draft treaty of 1874, because the Americans conceivably might accept it on its merits, as a fair bargain. But if distraction, apathy, and American disinterest in Canada held sway, the attempt would be fruitless. Brown had not failed as a diplomat. He had proved a competent and not unskilled negotiator – but diplomacy would not decide the issue. The United States was turned inward, to the great empires of western land and eastern industry that were hers to develop. Canada had not the power to make her look beyond.

Whatever Brown's hopes still, his treaty would never be approved. Reciprocity was a blind alley for Canadian Liberalism.

For the present, he was glad to put aside the whole question, to turn to his business and his farm and relax as far as possible after the long ordeal in Washington. Of course, he was with the family at Bow Park as much as he could be, though he had to stay in Toronto when Gordon went up to Thunder Bay on Lake Superior, to take his own holiday and look over some silver-mining property he was trying to develop.[128] The restful calm of the summer was only briefly broken in August, when the Dufferins visited Bow Park in the course of a vice-regal tour, and Anne managed a formal dinner party in the country, held in a tent, and graced with champagne and four other wines.[129] The Browns remained at the farm throughout September, as usual, and on returning to Toronto went into temporary quarters not far from Oak Lodge. They had given up their old house because they were building a large new one on Beverley Street, which would not be ready for some time.[130]

Meanwhile, a crisis seemed to be shaping up within the Reform party. Edward Blake was apparently engaged in something very like a revolt against the leadership of Alexander Mackenzie, and it might spread. Certainly there were disgruntled Liberals who felt that, as Prime Minister, Mackenzie was too narrowly humdrum, too dourly uninspiring, and still too subject to the former leader of the Grits, George Brown. But to a considerable extent the root of the trouble lay in the imposing but difficult person of Edward Blake himself.

He was a big man, somewhat fleshy, with grave, keenly discerning eyes behind small glasses, and a full face, clean-shaven but for a fringe of whiskers around his plump chin. He had a finely critical, highly trained mind; was surely the country's leading equity lawyer, and probably its best orator. Yet Blake needed fortitude to couple with his talents. He had ambition, a deep sense of public duty, and a strong desire to lead. But his pride was far too easily hurt; his sense of duty could not readily support the donkey-work and vexations of ordinary political activity; and while he wanted to lead, he was little prepared to accept lesser responsibilities first. In fact, his cabinet colleague, Richard Cartwright, went further, to declare him "constitutionally incapable of serving loyally under anybody".[131]

Be that as it may, Edward Blake was not one to suffer fools gladly. He was all too sure of the limitations of conscientious Alexander Mackenzie, the Prime Minister who had been a stonemason, and some said was a laborious stonemason still. Perhaps Blake, who had grown up in governing circles and made his own career by intellectual brilliance, could not appreciate the sheer, concentrated resolution that had given Alexander Mackenzie power to lead. Nevertheless, he could reasonably recall that Mackenzie had only reluctantly accepted the party leadership, and now bemoaned the burdens of the Prime Minister's post;[132] while he himself had first led Liberalism on the road to victory by becoming Premier of Ontario with Mackenzie serving under him. Of course, Blake might also have remembered that he had soon dropped the responsibilities of provincial office, and rejected the thankless role of leader of the federal opposition. Moreover, only strong urging had brought him into the cabinet when the new Dominion Liberal régime had been established; and then he had left office in February of 1874, as soon as the election results were sure.

Yet, by that autumn, Cincinnatus was willing to return again. Early in September Blake sent Mackenzie a carefully worded intimation that increasing pressures brought to bear on him had overcome his "personal reluctance to office", and that he was now willing to serve – as Prime Minister.[133] In short, if he could be captain, Edward Blake would play. But the close-grained Sarnia Grit had pride of his own, not to mention an angry feeling that the pressures from "influential quarters" that Blake said had pushed him forward might simply amount to a conspiracy to overthrow the present First Minister.[134] Mackenzie stiffly indicated he could not yield his place. His would-be successor hastily recoiled, stung and throbbing at having thus exposed himself to humiliating rejection.

The result was soon manifested. On Saturday, October 3, at a big Reform rally in Aurora, Ontario, Blake exploded in a mighty speech that broadly dissociated himself from Mackenzie's government policy and advocated a wonderful array of reforms from imperial federation to compulsory voting. He expressed his willingness to have British Columbia secede from Confederation rather than see the extravagant terms for building the C.P.R. fulfilled. He went on to stress the need of fostering a national spirit among Canadians – "four millions of Britons who are not free" – and to urge a federated Empire. He swept after the Senate, wanted it made elective; discussed election corruption, the ballot, and the franchise; and at length rode off on a hobby-horse of proportional representation. "I may be said to have made an imprudent speech," Blake ended finally; "at least it might be said if I were one of those who aspire to lead their fellow-countrymen as ministers." But to him it was permitted – as one "who prefers to be a private in the advance guard of freedom to a commanding place in the main body".[135] The nobility of that renunciation brought resounding cheers.

The Aurora Speech was an over-the-week-end sensation: a source of exciting stimulus to advanced Liberals, who could pick up what they wanted from Blake's assortment of reforms; a source of positive hope to defeated Tories, who could speculate happily on how it would embarrass their opponents; and a source of alarm and anxiety to old-line, ministerial Grits, who similarly had to speculate on what its consequences might be. George Brown himself commented to Mackenzie, "Blake you will see is out on the rampage! Look out for squalls!"[136] The Aurora proposals were "pleasant little additions to the burden of work which the Reform government already bears". As for Blake's conduct, "His character for discretion has been seriously lowered in public estimation by it – but I suppose, some bold, clever move might overcome that."[137] On the whole, however, Brown was inclined to minimize the significance of the Aurora outburst, and not to put the most sinister interpretations of plot and party schism on what he regarded as a temperamental error on Blake's part.[138]

None the less, Edward Blake was a powerful figure, whose opinions had to be treated seriously and circumspectly in public discussion. And so the *Globe* took up the Aurora Speech only after several cooling days, in two long editorials on October 7 and 8. The chief Grit organ graciously acknowledged the speech as "one of unusual power", with many ideas that, while not novel, bore "the stamp of vigorous and judicious thinking". The *Globe* was sure, however, that Mr. Blake did not want British Columbia's secession, but only to stress the impossibility of the original terms made by the Conservatives for building the Pacific railway, on which the Mackenzie ministry was now doing all that could reasonably be done.

As for the future relationship of Canada and the Empire, it was an open question. An imperial federal parliament had often been discussed: "Much in the abstract may be said in its favour, but its practicality is a very different affair." It was a subject for "interesting and harmless speculation" – though it was not clear whether encouraging a Canadian national sentiment would be compatible with the project of a grand federated empire. "In fact, however, neither a national nor an imperial spirit can be secured by mere resolutions or meaningless recommendations. It must grow, not by individuals every now and then saying to themselves 'we must be national', but by the people of a land generally feeling that they have a country, a history, and a destiny in common, of which they find increasing reason to be

proud." Sound words, perhaps, for all sorts of wishful nationalists to come.

Turning to Blake's internal, constitutional reforms, the *Globe*
took the cautious line to be expected. It denied that the constitution would be improved by electing Senators – "collision
with the more popular Assembly will follow naturally and
necessarily". The present Senate did manage to bring the House
of Commons to reconsider and revise legislation. This was all it
could accomplish, "and all which in any case we believe it ought
to aim at". The views Brown had upheld in supporting a nominated Senate at the Quebec Conference were echoed once again.
His paper urged a fair trial for the still new federal system,
before starting on more "constitution-mending".

So it was with compulsory voting – good in the abstract but
"positively impractical" – and with "fancy franchises" and
proportional representation. The *Globe*'s whole discussion was
reminiscent of Brown's stand against "organic changes" in 1859,
or against the original Grit radical programme for elective institutions in 1849-50. He and his journal had not become conservative; they had never been radical. This was their moderate
Victorian Liberalism still: believing in empirical, parliamentary
growth, suspicious of doctrinaire remaking of the constitution.

"Nations, institutions and sentiments grow, and grow slowly,"
concluded the *Globe*. "Our wisdom is to hasten slowly in constitution-tinkering, to develop our resources with all diligence,
bring the people of the different provinces together, [and]
increase our numbers. . . ." In the fullness of time, it added, a
developed Canada might make such changes in the constitution
and external relations as experience proved necessary. Right or
wrong, the fact was that this would be the Canadian programme
of the next half-century – not that of the Aurora Speech. In
this respect, Brown and the *Globe* remained a better guide to
the future than Private Blake of the advance-guard of freedom.

Nevertheless, the impact of Blake's speech still remained, in
the further left-wing stirrings it encouraged, and in the clashes
it now brought on between the *Globe* and the young nationalist
movement known as "Canada First", championed by another
formidable political enthusiast, Professor Goldwin Smith. Unquestionably, it would be some time before George Brown could
really feel that the commotion Blake had roused at Aurora had
fully worked itself out.

6

The Canada First group, who had eagerly heard Blake's call for a new national spirit, was a set of young idealists centred in Toronto who sought to infuse the federal union of 1867 with a vigorous Canadian nationalism. They were not sure whether this involved independence or imperial federation. They were not sure whether to found a "young Canada" party, to abjure all partyism as corrupting, or to try to purify the Liberal party. But they had ardour and initiative. They had established a weekly, the *Nation*, in April 1874, and on October 1 laid the corner-stone of the National Club in Toronto as their headquarters. And they had secured a powerful, wealthy patron in Goldwin Smith, sometime professor of modern history at Oxford, more recently of Cornell, who had been settled in Toronto since 1871.

Smith was almost incongruously out of place in the narrow limits of nineteenth-century Toronto. A prominent Manchester School Liberal and a talented controversialist, he had been a familiar member of that joint realm of English scholarship and politics where disputatious dons moved easily with the leading journalists and politicians of the day. Yet, fixing himself firmly in Toronto, he set about to waken a literature of current comment into life, to strive to raise the low, mean level of colonial politics, and to teach Canadians that only through ending their colonial dependence could they throw off their backwardness and rise to the majesty of nationhood. Whatever the details, his was a line of argument that thoroughly appealed to the idealists of Canada First. Goldwin Smith became their mentor, and the first president of the National Club.

He gave the club a glowing inaugural address forecasting Canadian independence, which was published in the *Nation* on October 15. But here the incongruity was that, for all Smith's talk of Canadian nationality, it was clear even before he left England that he assumed that Canada's ultimate destiny was absorption in the United States – rather a denial of nationhood.[139] Of course, in Canada's history many a proclaimed nationalist, when scratched, would reveal an absorptionist. Still there were others who considered that if Canadian independence also implied Canadian extinction, it was hardly a valid means of nation-building. George Brown was one of these. He believed that under existing circumstances the other side of the coin of independence was annexation; that a scarcely-formed Canada, not even linked from sea to sea, could not long survive separate on the American continent cut off from Great Britain.

Smith, indeed, would soon make clear that his zeal for Canadian nationality was only a passing phase, and take up the idea of continental union as the goal for Canada; not ultimately, but as soon as possible.[140] The fact was that as a confirmed Manchester School anti-imperialist he was essentially more concerned with the negative task of cutting colonial bonds than the positive problem of erecting a national structure, and as an "Anglo-Saxon" he inherently believed that Canada's assimilation in a broader English-speaking union of the New World was a proper fate for the struggling, disjoined Dominion. Accordingly, there was valid reason for those like Brown, who hoped for Canada to live and grow outside the American union, to oppose the exhortations to independence of "nationalists" like Goldwin Smith.

The reason seemed specially plain after the Aurora Speech had provided a meeting-ground for Canada Firsters and dissentient Liberals, thanks to Blake's call to cultivate a national sentiment, and his fervid reference to four million Britons who were not free. Actually, Blake's own answer had been a reconstruction of the bonds of empire through imperial federation; but it was the spirit rather than the content of Aurora that Goldwin Smith and his friends might seek to utilize. And if the emotional Edward Blake, swept on by his own eloquence, should be induced to become political leader of a nationalist Liberal movement, the result – from George Brown's standpoint – could be disastrous both to country and to party. Such a development had to be prevented. It had to be prevented at the source of danger by combating Goldwin Smith on his own favoured ground, the public press, by turning the power of the *Globe* against this considerable adversary – himself a master of invective – the "perpetually indignant" Mr. Smith.[141]

Of course, the *Globe* had contended against Goldwin Smith before: while he was still in England and writing forcefully to urge the mother country to cast off her useless colonial burdens, and more recently in Canada, where he had deplored the tyranny and venality of the Canadian party system and advocated non-partisan government with all the intensity of a natural partisan. The *Globe* scoffed at the notion that popular government could function without party; Smith denounced the power of the *Globe* as the very epitome of party tyranny.[142] And this, too, lay behind their clashes after the Aurora Speech.

Brown's tactics were to draw a sharp distinction between Edward Blake, the misguided Liberal, and Goldwin Smith, the false prophet of nationalism. Thus the *Globe*'s comments on Blake's speech were kept quite separate from its handling of Canada First – which soon received the main attention.[143] The enemies of Liberalism, it said bluntly, were making every effort to identify Blake with Canada First and its "foster parent", Professor Smith. But though both sought radical changes, the similarity ended there. Blake would reform Canada's imperial connections, Smith abolish them. The *Globe* opposed the first policy as unnecessary, the second as pernicious; and it regretted Blake's utterances precisely because they tended to rouse dissatisfaction that was capitalized on by Smith and Co.[144]

The Canada First movement itself, affirmed Brown's paper, was harmless enough. "Its apostles are of the mildest type of agitators, its literature is, to use the least offensive word, insipid." But Canada First had been adopted by Goldwin Smith and that meant "action at once aggressive and dangerous".[145] For Professor Smith was influential and cultivated, spoke and wrote admirably, and had wealth and leisure, as well as a love of expressing his opinions fearlessly – so that he should not object to similar treatment. And his course was essentially destructive: "We do not hesitate to say that in the early days of the Dominion, to preach the doctrine that a radical change in our political relations is desirable is about as injurious to the present prosperity and progress of the country as can possibly be conceived."[146] Where was the deep grievance against Britain to justify such a disturbance? Besides, when Canada was undertaking vast obligations of development, what would such an upheaval do to her stability and credit standing? And would independence come without resistance and convulsion – in which the Americans could step in? A little republic would not long persist beside the great one. Thus far, indeed, membership in the British Empire had worked to preserve Canada from American power and ambition.[147]

Furthermore, this country had a past, a tradition, and a connection. It was "not a new volume to be written by Goldwin Smith". His call for independence would be only the start of troubles. He was an unlikely leader of violent revolution, but that was the threat implied in his project. Should it happen, he and his fellow mischief-makers would be protected simply by their insignificance. They would not be worth the traitor's doom![148]

It was strong language, though no stronger than that current in the press of the day, and was used deliberately to impress the idea that, whatever Canada First thought it was doing, it was really playing with annexationist fire. Of course, the assailed parties reacted as strongly. Goldwin Smith wrote to the *Globe* acidly protesting the imputation of treason, along with the paper's complete lack of common sense and gentlemanly courtesy.[149] The *Nation* deemed Brown's paper "in savage earnest" in trying to cast the ascetic, academic Smith in the character of a leader of armed revolt – "an atrocious statement".[150] Replied the *Globe*, "We must acknowledge that at the time we had the feeling that the notion of Professor Smith 'raising the standard' and marching into Toronto at the head of his armed legions and surrounded by a brilliant staff of Canada First men was rather far-fetched and whimsical in no ordinary degree." Its "savagery" had had quite another meaning: "If people will make themselves ridiculous we can't help it."[151]

November had now arrived, however, without any fresh outbursts. The reverberations of the Aurora Speech seemed to be finally subsiding with no positive threats to the Reform party, and with Smith and the Canada Firsters still at least contained. "The interest expressed in the discussion has been unusually strong and general," Brown reported to Mackenzie, "and it is curious to hear the different objections to Blake's and Smith's opinions suggested from unexpected quarters."[152] He thought the party quite unshaken, and that "the safe policy of the old line Reformers has received a new endorsement from the country".[153] Meanwhile Mackenzie had been at work to conciliate Blake. The situation looked happier, without a doubt.

And so, in mid-December, George Brown could go back to Washington to survey the prospects of his draft reciprocity treaty, now that the congressional elections were over in the United States. The Democrats, traditionally the party of lower tariffs, had won control of the House; Brown's natural optimism swelled again.[154] But the new Congress would not meet till March. Thornton, moreover, seemed gloomy as ever, while Fish told him that the currency question monopolized everyone's thinking at present, and that there was "utter apathy" concerning the treaty.[155] Brown returned home in time for Christmas, still not giving up, but certain that nothing would happen for the moment. His own ambition, he admitted to Anne, was "dying out". "And would it contribute to home happiness to go in for a six months effort to make Yankee public sentiment and carry the treaty? I don't think it would – and shall not do it."[156]

Ontario election campaigns engrossed his attention through the early weeks of 1875, as Mowat was firmly returned to power. But before the end of January it grew clear that the trouble with Blake and the danger from Smith and his supporters was not yet over for the party. On January 27, in fact, a new daily paper appeared in Toronto: the *Liberal*. Backed by Edward Blake and his friends, it was clearly intended as the mouth-piece of advanced Liberalism, to press the party onward in reforms, and to challenge the hold of the older Grit Reformers, the Browns and Mackenzies, as well as contest the dominance of the *Globe* over the party press. Furthermore, Blake himself had been keeping very friendly company with the Canada Firsters.[157] In actuality, he had even approached Goldwin Smith about editing the *Liberal*; but the latter felt he had enough to do with the writing he had taken on for the *Nation*.[158] John Cameron, late of the London *Advertiser*, became editor instead.

Nevertheless, this venture by Blake and his supporters still was not pushed to the point of open party rupture. Under the circumstances, Brown evidently decided that salutary indifference was the best policy. The *Globe* virtually ignored the *Liberal*, and was restrainedly quiet on Blake. Yet on occasion it did hit out at some of his friends, such as David Mills, M.P. for Bothwell, a would-be Senate reformer ("Constitution-tinkering is his hobby").[159] In any case, however, George Brown had little to do now with the daily content of the *Globe*, since he was up in Ottawa for much of the spring of 1875.

He went to Ottawa just before the opening of parliament early in February. For he was a member of the legislature again, and this year he intended to take his seat in the Senate, as he had not been able to do the previous year. He met first with Mackenzie and Holton to talk over policy.[160] Dorion had become Chief Justice of Quebec, so that Holton was now virtually the senior Quebec Liberal, especially in the unfortunate absence of any really strong French Canadian in the cabinet. Blake was supposed to attend the meeting, but sent a letter giving his views instead.[161]

Then, when Dufferin regally opened the session on February 4, Brown was at his place in the upper house. The hallowed ritual of parliament, the tall, splendid chamber, the glittering uniforms of the Governor-General and his entourage – the new Senator found himself strongly moved by it all. "The House looked very handsome when the ceremony was at its height –" he wrote to Anne, "and made you feel that after all, Canada was *something*. I felt the old feeling creeping over me while I looked and pondered – and had a speech been in order just at that moment from the *juniorest* member, I think he would have been equal to it! Modest that – is it not?"[162] Modest or not, Brown was bound to feel that this was a fraternity in which, despite all drawbacks, he still belonged.

7

The Senator was receiving "invites" to Government House, beginning committee work, planning a speech on his draft reciprocity treaty. "I see very clearly that a great deal can be done with the Senate," he said. "Everybody is immensely civil – and after being on the shelf so long, I confess the thing is far from unpleasant."[163] Not displeasing, either, was Mackenzie's intimation that the question of a knighthood for him had been raised with Downing Street, in recognition of his work in Washington. "I answered that it was very pleasant to have the refusal –" George Brown told his wife, "and that of course you will have to determine the answer to be given – but I thought it very unlikely that we would conclude to accept it. . . . I am not a quarter of an inch taller. Are you? I would rather make a thundering good speech on Monday on the Treaty that will carry the legislature by storm and do no harm in the States than have a dozen knighthoods."[164]

On Monday, February 22, he had his try. His speech on the treaty was to all intents an official account of the negotiations carried on in Washington, replete with statistics to explain and defend the terms of the measure proposed. And so the Senate chamber was most unusually crowded, as members and spectators gathered to hear a full, authoritative report on reciprocity, and to see George Brown in action once again. He found it a considerable strain.[165] The Senate was so gravely quiet compared to the noisy, turbulent House he used to know. He had to watch what he said so carefully, conscious that it would be followed on both sides of the border, and he had to pile on facts and figures that he knew must weary his audience. Besides this, Brown was eight years out of practice.

Nevertheless, he spoke for two and a half hours, and thought it went "well enough".[166] Certainly, it was a lucid, judicious, and impressive account. And his speech rose with some of the old ardour at the end, when Brown declared that though the fate of the trade negotiations was settled for the present, the treaty was on record, and would no doubt form the basis of a future successful agreement. Until then, he warmly urged, Canadians should still follow the true wisdom of freeing their own trade: "Let the Americans load their industries with customs duties as they choose; let it be the firm policy of Canada to remove every barrier in the way of commercial extension, to repeal all duties on raw materials, on articles used in manufacturing, and on the common necessities of daily life . . . let them seek to develop their great national industries . . . let them open up new markets adapted to their traffic – and let the Canadian flag be found floating on every sea!"[167]

An inconclusive debate on trade policy was over by the end of the month, and after a brief trip home, Brown went on in March with more immediate problems such as the telegraph and cables bill and a New Brunswick schools question. But now the long-threatening "Blake matter" seemed to be coming to a head. By March 15 Brown had heard that friends of Blake were being sounded on the prospect of making a serious attack on the government. He thought it would blow over, "as almost every man of sense in the house acknowledged that it is right-down madness".[168] Nevertheless, he went to have a long talk with an old ally, Luther Holton, who now was somewhat a Blake sympathizer, or at least wanted to see the government reorganized. The Montreal Liberal had never taken kindly to Mackenzie's leadership, and had found one reason or another not to join the cabinet himself. Brown, at any rate, discovered that Holton strongly condemned the idea of a revolt. "But I am not quite sure," he added dubiously, "that he does not chuckle a little at having a crack at Mackenzie."[169]

The next day, he was up by half past six, to breakfast with Mackenzie himself. They discussed the problem in cordial agreement, as the firm old friends they were.[170] Yet, though Brown was optimistic that "the Blakeites begin to feel that they have made a decided mistake",[171] the real crisis only began on March 19, when Mackenzie introduced in the House of Commons a bill for building an Esquimalt and Nanaimo railway. This was part of the government's new bargain with British Columbia, to ease the original costly undertaking by the Conservatives to finish the whole Pacific railway within ten years. The Vancouver Island line would be a consolation prize for delaying and stretching out the programme of construction on the mainland. But to Edward Blake, feeling, as he had at Aurora, that almost any bargain with British Columbia was extravagant, the terms were still too high. He opposed the bill. It passed the House nevertheless; but in the Senate, where the Conservatives were strong, the defection of two Liberals to their side was sufficient to defeat it. That amounted to upsetting the government's entire railway policy, and might well lead Blakeites to full-scale revolt.

Gravely worried, the Reform party leaders strove to close the spreading gap. There were comings and goings at interviews across Ottawa in efforts to reach agreement. Blake would enter the cabinet under Holton, or would himself lead, but Mac-

kenzie still refused to yield the Prime Ministership.[172] Huntington, of Pacific Scandal fame, called on Brown to say that
Holton had taken offence at everybody and refused to go in, and
that Blake would enter only if Holton did.[173] Huntington, on
behalf of his French-Canadian colleagues, wanted Brown to
pacify Holton and then bring Mackenzie to offer both Blake
and Holton seats again. He also let it be known that he and his
Quebec friends sought to have Blake in the government quite
as much to keep Mackenzie in order as to silence the dissentients.
"I had the disagreeable task to perform tonight of letting Mack
understand that," Brown commented. "On the whole it is a
mess."[174]

On through March and into April the complex conversations
continued. Brown at least found Lord Dufferin "stiff for Mackenzie and dead against Blake".[175] But on April 6, he learned
from the Prime Minister that prospects were brightening.
Mackenzie had seen Blake on the fourth and brought him to
agree to consult with his wife and law partners about entering
the existing cabinet; and Holton would probably come too.
"Mackenzie professes immense gratitude for the aid I have
given him," reported Brown, "and is enormously delighted with
the success we have had."[176]

It seems that, as so often, Brown was being too optimistic
too soon. The negotiations with Blake continued for a whole
month more. But meanwhile the session ended in mid-April, and
hence the political danger was reduced. Moreover, back in
Toronto now, George and Gordon Brown kept the *Globe* and
its following as quiet on the problem as possible, ignoring the
gleeful badgering of the Conservative *Mail*, and the hopeful
forecasts by the Canada Firsters of a great new liberal-nationalist
movement. At length, in May, an agreement was reached that
would end the breach in Liberalism. Blake would accept Mackenzie's leadership, set aside constitutional reforms, and enter
the government as Minister of Justice. Mackenzie would have
to modify the railway terms for British Columbia still further,
and take a firm line with Britain in asserting Canada's rights to
control her own affairs. To such limits were the declarations of
Aurora reduced.

Once Brown had news of the definite agreement concluded in
Ottawa on May 18, the *Globe* was glad to observe that Blake
was "too able and influential a member of the party in power to
remain an outsider".[177] A few weeks later, when Blake spoke at
his acclamation in South Bruce, it was no less pleased to remark
that his speech gave evidence "that he can sink the doctrinaire in
the public servant".[178] Bygones would be bygones; but the old,

true, sensible Reformers had won, for they had had the great bulk of the party with them. That was the *Globe*'s conclusion. It seemed to be substantiated by the demise in June of the short-lived *Liberal*, which had never reached more than 5,000 daily circulation.[179] Brown's *Globe* was still undisputed ruler of the Canadian Reform press.

Moreover, the Conservatives had not managed to take advantage of the dissensions in Liberalism. The party was still firmly in power, with a good record of sound, careful administration, and what Brown, no doubt, would consider practical rather than visionary reforms behind it. Times were bad still, and long-run problems of trade and development were far from solved. But Prime Minister Mackenzie felt it safe to plan on a summer holiday in his native Scotland – and so did George Brown. The Brown family was going over for another extended stay. There was no problem of closing house, since they were still in temporary quarters, hoping to move into a completed new mansion on their return. June saw George Brown busy making arrangements for his absence at the *Globe* and Bow Park. And on July 2, the whole family left Toronto, to sail from Quebec aboard the *Polynesian*.

The trip really marked the passing of another phase in Brown's life. There would be no sharp change in his interests and activities on his return, but there was a point of transition here in his career. From the latter half of 1875 onward, his role as Liberal elder statesman became increasingly symbolic and nominal, decreasingly active and real. Gradually, though intermittently, he withdrew from political concerns, as he gave himself more and more to the development of his Bow Park stock-farm as the largest agricultural enterprise in Canada. In May of 1875 he had even refused Mackenzie's offer of the lieutenant-governorship of Ontario, made vacant by the death of its latest incumbent, John Crawford.[180] He preferred to stay plain George Brown and look after his own affairs.

To some extent, this growing withdrawal was merely continuing the trend of Brown's retirement from public life since 1867, a trend not really altered by his temporary service as a High Commissioner or his entrance into the Senate. Yet to some degree, as well, it demonstrated that Brown's influence was passing from the Canadian scene. The *Globe* did not lose its hold upon the public, but its director came to wield less weight in party counsels, and times were changing the import of his ideas.

One of the contentions of Blake's following had been that George Brown exercised far too much power over Mackenzie: that the Prime Minister had almost been an instrument for continuing Brown's rule over Liberalism. Actually, it was an empty charge. Mackenzie had a thoroughly determined mind of his own. He vigorously denied that Brown had interfered with his conduct of the leadership, and the record would seem to bear him out.[181] Not only had his old chief carefully refrained from pressing opinions on him; he had sometimes even failed to give advice when asked, through preoccupation with his own concerns.[182]

Yet because the two men were so close personally, and so much in harmony in their Scotch-Grit Liberalism, there could readily be the appearance of collusion between the responsible First Minister and the extra-parliamentary journalist.[183] Hence Blake, in drafting his own terms for entering the cabinet, had made one of them no interference by Brown.[184] In any case, his powerful and sensitive presence in the cabinet was bound to make some difference thereafter in Brown's relations with the Mackenzie régime. Blakeism had not won. But it had, perhaps, lessened the significance of Brownism.

And the significance of Brownism was decreasing in another way. Brown had stood for the mid-Victorian British Liberal ideal of free trade: for a low-cost economy essentially shaped to benefit the primary producers who were the basis of Canadian commercial activity; for lowering trade barriers through reciprocity, limiting the expenditures of government, and above all, for no protective tariff. The failure of his reciprocity negotiations, however, naturally reflected on his whole position regarding public policy. Moreover, when the terms of his draft treaty were known, there was considerable criticism of its free admission of certain American manufactures, indicating that a surprising amount of protectionist sentiment had emerged with the growth of industry in central Canada.

In fact, there would be a rising demand hereafter for policies of economic nationalism, for the fostering of national development by the American plan of protective tariffs and the high-cost economy that favoured home industries. This was a kind of nationalism that was as foreign to Blake or Goldwin Smith as it was to George Brown. But the future lay with it — not with Canada First or Senate reform. When Macdonald and the Conservatives whole-heartedly took up the American system, as they shortly did, the day of the mid-Victorian British Liberalism of Brown or Mackenzie was all but over. Another world was developing in Canada from 1875 onward: the later-nineteenth-century world of economic nationalism and aggressive imperialism, the expanding state and the entwining of government and protected business interests. It would be a distinctly different era. It could not be Brown's.

The Final Withdrawal

I

On July 14, 1875, the Browns arrived in Edinburgh, and a week later, George Brown himself went down to London. He had work to do at the *Globe* office in Cheapside: to go over the accounts of his English agency, hire a new sub-editor, and buy equipment for the new stereotyping process for his presses at home.[1] More than that, he was to see the imperial authorities about the Atlantic fisheries arbitration, which would go forward now that reciprocity negotiations with the United States had failed.[2] He spent a day at the Foreign Office and another at the Colonial Office, where he was quite taken with Lord Carnarvon.[3] There was a grand Colonial Office banquet at Greenwich, and a magnificent ball at the Duchess of Sutherland's, not to mention a pleasant chat with Gladstone, recalling the "old times" of the Confederation discussions just ten years earlier.[4] Yet Brown quickly closed this latest mission, and on July 28 caught the *Flying Scotsman* back to Edinburgh and the family group at Abden House.

Early in August, they all left for Oban, for the sparkling mountains, lochs, and sea coasts of Argyll. Alexander Mackenzie and his wife joined them briefly on the holiday, and while the men went fishing, the ladies drove about to view the romantic landmarks of the Western Highlands.[5] Then Browns and Nelsons boated down the Firth of Lorne and picnicked on the shore at Kerrara, and young Ginney, aged six, caught his first fish.[6] They went up to Ballachulich, to the sombre, brooding fastness of Glencoe. But much too soon it was time for George to go back to London to wind up business there. He had to return to Canada, the *Globe*, and Bow Park, leaving Anne and the children in Scotland until he could come back to them as early as possible in the winter. They made their parting before Brown set out for London. He went on to Liverpool to take ship on August 26. But Anne could not bear to let him sail without seeing him again, and so came down from Oban to say good-bye once more.[7]

His Atlantic crossing came frighteningly close to disaster. At midnight on September 2, when Brown's ship, the *Moravian*, was groping through fog a hundred miles east of Belle Isle, she ran full on an iceberg. A sudden yell – "Ice ahead!" – and then her bowsprit struck squarely, shattering to its base, and wrenching open the bow plates below.[8] It was fortunate that the Allan line steamer carried so long a bowsprit projecting from her raking bows, while, since it was late in the season, much of the berg had already been melted away. Thus the *Moravian*'s hull never reached the terrible mass of ice. Even so, the impact threw her nearly on her beam-ends, as she sheered away. And before she slowly righted herself water poured in through the damaged bow plates.

The rending crash at once woke Brown from his berth, then flung him right across the cabin as the ship rolled over on her side. Amid the roar of water, he was sure that she was sinking fast. "A million things rushed through the mind in these few dreadful seconds," he wrote later to his wife, "but the feeling of joy and thankfulness overtopped all other thoughts that Anne and our darlings were safe and away from the coming struggle for life." He rushed up on deck, the first passenger to scramble from below, and ran to the bridge to learn the true position. But there was no immediate danger, he found, and calm, disciplined steps were being taken to meet the emergency. Satisfied, he went aft to help reassure the other passengers, while the bow compartment was closed off and the pumps were put to work. The debris of the bowsprit and fore-rigging was cleared, the leaks checked as far as possible, and by one in the morning quiet had been restored. There was no panic among 400 passengers. "I have seen far more flutter on a railway train, from a shrill whistle of 'down brakes' because a cow had got on the track," Brown commented.[9] Still, he was glad enough to land safely at Quebec four days afterwards.

He found a deputation already waiting for him in Toronto, come there on behalf of the government of New Brunswick to buy some of his Bow Park shorthorns for distribution in that province. The reputation of his stock-raising farm had evidently spread; one of Brown's consuming interests, the improvement of the breed of cattle in Canada, was being realized through his steadily growing investment in Bow Park. On the present occasion, he disposed of twenty bull calves and ten young heifers for a bargain price of $7,000, and considered it "a wonderful cleaning-out of the herd – making room for the coming 138 youngsters!"[10]

At the *Globe* office, Gordon and the staff had everything in excellent order. Though times were still bad in Canada, his own business seemed "never better".[11] In fact, George Brown now undertook another drive to expand his paper's circulation. New lower postal rates enabled him to try a notable innovation. Hitherto subscribers who took papers by mail had had to pay the postage themselves. Henceforth the *Globe* would come post-paid, and at the same price (six dollars a year for the daily), which actually reduced its annual cost to a subscriber by about $1.20.[12] Again the venture seemed to pay. The daily's average circulation had been just over 20,000 at the end of August. It was 24,000 by mid-October.[13]

Furthermore, that autumn Brown carried through arrangements to launch a wholly new *Weekly Globe* for 1876.[14] It would have sixteen instead of eight pages, machine-folded, and printed with the new stereotyping equipment Brown had bought in England. Its contents would no longer be selected from the daily editions as in the past, but would be specially written for it. And there would be new features also: columns by cable from the *Globe*'s London office, full accounts of "manly sports", and a Ladies' Department presenting fashions, recipes, and family affairs. All for the same price of two dollars annually! The orders soon were pouring in.[15]

Politics, on the other hand, were fairly quiet for Brown – except for one incident that arose towards the end of September. On Saturday the twenty-fifth, with a delicious shudder of horror, the Toronto *Mail* printed a purportedly scandalous letter from George Brown to Senator John Simpson of Bowmanville, President of the Ontario Bank. It had been written three years earlier, during the general elections of 1872, and the *Mail* clearly meant it to be a disclosure of Liberal sin to equal or at least obscure the Conservative record of the Pacific Scandal in the same contest. As printed, the letter read: "The fight goes bravely on. . . . We have expended our strength in aiding the out-counties and helping our city candidates, but *a big push* has to be made on Saturday and Monday for the East and West divisions [of Toronto]. . . .*There are but half a dozen that can come down handsomely, and we all have done what we possibly can do, and we have to ask a few outsiders to aid us. Will you be one?*"

On the face of it, the sinister implications of this "big push" letter were somewhat dubious. To ask a wealthy party friend for contributions towards election expenses was in itself neither illicit nor unusual. What corrupt bargain or misuse of funds had been thus revealed? Eagerly, the Conservative *Mail*, the tottering *Leader,* and particularly the *West Durham News* of Bowmanville, proceeded to raise a fearsome structure of conjecture on this bare foundation. They conjured up a vast Liberal network of election bribery, supported by a Grit Sir Hugh Allen, John Simpson of the Ontario Bank. They marked the considerable increase of government deposits in that bank since Alexander Mackenzie and his party had taken office. They declared, in effect – in a mixture of virtuous alarm and immoral delight – "You're just as bad as we were said to be."[16]

Brown replied immediately. He published a signed statement in the *Globe* of Monday, September 27, declaring that Simpson had assured him that he had never received or seen the "big push" letter and had not contributed to the election fund it described. He, George Brown, however, had certainly written such a letter to three or four political friends at the time of the elections, and now assumed that a copy of one of these had been culled by the Conservative press. But far from regretting its publication, he asserted, he was glad to be able to show the real contrast with the Pacific Scandal. The Liberal fund in question had been raised to assist candidates in hotly contested ridings, or to back them in hopeless ones where little local aid would be forthcoming. The entire fund, only some $3,700, had been used thus for legitimate purposes such as travelling expenses for speakers and the circulation of campaign documents. Furthermore, this was the only general Reform fund collected for the elections of 1872, and consequently it amounted to a mere $45 for each of the 82 Ontario constituencies!

It was a complete refutation, for all who wanted to believe it. But those who did not could say that it was only a personal avowal from the ancient enemy of Tory truth and honour, the infamous George Brown. Still, however one might look at it, the Conservative case remained remarkably empty, and failed to produce one substantiating fact beyond the "big push" letter itself. Here was a very different situation from the reams of sworn testimony recorded in the case of the Pacific Scandal. One might also compare the Reformers' meagre $3,700 to the $180,000 Sir Hugh Allan actually admitted paying out, in the evidence taken on the Pacific Scandal: two cents on the dollar, the *Globe* said facetiously.[17] Of course, this sort of comparison might do less to indicate the Liberals' morality than their incapacity to raise a sizeable slush fund. It was more meaningful, as the *Globe* noted, to observe that the awful "big push" money was only equal to the legitimate cost of cabs John Hillyard Cameron had used in his Toronto constituency campaign alone![18]

Nevertheless, no one could settle conclusively how much Brown and the Liberals had actually raised from business men in 1872, or how they had used or abused it. The report presented was Brown's; the only objective facts were in the "big push" letter. The Conservative press exploited the situation to the full. Simpson himself, however, angrily denied the Conservative charges and sued the *West Durham News*. The greatly increased government deposits in his bank, it was contended, were simply the result of the Mackenzie ministry's reversing a policy that the Grits had long attacked; namely, giving the main use of government funds to the pet Tory Bank of Montreal.[19]

Undoubtedly one might then expect a Reform ministry to bank with its friends, without deducing any corrupt bargain from that act alone. And in any case, the entire weight of the presumptions in the "big push" case lay against the Conservatives. First, there was Brown's whole character and political career; he had faults, large faults, but deviousness and venality had not appeared among them. Second, elections normally cost money, quite legitimately, and the "big push" letter itself indicated no more than another passing of the hat. Third, John Simpson's own suit not only failed to disclose anything against him, but ended in the judgment that a criminal information could be laid against the editor of the *West Durham News* as the most lavish purveyor of the "scandal". And fourth, every Tory striving could not show that there was even an analogy here to the Pacific Scandal's linking of the C.P.R. charter with huge election disbursements. Accordingly, the "big push" excitement soon faded out, though it would be revived in a year's time to bother Brown once more.

In any event, he had other preoccupations in that autumn of 1875. Aside from implementing the changes at the *Globe*, and arranging for the meeting of the American Shorthorn Breeders' Association in Toronto early in December, Brown was diligently supervising the building of the new house on Beverley Street.[20] On a visit, Alexander Mackenzie expertly examined its brick- and stone-work, and pronounced it excellently done. "We will have," George proudly wrote to Anne, "as I always told you we would have – the best house in Toronto."[21] It would be commodious yet convenient, handsome but not ostentatious. It would be a family home. His letters overseas were full of the details: the croquet lawn, the rabbit-hutch for the children, the design of the iron railings, and the problem of the cornices in the main rooms – should they be moulded plaster or the new papier mâché?

And so the weeks of autumn passed. Gordon went to Kentucky for a holiday during December, and there was still more to do. As always, Brown missed Anne and the children "awfully". Yet, "I keep on working hard," he said gamely, "and find it very pleasant."[22] He went out only infrequently, sometimes just to play whist. He rather preferred to have a few friends in at home, such as Dr. Wilson and Professor Paxton Young of the University, for a quiet evening of talk.[23] On Christmas Day he particularly kept busy working, until it was time to go to dinner at Government House.[24] But New Year's came more easily, for he knew that in only a few weeks he would be away to Scotland. January of 1876, accordingly, was a whirlwind of preparations for his absence. And on the twenty-sixth Brown set sail.

2

In London again that February, he had a very different sort of mission to perform: to patent young Alexander Graham Bell's new system of "sound telegraphy". Brown knew the inventor of the telephone, then in his late twenties, as the son of his neighbour at Bow Park, Professor Melville Bell, a fellow Scot and authority on speech training who had settled outside Brantford several years before. Aleck Bell was a professor of vocal physiology himself at Boston University; but being in somewhat poor health, often used to come up to the family place at Tutelo Heights to rest and recuperate, and ponder on the experiments he was conducting in the transmission of sounds or speech along an electrified wire. By the previous summer, in fact, he had established the essential working principle of the telephone.[25] But he needed money to advance his plans, and especially to secure patent protection. And so in September of 1875 he approached his father's neighbour, the wealthy, well-known Senator Brown of Bow Park.[26]

Brown showed interest – perhaps stirred as much by Bell's enthusiasm as his invention. It was verbally agreed that he would bring his brother Gordon in and that the two of them would help support Bell in preparing and filing patent specifications. The anxious inventor was willing to grant them almost any rights in return.[27] Yet it must be remembered that this was an uncertain device of unrecognized significance. Brown obviously did not realize the potentialities within his grasp, when Bell offered him and his brother half interest in all the patents that he would take out abroad. The limits of Brown's interest, indeed, were shown by the fact that it took Bell until December to bring their verbal understanding to a written agreement. But on December 28 a letter signed by both George and Gordon obliged them each to pay Professor Alexander Graham Bell

$25 a month, up to a total of $300, while he was perfecting his inventions in telegraphy and preparing patent specifications.[28] It was little enough to venture. Yet the Bell telephone was a cloud a good deal smaller than a man's hand as yet, and hardly over the horizon.

One important factor in the agreement was that George Brown was soon leaving for England. He could thus apply for a British patent, and for others in Europe as well. It was important for Bell to apply first in England, before he filed specifications for an American patent, as otherwise his patent would not be valid under existing English law. Yet if he delayed too long in filing in the United States, rivals who had wind of his device might try to beat him there. Consequently, it was a still more anxious Bell who saw Brown to his ship in New York, late in January of 1876, and waited tensely for some word that his patent application had been entered in London.

By the time Brown got down to London, however, after his voyage and seeing his family in Edinburgh, it was nearly the middle of February. Again it was evident that he felt much less strongly about the ugent importance of patenting Bell's designs than did the inventor himself. Nevertheless, he and an associate in London, James McFarlane Gray, journeyed to the Patent Office together, to see if any discoveries in telegraphy recorded there would affect Bell's project.[29] After careful search they found none. The mercurial Gray was all for taking out a patent immediately, and in neighbouring countries as well. But Brown was cautious, wanted to consult with an expert in telegraphy first, and Gray suggested a Mr. Holmes of Chalk Town.

Off they went at once to see him. They stayed till 10:30 that night, while Holmes considered Bell's system. His authoritative judgment was, as Brown reported it, "that Bell has made a step in advance of everybody else – but that it is doubtful whether it would be workable on the ocean cable and quite certain that it would be of no commercial value on this side of the Atlantic (whatever it might be in the U.S.)."[30] Thus ruled the weight of British technical knowledge. Brown thought he would still consult his brother-in-law, Thomas Nelson, as an able, forward-looking business man – "but my present inclination is to go no further".[31]

He was also probably affected by a low opinion of his associate Gray, whose own eagerness likely did not help the cause. "Gray is a clever man –" he said, "very much so occasionally – but foggy. He is unquestionably as mad as a March hare."[32] And so Brown's interest in Bell's invention rapidly dwindled to nothing. Their agreement lapsed. But it lapsed in another sense, too, because an American friend of Bell's, fearful of waiting any longer, applied on his behalf for a United States patent only hours before a competitor filed a "caveat" in Washington in an attempt to block the way.[33] This had actually all taken place on February 14, when Brown was only beginning his investigations in London. Hence his own tentative try for a patent was invalidated anyway. But it is tempting, still, to speculate whether the Bell Telephone might not conceivably have been the Bell-Brown Telephone in Britain, British possessions, and over half the world.

Brown turned quickly from his venture with sound telegraphy to his real concern in London: the printing of a long prospectus on Bow Park for private distribution across Great Britain.[34] Its purpose was to attract shareholders; he planned to incorporate his cattle farm as a joint-stock company in order to raise short-horns on a scale beyond his capacity as an individual owner. What had begun as a relaxation and become a hobby was now a ruling enthusiasm, and George Brown always pushed his enthusiasms hard. As he wrote in his prospectus, he meant to expand Bow Park to supply "the vast demand for pure-bred stock now rapidly extending over the North American Continent".[35]

Already there were some 300 cattle on the 900 acres of Bow Park, and visitors were surprised by the "leviathan herd" of largely first-class animals.[36] There were extensive buildings, substantially built and neatly painted, laid out in ranges on a seven-acre plot: implement and engine sheds, stables for twenty-four horses, a row of box-houses for the shorthorns, and a capacious barn, 220 feet long. The large, well-fenced fields were linked by gravel roads, while the bulk of the acreage was intensively cultivated for the fodder crops that kept Bow Park close to self-sufficiency.[37] From twenty-two to thirty-five hands were employed, depending on the season. Brown estimated his whole estate to be worth about $450,000 — decidedly a valuable property for the year 1876.[38]

He was willing, however, to sell it to the proposed joint-stock company for $375,000. The company would be capitalized for $500,000; Brown himself would take payment in $200,000 worth of the shares and $175,000 in cash.[39] The rest of the capital raised by share subscription would go towards expanding the herd with the very best selected breeding stock. The former owner would continue to run the estate, in conjunction with Canadian and English boards of directors and the Company's permanent agent, resident in England. Brown was confident of annual profits from the sale of Bow Park pure-breds, and hence sure of dividends for the shareholders, even if cattle prices fell drastically. Great was the market, he believed, for high-bred shorthorns in America.[40]

As soon as his company prospectus was ready towards the end of February, he began vigorously campaigning after shareholders, only taking time off to do a little work for the *Globe* at the office in the City, or to pay brief visits back to Edinburgh. Of course, he had a broad field of prospects to begin with, both through his business contacts in England and Scotland and his familiarity now with leading cattle-breeders across the whole country. For example, the Canadian Senator Brown of Bow Park was already sufficiently well known among aristocratic shorthorn fanciers in England that the Duke of Manchester kept after him to come up to Kimbolton Castle at St. Neot's to inspect his herd.[41] Brown managed to drop in during one of his tours, duly admired the beautiful Duchess as well, and exchanged ideas with great Whig magnates like Lord Hartington.[42] He took these excursions into the ranks of the landed nobility quite matter-of-factly. The shorthorn was such a leveller of class distinction.

Well into spring he went on touring to raise capital for his company and examine cattle for prospective purchase. Times were still hard, and while everyone he saw agreed that his project would succeed, they all hesitated to make a move. "Not one has disapproved –" said Brown, "not one refused to cooperate – but they want someone to bell the cat, when they will all follow."[43] And then his Nelson brothers-in-law came in. Thomas took 500 shares, or $50,000 worth; William, $12,500.[44] Others did follow, until by the end of April $367,500 had been subscribed of the $400,000 capital that Brown had decided would be sufficient for the present.[45] The investors were largely centred in Scotland, particularly in Edinburgh. In the border country, cattle-breeders John Clay and his father had put up $10,000 between them; and the younger Clay, an agricultural expert who had already visited Bow Park, was hired as agent to buy and ship stock for the company in Britain.[46] Long afterwards, Clay remembered how George Brown's ardour had virtually swept cautious Scots into subscribing – his magnetic face and warm, finely-modulated voice, and the overpowering presence that almost prohibited doubts or second thoughts.[47]

In May, Brown could return to Canada to arrange for the actual chartering of the "Canada West Farm-Stock Association". It was to raise and sell pure-bred Clydesdales, sheep, pigs, and even chickens; but the shorthorn would remain its prime concern. Brown would be president, of course, and the vice-president would be his old Grit associate and Bow Park neighbour, David Christie, who now was Speaker of the Senate. Another old friend, Archibald McKellar, would serve as a Canadian director, while Thomas Nelson occupied a prominent place on the British board. And the whole scheme, in essence, consisted in applying capital, business skill, and technical knowledge to farming on a scale never seen before in Canada.[48]

Back in the Dominion that summer, Brown had to spend more time than he wanted in Toronto, though his family moved on to Bow Park late in June. But the *Globe* could not wholly be neglected; and Gordon, besides, had earned a holiday of his own.[49] They were even instituting something else for the newspaper: special early morning *Globe* trains, to Hamilton, first, and then to London, to carry the paper to out-of-town subscribers before breakfast. Brown thought it would be worth the considerable expense.[50] Then there was the house on Beverley Street, still under construction. But always his chief interest remained the Bow Park company.

By the autumn he had the organization in effective operation, and its future looked clear and inviting. George Brown had launched his last major enterprise, meant to crown the remainder of his days. Appearances, however, were sadly deceiving. Bow Park would end in utter failure – a failure inexorably connected with the final ending of Brown's own career.

3

Before settling down for a peaceful winter, he and his wife went down to Philadelphia to see the great American Centennial Exposition of 1876.[51] But the fall was not to pass away without other incident. Late in November, he found himself facing a charge of contempt of court, thanks to some reflections in the *Globe* on one of Her Majesty's justices of the Court of Queen's Bench in Ontario. The case really had begun some months before – and at its root was the famous "big push" letter once again.

During the summer, Chief Justice Harrison and Justices Morrison and Wilson of Queen's Bench had decided in favour of Senator John Simpson's application to have the editor of the *West Durham News* tried for malicious libel because he had charged Simpson with complicity in the alleged "big push" scandal. But in endorsing this decision Mr. Justice Wilson had added his own verbose opinion that George Brown's celebrated election letter of 1872 had, notwithstanding, been written "for corrupt purposes". What Wilson said, in fact, might really be called an extra-judicial tirade, since the *Globe* director was not before the court and his letter had not even been taken in evidence. But this in no way deterred his lordship from contending that he "might take notice of those matters which every person of ordinary intelligence is acquainted with", and asserting that Brown's call for a "big push" had simply been an invitation to bribery and corruption at the polls.[52]

It was all the more an odd performance, seeing that Wilson had nothing but assumption to go on − what "every person" knew − and not a word of evidence to contradict Brown's original denial of any sinister intent. Furthermore, Adam Wilson had once been a Liberal in politics, one whom Brown years before had helped to elect Mayor of Toronto and member for North York.[53] But nothing, of course, required him to love George Brown forever. And there was reason to think he had not loved him very long. There had been some friction between them after Wilson entered parliament in 1860, and he had been one of the "moderates" virtually tossed out of Sandfield Macdonald's government and on to the bench when Brown had forced its reconstruction in 1863. Perhaps then, Wilson was only now expressing an old, deep-rooted resentment. Perhaps he honestly believed that Brown was guilty in the "big push" episode. Or perhaps a combination of prejudice and assumption had brought him to pronounce as he had now, with all the prestige of his judicial authority surrounding him.

In any case, Brown at first ignored Wilson's gratuitous comments. But when the Conservative *Mail* and others seized on them delightedly (and there were by-elections going on), the *Globe* scathingly replied to the judge's "insolent and slanderous interpretation".[54] Once more it set out the arguments denying "big push" corruption; but more significantly, it also declared that, if as a result of this altercation the dignity of the judiciary should suffer, Wilson's own gross folly would be responsible. "We deeply regret being compelled to write of the conduct of any member of the Ontario bench in this fashion, but the offense was so rank, so reckless, so utterly unjustifiable. . . ."[55]

The response came, not from Wilson, but from a harried Mr. Wilkinson, the editor of the *West Durham News*, fearfully beset still by Simpson's action for libel. In a counter-attack that might help his own cause, Wilkinson filed a complaint against the managing director of the *Globe* for contempt of court in view of that journal's comments on Mr. Justice Wilson. The case did not come up for hearing until December 9. On that day, George Brown himself appeared in the courtroom before Chief Justice Harrison and Judge Morrison, to conduct his defence in person. He had a bad cold, but he was spoiling for the fight.

Vigorously he put forth his case, and took two days to do it, as he justified the *Globe*'s strictures on Wilson's conduct on grounds of explicit and unwarranted provocation. The judge, he roundly declared, had used his place to express opinions with "an indifference to evidence before the court and an indulgence in assumptions, surmises and insinuations totally unparalleled in the judicial proceedings of any Canadian court".[56] No one could claim that a judge might do no wrong or say what he pleased about anyone – and then condemn remonstrances as contempt of court! Indeed, he had searched the law books in vain to find any parallel for Wilson's behaviour in British courts for half a century, and he defied opposing counsel to find otherwise. Filled with conviction, vehemently delivered, this was an address in the best impassioned Brown style. The spectators had to be restrained from applauding.[57]

The hearings closed soon afterward, but judgment was not rendered until the end of December. At that time the judges disagreed, Harrison finding that there had been contempt, Morrison that there had not.[58] The charge accordingly came to nothing. Yet this was as clear as it had always been: that no one, not even a justice of the Crown with the majesty of the law behind him, could tread on George Brown with impunity.

A strike on the Grand Trunk, strongly condemned by the *Globe*, ushered in 1877. For a few days in early January Canada's main line of rail communication lay lifeless, until the management grudgingly rescinded a cut in wages. The mood of the times was sharp and rancorous. Depression was deep as the winter; and politics were becoming increasingly vehement as another federal election inevitably drew near. Mackenzie and his cabinet were still desperately striving to develop the Dominion amid world-wide depression, and to cut government expenditure at the same time. Macdonald and the Conservatives had quite recovered heart. They railed at the miserable failures of the Liberals and aggressively pushed their own recently proclaimed panacea for Canada's troubles, tariff protection. Of course, the free-trade *Globe* damned it, defended the Mackenzie régime against charges of incompetence and corruption, discovered fresh Tory scandals instead. Its tone was as edgy as the whole mood of the country; for now there was little that looked promising ahead.

Yet Brown himself remained largely concerned with matters

outside politics: the farm-stock company, *Globe* business, and the decorating of the new house. Parliament opened early in February; but it was a month later when he went up to Ottawa. There he at once consulted with Mackenzie, Holton, and other party friends in order to bring himself up to date,[59] since he might expect to have a prominent role in defending the government in the upper house.

The Senate, however, proved a remote Olympian haven compared to the battlefield of the Commons. Its sittings were short, its atmosphere relaxed, its consideration largely of legislative detail. It was worthy of remark, Brown felt, when "we old ladies" actually sat till 10:30 one evening and had a good debate.[60] Nevertheless, on March 19, war spread clearly to the upper house, when opposition forces there succeeded in carrying a motion condemning the Liberal government. George Brown spoke for an hour ("I made a capital speech," he modestly recorded), but the weight of Conservative appointments to the Senate for the six years after 1867 won the day.[61] Of course, under the cabinet system Mackenzie's government was only responsible to the verdict of the elected lower house. Yet it was a moral defeat, and Brown was glad at least to see the enemy majority in the Senate reduced from fifteen to ten in another vote the next day.[62]

His devotion to the Liberal cause and his liking for a good fight were still not sufficient to keep him in Ottawa long. He was too determined not to commit himself to political life again. Hence Senator Brown went back to Toronto after but three weeks in the capital, and only returned for the prorogation of parliament late in April.[63] Meanwhile Mackenzie and his colleagues had had a strenuous time in the Commons. Their large majority defeated every Conservative attack, but they closed the session breathless and exhausted.

Moreover, the situation was no better throughout the country as a whole. In British Columbia the failure of the Liberals' piecemeal building policy to produce the Pacific railway had brought angry talk of secession. In Ontario a Conservative programme that combined political picnics with speeches on protection had been succeeding all too well. In the Maritimes the Mackenzie ministry lacked really strong support. And in Quebec the upsurge of the Catholic clerical Ultramontane movement was badly harrying French-Canadian Liberals. Mackenzie constantly had to worry about the vulnerability of his *Rouge* associates to clerical attack. Strangely enough, he had even felt it necessary to complain to Brown a few months before that the *Globe* was being altogether too lenient and understanding in regard to priestly influence in Quebec, and was thus supplying comfort to the foes of Liberalism there![64]

His old friend, however, had even less concern for politics now that the summer season was beginning. The Brown family was in residence at Bow Park cottage before the end of May. George Brown himself was full of the farm company's affairs even while still in Toronto, and was up in his library of an evening, going over shorthorn herd books with Major Greig, one of the company directors.[65]

With the fresh capital provided, Bow Park was reaching new heights of well-groomed opulence. The fields were thick with fodder crops: rye, oats, peas, and corn. Nearly 400 shorthorns stood in sheltered paddocks, every animal inspected daily.[66] In the calving-house, each cow and and her calf had a box to themselves, and the full milk supply went to the offspring. The estate ran like the well-ordered agricultural factory it was: to the sound of bells, the clatter of farm machinery, and the coughing of the steam engine that pumped water, chopped feed, and cut wood for the winter.[67]

Visitors came from the United States and Europe to see Bow Park. It was part of the grand tour for British agriculturalists in North America. One such was James Macdonald, who in early August examined the farm for his forthcoming book, *Food from the Far West*. He found its buildings the most extensive he had seen throughout his wanderings across North America, and judged the Bow Park high-bred shorthorn herd to be probably the largest then in existence.[68] Only a few animals, he thought, were close to mediocre; the average was wholly creditable, and some were outstanding – for instance, Brown's Fourth Duke of Clarence, and the Grand Duchess of Oxford.[69] In a different vein, Macdonald looked to the growth of the new "dead meat" trade for the British market, which would do much to provide stimulus for the big cattle ventures such as this, when refrigeration methods on shipboard were improved.[70]

Bow Park was a great deal more than a factory enterprise, however. It was the ideal country home for the Brown family. There were the groves and tanglewoods to wander through, wild flowers and berries to collect, ponies, horses, and pets, boats along the Grand, and far vistas from grassy knolls and river banks for quiet contemplation. The children could roam freely there – Margaret, who was thirteen now, Oda, or Edith, eleven, and Ginney, nearly eight. As for George and Anne, it was constant joy to be at Bow Park. A twinge of sadness, known to generations of Canadians, came each year with the frosts of autumn, when it was time to close the family cottage and return to town once more.

4

In the autumn of 1877, the Browns were finally in possession of their proud new house. It stood at the corner of Beverley and Baldwin Streets, in what were then the quiet residential outskirts of north-west Toronto. It was not a notably large or extravagant mansion by the standards of Victorian Toronto plutocracy, but it was unquestionably substantial and distinguished. Built of red brick with carved stone trim, it rose three stories to a mansard roof. Elegant cast-iron railings set it off on the two street sides, while a high board fence and hedges enclosed the large gardens and range of outbuildings behind: the gardener's cottage, the stable, cow shed, and the chicken houses. Inside the house, the principal rooms displayed imported marble mantelpieces monogrammed with George's and Anne's initials, crystal chandeliers, panelled walls, and elaborately "enriched" ceilings. There was even a shower-bath, and water and gas were piped to dressing quarters throughout the house. They christened it "Lambton Lodge" (John Lambton, of course, was the great Liberal Earl of Durham), and happily looked forward to long, contented years in their new home.[71]

But outside its walls there seemed little contentment to be found in Canada, what with depression, unemployment, labour unrest, ever-falling public revenues, and clamour for protection. Brown's *Globe* still stood unshakably for the British Cobdenite principles of free trade and economic liberalism. Trade would right itself, it confidently proclaimed. The harvest had been good; the world-wide slump was a necessary purge after speculation and over-indulgence that would bring a return to economic health; and Canada was suffering far less than other countries.[72] Above all, the Grit organ denounced the Conservative proposal to import the American high-cost protective system, which certainly had not saved the United States from deep depression. It constantly argued that this "cure" would prove a far more permanent disaster than the present commercial malaise in a country inevitably committed to the production of low-cost goods for the world market.[73]

Despite all such contentions, distressed and impatient Canadians were less and less inclined to wait for economic recovery in nature's good time. *Something* must be done. Conservative talk of a "National Policy" and prosperity achieved through unspecified "adjustment" of the tariff sounded far more positive and hopeful than the *Globe*'s disquisitions on the infallible working of economic laws or the Mackenzie government's insistence that austerity and retrenchment offered the only possible way out. The discussion went on into the bleak winter of 1877-8, as the *Globe* repeatedly tried to sniff out signs of recovery and prove the soundness of the sensible Liberal policy.[74] But not for the first or last time, Vision threatened to be a far more effective appeal than Common Sense.

Furthermore, there were difficulties within the ministry itself. Mackenzie had never managed either to choose a strong team or to stamp his own leadership firmly on the cabinet. Blake was still a problem; Holton remained somewhat querulously outside, despite offers of portfolios. There were virtually only two ministers of sure ability, Richard Cartwright and David Mills – and perhaps a newly appointed French Canadian, young Wilfrid Laurier.[75] "I don't wonder at all at your groaning a little under the heavy burden you carry," Brown wrote sympathetically to Mackenzie.[76] And then the weighty Edward Blake once more determined to retire. He was miserably unhappy in office, and ill as well. In spite of every entreaty, he resigned in January 1878, just when the Liberal government faced the last session of parliament before a general election.

Parliament opened on February 7. George Brown came up to the Senate a week later.[77] He was invited to stay with the Mackenzies, where the two old associates could discuss the coming campaign together.[78] But he spent less than a week in Ottawa. Anne's brother John, who had married them, had died very suddenly, and she was grieving deeply.[79] Brown did not return to Ottawa, in fact, for almost a month.[80] When he did, he had missed much of the savage skirmishing preliminary to the election campaigns. Yet he did have one important assignment when he rejoined the parliamentary struggle in mid-March. The Conservative Senator D. L. Macpherson, prominent railway contractor and business man, had made telling attacks both in pamphlets and in the Senate on Liberal financial policy, which allegedly had brought the country close to bankruptcy. George Brown was chosen to answer him. He worked busily, gathering statistics on revenue and expenditure in order to compare the records of the Mackenzie and Macdonald administrations. And on March 21 he rose in the Senate to make still another powerful parliamentary speech.

One might wonder how the speech could manage to be powerful, packed as it was with figures and drafts of national balance sheets.[81] Yet it was delivered as always with Brown's intense air of conviction, and its mastery of evidence was almost devastating. He pounded at Macpherson's omissions, miscalculations, and mis-statements. When the other interrupted with explanations or objections, the remorseless orator leapt after him and beat him down further. He showed that the total deficit, the "bankruptcy" so much lamented, added up to less than two and a half million dollars under Liberal rule, and that in any case it was largely due to extravagant obligations incurred under the previous Conservative régime.

"Yes, there is a deficit," Brown exclaimed. "But it is because the right men are in the right place that the deficit is not infinitely greater. . . . And now, when the storm has well nigh passed, when the clouds begin to break – you! – you who caused all the trouble – glory that the revenue is reduced. . . . You cannot cloak your smothered delight that there is a deficit!" But what did this "fearsome thing" actually amount to? To the sum set aside for debt reduction – "The deficit, in fact, was caused by the reduction of the Public Debt. Is that a balance sheet in such times as the present to alarm anyone?"[82]

His speech was a great success, and was quickly put into pamphlet form at the *Globe* for distribution as campaign literature. The author himself went back to Toronto the next day.[83] He evidently felt he had done his parliamentary duty by his party, for he only briefly returned to Ottawa in mid-April, staying just long enough to earn his sessional indemnity.[84] Parliament did not finally close till May; but Brown still had no intention of enlarging his activities there.

At the *Globe* office now, he helped to launch the press campaign for the approaching summer of electioneering. The essential issue, his paper already had declared, "lay between a Revenue tariff and a Protective one".[85] By July there were daily articles on that theme. In summary, they offered the opinion that protection was wasteful, reactionary, pernicious, and unjust – conducive to bad relations with the United States, disloyalty to the Empire, and ultimate ruin for Canada. Even Bow Park might have to be set aside when George Brown was engaged on a crusade such as this!

Early in August the *Globe* announced that the elections would be held about September 19, and the pace, if possible, grew hotter.[86] Alexander Mackenzie was straining himself to the limit in speaking across the country; Cartwright and Mowat too; but they badly needed Blake, who was absent in England. About the only notable reinforcement was Wilfrid Laurier. The *Globe* said of him approvingly: "The French Canadian of today is not less loyal to his race and his tradition than is his Anglo-Saxon compeer. . . . And in the Minister of Inland Revenue, he has a representative who unites in a remarkable degree the spirit of French Canada with that love and close appreciation of the value of British institutions which distinguish the British statesmen."[87]

The need for help was plain, and Brown's ardour had been fully aroused. And so he agreed to step into the campaigning himself, for one last time, and take on several speeches across Ontario. It was arranged that he would set forth in mid-August, but for some reason his tour was delayed.[88] Not until September 11 did he open in St. Catharines, at an evening meeting in the City Hall. Rain was pouring down, but the hall was crowded to hear the former Liberal leader once again. He gave them a four-hour speech (the audience was "wonderfully patient", he thought), ripping into the absurdity of the Conservatives' "National Policy" of tariff protection for everyone – which meant privilege for everybody, or, more simply, inflation all round.[89] The true path of advance for Canada, he argued, lay through developing her agricultural interests and improving her farming techniques. Indeed, George Brown now seemed to lay more particular stress on agricultural development than he had during his earlier years in politics. Was it because he himself now was a farmer on a large scale, with a very sizeable investment in Canada's agricultural future?

Two days later he was in Bowmanville, and staying with John Simpson. Again the rain came down to spoil the grand procession arranged for him, the heavy, driving rain that marks the break from the sticky heat of early September to the cool crispness of Canadian autumn. But Brown gave another four-hour speech in the Town Hall, and moved on next day to Port Hope. He talked three and a half hours this time, chastising "this miserable will o' the wisp they called 'National Policy'!"[90] Yet much of his address was on the achievements of the Reform party in an earlier day; the veteran, perhaps, could not help dwelling on his own campaigns. Then he had a week-end's rest, and on September 16 was off to speak in Paris, where it was arranged that Anne would come over from Bow Park with their neighbour David Christie to hear him.[91]

Next day was election day, and Brown went back to Toronto to follow the proceedings at the *Globe* office. For the first time, the vote was by secret ballot; the results came in much faster. But as they did, they revealed an ever-growing tale of Liberal defeat – in fact, complete disaster. The Conservatives had swept the country, to win by as large a margin as the Liberals had in 1874. It was a "Waterloo of defeats", the *Globe* admitted, produced above all by the "seductive delusion" that protection would bring economic recovery.[92] And surely the paper was right, though Brown, Mackenzie, and the Liberals generally had never anticipated so startling an overturn. They had instead campaigned largely in the confidence of having done their best for the country: of having achieved effective measures of reform, provided honest, competent administration, and maintained cautious development and careful economy during grave depression. But this was their own "seductive delusion" – to assume that a country hungry for bold action and fresh hope would think their best was good enough.

Brown's own response was typical: no crying over spilled milk; hope for the best ahead. He could scarcely believe that the Canadian people would swallow protection for long. He was even inclined, at first, to advise Alexander Mackenzie not to resign but to carry on and meet parliament, in the hope that the victorious Conservative forces would fall apart there, once they had to face the necessity of giving specific content to their vague election catch-all, the National Policy.[93] The defeated Prime Minister, however, found good reasons for not making the attempt. Early in October he prepared to resign and hand the country back to Sir John Macdonald.

Bowing to that decision, Brown urged Mackenzie to come to Toronto and stay at Lambton Lodge, where they could gather "your best friends round you".[94] And he sent further characteristic words of advice to this particular old friend whose ideas and policies had always been so close to his own: "You have everything to be proud of, and nothing to be abashed about in your little disaster – try to feel this thoroughly and to show people that you do feel it."

"Don't mope –" he said in cheery affection, "I wish I were beside you now to poke you up."[95]

5

In November of 1878 George Brown turned sixty. With grey hair becoming white, and silvery whiskers framing his long, august-looking countenance, he had more the appearance of a grave and stately patriarch than the hearty, exuberant politician of earlier days. Indeed, this patriarchal image would come down to posterity, thanks largely to solemn engravings of the elder Brown, widely distributed by the *Globe*, that hung for years like Liberal icons in good Grit homes throughout the country. Yet the image was wrong, or at least superficial. The tall, white-headed figure in the black frock coat only looked austere and sombre in repose. And for him, that state was still very far from habitual.

For in these later years he continued to be vigorous, high-spirited, and full of quick enthusiasm. He tired more readily, no doubt; and he liked nothing better than to sit peacefully by the fireside with his wife. But there had always been this private tranquillity in Brown, who could relax so contentedly and completely within his own domestic world. Certainly, he seemed as physically strong as ever. At Bow Park he kept up his favourite pastime of collecting and piling stones in the fields, chatting away meanwhile with guests who found much less enjoyment in the sport.[96] At the *Globe* office he still liked to leap up the stairs four steps at a time – though Bob Gay, his old foreman, lamented that the Chief could no longer take six.[97] And it was in this era that he once settled a little friction with a badgering porter in the Montreal railway station by calmly picking up the man by the collar and the seat of his trousers and depositing him gently outside the station on the ground. The awestruck porter said afterwards that he had never felt so utterly helpless.[98]

Nevertheless, the years had had some mellowing influence on Brown. John Clay, agent for the farm-stock company in Britain, visited Bow Park and saw in its director "the manners of a Chesterfield", and "a kindly sort of sleepy eye that flashed as he spoke".[99] His methods remained autocratic, his nature uncompromising – but, said Clay, "In his home he was delightful, while on the farm he was one of the most charming men I ever met."[100] His conversation ranged widely. He talked not only of Canada and its politics, the promise of the great North West, or the state of American relations, but familiarly as well of Gladstone, Bright, and Cobden, and the overseas world of Britain and Europe. His flood of lively eloquence quite carried fascinated listeners away.[101]

But he could be particularly fascinating with children, gentle, direct, and playful as he was with them. His own three adored him. He was undoubtedly an indulgent father, though not a heedless one; he once wrote earnestly to his wife, "We must try hard to guide them wisely and firmly – but through the law of love."[102] Years later, when Margaret, Edith, and George were grown up with children of their own, they would treasure the memories of their father. Particularly they would remember watching at the windows of their Toronto home on winter evenings for a tall figure in an astrakhan cap to come briskly up the street. For then there would be laughter, games, and stories, and the crowning moments of the whole day.[103]

Of course, there was always a deep vein of seriousness in

Brown. It was expressed in his devoted Presbyterian faith, for instance. Yet there was nothing stern or narrowly pious about his religious outlook. He went to church regularly: in Toronto now, to St. James' Presbyterian, in Brantford, to Zion Church (where he would sit surrounded by his Bow Park farm hands like a laird with his tenantry) ;[104] it was not a matter of external obligation but a natural and necessary part of life itself. He felt little desire to probe into doctrine, but tried essentially to follow Christian precepts. His whole attitude came out clearly in a report he once sent to Anne in Scotland of the position Professor Paxton Young had taken during an evening's quiet discussion at their house.

"He said," recorded Brown a bit uncertainly, "that the longer he lived the more he felt that it was the spirit of Christianity rather than the letter that was to be looked to – and that a very large part of the duty of Christianity was to walk in love and charity to all men, to discharge all duties faithfully in every relation of life and make those around you happy. I think I have confessed to you feeling something like this – but the Christian system as taught by our own Presbyterian Church is so noble, so fine, so elevating, so admirably framed to make people good and happy and even prosperous in this world, as well as perfect them for that which is to come . . . that one shrinks from criticizing, even in his own mind, any part of it."[105]

Brown was wholly serious, as well, in his respect and care for learning. That might perhaps appear in his liking for the conversation and comradeship of academic figures such as Daniel Wilson, soon to be President of University College, or Paxton Young – or possibly in his testing his fourteen-year-old nephew, George Brown Ball, in Latin when he applied for a job at the *Globe* office.[106] It might be seen in his consistent concern for the development of public education, from common schools to university. And if he was a strong partisan of the state University of Toronto against denominational rivals, it was not merely because he believed in non-sectarian education, but because he thought that a single large provincial university could serve learning far more effectively than a number of small, divided colleges.[107] When Premier Mowat named him to the Senate of the University of Toronto in 1873, it meant almost as much to Brown as his appointment by Mackenzie to the Senate of the Dominion itself. Later, he remarked to Edward Blake, a graduate of Toronto, "Blake, do you know what the office is that I would most like to fill, if I were competent? I would like, if I were only a graduate, to be Chancellor of the University."[108]

One also might judge that journalism was severely serious

business to George Brown. At any rate, the *Globe* during his régime could rarely be accused of being light-hearted. There was sharp wit, biting irony, and derisive sarcasm; but any laughter was virtually always at someone's expense. Abusive, fierce, and ruthless: thus the *Globe* might seem to those who suffered at its hands – to Goldwin Smith, for instance, who described it as wielding "a literary despotism that struck without mercy".[109] And in the same way, Brown, through popular identification with his paper, might appear to be harsh, humourless, and perpetually indignant. People continued to assume that George Brown wrote every word in the *Globe*, even though it had long had a sizeable editorial staff, he was often away, and Gordon Brown for years had done far more to set the daily editorial tone. But the very success and power of the *Globe* helped to maintain a public image of Brown the dictator in its own inexorable and awesome mould.

And yet his paper was merely following the normal jungle conduct of contemporary Canadian journalism, where the life of less hardy news-sheets might be short as well as nasty and brutish. The pages of the *Globe*'s main rivals, from the *British Colonist* to the *Leader* (which died in 1876) or the *Mail*, showed no real difference in kind. Of course, each accused the other of forcing regrettable departures from gentlemanly behaviour – much as in the jungle world of competing sovereign states. But the first stone had been cast long before, in the obscure past, and if the *Globe* acquired an enduring name among its enemies for polemics and denunciation, it was essentially because it *was* enduring, outliving rival after rival while its dread reputation grew.

George Brown, then, accepted journalism as a fiercely serious business, always in the firm conviction of its public duty to expose wrong-doing and fight to the utmost for the true cause of the people – his own cause. Yet the staff on the *Globe* knew that the stern public image he accepted was far from being a valid picture of the Chief himself. Indeed, E. W. Thomson, who became principal editorial writer on the *Globe* in December 1878 and served till 1891, noted that Gordon Brown ("the greatest all-round editor I have yet had the pleasure of observing at work") actually inspired the bulk of the daily editorials during George Brown's later career – though Gordon, he added, was "a little too much given to ingenuity in vindictiveness".[110]

As a matter of fact, it was Thomson and William Inglis who were regularly writing the leading editorials by now. "We believed our indignation to be highly moral," Thomson later noted, "vituperative editorial was easy, and the vials of our wrath were poured out so freely [in the winter after the Conservative victory of 1878] that the Tories charged George Brown with penning all the the editorials himself. This was equivalent to describing them as ferocious in the extreme, and the relish of being confused with 'George' was not dashed by the lamentation of our opponents that the writing indicated him to be far gone in senility."[111]

By this time the *Globe*'s managing director was actually removing himself from any real concern with the day-to-day current of political events. Whenever Gordon was away and he presided at the editorial conferences, the staff could observe that he longer caught the significance of suggestions or verbal sketches of articles, as Gordon always did, but was inclined to leave things to the writers, and to treat the meeting as a formality, an opportunity for pleasant reflection on the past rather than consideration of the present.[112]

There was one occasion, as Thomson recalled, when someone mentioned to the Chief his old connection with penal reform and the Penitentiary Commission of 1849. This brought on a discourse on modes of punishment, and on capital punishment, which George Brown would still support. He lay back in his chair, "thrust out his long legs, contemplated his extensive boots, shook his white head solemnly, tightened his lips as though he would not say it, and then as if the spirit were too strong to be controlled, raised his eyes and burst out: 'Eh mon, but hangin's a grand thing for the criminal classes!' "[113] A qualification, perhaps, on Brown's early record of liberalism in penology!

He was the best of company at these meetings, amiable and easy-going, very far from the dictator. He kept an eager boyishness in his sixties. "No man was less a prig," concluded Thomson, "and this may have been a reason why some academic prigs hated him so ferociously, and, after his death, proceeded to stamp on his grave."[114] The reference could only have been to Goldwin Smith, whose own obituary review of the savage power that Brown had wielded would be savage to an extreme.

Impulsive, confident, peremptory, Brown was really what he had always been: downright and unequivocal in his loves and hates – kindly and affectionate, warlike and uncompromising. But perhaps contemporary Canada's one true humorous journal, *Grip*, would put it best in a piece of doubtful poetry not two years later:

> *His nature was a rushing mountain stream,*
> *His faults but eddies which its swiftness bred.*[115]

6

Bow Park was running into difficulties. The long-continuing depression had kept the market for pure-bred farm stock from developing as expected. The anticipated big Canadian demand did not materialize; Bow Park remained ahead of its time. The transatlantic "dead meat" trade was still hazardous and experimental, the British market scarcely worth the risk. And while there was some demand in the United States for high-bred stock, it was fickle and apt to be interrupted by restrictions placed on bringing cattle across the American border. Under these unfriendly circumstances, George Brown had simply gone on producing and hoping. But his company's shareholders in Britain were growing alarmed. Hearing nothing from Brown, they decided to send out John Clay on a mission of inquiry.[116]

He arrived in Toronto in January of 1879. "Are you here for peace or war?" Brown greeted him suspiciously. "For neither," Clay returned. "What we want is the truth, and if you had replied to letters and appeals there would have been no occasion for this trip."[117] On that, he was hospitably invited to stay at Lambton Lodge. Brown had nothing to hide. His faults, as usual, had been too much self-assurance and optimism; and he was as bad a correspondent as ever. He had put off writing and taken everything on himself, always expecting that things would get better and he could then send a good report to the shareholders.[118]

For more than two months Clay made Lambton Lodge his headquarters, while he and his host paid frequent visits to Bow Park and went over the accounts together. When he talked to Brown, the latter's enthusiasm and overflowing hopes effectively dispelled all worry. But the state of the farm itself brought deep misgivings – until, back "under the spell of Mr. Brown's eloquence the sun shone again".[119] Clay found that no animals at all were being sold, while debts and interest charges were mounting. The company was really drifting towards bankruptcy. Furthermore, George Brown was trying to manage far too much of the business himself, by wire; the other Canadian directors' roles were purely nominal. As for the vice-president, David Christie, his own farm nearby on the Paris Plains seemed rather run down, and when he and Brown came together they chiefly passed the time as two old party cronies, talking of early days and vanished backwoods politics.[120]

Still further, Clay considered that Brown's farming methods, however "advanced" and highly organized, were basically unwise for Bow Park.[121] Brown was a devotee of the soiling system, and ardently believed that because of Ontario's long winters it was far more efficacious to raise fodder crops and feed the herd in stalls throughout the year than to rely on uncertain grazing.[122] But this had required a large investment in storage barns and box-houses, while rich pastures stayed virtually unused. Moreover, Clay thought that the cattle, once supremely healthy, were weakening through being so generally penned up. Bow Park's graveyard, he noted, was full of valuable animals. In his judgment George Brown had failed to become a practical farmer.[123] He had farmed by the book, and nature was refusing to conform.

Nevertheless, the herd still had many fine, strong cattle. With careful management the situation might be saved. Brown had acquired an excellent herd manager the autumn before in John Hope from the Cotswolds, an expert in pure-bred cattle; but it was on the level above Hope that the direction needed changing. Brown, in fact, himself proposed that Clay take over, though the other was not eager for the job.[124] At any rate, he set off back to Scotland in the spring to lay his findings before the company shareholders. Brown's own answer was more capital to restore the finances.[125] If that were forthcoming, he would readily accept changes in the running of Bow Park.

These farm affairs had kept him from going up to the new Dominion Parliament, in session since February of 1879, and he did not attend the Senate until early May. Then he found Sir John Macdonald's restored Conservative régime already in trouble – or so he was glad to believe. The vaunted National Policy tariff was a mass of confusion. Even with sharp protective increases, the Tories had not been able to overcome the deficit themselves, and the farmers of Canada were turning away from the myth of agricultural protection. "The government party is completely demoralized," Brown wrote to his wife. "As it is they will muddle on until they break up from utter incompetence to grapple with the troubles they have piled up for themselves."[126]

It was highly wishful thinking; but a few weeks after the session ended, Mowat's sweeping victory in the Ontario provincial elections seemed to indicate that a reaction to Tory pretensions was setting in. The Conservatives had carried the province in 1878 with a majority of nearly two to one; now the Liberals triumphed in the same proportion. No wonder, then, that George Brown had no particular qualms about his party's future. As well as reigning in Ontario since 1872, the Grits had ruled the Dominion for almost five of the twelve years since

Confederation. Brown might well expect the alternation in office to continue. He could scarcely foresee that the Liberals would not again hold power in the Dominion until 1896, or that under the brilliant Blake, soon to succeed the supposedly plodding Mackenzie as federal leader, the party would have no real success whatever.

Another bright note came at the close of the session, when Brown was offered a knighthood, a Knight Commander of St. Michael and St. George. It was a belated result of former Prime Minister Mackenzie's efforts to have him honoured, and an exceedingly belated recognition of his vital role in the achievement of Confederation. No man in Canada deserved the honour more; yet it had been repeatedly delayed since Mackenzie had first intimated to Brown in 1875 that the recommendation was being made.[127] The imperial authorities had grown chary of granting colonial honours by that time, since some of their creations had pretty well tarnished their gleaming chivalry in the fumes of local politics: Sir Hugh Allan, Knight of the Pacific Scandal, for example. Accordingly, Dufferin and Carnarvon had moved very cautiously in regard to Brown, a man who had so many vociferous political opponents. The "big push" episode had even caused delay, until Dufferin was satisfied that it was safe to proceed.[128] His own relations with Brown grew cordial, and when the Governor-General departed from office in Canada late in 1878, he and the *Globe* director exchanged friendly personal messages of farewell.[129]

At length, in 1879 under a new Governor-General, the Marquis of Lorne, the imperial mechanism for producing knighthoods finally turned one out for Brown. On May 24, the Queen's birthday, he was ordered to appear in Montreal to receive the honour. He went, and he declined it.[130] Was it because the reward had come so late that his sensitive pride could not accept it, or because he refused to come in at the tail of some rather dubious predecessors? Quite likely both; but also, Brown had little taste for ceremonial distinctions in themselves. He had so expressed himself to his wife when Mackenzie had first mentioned the prospect of a title.[131] And long before, he had indicated his belief that official honours and social elevation did not accord well with either journalism or Liberalism in Canada.

Yet had he not, besides, a feeling that if it was something to be offered a K.C.M.G., it was still more to have declined? In any event, he composed a formal letter to Lord Lorne expressing his appreciation and the profound respect he felt for the Crown.[132] His old friend Daniel Wilson caught the proper note as he congratulated Brown the more on his refusal: "I am very glad that it is not because Her Majesty failed to recognize your true worth that you are still chief among H.M. Canadian Commoners, instead of being one of the rather too abundant colonial knights."[133]

But all this was by-play. The really important question that summer remained Bow Park. In Scotland, meanwhile, John Clay had reported on his findings to the shareholders.[134] There were bitter discussions, and angry charges levelled against Brown for the company's losses. Yet Thomas and William Nelson, two of the principal investors, stood by their brother-in-law. It was agreed that Clay would serve as manager for the company, to work with John Hope to put Bow Park on an even keel.[135] As he left for Canada again in August, Clay did not look forward to the task of replacing George Brown, particularly when he was bringing no more money out with him.[136] The Nelsons had succeeded in saving Brown's position as company president; but the other shareholders would not agree to put more funds into the enterprise.

Brown had been working hard to have the farm's affairs "cut and ready" for Clay's arrival.[137] His family were at Niagara for the summer, perhaps because he did not want them present for the rows that were almost sure to follow. For the former owner of Bow Park could never yield authority easily, he did not rate Hope as highly as Clay did, and he was much upset that no financial aid would be provided to ensure the farm's recovery.[138]

There was a gulf between the two men as the new régime got under way in September. There were jealousies and factions among the farm hands at Bow Park, as well.[139] But Brown seldom kept resentments long, except for his classic feud with Macdonald, and he recognized that Clay was labouring in a common cause. His spirits revived as the time for showing their stock at the fall fairs came round. Their Bow Park shorthorns did well from Ottawa to London, while the Clydesdales swept up awards across the border. Then in mid-October they ventured on a sale of some of their finest cattle in Chicago, and Brown, Clay, and Hope went there together to direct it. The results were disappointing, however. Yet Brown was almost incorrigibly cheerful and optimistic once more.[141]

November brought a new source of worry. The Americans were talking now of closing the border to Canadian cattle because of disease; and though the Bow Park stock was still healthy, Brown and Clay had to fear the loss of their one sizeable potential market. They made hasty preparations to send up to one hundred shorthorns to a farm leased near Chicago.[142]

But even as they were doing so, sheer calamity struck Bow Park.

About eleven o'clock on the night of December 2, the citizens of Brantford saw a lurid rosy light in the south-eastern sky. The fire bells rang, the engines turned out; but the news came quickly that it was Bow Park — and that was hopelessly too far. There, the great barn had inexplicably caught fire. Clay afterwards thought it was the work of an incendiary, one of the jealous old hands who had not accepted his and Hope's new authority. There was nothing to stop the flames; a fierce wind sent them roaring down the whole long range of buildings. All that could be done was to save the stock. The barn, the engine and implement sheds, the model stable, the box-houses: in all, seven of the ten main buildings burned to ashes before the wind changed and the wild night's destruction ceased. The cattle were saved, but sheep, pigs, and many of the work horses were lost.[143]

Brown was in Toronto, but arrived by train next day. He stood completely dazed as he surveyed the black sweep of desolation.[144] Then the cattle were moved to stalls in the Brantford Fair Grounds for the winter, while he strove to arrange finances to begin reconstruction of the farm. There was some $65,000 insurance on the property, but it was held with several companies, and disagreement arose over the settlement.[145] Under the circumstances, Brown had to meet the emergency needs of the estate from his own pocket. At this very moment he was engaged in a new programme of expansion at the *Globe*, and even a man of his reputed wealth found himself stretched thin. Yet he faced up to the heavy task "without a murmur", as Clay said.[146]

Things could always be worse. And soon they were. For three weeks Clay and Brown struggled through the rain and mud of a mild December to see all the cattle looked after, feed bought to replace that lost with the barn, and rebuilding started at Bow Park. And then on Christmas Day, of all days, disaster came again. The stable that had only been fitted up since the fire burned to the ground in the early hours of Christmas morning. Fourteen more horses were lost, the feed that had been gathered, the harness and equipment as well.[147] It was almost certainly the incendiary again; Clay even thought he knew him: "You could point your finger," he reported, painfully, "but you dare not utter a name."[148]

Anne's sister, Jessie Nelson, was staying at Lambton Lodge that winter, and was with George when the news arrived from Brantford. She saw him slump down into a chair and cry like a child.[149] It was the one agonizing blow too many in the series he had suffered. He did not go down to Bow Park this time. He never went there again.[150] He could not bear to see his beloved estate, his bold venture into pedigreed stock-raising in Canada far ahead of its time, end thus in complete ruin and tragedy. Yet the final round of his own tragedy was only now beginning.

7

March 25, 1880; four-thirty on a dull afternoon.[151] Brown was working quietly at the *Globe* office in his room that opened off the landing of the staircase up from King Street, which went on to the editorial rooms above. There was a tap at the door. He looked up from his desk to see a sallow little man, not much more than five feet tall, thin-faced, with a straggling moustache and goatee, standing uncertainly in his doorway. George Bennett was his name, the intruder mumbled, employed in the *Globe* engine-room for the past five years, and now discharged by the shop foreman for intemperance. He would like a certificate from Mr. Brown that he had served five years. He had the paper with him – fumbling for it – and if Mr. Brown would sign —.

Brown was impatient. He did not know the man. He did not know Bennett's record of drunkenness, neglect of duties, and wife-beating, or that he was now out on bail after being arrested for non-support.[152] Least of all did he know that Bennett, drinking heavily and brooding on his wrongs, had bought a revolver before coming to the *Globe* that day, and written down wild vows to kill his enemies at the newspaper office.[153] The one thing Brown did know was that he had been needlessly disturbed by this unprepossessing little creature, who had no doubt got what he deserved.

Gruffly he told Bennett to take his paper for signature to the head of the department where he had been employed. The foreman there had already refused to sign it, said Bennett, moving into the room and half closing the door behind him. Then take it to Mr. Henning, the *Globe* treasurer, who would have the record on the books – Brown grew uneasy. What did this man want? Bennett came forward to the desk. "Sign it – sign it," he demanded harshly. Brown rose. Angry refusal brought fierce insistence; the sound of rising voices could be heard in the editorial rooms. Now Brown's temper was soaring – when Bennett, white-faced and staring, suddenly snatched out his revolver and cocked it. *The little wretch might be meaning to shoot me,* flashed through Brown's mind.[154] Impulsively he leaped forward, grabbing for Bennett's wrist. There was a moment of mad struggle. The gun fired as Brown managed to deflect it downward. "Help, help – murder!" he shouted wildly. But his far greater strength quickly overcame his assailant. Forcing Bennett back out of the room and on to the landing, he held him there against the wall as he wrenched the still loaded weapon away.

The shot, the cry, and the noise of struggle brought three editorial staff members, Thomson, Ewan, and Blue, pounding down the stairs from above.[155] Aghast, they rushed to seize hold of Bennett, while Brown, grey and trembling, leaned against the wall. "Are you hurt, Mr. Brown?" Blue asked anxiously. "I don't know," Brown answered in a daze. Blue pointed sharply at the other's leg. "There," he said urgently. On the outside of the left thigh there was a clean hole in the broadcloth trousers. Brown slowly ran his hand down, and behind his leg a little lower. It came up stained with blood.[156]

They called the police and the doctor, while Brown went back into his room to lie down. Dr. Thorburn arrived and quickly dressed the injury. It seemed to be only a flesh wound, and quite superficial; the *Globe* director already appeared to be recovering, as he talked and joked about his "assassination" with excited members of the office staff.[157] Undoubtedly it would make a good news story for a rather dull day. He even walked down out of the building to take his usual hired carriage from the West End Cab Company home to Lambton Lodge.[158] He expected merely to have a short stay in bed while the wound healed. But he would never return to the *Globe* office.

8

At home, Anne settled her husband into bed; sadly shocked by what had happened, profoundly thankful that it was no worse. In the next few days messages of sympathy came in from all across the country. "The Czar of King Street has had a narrow escape," Goldwin Smith wrote less sympathetically to John A. Macdonald. "If he [Bennett] had used a horsewhip, perhaps the wave of public indignation would have been less universal."[159] Of course, Smith regarded the injury as slight, just as Brown did himself. But after four days the wound, instead of healing, was becoming inflamed and painful, while the invalid fretted to be out of the house and back at work.[160] On

March 30 he even held the annual shareholders' meeting of the
Globe Printing Company at Lambton Lodge, presiding from a
day-bed, much against his doctor's advice.[161] The picture given
to the meeting was a grey one. Because of heavy expenditure on
new equipment, the *Globe* had had only the barest credit
balance for the previous year, and it was decided to suspend
quarterly dividends for the year ahead.[162]

Undoubtedly the *Globe* was in difficulties; not desperate, but
serious, the result of the latest expansion that Brown had mapped
out for it. In the year gone by, its circulation had not been rising. In fact, in the summer of 1879 it had actually fallen from
a general level of about 24,000 for the daily to a low point of
20,000.[163] The paper's position was still unchallenged, and circulation had climbed again to about 23,000 by November of that
year.[164] But to George Brown that had not been good enough.
Perhaps the Tory sweep in 1878 had had something to do with
it; more probably it was the consequence of the long-drawn-out
depression. At any rate, in the autumn of 1879 Brown had decided
to try his usual aggressive answer that had worked so regularly
before: invest in new improvements to expand the journal's
circulation, and count on increased advertising to pay for the
outlay made.

And so, on November 1, it had been announced in the *Globe*
that a whole new version of the paper would come out on
January 1, 1880. The single great "blanket sheet" folded to
make four pages would disappear. In its place would be a new-
style journal of eight smaller pages, rising to sixteen when
warranted. This really meant the introduction of the multi-page
newspaper known today. The transformation would be possible
because completely new press machinery was being installed at
the *Globe*: the latest Bullock web presses, which could print, cut
and fold 28,000 eight-page units in an hour. A new font of type
had been ordered from Edinburgh to complete the wholesale
change. Yet the new *Daily Globe* would continue to sell for six
dollars a year, post-paid.[165] Still further, a new *Weekly Globe*
was announced a month later, enlarged from eighty to ninety-
six columns and printed on its own Bullock press, its price also
to remain unchanged at two dollars per annum.[166]

It was a sweeping venture at any time; remarkably so, considering the still lingering depression and the fact that Brown
had the debts and losses of Bow Park hanging over him. Perhaps even he would not have made the gamble had the fires at
Bow Park occurred a little earlier. But when they came in
December of 1879, he was already committed to his costly
expenditures on the *Globe*. All he could do was hope that they

would bring returns, and quickly. But meanwhile all his considerable wealth was tied up in the paper and his attempts to restore the devastated stock-farm. He could only hope and pray.

The new *Weekly Globe* had duly commenced with January of 1880.[167] But at the same time Brown had to announce that the machinery for the new daily issue was not ready, and it could not begin until late February.[168] Actually, it was mid-April before the multi-page *Daily Globe* finally appeared.[169] And all that time, through the first three months of 1880, Brown had been struggling with the problem of getting his new daily edition into operation. Circulation was advancing again, it was true. But he could not hope to recoup his expenses until the new *Globe* was actually on the streets. Of course, he had come through storms like this before: in 1861, for example, when the *Globe* had been expanded in advance of circulation while his Bothwell estate faced hard depression. Yet the strains at that time had brought him serious illness before his fortunes had fully recovered.[170] Now he was twenty years older, and suffering from a bullet wound that would not heal.

And so, as Brown lay ill at Lambton Lodge in early April, 1880, he was wracked with worry over his affairs, feverishly anxious to be up and doing, and, beyond that, full of the heartbreak of Bow Park. How could the losses there be made good? There was insurance, but it was still under dispute; and he and Clay had quarrelled further over how a settlement should be made.[171] There were unpaid farm debts still, the angry shareholders in Britain; and, apart from the land itself, the only saleable assets left to Bow Park were the cattle housed at Brantford. Brown had gone there in person late in January to try to help their public sale.[172] He had made an eloquent speech on what improved stock would do for Canada; but the audience proved chiefly curious, and still suspicious of newfangled Bow Park notions. "The Dominion maker was thirty years ahead of his time," Clay concluded gloomily.[173] The one chance remaining was the Chicago market. There John Hope at last managed to make a good sale in the middle of April.[174]

Perhaps things were finally looking up! The new *Globe* also came out in splendid form on April 15, with twelve pages. Brown's spirits came surging back as he rallied for the battle of recovery. He wired for Clay and made his peace: seemed almost his old self as he talked brightly of being back on duty in a week or two.[175] But it was already too late. He had been taxed too long and too severely. His physical defences had fatally broken.

For over a week his wound had been showing evidence of

gangrene.[176] Now his leg was swelling and becoming badly abscessed. Other doctors were called in; yet they could do nothing to check the spread of infection. Brown continued to be hopeful, cheerful despite steadily mounting pain. His appetite was failing, he slept poorly, and he was growing weak and feverish.[177] Still, there were periods of rally, as he fought back with all his courage and determination. Several times in fact, he was said to be much improved, in reassuring bulletins printed in the *Globe* through the latter days of April.[178] But each time his waning powers gave way, and he fell back exhausted. He could not eat; his massive body was wasting. And ruthlessly the poison in his system spread.

Old friends and associates wrote or called repeatedly: Alexander Mackenzie, Charles Clarke of Elora, men who had worked for him at Bow Park or the *Globe*.[179] An elderly printer, J. S. Smith, wrote recalling to his "dear friend" the distant day when they had tried the *Globe*'s first hand press together, and the young editor had proudly pronounced it good.[180] But by the end of April Brown was lapsing into delirium or coma, and his lucid periods were becoming shorter and full of suffering. There was little that his doctors or his heartsick wife and family could do but watch over him. Their pain was the greater because his conscious moments now were saddened by the sense of failure – above all, that he had not ensured the rich, contented future he had wanted so much for Anne and his three children.

One day his sister Marianne sat at his bedside as he seemed to be rousing again. He liked to talk whenever he could, and to hear news of the outside world as long as possible, for now he knew he was dying. "It's a troublesome world, George, isn't it?" said Marianne, as she made conversation.

He looked at her with the old quick flash of eye. "No," he answered keenly, "I have enjoyed my work, I've worked hard. It's been an intense pleasure to me." He spoke in a lively burst of energy, gesticulating as ardently as ever. "It's a grand thing to try to do one's duty – I have tried to do my duty in the sight of God. I've worked hard for my country, for my family and myself." His voice sank suddenly; his strength ebbed away. "But I have failed," he murmured. "I haven't accomplished what I would have liked."[181]

"We all fail," said Marianne to comfort him, "and God knows if we were seeking to do our duty when we fail."[182] He seemed more peaceful at the thought. He made no complaint about his physical suffering. He bore it in resignation, and without a word.

Outside, May was opening in the misty green of young spring

foliage. But in shadowed Lambton Lodge, George Brown's last conscious moments were slipping away. He was exquisitely tender with Anne and the children; he recognized them still when he could no longer speak.[183] Then coma became continuous. And on May 9, on a clear, still Sunday morning before dawn, all life ceased. George Brown was gone – with so much left undone.

So much left undone. The sense of failure that had burdened Brown's last illness still hung about his death. The irony was that he had scarcely recognized defeat before; he had been so constantly happy and successful in his all-important private world. Throughout his life he had gone on believing that virtually any problem could be dealt with if one simply faced up to it, reasoned out a course of action, and followed it through boldly to a conclusion. But not all problems could be solved by bold, decisive action; nor could hope and resolution always be enough. Of course, political defeats might have taught Brown so years earlier – if politics had meant enough to him. Instead, it was only at the very last that he came face to face with failure. Here was the irony and tragedy of his life.

There had been no tragedy and little failure in his election defeat and retirement at Confederation. He had already achieved the essential task that he had set himself in politics. No, the real defeat came only when his cherished private world stood in danger, and all his optimism, vigour, and self-confidence proved powerless to save it. Perhaps Brown never showed more courage than in the quiet forbearance of his final weeks, forbearance that he learned in the bitterness of suffering.

Yet, though he died believing he had not attained his goals, his failure was only transitory, only apparent. For Bow Park would be restored when Thomas Nelson took control and refinanced it, the *Globe* would certainly recover, and Anne and her children assuredly would never know want. Brown's own world endured, after all. But what of the world outside? What of the institutions he had done so much to mould in Canada: the press, the Liberal party, Confederation itself? His work here would no less endure. He had shaped an irresistible sectional movement – largely through the power of the newspaper he had also made – and used it to achieve a great national purpose, federal and transcontinental union. Through nearly forty years George Brown had fixed his mark on Canada. It was a mark beyond all erasing.

9

On May 12, in the bright spring sunshine, a slow, solemn procession moved through the hushed and crowded streets of Toronto towards the burying-ground on the outskirts known as the Necropolis.[184] Only the tolling of church bells broke the stillness. Businesses had closed; the visiting D'Oyly Carte Company had cancelled their performance of the new Gilbert and Sullivan opera, *The Pirates of Penzance*.[185] As the long funeral procession passed – lines of carriages, delegations from across the country, two hundred *Globe* employees past and present – ordinary citizens silently fell in behind, to follow onward to the cemetery.[186] There, two of Brown's oldest political comrades, Alexander Mackenzie and Antoine Aimé Dorion, led the pall-bearers. Luther Holton had died but two months earlier; Oliver Mowat was abroad; but the others included personal friends, Daniel Wilson and David Christie; party colleagues, Edward Blake and Richard Cartwright; and former enemies, Alexander Campbell and William Howland.[187] Most eyes, however, were on the little group of Anne Brown and her children, standing desolate at the graveside, as Reverend Dr. King conducted the final ceremony, and laid her husband to rest beside his parents and his sister Catherine.

George Bennett would hang for murder. To the last he denied ever having premeditated the shooting of George Brown – victim of an almost irrelevant accident.[188] And surely, if Bennett had fired the shot, there had been other destructive influences at work to make the wound that he inflicted fatal: Bow Park, Brown's own worries and exertions, all that had preyed upon his mind. Yet the best skill of Bennett's talented lawyer, Nicholas Flood Davin, could not prevent a verdict of murder. The medical evidence that Brown had died from infection spread by the wound seemed overwhelming.[189] Besides, there were the damning documents Bennett had carried with him on the day of the shooting, in which he swore to kill his enemies.[190] Another age might still not have hanged him. But few then would have voted for any other judgment.

Afterwards, when it was all over, the following years went on much as George Brown might have wished. The family remained at Lambton Lodge, while Gordon Brown took over the *Globe* and Thomas Nelson and John Clay made Bow Park thrive again.[191] Soon, moreover, Margaret and Edith Brown entered the University of Toronto, to become two of its first women graduates. Yet Anne still yearned for Scotland, and now there was no George to hold her to Canada. She would return to Edinburgh; her girls would marry there; while young George Mackenzie Brown would go on to Oxford and afterwards join the Nelson publishing house. Later, he would briefly sit in parliament for Edinburgh, and become managing director of Nelson's — to work in close association with a leading Nelson author and future Governor-General of Canada, John Buchan, Lord Tweedsmuir. As for Anne Brown, she often spent summers at Oban in her later years, where in time the widow of another noted Canadian appeared, Lady Macdonald. It was said that the two elderly ladies ignored each other as their carriages passed, staring stiffly ahead, faithful still to their husband's old enmity.[192]

Yet George Brown's brother and sisters and their children remained firmly rooted in North America. George Brown, too, lay where he belonged, in the city and the country he had made his own. It was far from quiet Alloa, his birth-place, and from Edinburgh, his boyhood home. But what could be more a man's country than that which he himself had helped to build?

Note on Sources

As might be expected, this second volume on the life of Brown is based essentially on the same body of contemporary material in manuscripts, newspapers, and public records as the first. It should not be necessary, therefore, to repeat what has already been said regarding sources in *Brown of the 'Globe': the Voice of Upper Canada*, but merely to note additional materials or those that have been particularly stressed in this concluding work.

Among manuscript sources, the George Brown Papers (Public Archives of Canada, Ottawa) and the largely complementary Alexander Mackenzie Papers (Queen's University Archives, Kingston; microfilm copy at the Public Archives of Canada) remain of prime importance. But in the Brown Papers, the letters of George Brown to his wife, Anne, are of special value — as the many quotations in the text will show. This rich fund of closely personal information, lacking for Volume I, not only offers insight into Brown's private thoughts and feelings, but also provides a running commentary on many of the political issues in which he was involved, since he wrote to his wife so regularly and fully whenever he was away from home.

It is only unfortunate that so few of Anne Brown's replies have been preserved, for obviously her side of the correspondence was as detailed and affectionate as her husband's. The explanation is quite characteristic of both of them. George Brown could not bear the thought of other eyes than his seeing Anne's letters, and hence destroyed them after a few days, always making sure that he had a fresh batch to carry about with him in his pockets. (See George Brown to Anne Brown, December 12, 1875.) Anne Brown, on the other hand, saved almost everything that came from George, bundling the letters up, and often annotating them on the outside.

In consequence, the letter or two from Anne to her husband that still remain evidently have survived because he returned them to her, for one reason or another, with comments of his own — as, for instance, when in agitation she signed one of them "George", and he sent it back to her as proof, because she could not believe that she had done so! (See Anne to George Brown, February 28, 1865; George to Anne Brown, March 2, 1865.) That Anne was as interesting and lively a correspondent as George, however, is well substantiated by other letters to her relatives in Scotland, which are still in family hands at Ichrachan House in Argyllshire.

Other manuscript sources of notable value for this second volume are the John A. Macdonald Papers, Public Archives of Canada, and, at the Department of Public Records and Archives of Ontario, Toronto, the Edward Blake, the Richard Cartwright, and the Alexander Campbell Papers. This list does not exclude the other collections that have already been noted in Volume I; nor does it include a variety of other manuscripts utilized here and there in Volume II to which references will be found in the chapter notes below. One other source used in connection with the printers' strike of 1872 perhaps deserves particular mention here, since to the writer's knowledge it has not been examined in detail before: the Minute Books of the Toronto Typographical Society, in two volumes, 1859-1871 and 1872-1883.

The relevant public records, other than those for which copies were found in the Brown or Macdonald Papers, were largely dealt with through printed parliamentary journals and appendices, the G Series at the Public Archives (dispatches from the Secretary of State for the Colonies to the Governor-General of Canada), and Series C.O. 42 (dispatches from the British North American provinces to the Colonial Office), examined at the Public Archives or the Ontario Archives on microfilm copies. The Edward Cardwell Papers in the Public Record Office, London, also supplied significant information. Another useful source, which might be called "semi-official", was the published *Dufferin-Carnarvon Correspondence, 1874-1878*, edited by C. W. de Kiewiet and F. H. Underhill (Champlain Society, Toronto, 1955). This was supplemented by the Earl of Dufferin Papers on microfilm in the Public Archives.

In regard to newspapers, the Toronto *Globe*, of course, was stressed above all, balanced or offset by its chief rivals, the Toronto *Leader* and, later, the Toronto *Mail*. Montreal, Quebec, Halifax, Saint John, Hamilton, and London papers were examined for specific points, largely through files microfilmed by the Canadian Library Association. George Brown's parliamentary and public speeches generally had to be obtained through detailed press reports. There was no official Hansard until after Confederation. But some of his more important addresses were reprinted in pamphlets, which have been cited in the notes below.

Notes

Chapter 1

Pages 1 to 35

1 *Globe* (Toronto), January 2, 1860.
2 Public Archives of Canada, George Brown Papers, Mowat to Brown, December 15, 1859.
3 *Globe*, January 2, 1860.
4 *Ibid.*
5 *Ibid.*
6 *Ibid.*, January 5, 13, 1860.
7 *Ibid.*, December 28, 1859.
8 Captain C. H. Rhys, *A Theatrical Trip for a Wager* (London, 1861), p. 71.
9 *Ibid.*
10 Brown Papers, George Brown to Anne Brown, October 1, 1863.
11 *Globe*, January 2, 1860.
12 *Ibid.* All the references to the *Globe*'s improvements in this paragraph are from the same article of January 2, 1860.
13 *Ibid.*
14 See pp. 288-97 below.
15 No *Globe* circulation figures are available for early 1860, but this seems a safe estimate, since the nearest total given, on July 19, 1861, was 27,996.
16 *Globe*, December 20, 27, 1861.
17 Robert Sellar, *George Brown, the Globe and Confederation* (Toronto, 1917), p. 6. See also *Brown of the Globe*, vol. 1, pp. 178-9.
18 Typescript history of the *Globe* (no author, but probably M. E. Hammond) in the office of the *Globe and Mail*, Toronto, p. 47; W. J. Rattray, *The Scot in British North America* (4 vols., Toronto, 1880-3), vol. 2, p. 1124.
19 *Globe*, January 7, 1860.
20 *Ibid.*, August 16, 1860.
21 *Ibid.*, August 16, 20, 1860.
22 *Ibid.*, January 16, 1860.
23 J. P. Robertson, *A Political Manual of the Province of Manitoba and the North West Territories* (Winnipeg, 1887), p. 162.
24 *Globe*, November 25, 1859.
25 *Ibid.*, January 26, 1860.

26 *Ibid.*
27 *Ibid.*, January 27, 1860.
28 *Ibid.*, February 10, 1860.
29 Public Archives, William McDougall Letters, vol. 2, "Constitutional Reform Association Minute Book" (two torn-out sheets only, thus headed, covering from November 11, 1859 to January 15, 1860).
30 *Address of the Constitutional Reform Association to the People of Upper Canada* (Toronto, 1860), n.p.
31 *Ibid.*
32 *Ibid.*
33 *Globe*, January 4, 1860.
34 Brown Papers, Holton to Brown, October 14, 20, 28, 1859. *Weekly Globe*, November 4, 1859. Isobel Skelton asserts, without giving her evidence, that D'Arcy McGee wrote the Lower Canadian Liberals' "federation manifesto" (*The Life and Times of Thomas D'Arcy McGee* (Gardenvale, 1925), p. 373). However, Holton in his letter to Brown of October 20 claims first authorship.
35 Public Records and Archives of Ontario, Charles Clarke Papers, Sheppard to Clarke, November 27, December 4, 1859. See *Brown of the Globe*, vol. 1, pp. 311-25.
36 *Leader* (Toronto), December 16, 1861; *Globe*, January 28, 1860.
37 The increasingly general use of this term for Upper Canada Reformers becomes evident in the *Globe* during 1860; it no longer connotes "radical" in a rather pejorative sense. For example, see its use in editorial of July 2, 1860.
38 Public Archives, Alexander Mackenzie Papers (microfilm), Brown to Holton, September 24, 1859. See also *Brown of the Globe*, vol. 1, p. 318.
39 *Globe*, March 2, 1860.
40 *Ibid.*, March 7, 1860.
41 *Ibid.*
42 P. C. Cornell, *The Alignment of Political Groups in Canada, 1841-1867* (Toronto, 1962), p. 108. I have included Hogan with the Liberals since he had been

elected (and he largely voted) with them.

43 *Globe*, March 6, 1860.

44 *Ibid.*

45 *Ibid.*, March 2, 1860.

46 *Ibid.*

47 *Ibid.*, April 6, 1860.

48 *Ibid.*, March 2, 1860.

49 *Ibid.*, April 6, 1860.

50 *Leader*, March 14, 1860; *Globe*, March 2, April 6, 1860.

51 *Globe*, April 6, 1860.

52 *Ibid.*

53 *Ibid.*, March 2, 1860.

54 W. S. Wallace, *Murders and Mysteries* (Toronto, 1931), pp. 255-71.

55 *Leader*, March 14, 1860.

56 *Ibid.*, March 21, 22, 1860.

57 Clarke Papers, Sheppard to Clarke, March 19, 1860. See also Ontario Archives, William Lyon Mackenzie–Charles Lindsey Papers, D. Christie to Mackenzie, May 4, 1860.

58 Clarke Papers, Sheppard to Clarke, March 19, 1860.

59 *Ibid.*

60 *Leader*, March 14, 23, 1860.

61 *Ibid.*, March 23, 24, 28, 1860.

62 Foley to Editor of the *Globe*, April 11, 1860; *Globe*, April 16, 1860.

63 *Leader*, March 19, 1860.

64 *Globe*, March 29, April 6, 1860.

65 Mackenzie Papers, Brown to Mackenzie, March 28, 1860.

66 *Ibid.*

67 *Globe*, April 6, 1860.

68 *Ibid.*

69 *Ibid.*

70 Quoted in *Leader*, March 30, 1860.

71 Mackenzie Papers, Brown to Mackenzie, March 28, 1860; *Globe*, April 6, 1860.

72 *Globe*, *ibid.*

73 This is a deduction from reports of his "indisposition" in both *Globe* and *Leader*, as immediately below.

74 *Leader*, April 14, 1860.

75 *Ibid.*, April 18, 1860; *Globe*, April 19, 1860.

76 *Leader*, April 24, 1860; *Globe*, April 20, 1860.

77 Thompson's *Mirror of Parliament* (Quebec, 1860), Nos. 35, 36.

78 *Globe*, May 3, 1860.

79 *Journals of the Legislative Assembly of the Province of Canada* (1860), pp. 336-7.

80 *Ibid.*

81 *Globe*, May 9, 1860.

82 See the *Globe*'s renewed emphasis in articles of late May and into June, 1860, on "French domination", and its extracts from Upper Canadian press in this regard.

83 *Globe*, May 9, 1860.

84 *Ibid.*, May 12, 1860. A similar statement on June 23 extended the limits "from Newfoundland to Vancouver's Island".

85 J. G. Hodgins, *Documentary History of Education in Upper Canada* (28 vols., Toronto, 1894-1910), vol. XV, p. 98. See also J. S. Moir, *Church and State in Canada West* (Toronto, 1957), pp. 118-20.

86 H. H. Langton, *Sir Daniel Wilson, A Memoir* (Edinburgh, 1929), p. 16.

87 Brown Papers, Wilson to Brown, January 4, 1860.

88 *Ibid.*, April 30, 1860.

89 Hodgins, *op. cit.*, Ryerson's statement to the Committee, p. 125.

90 *Ibid.*, p. 126.

91 *Ibid.*, Brown's examination of Ryerson, pp. 140-9.

92 *Globe*, April 20, 1860; Victoria University Archives, Egerton Ryerson Papers, Ryerson to Mrs. Ryerson, April 25, 1860.

93 C. B. Sissons, *Egerton Ryerson, his Life and Letters* (2 vols., Toronto, 1947), vol. 2, p. 419.

94 Brown Papers, Wilson to Brown, May 11, 1860.

95 *Ibid.*, Sandfield Macdonald to Brown, May 18, 1860. See *Montreal Gazette*, May 15, for the opening of the controversy. The texts of all the letters exchanged were published in the *Globe* of June 2 and July 9, 1860.

96 Brown to Sandfield Macdonald, July 5, 1860, published in *Globe*, July 9, 1860.

97 Mackenzie Papers, Brown to Mackenzie, August 3, 1860.

98 *Leader*, August 2, 1860. See also May 16, 1860; and *Globe*, August 1, 6, 8, 11, 1860.

99 *Leader*, August 2, 1860.

100 *Ibid.*, August 3, 4, 1860.

101 *Ibid.*, August 7, 1860.

102 *Ibid.*

103 *Globe*, August 16, 17, 18, 20, 1860.

104 Ontario Archives, George Sheppard–William Buckingham Correspondence, Sheppard to Buckingham, November 26, 1860.

105 Mackenzie Papers, Brown to Holton, August 3, 1860.

106 *Globe*, August 20, 1860.

107 D. G. Creighton, *John A. Macdonald: The Young Politician* (Toronto, 1952), pp. 301-2.

108 *Globe*, September 10, 1860.

109 *Ibid.*, September 2, 1860.

110 *Ibid.*

111 *Ibid.*, September 8, 1860.

112 *Ibid.*, September 8, 10, 12, 14, 1860.

113 See *Brown of the Globe*, vol. 1, p. 133. Brown later wrote to the Roman Catholic archbishop of Toronto, John Joseph Lynch, "I have no sympathy with the Orange Order. I regard its introduction into Canada and propagation here as little less than a crime." (Toronto Archdiocesan Archives, Lynch Papers, Brown to Archbishop Lynch, March 12, 1873).

114 *Globe*, September 7, 12, 14, 1860.

115 *Ibid.*, September 17, 1860.

116 *Ibid.*
117 Brown Papers, McGee to Brown, October 1, 1860.
118 Mackenzie Papers, Brown to Holton, September 27, 1860.
119 *Ibid.*
120 *Ibid.*
121 *Ibid.*, October 5, 1860.
122 *Ibid.*, November 27, 1860.
123 Mackenzie Papers, Brown to Mackenzie, December 5, 1860.
124 *Globe*, December 19, 1860; January 1, 1861.
125 Brown Papers, Brown to Foley, January 3, 1861.
126 *Globe*, January 16, 24, 31, 1861.
127 Brown Papers, incomplete draft in George Brown's handwriting. No date, but internal evidence places it near the end of 1860.
128 *Ibid.*, Holton to Brown, November 16, 1860.

Chapter 2

Pages 36 to 70

1 *Globe*, January 14, 1861.
2 *Ibid.*, January 8, 1861.
3 *Ibid.*, January 12, 1861.
4 *Ibid.*, January 8, 1861.
5 *Ibid.*, February 21, 1861.
6 *Ibid.*, January 8, February 21, 1861.
7 *Ibid.*, January 5, 1861.
8 *Ibid.*, January 3, 1861.
9 For example, the Brantford *Courier*, quoted in *Globe* for January 3, 1861.
10 *Address of the Constitutional Reform Association to the People of Upper Canada*, n.p.
11 *Globe*, January 5, 1861.
12 *Ibid.*
13 Mackenzie–Lindsey Papers, Tilley to Lindsey, September 5, 1860.
14 *Globe*, February 5, 1861.
15 *Ibid.*, February 14, 23, 1861.
16 The Conservative Minister of Finance, Alexander Galt, himself had estimated in January that Lower Canada would have 1.3 million to Upper Canada's 1.5 million. Mackenzie–Lindsey papers, Galt to Lindsey, January 3, 1861.
17 Brown to Holton, May 2, 1861; quoted in Alexander Mackenzie, *The Life and Speeches of Hon. George Brown* (Toronto, 1882), p. 197; *Globe*, April 4, 8, 1861.
18 *Globe*, March 12, 1861.
19 Brown to Holton, May 2, 1861, *loc. cit.*
20 *Globe*, April 23, 1861.
21 Brown to Holton, May 2, 1861, *loc. cit.*
22 Brown Papers, Holton to Brown, March 16, 1861.
23 Brown to Holton, May 2, 1861, *loc. cit.*
24 *Ibid.*
25 *Ibid.*, Brown Papers, George Brown

to Anne Brown, October 14, 1865.
26 *Globe*, June 8, 1861.
27 Brown Papers, McDougall to Brown, April 1, 1861.
28 *Globe*, April 11, 1861.
29 Brown Papers, McDougall to Brown, April 1, 1861.
30 *Ibid.*
31 *Ibid.*
32 *Ibid.*
33 *Ibid.*, Mowat to Brown, May 13, 1861.
34 *Ibid.*, McDougall to Brown, April 1, 1861.
35 *Ibid.*, Holton to Brown, March 16, 1861.
36 *Globe*, June 8, 1861.
37 *Ibid.*
38 *Ibid.*
39 *Ibid.*, June 18, 1861.
40 *Ibid.*, June 20, 1861.
41 *Ibid.*
42 *Ibid.*, June 29, 1861.
43 *Ibid.*
44 *Ibid.*, July 6, 1861.
45 *Ibid.*, July 8, 1861.
46 *Leader*, June 7, 1861. For Crawford's election address see *ibid.*, June 26, 1861.
47 Public Archives, John A. Macdonald Papers, vol. 337, Ryerson to Macdonald, July 12, 1861.
48 *Globe*, July 11, 1861.
49 *Ibid.*
50 P. G. Cornell, *op. cit.*, pp. 48-9, 109. See also Brown Papers, Brown to Dorion, July 19, 1861.
51 *Globe*, May 1, 1861.
52 Ryerson Papers, Macdonald to Ryerson, June 6, 1861. See also [Conservative] *Voters Guide for 1861*, Macdonald Papers, vol. 297; Kingston *Chronicle and News*, July 12, 1861.
53 Sissons, *Ryerson*, vol. 2, p. 436.
54 Cornell, *op. cit.*, p. 109.
55 *Ibid.*
56 Evidently Sicotte was seeking to find a new western majority for the French to work with, while Cauchon thought the existing "game" played out. See Brown Papers, McDougall to Brown, April 1, 1861.
57 *Ibid.*
58 *Ibid.*, Brown to Dorion (copy), July 19, 1861.
59 *Ibid.*, Dorion to Brown, July 27, 1861.
60 *Ibid.*
61 *Ibid.*, Brown to Dorion (copy), "July 1861". Internal evidence would date this private note as written at the same time as Brown's more formal letter of July 19 cited above.
62 *Ibid.*, Dorion to Brown, July 27, 1861.
63 *Ibid.* See also Brown Papers, Holton to Brown, July 25, 1861.
64 *Globe*, August 10, 1861. One might note at this point a letter from D. H. Feehan to John A. Macdonald of July 29, 1861 (Macdonald Papers, vol. 337), reporting on Brown's state of mind after

the election. Feehan claimed Brown had said that very afternoon, "My policy is the dissolution of the union – it must come to that." This statement of "extreme views" might have reflected momentary exasperation on Brown's part (he would just have received Dorion's letter rejecting any renewal of east-west Reform unity) or it might have been coloured, in reporting, by Feehan's own strong Conservative predilections. But it remains clear in any case that the *Globe* did not make dissolution a policy, and that Brown and his associates did not discuss any such possibility. Whether valid or not, therefore, this isolated piece of evidence of "dissolutionism" in Brown's thinking had no future bearing.

65 *Globe*, August 27, September 2, 7, 12, 1861.
66 *Ibid.*, January 1, 1861.
67 *Ibid.*, August 23, 1861.
68 *Ibid.*, September 7, 1861.
69 Crown Grant to the Hon. George Brown, Township of Zone, County of Kent, recorded August 22, 1861, Lib. HZ, Folio 211; in author's possession.
70 *Globe*, October 4, 29, 1861.
71 *Ibid.*, November 7, 1861.
72 *Ibid.*, September 23, 1861.
73 See L. B. Shippee, *Canadian-American Relations, 1849-1874* (New Haven, 1939), pp. 114-16, and Robin Winks, *Canada and the United States: the Civil War Years* (Baltimore, 1960), pp. 12-21, for these assessments of Canadian attitudes.
74 *Globe*, May 3, 1861; Winks, *op. cit.*, p. 44.
75 Winks, *ibid.*
76 *Ibid.*, pp. 29, 57.
77 *Ibid.*, pp. 34-42, 65-7.
78 George Brown, speech to the Toronto Anti-Slavery Society of February 3, 1863, published in Mackenzie, *op. cit.*, pp. 292-3; *Globe*, August 7, 1861.
79 *Globe*, July 26, August 21, 31, 1861.
80 *Ibid.*, August 15, December 31, 1861; June 21, 1862; October 4, 1864.
81 *Ibid.*, November 18, 26, 1861.
82 *Ibid.*, November 26, 1861.
83 *Ibid.*, December 10, 1861.
84 *Ibid.*, December 12, 13, 1861.
85 J. J. Talman, "A Canadian View of Parties and Issues on the Eve of the Civil War," *Journal of Southern History*, vol. 5, No. 2, pp. 245-53. See also Clarke Papers, Sheppard to Clarke, January 24, March 19, 1861; *Leader*, December 16, 1861.
86 *Globe*, December 14, 1861.
87 *Leader*, December 11, 13, 14, 1861.
88 *Globe*, December 9, 17, 1861.
89 *Leader*, December 12, 13, 16, 1861.
90 *Globe*, December 16, 1861.
91 *Ibid.*, December 16, 1861.
92 *Ibid.*
93 *Ibid.*, December 17, 18, 1861.
94 *Ibid.*, December 21, 1861.
95 *Ibid.*, December 23, 1861.
96 Winks, *op. cit.*, p. 85.
97 *Ibid.*, p. 86.
98 *Globe*, December 26, 1861.
99 *Ibid.*, December 30, 1861.
100 *Ibid.*, January 1, 1862.
101 *Leader*, January 8, 10, 1862.
102 See Sheppard–Buckingham Correspondence, Sheppard to Buckingham, February 17, 1862; July 21, 1864; March 16, 1867.
103 *Globe*, February 11, 1862; *Leader*, February 10, 1862.
104 *Leader*, March 10, 1862.
105 *Globe*, October 1, 1861.
106 R. G. Trotter, *Canadian Federation* (Toronto, 1924), pp. 189-90.
107 *Globe*, February 15, 1862.
108 *Ibid.*
109 *Ibid.*
110 G. P. de T. Glazebrook, *A History of Transportation in Canada* (New Haven, 1938), pp. 192-3.
111 E. W. Watkin, *Canada and the United States: Recollections, 1851-1886* (London, 1887), pp. 11-13, 451.
112 *Globe*, October 1, 1861; February 24, 1862.
113 *Ibid.*, January 1, 1862.
114 Public Archives, Governor-General's Correspondence, G464, Monck to Newcastle, January 7, February 2, 1862.
115 Brown to Holton, February 19, 1862, quoted in Mackenzie, *op. cit.*, p. 198.
116 *Globe*, January 1, 1862.
117 *Ibid.*
118 *Ibid.*, March 5, 1862.
119 *Ibid.*, August 15, 1861; February 12, 1862.
120 *Ibid.*, October 8, 1861; March 4, 1862.
121 *Ibid.*, March 5, 1862.
122 *Ibid.*
123 *Ibid.*
124 Brown Papers, McDougall to Brown, March 27, 1862.
125 *Globe*, April 1, 1862.
126 *Ibid.*, April 10, 1862.
127 *Ibid.*, May 7, 1862.
128 *Ibid.*, May 5, 1862.
129 *Globe*, May 1, 13, June 2, 1862.
130 *Journals of the Assembly* (1862), p. 229.
131 Creighton, *The Young Politician*, p. 331.
132 Watkin, *op. cit.*, p. 95.
133 *Ibid.*
134 Brown Papers, McDougall to Brown, March 27, 1862; Mowat to Brown, May 7, 1862; Mackenzie to Brown, May 22, 1862.
135 *Ibid.*, J. K. Edwards to Brown, May 24, 1862.
136 *Globe*, June 2, 1862.
137 *Ibid.*
138 Brown Papers, Edwards to Brown, May 24, 1862.
139 *Ibid.*; and Shuter Smith to Brown, May 24, 1862, Brown Papers.

140 *Ibid.*, McDougall to Brown, May 23, 1862.
141 *Ibid.*, Mowat to Brown, May 23, 1862.
142 *Ibid.*, Edwards to Brown, May 24, 1862.
143 *Ibid.*, Mowat to Brown, May 23, 1862.
144 *Ibid.*.
145 *Ibid.*, Blair to Brown, May 24, 1862.
146 *Ibid.*, Mackenzie to Brown, May 22, 1862.
147 *Ibid.*, May 31, 1862.
148 *Globe*, May 28, 1862.
149 *Ibid.*
150 Mackenzie Papers, Brown to Holton, May 29, 1862.
151 *Ibid.*
152 *Ibid.*
153 *Ibid.*
154 Brown Papers, Holton to Brown, June 1, 1862.
155 Mackenzie Papers, Brown to Holton, June 2, 1862.
156 *Ibid.*
157 *Ibid.*
158 *Ibid.*
159 *Ibid.* See also Brown Papers, Holton to Brown, June 6, 1862.
160 *Globe*, June 4, 1862.
161 Mackenzie Papers, Brown to Holton, June 2, 1862.
162 *Ibid.*
163 See mention of Brown's plan in Brown Papers, Holton to Brown, February 24, 1862; see also *Globe*, July 8, 1862.
164 *Globe*, January 21, 1862.
165 Typescript history of the *Globe*, p. 98.
166 Macdonald Papers, vol. 188, Brown to D. Shaw, September 3, 1862.
167 *Ibid.*
168 *Ibid.*, Shaw to Brown, July 28, 1862.
169 *Ibid.*
170 *Ibid.*, Brown to Shaw, September 3, 1862.
171 *Ibid.*
172 *Brown of the Globe*, vol. 1, pp. 10-11.

Chapter 3

Pages 71 to 102

1 Brown Papers, McGee to Brown, August 5, 1862.
2 Mackenzie Papers, Brown to Holton, September 3, 1862; *Globe*, August 8, 9, 1862.
3 *The Times* (London), June 6, 1862.
4 Assessment based on *Globe* for April 10, May 22, June 21, July 12, 1862.
5 *Ibid.*, August 9, 1862.
6 *Ibid.*
7 Mackenzie Papers, Brown to Holton, September 3, 1862.
8 *Ibid.*

9 *Ibid.*
10 *Ibid.*
11 *Ibid.*
12 *Globe*, February 7, 1862; see also Brown Papers, Brydges to Brown, February 11, 1862.
13 *Globe*, August 23, 1862; October 2, 1863.
14 Mackenzie Papers, Brown to Holton, September 3, 1862.
15 *Ibid.*
16 *Ibid.*
17 *Ibid.* Galt was evidently wholly convinced, ready for a stiff dose.
18 *Ibid.*
19 *Ibid.*
20 *Ibid.*
21 *Ibid.*
22 Daniel Wilson, *William Nelson* (Edinburgh, 1889), p. 143.
23 Brown–Nelson Family Papers (Ichrachan House, Argyll), Thomas Nelson to Anne Nelson, August 11, 1862.
24 *Ibid.*, letters of Anne Nelson, 1848-62.
25 *Ibid.*, Anne Nelson's journal for 1851.
26 *Ibid.*, Jane Currie to Anne Nelson, October 20, 1862.
27 Brown Papers, George Brown to Anne Brown, October 1, 1864.
28 *Ibid.*
29 *Ibid.*
30 Brown–Nelson Papers, George to Anne, "Tuesday morning", Edinburgh. From internal evidence, written shortly before their marriage.
31 *Ibid.*, Peter McDowall to Anne Brown, May 1872.
32 Brown Papers, George Brown to Anne Nelson, November 12, 1862; *ibid.*, G. D. Englehart to Brown, November 13, 1863.
33 Brown–Nelson Papers, undated press clippings on the wedding.
34 *Ibid.*, Margaret Nelson to Anne Brown, n.d.
35 *Ibid.*, John Nelson to Anne Brown, November 28, 1862.
36 Brown Papers, George to Peter Brown, December 19, 1862.
37 *Ibid.*
38 *Ibid.*
39 *Ibid.*
40 *Globe*, December 27, 1862.
41 *Ibid.*
42 *Ibid.*
43 *Ibid.*
44 *Ibid.*
45 Brown–Nelson Papers, Thomas Nelson to Anne Brown, July 17, 1863.
46 Mackenzie Papers, Brown to Holton, January 5, 1863.
47 Brown Papers, Mowat to Anne Brown, May 28, 1880.
48 Brown had suffered from sciatica during his visit to Britain, and it recurred from time to time thereafter, as his letters to his wife indicate.
49 *Globe*, December 27, 1862.

50 Brown–Nelson Papers, undated press clippings on Brown's wedding.
51 Brown Papers, George to Anne Brown, February 21, 1865.
52 *Globe*, July 31, 1862.
53 Mackenzie Papers, Brown to Holton, January 5, 1863.
54 *Ibid.* See also Brown to Holton, February 12, 1863.
55 This is repeatedly made evident in Brown's letters to his wife.
56 Mackenzie Papers, Brown to Holton, February 12, 1863.
57 *Ibid.*
58 Brown Papers, Holton to Brown, February 19, 1863.
59 Mackenzie Papers, Brown to Holton, February 12, 1863.
60 *Ibid.*
61 *Ibid.*
62 Brown Papers. Letter is dated by postmark February 26, but written late on 25th.
63 Mackenzie Papers, Brown to Holton, January 5, 1863.
64 Brown Papers, George to Anne Brown, February 26, 1863.
65 *Ibid.*
66 *Ibid.*, "Norwich, Friday Morning" (February 27, 1863).
67 *Ibid.*, "Ingersoll, Monday Morning" (March 2, 1863).
68 *Ibid.*, February 27, 1863.
69 *Globe*, March 5, 6, 1863.
70 *Ibid.*, March 10, 1863.
71 *Ibid.*
72 *Ibid.*
73 Brown Papers, George to Anne Brown, April 4, 1863.
74 *Ibid.*
75 Mackenzie Papers, Brown to Holton, March 7 (misdated "February 7"), 1863.
76 *Ibid.*, March 31, 1863.
77 *Ibid.*, February 12, 1863; *Globe*, October 9, 1862.
78 *Globe*, October 15, 1862; January 19, 1863.
79 *Ibid.*, February 21, 24, 1863.
80 Moir, *op. cit.*, p. 174.
81 *Leader*, March 18, 1863; *Globe*, March 16, 1863.
82 *Globe, ibid.*
83 *Canadian Freeman* (Toronto), March 9, 1863.
84 *Journals of the Legislative Assembly* (Seventh Parliament, 1863), p. 129.
85 *Ibid.*
86 *Globe*, March 9, April 6, 1863.
87 Sissons, *op. cit.*, vol. 2, p. 483.
88 Macdonald Papers, vol. 188, Cameron to Macdonald, March 16, 1863.
89 Mackenzie Papers, Brown to Holton, March 31, 1863.
90 *Globe*, May 2, 1863.
91 For example, see Mackenzie Papers, Mackenzie to Brown, May 31, 1862.

92 *Ibid.*, Brown to Holton, March 31, 1863.
93 Macdonald Papers, vol. 338, Ryerson to Macdonald, May 23, 1863.
94 *Globe*, May 8, 1863.
95 *Ibid.*
96 *Journals of the Legislative Assembly* (Seventh Parliament, 1863), p. 325.
97 Brown Papers, George to Gordon Brown, May 11, 1863.
98 *Ibid.*
99 *Ibid.*
100 *Ibid.*
101 *Ibid.*
102 *Ibid.*
103 *Globe*, May 22, 1863.
104 Brown Papers, George to Anne Brown, June 4, 1863.
105 *Globe*, June 17, 1863.
106 Cornell, *op. cit.*, p. 110.
107 *Ibid.*
108 Mackenzie Papers, Brown to Holton, June 26, 1863.
109 *Ibid.*
110 *Montreal Gazette*, June 10, 1863; *La Minerve* (Montreal), June 9, 1863.
111 Mackenzie Papers, Brown to Holton, June 26, 1863.
112 *Globe*, July 1, 1863.
113 *Ibid.*, February 5, 1863.
114 Brown–Nelson Papers, Thomas Nelson to Anne Brown, July 17, 1863.
115 *Ibid.*, Brown to Margaret Nelson, July 2, 1863.
116 Brown Papers, George to Anne Brown, July 25, 1863.
117 *Ibid.*
118 *Globe*, August 14, 1863.
119 *Journals of the Assembly* (Eighth Parliament, 1863), p. 20.
120 *Ibid.*, pp. 57-8.
121 *Globe*, August 31, 1863.
122 *Ibid.*, September 18, 1863.
123 *Ibid.*, October 7, 1863.
124 *Ibid.*, October 12, 1863.
125 *Ibid.*, October 13, 1863.
126 *Appendices to the Journals of the Legislative Assembly of the Province of Canada*, vol. XVII, No. 3 (1859), Appendix 3.
127 *Globe*, August 15, October 13, 1863.
128 *Ibid.*
129 Brown–Nelson Papers, Brown to Margaret Nelson, October 2, 1863.
130 *Ibid.*
131 Brown Papers, George to Anne Brown, October 9, 1863.

Chapter 4

Pages 103 to 146

1 *Globe*, January 12, 20, 27, 1864.
2 Winks, *op. cit.*, p. 140.
3 *Globe*, November 14, 16, 1863.

4 *Ibid.*, January 2, 1864.
5 Brown Papers, Brown to Sandfield Macdonald, January 25, 1864 (draft).
6 *Ibid.*; *Globe*, October 19, 1863.
7 *Globe*, June 9, 1854.
8 *Ibid.*, October 19, 1863.
9 *Globe*, November 12, 1850; March 2, 1857; January 22, 1863.
10 *Ibid.*, July 27, 1863.
11 *Ibid.*, May 23, 1863.
12 Watkin, *op. cit.*, p. 173.
13 Mackenzie Papers, Brown to Holton, September 3, 1862; *Globe*, July 3, 1863.
14 *Globe*, January 27, 1864.
15 *Ibid.*
16 *Brown of the Globe*, vol. 1, pp. 167-8.
17 *Globe*, April 7, 1863.
18 *Ibid.*, January 29, 1863. See also January 12, 1863.
19 *Ibid.*, July 11, 1863.
20 *Ibid.*, February 3, 1863.
21 *Ibid.*
22 *Ibid.*
23 *Ibid.*, July 24, 1863.
24 *Ibid.*
25 *Ibid.*, January 6, 1863.
26 Brown–Nelson Papers, notes of family birthdays recorded by Anne Brown.
27 Mackenzie Papers, Brown to Holton, January 19, 1864.
28 *Ibid.*
29 *Ibid.*
30 Brown Papers, Sandfield Macdonald to Brown, January 21, 1864.
31 *Ibid.*
32 Public Archives, Sandfield Macdonald Papers, Brown to Macdonald, January 25, 1864.
33 *Ibid.* See also Mackenzie Papers, Brown to Holton, June 26, 1863, and January 29, 1864.
34 Brown Papers, Holton to Brown, November 1, 1863.
35 Mackenzie Papers, Brown to Holton, October 23, 1863.
36 Brown Papers, Holton to Brown, December 6, 1863.
37 Mackenzie Papers, Brown to Holton, January 19, 1864.
38 *Ibid.*
39 E. R. Cameron, *Memoirs of Ralph Vansittart* (Toronto, 1924), pp. 119-20, 137, 152.
40 Mackenzie Papers, Brown to Holton, January 29, 1864.
41 *Ibid.*
42 *Ibid.*, February 6, 1864.
43 *Ibid.*
44 Cornell, *op. cit.*, pp. 55-6.
45 Mackenzie Papers, Brown to Holton, January 29, 1864.
46 Macdonald Papers, vol. 191, C. J. Brydges to Macdonald, February 24, 1864.
47 *Ibid.*
48 *Ibid.*
49 *Ibid.*
50 Cameron, *op. cit.*, p. 138.

51 Macdonald Papers, vol. 191, Brydges to Macdonald, February 24, 1864.
52 Brown Papers, George to Anne Brown, February 22, 1864.
53 *Ibid.*, February 25, 1864.
54 *Ibid.*, February 27, 1864.
55 *Ibid.*, February 29, 1864.
56 *Ibid.*, March 1, 1864.
57 *Ibid.*
58 *Ibid.*, March 2, 1864. It should be noted that Brown had remained in contact with McGee even after the latter had declared war on the reconstructed Sandfield Macdonald ministry that had ejected him. (See Cameron, *op. cit.*, p. 120.) Brown had also consulted McGee before moving his constitutional resolution in October 1863, and gained his support for it from that time forward (*ibid.*, pp. 138, 146).
59 *Ibid.*, March 4, 1864.
60 *Ibid.*, March 12, 1864.
61 *Ibid.*, February 29, 1864.
62 *Globe*, March 15, 1864.
63 *Appendices to the Journals of the Assembly* (1859), Appendix 3.
64 *Globe*, March 15, 1864.
65 *Ibid.*
66 *Ibid.*
67 *Ibid.*
68 *Ibid.*
69 *Ibid.*
70 *Ibid.*
71 *Ibid.*
72 Brown Papers, George to Anne Brown, March 15, 1864.
73 *Leader*, March 18, 1864.
74 *Globe*, March 30, 1864; Public Archives, Colonial Office Papers (microfilm) C.O. 42, vol. 640, Monck to Newcastle, March 31, 1864.
75 *Globe*, March 19, 1864.
76 Quebec *Chronicle*, March 31, 1864.
77 *Globe*, March 31, 1864.
78 Brown Papers, George to Anne Brown, March 30, 1864.
79 J. Young, *Public Men and Public Life in Canada* (Toronto, 1902), pp. 203-4.
80 Brown Papers, George to Anne Brown, May 13, 1864.
81 *Ibid.*, Holton to Brown, April 3, 1864.
82 *Ibid.*
83 *Leader*, March 15, 1864; *Globe*, March 15, 1864.
84 Brown Papers, George to Anne Brown, May 14, 1864.
85 *Ibid.*
86 *Ibid.*, May 16, 1864.
87 *Ibid.*
88 *Ibid.*
89 *Globe*, May 20, 1864.
90 Brown Papers, George to Anne Brown, May 18, 1864.
91 *Journals of the Assembly* (1864), pp. 225-6.
92 Brown Papers, George to Anne Brown, May 20, 1864.
93 *Globe*, May 21, 1864.

94 C. Martin, *Foundations of Canadian Nationhood* (Toronto, 1955), p. 310.
95 Brown Papers, George to Anne Brown, May 20, 1864.
96 *Globe*, May 24, 1864.
97 *Ibid.*, June 15, 1864.
98 *Journals of the Assembly* (1864), p. 384.
99 *Globe*, May 24, 1864.
100 *Journals of the Assembly* (1864), p. 384.
101 Brown Papers, George to Anne Brown, May 24, 1864.
102 *Ibid.*, June 2, 1864.
103 *Ibid.*
104 *Ibid.*
105 *Ibid.*, June 11, 1864.
106 *Ibid.*, June 13, 1864.
107 *Ibid.*
108 *Ibid.*
109 *Ibid.*
110 *Ibid.*
111 Cornell, *op. cit.*, p. 56.
112 *Journals of the Assembly* (1864), pp. 389-90.
113 *Speech of the Hon. Geo. Brown, M.P.P., when Re-elected by Acclamation for the South Riding of Oxford, on the Coalition of 1864* (first published in the *Globe*, July 14, 1864, and republished as a pamphlet, n.d.), p. 9. This is a useful document presenting Brown's own synopsis of the negotiations leading to a government pledged to seek federation – to be used in conjunction with the official "Ministerial Explanations" of June 22, 1864, Brown's letters to his wife, and Brown's own speech of explanation in the Assembly of June 22 (printed in the *Globe* of June 23, 1864). These are leading sources for analysing Brown's personal role in the negotiations, though a variety of other items have also been drawn on here.
114 Ministerial Explanations. These are published both in Sir Joseph Pope's *Memoirs of the Right Honourable Sir John Alexander Macdonald, G.C.B.* (Musson, Toronto, n.d.), pp. 681-7, and in J. H. Gray, *Confederation of Canada* (Toronto, 1872), pp. 20-8; but there are minor discrepancies between the two texts. There are also printed copies in the Macdonald Papers, vol. 46, the source of Pope's own version, and in C.O. 42, vol. 641, enclosed in Monck's dispatch of June 30 to Cardwell. The latter seems to be the better copy. The Macdonald Paper version varies from it, containing, e.g., "federation principle" instead of "federative principle" (see note 125 below) and leaves out the phrase "constituted on the well understood principles of Federal Government", which is written in by hand. This phrase is *in* the C.O. 42 version, however; thus it has been used here as the authority.
115 *Ibid.*
116 *Globe*, June 16, 1864.

117 *Ibid.*
118 C.O. 42, vol. 641, Monck to Cardwell, June 30, 1864, and enclosure, Memorandum "B". Monck had also suggested a coalition of parties on the fall of the Sandfield Macdonald ministry in March. In the Brown Papers are proof sheets of a brief biographical sketch of Brown's life (no author, no date) annotated in George Brown's own hand, concerning Monck's proposal. Brown there comments: "I had a full understanding with Lord Monck all this time, and his appeal was with a knowledge of the course I would take."
119 Brown Papers, George to Gordon Brown, May 11, 1863.
120 Macdonald Papers, Macdonald to S. I. Lynn, April 10, 1866.
121 Ministerial Explanations.
122 Brown Papers, George to Anne Brown, June 18, 1864.
123 Ministerial Explanations.
124 *Ibid.*
125 *Ibid.*
126 *Globe*, June 18, 1864.
127 *Leader*, June 18, 1864.
128 *Globe*, June 18, 1864.
129 *Leader*, June 18, 1864.
130 Brown Papers, George to Anne Brown, June 17, 1864.
131 *Leader*, June 18, 1864.
132 Ministerial Explanations; *Globe*, June 20, 1864.
133 Ministerial Explanations.
134 *Parliamentary Debates on the Subject of the Confederation of the British North American Provinces* (Quebec, 1865), p. 194.
135 Ministerial Explanations; Brown's *Speech in South Oxford*, p. 17.
136 Ministerial Explanations.
137 *Speech in South Oxford*, p. 13.
138 Ministerial Explanations.
139 *Speech in South Oxford*, pp. 10-11.
140 *Ibid.*, p. 11.
141 *Ibid.*
142 *Ibid.*, p. 13; *Globe*, June 22, 1864.
143 Ministerial Explanations.
144 Brown Papers, George to Anne Brown, June 20, 1864.
145 *Ibid.* (A note written half an hour previous to the letter cited immediately above.)
146 *Globe*, June 22, 1864.
147 *Ibid.* Minutes of the meeting are printed in Mackenzie, *Brown*, pp. 92-3.
148 Ministerial Explanations.
149 Brown Papers, McGee to Brown, June 22, 1864.
150 *Ibid.*, Monck to Brown, June 21, 1864.
151 *Ibid.*, George to Anne Brown, June 20, 1864.
152 Ministerial Explanations.
153 Brown Papers, George to Anne Brown, June 23, 1864.
154 *Globe*, June 23, 1864.
155 *Ibid.*

156   *Ibid.*
157   *Ibid.*
158   *Ibid.*
159   *Ibid.*, see also *Speech in South Oxford*, p. 12.
160   *Globe*, June 23, 1864.
161   *Ibid.*
162   *Ibid.*
163   *Ibid.*
164   *Ibid.*
165   *Ibid.*
166   *Ibid.*
167   *La Minerve*, June 21, 1864.
168   Brown Papers, George to Anne Brown, June 23, 1864.
169   *Ibid.*, June 27, 1864.
170   *Globe*, June 23, 1864.
171   Brown plainly saw "vistas of nationhood" at this time. In his speech to his constituents in South Oxford, on July 11, he said: "It cannot be that these great Provinces shall always be permitted to hold their present relations to the mother country. We cannot expect that Britain will always, without consideration, send her navy to guard our shores . . . [and] stand ready to defend us against attack. We must look forward to the day when the whole of British America shall stand together; and, in close alliance and heartiest sympathy with Great Britain, be prepared to assume the full duties and responsibilities of a great and powerful nation." (*Speech in South Oxford*, p. 17).

Chapter 5

Pages 147 to 186

1   Brown Papers, George to Anne Brown, July 7, 1864.
2   *Speech in South Oxford*, p. 11.
3   See *Leader*, July 8, and especially July 2, 1864, for continued Conservative press antipathies.
4   Circular for North Ontario signed by John A. Macdonald, quoted in Pope, *op. cit.*, p. 276.
5   Brown Papers, George to Anne Brown, July 20, 1864.
6   *Ibid.*, July 28, 1864.
7   *Ibid.*
8   *Ibid.*
9   *Ibid.*
10   *Ibid.*, August 5, 1864.
11   C.O. 42, vol. 642, Monck to Cardwell, August 26, 1864.
12   Brown Papers, George to Anne Brown, July 10, 18, August 1, 1864.
13   *Ibid.*, August 8, 1864.
14   *Ibid.*
15   *Ibid.*, August 15, 1864.
16   *Ibid.*
17   *Ibid.*, August 8, 1864.
18   *Ibid.*, August 15, 1864.
19   *Ibid.*, August 26, 1864.
20   *Ibid.*, August 28, 1864.
21   *Ibid.*, August 29, 1864.
22   *Ibid.*, September 13, 1864.
23   *Ibid.*
24   *Ibid.* Until the next reference below, ensuing quotations are drawn from this source.
25   There is some question as to the order in which Canadian speakers addressed the Charlottetown Conference. Reports in the Charlottetown *Monitor* and Saint John *Telegraph* gave the sequence as Cartier, September 2, Macdonald on Saturday the 3rd, and both Brown and Galt on Monday, September 5. This "timetable" has been followed in W. M. Whitelaw, *The Maritimes and Canada before Confederation* (Toronto, 1934), pp. 220-4, and Creighton, *The Young Politician*, pp. 365-7. But George Brown in his long letter to his wife of September 13, 1864, gives the order as Cartier and Macdonald on the 2nd, Galt on the 3rd, and Brown on the 5th. This is the version that has been followed here. Admittedly Brown wrote a week afterward, but he was an actual participant, while the press was excluded from the Conference (and complained against the policy of secrecy), so that their information was decidedly second-hand. Furthermore, Brown's sequence for the proceedings of this scantily-documented conference is borne out by the remarks of another participant, Jonathan McCully of Nova Scotia, in a speech in Toronto in November of 1864. (See Edward Whelan, *The Union of the British Provinces* (Charlottetown, 1865), p. 167.) This same sequence has also been followed by P. B. Waite in *The Life and Times of Confederation* (Toronto, 1962), pp. 76-8.
26   Brown Papers, George to Anne Brown, September 13, 1864. Until the next reference below, the account and all quotations are from this source.
27   Brown's speech in Toronto, November 3, 1864, quoted in Whelan, *op. cit.*, p. 189.
28   This, at any rate, was the *Globe*'s opinion on August 10, 1864. Moreover, Chester Martin (*Foundations of Canadian Nationhood*, p. 331) terms Brown the "apostle" of Maritime union "as the basis of sectional representation in the upper house" of a new federal parliament. This may also be supported by the fact that, at the subsequent Quebec Conference, Brown himself moved for the Maritimes to be represented in the upper house as one sectional block equal to each of the Canadas – a motion of October 17 to be found in the original Quebec Conference notes and minutes in the Macdonald Papers, vol. 46, but not identified in the record edited and published by Joseph Pope, known usually as *Confederation Documents* (Toronto, 1895). See also Notes by A. A. Macdonald in the Macdonald Papers, vol. 46.

29 Gray, *op. cit.*, p. 33.
30 Brown Papers, George to Anne Brown, September 12, 1864.
31 Gray, *op. cit.*, pp. 34-5.
32 *Ibid.*, p. 35.
33 Whelan, *op. cit.*, p. 53.
34 Brown Papers, George to Anne Brown, September 19, 1864.
35 *Ibid.*
36 *Ibid.*, September 12, 1864.
37 *Ibid.*, September 19, 1864.
38 *Ibid.*, September 12, 1864.
39 *Globe*, September 21, 1864.
40 *Ibid.*, September 13, 21, 1864.
41 Brown Papers, George to Anne Brown, September 23, 1864.
42 *Ibid.* See also *Globe*, September 5, 17, 1864. The London *Spectator* of August 20 gave the true accolade for the South Oxford speech: "Mr. Brown talks like an English statesman, without a trace of bombast or dreamy oratory . . ."
43 Brown Papers, George to Anne Brown, October 1, 1864.
44 *Ibid.*
45 *Ibid.*
46 *Ibid.*
47 *Globe*, December 1, 1864; March 5, 1894.
48 Brown Papers, George to Anne Brown, October 1, 1864.
49 *Ibid.*
50 *Ibid.*, October 10, 1864.
51 *Ibid.*
52 *Globe*, October 11, 1864.
53 *Montreal Gazette*, October 28, 31, 1864.
54 Pope, *Confederation Documents*, pp. 5-11, 61.
55 Macdonald Papers, vol. 46, printed memorandum, "Confederation of British America". See *Globe*, September 26, 27, October 4, 1864.
56 Brown Papers, George to Anne Brown, September 23, 1864. It is possible that Brown himself drafted this outline; it reflects his style and general views. But in that case he was most impersonal and unusually modest in not referring to its authorship in sending it to his wife.
57 *Globe*, October 12, 1864.
58 *Ibid.*, October 22, 1864.
59 Brown Papers, George to Anne Brown, October 17, 1864.
60 *Ibid.*
61 Pope, *Confederation Documents*, p. 7.
62 *Ibid.*, p. 59.
63 *Ibid.*, p. 60.
64 *Ibid.*, pp. 60-1.
65 *Ibid.*, p. 14. See also Macdonald Papers, vol. 46, Quebec Conference minutes of October 17, omitted in Pope, which indicate that Brown moved the amendment establishing the principle of three equal blocks of seats for Upper and Lower Canada, and for Nova Scotia, New Brunswick and Prince Edward Island combined. When this was accepted, it was then agreed that each block would consist of twenty-four seats (Nova Scotia and New Brunswick each to have ten, Prince Edward Island four) and that Newfoundland might also enter with four members of its own.
66 Brown Papers, George to Anne Brown, October 15, 1864.
67 *Ibid.*, October 17, 1864.
68 *Ibid.*
69 *Ibid.*
70 *Ibid.*
71 See Brown's speech in Toronto of November 3, 1864, quoted in Whelan, *op. cit.*, p. 193. See also Waite, *op. cit.*, p. 82, and John Lewis, *George Brown* (Toronto, 1910), p. 164.
72 *Brown of the Globe*, vol. 1, pp. 161-2. See also Brown's speech of November 3, 1864, *loc. cit.*, and *Globe*, October 4, 8, 20, 1864.
73 Brown did not approve the ensuing resolution to leave the choice of the first federal legislative councillors to the present provincial governments; but he was outvoted 9 to 3, within the Canadian cabinet, before Canada endorsed the principle of appointment by the existing régime — in which the Conservatives obviously had the majority! And Brown's effort then to leave the mode of choosing councillors to each province to arrange later, in its own way (for the Grits could plainly dominate Upper Canada by itself), was also defeated. Quite evidently, party calculations and concerns had momentarily re-emerged. See Macdonald Papers, vol. 46, Quebec Conference minutes for October 19, 1864.
74 Pope, *Confederation Documents*, p. 19.
75 *Ibid.*, p. 72.
76 *Ibid.*, p. 74.
77 *Ibid.*, pp. 75-6.
78 *Ibid.*, p. 76.
79 *Ibid.*, p. 77.
80 See chapter 1, p. 11 above.
81 *Globe*, August 1, September 16, December 9, 1864; Whelan, *op. cit.*, p. 197.
82 *Brown of the Globe*, vol. 1, p. 321.
83 *Globe*, August 1, 1864.
84 "French Canadianism" was used in the *Globe* pejoratively, to signify a dominating influence, not neutrally, to mean a culture or way of life. Thus George Brown would use it in writing to his wife — see note 95 below.
85 *Globe*, December 9, 1864; *Confederation Documents*, pp. 75-6.
86 Whelan, *op. cit.*, p. 197; *Confederation Documents*, p. 80.
87 Pope, *Confederation Documents*, p. 85.
88 Whelan, *op. cit.*, p. 197.
89 *Ibid.*; *Globe*, August 1, 1864.
90 *Globe*, September 16, 1864.
91 Brown Papers, George to Anne Brown, October 21, 1864.
92 *Ibid.*

93 *Ibid.*, October 17, 1864.
94 *Ibid.*
95 *Ibid.*, October 27, 1864. See note 84 above.
96 *Ibid.*
97 *Ibid.*, October 31, 1864.
98 *Ibid.*, June 18, 1864.
99 *Globe*, November 3, 1864.
100 *Ibid.*
101 *Ibid.*
102 *Ibid.*
103 *Montreal Herald*, October 29, 1864.
104 Whelan, *op. cit.*, p. 130.
105 *Ibid.*, pp. 187-8. See pp. 188-203 for following quotations from Brown's Toronto speech.
106 *Ibid.*
107 Brown Papers, George to Anne Brown, November 7, 1864.
108 *Globe*, November 5, 1864.
109 Brown Papers, George to Anne Brown, November 11, 1864.
110 *Ibid.*, November 7, 1864.
111 C. R. W. Biggar, *Sir Oliver Mowat*, 2 volumes (Toronto, 1905), vol. 1, p. 133.
112 Brown Papers, George to Anne Brown, October 27, 1864.
113 *Ibid.*, November 11, 1864; Macdonald Papers, vol. 188, Brown to Macdonald (telegram), November 16, 1864. William McDougall was evidently annoyed by the haste of Brown's decision, since he had had his eye on the Postmaster-Generalship for himself. McDougall Letters, Brown to McDougall, December 1, 1864.
114 C. P. Stacey, *Canada and the British Army*, 1846-1871 (London, 1936), pp. 165-6.
115 *Ibid.*, p. 167.
116 *Ibid.*, pp. 167-8.
117 *Globe*, November 19, 1864. It appears that Brown did not share in the final drafting of the council minute on the defence proposals he had to take up in England. It was finished on the same day that he left Quebec, November 16, and presumably he was busy then with his own preparations. At any rate he made complaints about it to both McDougall and Macdonald. (See his letter to McDougall of December 1, mentioned in note 113 above, and that to Macdonald of "Saturday evening" before he left, in the Macdonald Papers, vol. 188.) His complaints, however, concerned form more than content — essentially that his own concern with the defence question was not acknowledged — though he also did not like Upper Canada's defences being left for the future. Yet he told Macdonald he was "entirely in accord" with the basic grounds and the goal of the minute.
118 McDougall Letters, Brown to McDougall, December 1, 1864.
119 Brown Papers, George to Anne Brown, November 11, 1864.
120 *Ibid.*, December 3 and 5, 1864. See also C.O. 42, vol. 643, Monck to Cardwell,

November 7, 1864, and Cardwell to Monck (draft), December 3, 1864.
121 Brown Papers, George to Anne Brown, December 5, 1864.
122 *Ibid.*, December 5, 6, 8, 1864.
123 *Ibid.*, December 6, 1864.
124 *Ibid.*
125 *Ibid.*, December 10, 15, 1864.
126 *Ibid.*, December 14, 1864.
127 Macdonald Papers, vol. 188, Brown to Macdonald, December 22, 1864.
128 *Ibid.*
129 Legislative Library of Ontario, *Province of Canada, State Book AB, Documents Relating to the Opening of the North West Territories to Settlement and Cultivation* (Quebec, 1865).
130 *Ibid.*
131 *Ibid.*
132 *Ibid.*
133 Brown Papers, Viscount Bury to Brown, December 13, 1864; George to Anne Brown, December 5, 10, 15, 1864.
134 *Ibid.*, R. C. Fisher to Brown, December 10; George to Anne Brown, December 15, 1864.
135 *Ibid.*, George to Anne Brown, December 13, 1864.
136 *Ibid.*, December 16, 1864.
137 Quoted in Frances E. O. Monck, *My Canadian Leaves* (London, 1891), p. 264.
138 Winks, *Canada and the United States*, p. 318.
139 *Globe*, January 28, 1864.
140 Brown Papers, George to Anne Brown, February 7, 1865.
141 *Ibid.*
142 All quotations from Brown's speech are taken from *Parliamentary Debates on the Subject of the Confederation of the British North American Provinces* (Quebec, 1865), pp. 84-115.
143 Brown Papers, George to Anne Brown, February 9, 1864.
144 *Ibid.*, March 4, 1865.
145 *Confederation Debates*, p. 1027.
146 Brown Papers, George to Anne Brown, March 14, 1865.

Chapter 6

Pages 187 to 220

1 Brown Papers, George to Anne Brown, February 21, 1865.
2 *Ibid.*, February 23, 1865.
3 F. N. Walker, "George Brown, Man of Many Faculties and Friends", typescript copy, Toronto, 1952, in author's possession.
4 Brown Papers, George to Anne Brown, March 6, 1865.
5 *Ibid.*, February 27, 1865.
6 *Ibid.*
7 *Ibid.*, Anne to George Brown, February

28, 1865.

8 *Ibid.*, George to Anne Brown, March 2, 1865.

9 *Ibid.*, references in George Brown's letters of March 1, 6, 8, 10, 1865.

10 *Ibid.*, March 1, 1865.

11 *Ibid.*

12 *Ibid.*

13 *Ibid.*, March 13, 1865.

14 *Ibid.*, March 7, 9, 1865.

15 *Ibid.*, March 4, 1865.

16 *Ibid.*, Tilley to Brown, November 2, 1864.

17 *Ibid.*

18 *Ibid.*, George to Anne Brown, March 8, 1864.

19 *Ibid.*, March 13, 1865.

20 *Ibid.*

21 *Ibid.*, March 17, 1865.

22 *Ibid.*, March 20, 1865.

23 *Ibid.*, March 21, 1865.

24 *Ibid.*, March 20, 21, 1865.

25 *Globe*, March 9, 1865; Stacey, *op. cit.*, p. 171.

26 *Globe*, March 27, 1865.

27 *Ibid.*, March 17, 1865.

28 Brown Papers, George to Anne Brown, March 20, 1865.

29 *Ibid.*, March 23, 24, 1865.

30 *Ibid.*, March 22, 23, 1865.

31 *Ibid.*, March 23, 1865.

32 See Brown's statement to Parliament of August 9, 1865 (in *Globe* of August 10). The agreement "ratified by Sir Etienne Taché in March" is also referred to in Brown's letter to Macdonald of August 5, 1865, during the ministerial reconstruction of that month. See Macdonald Papers, vol. 188.

33 Brown Papers, George to Anne Brown, March 24, 1865.

34 Typescript history of the *Globe*, p. 74.

35 Macdonald Papers, vol. 188, Brown to Shaw, September 3, 1862.

36 Brown Papers, George to Anne Brown, June 22, 1866.

37 Macdonald to Pope, quoted in Pope, *Macdonald*, p. 300.

38 Brown Papers, George to Anne Brown, June 26, 1866.

39 *Ibid.*, April 28, 1865.

40 *Ibid.*, April 28, May 6, 1865.

41 *Ibid.*, May 18, 1865.

42 *Ibid.*, May 20, 1865.

43 *Ibid.*, May 6, 1865.

44 *Ibid.*

45 *Ibid.*

46 *Ibid.*

47 *Ibid.*, May 13, 1865.

48 *Ibid.*, May 6, 1865.

49 *Ibid.*, May 13, 1865.

50 *Ibid.*, June 3, 1865.

51 *Ibid.*, May 18, 1865.

52 *Ibid.*

53 *Ibid.*, May 20, 1865.

54 *Ibid.*, May 25, 1865.

55 *Ibid.*, May 27, 1865.

56 *Ibid.*

57 *Ibid.*, May 13, 1865.

58 *Ibid.*, May 25, 1865.

59 *Ibid.*

60 *Ibid.*, June 1, 1865.

61 *Ibid.*; Pope, *op. cit.*, p. 300; O. D. Skelton, *The Life and Times of Sir Alexander Tilloch Galt*, p. 385.

62 Brown Papers, George to Anne Brown, June 1, 1865.

63 *Ibid.*

64 *Ibid.*, first sheet missing, but date may be set as June 8, 1865, by internal evidence.

65 *Ibid.*

66 *Ibid.* For a summary of the matters agreed on by the Imperial and Canadian representatives see C.O. 42, vol. 647, document of June 20, 1865, signed by Gladstone, Cardwell, Somerset, de Grey, Macdonald, Brown, Cartier, and Galt.

67 Brown Papers, George to Anne Brown, July 13, September 12, 1865.

68 *Ibid.*, August 1, 4, 1865.

69 *Ibid.*, August 4, 1865.

70 *Ibid.*, George to Gordon Brown, May 11, 1863; Monck to Brown, May 21, 1864.

71 *Ibid.*, George to Anne Brown, August 4, 1865.

72 *Ibid.* See also Brown Papers, "Memorandum of a Conversation between the Governor-General and Mr. Brown, August 3, 1865".

73 Cartwright, *Reminiscences*, p. 41.

74 Brown Papers, George to Anne Brown, August 4, 1865.

75 *Ibid.* Quotations that follow pertaining to this interview (down to the next reference) are also taken from the same source.

76 *Ibid.*

77 Macdonald Papers, vol. 51, "Ministerial Negotiations for the Reconstruction of the Government consequent on the Death of Sir Etienne Taché".

78 *Ibid.*

79 Brown Papers, George to Anne Brown, August 4, 1865. See also *ibid.*, Macdonald to Brown, August 4, 1865.

80 *Ibid.*, George to Anne Brown, August 4, 1865.

81 *Ibid.*

82 *Ibid.*, "12 noon", August 4, 1865 (i.e., this is a second letter of the same day).

83 Macdonald Papers, "Ministerial Negotiations", Brown to Macdonald, August 4, 1865.

84 *Ibid.*, Macdonald to Brown, August 5, 1865.

85 *Ibid.*, Brown to Macdonald, August 5, 1865.

86 Creighton, *The Young Politician*, p. 419.

87 *Confederation Debates*, p. 708.

88 See Brown to Macdonald, "Quebec, Monday", quoted in Pope, *Macdonald*, p. 306. It is Pope who terms Macdonald's action "inadvertence" — and talks of Brown's "morbid jealousy" (p. 304). But Cartwright (*op. cit.*, pp. 40-3) declares that Macdonald was in "temporary eclipse" during 1865, "thoroughly alarmed" over the increasing good understanding between his old ally, Cartier, and Brown, and working diligently to weaken Brown's position in the government. Both these sources are obviously biased. Lacking more precise evidence, I have steered between them.

89 Sellar, *op. cit.*, p. 22. Brown made this point particularly clear when on his resignation in December 1865 he told Sellar's brother, Thomas, then Montreal correspondent of the *Globe*, that he "could not stand any longer the gross maladministration going on — offices and favours to the undeserving and jobs for supporters. The whole aim was to keep in power and help favourites, and he was glad to be quit of them." This is quoted from a note by Robert Sellar, found in his own copy of Alexander Mackenzie's *Brown*, and now in the Public Archives of Canada.

90 Skelton, *op. cit.*, p. 401.

91 Macdonald Papers, vol. 230, Macdonald to McDougall, July 8, 1864.

92 *Globe*, August 10, 1865.

93 Gray, *op. cit.*, p. 296. Cartier and Macdonald were "by courtesy further admitted" (*ibid.*, p. 297); Cartier attended but not, apparently, Macdonald. See *Globe*, correspondent's reports, September 18, 19, 1865. Pope (*op. cit.*, p. 310) treats Macdonald and Cartier both as regular members.

94 Gray, *op. cit.*, p. 298.

95 Brown Papers, George to Anne Brown, September 16, 1865.

96 *Ibid.*, October 10, 1865.

97 *Ibid.*, October 13, 1865.

98 *Ibid.*

99 *Ibid.*, November 8, 1865. Note that Brown informed Monck that the cabinet decision came on November 7, and in response to a request from Lieutenant-Governor Gordon of New Brunswick. *Ibid.*, Brown to Monck, December 25, 1865.

100 *Ibid.*, George to Anne Brown, November 8, 1865.

101 *Ibid.*, November 13, 1865.

102 *Ibid.*, November 18, 1865.

103 See p. 157 above, and also note 28 to chapter 5.

104 Brown Papers, Gordon to George Brown, March 17, 1865.

105 *Ibid.*

106 Public Archives, G 174, Cardwell to Monck, June 24, 1865.

107 Brown Papers, Monck to Brown, October 28, 1865.

108 Public Record Office 30/48, Cardwell Papers, Gordon to Cardwell, January 15, 1865.

109 *Ibid.*

110 *Ibid.*, December 19, 1864. It may be noted that on March 22, 1865, Gordon

affirmed to Cardwell (*ibid.*) that Brown largely shared his own views regarding the absurdity of "seven parliaments and seven responsible governments" for three million people. But here, surely, Gordon was straining words to fit his case. Because of French Canada (and his own Upper Canada sectionalism) Brown had repeatedly recognized the necessity of federal union. The true key words were "seven *responsible* governments" — since Brown had not thought that system was required for the local legislatures in Confederation.

111 *Ibid.*, Gordon to Cardwell, November 20, 1865.

112 *Ibid.*

113 Brown Papers, George to Anne Brown, November 18, 1865.

114 *Ibid.*

115 Creighton, *op. cit.*, p. 428. See also Waite, *op. cit.*, p. 252, and *Morning News* (Saint John), March 14, 1866.

116 Brown Papers, Brown to Monck, December 25, 1865.

117 *Ibid.* See also Waite, *op. cit.*, p. 220.

118 *Morning Chronicle* (Halifax), April 16, 1866. See also Brown Papers, draft reply of Brown to Tupper, to telegram, Tupper to Brown, April 13, 1866.

119 Brown Papers, Brown to Monck, December 25, 1865.

120 C.O. 42, vol. 649, Copy of Report of Committee of Executive Council, July 15, 1865. See also Macdonald Papers, vol. 188, notes in Macdonald's handwriting on Brown's views of Washington mission, "July 15".

121 Brown Papers, Brown to Monck, December 25, 1865.

122 *Ibid.*

123 Skelton, *op. cit.*, p. 400.

124 Brown Papers, Sumner to Brown, June 7, 1850.

125 Rush Rhees Library, Seward Papers, Brown to Seward, June 30, 1862.

126 Brown Papers, Brown to Monck, December 25, 1865.

127 Macdonald Papers, vol. 188, notes by Macdonald, beginning "July 15" [1865], on discussions with Brown regarding policy for reciprocity negotiations.

128 Brown Papers, Brown to Monck, December 25, 1865.

129 *Ibid.*

130 *Ibid.*

131 *Ibid.*

132 *Ibid.*

133 *Ibid.*

134 *Ibid.* The Washington press dispatch of November 30 appears as a clipping in the Brown Papers. See also, *ibid.*, Galt to Brown, December 5, 1865.

135 *Ibid.*, Brown to Monck, December 25, 1865. See also, *ibid.*, printed confidential government "Memorandum" of February 20, 1866, on the course of the reciprocity negotiations. Brown's own account is not

essentially at variance with this, but has been given priority in any case because of the need to understand his own viewpoint, in order to explain his reactions.

136 Brown Papers, George to Anne Brown, December 14, 1865.
137 *Ibid.*, Brown to Monck, December 25, 1865.
138 *Ibid.*
139 *Ibid.* The tenses in the quotation have been altered to put it into direct discourse.
140 *Ibid.*
141 *Ibid.*
142 *Ibid.*
143 *Ibid.*
144 *Ibid.*
145 *Ibid.*
146 *Ibid.*
147 *Ibid.* See also manuscript memorandum by Galt, December 18, 1865, in Brown Papers.
148 *Ibid.*, Brown to Monck, December 25, 1865.
149 Order-in-Council of December 22, 1865, included in Memorandum of February 20, 1866, *loc. cit.*
150 Brown Papers, telegram, George to Anne Brown, December 19, 1865. He added: "Happily we don't part in anger."
151 *Ibid.*, George to Anne Brown, telegram December 21, 1865. Cartier to Brown, *ibid.*, December 19, 1865.
152 Cartwright, *op. cit.*, pp. 40-1.
153 Brown Papers, Cartier to Brown, 2:30 p.m., December 19, 1865.
154 Macdonald Papers, Brown to Cartier, December 19, 1865.
155 Brown Papers, Cartier to Brown, 4:30 p.m., December 19, 1865.
156 *Ibid.*
157 Brown's speech in explanation of his resignation, in parliament, June 15, 1866, quoted in Gray, *op. cit.*, p. 321.
158 W. Buckingham and G. W. Ross, *The Hon. Alexander Mackenzie, His Life and Times* (Toronto, 1892), pp. 201-3.
159 Brown Papers, Monck to Brown, January 18, 1866.
160 *Globe*, February 8, 1866.
161 Brown's speech on his resignation, Gray, *op. cit.*, p. 321.

Chapter 7

Pages 221 to 259

1 Captain John A. Macdonald, *Troublous Times in Canada* (Toronto, 1910), p. 16.
2 *Globe*, March 3, 1866.
3 C. P. Stacey, "Fenianism and the Rise of National Feeling in Canada", *Canadian Historical Review*, September 1931, p. 244.
4 *Globe*, March 12, 13, 14, 1866.
5 Brown Papers, McGee to Brown, "Wednesday evening, 6 o'clock", by

internal evidence, written in March 1866.
6 *Ibid.*, Monck to Brown, March 14, 1866.
7 *Ibid.*, McGee to Brown, "Wednesday evening, 6 o'clock".
8 H. A. Davis, "The Fenian Raid on New Brunswick", *Canadian Historical Review*, December, 1955, pp. 322-4.
9 *Ibid.*, p. 330.
10 *Ibid.*, p. 322.
11 *Globe*, May 10, 1866.
12 *Ibid.*, May 7, 1866.
13 *Ibid.*, June 1, 1866.
14 *Ibid.*, June 2, 1866.
15 Typescript history of the *Globe*, p. 75.
16 *Globe*, June 6, 1866.
17 *Ibid.*, June 12, 1866.
18 Brown Papers, George to Anne Brown, June 14, 1866.
19 *Ibid.*, June 4, 1866.
20 *Ibid.*
21 Gray, *op. cit.*, pp. 311-25.
22 *Ibid.*, pp. 314-21.
23 Brown Papers, George to Anne Brown, June 15, 1866.
24 *Ibid.*, June 22, 1866.
25 *Ibid.*
26 This may be inferred from the manner in which Macdonald later described the ending of his cordial relations with Brown. See Pope, *Memoirs*, p. 281.
27 See, for example, A. L. Burt, ed., "Peter Mitchell on John A. Macdonald", *Canadian Historical Review*, September 1961, pp. 209-27.
28 Brown Papers, George to Anne Brown, June 19, 1866.
29 *Ibid.*
30 *Ibid.*, June 18, 1866.
31 *Ibid.*, June 19, 1866.
32 *Ibid.*, June 20, 1866.
33 *Ibid.*, June 26, 1866.
34 *Ibid.*, June 20, 1866.
35 *Ibid.*, June 26, 1866.
36 *Ibid.*
37 *Ibid.*
38 *Ibid.*, June 26, July 4, 1866.
39 Dorion at this time failed completely with a motion to refer Confederation to the people.
40 Brown Papers, George to Anne Brown, July 4, 1866.
41 *Ibid.*
42 Speech of July 10, quoted in *Globe*, July 14, 1866.
43 *Ibid.*
44 *Ibid.*
45 *Ibid.*
46 *Globe*, July 7, 1866.
47 *Ibid.*, June 28, July 5, 1866.
48 Skelton, *Galt*, p. 398.
49 Brown Papers, George to Anne Brown, July 9, 11, 1866.
50 *Ibid.*, July 7, 1866.
51 *Ibid.*, July 10, 1866.
52 *Globe*, July 12, 1866.
53 *Journals of the Assembly* (1866), p. 128.

54 Brown Papers, George to Anne Brown, July 12, 1866.
55 *Ibid.*, July 25, 1866.
56 *Ibid.*
57 *Ibid.*
58 *Ibid.*, July 26, 1866.
59 *Globe*, July 28, 1866.
60 *Ibid.*, August 3, 1866.
61 *Ibid.*
62 *Ibid.*, July 28, 1866.
63 *Ibid.*, August 4, 8, 1866.
64 *Ibid.* Brown also expressed his dislike for the guarantee given to minority educational rights in the provinces under the projected federal constitution. It invited interference in a province's local affairs and "fettered" the majority. He had fought unsuccessfully against a guaranteeing resolution at the Quebec Conference, he said, and now saw his efforts justified. A minority's best protection was the majority's sense of justice. See *Globe*, August 8, 1866.
65 Brown Papers, George to Anne Brown, August 6, 1866.
66 *Ibid.*
67 *Ibid.*
68 *Leader*, August 8, 1866.
69 *Globe*, August 8, 1866.
70 Brown Papers, George to Anne Brown, August 8, 1866.
71 *Ibid.*
72 *Ibid.*, July 26, 1866.
73 *Ibid.*, July 12, 1866.
74 *Globe*, April 2, 1866.
75 Concern for the future financial security of his family is a recurrent theme in George Brown's letters to his wife in the Brown Papers.
76 *Canada Farmer* (Toronto), January 15, 1876. John Clay, *My Recollections of Ontario* (Chicago, 1918), p. 15.
77 Ontario Archives, Deed Copy Book, Brant County, Brantford Township, volume F, 1865-67, item 3426.
78 *Ibid.*, item 3459.
79 *Ibid.*, items 3550, 3480.
80 Ontario Archives, Abstract Index of Deeds, Brant County, Brantford Township (microfilm copy) volumes B-C, Liber L, item 6040 (1873).
81 *Globe*, August 21, September 11, 12, 18, 1866.
82 *Ibid.*, August 16, 17, 22, September 5, 1866. It might be added that D'Arcy McGee himself, deeply concerned over Fenianism, was dissatisfied with Macdonald's administration of the Militia Department and proposed that it be turned over to Galt. See Isobel Skelton, *McGee*, p. 525.
83 *Globe*, September 5, 1866.
84 Brown Papers, George to Anne Brown, July 9, 1866.
85 *Globe*, September 19, 1866.
86 *Ibid.*, September 19, October 6, 1866.
87 *Ibid.*, October 2, 1866.
88 *Ibid.*, April 25, 1867.
89 *Ibid.*, November 13, 14, 15, 20, 1866.

90 See *ibid.*, December 3, 1866, for *Globe*'s general assurance (in replying to annexationist kite-flying in the American press) that Canada's fears over trade losses and Fenian dangers had proved groundless — and that Confederation would meet the needs of the future.
91 Mackenzie Papers, Brown to Holton, January 17, 1867.
92 *Ibid.*
93 *Ibid.* Holton replied to Brown (Brown Papers) on January 19, "If Confederation does come I shall even be reconciled to it."
94 *Globe*, February 11 *et seq.*, to March 15, 1867.
95 Mackenzie Papers, Brown to Mackenzie, March 12, 1867.
96 *Ibid.*
97 *Globe*, February 27, 1867.
98 *Ibid.*
99 *Ibid.*, February 26, 1867.
100 *Ibid.*, February 22, March 11, 1867.
101 *Ibid.*
102 *Ibid.*, March 2, 1867. The *Globe*'s Ottawa correspondent reported (March 1) that the government that day had received the official copy of the bill.
103 *Leader*, March 6, 1867; *Weekly Globe*, June 7, 1867.
104 *Globe*, March 5, 1867.
105 *Leader*, March 4, 1867.
106 *Globe*, March 2, 1867.
107 *Ibid.* Put into direct discourse.
108 Mackenzie Papers, Brown to Mackenzie, May 13, 1867.
109 Brown Papers, Parker to Brown, March 4, 1867.
110 *Ibid.*, D. Macdonald to Brown, April 18, 1867.
111 See also *ibid.*, J. Young to Brown, April 9, 1867.
112 *Globe*, March 20, April 4, 1867.
113 *Ibid.*, April 12, 1867.
114 *Ibid.*
115 *Ibid.*, April 19, 1867. See also *Globe*, March 5, April 24, 1867.
116 *Ibid.*, April 24, 1867.
117 *Ibid.*
118 *Leader*, May 2, 1867.
119 Mackenzie Papers, Brown to Holton, May 13, 1867.
120 *Ibid.*
121 *Globe*, May 15, 1867.
122 *Ibid.*
123 Mackenzie Papers, Brown to Holton, June 10, 1867.
124 Brown Papers, Holton to Brown, May 31, 1867.
125 *Ibid.* "It is our constitution," Holton said. See also *ibid.*, June 1, 1867.
126 *Ibid.*, Holton to Brown, May 16, 1867. See also *ibid.*, May 1, 1867.
127 Mackenzie Papers, Brown to Holton, June 10, 1867.
128 Brown Papers, Holton to Brown, June 21, 1867.
129 *Weekly Globe*, June 21, 1867.

130 *Ibid.*

131 Mackenzie Papers, Brown to Holton, June 10, 1867.

132 *Ibid.*, June 19, 1867.

133 *Globe*, June 26, 1867.

134 Mackenzie Papers, Brown to Holton, July 2, 1867.

135 *Globe*, June 29, 1867. The following account of the Convention, and all quotations down to the next note below, are taken from the complete report of the proceedings given in the *Globe* of this date. See also account in Young, *Public Men*, pp. 349-63, and Appendix VI, pp. 396-404, for list of delegates, their homes and occupations. Young was present as a delegate.

136 Sir George Ross, *Getting into Parliament and After* (Toronto, 1913), p. 20. Ross was also present. See also Macdonald Papers, vol. 340, A. Cameron to Macdonald, June 29, 1867, for an unfriendly version of this same scene.

137 *Globe*, June 29, 1867. The following quotations, down to the next note, are similarly taken from this source.

138 Young, *op. cit.*, p. 361.

139 *Globe*, June 29, 1867.

140 *Ibid.*, July 2, 1867.

141 The following account of Brown's activities on the eve of Confederation is taken from a memoir written by Robert Gay himself, which appeared in *East and West* (Toronto), June 25, 1904.

142 *Globe*, July 2, 1867.

143 Gay, *loc. cit.*

144 *Ibid.*

145 Brown Papers, Monck to Brown, November 13, 1868.

146 *Globe*, July 2, 1867.

147 Mackenzie Papers, Brown to Holton, July 2, 1867.

148 *Ibid.*

149 Brown Papers, Holton to Brown, July 4, 10, 1867.

150 Mackenzie Papers, Brown to Holton, July 5, 1867.

151 Brown Papers, Holton to Brown, July 16, 1867.

152 Mackenzie Papers, Brown to Holton, July 5, 1867; *Globe*, July 10, 1867.

153 Mackenzie Papers, Brown to Holton, July 5, 1867.

154 *Globe*, July 19, 1867.

155 Brown Papers, Mackenzie to Brown, August 21, 1869.

156 *Globe*, July 23, 1867.

157 Brown Papers, George to Anne Brown, July 25, 1867; *Globe*, July 25, 1867.

158 *Globe*, August 15, 1867.

159 Macdonald Papers, vol. 230, J. S. Macdonald to J. A. Macdonald, August 13, 1867.

160 *Globe*, August 19-26, 1867.

161 *Ibid.*, August 27, 1867.

162 Mackenzie Papers, Brown to Mackenzie, August 20, 1869.

163 *Globe*, August 28, 1867.

164 Mackenzie Papers, Brown to Mackenzie, August 20, 1869.

165 *Ibid.*, Mackenzie to Brown, August 28, 1867.

166 Brown Papers, C. Clarke to Brown, August 29, 31, 1867.

167 Mackenzie Papers, Brown to Mackenzie, October 3, 1868; Clarke Papers, Brown to Clarke, October 31, 1868.

168 *Globe*, August 30, 31, 1867.

169 John Squair, *The Townships of Darlington and Clarke* (Toronto, 1927), pp. 157-8.

170 *Globe*, September 20, 1867.

171 Ontario Archives, R. J. Cartwright, Papers, Macdonald to Cartwright, November 17, 1869.

172 Mackenzie Papers, Brown to Mackenzie, October 3, 1867.

173 *Ibid.*

174 See Brown Papers, Brown to Mrs. Nelson (Anne's mother), April 22, 1867, for evidence of how a trip to Scotland had had to be put off through the year.

Chapter 8

Pages 260 to 300

1 Brown Papers, George to Anne Brown, January 5, 1868 (misdated 1867).

2 Mackenzie Papers, Brown to Mackenzie, October 3, 1867.

3 Brown Papers, George to Anne Brown, January 5, 1868.

4 *Ibid.*, January 16, 1868.

5 *Ibid.*

6 *Ibid.*, January 30, February 23, 1868.

7 *Ibid.*, January 30, 1868.

8 *Ibid.*, February 16, 1868.

9 *Ibid.*, February 16, March 12, 19, 1868. See also Mackenzie Papers, Brown to Mackenzie, August 20, 1869.

10 Brown Papers, George to Anne Brown, February 16, 1868.

11 *Ibid.*, March 16, 1868. This is confirmed by Cartier. See Macdonald Papers, vol. 202, Cartier to Macdonald, May 15, 1868.

12 Archives of the Province of Quebec, Collection Chapais, Brown to Cartier, February 17, 1868.

13 *Ibid.*

14 Brown Papers, Cartier to Brown, February 27, 1868.

15 *Ibid.*, George to Anne Brown, March 8, 1868.

16 *Ibid.*, March 12, 1868.

17 *Ibid.*, March 12, 19, 1868.

18 *Ibid.*, March 8, 1868.

19 *Ibid.*, March 19, 1868. Brown replied to Cartier on March 10.

20 *Ibid.*, Cartier to Brown, March 14, 1868.

21　*Ibid.*, Mackenzie to Brown, March 21, 1868.
22　*Ibid.*, March 21, 23, 1868.
23　*Ibid.*, George to Anne Brown, March 29, 1868.
24　*Ibid.*, April 7, 1868.
25　*Ibid.*, March 2, 8, 16, 23, 1868.
26　*Ibid.*, August 5, 1868.
27　*Ibid.*, July 30, 1868.
28　*Ibid.*
29　*Ibid.*, July 31, 1868.
30　*Ibid.*, August 1, 1868.
31　*Ibid.*
32　*Ibid.*, August 4, 1868.
33　*Ibid.*
34　*Ibid.*, August 5, 1868.
35　*Ibid.*, August 5, September 1, 3, 1868. See also *ibid.*, deed, F. W. Goddard and G. Brown, of April 26, 1870, regarding house and land in Lambeth, probated to Brown in 1868.
36　*Ibid.*, September 3, 1868. Brown's considerable library, largely on history and politics, is at Ichrachan House today.
37　See *Globe*, November 27, 1868, for announcement.
38　See *Globe* for latter half of October 1868. Part of page one continued to be occupied by advertisements, however; and the proportion varied up and down during the rest of Brown's life.
39　*Globe*, November 27, 1868.
40　See advertisements in *Globe* through January 1869.
41　*Ibid.*, November 27, 1868.
42　*Ibid.*
43　Typescript history of the *Globe*, p. 83.
44　*Globe*, October 12, November 4, 1868.
45　Brant County, Brantford Township, Abstract Index of Deeds, vols. B-C, Liber L, 6040, March 27, 1868.
46　*Globe*, December 16, 1868.
47　*Ibid.*
48　*Ibid.*, January 25, 1869.
49　*Ibid.*
50　*Ibid.*, January 1, 1869.
51　*Ibid.*, January 4, 21, 1869.
52　Brown Papers, George to Anne Brown, March 8, 1868.
53　*Leader*, March 12, 1869.
54　*Globe*, March 26, 27, 1869.
55　*Ibid.*, April 5, 1869. See also new *Globe* series on North West, beginning May 28, 1869.
56　Brown Papers, Monck to Brown, November 13, 1868.
57　*Globe*, June 24, July 3, 1869.
58　*Ibid.*, June 5, 1869.
59　*Ibid.*, June 11, 1869.
60　*Ibid.*, July 30, 1869.
61　*Ibid.*, September 23, 1869.
62　Brown Papers, Mackenzie to Brown, July 22, 1869.
63　*Ibid.*, August 21, September 1, 1869. See also *ibid.*, Holton to Mackenzie, August 25, 1869.
64　Mackenzie Papers, Brown to Mackenzie, August 20, 1869.
65　*Ibid.* See also *ibid.*, Mackenzie to Brown, May 19, 1869.
66　*Ibid.*, Brown to Mackenzie, August 20, 1869.
67　*Ibid.*
68　*Ibid.*
69　*Ibid.*
70　Brown Papers, Mackenzie to Brown, August 21, 1869.
71　Brown–Nelson Papers. Notes of family birthdays recorded by Anne Brown.
72　*Globe*, September 20, November 18, 1869.
73　*Ibid.*, November 17, 1869.
74　*Ibid.*, November 23, 1869.
75　*Ibid.*, December 31, 1869.
76　*Ibid.*, June 5, July 26, August 31, September 23, October 14, 1869.
77　*Ibid.*, December 31, 1869.
78　*Ibid.*, January 7, 1870.
79　*Ibid.*, January 4, 6, 7, 1870.
80　*Ibid.*, January 7, 1870.
81　*Ibid.*
82　*Ibid.*, January 12, 1870.
83　*Ibid.*, January 18, 1870.
84　*Ibid.*
85　*Ibid.*, February 18, 25, 1870.
86　*Ibid.*, March 7, 1870.
87　*Ibid.*, March 30, 1870.
88　*Ibid.*
89　*Ibid.*, March 31, April 1, 1870.
90　*Ibid.*, February 5, 1870.
91　*Ibid.*
92　*Ibid.*, April 13, 1870.
93　*Ibid.*, April 16, 1870.
94　*Ibid.*
95　*Ibid.*, April 22–May 2, 1870, *passim*.
96　*Ibid.*, May 4, 14, 1870. See also *ibid.*, July 25, 1870.
97　Brown Papers, George to Anne Brown, January 16, 18, 19, 1870. Contracts were secured. Hugh Baines was named the managing director of the Steel, Iron and Railway Works Company, which after two successful years was sold to the Canadian Car Company. See *Globe* for October 3, 1872.
98　*Ibid.*, May 11, 1870.
99　Mackenzie Papers, Brown to Mackenzie, April 29, 1870.
100　*Globe*, April 15, 1880.
101　*Ibid.*, September 6, 1870.
102　Brown Papers, George to Anne Brown, September 15, 1870. He had also entertained the young Canadian Press Association at Bow Park, and addressed their banquet in Brantford on July 19. A. H. U. Colquhoun *et al.*, *A History of Canadian Journalism* (Toronto, 1908), p. 66.
103　*Globe*, October 21, 1870.
104　Letter from Brydges in *ibid.*, October 19, 1870.
105　Charles Clarke, *Sixty Years in Upper Canada* (Toronto, 1908), pp. 154-5.
106　*Globe*, October 31, 1870.

107   Mackenzie Papers, Brown to G. Buckingham, February 4, 1870.
108   *Globe*, December 8, 1870.
109   Macdonald Papers, *Letter from the Hon. George Brown to John O'Donohue, Patrick Hughes, J. D. Merrick, and Thomas McCrossen, Esqs., March 9, 1871.*
110   *Globe*, March 9, 1871.
111   Clarke Papers, October 31, 1868.
112   Macdonald Papers, vol. 230, J. S. Macdonald to J. A. Macdonald, May 29, 1871.
113   *Globe*, March 28, 1871.
114   *Ibid.*, March 29, 1871.
115   D. G. Creighton, *John A. Macdonald, The Old Chieftain* (Toronto, 1955), p. 104.
116   Brown Papers, George to Anne Brown, June 8, 1871.
117   *Ibid.*
118   Mackenzie Papers, Brown to Mackenzie, April 24, 1872.
119   Brown Papers, George to Anne Brown, June 8, 1871.
120   *Ibid.*, June 15, 1871.
121   *Ibid.*, June 22, 25, 1871.
122   *Ibid.*, July 2, 1871.
123   *Ibid.*, July 6, 1871.
124   *Ibid.*, July 2, 1871.
125   *Ibid.*, July 22, 1871.
126   *Ibid.*, July 17, 1871.
127   Macdonald Papers, vol. 230, J. S. Macdonald to J. A. Macdonald, September 10, 1871.
128   *Ibid.*, November 6, 1871.
129   Clarke, *op. cit.*, p. 169.
130   *Ibid.*, p. 171.
131   *Ibid.*
132   *Ibid.*, p. 174.
133   Quoted in Pope, *Macdonald*, p. 503, Macdonald to J. Carling, December 23, 1871.
134   *Globe*, March 4, 1872.
135   Minutes of the Toronto Trades' Assembly, February 2, 1872, typed copies in possession of the Toronto District Labor Council.
136   *Globe*, February 16, 1872.
137   *Ibid.*, March 16, 1872.
138   *Leader*, March 16, 1872.
139   Minutes of the Toronto Typographical Union, for May 9, 1886. From the Manuscript Minute Books of the Union for 1859-1871 and 1872-1883, made available to the author through the kind interest of Mr. L. Zolf.
140   This is an estimate based on annual reports of the Typographical Union (in the first of the above Minute Books), as presented in January of 1868 (75 members), 1869 (129) and 1870 (162). Unfortunately, the reports thereafter were not copied into the minutes.
141   Minutes of the Union for February 17, 1872.
142   *Globe*, March 22, 1872.
143   Minutes of the Union for March 2, 1872.

144   *Globe*, February 16, 1872.
145   *Ibid.*
146   *Ibid.*
147   *Ibid.*, June 17, 1848; September 11, 1852; May 10, 11, 1854; May 17, 1867.
148   *Ibid.*, February 7, May 11, 1867. See also May 10, October 4, 1864; and *Weekly Globe*, September 13, 1867.
149   *Globe*, July 2, 1853; June 6, 1854. See also H. A. Logan, *Trade Unions in Canada* (Toronto, 1948), p. 26.
150   J. M. Conner, *Toronto Labour Souvenir* (Toronto, 1928), p. 46; *Leader*, April 1, 1872.
151   *Leader*, ibid.
152   Logan, *op. cit.*, p. 35.
153   Sellar, *Brown, Globe and Confederation*, p. 6. Sellar asserts that Brown generally gave higher wages and lighter work than any union office.
154   Minutes of the Union for February 14, 1866.
155   *Globe*, April 2, 1872.
156   *Ibid.*
157   *Ibid.*, March 22, 1872.
158   *Ibid.*
159   Circular quoted in *Globe*, April 2, 1872.
160   Minutes of Union for March 13, 1872.
161   *Ibid.*
162   *Ibid.*
163   *Ibid.*
164   *Globe*, April 2, 1872.
165   *Ibid.* See also *Leader*, March 22, April 3, 1872.
166   *Globe*, March 22, 1872.
167   *Ibid.*
168   *Ibid.*, March 25, 1872.
169   *Globe*, April 2, 1872.
170   *Ibid.*
171   *Ibid.*, March 22, 1872.
172   *Leader*, March 18, 19, 23, April 3, 9, 1872.
173   Creighton, *The Old Chieftain*, pp.116, 118, 124.
174   *Leader*, March 29, 30, April 1, 1872.
175   Speech by Beaty quoted in *Leader*, April 4, 1872.
176   B. Ostry, "Conservatives, Liberals, and Labour in the 1870's", *Canadian Historical Review*, June 1960, p. 106. Note also Beaty's election appeal to the "Working Men of East Toronto", *Leader*, July 22, 1872.
177   *Leader*, April 4, 1872.
178   Brown Papers, see letters and telegrams from printers seeking employment and Brown's agents seeking printers, for late March and early April, 1872.
179   *Ibid.*, Alex. Jacques to Brown, March 25, 1872.
180   *Globe*, April 19, 1872. Testimony given in magistrate's examination of strikers. D. G. Creighton ("George Brown, Sir John Macdonald and the 'Workingman' ", *Canadian Historical Review*,

December 1943, p. 369) speaks of a "private detective", but the *Globe* reference would indicate that he was a government employee, and used here with his superior's knowledge.

181   *Globe*, March 29, 1872.
182   *Leader*, March 27, 28, 1872.
183   *Globe*, April 8, 1872.
184   *Ibid.*, March 30, 1872.
185   *Ibid.*, April 19, 1872.
186   *Ibid.*
187   *Ibid.*, May 20, 1872.
188   *Ibid.*, May 8, 1872. See also *ibid.*, July 8, 1872.
189   *Ibid.*, June 7, 1872.
190   Minutes of Union for June 1, 1872.
191   Creighton, "Brown, Macdonald and 'Workingman' ", p. 374.
192   Letter to *Globe*, July 13, 1872.
193   *Ibid.* See also *ibid.*, July 10, 1872, and Ostry, *loc. cit.*, pp. 114-15.
194   Minutes of Toronto Trades' Assembly for July 5, 1872.
195   *Globe*, August 13, 1872.
196   Brown Papers, George to Anne Brown, August 12, 1872.
197   *Globe*, August 12, 1872.
198   *Ibid.*, August 17, 1872.
199   Ostry, *loc. cit.*, p. 117; *Ontario Workman* (Toronto), September 5, 1872.
200   Brown Papers, George to Anne Brown, August 22, 1872.
201   *Globe*, August 29, 1872.
202   Brown Papers, George to Anne Brown, August 29, 1872.
203   Even in Beaty's own East Toronto constituency, a correspondent privately told Macdonald's colleague, Alexander Campbell, "Money carried the day." Ontario Archives, A. Campbell Papers, C. J. Campbell to A. Campbell, August 18, 1872.

Chapter 9

Pages 301 to 337

1   Brown Papers, George to Anne Brown, August 12, 14, 1872; August 23, 1873.
2   *Ibid.*, August 12, 14, 1872.
3   Letter from T. E. Gillespie (a former farm hand at Bow Park) to F. P. Adams, February 25, 1904, in clippings and letters kindly presented to the author by Mrs. Frank Yeigh, Toronto.
4   Brown Papers, George to Anne Brown, September 17, 1872.
5   *Globe*, October 29, 1872.
6   *Ibid.*, October 18, 1872.
7   Biggar, *Mowat*, vol. 1, pp. 152-3.
8   Dale Thomson, *Alexander Mackenzie, Clear Grit* (Toronto, 1960), p. 144.
9   *Ibid.*
10   *Ibid.*, p. 145.
11   *Mail* (Toronto), October 25, 1872.
12   *Globe*, December 19, 1872.
13   *Mail*, February 1, 1873.
14   See Brown Papers, E. Penny to Mackenzie, December 10, 1872; and Campbell Papers, J. Beaty to J. A. Macdonald, November 4, 1872.
15   *Ibid.*, Mackenzie to Brown, March 5, 7, 1873.
16   *Mail*, April 3, 1873.
17   *Globe*, April 7, 1873.
18   *Ibid.*, April 8, 1873.
19   This may be presumed from the fact that Penny's letter of December 10 to Mackenzie was obviously passed on to Brown, since it was among his papers.
20   Creighton, *The Old Chieftain*, p. 153.
21   *Ibid.*, p. 154.
22   *Globe*, May 5, 1873; *Mail*, May 7, 1873.
23   *Globe*, May 8, 10, 1873.
24   *Ibid.*, May 20, 1873.
25   *Mail*, May 17, 28, June 2, 4, 1873.
26   *Globe*, May 20, 31, June 3, 11, 1873.
27   *Globe*, July 3, 1873.
28   *Ibid.*
29   *Ibid.*, July 4, 1873. The "incriminating" documents were published simultaneously by the Montreal *Herald* and the Toronto *Globe*.
30   *Ibid.*, July 18, 1873.
31   *Ibid.*, July 9, 1873.
32   *Ibid.*
33   Brown Papers, George to Anne Brown, June 12, August 13, 23, 1873.
34   *Ibid.*, July 23, August 7, 1873.
35   *Ibid.*, August 7, 1873.
36   *Ibid.*
37   *Ibid.*
38   *Ibid.*
39   *Ibid.*, Mackenzie to Brown, July 21, 1873.
40   Thomson, *op. cit.*, pp. 155-6; Creighton, *The Old Chieftain*, pp. 171-2.
41   Thomson, *op. cit.*, pp. 156-8.
42   Mackenzie Papers, Brown to Mackenzie, August 9, 1873.
43   *Ibid.*
44   *Ibid.*
45   *Ibid.*
46   *Ibid.*, August 14, 1873.
47   *Ibid.*
48   Public Archives, Earl of Dufferin Papers (microfilm), Kimberley to Dufferin, August 14, 1873. It is not surprising that Dufferin later told Kimberley of his dislike for Brown — and that Mackenzie was Brown's puppet. *Ibid.*, Dufferin to Kimberley, October 10, 1873.
49   *Ibid.*, Dufferin to Langevin, August 3, 1873.
50   See *Globe* for two weeks following August 14, 1873. Note also Creighton, *The Old Chieftain*, p. 166, regarding rising protest.
51   Mackenzie Papers, Brown to Mackenzie, August 14, 1873.
52   Brown Papers, George to Anne Brown, August 13, 1873.

53   *Ibid.*, August 9, 1873.
54   *Ibid.*, August 23, 1873.
55   *Globe*, September 20, 1873.
56   Quoted in *ibid.*, October 13, 1873.
57   *Ibid.*, November 3, 1873.
58   *Ibid.*, November 6, 1873.
59   Brown Papers, Mackenzie to Brown, November 5, 1873.
60   *Ibid.*, November 13, 1873.
61   *Ibid.*, Letters Patent, Summons to the Senate of Canada, December 20, 1873.
62   *Globe*, January 13, 1874.
63   C. W. de Kiewiet and F. H. Underhill, eds., *Dufferin–Carnarvon Correspondence, 1874–1878* (Toronto, 1955), p. 3, Dufferin to Carnarvon, February 26, 1874.
64   Brown Papers, Mackenzie to Brown, December 22, 1873.
65   Brown's speech to the Senate on the reciprocity negotiations, February 22, 1875, given in Mackenzie, *Brown*, pp. 355-6. See also *Dufferin–Carnarvon Correspondence*, p. 8, Dufferin to Carnarvon, March 13, 1874, which credits "the original idea" to Brown.
66   Mackenzie Papers, Brown to Mackenzie, February 9, 1874.
67   Dufferin Papers, Rothery to Dufferin, January 27, 1874.
68   Brown Papers, George to Anne Brown, February 12, 1874.
69   *Ibid.*, February 14, 1874. "Ginney" was his son's nickname.
70   *Ibid.*, February 12, 1874.
71   *Ibid.*, Brown to Mackenzie, April 1, 1874.
72   *Ibid.*, George to Anne Brown, February 18, 1874.
73   *Ibid.*, February 12, 1874.
74   *Ibid.*
75   *Ibid.*, February 14, 1874.
76   *Ibid.*
77   *Ibid.*, February 18, 1874.
78   *Ibid.*, February 12, 1874.
79   *Dufferin–Carnarvon Correspondence*, pp. 2-3, Dufferin to Carnarvon, February 26, 1874.
80   *Ibid.*, p. 8, Dufferin to Carnarvon, March 13, 1874.
81   Mackenzie Papers, Brown to Mackenzie, February 23, 1874.
82   Brown Papers, Brown to Mackenzie, April 1, 1874.
83   See Shippee, *Canadian–American Relations*, p. 461, and Mackenzie Papers, Brown to Mackenzie (telegram), February 15, 1874, on Thornton's hopes; Mackenzie Papers, Mackenzie to Brown, April 15, 1874, on their decline.
84   Brown Papers, Brown to Mackenzie, draft, April 1, 1874.
85   *Ibid.*
86   *Ibid.*
87   *Ibid.*
88   *Ibid.*
89   Excerpts from Fish's diary, March 28, 1874, Allan Nevins, *Hamilton Fish* (New York, 1936), Appendix II, pp. 919-20.
90   Dufferin Papers, Dufferin to Mackenzie, March 30, 1874.
91   Public Archives, Mackenzie Letterbooks, vol. III, Mackenzie to Brown, March 28, 1874; Thomson, *op. cit.*, p. 204.
92   Mackenzie Papers, Mackenzie to Brown, April 15, 1874.
93   Mackenzie Papers, Brown to Mackenzie, April 22, 1874.
94   *Ibid.*
95   *Parliament of Canada, Sessional Papers, 1875*, No. 51, "Report of Committee of the Privy Council, March 26, 1874". See also *Dufferin–Carnarvon Correspondence*, p. 20, Dufferin to Carnarvon, March 27, 1874.
96   Fish's diary, April 27, 1874, Nevins, *op. cit.*, p. 919.
97   Dufferin Papers, Brown to Dufferin, April 28, 1874.
98   Brown Papers, Brown to Dufferin, May 17, 1874.
99   *Ibid.*, George to Anne Brown, May 10, 1874.
100   *Ibid.*, May 15, 1874.
101   *Ibid.*, J. W. Clendenning to Brown, April 30, 1874.
102   *Ibid.*, George to Anne Brown, May 6, 15, 1874.
103   *Ibid.*, Brown to Mackenzie, May 22, 1874.
104   *Ibid.*, George to Anne Brown, May 21, 1874.
105   Mackenzie Papers, Brown to Mackenzie, telegrams, May 23, 24, 1874.
106   *Ibid.*, May 25, 1874.
107   *Ibid.*
108   Brown Papers, George to Anne Brown, May 27, 1874.
109   *Ibid.*
110   Mackenzie Papers, Brown to Mackenzie, telegram, May 30, 1874. See also *ibid.*, Mackenzie's memorandum to Brown of May 29, 1874.
111   *Ibid.*, Brown to Mackenzie, telegram, June 7, 1874.
112   Brown Papers, George to Anne Brown, June 7, 1874.
113   *Ibid.*, June 8, 9, 10, 1874.
114   *Ibid.*, June 10, 1874.
115   *Ibid.*
116   *Ibid.*, June 12, 1874.
117   *Ibid.*
118   *Ibid.*
119   *Ibid.*
120   *Ibid.*
121   *Ibid.*, June 13, 1874.
122   Mackenzie Papers, Brown to Mackenzie, telegram, June 15, 1874.
123   Brown Papers, George to Anne Brown, June 18, 1874.
124   *Ibid.*, June 20, 1874.
125   *Ibid.*
126   This may be seen from the response of numerous influential Republican journals, Boards of Trade, business men, and politicians who were certainly not

Democrats or low-tariff advocates.

127   The tone of Fish's diary indicates that he was serious about the negotiations but by no means strongly committed to them.
128   Mackenzie Papers, Gordon Brown to Mackenzie, June 20, 1874.
129   Brown Papers, Anne Brown to Mrs. Nelson, August 28, 1874.
130   Mackenzie Papers, Brown to Mackenzie, October 30, 1874.
131   Cartwright, *Reminiscences*, p. 134.
132   Ontario Archives, Blake Papers, Mackenzie to Blake, May 28, 1874.
133   *Ibid.*, Blake to Mackenzie, September 6, 1874.
134   Thomson, *op. cit.*, p. 214.
135   Blake's speech was published as a pamphlet, *A National Sentiment* (Ottawa, 1874).
136   Mackenzie Papers, Brown to Mackenzie, October 6, 1874.
137   *Ibid.*, October 30, 1874.
138   *Ibid.*
139   Elizabeth Wallace, *Goldwin Smith* (Toronto, 1957), pp. 54, 192, 255.
140   *Ibid.*, p. 263.
141   *Ibid.*, p. 284. Smith had sought to have Blake at the laying of the National Club's cornerstone, and was in close, friendly communication. See Blake Papers, Smith to Blake, October 5, 20, 1874.
142   *Globe*, February 6, 8, 17, 1873; October 6, 1874. See *Canadian Monthly*, February 1873, p. 141, March, 1873, (articles by Smith), and Smith's inaugural speech to the National Club in the *Nation* (Toronto), October 15, 1874.
143   *Globe*, October 5, 19, 27, November 7, 14, 1874.
144   *Ibid.*, October 23, 1874.
145   *Ibid.*, October 19, 1874.
146   *Ibid.*
147   *Ibid.*, October 17, 19, 1874.
148   *Ibid.*, October 27, 1874.
149   *Ibid.*, November 7, 1874. Smith in the *Nation* repeatedly denounced the *Globe* for descending to personal attacks. The *Globe* answered that he could not have both "the advantage of publicity and the immunity of the anonymous" (February 4, 1875).
150   *Nation*, November 12, 1874. See also *ibid.*, November 19, 1874, which charged the *Globe* with "knavery, lying, injustice, tyranny, hypocrisy", and termed Brown "the would-be dictator".
151   *Globe*, November 14, 1874.
152   Mackenzie Papers, Brown to Mackenzie, October 30, 1874.
153   *Ibid.*
154   Brown Papers, George to Anne Brown, December 15, 1874.
155   *Ibid.*, December 16, 17, 1874.
156   *Ibid.*, December 15, 1874. Brown, nevertheless, made another brief trip to Washington, late in January of 1875, to see Thornton and test the new Congress. He returned unhopeful. Mackenzie Papers,

Brown to Mackenzie, January 25, 1875.
157   Blake was evidently party to a suggestion – rejected – that Smith run for parliament. Blake Papers, Smith to Blake, November 27, 1874.
158   Wallace, *op. cit.*, p. 77. See also Blake Papers, Smith to Blake, July 7, 1875.
159   *Globe*, March 4, 5, 1875. Smith and the *Nation* kept up a vigorous fight against the *Globe*'s "dictatorship", however, echoed by some Liberal journals but equally by old Conservative and "moderate" rivals. See *Nation*, January 29, February 5, 26, March 5, 1875. See also *Liberal* (Toronto), February 19, March 11, 1875, and *Globe*, January 4, February 20, March 27, 1875.
160   Brown Papers, George to Anne Brown, February 4, 1875.
161   *Ibid.*
162   *Ibid.*
163   *Ibid.*, February 19, 1875.
164   *Ibid.*
165   *Ibid.*, February 22, 1875. Misdated "12th", but written in haste, and clearly on the 22nd by internal evidence.
166   *Ibid.*
167   Speech published in Mackenzie, *op. cit.*, p. 374.
168   Brown Papers, George to Anne Brown, March 15, 1875.
169   *Ibid.*
170   *Ibid.*
171   *Ibid.*, March 18, 1875.
172   Mackenzie Papers, Blake to A. Jones, March 20, 1875. See also Mackenzie Letterbooks, vol. II, Mackenzie to Brown, March 29, 1875.
173   Brown Papers, George to Anne Brown, March 27, 1875.
174   *Ibid.*
175   *Ibid.*, April 6, 1875.
176   *Ibid.*
177   *Ibid.*, May 20, 1875.
178   *Ibid.*, June 4, 1875.
179   Blake Papers, John Cameron to Blake, May 17, 1875. Mackenzie Papers, Brown to Mackenzie, July 15, 1875.
180   Mackenzie Papers, Brown to Mackenzie, May 15, 1875.
181   Mackenzie Letterbooks, vol. III, Mackenzie to John Cameron, October 18, 1874. See also Mackenzie Papers, Mackenzie to C. R. Black, May 20, 1880: "He [Brown] was said to control my Government; so scrupulous was he about not influencing me that he never wrote me on public affairs unless I addressed him on some special case." See also Thomson, *op. cit.*, pp. 177, 218, 276.
182   See Mackenzie Papers, Brown to Mackenzie, October 30, 1874; November 13, 1875. Even as early as March 21, 1870 (*ibid.*) Brown told Mackenzie he was too out of touch to advise him on the question of party reorganization in Ottawa. See also *ibid.*, March 14, 1870.
183   On the harmony of the views of

Brown and Mackenzie see *ibid.*, April 29, 1870; on their friendship, *ibid.*, May 15, 1875; on Brown's admiration for Mackenzie, *ibid.*, July 15, 1875.
184 Blake Papers, undated memorandum by Blake on terms to be discussed with Mackenzie, evidently before rejoining the cabinet. See W. R. Graham, "Liberal Nationalism in the Eighteen-Seventies", *Canadian Historical Association, Annual Report*, 1946, note 39, p. 111.

Chapter 10

Pages 338 to 373

1 Mackenzie Papers, Brown to Mackenzie, July 15, 1875.
2 Brown Papers, George to Anne Brown, July 22, 1875.
3 *Ibid.*, July 24, 1875.
4 *Ibid.*, July 22, 23, 1875.
5 Brown–Nelson Papers, Anne Brown's diary for 1875.
6 *Ibid.*
7 Brown Papers, George to Anne Brown, August 19, 1875.
8 The following account of the *Moravian*'s collision, together with the quotations, is taken from Brown's letter to his wife of September 12, 1875, *ibid.*
9 *Ibid.*
10 *Ibid.*
11 *Ibid.* See also *ibid.*, October 10, 14, 21, 1875.
12 *Globe*, September 25, 1875.
13 *Ibid.*, October 29, 1875.
14 *Ibid.*, October 1, 1875, *et seq.*
15 Brown Papers, George to Anne Brown, December 12, 30, 1875.
16 *Mail* (Toronto), September 27, 29, 1875; *Leader*, September 28, 1875; a copy of the *West Durham News* for September 24, 1875, is in the Dufferin Papers.
17 *Globe*, September 30, 1875.
18 *Ibid.*
19 *Ibid.* See also *Weekly Globe*, July 4, 1876, on Simpson's case against the *West Durham News*, and the judgment delivered in his favour on June 29, 1876.
20 *Ibid.*, November 10, December 2, 1875.
21 Brown Papers, George to Anne Brown, September 19, 1875. See also *ibid.*, October 4, 14, November 11, 21, 1875.
22 *Ibid.*, October 10, 1875.
23 *Ibid.*, December 12, 1875.
24 *Ibid.*, December 26, 1875.
25 T. B. Costain, *The Chord of Steel* (New York, 1960), pp. 149-51.
26 Catharine Mackenzie, *Alexander Graham Bell* (Boston, 1928), p. 103.
27 Costain, *op. cit.*, p. 169.
28 C. Mackenzie, *Bell*, pp. 107-8. But see also Brown Papers, George to Anne Brown, December 30, 1875, which suggests that Brown had really undertaken to patent

Bell's "harmonic telegraph", not the telephone. Bell, however (see Mackenzie, *Bell*, p. 112), clearly thought Brown was patenting his telephonic device. It seems likely that Brown was to seek patents for both.
29 Brown Papers, George to Anne Brown, February 16, 1876.
30 *Ibid.*
31 *Ibid.*
32 *Ibid.* See also *ibid.*, February 18, 1876.
33 Mackenzie, *Bell*, p. 112.
34 *Strictly Private and Confidential Memo* [sic], printed Prospectus on Bow Park, London, February 22, 1876. In author's possession.
35 *Ibid.*
36 John Clay, *New World Notes* (Kelso, 1875), p. 89.
37 *Canada Farmer*, January 15, 1876.
38 Prospectus on Bow Park.
39 *Ibid.*
40 *Ibid.*
41 Brown Papers, Manchester to Brown, March 9, 11, 1876.
42 *Ibid.*, George to Anne Brown, March 14, 1876.
43 *Ibid.*, March 15, 1876.
44 Brown–Nelson Papers, T. Nelson to R. Gregg, April 4, 1876.
45 *Ibid.* See also Prospectus.
46 John Clay, *My Recollections of Ontario* (Chicago, 1918), p. 27.
47 John Clay, *My Life on the Range* (Chicago, 1924), p. 7.
48 Prospectus.
49 Brown Papers, George to Anne Brown, July 27, 1876.
50 *Ibid.*
51 *Ibid.*, September 28, 1876.
52 *Globe*, July 8, 1876.
53 See p. 4 above.
54 *Globe*, July 8, 1876.
55 *Ibid.*
56 *Ibid.*, December 11, 1876.
57 *Ibid.*, December 11, 12, 14, 1876.
58 *Ibid.*, December 30, 1876.
59 Brown Papers, George to Anne Brown, March 6, 1877.
60 *Ibid.*, March 10, 1877.
61 *Ibid.*, March 20, 1877.
62 *Ibid.*
63 *Ibid.*, March 27, April 27, 1875.
64 Mackenzie Papers, Mackenzie to Brown, January 25, 1877.
65 Brown Papers, George to Anne Brown, May 29, 1877.
66 James Macdonald, *Food from the Far West* (London, 1878), p. 245.
67 *Canada Farmer*, January 15, 1876.
68 Macdonald, *op. cit.*, p. 245.
69 *Ibid.*, p. 246.
70 *Ibid.*, pp. 251-6.
71 For description of features of the house, see George Brown's "progress reports" in letters to his wife, Brown Papers, 1875-7, *passim*.

72 *Globe*, October 26, 1877.

73 *Ibid.*, September 3-8, 12, 1877.

74 *Ibid.*, November 20, December 14, 24, 1877.

75 Brown in 1875 had written to Mackenzie favouring the choice of Laurier for the cabinet — "the young, vigorous, popular and eloquent man of the present moment". Mackenzie Papers, Brown to Mackenzie, November 13, 1875.

76 *Ibid.*, November 18, 1877.

77 Brown Papers, George to Anne Brown, February 14, 1878.

78 *Ibid.*, February 18, 1878.

79 *Ibid.*

80 *Ibid.*, March 16, 1878.

81 *Speech of the Hon. George Brown in the Canadian Senate, March 21, 1878, on the Public Finances of the Dominion* (Toronto, 1878).

82 *Ibid.*, pp. 23-4.

83 Brown Papers, George to Anne Brown, March 20, 1878.

84 *Ibid.*, April 17, 1878.

85 *Globe*, March 2, 1878.

86 *Ibid.*, August 9, 1878.

87 *Ibid.*, July 4, 1878.

88 Brown Papers, George to Anne Brown, August 9 (19?), 1878.

89 *Ibid.*, September 12, 1878; *Globe*, September 12, 1878.

90 *Globe*, September 16, 1878.

91 Brown Papers, George to Anne Brown, September 15, 1878.

92 *Globe*, September 18, 19, 1878.

93 Mackenzie Papers, Brown to Mackenzie, October 1, 1878.

94 *Ibid.*, October 3, 1878.

95 *Ibid.*, October 1, 1878.

96 Clay, *Recollections*, p. 14.

97 E. W. Thomson in *Transcript* (Boston), undated clipping in collection donated to the author by Mrs. Frank Yeigh.

98 Undated newspaper clipping from Yeigh collection.

99 Clay, *Recollections*, p. 14.

100 *Ibid.*

101 *Ibid.*

102 Brown Papers, George to Anne Brown, March 8, 1877.

103 Recollections of Dr. George Barbour, Cincinnati, from his mother, George Brown's daughter, Margaret, told to the author in July 1959.

104 Undated clipping from Stratford *Times*, Yeigh collection.

105 Brown Papers, George to Anne Brown, December 12, 1875.

106 Recollections of the late George Brown Ball, Richmond Hill, nephew of George Brown, told to the author in June, 1955.

107 See, for example, Brown's fight against the "divisionist" University Bill of 1853 (*Brown of the Globe*, vol. 1, p. 170), or his stand on the University Committee of 1860 (above, p. 25).

108 *Memorials of Chancellors W. H. Blake, Bishop Strachan, Professor H. H. Croft and Professor G. P. Young presented to the University of Toronto* (Toronto, 1894). Includes speech by Edward Blake.

109 See Goldwin Smith's review of Alexander Mackenzie's biography of Brown in *The Bystander* (Toronto), vol. III, January 1883, pp. 70-8.

110 E. W. Thomson, *loc. cit.*

111 *Ibid.*

112 *Ibid.*

113 Quoted by Thomson, *loc. cit.*

114 *Ibid.*

115 *Grip* (Toronto), May 15, 1880.

116 Clay, *Recollections*, p. 28.

117 *Ibid.*

118 Clay, *Life on the Range*, p. 7.

119 Clay, *Recollections*, p. 29.

120 *Ibid.*, p. 32.

121 *Ibid.*, pp. 15, 17, 58-9.

122 *Canada Farmer*, January 15, 1876.

123 Clay, *Life on the Range*, pp. 9-10.

124 Clay, *Recollections*, p. 35.

125 *Ibid.*

126 Brown Papers, George to Anne Brown, May 7, 1879.

127 *Ibid.*, February 19, 1875.

128 *Dufferin–Carnarvon Correspondence*, p. 358, Dufferin to Carnarvon, July 20, 1877.

129 Brown Papers, Dufferin to Brown, September 21, 1878, Brown to Dufferin, October 4, 1878.

130 *Ibid.*, George to Anne Brown, telegram, May 24, 1879.

131 *Ibid.*, George to Anne Brown, February 19, 1875.

132 *Ibid.*, Brown to Lorne (draft), June 21, 1879.

133 *Ibid.*, D. Wilson to Brown, May 26, 1879.

134 Clay, *Recollections*, p. 36.

135 *Ibid.*

136 *Ibid.*

137 Brown Papers, George to Anne Brown, July 31, 1879.

138 Clay, *Recollections*, p. 37.

139 *Ibid.*

140 *Ibid.*, p. 38.

141 *Ibid.*, p. 40.

142 *Ibid.*, p. 40-1.

143 *Mail*, December 4, 1879.

144 Clay, *Recollections*, p. 41.

145 *Ibid.*, p. 42; *Globe*, December 4, 1879.

146 Clay, *Recollections*, p. 42.

147 *Mail*, December 26, 1879.

148 Clay, *Recollections*, p. 43.

149 *Ibid.*, p. 43.

150 *Ibid.*, p. 44.

151 The chief source for the following description of Brown's shooting is the *Globe* for March 26, 1880. But other sources have also been used, particularly the reminiscences of Archibald Blue (one of the *Globe* staff who answered Brown's call

for help), which were printed in that journal for July 2, 1904.

152 *Globe*, March 26, 1880.

153 From evidence at the trial of Bennett, proceedings of which were printed in the *Globe* for June 23, 1880.

154 *Ibid.*, March 26, 1880.

155 *Ibid.*, July 2, 1904.

156 *Ibid.*

157 Typescript history of the *Globe*, p. 118.

158 The cab company's card for the day, initialled by Brown, is in the Brown Papers. He dismissed the cab that day at 7:10 p.m.

159 Smith to Macdonald, March 27, 1880, in Joseph Pope, *Correspondence of Sir John Macdonald* (Toronto, n.d.), p. 273.

160 Proceedings of Bennett's trial, *Globe*, June 23, 1880.

161 *Globe*, March 31, 1880.

162 *Ibid.* Current debts, due to expenditure on new plant, were, in fact, $61,308.

163 See *Globe* for July and August 1879.

164 *Ibid.*, November 21, 1879.

165 *Ibid.*, November 1, 1879.

166 *Ibid.*, December 2, 1879.

167 *Weekly Globe*, January 2, 1880.

168 *Globe*, January 2, 1880.

169 *Ibid.*, April 15, 1880.

170 See above, pp. 40-1.

171 Clay, *Recollections*, p. 45.

172 *Ibid.*, p. 44.

173 *Ibid.*, p. 46.

174 *Ibid.*, p. 45.

175 *Ibid.*

176 Trial proceedings, *Globe*, June 23, 1880.

177 *Ibid.*

178 For example, *ibid.*, April 24, 26, 30, 1880.

179 See the Brown Papers, which also include messages from Lorne, Dufferin, and a "devoted friend", Archbishop Lynch.

180 *Ibid.*, J. S. Smith to Brown, April 7, 1880.

181 *Ibid.*, notes of a conversation between "Mrs. Ball and Mr. Brown, Tuesday, 20th April, Afternoon".

182 *Ibid.*

183 Mackenzie, *Brown*, p. 143.

184 *Globe*, May 13, 1880.

185 *Ibid.*, May 10, 1880.

186 *Ibid.*, May 13, 1880.

187 *Ibid.*

188 Report of Bennett's execution, *Globe*, July 24, 1880.

189 Trial proceedings, *ibid.*, June 23, 1880.

190 *Ibid.* See also A. R. Hassard, *Famous Canadian Trials* (Toronto, 1924), pp. 158-172.

191 Gordon Brown, however, gave up management of the *Globe* at the end of 1882, because of disagreements with the directors of the Printing Company, who hired John Cameron, of the defunct *Liberal*, in his stead. (See Sir John S. Willison, *Reminiscences, Political and Personal* (Toronto, 1919), p. 80.) Gordon Brown became Registrar of the Surrogate Court in Toronto, and died there in 1896.

192 Tradition reported by the late George Brown Ball. Anne Brown died in Edinburgh in 1906.

Index

The Globe.

TORONTO, MONDAY, JULY 1.

CONFEDERATION DAY!

The Union of the Provinces of Canada, Nova Scotia and New Brunswick, under the new Constitution, takes effect to-day. We heartily congratulate our readers on the event, and fervently pray that all the blessings anticipated from the measure, by its promoters, may be fully realized.

So far as the people of Upper Canada are concerned, the inauguration of the new Constitution may well be heartily rejoiced over as the brightest day in their calendar. The Constitution of 1867 will be famous in the historical annals of Upper Canada, not only because it brought two flourishing Maritime States into alliance with the Canadas, and opened up new markets for our products, and a direct railway route to the Atlantic through British territory, but because it relieved the inhabitants of Western Canada from a system of injustice and demoralization under which they had suffered for a long series of years.

The unanimity and cordiality with which all sections of the people of Canada accept the new Constitution, gives the happiest omen of its successful operation. And, assuredly, if the people of the United Provinces are true to themselves and exercise a persistent and careful control over all public proceedings, there is not a shadow of doubt as to success. The only danger that threatens us is, lest the same men who have so long misgoverned us, should continue to misgovern us still, and the same reckless prodigality exhibited in past years should be continued in the future; but this we do not fear. We firmly believe, that from this day, Canada enters on a new and happier career, and that a time of great prosperity and advancement is before us.

EAST YORK.—The Tories are trying to bring out Mr. T. A. Milne for this County.

We regret to announce the death of the Hon. Thos. H. Haveland, Legislative Councillor of Prince Edward Island, President of the Bank of Prince Edward Island and Mayor of Charlottetown.

WEST PETERBOROUGH.—Mr. John Walton, we are happy to see, has consented to be a candidate for the Legislature of Ontario, in this county, and we do not doubt that he will be entirely successful.

MINION, and Toronto again becomes the Seat of Government of Upper Canada under its new name of the Province of Ontario. Toronto has bestirred herself to make the holiday befitting the occasion; and, although various circumstances have militated against the preparations, yet sufficient is announced to secure that the day shall be remembered among us as an eventful one in our history.

Ere this fairly reaches our readers, more than item in the day's programme will have become an event of the past. Hours before these lines are read, the bells of St. James' broke the midnight silence to convey the joyful news to the city that the important era had arrived; and at four a. m. a detachment of the 10th Royals were to assemble at the drill shed, and hoist the Union Jack on the new flagstaff erected in front of the shed. The 10th Royal regimental colours were also to be hoisted at the north end of the shed at the same time. The Union Jack will be saluted with 21 guns immediately afterwards.

At 6 o'clock a.m., an immense ox will be roasted by Capt. Woodhouse, of the barque *Lord Nelson*, at the foot of Church street. The animal, which was a very fine one, was purchased by subscription from Mr. Joseph Lennox, of Yorkville. The roasting will occupy a large portion of the day, and the meat will afterwards be distributed among the poor of the city.

At half-past nine, an interesting meeting will be held in the lecture room of the Mechanics' Institute. The meeting will be held under the auspices of the Toronto branch of the Evangelical Alliance, and Christian persons of all denominations are invited to attend at that hour to invoke the divine blessing on the new Dominion. Brief addresses are expected from the Hon. Vice-Chancellor Mowat, President of the Alliance, and the Rev. Messrs. Baldwin, Dewart and others.

At half-past ten, a grand review will be held on the grounds west of Spadina avenue. The volunteers muster at their head quarters at 9 a. m., and are expected to be on the ground in time to receive the General, punctually at 10:30. The 13th Hussars, 17th infantry, two batteries of regular and one of volunteer artillery, Queen's Own, 10th Royals, and Grand Trunk Volunteer battalions, and Captain McLean's Fort artillery company, will take part in the review. Line will be formed prior to the arrival of General Stisted, and immediately on his entry on the field, a *feu de joie* will be fired by the infantry, and a royal salute by the artillery.

In the afternoon, a pic-nic and festival in aid of the building of St. Patrick's School House and temporary church on Dummer street, will take place on the Government grounds.

The Directors of the Horticultural Society have prepared a most attractive evening's entertainment. The bands of the 17th and 13th Hussars will be present, and a programme is arranged which will no doubt draw large crowds. After the concert, the bands will supply music for dancing.

About 9 o'clock in the evening, fireworks will be let off in the Queen's Park. The avenues leading to the Park will be illuminated with lanterns, and a band will be present to add to the enjoyment of the occasion. In addition to these doings in the city, the Great Western advertise cheap rates to different points curation to this city from the different stations; and the steamer *City of Toronto* leaves at 7 o'clock, with a party of excursionists for Lewiston, the Falls and Buffalo.

The *Rothesay Castle* will make three trips around the Island, for the accommodation of excursionists favouring short lake trips, at one, two and three o'clock.

In addition, illuminations and fire-works will be indulged in to a considerable extent. The Post Office, Gas House, and other buildings, have undergone the gas-fitters' manipulation; while in front of the Queen's, and at other points, a number of fireworks will be displayed.

IN YORKVILLE,

On its being entered, the bed was lot fire and a soldier lying on it drunk.

An Advertising Journal, for gratis circulation, has appeared.

A telegram from Capt. Kerr, of the *American*, Anticosti, June 26th, says

"I send mails and specie off to-night Gaspe, to catch the steamer downward Father Point on Saturday night. The venue cutter *Canadienne* is here. schooners loaded, have been sent a Quebec. Weather fine. I have lift the cargo thrown overboard."

Another telegram says all the passe are well.

Great preparations are making for day.

There are now 48,688 bushels of whe 43,967 barrels of flour in store and hands of millers—a good deal less th time last year. This having been a Obligation, little business was done produce market.

One hundred and fifty-eight cable eighty-four steerage passengers sailed *Austrian*.

Latest from Euro

(By Atlantic Cable).

LONDON, June 29, noon.—Additio telligence, relative to the loss of the States sloop-of-war *Sacramento*, has be ceived. The crew escaped to the sh small boats. No lives lost.

LONDON. June 29.—A public bre was given to Wm. Lloyd Garrison t A large number was present. The pri speakers were John Bright and the D Argyle. Friendly toasts were drank the affair was a perfect ovation.

Atlantic and Great Western consol shares, 25¼; U. S. 5.20'z, at Fran closed at 77½ for issue of 1862.

Financial and Commercial.

LONDON, June 29, noon.—Consols Bonds, 72¾; Erie, 42¾; Ill C, 79¼; W, 24¾. Tin, 86s 6d for straits and. Linseed, 64s 6d for Calcutta. Linseed firmer, at £10 10s per ton for thin obj.

LIVERPOOL, June 29, noon.—Cotto and unchanged; sales to-day 10,000 Breadstuffs unchanged. Corn 38s fo Lard, 48s 3l. Tallow firmer, at Othes articles unchanged.

LONDON, June 29, 2 p.m.—Gover says that the state of Ireland at the time forbids the adoption of any Bill in her behalf.

Consols, 94½; Ill C, 79; Erie, bonds, 73; A & G W, 24¾.

LIVERPOOL, June 29, 2 p.m.—Chee vanced 1s; tallow advanced 9d. No changes.

bonds, 72¾; Ill C, 79¼; Erie, 43.

LIVERPOOL, June 29, evening.—C breadstuffs and provisions unaltered. turpentine, 30s; tallow, 44s; Calcut seed, 64s. Other articles unchanged.

STEAMSHIP "NORTH AMERIC

(Despatch to H. & A. Allan & C

ANTICOSTI, Wednesday night, June I send the mails and specie off to-nig